Speech Methods and Resources

Under the Advisory Editorship of J. Jeffery Auer

Speech Methods and Resources

A Textbook for the Teacher of Speech Communication
Second edition

edited by Waldo W. Braden
Louisiana State University

Harper & Row, Publishers
New York Evanston San Francisco London

Speech Methods and Resources: A Textbook for the Teacher of Speech Communication, Second edition
Copyright © 1972 by Waldo W. Braden

Standard Book Number: 06–040901–0

Library of Congress Catalog Card Number: 70–174524

Contents

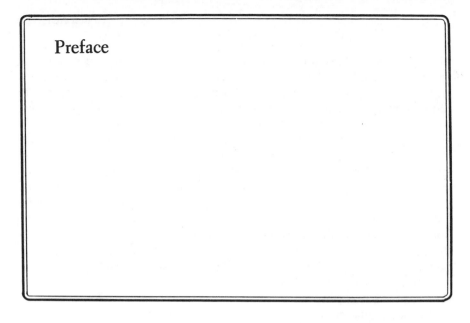

Preface

Our goals and point of view in preparing the second edition of *Speech Methods and Resources* remain the same as when we conceived the book in 1961. It is planned for persons who intend to teach speech either in high school or in college. It is written especially for those who are about to have the exciting experience of teaching for the first time, for those who are called upon to teach basic or general courses, and for those who direct extracurricular activities. It is probable that the book will find many of its readers among students enrolled in college courses in speech education and teacher training. We hope that others as well will discover here worthwhile suggestions and new insights. It should be stressed that the book is not planned for specialists or for those who limit their teaching to specialized areas such as radio or speech correction, though most of the specialized areas are discussed by specialists in those areas.

The word *resources* in the title implies a second purpose—that is, the pulling together of useful materials, helpful readings, courses of study, and visual aids. This aspect of the book should provide ready references when a teacher is searching for ideas and procedures.

At all times we have attempted to be specific in suggesting methods and assignments; consequently, we have been prescriptive, directive, and at times even persuasive. But at the same time we make no claim to having final answers to the problems of speech pedagogy. Perhaps there are no final or simple solutions to many of these which vary inevitably from teacher to teacher, from class to class, and even from institution to institution. Remembering our own first days in the classroom, we know that the beginning teacher often seeks concrete suggestions instead of abstract generalizations. We offer each recommendation as a starting point, a point of view, *a* way (not *the* way) to meet a problem. We urge the beginner to work from these vantage points to formulate his own speech philosophy and to think creatively about how to conduct courses and about how to motivate students to develop understanding and skill in the use of speech.

This edition is a cooperative effort of 10 faculty members of the Department of Speech of Louisiana State University. Our training has been acquired in several of the major institutions and under some of the foremost speech educators. To each of these persons we owe much. Our total experience encompasses teaching at all levels of instruction from elementary school to the university. Although at present each contributor teaches advanced courses in his special field, we also have had our turns at serving as general teachers of speech. Each semester most of the contributors teach at least one section of a basic speech course at Louisiana State University. Through actual participation we are familiar with the demands of extracurricular activities: directing plays, supervising discussion and debate, planning radio and television programs, and organizing assembly activities. In addition, for many years we have counseled high school teachers in planning courses and in promoting speech activities. In spite of diversity of backgrounds and experience, we hold that working closely together in an integrated department has added to our strength and has given us a unified point of view which we have tried to express in this book.

We wish to express our appreciation to G. W. Gray, L. Stanley Harms, and Clinton Bradford who helped with the first edition. We are pleased to welcome as new contributors Stuart I. Gilmore, John H. Pennybacker, and J. Donald Ragsdale.

It is obvious that so many different persons contributing so many chapters to such a work would inevitably have drawn heavily on a great number of persons. So numerous have these sources been that it is impossible to recognize them by name or with reference to their several contributions. Individually and collectively we are deeply indebted to them for their help and encouragement.

Waldo W. Braden
Editor

1. The Scope of Speech Education: An Overview

Waldo W. Braden

A TRADITION

The teaching of speech has a long and distinguished tradition, dating back perhaps as far as three thousand years. Definite evidence exists that in the fifth century B.C. the Greek rhetorician Corax established himself as a teacher on the island of Sicily when his compatriots discovered that they could not maintain themselves or their causes in court without training in speechmaking. They learned the hard way that how you say it contributes significantly to what you say. Soon young men all over the Greek world made the same discovery about politics; consequently, they eagerly sought out those who presided over the art that makes men eloquent. They were avid students and learned their lessons well. In time they developed an Attic oratory which became the model of speaking for the Western world. The Greek sophists, the Attic orators, Plato, Isocrates, and Aristotle each had a part in developing and in putting rhetoric and persuasive speaking on a firm foundation. Furthermore the Greeks developed and systematized the poetics, the source of the theory of the drama.

Pointing us in the direction that we have traveled since those ancient times, Greek thinkers and teachers provided a philosophy and ideals that continue to inspire and direct our efforts in speech education even today. As early as 354 B.C. Isocrates (436–338 B.C.), "the old man eloquent," gave an excellent statement of the value of speech.[1]

[1] Isocrates (253–257), trans. George Norlin, *Antidosis*, Cambridge: Harvard Univ. Press, 1929, vol. 2, p. 827.

Because there has been implanted in us the power to persuade each other and to make clear to each other whatever we desire, not only have we escaped the life of wild beasts, but we have come together and founded cities and made laws and invented arts; and, generally speaking there is no institution devised by man which the power of speech has not helped us to establish. For this it is which has laid down laws concerning things just and unjust, and things honourable and base; and if it were not for these ordinances we should not be able to live with one another. It is by this that we confute the bad and extol the good. Through this we educate the ignorant and appraise the wise; for the power to speak well is taken as the surest index of a sound understanding, and discourse which is true and lawful and just is the outward image of a good and faithful soul. With this faculty we both contend against others on matters which are open to dispute and seek light for ourselves on things which are unknown; for the same arguments which we use in persuading others when we speak in public, we employ also when we deliberate in our thoughts; and, while we call eloquent those who are able to speak before a crowd, we regard as sage those who most skillfully debate their problems in their own minds. And, if there is need to speak in brief summary of this power, we shall find that none of the things which are done with intelligence take place without the help of speech, but that in all our actions as well as in all our thoughts speech is our guide, and is most employed by those who have the most wisdom.

Since those glorious Hellenic days, teachers and scholars have continued to work at the development of sound theory and effective teaching methods. The roll is long. In Rome, where rhetoric was later in developing, Cicero and Quintilian wrote treatises on the subject. Significant in their day, but long forgotten now, are men like Theon, Hermogenes, and Aphthonius. The church fathers, particularly Saint Augustine, found the subject important and consequently adapted it to preaching. With the passing centuries, Cassiodorus, Isidore of Seville (Spain), Alcuin, Ramus, and Vossius shaped and redirected the course of speech education. In the Middle Ages rhetoric, of course, was one of the seven liberal arts. Among the early teachers of English rhetoric were Thomas Wilson, Francis Bacon, John Ward, John Lawson, Hugh Blair, George Campbell, and Richard Whately. Another significant group of English speech teachers were the elocutionists: John Mason, Thomas Sheridan, Joshua Steel, John Walker, and Gilbert Austin. In our own early history John Witherspoon, signer of the Declaration of Independence, and John Quincy Adams, later the sixth president of the United States, were teachers of speechmaking before they became famous in politics. Later in the past century and in the first quarter of the present century, George Pierce Baker, Smiley Blanton, Ralph B. Dennis, A. M. Drummond, Solomon Henry Clark, William T. Foster, James M. O'Neill, Frank M. Rarig, Lew Sarett, Thomas Clarkson True-blood, James A. Winans, and Charles Henry Woolbert distinguished themselves as speech teachers and authors of significant textbooks; they had much to do with the present emphasis and the development of modern departments of speech. In the twentieth century teachers of speech have established themselves in hundreds of colleges and universities as well as in great numbers of high schools. As a discipline the teaching of speech communication can claim a longer existence than many other subjects in the curriculum.

WHAT DOES SPEECH INVOLVE?

Some persons are confused about what the speech communication teacher does. They may think of him as a teacher of elocution, whose main concern is voice lessons, breathing drills, and graceful posture. Some may refer to him as a coach—like an athletic coach—who trains students to win contests. On occasion a hypercritical person may associate with him the word *sophist*, believing that a speech teacher deals in tricks of persuasion, in memory training, and in human relations. But none of these impressions gives a fair picture of the modern speech teacher or of the field of speech education.

Before undertaking a study of speech methods a novice teacher should first get a broad view of the field. To this purpose the present discussion is devoted.

Seven Areas of Academic Instruction

In ancient Greece the study of speech was limited to persuasive speaking and the drama. From that simple beginning speech has expanded into a wide and varied subject. Karl Wallace, life-long student of the field, in attempting to "describe compactly" the field of speech says that it is an "area of study whose twin aims are to understand the functions, processes, and effects of oral communication and to teach the principles and methods that make the spoken word effective. It is a field populated by persons who are devoted to knowledge and to teaching."[2]

Following is a brief description of seven areas of the field today.

Public address, which developed from rhetoric, is concerned with principles and practices of speechmaking. The area takes as its purpose "to make inquiry and to disclose information" and "to ascertain truth and advocate it."[3] It embraces public speaking, business speaking, argumentation, discussion, and debate. At more advanced levels it includes the history and criticism of oratory, rhetorical theory, rhetoric, and speech criticism.

Oral interpretation, sometimes called *oral reading, interpretative read-*

[2] Karl Wallace, "The Field of Speech, 1953, An Overview," *Quarterly Journal of Speech*, April, 1954, 40:117.
[3] "A Program of Speech Education," *Quarterly Journal of Speech*, October, 1951, 37:353.

ing, or *interpretation*, teaches the student how to read aloud good literature: prose, poetry, and drama. The single performer may read from a
manuscript or book or he may recite from memory. He strives to communicate orally the written symbols to his listeners, hoping to give them
understanding, enjoyment, and stimulation. Also considered a part of this
field are choral reading and group play reading, in which several persons
join to present orally a piece of literature.

Theater or dramatics, which finds its parent source in the poetics of
ancient Greece, concentrates on the understanding, appreciation, and
presentation of plays. The field embraces both theoretical and applied
courses. Among the former are dramatic theory, history of the theater,
dramatic literature, and dramatic criticism. On the practical side are acting,
directing, design, makeup, costuming, and stagecraft.

Speech correction and audiology has as its main concern the study and
treatment of the speech handicapped. Persons working in this area attempt
to understand and to correct functional and organic difficulties involving
articulation-enunciation, abnormal voice quality, stuttering, cleft palate,
aphasia, and hearing problems.

Speech science, sometimes taught under a title such as *experimental
phonetics*, investigates the physical characteristics of speech and communication.

Phonetics and linguistics, allied with and closely related to speech
science, involves the study of language and speech sounds. In some institutions, linguistics is taught as a separate field in departments of English or
foreign languages or in a department of its own.

Radio and television considers appreciation, programing, script writing,
and program production in the mass media involved. Engineering phases
of the field are usually not considered in departments of speech.

Extracurricular Speech Activities

In addition to classroom instruction, the speech teacher is usually concerned with several extracurricular speech activities. When other teachers
have finished the school day and departed for home, the speech teacher
may be doing some of his most important teaching. The enthusiastic
teacher will welcome the opportunity to work directly with a select group,
which may include some of the most talented students in the school. Both
students and teachers strive for superior achievement. It often happens
that the students become so enthusiastic about participation, particularly
when interschool competition is involved, that they exercise considerable
influence on the school authorities to increase classroom instruction in
speech.

Extracurricular speech activities fall under four main headings. First
there are the speaking events, sometimes referred to as *forensics*, which

include discussion, debating, student legislatures, original oratory, oratorical declamation, after-dinner speaking, extempore and impromptu speaking. Generally these activities are organized around interschool competition on a district, state, regional, and even national basis.

The second major area involves dramatics or play production. It is difficult to find a high school or college where at least two or three plays are not presented each year. In many states, one-act play contests are held. The dramatics club or players' guild frequently serves as a social and producing group.

Interpretative reading, declamation, and choral reading (verse choirs) compose a third type of activity. In some regions, festivals and contests are conducted.

The fourth type of activity embraces radio and television programing. Under the direction of a faculty advisor students may write, direct, and produce shows. Such programs are greatly facilitated when a local station releases time once or twice a week to students for presenting programs on the air.

The Speech and Hearing Clinic

Throughout this country there has been a growing awareness of the need to give attention to the handicapped. Developing out of this concern has come the program of speech and hearing therapy (speech correction, speech pathology, and audiology). This work is usually done in clinics. The personnel in these centers diagnose, counsel, and retrain speech defectives. They also advise parents on how to provide a positive environment for the handicapped. Many public schools and colleges are developing extensive programs to satisfy such needs. Some clinics operate completely independent of a school system—sometimes as part of a hospital, sometimes as a completely independent center. Service organizations such as an Easter Seal group, a Junior League, or a civic club may sponsor and finance these units.

The Characteristics of a Good Speech Program

A good speech program is based on at least four important considerations.

1. A good speech program is consistent with the social, political, and economic demands of a democratic society. It strives to develop the maximum potentialities of the student in order that he may be effective both as an individual and as a citizen. With reference to each activity and to each project, the teacher justifies his choice by the touchstone: how does it contribute to a productive, happy, and successful life? His goal is not to teach the student how to exploit or to deceive his fellow beings or how to achieve quick success. Rather, the courses are focused on the communica-

tion of ideas and are consistent with good current practice. As a result the student becomes a careful and systematic observer, listener, and evaluator of what he hears in daily conversation, on radio and television, and in the public forum.

2. A good speech program is student centered—that is, student development comes first. Early in each course the teacher diagnoses the students' interests, needs, abilities, and capabilities. Using self-inventories, diagnostic tests, attitude tests, autobiographical speeches, and personal conferences, the teacher studies his students and plans the course of study accordingly. "Teaching can thus proceed in terms of the maximum benefits to the greatest number as well as be made specific to individual needs."[4]

3. The good speech program provides training for students at all levels. It is not limited either to gifted persons with special aptitudes or to the handicapped or to any certain age group. Nor is it confined to any one phase such as platform speaking, oral reading, or acting. It is available to those who need it, regardless of whether they intend to be housewives, farmers, mechanics, scientists, doctors, lawyers, or ministers. It attempts to keep pace with the demands of community living and rapidly developing technology.

4. A good speech program receives as much time and emphasis and requires a teacher as highly trained and as competent as any other subject in the curriculum. It is offered on the same bases and demands as much work and effort from the student as any other subject. It combines the presentation of principles with sufficient practice to result in understanding and mastery. Although in many of its phases it attempts to develop a skill, it is based on thorough study and application of theory that has been accumulated through the centuries.

ELEMENTS OF A SUCCESSFUL SPEECH COURSE

The four necessary ingredients or elements of any effective course in speech communication are a well-trained teacher, a guiding philosophy, a course plan, and a meeting place and equipment.

A Well-Trained Teacher

The vitality of any course depends on the personality, character, knowledge, and training of the teacher. The effective teacher of speech is broadly educated. He has a strong liberal-arts background including history, political science, economics, sociology, literature, foreign language, logic, psychology, and science. In addition he is well read in the best literature in the

[4] Harry G. Barnes, Teaching the Fundamentals of Speech at the College Level," *Speech Teacher*, November, 1954, 3:246.

English language. He continues reading the best books as they become available.

In his own field he is thoroughly familiar with the fundamental processes of speech, public speaking, argumentation, interpretation, dramatics, and other speech activities. Furthermore, he should be able to direct one or more extracurricular activities: discussion and debate, interpretative reading, radio, or dramatics. A knowledge of phonetics, communication theory, semantics, and speech science will enrich his teaching. Training in speech correction will enable him to work with functional defects of articulation and to advise handicapped students.

The alert teacher is well informed about current affairs. As a daily habit he reads a good newspaper, the *New York Times* or the *Christian Science Monitor*, for example, several good news magazines, and other periodical literature. In this age of radio and television he cannot hope to keep up with his students without hearing and viewing several news programs and public service features each week.

The well-trained teacher of speech has a high degree of proficiency in oral communication. He is likely to be considered a model by his students: consciously and unconsciously they will imitate him. As minimum essentials he should have good articulation, acceptable pronunciation, a clear and distinct voice, and a pleasing manner. He should be free of distracting mannerisms, speech defects, and vocal abnormalities. For effective teaching he should have an extensive vocabulary and good diction. He should be an effective public speaker, able to present his ideas cogently and forcefully in the classroom and in the public forum. In addition, he should excel in one or more speech activities: debating, oral interpretation, radio speaking, or acting. In other words, he should be able to practice what he preaches.

The good teacher is also a man of good will and good character. His students recognize him as a person who is sincerely interested in their welfare and their improvement. They respect his honesty, his enthusiasm, his fairness, and his straightforward manner of handling their personal problems. They accept his criticism as just and deserved. The teacher establishes in his classroom an optimistic and encouraging atmosphere in which the student wants to improve.

A Guiding Philosophy

The second minimum essential is a carefully thought out philosophy. The teacher has a sense of direction and understanding of what he hopes to achieve and why he thinks his goals are important. He will draw his tenets from the rhetorical tradition, philosophical concepts, current educational philosophy, and his school and departmental objectives.

In thinking through what has been referred to as a sense of direction, he should recognize what Claude Kantner has called "the two-way relation" which exists between the student's proficiency in speech and his store of information. In communicating, the student speaker depends on "everything that he has done and learned—in short, what he is." Conversely, he is limited in his ability to use what he has learned by his ability to express himself. The function of the teacher of speech is to educate the student in "how to tap and organize and present orally these latent resources.[5] By careful direction a speech course should force the student to draw on his total education, to synthesize what he is learning, to think deeply, and to read widely. He may, through speech, learn the necessity for broad learning, careful preparation, and honest thinking.

A Course Plan or Syllabus

Out of a teaching philosophy should grow a means of implementation—a course plan that takes into account (1) the course objectives, (2) the needs and abilities of the student, (3) the time allotted for the course, (4) the amount of equipment available, and (5) the physical limitations of the meeting place.

From the beginning, the student is entitled to know the teacher's philosophy as well as the plan of the course. Therefore he should early be given a syllabus indicating what is expected of him and the sequence of assignments.

The plan should start with the student where he is and keep him constantly developing greater proficiency. The basic course in speech should be built around these interrelated elements: (1) the presentation of principles, (2) opportunities to practice or to perform, (3) constructive criticism, and (4) some type of testing or evaluation.

A Meeting Place and Equipment

Winston Churchill, in discussing the rebuilding of the chamber where the House of Commons meets, once said, "We shape our buildings and afterwards our buildings shape us." Indeed the speech teacher is fortunate when he is invited to help "shape" the place where he is to teach. But since too often he has no control over these matters, he finds that the surroundings impose limitations on what he can achieve. In other words, the room "shapes" the presentation.

Like many other subjects in the curriculum, speech in its various forms has some specialized needs as to its meeting place and the equipment required for effective teaching.

The Meeting Place.   What is the best type of classroom? Like any other

[5] Claude E. Kantner, "Speech and Education in a Democracy," *Southern Speech Journal*, September, 1951, 17:14–22.

subject that involves oral presentations, a speech class requires good acoustics, adequate lighting, satisfactory ventilation, comfortable chairs, and a blackboard. Boase and Glancy, who have made a careful study of the matter, recommend the following room for teaching speech communication:

The classroom should be large enough to accommodate from twenty-five to thirty students comfortably. Either tables and chairs or tablet armchairs are preferable to stationary desks. Indeed, if the school wisely selects tables, a trapezoidal type makes possible highly flexible arrangements—round table, T shape, etc.—contributing to optimum workshop and discussion conditions. At the front, a raised platform with a speaker's stand should replace the traditional teacher's desk. Although the entire school should receive acoustical treatment and be liberally equipped with conduit for microphone and loudspeaker connections, such provisions are imperative in the speech area. Liberal spacing of microphone in-puts in the ceiling and along the walls promotes easy and unobtrusive recording of speeches, oral readings, discussions, debates and radio plays.[6]

Most teachers feel that a chart rack, a movable blackboard, and a bulletin board are also essential. It is also necessary to have, either in the room or nearby, storage facilities for such items as stage lights, makeup, audiovisual equipment, and other supplies.

Equipment. Modern speech teaching makes essential the following equipment: a good portable tape recorder, a phonograph, a public-address system, a radio, and a television set. Also extremely useful in teaching speech communication is the videotape recorder. Particularly are these required in oral activities, recording performances, playing records, and viewing and listening to radio and television programs, if training is to be functional and realistic. The teacher must have, in addition, an adequate supply of tapes and a carefully selected library of recorded readings and speeches. It is also extremely helpful to have recorded outstanding examples of student work.

If at all possible the teacher should have a stop watch (although sometimes an ordinary kitchen timer will suffice) to time speeches, readings, and radio programs. The effective speaker should always be aware of the necessity of staying within time limits.

The specialized courses, such as speech correction, radio and television, and dramatics, require highly specialized types of space and specifically designed equipment. Play production in a gymnasium is extremely difficult. Scenery, costumes, spotlights, and makeup are minimum essentials. Radio and television programs cannot be produced in just any room—an improvised studio is a must.

[6] Paul H. Boase and Donald R. Glancy, "And Gladly Will They Learn, and Gladly Teach," *Speech Teacher*, November, 1966, 15:268–269.

PROFESSIONAL AFFILIATIONS

Because educational theory, methods, and practices are changing rapidly, it behooves the good teacher to make every effort to keep current with the new developments and equipment. After finishing collegiate training the teacher may, of course, participate in in-service training, workshops, short courses, and an occasional summer session or sabbatical leave at a major institution. The more ambitious person will want to pursue a graduate degree. But to stay professionally alive from day to day the alert teacher participates in one or more professional associations and reads several professional journals.

A good association has much to offer to a teacher. It will maintain an active national office staffed by competent professional administrators, publish one or more professional journals and directories, distribute professional literature, operate a teacher placement service, hold an annual convention and perhaps some workshops, establish liaison with other professional groups, represent the members at public hearings, establish standards, and encourage professional competency. These services are important to a discipline and its members.

Available to the teacher of speech communication are numerous national, regional, and state associations devoted primarily to the discipline (for up-to-date lists and addresses see annual *Directory of Speech Communication Association*). In addition the several honorary societies function as service and recognition groups (for list and description see *The Speech Teacher*, November, 1968, 18: 346–348).

Selected Major Associations

American Educational Theatre
  Association
815 17th Street N.W.
Washington, D.C. 20006

American Forensic Association
Dan P. Millar, Executive Secretary
Department of Speech
Bowling Green State University
Bowling Green, Ohio 43402

American Speech and Hearing
  Association
9030 Old Georgetown Road
Washington, D.C. 20014

Association for Professional
  Broadcast Education

1771 North Street N.W.
Washington, D.C. 20036

National Association of Educational
  Broadcasters
1346 Connecticut Avenue
Washington, D.C. 20036

Speech Communication Association
Statler Hilton Hotel
New York, New York 10001

International Communication
  Association
Michael Sineoff, Executive Secretary
Ohio University
Athens, Ohio 45701

Regional Associations

Central States Speech Association
Southern Speech Communication
  Association

Speech Association of the Eastern
  States
Western Speech Association

Honorary Organizations

Alpha Epsilon Rho
  (radio and television)
Alpha Psi Omega
  (dramatics)
Delta Psi Omega
  (dramatics)
Delta Sigma-Rho-Tau Kappa Alpha
  (forensics)
International Thespian Society
  (dramatic arts in high school)
National Collegiate Players
  (theatre arts)
National Forensic League
  (forensic society for high school
  students)

Phi Beta
  (for collegiate women studying in
  the fields of music or speech)
Phi Rho Pi
  (forensics for junior colleges)
Pi Kappa Delta
  (forensics)
Sigma Alpha Eta
  (speech pathology and audiology)
Sigma Epsilon
  (speech education)
Theta Alpha Phi
  (dramatics)
Zeta Phi Eta
  (for professional women in field of
  speech)

Selected Journals in Speech Communication and Related Fields[7]

The Afro-Asian Theatre Bulletin
  (AETA)
American Speech
Bibliographic Annual in Speech
  Communication (SCA)
Central States Speech Journal
  (CSSA)
Classical Journal
The Drama Review
Educational Broadcasting Review
  (NAEB)
Educational Theatre Journal
  (AETA)
Elementary English (NCTE)
ETC (ISGS)
The Forensic (PKD)
Journal of the American Forensic
  Association (AFA)
Journal of Black Studies
Journal of Broadcasting (APBE)
Journal of Communication (ICA)
Journal of Communication Disorders
Journal of English as a Second
  Language (ALI)

Journal of Speech and Hearing
  Disorders (ASHA)
Journal of the U.S. Institute for
  Theatre Technology (USITT)
Journal of the University Film
  Association
Language and Language Behavior
  Abstracts
The Latin American Theatre Review
  (AETA)
Players Magazine
Philosophy and Rhetoric
Publication of the Modern Language
  Association (MLA)
The Quarterly Journal of Speech
  (SCA)
The Southern Speech Journal
  (SSCA)
Speaker and Gavel (DSR-TKA)
Speech Monographs (SCA)
The Speech Teacher (SCA)
TESOL Quarterly (TESOL)
Theatre Documentation (TLA)
Today's Speech (SAES)
Western Speech (WSA)

7 See SCA Annual Directory for addresses of editors.

EXERCISES

1. Questions for discussion:
   a. Should teachers of speech have a code of ethics similar to that of doctors? What items should be covered in such a code?
   b. How should speech fit into a liberal or general education? Are there courses offered by departments of speech that are inconsistent with goals of liberal arts?
   c. How does the teaching of speech differ from other subjects in the curriculum of a high school and of a college? In method and subject matter? To what subjects is it similar?
   d. Should the superior student take speech communication? What should the speech teacher say to the guidance counselor who argues that speech is not challenging enough for the bright student?
   e. What should be the reaction of the speech communication teacher to having only the slower students directed to the speech communication class?
2. Prepare a chart in which you classify all the courses in speech under the seven headings given on pp. 3–4 (for a list of courses consult several college catalogs). In case you find subject titles that do not fit under any of the seven given, list additional categories. For example, see W. Arthur Cable, "The Field of Speech," *Quarterly Journal of Speech*, June, 1930, 16: 342–343. How does your chart differ from the one Cable prepared in 1930? What new subjects have come into the curriculum since that date? Be prepared to defend your classification.
3. Discuss speech communication as a behavioral science. How would a course taught as a behavioral science differ from one taught as a liberal art?
4. Prepare a written analysis of a good teacher you have had (a speech teacher, if possible). Consider the following:
   a. How he aroused interest in his subject.
   b. His motivational techniques.
   c. His philosophy of teaching.
   d. His handling of routine class matters, assignments, discipline.
   e. What was unique about his methods?
5. Discuss how and why speech training is important in various lines of endeavor: scientists, doctors, lawyers, engineers, housewives, secretaries, farmers, teachers, factory foreman, shop stewards, etc. Each member of the class may select one and interview a representative to get first-hand information. Report your findings in not more than 10 minutes.
6. Investigate the various state requirements for teacher certification. Also investigate the requirements for certification for a speech correctionist.
7. Assignment in learning about prominent personalities in the field: Prepare a 3-minute report on a leading figure in speech education. Each member of the class should select a different person. For information consult the leading speech publications as well as biographical sources. Below are several suggestions.
   a. Ancient world: Aristotle, Corax, Cicero, Gorgias, Isocrates, Longinus, Ptah-Hotep, Protagoras, Plato, and Quintilian.
   b. England: Hugh Blair, Francis Bacon, George Campbell, Thomas Sheridan, Richard Whately, and Thomas Wilson.
   c. United States, prior to 1900: John Quincy Adams, Edward T. Channing, Chauncey Goodrich, John Witherspoon, Ebenezer Potter, and James Rush.
   d. United States, early twentieth century: George Pierce Baker, Charles Woolbert, James O'Neill, Solomon Henry Clark, A. E. Phillips, and James A. Winans.
   e. United States, contemporary: Bower Aly, J. Jeffery Auer, A. Craig Baird, Gladys Borchers, W. Norwood Brigance, Lionel Crocker, A. M. Drummond, G. W. Gray,

Kenneth Hance, Hubert Heffner, Franklin Knower, Wendell Johnson, James Mc-Burney, Alan Monroe, Elwood Murray, Wayland Maxfield Parrish, Loren Reid, Karl Wallace, Andrew Weaver, C. M. Wise, and Frank Whiting.

REFERENCES

Books of Speech Methods

BALCER, CHARLES L. AND SEABURY, HUGH F., *Teaching Speech in Today's Secondary Schools*, New York: Holt, Rinehart & Winston, 1965.

BROOKS, KEITH (ED.), *The Communicative Arts and Sciences*, Columbus, Ohio: Charles E. Merrill, 1967.

ECROYD, DONALD H., *Speech in the Classroom*, Englewood Cliffs, N.J.: Prentice-Hall, 1969.

FESSENDEN, SETH A., JOHNSON, ROY IVAN, LARSON, P. MERVILLE, AND GOOD, KAYE M., *Speech for the Creative Teacher*, Dubuque, Ia.: William C. Brown, 1968.

HUCKLEBERRY, ALAN W. AND STROTHER, EDWARD T., *Speech Education for the Elementary Teacher*, Boston: Allyn & Bacon, 1966.

LEWIS, GEORGE L., EVERETT, RUSSELL I., GIBSON, JAMES W., AND SCHOEN, KATHRYN T., *Teaching Speech*, Columbus, Ohio: Charles E. Merrill, 1969.

NELSON, OLIVER W. AND LARUSSO, DOMINIC A., *Oral Communication in the Secondary School Classroom*, Englewood Cliffs, N.J.: Prentice–Hall, 1970.

OGILVIE, MARDEL, *Teaching Speech in the High School: Principles and Practices*, New York: Appleton-Century-Crofts, 1961.

PHILLIPS, GERALD M., et al., *The Development of Oral Communication in the Classroom*, New York and Indianapolis: Bobbs-Merrill, 1970.

REID, LOREN, *Teaching Speech*, New York: McGraw-Hill, 1971.

REID, RONALD (ED.), *Introduction to the Field of Speech*, Glenview, Ill.: Scott, Foresman, 1965.

ROBINSON, KARL F. AND KERIKAS, E. J., *Teaching Speech: Methods and Materials*, New York: McKay, 1963.

Teacher's Guide to High School, Indiana State Department of Public Instruction, 1966. (Available from Speech Communication Association.)

A Philosophy of Speech Communication

AUER, J. JEFFERY, "Speech Is a Social Force," *NEA Journal*, November, 1960, 49:21.

BASKERVILLE, BARNET, "I Teach Speech," *AAUP Bulletin*, Spring, 1959, 49:58–69.

BRADEN, WALDO W., "Teachers of Speech as Communicators," *Speech Teacher*, March, 1966, 15:91–98.

BRADEN, WALDO W., "An Uncommon Profession," *Southern Speech Journal*, Fall, 1970, 36:1–10.

GUNDERSON, ROBERT, "In Behalf of Rhetoric," *NEA Journal*, January, 1963, 52:12–13.

HARSHBARGER, H. CLAY, "Our Common Bond: Rhetoric and Poetics," *Speech Teacher*, March, 1969, 18:91–98.

HOSTETTLER, GORDON F., "Speech as a Liberal Study," In Goodwin F. Berquist, Jr. (ed.), *Speeches for Illustration and Example*, Glenview, Ill.: Scott, Foresman, 1965.

MC LAUGHLIN, TED J., "The Responsibility of Speech Departments in a Time of Revolt," *Speech Teacher*, January, 1967, 16:51–55.

REID, LOREN, "The Discipline of Speech," *Speech Teacher*, January, 1967, 16:1–10.

WALLACE, KARL R., "More than We Can Teach," *Speech Teacher*, March, 1957, 6:95–102.

WALLACE, KARL R., SMITH, DONALD K., AND WEAVER, ANDREW T., "The Field of Speech: Its Purposes and Scopes in Education," *Speech Teacher*, November, 1963, 12:331–335.

YEOMANS, G. ALLAN, "Speech Education: A Terrible Responsibility," *Vital Speeches of the Day*, March 15, 1964, 30:348–352.

YEOMANS, G. ALLAN, "Why Major in Speech?" *Vital Speeches of the Day*, March 1, 1967, 33:303–305.

Great Teachers of Speech Communication[8]

Babcock, Maud May

BABCOCK, MAUD MAY, "Teaching Interpretation," *Quarterly Journal of Public Speaking*, July, 1915, 1:173–176.

SMITH, JOSEPH F., "Maud May Babcock, 1867–1954," *Speech Teacher*, March, 1962, 11:105–107.

SMITH, JOSEPH F., "Maud May Babcock," *Speech Teacher*, November, 1962, 11:304–307.

Baird, Albert Craig

BAIRD, ALBERT CRAIG, "Responsibilities of Free Communication: The Quality of Our Political Discourse," *Vital Speeches of the Day*, September 1, 1952, 18:699–701.

HITCHCOCK, ORVILLE A., "Albert Craig Baird," in Loren Reid (ed.), *American Public Address*, Columbia, Mo.: University of Missouri Press, 1961, pp. xi–xix.

MITCHELL, ANNE G., "A. Craig Baird, Editor and Teacher," *Speech Teacher*, January, 1969, 18:1–8.

Baker, George Pierce

BAKER, GEORGE PIERCE, "The 47 Workshop," *Quarterly Journal of Speech Education*, May, 1919, 5:185–195.

DEVRIES, DONNA, "George Pierce Baker," *Western Speech*, Winter, 1959, 23:24–26.

Bassett, Lee Emerson

BASSETT, LEE EMERSON, "From Doghouse to Doctorate," *Western Speech*, March, 1951, 15:11–18.

BASSETT, LEE EMERSON, "Speech in the West, 1949: Elocution Then, Oral Interpretation Now," *Western Speech*, March, 1949, 13:3–8.

BLATTNER, HELENE, "Lee Emerson Bassett," *Western Speech*, Spring, 1961, 25:101–102.

MOUAT, LAWRENCE H., "Lee Emerson Bassett," *Speech Teacher*, November, 1962, 11:299–302.

Borchers, Gladys L.

BORCHERS, GLADYS L. "Speech Education: An Overview: Philosophy, Objective, Content," in Keith Brooks (ed.), *The Communicative Arts and Sciences of Speech*, Columbus, Ohio: Merrill, 1967, pp. 512–521.

---

[8] We can learn much from a study of the great teachers of the past. The list given below is confined to persons who have made significant contributions during the present century. Several are founders of the Speech Association of America. Many of them wrote significant textbooks and had wide influence on speech education. In each case a significant article by the person is included first. Many other persons could be included, but are not because biographical articles on them are not readily available. All on the present list are retired or deceased.

WEAVER, ANDREW THOMAS, "Gladys L. Borchers: Teacher of Speech," *Speech Teacher*, January, 1964, 13:1–5.

Brigance, William Norwood

BRIGANCE, WILLIAM NORWOOD, " 'Good' People, and Teachers of Speech," *Speech Teacher*, September, 1952, 1:157–162.
PHILLIPS, MYRON, "A Great Teacher Passes—William Norwood Brigance," *Speech Teacher*, March, 1960, 9:91–94.
TOMPKINS, PHILIP K., "W. Norwood Brigance's Advice to a Young Writer," *Central States Speech Journal*, February, 1965, 16:35–37.

Dennis, Ralph

BARRY, JAMES J., "Ralph Brownell Dennis," *Central States Speech Journal*, November, 1950, 2:1–5.
DENNIS, RALPH, "One Imperative Plus," *Quarterly Journal of Speech Education*, June, 1922, 8:218–223.
DONNER, STANLEY T., "Ralph Dennis: A Great Teacher," *Speech Teacher*, September, 1962, 11:214–220.
GILBERT, EDNA, "Ralph Dennis," *Speech Teacher*, November, 1962, 11:294–297.
RARIG, FRANK M., "Ralph Dennis," *Quarterly Journal of Speech*, April, 1943, 29:234–240.

Dolman, John, Jr.

DOLMAN, JOHN, JR., "Educational Dramatics," *Quarterly Journal of Speech Education*, April, 1921, 7:158–161.
KERSHNER, A. G., JR., "John Dolman, Jr.," *Speech Teacher*, November, 1962, 6:290–292.

Drummond, Alexander M.

CURVIN, JONATHAN, "Alexander M. Drummond," *Speech Teacher*, January, 1963, 12:10–12.
DRUMMOND, ALEXANDER M., "A Dramatist Looks at Public Speaking," *Quarterly Journal of Speech*, October, 1948, 34:342–346.
HUDSON, HOYT H., "Alexander M. Drummond," in *Studies in Speech and Drama*, Ithaca, N.Y.: Cornell University Press, 1944, pp. 3–13.

Gray, Giles W.

GRAY, GILES W., "Some Teachers and the Transition to Twentieth Century Speech Education" (Trueblood, Baker, S. H. Clark, Winans and Woolbert), in Karl Wallace (ed.), *History of Speech Education in America*, New York: Appleton-Century, Crofts, 1954, pp. 422–446.
GRAY, GILES W., "How Much Are We Dependent upon the Ancient Greeks and Romans?" *Quarterly Journal of Speech Education*, June, 1923, 9:258–279.
PETERSON, GORDON E., "Giles Wilkeson Gray," *Speech Teacher*, January, 1961, 10:10–12.

Johnson, Gertrude

JOHNSON, GERTRUDE, "Dramatic Production and the Educational Curriculum," *Quarterly Journal of Speech Education*, March, 1919, 5:156–170.
SKINNER, E. RAY, "Gertrude Johnson: Pioneer in the Oral Interpretation of Literature," *Speech Teacher*, September, 1965, 14:226–229.

O'Neill, James M.

COVELLI, EUGENE F., "James Milton O'Neill: Father of the Modern Speech Movement," *Speech Teacher*, September, 1964, 13:176–183.

O'NEILL, JAMES M. "The Professional Outlook," *Quarterly Journal of Public Speaking*, January, 1916, 2:52–63.

ROUSSEAU, LOUSENE, "Great Teachers of Speech: James Milton O'Neill," *Speech Teacher*, March, 1961, 10:95–99.

Parrish, Wayland Maxfield

HOCHMUTH, MARIE, "Great Teacher of Speech: Wayland Maxfield Parrish," *Speech Teacher*, September, 1955, 4:159–160.

MURPHY, RICHARD, "Wayland Maxfield Parrish," *Speech Teacher*, November, 1962, 11:307–310.

PARRISH, WAYLAND MAXFIELD, "The Tradition of Rhetoric," *Quarterly Journal of Speech*, December, 1947, 33:464–467.

Rarig, Frank M.

MC BRIDGE, MALCOLM R., "Great Teachers of Speech: Frank M. Rarig," *Speech Teacher*, November, 1955, 4:231–232.

RARIG, FRANK M. "Our Speech and Our Inter-personal Relations," *Quarterly Journal of Speech*, December, 1948, 34:439–444.

THOMPSON, DAVID W., "Frank M. Rarig," *Speech Teacher*, November, 1962, 11:292–294.

Ryan, John P.

REID, LOREN, "John P. Ryan's Art of Teaching," *Speech Teacher*, November, 1959, 9:288–299.

RYAN, JOHN P., "The Department of Speech at Grinnell," *Quarterly Journal of Public Speaking*, July, 1917, 3:203–209.

Trueblood, Thomas C.

MARSHMAN, JOHN T., "Fulton of Fulton and Trueblood," *Central States Speech Journal*, March, 1951, 2:46–54.

OKEY, LOREN LAMONT, "Thomas Clarkson Trueblood, Pioneer, 1856–1951," *Speech Teacher*, January, 1962, 11:10–14.

OKEY, LOREN LAMONT, "Trueblood of Fulton and Trueblood," *Central States Speech Journal*, December, 1951, 3:5–10.

TRUEBLOOD, THOMAS C., "Pioneering in Speech," *Quarterly Journal of Speech*, December, 1941, 27:503–511.

Weaver, Andrew Thomas

HABERMAN, FREDERICK, W., "Andrew Thomas Weaver," *Speech Teacher*, March, 1963, 12:85–91.

WEAVER, ANDREW THOMAS, "The Case for Speech," *Quarterly Journal of Speech*, April, 1939, 25:181–188.

WEAVER, ANDREW THOMAS, "Seventeen Who Made History: The Founders of the Association," *Quarterly Journal of Speech*, April, 1959, 45:195–199.

Wichelns, Herbert A.

HUNT, EVERETT L., "Herbert A. Wichelns and the Cornell Tradition of Rhetoric as a Humane Study," in *The Rhetorical Idiom*, Ithaca, N.Y.: Cornell University Press, 1958, pp. 1–4.

WICHELNS, HERBERT A., "Our Hidden Aims," *Quarterly Journal of Speech*, November, 1923, 9:315–323.

Winans, James A.

CROCKER, LIONEL, "The Break with Elocution: The Origin of James A. Winans' *Public Speaking*," *Today's Speech*, April, 1958, 6:23–26.
CROCKER, LIONEL, "The Evolution of *Public Speaking* by James A. Winans," *Southern Speech Journal*, September, 1942, 8:4–8.
WICHELNS, HERBERT A., "James Albert Winans," *Speech Teacher*, November, 1961, 10:259–264.
WINANS, JAMES A., "The Sense of Communication," *Southern Speech Journal*, September, 1943, 9:3–11.

Wise, Claude M.

SHAVER, CLAUDE L., "Claude M. Wise," *Southern Speech Journal*, Spring, 1969, 34:225–228.
WISE, CLAUDE M., "Departments of Speech: A Point of View," *Southern Speech Journal*, Fall, 1954, 20:1–6.
WISE, HARRY S., "C. M. Wise, a Biographical Note," *Essays in Honor of Claude M. Wise*, Sponsored by the Speech Association of America, Hannibal, Mo.: Standard Printing Co., 1970, pp. 1–2.

Woolbert, Charles Henry

NELSON, SEVERINA E., "Charles Henry Woolbert," *Speech Teacher*, November, 1962, 11:302–304.
TRAUERNICHT, MAXINE, "Woolbert as a Teacher," *Speech Teacher*, September, 1960, 9:200–206.
WEAVER, ANDREW T., "Charles Henry Woolbert," *Quarterly Journal of Speech*, February, 1930, 16:1–9.
WOOLBERT, CHARLES HENRY, "The Teaching of Speech as an Academic Discipline," *Quarterly Journal of Speech Education*, February, 1923, 9:1–18.

2. Teaching Public Speaking

Waldo W. Braden

This chapter is based on the assumption that the person who is enrolled in a speech methods class or who is seeking a new point of view is already thoroughly acquainted with *what* to teach and that his main interest is in *how* to teach. The prospective teacher who does not understand speech theory is advised first to study several basic textbooks in the field.

The effective teacher must know what he is teaching before he considers how to teach.

SOME FIRST CONSIDERATIONS

A Definition

As discussed in this chapter, *public speaking* refers to the process a speaker uses on a given occasion to communicate with an audience. Motivated by utilitarian purposes, the oral communicator seeks to gain a response from his listeners, that is, understanding, amusement, appreciation, intensification of attitudes, mental agreement, or action. Coming within his scope are definition, exposition, demonstration, eulogy, commendation, conviction, and persuasion. The subject may be taught under varying course titles: public speaking, fundamentals of public speaking, extemporaneous speaking, business speaking, speech composition, communicative speech, oral communication, effective speaking, and even oral English.

This chapter makes no attempt to discuss all the activities that might be included under these titles or in textbooks on the subject; the reader is advised to look elsewhere for suggestions concerning the teaching of conversation, discussion, debate, oral reading, radio-television speaking, and parliamentary law.

The Place of Public Speaking

The teacher should be aware of the nature of his subject and of its place in the curriculum. Usually operating in high school and college are four tendencies that affect planning and implementing courses in public speaking.

First, public speaking is generally the first speech course, or a major part of the first speech course, in which the student enrolls. Actually speechmaking is the "backbone of many courses presented under the title of fundamentals of speech."[1] James W. Gibson and his colleagues confirmed this conclusion in a nationwide survey of 564 colleges and universities. They reported that "the basic course in the vast majority of the reporting schools continues to take a public speaking or fundamentals approach, to use textbooks oriented toward public speaking, to emphasize the construction and delivery of informative and persuasive speeches. . . ."[2] A recent summary of the status of speech in the secondary schools of several widely scattered states suggests that these same conclusions apply to the high schools.[3]

Second, enrollments in public speaking courses are usually larger than in any other speech course. In many high schools it is the only course offered. In many colleges it is the bread-and-butter course to which many departments send students; they frequently come from agriculture, commerce, forestry, engineering, prelaw, premedicine, and liberal arts. Many schools require it for graduation. Consequently, it is likely to be a multisectional course taught by many different teachers.

Third, public speaking is frequently the only speech course the majority of enrollees will take. As a terminal course, it provides them with their sole opportunity to develop wholesome speech attitudes, to gain an understanding of speech principles, and to master essential oral skills. On the basis of what is accomplished within this single course, the teacher and the department are often judged by their colleagues.

Fourth, public speaking requires mastery of the total communicative process, involving the five canons of rhetoric: invention, organization, style, memory, and delivery. Through the centuries, experience suggests that

---

1 Harry G. Barnes, "Teaching the Fundamentals of Speech at the College Level," *Speech Teacher*, November, 1954, 3:248.
2 James W. Gibson, Charles R. Gruner, William D. Brooks, and Charles R. Petrie, Jr., "The First Course in Speech: A Survey of U.S. Colleges and Universities," *Speech Teacher*, January, 1970, 19:13–20.
3 William D. Brooks, "The Status of Speech in Secondary Schools: A Summary of State Studies," *Speech Teacher*, November, 1969, 18:276–281.

concentration on any one or two of these aspects at the expense of the others results in an incomplete and meaningless knack. What obligation does this factor impose? It means the teacher must include within the course all the elements of speechmaking.

GOALS AND MATERIALS

Selecting Course Goals

A course in public speaking usually has three types of general objectives:

To instill wholesome attitudes and values concerning public speaking and its importance in a democratic society;
To teach the principles of public speaking;
To develop communicative skills or competences.

Under the development of wholesome attitudes and values the instructor should give attention to the following:

1. Appreciation of the place of public speaking in a democratic society
2. Recognition of the social responsibilities of a public speaker
3. Development of an urge to communicate
4. Understanding that proficiency in speaking comes through careful and thoughtful study of principles and their applications and practice
5. Desirability of eliminating unfavorable speech attitudes such as the following:
   a. Inferiority, social inadequacy, and fear of speaking in public.
   b. Superiority or overconfidence.
   c. Unconcern about the importance of eliminating distracting habits and mannerisms.
   d. Belief that knowledge of a topic "infers the ability to speak."
   e. Belief that public speaking is solely a means for personal gains without considering social goals.
6. The importance of freedom of speech in a democratic society

To teach the rhetorical principles, the teacher should plan the instruction to embrace essential elements of the speaking process including:

1. Finding a speech topic
2. Analyzing the subject and determining sound premises
3. Organizing a speech
4. Developing a subject, including the use of forms of support
5. Adapting speech materials to the needs and demands of the listeners and of the occasion
6. Phrasing the speech in clear, appropriate, vivid, and impressive language
7. Employing acceptable pronunciation and effective voice control
8. Using appropriate bodily activity in the communicative process
9. Gaining an understanding of how to get attention, to hold interest, to stimulate attitudes, and to elicit understanding and action
10. Training in critical listening
11. Making intelligent judgments about speeches and speakers

In the development of speech communicative skills or competences the instructor should strive to achieve the following:

1. Self-analyses resulting from criticism
2. Insight into principles through practice
3. Development of proficiency in oral communicative techniques
4. Establishment of sound speechmaking techniques

Teaching Materials and Types of Assignments

Before attempting to plan a course in public speaking the teacher should take an inventory of the following resources and materials available for teaching:

1. The textbook
2. Outside readings
3. Printed speech models
4. Recordings of speeches
5. Live speeches delivered in face-to-face situations
6. Videotapes and videotape equipment
7. Films and filmstrips
8. Other visual aids—charts, flannel board
9. Workbooks
10. Handouts—summaries, examples
11. Attitude and psychological tests
12. Study questions
13. Voice recordings
14. Self-analyses by students
15. Personal conferences
16. Listening reports
17. Research assignments
18. Classroom discussion
19. Rehearsals or speech practice before civic groups, etc., in practice or laboratory section, with recordings, with videotapes
20. Performance

The well-planned course makes use of a variety of these items to keep the presentation interesting and impelling.

PLANNING AND ARRANGING ASSIGNMENTS

In a public speaking course there are many ways to achieve the course objectives through planning exercises and ordering them. In this section we consider the following: (1) the principles approach, (2) the activities approach, (3) the inductive approach, and (4) the combination approach.

The Principles Approach

In this scheme the instructor develops each assignment around a speech principle or concept. One widely used textbook explains that it "provides information on the speaking process, purposes, and situations and practical suggestions for applying this information. The authors hope that by relating these instructions to your speaking experience in the classroom and elsewhere, you will progress toward the goal of effective speech.[4] Below are three exercises which illustrate assignments of this type.

The first example, planned for early in the course; is to help the student master simple speech organization:

Student Assignments

1. Prepare a 3- to 5-minute speech in which you explain the operation of some apparatus. Actually bring the apparatus to class for demonstration. Divide your explanation into three steps or points. Follow this procedure: after a brief introduction, give a preview of your points. As you present each point, write it on the blackboard. In your conclusion, review the points developed by pointing to them as you repeat them orally. Prepare a written outline.
2. Bring to class a full-page colored magazine advertisement in which the advertiser utilized one or two of the principles of motivation discussed in Chapters 10 and 11 in Gray and Braden's *Public Speaking, Principles and Practice*, 2nd edition (Harper & Row, 1963). Be prepared in a 5-minute report to analyze those factors for the class. Distinguish between factors used for motivation and those to capture attention. Tell why you think these factors are particularly effective or ineffective. Show how these same factors may be utilized in public speaking. Concentrate on two or three appeals.
3. Deliver a 5-minute persuasive appeal in which you attempt to move your classmates to action on some personal or community problem (donate to the Red Cross, join the Army, vote for Joe Smith, etc.). Select a specific goal well within the reach of your listeners. Organize the talk around a deductive pattern. Use at least three types of supporting material. Prepare a written outline in which you identify the type of supporting materials to be used.

Student assignment 1 gives the student the dual task of manipulating an apparatus and putting his organization in ordal form. In addition, the resulting activity should relieve tension, thereby helping to overcome stage fright.

The second assignment is planned to lead the student to a better understanding of the factors of attention and interest and the principles of motivation.

Notice that student assignment 2 requires the student to apply the principles under consideration in a wider context than that presented in the textbook. To complete the assignment, the student must do three things: First, study the assigned reading in order to know for what to look; second, apply what he has learned in attempting to select an advertisement for analysis, in attempting to isolate one or two appeals, and to determine how they may be used in a speech; third, make an oral presentation of his analysis.

The third student assignment seeks to help the student comprehend the elements of a persuasive speech. This particular problem focuses on speech organization and the use of supporting materials. This assignment requires the student to read the textbook and, in addition, to weigh his supporting

[4] Alan Monroe, *Principles and Types of Speech*, 6th ed., Glenview, Ill.: Scott, Foresman, 1967, pp. vi–vii.

materials carefully. Furthermore, the students are prepared for the speech criticism, for they know the bases on which the teacher is going to evaluate the exercise.

A course developed from this point of view embraces a progressive series of speaking assignments, graduated in difficulty. The mastery of a given principle is followed by the study of a second, a third, until the student masters all aspects of speechmaking. The assignments may be arranged in a sequence such as the following:

1. Nature of stage fright
2. Selecting a subject
3. Analyses of the audience and the occasion
4. Simple speech organization
5. Finding and using speech materials
6. Complex organization
7. Forms of support
8. Language
9. Voice and pronunciation
10. Persuasion

The Activities Approach

In this approach the teacher plans the assignment around an activity, a type of speech, or a general end. One writer explains this approach as follows: "Activities refers to speech forms such as public speaking, informal speech, discussion, and debate. In this approach, the teacher centers the work units or lessons on speech activities. The student studies speech subject matter, fundamentals, and the principles unique to each activity as a means of performing an experience."[5] Notice that this statement puts particular emphasis on the whole method of learning; it suggests that principles presented in isolation are not so meaningful as when they are viewed in the total speech situation. A course following this plan may involve the following:

1. Visual-aid speech
2. Demonstration talk
3. Speech of explanation
4. Speech of opinion
5. Eulogy
6. Good-will speech
7. Inspirational talk
8. Sales talk
9. Speeches of special occasions
10. After-dinner speech
11. Campaign speech
12. Persuasive speech
13. Radio speech
14. Manuscript speech

The Inductive Approach

Assignments may involve an experimental approach that uses many of the same methods and exercises except that it requires the student to search out the principle inductively. He is directed to seek an understanding of the principle through a careful study of speech models and the observation of speaking performances. He is motivated to ask such questions as, "Why

[5] J. W. Patterson, "The Activities Approach in the First Course," *Speech Teacher*, September, 1969, 18:223.

does the speaker succeed or not succeed?" or "What is the principle involved?" Mary Louise Gehring explains this method as follows:

Speeches—printed, recorded, or "live"—are presented to the students, who must then use their own analytical abilities to derive the rhetorical principles involved. Hopefully, this process encourages creative thinking. There is no pat formula but an individual realization of a concept. The inductive approach rarely produces "parrots," but it can result in a view of rhetoric which is little more than a hodge-podge of personal opinions. To avoid this result, the teacher must select the models carefully and guide their analysis wisely.[6]

This method is utilized in the book *Speech Practices, A Resource Book for the Student of Public Speaking*, by Braden and Gehring (Harper & Row, 1958). This book includes several speeches and speech excerpts followed by a series of questions designed to stimulate the discovery of the principle. Emphasis is not on imitation, but on active reading and listening.

To summarize, the approach makes use of many speech models, listening assignments, outside reports on other speakers, and assignments that invite the student to attempt to utilize new techniques.

The assignments given below illustrate this approach.

Student Assignments

1. Deliver a 5-minute talk on the analysis of the audience and the occasion. Analyze for your classmates how a speaker that you have heard in a face-to-face situation succeeded or failed because of good or poor adjustment. You may wish to speak on a topic similar to the following:
   a. How a poor audience analysis caused a speaker to fail
   b. How on-the-spot adjustment to the speaking situation saved the day
   c. How an unforeseen incident wrecked a speech
   d. How an inappropriate subject embarrassed a speaker
   e. How a speaker's appearance or platform deportment contributed to ineffectiveness
   f. How a speaker made a difficult subject meaningful
   g. A difficult subject that caused a speaker trouble
   h. How courage scattered a mob
   i. How a famous speaker coped with a difficult speaking situation
   j. My pet peeves about speakers
2. Evaluate for your classmates one of your own speaking experiences. You may wish to consider a topic such as one of the following:
   a. How a lack of self-confidence caused me to fail
   b. How I succeeded because of my speaking ability
   c. The day I wished for eloquence
   d. How I prepared for a speaking contest
   e. How I won (or lost) a speech contest
   f. Why I am taking this course
   g. The problem I hope to solve in this course
   h. My ideal speaker
   i. A speech I shall never forget
   j. How I talked my way out of a tight spot

[6] Mary Louise Gehring, "The Inductive Approach to Speech Models," *Speech Teacher*, January, 1967, 16:16.

3. Prepare a 10-minute report on one of the following topics or a similar one:
   a. How a famous speech was prepared
   b. How a prominent speaker prepares his speeches
   c. How poor speech preparation caused a speaker to fail
   d. A sure-fire method of speech preparation
   e. Famous speech ghost writers
   f. Ghost writing today
   g. Speech writing teams of recent presidents
4. Interview a local minister or some prominent local speaker concerning his methods of speech preparation. (Your instructor will tell you whether the results of the interview are to be submitted orally to the class or in written report.) Ask the interviewee such questions as the following:
   a. How does the speaker get ideas for speeches?
   b. Does he keep a speech material file or scrapbook?
   c. What sources has he found the best for supplying ideas and materials for speeches?
   d. What steps does he follow in preparing a speech?
   e. In his preparation, does he prepare an outline? Does he prepare a complete manuscript and memorize it?
   f. Does he rehearse it orally? Does he have anyone who acts as critic? Does he use a speech recorder in speech preparation?
   g. Does he have any advice about speech preparation to give beginning speakers?

Notice that each exercise involves the analysis of an actual performance or speech experience. In the process the student becomes a creator, an inventor, a critic through observation, analysis, and synthesis.

The Combination Approach

Seldom does a given course follow exclusively any one of the three methods. More likely the total course plan combines aspects of all three. Notice how all three are utilized in the following syllabus.

Course Outline for Semester Course

(Basic Text: Waldo W. Braden, *Public Speaking: The Essentials*, New York: Harper & Row, 1966.)
   I. Introduction
      A. Getting acquainted
         1. Speech of introduction: In 2 to 3 minutes introduce yourself to the class, giving several facts about your background and favorite activities which will help your classmates to know you.
         2. Reading assignment: Braden, Chapter 1, "Your Approach to Speech-making," pp. 1–10.
         3. Speaking assignment: In 2 to 3 minutes tell the class about your hobby or favorite pastime, encouraging members of the class to ask you questions.
         4. Reading assignment: Braden, Chapter 1, pp. 10–22.
         5. A 20-minute test on Chapter 1.
      B. Class projects
         1. Class visit to the library: To learn how to use it (if times permits).
         2. Resource inventory: The class will be divided into teams of 4 to 6

students. The goal is to take an inventory of resources available to the speaker in your community. Each team will concentrate on one of the following:

    a. Available periodicals in school and community library. Members will present 2-minute reports on unfamiliar magazines.

    b. Available newspapers (in addition to local ones). Members will make 2-minute reports on different papers. If possible, report on newspapers such as the *New York Times* or the *Christian Science Monitor*.

    c. The rating of reference works in the library. Interview librarians and consult Constance Winchell, *Guide to Reference Works*.

    d. Radio and television as source of speech materials.

3. Reading assignment: Braden, Chapter 2, "Resources for Subjects and Materials."

4. Preparation: Compile a list of 50 speech topics which you think would be appropriate for class talks. You may wish to organize your selection around topics suggested by "Sources of Speech Subjects," p. 32.

II. The Informative Speech

  A. Speech on a simple operation

    1. Speaking assignment: In 2 to 4 minutes demonstrate how to do some simple operation such as using a can opener, swinging a golf club, or doing a dance step. Divide your presentation into 2 or 3 steps. Prepare a simple outline that conforms to suggestions found in the chapter.

    2. Reading assignment: Braden, Chapter 3, "How to Organize a Speech."

    3. Class: The class will discuss the problems of preparing an outline. Several members of the class will put their outlines on the blackboard.

    4. Optional assignment: From the scrambled sentences given on p. 62 under the title of "Sharpening a Pocket Knife," prepare an outline.

  B. Speech on a machine's operation

    1. Speaking assignment: In 2 to 4 minutes explain the operation of some machine. Divide your explanation into 3 or 4 steps or points. Prepare a written outline. Follow this procedure in your speech.

      a. Give a brief introduction in which you attempt to arouse interest in your subject.

      b. Give a brief preview of the points you intend to develop.

      c. As you present each point, write it on the chalkboard.

      d. In your conclusion, review the points.

    2. Reading assignment: Braden, Chapter 4, "Mastering Your Speech."

    3. A 20-minute test over textbook.

  C. Speech on adapting to an audience

    1. Speaking assignment: Deliver a 2- to 4-minute talk on adapting a talk to the audience. Analyze for your classmates how a speaker that you have heard (if possible, in a face-to-face situation) succeeded or failed because of good or poor adjustment. You may wish to speak on a subject similar to one of the following:

      a. How a poor audience analysis caused a speaker to fail.

      b. How on-the-spot adjustment to the speaking situation saved the day.

      c. How an unforeseen incident wrecked a speech.
      d. How an inappropriate subject embarrassed a speaker.
      e. How "talking down" to an audience caused a speaker to fail.
      f. How a speaker used "the facts of interest" to win an audience.
  2. Reading assignment: Braden, Chapter 5, "Selling Yourself to Your Listeners."
  3. A 20-minute test over textbook.
D. Speech on communication without words
  1. Speaking assignment: Demonstrate how to communicate without words. You may wish to do one of the following:
      a. Act out a message for your classmates.
      b. Demonstrate in pantomime correct and incorrect platform habits.
      c. Give several hand signals that are commonly recognized.
      d. With 2 or 3 other students act out, without words, a message.
      e. Convey the thought of a well-known saying by gestures.
  2. Reading assignment: Braden, Chapter 6, "Effective Delivery," pp. 109–118.
E. Speech on a current event
  1. Speaking assignment: Present a 1- to 2-minute current event. This speech will be recorded for study and analysis.
  2. Reading assignment: Braden, Chapter 6, "Effective Delivery," pp. 119–127.
  3. Class: Each student will evaluate his own recording. Each will also ask a classmate to make a similar evaluation of the recording.
  4. Class discussion: The class will consider the topics "What is good voice quality?" and "What can a student do to improve his voice quality?" In addition, the instructor will discuss substandard pronunciation and point out words with which the class members have difficulty.
F. Speech for clarity
  1. Speaking assignment: Present a 3- to 5-minute informative speech in which you make use of the blackboard or a chart. Remember that the goal is to be *clear*. Prepare a written outline.
  2. Reading assignment: Braden, Chapter 9, "How to Be Clear."
  3. Class: Class members will be encouraged to ask questions at the end of each speech. (See Braden, pp. 185–190.) Each member of the class is to write in not less than 200 words an evaluation of his feedback.
  4. A 20-minute test over textbook.
G. Speech on an extended example
  1. Speaking assignment: Present a 3- to 5-minute speech built around an extended example, that is, phrase a central thought or proposition and then tell a story or give a single instance to develop it. (See Braden, speaking assignment numbers 1 and 2, pp. 165–166.) Attempt to apply one of the following techniques:
      a. Find a new and different approach (see Braden, pp. 150–152).
      b. Dramatize what you say (see Braden, pp. 157–160).
      c. Keep your listeners guessing (see Braden, pp. 160–161).
      d. Use humor to create and hold interest (pp. 161–163).
  2. Reading assignment: Braden, Chapter 8, "How to Be Interesting."
H. Speech on a sales talk
  1. Speaking Assignment: Deliver a 3- to 5-minute sales talk. Be sure to

make use of the motives found in Braden, pp. 211–213 of text. Prepare a written outline.
2. Class: The class members will make a list of motives used in each
speech.
3. Reading assignment: Braden, Chapter 9, "How to Be Clear."
4. Class: Class members will be encouraged to ask questions at the end
of each speech (see Braden, pp. 185–190). Each member of the
class is to write in not less than 200 words an evaluation of his feedback.
4. A 20-minute test over textbook.
I. Speech on a selected topic
1. Speaking assignment: A class committee of 3 will prepare a list of 30
topics on the general theme selected by the class. Each topic will be
phrased in question form. In class each member of the class will be
permitted to draw 3 topics when his turn to speak comes. He will
put 2 back into the receptacle and speak on the third for not more
than 3 minutes.
2. Reading assignment: Braden, review pp. 52–61 and Chapter 10,
"How to Be Persuasive," pp. 194–202.
3. Optional assignment: The instructor will prepare a list of topics
based upon the subjects discussed in the local newspaper during
the previous week.
J. A formal address
1. Speaking assignment: Deliver a 5-minute (750 words) manuscript
formal address. This speech is to be carefully written and polished.
You may either read the speech from manuscript or deliver it from
memory. The delivery is to be polished.
2. Reading assignment: Braden, Chapter 10, "How to Be Persuasive,"
pp. 203–216.
III. Evaluation
A. Speech evaluation
1. Class: Each member of the class will evaluate one of the speech
models found in Braden, pp. 223–243. You may be asked to evaluate
it in a theme in terms of the previous chapters or you may present
a 5-minute oral appraisal.
2. Reading assignment: Braden, pp. 223–243.
B. Review
C. Final written examination

SUPPLEMENTING ACTIVITIES

The Common Materials Approach

The common materials approach to teaching speech is a method which
centers speaking performances of a class on a single theme or subject. It is
known by such other labels as case study, controlled materials, selected
issues, great issues, or controlled research method.

A class using this approach may unfold in two ways. First, the students
may make use of a book of readings or source materials in addition to the

regular textbook. Two such books are Herbert W. Hildebrandt's *Issues of Our Times: A Summon to Speak* (Macmillan, 1963) and Paul D. Brandes and Theodore J. Walwick's *A Research Manual for the Performances Course in Speech* (Harper & Row, 1966). These books are collections of miscellaneous materials including speeches, letters, diaries, essays, and reports. The student uses the source book in preparing his speeches or he may turn to the bibliography for suggestions of further readings.

A second approach is to have all students in a class pursue a common theme, such as freedom of speech, civil rights, or black rhetoric. The class may concentrate its study around a paperbound casebook, organized around a central topic. Some examples are the following:

BOASE, PAUL H., *The Rhetoric of Christian Socialism*, New York: Random House, 1969.
BOSMAJIAN, HAIG A. AND BOSMAJIAN, HAMIDA, *The Rhetoric of the Civil Rights Movement*, New York: Random House, 1969.
HAIMAN, FRANKLYN S., *Freedom of Speech, Issues and Cases*, New York: Random House, 1968.
JOHANNESEN, RICHARD L., *Ethics and Persuasion, Selected Readings*, New York: Random House, 1968.
LOMAS, CHARLES W., *The Agitator in American Society*, Englewood Cliffs, N.J.: Prentice-Hall, 1968.
PENNYBACKER, JOHN H. AND BRADEN, WALDO W., *Broadcasting and the Public Interest*, New York: Random House, 1969.

After selecting a subject the group assembles a bibliography and devotes all assignments to exploration of the topic. Sometimes a class may be divided into three or four subgroups with each pursuing a different topic. The instructor may choose to use this method for only a portion of the semester.

The objectives of the method are as follows:

1. The student is forced to consider more challenging material.
2. The student does more extensive research since he devotes several assignments to one theme.
3. The limited material permits the instructor to check the student's analysis and documentation more carefully.
4. The teacher can prevent plagiarism and careless analyses.
5. The student can be better indoctrinated with reference to such subjects as free speech.

This method may be used in the discussion, debate, persuasion, or interpretative reading course.

The Use of Speech Models and Examples

One good way to enrich a course in speech communication is through the study of speech models and examples which may include the great eloquence of the past, the speeches of classmates, those delivered in the public forum, and those published in such publications as the bimonthly magazine *Vital Speeches of the Day* or in *Representative American Speeches* (H. W. Wilson). The Greeks and Romans found this method of instruction effective. Saint Augustine declared that he "would rather send a student to read and listen to and exercise himself in imitating eloquent men" than to send him to teachers of rhetoric. Today, of course, a wide variety of material exists to assist the teacher in locating and using speech models.

The study of a speech model or example supplements the presentation of theory and development of skills and adds a liberal flavor to the learning process. A. Craig Baird, eminent educator, has explained this influence as follows:

What are these liberal objectives which speech courses should support . . . Behind the immediate patterns of training in communicative techniques lies the student's increasing understanding of knowledge and of his intellectual heritage. Central in his academic experience should be his insight into the historic records and into those of his day in the library, laboratories, lecture halls, and elsewhere. Such vistas of knowledge and ideas should lead, in theory at least, to his adaptation to the spirit of inherited wisdom and his impulse to help transmit and further illuminate these permanent values. This student on his way to liberal education is challenged to further exploration of a given field or problem, and so he enters into a wider perspective of related subject matter areas. His readings, discussions, essays, and intellectual reaction to all that he hears and absorbs should lead to his creative as well as reproductive contributions. His intellectual competency should be more and more marked by logical, aesthetic, social, and ethical qualities. His liberal character is humane as well as scientific. Something of a philosophic cast begins to emerge. His view of a better world, for example, guides him toward advocacy of intellectual and political freedom, equality of opportunity for all, and similar tenets of Western Civilization. His training in theory at least, begins to fit him "to perform justly and magnanimously all the offices both private and public in Peace and War."[7]

The advantages of studying the speeches of others are numerous.

1. It provides a greater understanding of the theory of speech communication. An abstract principle becomes meaningful when its application is observed in speech.

2. Reading masterpieces inspires the novice to want to excel; imitation has long been a significant means of education.

3. The speeches of others are a fruitful source of ideas and speech materials. After reading the speech of an Edmund Burke, Ralph Waldo Emerson, or Martin Luther King, the student may gain new views of his own time or find a statement that has meaning and force in his own affairs.

[7] A. Craig Baird, "Speech Models and Liberal Education," *Speech Teacher*, January, 1967, 16:11–15.

4. The study of speeches sharpens the student's ability to make critical judgments. It gives him a reference for comparison and provides him with an opportunity to observe how great minds work.

5. Because speeches reflect the times of which they are a part, their study develops an appreciation for the place of public address in a free society. Delivered at dramatic moments in history, the eloquence of Webster, Lincoln, Wilson, and F. D. Roosevelt expresses the democratic ideal in memorable words.

The teacher who builds a unit of a beginning course around the study of speech example needs to plan his presentation carefully. What he does will, of course, depend on his goal. In directing the students' study, this teacher will want to consider the following possibilities:

1. Discuss how the unit fits into the syllabus, making clear to the students the objectives.
2. Give suggestions concerning how to read or listen to and analyze a speech; that is, the minimum essentials of rhetorical criticism.
3. Discuss the background of the speech, giving attention to the historical forces that influenced the speaker and audience.
4. Analyze the immediate occasion (time and place) and the composition of the audience.
5. Provide a series of questions to help the student in finding the important points.

Some typical assignments using speech examples are the following:

Student Assignments

1. Prepare a written critique of the speech of a classmate.
2. Observe the speaking of a prominent minister, politician, or educator.
3. Write an evaluation of the strategy of a famous speech.
4. Build a speech around an important thought taken from a speech.
5. Analyze a speech and evaluate one of the following: appropriateness of the subject, the structure (organization), the language, audience adjustment, the proofs, immediate effect, and long-range influence.
6. Check the text of a speech you have heard against what is reported in the press or on television and radio.
7. Memorize and deliver a famous speech in the costume of the day.
8. Interview a well-known speaker on how he prepares a speech.

LIST OF FAMOUS SPEECHES[8]

WILLIAM JENNINGS BRYAN, "Cross of Gold," July 8, 1896.* Excellent use of emotional and ethical appeal. (3, 4, 7, 9, 10, 11, 18)

[8] These selections of famous speeches are often cited as speech models. Most of the speeches listed above are short, readily available, and interesting to students. They can be discussed within a single class period without extensive explanation of the historical background. Most of them are considered outstanding examples of eloquence. The members in parenthesis after each speech indicate where the speech can be found in the following list of collections. Each speech is available in many other places. An asterisk indicates that the speech is available in recorded form.

RUSSELL CONWELL'S "Acres of Diamonds," delivered from 1875 to 1925. Excellent use of illustrations. (2, 4)

JONATHAN EDWARDS, "Sinners in the Hands of Angry God," July 8, 1741. Interesting organization, powerful emotional appeal, excellent use of figurative language. (3, 10)

RALPH WALDO EMERSON'S "The American Scholar," August 31, 1837. Good organization, full of provocative quotations, excellent use of language. (3, 7, 10, 11)

HENRY W. GRADY'S, "The New South," December 22, 1886. Adjustment to hostile audience, excellent use of examples, effective introduction. (3, 7, 10)

PATRICK HENRY'S, "Liberty or Death," March 23, 1775.* Inductive development, dramatic use of language, strong emotional appeal. (3, 4, 7, 9, 10, 11, 18)

ROBERT G. INGERSOLL'S, "At His Brother's Grave" and "Decoration Day Address," Unusual style, rhythm, and poetic quality. (3)

MARTIN LUTHER KING'S, "I Have a Dream," August 28, 1963. Excellent use of parallel structure, rhythmic style, excellent use of emotional appeal. (9, 10, 11, 16)

ABRAHAM LINCOLN'S, "First Inaugural Address," March 4, 1861,* "Gettysburg Address," November 19, 1863, and "Second Inaugural Address," March 4, 1865.* Simple language, chronological order, simple but eloquent language, excellent for memorization. (3, 4, 7, 9, 10, 18, 19)

DOUGLAS MAC ARTHUR'S, "Old Soldiers Never Die," April 19, 1951.* Strong use of emotional and ethical appeal, excellent speech to stir discussion. (2, 4, 7, 10, 18, 17)

WENDELL PHILLIP'S, "Toussaint L'Ouverture," and "Murder of Lovejoy." Good audience adjustment, effective use of emotional appeal. (2, 3, 11)

ADLAI E. STEVENSON, "Acceptance Speech—1952," July 21, 1952. Powerful emotional appeal and excellent choice of language. (4, 7, 10, 13)

BOOKER T. WASHINGTON, "Atlantic Exposition Speech," September 18, 1895. Audience adjustment, clever use of story (see introduction). (3, 7, 10)

FRANKLIN ROOSEVELT, "The First Inaugural Address," March 4, 1932* and "Declaration of War Against Japan," December 8, 1941.* Direct and forceful style, forceful use of detail, powerful emotional appeal. (2, 4, 7, 9, 10, 15)

THEODORE ROOSEVELT, "The Man with the Muckrake," April 14, 1906. Deductive organization, for support uses specific instances, comparison, careful use of language. (3, 7, 10, 17)

WILLIAM SHAKESPEARE, Speech of Mark Anthony from play Julius Caesar. Adjustment to hostile audience. (9)

DANIEL WEBSTER, "Knapp-White Murder Case," August 20, 1830 and "Reply to Hayne," January 26–27, 1830. Graphic use of vivid detail, effective use of several types of argument, evidence, and specific methods of refutation. (3, 4, 7)

COLLECTIONS OF SPEECHES

1. ALY, BOWER AND ALY, LUCILE F., *American Short Speeches*, New York: Macmillan, 1968.

2. ALY, BOWER AND ALY, LUCILE F., *Speeches in English*, New York: Random House, 1968. Ten orators with a speech from each. A biographical sketch, explanation of speaker, and the speech, critical analyses, and suggestions for the readings are enclosed for each speaker.

3. BAIRD, A. CRAIG, *American Public Addresses, 1740–1952*, New York: McGraw-Hill, 1956. Twenty-six speakers, 38 speeches, and excellent introduction, "The Study of Speeches."

4. BENEDICT, STEWART H., *Famous American Speeches*, New York: Dell, 1967. Twenty speakers, 23 speeches in inexpensive paperback.

5. BRADEN, WALDO W. AND GEHRING, MARY LOUISE, *Speech Practices: A Resource Book for Student of Public Speaking*, New York: Harper & Row, 1958. Contains many excerpts from famous speakers as well as students. Study questions designed to draw out recognition of rhetorical principle.
6. BRANDT, CARL G. AND SHAFTER, EDWARD M., JR., *Selected American Speeches on Basic Issues, 1850–1950*, Boston: Houghton Mifflin, 1960.
7. CAPP, GLENN R., *Famous Speeches in American History*, New York and Indianapolis: Bobbs-Merrill, 1963. Fourteen speakers, 18 speeches with excellent discussion on speaker, the occasion, and the speech. Includes some teaching aids.
8. GRAHAM, JOHN, *Great American Speeches*, New York: Appleton-Century-Crofts, 1970. Twenty-four speeches from 24 speakers (those recorded in Caedmon Series, see #18 below) and several critical essays.
9. HIBBITT, GEORGE, *The Dolphin Book of Speeches*, New York: Doubleday, 1965. Inexpensive paperback with over 60 speeches ranging from those of Socrates to John F. Kennedy.
10. LINSLEY, WILLIAM A., *Speech Criticism: Methods and Materials*, Dubuque, Ia.: William C. Brown, 1968. Seven essays on rhetorical criticism and 31 speeches.
11. OLIVER, ROBERT T. AND WHITE, EUGENE E., *Selected Speeches from American History*, Boston: Allyn and Bacon, 1969. Twenty-two speakers with a speech from each. Includes excellent introductory chapter on study of speeches as well as provocative study materials.
12. PETERSON, HOUSTON, *A Treasury of the World's Great Speeches*, New York: Simon and Schuster, 1954. One hundred twenty-five speakers and 160 speeches and parts of speeches from Moses to Eisenhower.

RECORDED SPEECHES

13. *Adlai Stevenson, the Man, the Candidate, the Statesman* (Macmillan).
14. *Churchill in His Own Voice and Voices of His Contemporaries* (Caedmon Records).
15. *F.D.R. Speaks, Authorized Edition of Speeches, 1938 to 1945.* (Washington Records, W-FDR).
16. *Freedom March on Washington, August 28, 1963* (20th Century-Fox Records, TFM 3110).
17. *General Douglas MacArthur Address Before Congress, April 19, 1951.* "Old Soldiers Never Die" (CMS Records).
18. *Great American Speeches*, Caedmon, Vol. I, 1775–1886 (TC 2016); Vol. II, 1898–1918 (TC 2031); Vol. III, 1931–1947 (TC 2033); Vol. IV, 1950–1963 (TC 2035).
19. *Raymond Massey Reads the Writings and Speeches of Abraham Lincoln* (Living Literature).

Impromptu Speaking

The proficient speaker must be able to respond fluently when he is called upon without prior notice. Somewhere in the beginning course, perhaps during the second half of the term, the instructor should include some units upon impromptu speaking, that is, speaking without formal preparation. Many textbooks provide a simple explanation in a page or two of what the speaker should do when called upon to think upon his feet.

The best instruction comes through giving the student an assignment demanding an impromptu talk. In this unit the instructor can do his best teaching through his criticism. He may choose to give group critiques, instead of focusing upon an individual.

Below are several assignments which provide realistic impromptu situations.

Student Assignments

1. Prior to class the teacher places a list of topics on the blackboard. The students are permitted to select one topic and speak upon it.
2. The "bag of tricks":[9] The teacher places in a sack or closed receptacle a number of simple objects: toy, dog, spoon, knife, rock, toy bell, newspaper clipping, etc. The student draws an object and talks about it, or he may tell a story about it.
3. Current events or Russian roulette: The class is told that topics will be framed from lead stories in three or four days of newspapers (give name of paper). Topics are put on strips of paper, placed face down on table in classroom. The student has an opportunity to draw three topics, one at a time. If he chooses, he may speak upon the first or return it to the table. He has the same option for the second, but if he returns it, he must speak upon the third topic.
4. Student topics: Students frame the topics, which are placed on the table. The student speaker draws three, selects one, and speaks upon it.
5. Extemporaneous impromptu speaking assignment:
   a. Selecting a subject for the unit. As a class you are to select a general proposition similar to the intercollegiate debate question or some other broad subject such as capital punishment, socialized medicine, or relations with China. The topic should be worded in the form of a proposition and partiitioned carefully.
   b. Extemporaneous speaking phase. The class will be divided into groups of 5 or 6; each group will be assigned a phase of the proposition and on an assigned day will conduct a symposium with each member delivering a 5-minute speech on some limited aspect. Following the formal speeches the discussion will be opened to questions from the floor.
   c. Impromptu speaking phase. After each group has presented its phase, the instructor (or a class committee) will prepare a list of topics for impromptu speaking. When your turn comes, your instructor will give you a topic to discuss. At the close of your speech you will be expected to answer questions from the floor.
   d. Group evaluation. After each member of the class has delivered an impromptu speech, each member will be asked to rank his classmates in a rank order, listing them from the student who has been the most effective to the least effective in the two assignments. Ranks can be averaged by a class committee to determine final rating.
6. The Hendrix system:[10]
   It is important that the topics not be so specific as to require detailed supporting materials. Each topic should be prepared on a separate slip of paper.
   Phase two of the impromptu assignment is the distribution of the topics to the students. . . . The topics may be stockpiled in a large envelope placed on a classroom desk in front of the class or out in the hall. The first speaker is called

[9] Lynne S. Gross, "Creative Speaking from a 'Bag of Tricks,'" *Speech Teacher*, January, 1970, 19:76–77.
[10] J. A. Hendrix, "The Impromptu Classroom Speech," *Speech Teacher*, November, 1968, 17:334–335.

to this "preparation desk" for a few minutes of preparation while the teacher is giving instructions for the assignment. When the teacher has finished, the first speaker rises to deliver his impromptu speech. Before he begins to speak, however, the second speaker takes his place at the preparation desk and may use all the time taken by the first speech to select his topic and prepare his own speech. With a 2- to 3-minute time limit on all speeches, this procedure insures roughly equal preparation time for all students.

7. The geometric form: Professor Thomas R. King explains this procedure as follows:

The teacher prepares for the lesson by drawing on 4 × 6 or 5 × 8 index cards a number of geometric figures. . . .

To start the period the teacher asks his students to get out pencils and paper. He then places one of the cards on the rostrum and asks one of the students to tell the rest of the class how to draw the figure on the card. The speaker tries to get each class member to draw a figure that is exactly the same size and shape as the one on the card. The only limitations on the speaker are that he must not pick up the card and show the figure to the audience or draw the figure on the chalk board. The speaker may use gestures if he wants to and identify the figures by any labels from geometry which he wishes to use. The audience may not talk back to the speaker or show him what they have drawn. When each speaker finishes, the teacher compares for all to see the original figure and drawings by class members.[11]

Listening

Teaching of listening in the beginning speech communication course is a little like talking about the weather. Many persons talk about the subject, but too few have come up with practical suggestions about how to improve it in the classroom.[12] The subject has been called to the attention of speech teachers[13] largely through the efforts since 1948 of Professor Ralph G. Nichols of the University of Minnesota. Most of the textbooks directly or indirectly quote him concerning the nature and problems associated with this complex process. There seems to be little point of repeating here the principles of listening, already discussed adequately elsewhere.[14] Instead the focus is upon how to teach this skill.

Lewis and Nichols suggest that "the best approach to classroom training in listening appears to be through a coordination of listening and speech instruction. In schools where no immediate opportunity exists to institute a course labeled "listening," the next best alternative has frequently seemed

[11] Thomas R. King, "An Inductive Opening Exercise," *Speech Teacher*, January, 1969, 18:21–22.

[12] Sam Duker, *Listening Bibliography*, Metuchen, N.J.: Scarecrow Press, 1964. Annotated list of 880 articles.

[13] Nichols' articles are too numerous to mention. See especially Ralph G. Nichols and Leonard A. Stevens, *Are You Listening?* New York: McGraw-Hill, 1957; Ralph G. Nichols, "Do We Know How to Listen? Practical Helps in a Modern Age," *Speech Teacher*, March, 1961, 10:118–124. Also reprinted in (J. Jeffery Auer, ed.), *The Rhetoric of Our Times*, New York: Appleton-Century-Crofts, 1969, pp. 227–236.

[14] Seth A. Fessenden, *et al.*, *Speech for the Creative Teacher*, Dubuque, Ia.: William C. Brown, 1968, chap. 10, "Toward Better Listening"; Giles W. Gray and Waldo W. Braden, *Public Speaking, Principles and Types*, 2nd ed., New York: Harper & Row, 1963, chap. 7, "Listening."

to be the dovetailing of listening assignments into routines already established in speech classes."[15]

Substantial evidence has been accumulated to show that to improve listening the teacher must motivate the student and then provide positive reinforcement to improve listening. Enrolling in a speech class in which the student may evaluate speeches is not enough. Neither are talking and reading about the subject, although a necessary first step, sufficient for improvement. Reading the chapter in the textbooks, hearing a record or videotape on the subject, or exchanging views on "who are the good listeners" will not turn what Nichols calls "bad listeners" into "good listeners."

Recently in attempting to learn more about how to teach listening Johnson and Richardson conducted a meanful experiment at Auburn University. The procedures that they found successful in improving the listening scores on the *Brown-Carlsen Listening Comprehension Test* suggest two methods that can be adapted to the speech communication class.[16]

The first method, which they call "a lecture method of listening training and practices," employed six 10-minute lectures on tape. These were administered one per week for six consecutive weeks. The first one discussed listening techniques and the remaining five comprised practice material based upon speech theory. Some teachers might have stopped with the playing of the tapes, but Johnson and Richardson, eager to provide positive reinforcement, followed each lecture with a 10-item multiple choice test which was graded, counted as a part of the course grade, and returned to the student at the next period. In other words, they incorporated (1) theory, (2) practice, and (3) *immediate* reinforcement.

The second method which Johnson and Richardson termed "a listener-oriented method of speaker evaluation" is equally applicable to the classroom situation. For each assigned speech the student speaker was required to prepare 5 to 10 questions requiring short answers. After the scheduled speeches were delivered on a given day, the instructor administered a test over only one of the speeches. But not knowing which one would be chosen, the students were encouraged to listen more carefully to all speeches. To provide the necessary immediate reinforcement, the quizzes were graded, counted as a part of the course grade, and returned to the students at the next class period.

Johnson and Richardson found little difference in the two methods; each produced about the same results. However, they demonstrated in developing listening skills that the two methods were far superior to the

[15] Thomas R. Lewis and Ralph G. Nichols, *Speaking and Listening*, Dubuque, Ia.: William C. Brown, 1965, p. 7.
[16] Martha Johnson and Don Richardson, "Listening Training in the Fundamentals of Speech Class," *Speech Teacher*, November, 1968, 17:293–296.

method followed in the usual speech class of having and evaluating speeches.

To summarize, it seems that to integrate listening into a course, it should incorporate (1) motivation, (2) an understanding of theory, (3) forced practice, and (4) reinforcement (grades and rewards). The resourceful teacher can easily fit assignments similar to those of Johnson and Richardson into the typical syllabus for the first course.

Teachers interested in testing the listening abilities of their students should become familiar with the STEP listening test (Princeton, N.J., Educational Testing Service, 1957), the Brown-Carlsen Listening Comprehension Test (Harcourt Brace Jovanovich, 1965). The latter purports to measure immediate recall, following directions, recognizing transitions, recognizing word meaning, and lecture comprehension. The availability of alternate forms of this test make possible pre and post testing. Although questions have been raised concerning whether this test embraces all the factors of this complex skill (or skills),[17] it has been the more widely used and the most readily available instrument for evaluating listening.

EXERCISES

1. Prepare a complete syllabus for a beginning semester course in speech communication for either a high school or college class. Plan it for a group of 20 students. Include specific speaking and reading assignments. You may use a single or a multi-book approach. Also prepare midsemester and final examination questions.
2. Prepare a syllabus for a unit in speechmaking to be included in a fundamentals course or an activity course. Plan it for a class of 20 for no more than 6 weeks. Explain its relationship to other units of the course.
3. Observe a class in public speaking and summarize your observations in a written report. Consider the following:
   a. How the instructor makes assignments.
   b. How the instructor attempts to motivate the student to improve.
   c. The order of activities in the class.
   d. How the instructor conducts class discussion.
   e. How the instructor stimulates questions.
   f. How the instructor gives speech criticism.
4. Prepare a rating blank for evaluating the teacher of public speaking. Use a form similar to that found on p. 330.
   In less than 10 minutes explain and defend your rating blank before your methods class. In light of comments and suggestions from your classmates and teacher, revise the rating sheet.
   Use your rating sheet in evaluating a classmate who is teaching a unit on public speaking.
5. Evaluate 10 textbooks for beginning speech, using the criteria suggested in this

[17] Sam Duker and Charles R. Petrie, Jr., "What We Know About Listening: Continuation of a Controversy," *Journal of Communication*, December, 1964, 14:245–252. Also see Charles M. Kelly, "An Investigation of the Construct Validity of Two Commercially Published Listening Tests," *Speech Monographs*, June, 1965, 32:139–143.

chapter. After evaluating the 10 books, select the one you would like to use in a course in public speaking and defend your selection in not more than 1000 words.

6. Questions for discussion:
    a. Should the teacher give students a list of speech topics or should he require them to seek their own topics?
    b. Should the student have the right to determine the nature and content of the course? For example, should the instructor use only assignments that are popular with the students?
    c. How much "freedom of speech" should the student be given in the public speaking course?
    d. Should the teacher insist on the student speaker stirring up a genuine response from his classmates?
    e. Should the student be permitted to deliver classroom speeches to imaginary listeners? For example, at the beginning of a speech the student prefaces his remarks with "Now imagine that you are the board of directors of a large corporation" or "this speech was prepared for the Ladies Aid Society."
    f. Should the student be permitted to use notes? Advantages? Disadvantages?
    g. Should the student be permitted to use a lectern? Advantages? Disadvantages?
    h. Should classmates be encouraged to heckle a student speaker?
    i. Should the student be encouraged to speak extemporaneously? What are the disadvantages in memorizing each talk delivered in class?
    j. Should the student be permitted to talk on a subject of which the teacher disapproves or with which the teacher disagrees? How should the teacher handle criticism of subjects of these types?
    k. What should be the teacher's attitude toward the sources of information used by the students? Should the teacher discourage speeches that are based exclusively on material from a single article in a magazine digest or from pamphlets of a pressure group?
    l. Should the teacher concern himself with sound thinking as well as fluency and polished delivery?
    m. What should the teacher do when he knows that a student has misinterpreted facts? Falsified facts? Misunderstood facts?
    n. How should the teacher grade the student who delivers effective speeches, but who does not study the assigned readings?
    o. What should the teacher do when a student blocks or goes blank during a speaking performance?
    p. How should the teacher handle the student who refuses to give oral speaking assignments?
    q. Should the teacher attempt to teach attitudes? Should he be concerned with how the student is to use public speaking after he leaves the class?
    r. What percentage of the final grade should be based on midsemester and final examinations?
7. Prepare a research paper on a topic such as the following:
    a. Should speech communication be a compulsory or elective subject? In junior high school? In college? Write on only one.
    b. Is it desirable to combine the teaching of speech communication with English? With social studies? With other subjects? What are the advantages and disadvantages?
    c. Should speech be taught in the elementary grades? As a separate course?
    d. How can extracurricular speech activities and the formal course in speech communication be coordinated?

e. How have teaching objectives and methods of speech changed in the past 50 years? Compare a current textbook with one published in 1900 or before.

f. What influence have Greek writers in rhetoric had on modern speech communication theory and teaching methods?

REFERENCES

BRANDES, PAUL D., "The Common Materials Approach to the Teaching of Speech," *Speech Teacher*, November, 1967, 16:265–268.

DEDMON, DONALD N. AND FRANDSEN, KENNETH D., "A 'Required' First Course in Speech: A Survey," *Speech Teacher*, January, 1964, 13:32–37.

HANCE, KENNETH G., "The Character of the Beginning Course: Skill and/or Content," *Speech Teacher*, September, 1961, 10:220–224.

HILDEBRANDT, HERBERT W., "A Rationale for Non-Fragmented Topics," *Speech Teacher*, November, 1967, 16:259–264.

HILDEBRANDT, HERBERT W. AND SATTLER, WILLIAM M., "The Use of Common Materials in the Basic College Speech Course," *Speech Teacher*, January, 1963, 12:18–25.

JOHNSON, ROBERT C., "Teaching Speech Ethics in the Beginning Speech Course," *Speech Teacher*, January, 1970, 19:58–61.

JULEUS, NELS G., "A Plan for Teaching Speech Preparation," *Speech Teacher*, March, 1965, 14:107–109.

OLIVER, ROBERT T., "The Eternal (and Infernal) Problem of Grades," *Speech Teacher*, January, 1960, 9:8–11.

SAWYER, THOMAS M., JR., "A Grading System for Speech Classes," *Speech Teacher*, January, 1960, 9:12–15.

Symposium on Using Speech Models, *Speech Teacher*, January, 1967, 16:11–27: A. Craig Baird, "Speech Models and Liberal Educations." Haig A. Bosmajian, "Using Readings in Speech." Mary Louise Gehring, "The Inductive Approach to Speech Models." Harry P. Kerr, "Using *Opinion and Evidence*: The Case Method." Eugene E. White, "Supplementing Theory and Practice."

WHITE, HOLLIS L., "The Common Materials Approach: A Negative View," *Speech Teacher*, November, 1967, 16:279–283.

WOOD, ROY V. ET. AL., "The Effect of Learning About Techniques of Propaganda on Subsequent Reaction to Propagandistic Communications," *Speech Teacher*, January, 1970, 19:49–53.

Books of Speech Models

ALY, BOWER AND ALY, LUCILE, *American Short Speeches*, New York: Macmillan, 1968.

ALY, BOWER AND ALY, LUCILE, *Speech in English*, New York: Random House, 1968.

ARNOLD, CARROLL C., EHNINGER, DOUGLAS, AND GERBER, JOHN C., *The Speaker's Resource Book*, Glenview, Ill.: Scott, Foresman, 1961.

AUER, J. JEFFERY, *The Rhetoric of Our Times*, New York: Appleton-Century-Crofts, 1968.

BAIRD, A. CRAIG, *American Public Address, 1740–1952*, New York: McGraw-Hill, 1956.

BERQUIST, GOODWIN F., JR., *Speeches for Illustration and Example*, Glenview, Ill.: Scott, Foresman, 1965.

BLACK, EDWIN AND KERR, HARRY P., *American Issues: A Sourcebook for Speech Topics*, Harcourt Brace Jovanovich, 1961.

BOSMAJIAN, HAIG A., *Readings in Speech*, New York: Harper & Row, 1965.

BRADEN, WALDO W. AND GEHRING, MARY LOUISE, *Speech Practices: A Resource Book for the Student of Public Speaking*, New York, Harper & Row, 1958.

BRANDT, CARL G. AND SHAFTER, EDWARD M., JR., *Selected American Speeches on Basic Issues, 1850–1950,* Boston: Houghton, Mifflin, 1960.

CAPP, GLENN R., *Famous Speeches in American History,* New York and Indianapolis: Bobbs-Merrill, 1963.

GRAHAM, JOHN, *Great American Speeches, 1898–1963,* New York: Appleton-Century-Crofts, 1970.

HAIMAN, FRANKLYN S., *Freedom of Speech: Issues and Cases,* New York: Random House, 1965.

HILDEBRANDT, HERBERT W., *Issues of Our Time: A Summons to Speak,* New York: Macmillan, 1963.

KERR, HARRY P., *Opinion and Evidence, Cases for Argument and Discussion,* Harcourt Brace Jovanovich, 1962.

LASER, MARVIN, CATHCART, ROBERT S., AND MARCUS, FRED H., *Ideas and Issues: Readings for Analysis,* New York: Ronald Press, 1963.

LINKUGEL, WIL A., ALLEN R. R., AND JOHANNESEN, RICHARD L. *Contemporary American Speeches, A Sourcebook of Speech Forms and Principles,* 2nd ed., Belmont, Calif.: Wadsworth, 1969.

OLIVER, ROBERT T. AND WHITE, EUGENE E., *Selected Speeches from American History,* Boston: Allyn & Bacon, 1966.

REIN, IRVING J., *The Relevant Rhetoric,* New York: Free Press, 1969.

SCOTT, ROBERT L. AND BROCKRIEDE, WAYNE, *The Rhetoric of Black Power,* New York: Harper & Row, 1970.

SMITH, ARTHUR, *Rhetoric of Black Revolution,* Boston: Allyn & Bacon, 1969.

THONSSEN, LESTER, *Representative American Speeches,* New York: Wilson. Issued annually since 1938. From 1938 through 1959 A. Craig Baird served as editor.

THONSSEN, LESTER AND FINKEL, WILLIAM L., *Ideas That Matter: A Sourcebook for Speakers,* New York: Ronald Press, 1961.

WILLIAMS, JAMYE AND WILLIAMS, MCDONALD, *The Negro Speaks,* New York: Noble & Noble, 1970.

WRAGE, ERNEST J. AND BASKERVILLE, BARNET, *American Forum: Speeches on Historic Issues, 1788–1900,* New York: Harper & Row, 1960.

WRAGE, ERNEST J. AND BASKERVILLE, BARNET, *Contemporary Forum: American Speeches on Twentieth-Century Issues,* New York: Harper & Row, 1962.

Distributors of Spoken Records

Caedman Records, Inc., 505 Eighth Ave., New York 10018.

Columbia Records Special Services, 1400 Fruitridge Avenue, Terre Haute, Indiana 47805.

Educational Audio Visual, Inc., Pleasantville, New York 10570.

Educational Record Sales, 157 Chambers St., New York 10007.

Enrichment Teaching Materials, 71 West 23rd Street, New York 10010.

RCA Educational Sales, 1133 Avenue of the Americas, New York 10036.

Spoken Arts, Inc., 59 Locust Ave., New Rochelle, New York 10801.

Stanley Bowmar Co., Inc., Valhalla, New York 10595.

Valiant I.M.C., 237 Washington Avenue, Hackensack, New Jersey 07602.

3. Some Persistent Problems in Teaching Speech Communication

Waldo W. Braden

The writer now has served as an administrator for 12 years. It occurs to him that in many respects the problems he encounters repeatedly in that capacity are much the same as those that persist at other levels. At the beginning of each term he finds himself repeating much of what he has said at the opening of the previous term. Teachers have a way of becoming so involved in their specialized subjects that they forget routine matters concerning housekeeping, recordkeeping, record and administrative procedures. Senior staff members are bored (but forgetful) to hear the same advice again; the novice teachers have questions which they are timid to ask—for fear that their inexperience will become more evident than it already is.

Below are some of these persistent problems that frequently need mentioning:

1. Meet the class on time at the scheduled place.
2. Keep complete and accurate records.
3. Post and maintain office hours.
4. Keep the physical appearance of the classroom attractive.
5. Leave the furniture and equipment in an acceptable arrangement for the next class.
6. Treat the service personnel with respect and kindness.
7. Request equipment and supplies far enough ahead to have them available when needed.
8. Dress acceptably and maintain a friendly but appropriate atmosphere in the class.
9. Treat all students alike; demand respect but be a person of good will.
10. Cooperate with other teachers in promoting the welfare of the students.

MOTIVATING THE STUDENT

The speech class provides the teacher with many opportunities for motivation. The successful teacher knows how to activate these springs of action and keep his student marching toward the attainment of effective and good speaking. The student learns more rapidly when he sees the importance of a subject and when he finds it satisfying than when he is forced to study against his will. Below are four principles that are probably basic to motivation:

1. The student should understand and appreciate that the activity is important and worthy of effort.
2. The student should experience satisfaction and pleasure in participating in the activity.
3. The student should feel that the goal is attainable, and he should be able to notice his progress.
4. The student should receive positive encouragement in his efforts.

In order to meet these conditions the teacher must carefully lay out his plan for the term. First he should establish that he is a man of good will who is sincerely eager to help the student improve. He must be considerate in his remarks about each performance, must treat all students alike, and make it known that he believes in the worth of the individual. In other words, he must sell himself.

Second, the teacher must emphasize the importance and worth of speech communication training. Latin went out of the curriculum largely because students did not understand the importance of studying a "dead language." The teachers should assemble arguments and instances of how the subject will make important contributions to the student. In addition to emphasizing personal benefits, the teacher should stress socially oriented motives including those relating speech communication to citizenship training and more effective participation in a democratic government. In a word the teacher must sell his subject.

A third aspect of motivation includes the creation and fostering of a pleasant, desirable, and expectant atmosphere. Coming to class and participating in assignments must be made exciting, stimulating, and satisfying. The teacher should promote the attitudes that the class consists of (1) mutual efforts of (2) equal partners who are (3) striving to accomplish a group goal. Each student is important in this group effort. For example, the teacher may suggest that to present an ill-prepared speech is to let the group down and that each student is his brother's keeper in that he is eager to have a fellow classmate improve. Whenever possible the teacher assigns *group* tasks to promote togetherness and a sense of belonging to an important group. Group dynamics are utilized whenever possible.

THE FIRST MEETINGS OF THE CLASS

Much of the success of a speech communication class may depend upon how the teacher handles the first three or four class periods. Many students enroll in the subject with apprehension. As many as 75 percent may believe that their greatest problem is stage fright. Some have been forced into the subject by a curriculum requirement, an administrative regulation, or even by an overdirective parent or adviser. The student may regard the subject and particularly the teacher as real threats to his future, preventing him from taking advanced courses, from graduation, from initiation into a fraternity or sorority, from getting a good job, or even from receiving parental aid or social approval. If speech communication is to live up to its potential, then the teacher must make a good start by relieving fears and anxieties, providing satisfactory orientation, and starting the student off with the belief that he can complete the course satisfactorily.

Introducing the Subject

At the first class meeting, the instructor should set the tone for the remainder of the semester:

1. He should carefully present an overview of what the course will entail. Many instructors distribute a syllabus which outlines the activities and assignments for the entire term. Students like to have a time schedule if possible.

2. He should also carefully explain the "rules of the game," that is, the requirements of the course and obligations of the student—(a) attendance, (b) excused absences, (c) examinations, (d) makeup speeches, (e) out-of-class assignments such as required attendance at forums and plays, and (f) acceptable dress and behavior.

3. He should encourage a frank discussion of the rules. At this moment the teacher should demonstrate that questions and class participation are welcome and encouraged. The teacher must meet frank questions with frank but considerate answers (omit sarcasm and attempts to be clever at the expense of the student).

4. In his orientation the teacher should establish what benefits accrue from the study and mastery of the principles and skills of speech communication. Yes, he should give a good will and sales talk combined to establish that the subject is important and beneficial.

The First Student Participation

The opening assignment should be planned to achieve three purposes: (1) to give the student an opportunity to know classmates; (2) to provide the teacher with insight into needs and abilities of the student; and (3) to start the student out with a successful experience.

Some typical opening assignments are the following:

a. The student introduces himself.
b. The student introduces a classmate (after a conference with him).
c. A pantomime.
d. Short speech (2 or 3 minutes) on a hobby, petty peeve, exciting experience.
e. Short speech on a proverb.
f. A reading of a favorite piece of literature.

During this first performance the instructor should encourage students to volunteer. He should probably not assign grades or give direct criticisms of each presentation. Any comments made should be encouraging and demonstrate to the student that he is in a friendly atmosphere.

Withholding criticism of individual performances during the two or three assignments, the instructor may discuss two or three speakers at one time, emphasizing group achievement.

HANDLING VARYING ABILITIES

It is not uncommon to have in a single class persons with a wide range of abilities and experience. One student may have done considerable speaking and performing in a Future Farmers group or in the local community theatre, while another has never appeared in public, and has consistently avoided speech classes or situations that demanded individual response. It is entirely possible that the superior student may be more effective when he enrolls than another member will be at the end of the semester. Does this disparity mean that the experienced speaker is assured of an A and the timid student is destined to receive a low grade? To permit this impression to persist is to encourage low morale, friction among the students, and unsatisfactory performance.

1. To meet the problem of varying abilities, the teacher may insist that *improvement* is necessary of all class members. In other words, the experienced person must show development as well as the inexperienced one.

2. A given assignment may include activities of varying difficulty. The proficient student is assigned the more difficult tasks. For example, he may prepare a speech to demonstrate the requirement of assignment. The teacher feels free to analyze the speech in considerable detail in order to show the other students what they should strive for.

3. The syllabus may incorporate peer group instruction in which the better students help the less fortunate ones. For example, a classmate may rehearse a colleague before an assignment is given in class or he may help administer drill materials.

4. The talented student is given an extra assignment. In addition to class participation, he is encouraged to join the speaker's bureau or to prepare reports on additional readings or to complete outside projects.

5. Students may be subdivided on the basis of ability and experience into subgroups in order to pursue specialized projects. If teacher aids are available, two groups may perform at the same time. While group A works on performance, group B does voice and diction drills or perhaps listens to recordings or participates in videotaping.

EXTENDING THE PERIMETERS OF THE CLASSROOM[1]

If the learning process is confined to what can be mastered during the actual minutes of a class meeting, then education is indeed a slow process. Actually the time spent during a 50-minute period only opens a door or introduces the possibilities of a subject or stirs the student's desire for engaging in further activity. John S. Gibson, Director of the Lincoln-Filene Center for Citizenship and Public Affairs at Tufts College, made this point as follows:

Only in this way can all patterns of education be joined and can students really believe that the school is sincere in its broader educative function. . . . All of this relates to our constant attempt to develop connective links between the curriculum in the school—especially in the social studies, the humanities, and the performing arts—and the real world and the real problems confronting the students. It means bringing that real world into the classroom and drawing upon the community at large as a learning environment. . . .

The teaching-learning process must maximize all possibilities for involving the student in that process, and in many ways. Inquiry and discovery, role playing and gaming, group discussions and multisided debates are very much in order rather than asking students to read, to listen, and to answer the questions at the end of a chapter. We are hardly going to advance a behavioral objective called enlightened participation if we do not honor the process of enlightened participation in the classroom.[2]

How can the teacher of speech communication bring "the real world into the classroom" and draw "upon the community at large as a learning environment?" Below are six suggestions taken from recent issues of the *Speech Teacher:*

The Interview Speech. Dorothy Q. Weirich, of Webster Grove (Missouri) High School explains how her classes utilize this assignment:

The assignment must be presented with care. The students are instructed to select for an interview a person whose business, profession, hobbies, or ideas are interesting. An appointment, either by letter or by telephone, is made. The student, aided by class instruction, prepares for the interview. After the inter-

---

[1] The author is indebted to M. E. Scheib for this title. See *Speech Teacher*, September, 1967, 16:215–216.
[2] John S. Gibson, "Needed: A Revolution in Citizenship Education," *Vital Speeches of the Day*, May 15, 1969, 35:473–478.

view has been conducted, the student presents the material he has secured in a speech before the class. Finally, he is required to write a note of appreciation for the interview. . . . My students have interviewed personalities ranging from Helen Hayes, Guy Lombardo, Stan Musial, the Governor of Missouri to a bum on Market Street (St. Louis' own Skid Row)! The bum, a graduate of Princeton, but a human derelict, had a profound effect on an impressionable adolescent, who in turn had a profound effect on a good speech class.[3]

Henrietta H. Cortright of Seaholm High School, Birmingham, Michigan uses the interview assignment in slightly different but effective form. She instructs her students as follows:

Select a vocation. Investigate education, training, and work experience needed to qualify for your chosen vocation. Consider your potentialities for success. Evaluate responsibilities, openings, and opportunities for advancement as well as hours, duties, and financial remuneration. After exhausting familiar sources of information—libraries, counselor, parents, adult friends—if possible, arrange an appointment with someone in that vocation.

Rehearse, then conduct interview with a classmate who will role play the employer. Give classmate fifteen questions to ask concerning the vocation and your qualifications. Assume yourself ten years older. Have clothes, appearance, action, and language appropriate for that age and occasion. Carry names, addresses, and phone numbers of two character and two professional references. For use outside the classroom, of course, permission must be obtained from references.[4]

The Speaker's Bureau. Speaking to a classroom audience may of course be limiting. In order to broaden the students' experience, some teachers arrange speaking engagements for students with outside groups. Daniel I. Munger of McCluer High School, Florissant, Missouri, explains how he operates the speaker's bureau:

Student speeches were prepared in the conventional manner. A special bulletin was addressed to faculty supervisors of "advisories" (25-minute homerooms) listing the speeches available. Invitations were received for speaking appointments and a speaking schedule was implemented.

After appearing before 30 or 40 audiences speakers began to find ways to retain "freshness" in presentation. They became sufficiently fluent and polished that they could study audience reaction and discover how each audience is different. As they learned to adapt to varying audiences, the students found that traits of audience behavior could be isolated, systemized, and exploited by a speaker. Also a comparison of written comments from the many audiences provided a depth and variety of criticism for student reflection.[5]

Speech on Location. Not all speech must be presented within the

[3] Dorothy Q. Weirich, "The Interview Speech," *Speech Teacher*, March, 1968, 17:173.
[4] Henrietta H. Cortright, "Interview for Life Work," *Speech Teacher*, March, 1968, 17:173.
[5] Daniel I. Munger, "Student Speaker's Bureau," *Speech Teacher*, March, 1968, 17:176.

confines of a given classroom. The field trip idea may contribute to instruction. Marjory W. Carr of Santa Fe (New Mexico) High School attempts to make her students aware of "the cultural heritage" of their community. At the same time she provides them with realistic speaking experiences.

Each student is asked to deliver an informative talk upon the fine art or folk art of the community—if possible on location.

Subject matter comes from our three cultures—Indian, Spanish, and Anglo. Both fine art and folk art in painting, sculpture, music, weaving, wood carving, silvercrafting, pottery, church art, dance, and architecture are acceptable. . . .

Resource material may come from publications or personal interviews. Biographical material is permissible only as it affects the work being discussed. Speakers are given one month of research time while other assignments are covered in the classroom.

This assignment has been delivered in the art museum, the folk art museum, the museum of Indian ceremonial art, churches, an artist's studio, the opera amphitheater, or in the classroom depending on the speaker's choice of topic. Since our community is relatively small, a school bus keeps us within our schedule.[6]

Campaign Speeches.   The speech teacher must keep before the students the vital role of speech communication in democratic decision-making. Often during a state or national election he may focus attention on the speaking of political figures. Using what she called a "political advocacy speech," Carol Cole has accomplished these objectives as follows:

Each student's objective is to persuade the class to accept a candidate running for political office. The assignment requires that the students develop a rationale for the support of a particular candidate and communicate that rationale to their audience. These speeches often include the previous experience of the candidate, the past voting record of the candidate (if an incumbent), the campaign promises of the candidates, excerpts from speeches of the candidate, and statements of why this candidate is favored by the student over the other candidates running for the office. Concluding the assignment with a mock election adds to the excitement. . . . The assignment can provide a starting point for discussion of political issues and persuasive techniques. The speech can also illustrate the importance of political speaking in public address.[7]

Speaker's Notebook.   Keeping the student's attention focused on progress is sometimes a problem. Barbara L. Clemmons of Ocala (Florida) High School makes her teaching more vital and meaningful by requiring each student to keep a notebook. She explains:

In it he records his personal objectives for speech learning. It is understood

---

[6] Marjory W. Carr, "Informative Talk on the Fine Arts," *Speech Teacher*, March, 1968, 17:179.

[7] Carol Cole, "Political Advocacy Speech," *Speech Teacher*, January, 1969, 18:80–81.

that as he learns more about speech he may, and probably will, alter these objectives.

The next item recorded in the notebook is my critique on each speaking assignment. It is impossible to remember completely each student's former criticisms without having them available for reference. With the notebook I am able to evaluate progress, noting improvement as well as faults.

Following my critique the speaker writes a summary of student criticisms and his own reactions, relating them to his goals. He is encouraged to review all comments on his previous speeches before his next experience.[8]

Telelecture. One excellent method of providing your students with a wider experience is to bring guest lecturers or resource persons to class for special representations. But even when such a person cannot take time to visit a group, the guest can become available through the use of a telelecture or amplified telephone conversation. Yeomans and Lindsey explain this technique as follows:

What is telelecture? It is a low-cost technique designed to reach larger audiences and overcome the problems of distance and time in bringing in outside resources. It brings the lecturer to the audience by means of a telephone call. His voice is amplified over loudspeakers, and equipment is usually available for members of the audience to talk directly with the lecturer. The speaker's picture may be projected on to a screen, thus supplementing his voice in making his presence felt.[9]

ADMINISTRATIVE PROBLEMS

Class Size

The optimum class size depends on the type of course and the number of assignments desired. The survey or lecture course can accommodate many more persons than the performance course in which each member is expected to deliver oral exercises. A recent survey of over five hundred junior colleges, colleges, and universities found that in over 70 percent of these institutions the class size for courses carrying three semester hours credit ranged from 17 to 22 students.[10] Speaking assignments are held to 4 or 5 minutes. On this type of schedule at least three class periods are required to complete a performance assignment.

High school classes meeting five days a week should not exceed numbers

8 Barbara L. Clemmons, "Reaction Notebook," *Speech Teacher*, March, 1968, 17:177.
9 G. Allan Yeomans and Henry C. Lindsey, "Telelectures," *Speech Teacher*, January, 1969, 18:65–67.
10 James W. Gibson *et al.*, "The First Course In Speech: A Survey of U.S. Colleges and Universities," *Speech Teacher*, January, 1970, 19:13–20.

recommended for colleges. Obviously, much more can be accomplished with sections numbering 12 to 15 students.[11]

The Length of Speaking Assignments

Closely related to the topic just discussed is the matter of the length of the speaking assignments. Is it better to use long or short speeches? One authority recommends, "At the beginning of the course short and frequent speeches are more conducive to progress. . . . than long speeches." From the standpoint of the principles of repetition and accumulation of learning, more frequent appearances should result in the establishment of sound habits. Many teachers feel that each student should have the opportunity to participate at least once a week. A little figuring will demonstrate how difficult it is to hear and comment on more than seven five-minute speeches in a 50-minute period.

Amount of Time Devoted to Performance, Class Discussion, and Criticism

In his extensive survey of the first course in speech Hargis found that in 229 departments an average of 59 percent of the time was devoted to student performance, 15 percent to criticism, 12 percent to lectures, and 12 percent to discussion.[12] An extensive study of speech in the high schools of Ohio revealed that the teacher estimated "that about one-half of the class time was devoted to student performance, one-fourth to lecture or instructor-led class discussion and one-fourth to tests, and in-class preparation or study."[13] The beginning instructor is likely to devote too much time to lecturing, forgetting that principles may be emphasized through performance and criticism and that a good textbook, clearly written, need not be discussed at length in class.

To make the Hargis statistics more meaningful and applicable to class procedure, let us use them to suggest a basis for allotting the time of a single 50-minute class period. Accordingly the period would be divided as follows: (1) 30 minutes to performance; (2) 14 minutes to criticism and discussion; (3) 6 minutes to lecturing.

Now let us look at these statistics in a second way—from the point of view of a typical high school class and of a typical college class. In a high school class in which 90 periods (18 × 5) are available during a semester,

[11] Henrietta H. Cortright, Doris S. Niles, and Dorothy Q. Weirich, "Criteria to Evaluate Speech I in the Senior High School," Speech Teacher, September, 1968, 17:217–224.

[12] Donald E. Hargis, "The First Course in Speech," Speech Teacher, January, 1956, 5:29–30.

[13] Charles R. Petrie, Jr. and Thomas R. McManus, "Status of Speech in Ohio Secondary Schools," Speech Teacher, January, 1968, 17:24.

65 periods would be devoted to performance and criticism and 25 to tests, lectures, and discussion. For a typical semester college class (18 × 3) the 54 periods might be divided as follows: 39 periods for performance and criticism and no more than 15 periods for other activities. Of course these illustrations are only rough guides. Each class must be planned in terms of students' needs and abilities.

Scheduling Speaking Performance

Six methods of scheduling speaking assignments may be used.[14]

1. Alphabetical order. The roll book method.
2. Volunteering. The student speaks according to his own preference. Caution: Don't permit the timid student always to wait until others have talked.
3. The teacher's preference. The teacher determines the order, calling on the student according to his own preferences.
4. Assigned order. A rotating scheme may be used to bring a different member up first for each assignment. Members may be rotated forward one place for each period as follows:

Order	First Assignment Student	Second Assignment Student	Third Assignment Student
1	A	B	C
2	B	C	D
3	C	D	A
4	D	A	B

A second scheme is to divide the class into two or three groups, letting a different group open each new assignment; that is, if Group A leads off today, Group B will open the next assignment.

5. Drawing for order by lot.
6. A student-arranged program. The class operates under a chairman who is responsible for arranging the speaking order after consultation with other members.

The question arises as to which method should be used to determine speaking order. Certainly the wise instructor wants a scheme that is fair to all students, maintains class morale, and results in maximum improvement. Before attempting to suggest which methods are best, let us list some of the problems that instructors sometimes encounter with reference to speaking order:

1. Timid students often hold back, waiting for the more aggressive ones to show them how to carry out the assignment.
2. Lazy or procrastinating students are likely to put off speaking until the last day.

[14] The methods were suggested to author by Horace Rodman Jones, "The Development and Present Status of Beginning Speech Courses in Colleges and Universities in the United States," unpublished Ph.D. dissertation, Northwestern University, 1952. This material is used by special permission of Dr. Jones.

3. Students who speak on the first day are at the disadvantage of preparing their speeches before they have heard the teacher's criticism or class discussion of other performers. Furthermore, the teacher may grade all students in terms of the opening speeches.
4. The students who speak near the end of the roll have the advantage of extra time for preparing and polishing their speeches.
5. The students who speak the last day are likely to get less criticism than earlier speakers.

These problems suggest that the volunteer system has some serious disadvantages. Calling on the students in alphabetical order is a little better. Actually any of the last four systems provide a means of having different students try at leading off. No student is permitted to dominate the class or to monopolize a favorite position. Some teachers argue that the student should know exactly when he is to speak. They feel that such scheduling permits the student to prepare more adequately and to develop a greater urge to communicate.[15]

Bases for Grading

One of the most difficult and trying aspects of teaching public speaking is estimating the grades of the students. Grading in speech courses is made difficult because many intangible factors are involved in a speaking performance. Grading may be approached from several points of view.

Improvement.   This criterion is how much the student improves during the term. Under this system the poor speaker who makes progress may earn a higher grade than the good speaker who shows no improvement.

Comprehension of the Textbook.   The grade on this basis depends on the student's marks on written assignments, tests, and class discussions.

Effort Expended.   How hard does the student try? Does the student work diligently on the various class assignments? These and similar questions receive consideration under this standard. One well-known teacher explains, "Students should be given special credit for genuine effort. An honest try along with a cooperative attitude should be recognized in some measure. Effort may be reflected in class attendance, readiness to speak on the assigned day, promptness in handing in assignments, listening behavior, and careful preparation of speeches."[16]

Ability.   The student with experience and natural aptitude is favored by this system. This standard is likely to have an important place in courses of a professional nature or in courses involving departmental majors.

Class Attendance and Punctuality.   Generally this standard operates in a negative sense. Students who have excessive absences or who are habitually tardy are penalized.

15 G. E. Densmore, "The Teaching of Speech Delivery," *Quarterly Journal of Speech*, February, 1946, 32:67–71.
16 E. C. Buehler, *Teacher's Guide and Syllabus for Course 1: Fundamentals of Speech*, Lawrence: Univ. of Kansas, 1958, p. 5.

Achievement. Actually the teacher may approach this standard from two points of view. He may measure the student against an idealized or theoretical standard. At the close of the class, he may ask how the student compares to his yardstick.

A second approach is to measure achievement in terms of the immediate class—that is, with reference to the rate of improvement of other class members.

Attitude of the Student. Under this heading the teacher considers such qualities as cooperativeness, respect for authority, courtesy, willingness to carry out assignments, acceptance of criticism, and interest in the class projects.

Combination of Several or All of These. The good teacher uses several of these standards and attempts to get as many ratings as possible to determine the final grade.

REFERENCES

AUER, J. JEFFERY, "Speech Is a Social Force," *NEA Journal,* November, 1960, 49:21–23.

BRADEN, WALDO W. (ED.), "Effective Projects and Assignments for Teaching Public Speaking in High School," *Speech Teacher,* March, 1968, 17:173–179.

BROOKS, WILLIAM D. AND PLATZ, SARAH M., "The Effects of Speech Training upon Self-Concepts as a Communicator," *Speech Teacher,* January, 1968, 17:44–49.

BUEHLER, E. C., "The First Seven Days of the College Beginning Speech Class," *Speech Teacher,* November, 1958, 7:302–308.

BYERS, BURTON H., "Speech and the Principles of Learning," *Speech Teacher,* March, 1963, 12:136–140.

CROWELL, LAURA, "The Process-Inquiry Speech," *Speech Teacher,* September, 1952, 1:167–175.

GRIFFITH, FRANCIS, "The Ideal Speech Program in the Secondary School," *Speech Teacher,* January, 1963, 12:34–36.

HARDING, H. F., "The 1968 Presidential Campaign and Teachers of Speech," *Speech Teacher,* March, 1968, 17:150–155.

HORKAN, VINCENT J. AND OKEY, L. LAMONT, A *Guide to Speech,* New York: Noble & Noble, 1959.

HUCKLEBERRY, ALAN W. AND STROTHER, EDWARD S., "Saving Time in the Speech Class," *Speech Teacher,* March, 1969, 18:124–128.

KENNER, FREDA, "Motivating Students," *Speech Teacher,* November, 1969, 18:263–264.

KNOWER, FRANKLIN H., "The College Student Image of Speech, Communication, and Speech Instruction," *Speech Teacher,* March, 1966, 15:108–112.

MC CROSKEY, JAMES C., "The Effect of the Basic Speech Course on Student's Attitudes," *Speech Teacher,* March, 1967, 16:115–117.

OGILVIE, MARDEL AND SEARLES, MYRTLE, "The Important Place of 'Sharing Ideas,'" *Speech Teacher,* November, 1960, 9:287–289.

PHELPS, WALDO W., "The Panel-Forum as a First Assignment in the Secondary School Speech Fundamentals Class," *Speech Teacher,* September, 1952, 1:163–166.

REID, LOREN, "On First Teaching Speech," *Speech Teacher*, January, 1952, 1:1–8.

YEOMANS, G. ALLAN, "Speech Education: A Terrible Responsibility," *Vital Speeches of the Day*, March 15, 1964, 30:348–352.

YEOMANS, G. ALLAN AND LINDSEY, HENRY C., "Telelectures," *Speech Teacher*, January, 1969, 18:65–67.

4. Teaching Discussion

Owen Peterson

Although almost every school with a speech program provides some kind of training in discussion, arrangements for teaching this form of public address vary greatly. At some institutions, training is wholly extracurricular. At others, units of study in discussion are included in fundamentals courses. Some schools offer separate courses in discussion or combine discussion and debate in a single course. At the college and university level, entire sequences of courses in discussion may be available to the student. Supplementing formal classroom instruction at many schools is an extracurricular program that includes discussion training.

THE DISCUSSION PROCESS

Relationships

In designing the type of discussion training to be offered, the speech teacher should recognize that debate and discussion are closely related activities. Three similarities are particularly important: (1) Both the debater and the discussant strive for the same basic goal, finding the best solution to a problem and, although their methods differ, both pursue essentially the same investigative process to achieve this objective; (2) both consider similar types of problems; (3) both employ many of the same speech techniques.

The most important resemblance between debate and discussion probably is the reflective thought process followed in both activities—an adaptation of principles formulated by John Dewey.[1] The process consists of the following steps:

1. Realization of a felt difficulty
2. Confirmation of the felt difficulty
3. Discovery of the factors and causes of the problem
4. Formulation of a series of hypotheses concerning possible solutions
5. Weighing the possible solutions
6. Determination and verification of the best solution

In practice, problem solving usually begins with interchange between two or more persons about a condition that they believe requires modification or improvement (realization of a felt difficulty). Logically, the first step in investigating this condition is to make certain that a problem actually exists (confirmation of a felt difficulty). After determining that the situation warrants further study, the interested persons seek to obtain exact and detailed information (discovery of factors and causes of the problem). Having determined the nature, scope, and causes of the problem, the group is ready to seek remedies (formulation of a series of hypotheses concerning possible solutions) and, subsequently, to compare the several proposed remedies (weighing the possible solutions). Finally, the group tries to agree on the best single plan or combination of solutions (determination of the solution to be followed). Ideally, the group would go one step further and periodically review and reevaluate the solution after it has been implemented.

While both discussion and debate are based on a pattern of reflective thought, the essential difference between the two activities lies in the attitudes of the participants. At any stage in the reflective thought process, debate may supplant discussion. (See chart on p. 56.) Controversy may arise over whether a problem actually exists, over the nature and seriousness of the situation, over the relative merits of the proposed remedies, or over the advantages and disadvantages of a particular solution. So long as the investigators, in spite of minor disagreement from time to time, cooperatively seek to understand and solve the problem, the process is discussional in nature. However, when the participants recognize that cooperation is no longer possible and, instead, seek to demonstrate the superiority of their respective points of view, the situation becomes one of debate.

Because of the problem-solving nature of both discussion and debate, the types of questions that lend themselves well to each approach are similar. Informative, stimulating, and entertaining messages are better suited to the public speaking situation than to the round table or debate platform. However, questions involving differences of opinion, values, or

[1] John Dewey, *How We Think*, Lexington, Mass.: Raytheon/Heath, 1933, pp. 71–78, 91–101.

Relation of Discussion and Debate to the Reflective Thought Process

Dewey Reflective Thought	Discussion	Debate
	(Usually predetermined)	(Usually predetermined)
1. Realization of a felt difficulty		

2. Confirmation of felt difficulty	I. Is there a problem?
	  A. What is the nature of this problem?
		I. Is there a need for a change from the status quo?
		  A. Does a problem exist?

3. Discovery of factors and causes of the problem	B. What are the causes of the problem?	B. What are the causes of the problem?
4. Formulation of a series of hypotheses concerning possible conclusions	II. What solutions can be proposed to meet the problem?	C. Will solutions other than the affirmative proposal solve the problem?
5. Weighing the possible solutions	III. What are the advantages and disadvantages of the various solutions?	II. Is the affirmative proposal practicable? III. Is the affirmative proposal desirable?
6. Determination of the solution to be followed	Decision: What is the best solution?	Decision: Should the affirmative proposal be adopted?

interpretations are well adapted to either discussion or debate if properly framed.

Discussion and debate also involve similar skills and techniques. Effective participation in either activity demands thorough investigation of the question, ample supporting evidence, logical thought processes, adaptability and flexibility, and good speaking habits. In teaching debate and discussion, the instructor should keep in mind these similarities.

Aims and Goals

The teacher's first step in planning a course or unit of study in discussion must be to formulate the objectives he hopes to achieve. Until he has done this, he cannot plan a course of study that will accomplish the ends he envisions. Among his objectives may be the following:

1. To develop an understanding and appreciation of the nature, values, and uses of discussion.
2. To develop a mastery of the techniques of effective discussion leadership and participation.
3. To familiarize the student with the materials and methods of research.
4. To stimulate interest in and understanding of significant contemporary problems and issues.
5. To develop ability to think clearly, critically, and analytically.
6. To increase the effectiveness of the individual's participation in democratic society.
7. To aid the student in adapting to his social, political, and professional environment.
8. To develop effective speech habits.

Although discussion techniques are often used for therapeutic and other purposes in sensitivity sessions, group psychotherapy, and related activities, the speech teacher should bear in mind that his purpose is to teach the student to communicate effectively in group situations, not to rid him of his neuroses or solve his emotional problems. The latter tasks belong to the trained clinical psychologist or psychiatrist, not the speech teacher.

Teaching Materials and Aids

Many excellent textbooks in discussion are available at both high school and college levels.[2] Textbooks devoted exclusively to discussion may be used or the instructor may prefer a single volume that treats both discussion and debate. In addition, many public speaking and fundamentals texts include chapters on discussion. In selecting a text, the teacher undoubtedly will wish to study several works before making a final decision. Examination copies can be secured from most publishers on request. A valuable aid in selecting a textbook is the "Check List of Books,

---

[2] See p. 72 for a list of textbooks on discussion and debate.

Equipment and Supplies in the Field of Speech," published annually by the Speech Communication Association. Copies of this booklet can be obtained free of charge simply by writing to the Executive Secretary of that organization.

After selecting a textbook, the instructor should investigate available specialized publications and collections of materials on questions suitable for discussion. Four particularly helpful collections are *The Reference Shelf Series*.[3] *N.U.E.A. Debate Handbook*,[4] *Congressional Digest*, and *The Annals of the American Academy of Political and Social Science*. Each of these publications also will prove valuable in studying debate propositions.

Each *Reference Shelf* volume is devoted to a significant controversial question and contains articles by reputable authorities on both sides of the problem, as well as an extensive bibliography. The *Congressional Digest* also brings together articles reflecting conflicting opinions on a single public issue. Each year the editor devotes issues to the college and high school national debate propositions, usually including an analysis of the problem. *The Annals of the American Academy of Political and Social Sciences* consists of a collection of articles by recognized experts on a single important problem. Since these problems often lend themselves well to discussion and debate, this journal may prove a valuable addition to the forensics library.

If the teacher wishes to secure a collection of models for debate and discussion, he will be interested in *The University Debaters Annual*.[5] Published annually from 1915 through 1952, each volume contains the texts of several speeches as they were actually delivered in intercollegiate forensic contests.

In addition to these collections, several other handbooks are published in editions devoted to the current national high school and college debate and discussion questions. These manuals are assembled exclusively for discussants and debaters and usually contain definitions of the principal terms of the questions, analyses of the problems, excerpts from published articles and speeches on the subject, bibliographies, and similar items related to the national topics.

While such handbooks may at first appear to be a boon, leading teachers generally agree that there are several dangers in using *some* of these volumes. Properly used, the manual can be a valuable aid, especially if library facilities are inadequate; for it does provide information in a compact source and at a moderate cost. However, if the teacher truly believes that training in discussion should develop ability to think clearly, critically, and

[3] Published by H. W. Wilson Company, New York.
[4] Published by the Committee on Discussion and Debate, National University Extension Association, Charley A. Leistner, Univ. of Oregon, Eugene, Ore.
[5] Published by H. W. Wilson Company, New York.

analytically, and should familiarize students with the materials and methods of research, he will view with caution handbooks that pretend to provide the student with a complete analysis and supporting material. Such a handbook too often becomes a substitute for individual thought and investigation. Instead of trying to find the issues and arguments himself, the student is inclined to accept the compiler's analysis; instead of reading widely in an effort to discover a variety of opinions and evidence, he finds it easier to rely almost exclusively on the excerpts contained in the manual.

In addition to these two potential hazards, the instructor should remember that he has no assurance of the authoritativeness or reliability of the analyses and materials set forth in some handbooks. A final disadvantage is that while the material may have been fairly recent at the time of publication, much of it may become outdated quickly.

In summary, if a manual or handbook is utilized the teacher should exercise care in choosing the volume, he should anticipate the problems that may arise from its availability, and he should so control its use that the value of the student's experience will not be seriously jeopardized.

Teaching Conditions and Facilities

Almost all speech teachers agree that frequent performance experiences are essential to improvement in speaking. Thus, in order to give each student ample opportunity for practice and evaluation, the class in discussion must be limited in size. In addition, certain arrangements within the classroom facilitate better performance in this activity.

Since discussion normally occurs in democratic and relaxed surroundings, the teacher should plan and conduct the class in such a way that freedom of expression and informality are encouraged. While the attitude of the instructor probably is the most important factor in establishing this atmosphere, the seating of the students around a large table or in a circle or semicircle in comfortable surroundings may aid substantially. If possible, the class should be limited to 20 to 24 students. Since good discussion seldom occurs in groups of more than 8 or 10 persons, a small class permits each student to participate in several discussions and enables the instructor to schedule a series of performances involving every class member over a short span of time.

PLANNING THE UNIT OR COURSE OF STUDY

Since the conditions under which discussion is taught vary widely depending on the age, ability, and experience of the students and the amount of time to be devoted to this activity, no effort is made here to set down a day-by-day course outline. The following list of study units and exercises, however, may prove helpful to the teacher in planning a unit or course in discussion.

Suggested Study Units

   I. The nature and importance of discussion
     A. Definition of discussion
     B. The uses of discussion
     C. Differences from conversation, debate, and public speaking
     D. Attitudes of discussion participants
     E. The role of the leader or moderator
  II. Types of discussion
     A. Round table
     B. Panel
     C. Symposium
     D. Forum
     E. Business conference
     F. Committee
     G. Case method
 III. Selecting discussion topics
     A. Criteria for selecting discussion topics
     B. Phrasing discussion questions
 IV. Analysis of the discussion question
     A. Defining terms
     B. History and background
     C. Establishing goals, standards, or criteria
     D. Analyzing the problem
       1. Definition of an issue
       2. Locating issues
     E. Finding possible solutions
     F. Method of determining the best solution in light of goals, standards, or criteria
  V. Gathering evidence and information for discussion
     A. Sources
     B. Types
     C. Taking notes
 VI. Argument
     A. Kinds
     B. Uses
 VII. Evaluating evidence and argument
     A. Evaluating sources
     B. Evaluating evidence
     C. Testing argument
VIII. Discussion outlines
     A. The group outline
       1. Purpose
       2. Parts and form
       3. Preparation
     B. The individual outline
 IX. The qualities of an effective discussion leader
     A. The leader's role in discussion
     B. Traits of good leadership

X. The qualities of an effective discussion participant
  A. The participant's role in discussion
  B. Traits of good discussion participation
XI. Special techniques
  A. Role-playing
  B. Buzz groups
  C. Brainstorming
  D. Agree-disagree discussion guide
  E. Sociodrama

For examples of how specific course outlines and assignments may be developed, see pp. 70–71 at the end of the chapter.[6]

Student Assignments

1. Select and phrase discussion topics.
2. Prepare a bibliography on a discussion question.
3. Prepare a scrapbook of clippings on the discussion question.
4. Prepare a group discussion outline.
5. Prepare an individual discussion outline.
6. Listen to a radio or television discussion.
7. Prepare a short speech defining the terms of a discussion question.
8. Prepare and deliver a speech giving the history and background of a discussion question.
9. Participate in a classroom discussion.
10. Record and play a class discussion for evaluation by the class.
11. Write a critique of a classroom discussion.
12. Write a critique of a student's own participation in a classroom discussion.
13. Write a resolution embodying the conclusion of a discussion group.
14. Present a discussion before another class or some community or school club or organization.

PRINCIPLES FOR TEACHING DISCUSSION

Regardless of the length or scope of the unit on discussion, several principles should guide the instructor in planning and teaching this type of speaking. If the activity is to be of maximum value to the student, certain principles should be recognized: (1) instruction should not emphasize techniques at the expense of content; (2) discussion performances should be as realistic as possible within the restrictions of the classroom situation; (3) evaluation and criticism of classroom discussions are important in teaching discussion. Although these principles seem fairly obvious at first glance, a more detailed examination of each will reveal some of the peculiar problems that the discussion teacher faces.

[6] See also Paul W. Keller, "A Secondary School Course in Discussion"; J. Walter Reeves, "A Secondary School Course in Argumentation"; and Karl F. Robinson and John W. Keltner, "Suggested Units in Discussion and Debate for Secondary Schools," *Bulletin of the National Association of Secondary School Principals*, May, 1952, 36:72–78.

Techniques versus Content

Discussion requires an understanding and mastery of a body of speech techniques not wholly like those of any other speaking activity. However, as in teaching other forms of public speaking, the instructor has an obligation to see that student performance is based on a complete understanding of his subject. The teacher—and the student—should guard against becoming so interested in acquiring effective techniques that they neglect the importance of substantial content. The very nature of discussion contributes to this possibility: Knowing that discussion is a pooling of the ideas and information of several members of a group and that many differences are resolved through compromise, students frequently are tempted to assume that a hazy and imprecise knowledge will suffice them. What I don't know, the student reasons, someone else can supply. When we disagree, he continues, we will compromise. Training in this kind of discussion is virtually worthless. Two heads are better than one only if the combined wisdom of the two exceeds that of either one. A pooling of ignorance results only in greater ignorance. A compromise between two degrees of inaccuracy does not produce accuracy.

A single example should serve to illustrate the importance of accurate and precise information. Let us assume that a committee has been appointed to plan the annual class dance. At one point in the discussion the committee is attempting to determine how much money will be required. All agree that the major expense is the cost of the band, but no one knows how much this item will be. John, who postponed investigating the subject, guesses that the band will cost at least $600. Tom, who assumed that someone else would find out, thinks he recalls that the cost was only $200 the previous year. When no one else can contribute information, Mary, in her best discussion manner, suggests that they compromise on the sum of $400. Obviously, this proposal is no solution to the impasse. If John is right, the estimate is too low; if Tom is right, it is too high; and there is no assurance that any of the three figures is even close to accurate. Clearly, the compromise is of no help whatever. Without precise, accurate, up-to-date information, further deliberation is a waste of time. No matter how objective, cooperative, tactful, friendly, and eloquent the participants may be, until the cost of the band is known the group cannot determine its budget.

Although the above example is fairly obvious, there is no substitute for knowledge regardless of the complexity of the topic under discussion. Robert S. Cathcart points out: ". . . No amount of cooperation ever produced valid solutions in a group in which the individuals were incapable of sound logical reasoning. There is no magic about a group that gives it powers above and beyond the mental abilities of its members. . . . Certainly no amount of cooperation alone can adequately substitute for any lack of inquiry, constructive thinking, and criticism."[7] Thus, as a first duty the teacher must impress on his students the need for thorough investigation and penetrating study of the problem.

Realism

Even under the most favorable conditions, the classroom remains an artificial situation for the presentation of speeches. However, this limitation should not prevent the instructor from seeking to provide practice that is realistic. Four aspects of classroom discussions toward which a realistic approach is important are (1) the selection of subjects, (2) the observance of time limits set for class performances, (3) the objective of discussion, and (4) the attitudes of the participants in classroom exercises.

Selection of Meaningful Subjects.   Most textbooks include among the criteria to be followed in the selection of discussion questions tests of worth or significance and interest to the participants. If the instructor adheres to these standards in guiding his class in the choice of topics, he may discover, especially with younger students, that their interests often are not very significant. How should the teacher handle this seeming dilemma? Should he permit the class to discuss trivial matters or lead them to struggle with problems of greater importance but less immediate interest?

If approached realistically, the problem is not so difficult to resolve as might first appear. To answer this question, the teacher should consider the types of questions his students are likely to discuss as adult citizens. After graduation, they are not likely to participate in any serious or systematic discussion of topics they consider dull or trivial. Most likely their formal discussion activities will be related to their vital concerns, whether these be school, community, business, religious, or social matters. Any approach to teaching discussion that ignores this factor of interest is unrealistic. John Keltner cites as an example, "How close to reality could an imposed classroom discussion of the economic crisis be unless the members of that group were themselves, *in their own perceptions,* deeply involved in this crisis?" "Discussion," he continues, "which occurs as a result of the *perceived needs in a given situation* is the kind which is 'realistic.' "[8]

To ignore the test of worth or significance in selecting discussion topics also would be unrealistic. After graduation the student is not likely to participate in discussions dealing with inconsequential matters. Since adult discussion groups usually are organized to consider matters affecting the welfare of the community, state, or nation or some business, social, educational, political, or religious group within the community, students should

[7] Robert S. Cathcart, "The Case for Group Discussion Contests," *Speech Teacher,* November, 1957, 6:316–317.

[8] John Keltner, "The Laboratory Method of Discussion Training at Kansas State College," *Speech Teacher,* September, 1958, 7:201.

be encouraged to reflect on questions of comparable importance. Questions such as "What should be done to improve the appearance of school hallways?" and "What is the best way to find a parking place on campus?" are better suited to individual investigation and reports than to group study and discussion by seven or eight persons. These may be problems, but they are unrealistic *discussion* problems. The teacher should ask his students to discuss "the public problems of the educated citizen."[9] Donald K. Smith defines these as "questions of public policy, questions of personal standards or values which have implication to the ordering of social life, and questions which propound knotty intellectual issues."[10]

While high school students undoubtedly will deal with less complex questions than those selected by college and university undergraduates, nevertheless the instructor should discourage the discussion of trivial issues. This principle does not mean that the class must concern itself only or even primarily with remote questions of international scope and implication. In every school and community, there are many problems that are both interesting and important. These include questions such as:

What can be done to promote more intelligent voting?
How effective are present laws in controlling corruption in government?
What can be done to improve our mental hospitals?
What changes are needed in our laws dealing with narcotics?
How can teaching and grading methods at X be improved?
What voice should students have in determining educational policies?
What should be done to reduce juvenile delinquency in (city, state, school)?
What are the limits of dissent that democracy can tolerate?

The above questions[11] indicate only a few of the many possible significant topics that most students probably would find interesting and challenging to discuss.

Imposing Realistic Time Limits. Another question the teacher of discussion faces is, "How confining should time limits be for classroom discussion performances?" The writer once worked with a group of students preparing a discussion of the pros and cons of progressive education to be presented over a commmercial broadcasting station in 10 minutes. Although a 10-minute program was presented, it definitely was not discussion. To attempt to confine discussion performances to a severely limited period of time and expect the experience to be meaningful or to result in satisfactory solutions to significant problems simply is unrealistic. The fact is that outside the classroom most discussion groups will continue as long as is necessary to achieve their goals. For example, if a PTA committee has set aside an hour for discussion of a problem and at the end of that time

9 Donald K. Smith, "The Discussion Course at Minnesota: A Liberal Arts Approach," *Speech Teacher*, September, 1958, 7:195.
10 *Ibid.*
11 For additional suggested questions see Marilyn Myers and Lionel Crocker, "One Hundred Questions for Public Discussion," *Speech Teacher*, November, 1953, 2:266–272.

finds that no decision has been reached, rather than jumping to a hasty conclusion the committee probably will schedule an additional meeting. Representatives of labor and management attempting to settle a controversy will not give up because time has expired; if progress is being made, they will continue the discussion. It is equally important in the classroom that the students not feel under compulsion to reach a satisfactory solution in a limited period. In practice, this usually results in superficial analysis, compromises in which the participants believe only half-heartedly, and other expedients which, while they do not lead to a satisfactory solution of the problem, will guarantee that *some* solution has been reached before the deadline.

Better discussion usually results if the participants are asked to begin discussion of a problem and progress as far as they can in the time available. If the topic has been well chosen in light of the time set aside for discussion, the group probably will reach a solution; but if a solution is not reached no penalty should be attached. The instructor must always bear in mind that in spite of careful choice of subject to suit the time available, differences of opinion among the participants may unexpectedly delay the group. Surely students should not be penalized for having to cope with disagreement, a very common discussion phenomenon. The group that has faced, resolved, and overcome conflict has had a far more valuable and realistic experience in discussion than the group that progresses from introductory remarks to final summary without a ripple of disagreement.

A somewhat different problem is posed by radio or television discussion programs where a specified number of minutes is available. Many schools present such programs regularly over educational or local commercial broadcasting stations.[12] That such training is valuable is unquestioned; however, the teacher is well advised to treat this type of activity more as a public performance or program than as a discussion. An important factor in preparing a discussion for broadcast is timing. To satisfy the listening public, the presentation of a solution within the time available is desirable. But in attempting to plan the discussion so that a solution is reached before the program ends, the instructor runs the risk that practice may cause a loss of spontaneity and interest among the participants during the actual performance. Just about the only satisfactory solution to this problem is for the teacher to meet with the discussants, talk over the general nature of what they plan to say without going into specific details or proposals, and attempt to allocate tentatively the amount of time that the group will give to each aspect of the question. This guidance may prove helpful to both the moderator and the participants in keeping the discussion moving toward its goal. However, even in this type of situation it is

---

[12] Wayne E. Brockriede and David B. Strother discuss an interesting experiment in televising debate and discussion in "Televised Forensics," *Speech Teacher*, January, 1957, 6:30–35.

advisable for the teacher to make certain that the participants realize that their primary aim is good discussion rather than simply finding a solution on time.

Emphasizing the Cooperative Nature of Discussion. Although most standard discussion textbooks point out that the goal of a discussion is to find, through the exchange of information and ideas, a solution or answer acceptable to *all* members of a group, in practice it often is difficult to impress on students the importance of this concept. When controversy that cannot easily be resolved develops, student discussion groups frequently express a desire to vote to settle the disagreement. The first reason for avoiding this practice is simply that "might" does not necessarily make "right." The mere fact that the majority believe one point of view to be correct does not prove the superiority of their argument. A second reason for avoiding the ballot as a means of settling differences is that in many discussion situations voting, instead of solving the controversy, may serve only to alienate some members of the group. In a nonclassroom discussion, the losers may decide that since their views are so little regarded, they—and sometimes the organizations they represent—are under no obligation to support the plan evolved by the victors.

Developing Realistic Participation Attitudes. Among desirable attitudes that the instructor should stress, two traits important to effective discussion are likely to be misunderstood by the student. These qualities are objectivity (or open-mindedness) and cooperation.

The inclusion of objectivity in a list of desirable discussion attitudes will not be questioned by most students. The difficulty arises when, after the instructor has stressed the importance of thorough study of the question and the necessity of remaining open-minded while preparing to participate, the alert student asks, "How can you study a problem without beginning to formulate ideas and opinions?" The answer is that most people cannot. The teacher of discussion must realize this fact and not ask the impossible. The student undoubtedly will have many preconceived attitudes and ideas when discussion begins. However, if discussion is to be successful he must regard these conclusions as tentative. His attitude should be: I have several opinions on this subject; however, the other members of the group will have materials I have overlooked. I hope that by sharing our ideas and information, all of us will be able to come to a better understanding and solution of the problem.

In stressing the importance of a cooperative attitude, the teacher should be careful not to encourage insincerity and slipshod thinking. If too great a premium is placed on agreeableness, students may be led to forsake their own convictions. This teaches not discussion, but hypocrisy. For the classroom experience in discussion to be realistic the student must feel free to dissent without penalty. Furthermore, when a discussant remains unconvinced in spite of the arguments of other members of the group, he should not be penalized because of the failure of others to change his convictions. Since penetrating discussion frequently results from controversy, the participant must feel free to voice his disagreement. This, of course, should not be interpreted as an invitation to stubborn obstructionism.

Importance of Evaluation and Criticism

The effectiveness of the course or unit in discussion is determined to a great extent by the ability of the instructor to provide the student with frequent and perceptive critical comment on his performance.

Desirable Characteristics of Discussion Criticism. Since the instructor's purpose in criticizing performances is to encourage and guide the student in his effort to master the skills and techniques of discussion, his comments should (1) motivate improvement by stressing student strengths as well as weaknesses, (2) encourage a cooperative discussion attitude, and (3) be based on an understanding of human behavior, a knowledge of discussion methods, and familiarity with a variety of subjects.

In evaluating student performances, the instructor's criticism should not concern itself solely with negative factors. Praise is a strong motivational device and for that reason alone the instructor should make every effort to find something commendable in each student's discussion participation. However, if the student is to make substantial improvement the teacher must always provide concrete suggestions for the correction of weaknesses.

In evaluating discussion performances, a question of concern to teachers for some time has been whether individual grades and ratings create a competitive atmosphere incompatible with the cooperative nature of the discussion situation. Convinced that competition for ratings destroys cooperativeness, some teachers prefer to score discussion performances on a group basis, assigning a single group grade to each participant. While this procedure encourages cooperation, it often results in injustice. The outstanding participant in a poor group may be penalized for the inadequacy of others. To contend that he should have raised the level of discussion may be unrealistic; it is possible that his efforts were the best possible under the circumstances.

Another approach that some instructors favor is to grade the discussion performance on both a group and an individual basis. After the discussion has been completed, the teacher determines the general effectiveness of the group in comparison to past efforts and to the performances of other groups and arrives at a grade for the entire group. He then reflects carefully on the contributions of each member of the group and assigns individual grades as well.

In spite of the cooperative nature of discussion, a strong case can be made for grading participants on an individual, competitive basis. Cooperation and competition are not necessarily incompatible. The typical American competes daily for approval, acceptance, advancement, and promotion through cooperation. His success is largely determined by his ability to fit in and get along well in the classroom, on the job, in the neighborhood, or at the club. In each of these spheres of activity he competes for approval and recognition by cooperating effectively. Furthermore, the very element of competition in cooperative activities often motivates better cooperation. Not wanting to impair his status, to lose his position, or to deprive himself of opportunities for advancement, the individual seeks to increase his contribution to the success and welfare of the group.

Just as competition and cooperation are compatible in our daily lives, so are they compatible in discussion. The very nature of the discussion situation encourages both. Organized to seek a mutually satisfactory answer to a problem, the discussion group places a high premium on cooperation. Yet, regardless of whether a teacher or critic-judge is present, the individual knows that he is being evaluated, rated, or sized up by others in the group or in the audience. To obtain the acceptance and recognition he seeks, the wise discussant will strive to cooperate as effectively as he can. Thus the very fact that he is competing (for acceptance, a high grade, praise, recognition) may actually encourage a more cooperative attitude.

Finally, if students are to develop appreciation of the nature and worth of discussion as a problem-solving tool, the teacher must become a highly perceptive critic. He must be able to distinguish the cooperative participant from the "yes man," the sincere dissenter from the obstructionist, the well-informed contributor from the mere talker, and the original thinker from the repeater or rephraser. In other words, the teacher must be a keen student of human behavior as well as an expert on discussion techniques and the many problems that are discussed. If the instructor is poorly informed on the questions discussed, he cannot hope to separate biased, irrelevant, and incomplete data from objective, pertinent, and substantial information. If the teacher rewards insincerity, inadequate preparation, and faulty thinking, he cannot expect to instill in his students an appreciation for the true values of discussion. Thus upon his ability as a critic and evaluator largely depends the worth of the course or unit in discussion.

Methods of Evaluating Discussion. In an effort to assist the critic or observer in understanding and measuring discussion behavior, experts have developed a variety of evaluation procedures. The teacher of discussion should be acquainted with several of these techniques in order to insure the best possible approach in evaluating student performances. Among the methods the instructor may wish to adopt are the following:[13]

[13] A detailed discussion of these and other methods of evaluating discussion may be found in Waldo W. Braden and Earnest S. Brandenburg, *Oral Decision-Making*, New York: Harper and Row, 1955, pp. 335–361. See also Earnest Brandenburg and Philip Neal, "Graphic Techniques for Evaluating Discussion and Conference Procedures," *Quarterly Journal of Speech*, April, 1953, 39:201, and Henry L. Ewbank and J. Jeffery Auer, *Discussion and Debate, Tools of a Democracy*, 2nd ed., New York: Appleton-Century-Crofts, 1951, pp. 357–373.

1. *The critic-observer approach*, in which a single critic, usually the teacher, observes and evaluates the content or value of the participants' contributions and the techniques and skills employed by the leader and the discussants. With this approach, the critic-observer usually uses a rating blank, scores each participant on every item in a list of desirable qualities, and explains the reasons for his score.

2. *The feedback approach*, which is simply a chronological review of the discussion supplemented by evaluation of the effectiveness of the contributions and techniques of the participants.

3. *The audience-reaction approach*, which consists of assigning selected members of the audience to observe and evaluate specified individuals, techniques, or portions of the discussion.

4. *The participation approach*, which seeks to measure the frequency and nature of individual participation throughout the discussion. The critic may simply count the number of contributions by each person; he may prepare a chart of the seating arrangement and, by the use of arrows to indicate the persons to which each speaker's remarks were directed, attempt to learn something about the flow of participation; or, in addition to counting each speaker's contributions, he may attempt to characterize types of contribution with a set of symbols (for example, he might use O to designate an original contribution, S for supporting information, I for irrelevancy, Q for question, and so forth).

5. *The self-evaluation approach*, in which, at assigned intervals during the discussion, each member is asked to mark quickly a check sheet indicating his interest, attitude, and/or understanding of the topic under consideration at that moment.

6. *The discussion-profile approach*, in which a critic shows trends in the quality, relevancy, or interest of the discussion by preparing a simple line graph with explanatory annotations (for example, as interest increased or the quality of contributions improved, the critic's line would rise; if interest diminished or the group got off the issue the line would fall).

While it by no means includes all of the possible methods of evaluating discussion, the above list does suggest the variety of approaches that may be used. Familiarity with several approaches, and the use of different methods from time to time, should aid both student and teacher in learning more about what occurs during a discussion and in determining ways to improve discussion participation.

A ONE-SEMESTER COLLEGE COURSE IN DISCUSSION AND CONFERENCE SPEAKING

This course is planned to teach the theory and practice of discussion and conference speaking. During the term each member of the class will participate in five discussions. The class will be divided into groups of 5 to 7 students. The groups or panels will function as units during the remainder of the term. The chairmanship will shift with each discussion, and no person may act as chairman more than once.

Special Reports. During the term each member is responsible for reviewing for the class one current article in discussion. These reports are to be no more than 10 minutes long. They should be carefully prepared for oral presentation. Members of the class will be held responsible for these reports.

Course Outline

(Basic Text: Laura Crowell, *Discussion: Method of Democracy*, Glenview, Ill.: Scott, Foresman, 1963.)

1. Speech of introduction: Give a brief speech of introduction, telling who you are and why you are taking the course.
   Reading assignment: Crowell, Chapters 1, 2 and 14.
2. Speech on a thought-provoking statement
   Speaking assignment: Deliver a 2- to 3-minute talk on some thought-provoking statement you have read. Or you may speak on the topic: the importance of discussion in the life of the average citizen (include actual examples of how discussion is used in your home community).
   Reading assignment: Crowell, Chapters 4 and 5.
3. Speaking assignment: Present a speech of definition (2 to 3 minutes long). Define one of the terms found in Chapters 4 and 5 of Crowell. Consult an outside source in preparing your definition. Include in your definition a specific example in order to make your term clear and meaningful.
4. Discussion: The class will be divided in groups of 5 to 7 persons. Each group will discuss a school or local problem. Each group will be allowed 45 minutes for its presentation. Members not participating will write critiques of the performance.
5. Reading assignment: Crowell, Chapters 3 and 6.
   Written assignment: Prepare a list of 20 topics suitable for the class to discuss. Classify them under the following headings: school, local, state, and national.
6. Writing assignment: Prepare a discussion outline for one of the topics you selected on the previous day.
   Reading assignment: Review Crowell, Chapter 6.
7. Discussion assignment: Each group will present another discussion in 45 minutes.
   Reading assignment: Crowell, Chapter 7.
8. Examination.
9. Reading assignment: Crowell, Chapters 9 and 10.
10. Panel discussions: All groups will consider a common topic, but each group will consider a different phase. After 40 minutes of discussion by a group the audience will be permitted to ask questions and contribute any comments.
11. Reading assignment: Crowell, Chapters 11 and 12. Special reports on a discussion you have heard. These reports should not be more than 10 minutes long.

12. Symposia on current problems: One member will present a problem in 7 to 10 minutes. Each member of the group will present a solution to the problem in 5 minutes. After each member has had an opportunity to speak, members of the audience will be permitted to ask questions and make comments.
13. Reading assignments: Crowell, Chapter 13.
14. Discussion-progression:
    a. The class will select a vital problem for discussion.
    b. Each class group will investigate a phase of the problem. When the committee has thoroughly analyzed the problem it will draft a written report in the form of a resolution for presentation to the entire class. If the group is unable to reach unanimous agreement, the minority may also draft a report.
    c. The class will assume the form of a legislative council with a presiding officer and clerk. After the reports are heard by the council, a course of action will be determined. In the process the group will probably engage in legislative debate.
15. Final examination: over the entire book.

EXERCISES

1. Plan a one-semester course in discussion. In your plan, include a lesson for each day, giving the assigned readings, objectives, and classroom activities.
2. Plan a 4-week unit on discussion. Include the following:
    a. Objectives.
    b. Assigned readings and projects.
    c. Classroom activities.
    d. A unit examination.
3. After reading several of the articles listed in the references, write a 500-word paper on one of the following:
    a. Discussion is the most democratic form of speech.
    b. Attitudes are more important than subject matter in discussion.
    c. It is unlikely that a good debater could be an effective discussant.
    d. Discussion is impractical in resolving highly controversial issues.
4. Prepare a list of 10 discussion questions well suited to a group of high school (or college) students.
5. Observe a high school (or college) class in discussion. Give attention to the following:
    a. Course objectives and how they are revealed.
    b. How the teacher makes assignments.
    c. Efforts to motivate the students.
    d. Student attitudes toward the assignments and class activities.
    e. The progress made by the group.
6. Prepare a rating blank for evaluating discussion.
7. Attend a discussion (presented either in class or outside). Using a prepared rating blank, evaluate the discussion.
8. Compare several high school or college discussion textbooks. Select the textbook you think presents the best treatment of the subject. In a short paper, justify your choice.

REFERENCES

Discussion and Debate

AUER, J. JEFFERY, "Tools of Social Inquiry: Argumentation, Discussion, and Debate," *Quarterly Journal of Speech*, December, 1939, 25:533–539.

BAIRD, A. CRAIG, "Argumentation as a Humanistic Subject," *Quarterly Journal of Speech*, June, 1924, 10:258–264.

CAPP, GLENN R., "Discussion and Debate in Life Activities," *Bulletin of the National Association of Secondary School Principals*, January, 1954, 38 (199):67–70.

EWBANK, HENRY LEE, "Bibliography on Periodical Literature on Debating and Discussion," *Quarterly Journal of Speech*, December, 1938, 24:634–641.

HOWELL, WILLIAM S. AND BREMBECK, WINSTON L., "Experimental Studies in Debate, Discussion, and General Public Speaking," *Bulletin of the National Association of Secondary School Principals*, May, 1952, 36 (187):175–192.

MC BURNEY, JAMES H., "The Role of Discussion and Debate in Democratic Society," *Bulletin of the National Association of Secondary School Principals*, May, 1952, 36 (178):22–26.

REUTTER, D. C., "Providing High School Students with Debate and Discussion Topics," *Speech Teacher*, September, 1963, 12:233–239.

ROBINSON, KARL F., "Suggested Units on Discussion and Debate for Secondary Schools," *Quarterly Journal of Speech*, October, 1946, 32:385–390.

THOMPSON, WAYNE, "Discussion and Debate: A Reexamination," *Quarterly Journal of Speech*, October, 1944, 30:288–299.

TIMMONS, WILLIAM M., "Discussion, Debating, and Research," *Quarterly Journal of Speech*, October, 1941, 27:415–421.

Discussion

ANDERSEN, MARTIN P. (ED.), "Roles of the Teacher of Discussion," *Quarterly Journal of Speech*, April, 1960, 46:176–188.

ARNOLD, CARROLL C., "Teaching Discussion for the Development of Democratic Behavior," *Bulletin of the National Association of Secondary School Principals*, January, 1954, 38 (199):83–86.

BARNLUND, DEAN C., "Our Concept of Discussion: Static or Dynamic?" *Speech Teacher*, January, 1954, 3:8–14.

BECKER, SAM L., "Rating Discussants," *Speech Teacher*, January, 1956, 5:60–65.

CATHCART, ROBERT S., "Leadership as a Secondary Function in Group Discussion," *Speech Teacher*, September, 1962, 11:221–226.

CROWELL, LAURA, "Rating Scales as Diagnostic Instruments in Discussion," *Speech Teacher*, January, 1953, 2:26–32.

GIFFIN, KIM AND LASHBROOK, BRAD, " 'Group Action' in Perspective," *Speech Teacher*, March, 1960, 9:127–130.

HOWELL, WILLIAM S. AND SMITH, DONALD K., "Discussion Re-examined," *Central States Speech Journal*, Fall, 1953, 5:3–7; Spring, 1954, 5:21–24.

KELLER, PAUL W., "A Secondary School Course in Discussion," *Bulletin of the National Association of Secondary School Principals*, May, 1952, 36 (187):45–56.

KELTNER, JOHN, "The Laboratory Method of Discussion Training at Kansas State College," *Speech Teacher*, September, 1958, 7:199–208.

KELTNER, JOHN AND HAIMAN, FRANKLYN, "Discussion as a Tool in Acquiring and Using Knowledge," *Bulletin of the National Association of Secondary School Principals*, January, 1954, 38 (199):111–116.

MORTENSON, CALVIN D., "Should the Discussion Group Have an Assigned Leader?" *Speech Teacher*, January, 1966, *15*:34.

SCHEIDEL, THOMAS M. AND CROWELL, LAURA, "Idea Development in Small Discussion Groups," *Quarterly Journal of Speech*, April, 1964, *50*:140–145.

UTTERBACK, WILLIAM E., "Evaluation of Performances in the Discussion Course at Ohio State University," *Speech Teacher*, September, 1958, *7*:209–215.

WATKINS, LLOYD, "Some Problems and Solutions in Teaching Group Discussion," *Speech Teacher*, September, 1961, *10*:211–214.

Textbooks

BARNLUND, DEAN C. AND HAIMAN, FRANKLYN S., *The Dynamics of Discussion*, Boston: Houghton Mifflin, 1960.

BORMANN, EARNEST G., *Discussion and Group Methods: Theory and Practice*, New York: Harper & Row, 1968.

GULLEY, HALBERT E., *Discussion, Conference, and Group Process*, 2nd ed., New York: Holt, Rinehart and Winston, 1968.

HAIMAN, FRANKLYN S., *Group Leadership and Democratic Action*, Boston: Houghton Mifflin, 1951.

HARNACK, R. VICTOR AND FEST, THORREL B., *Group Discussion: Theory and Technique*, New York: Appleton-Century-Crofts, 1964.

POTTER, DAVID A. AND ANDERSEN, MARTIN P., *Discussion: A Guide to Effective Practice*, 2nd ed., Belmont, Calif.: Wadsworth, 1970.

SATTLER, WILLIAM M. AND MILLER, N. EDD, *Discussion and Conference*, 2nd ed., Englewood Cliffs, N.J.: Prentice-Hall, 1967.

SMITH, WILLIAM S., *Group Problem-Solving Through Discussion: A Process Essential to Democracy*, New York and Indianapolis: Bobbs-Merrill, 1965.

UTTERBACK, WILLIAM E., *Group Thinking and Conference Leadership*, rev. ed., Boston: Houghton Mifflin, 1964.

WAGNER, RUSSELL AND ARNOLD, CARROLL C., *Handbook of Group Discussion*, 2nd ed., Boston: Houghton Mifflin, 1966.

5. Teaching Debate

Owen Peterson

Debate is justly recognized as one of the most important forms of public address in a democratic society. For it is in the give-and-take of debate that the goals, directions, problems, and remedies of society are most thoroughly examined, analyzed, and dissected, revealing all of the flaws, virtues, failures, gains, obstacles, and alternatives. In view of the importance of debating in the political, social, religious, and economic aspects of our lives, it is not surprising that most high schools and colleges provide training in this form of oral communication.

Debate, as explained in Chapter 4, is closely related to discussion and to the reflective thought pattern. It becomes important in the democratic process when the cooperative approach of discussion is no longer possible in dealing with a problem and the various alternatives must be presented to the public or some determining body for a choice.

AIMS AND GOALS

Like discussion, debate should acquaint the student with research methods and materials, should stimulate his interest and knowledge of contemporary issues, should improve his skill in analysis and reasoning, and, thereby, better equip him to fulfill his social, professional, and political responsibilities.

In addition, debate training seeks:

1. To develop an understanding and appreciation of the uses, values, and nature of debating.

74

2. To familiarize the student with the effective use of persuasive devices.
3. To develop proficiency in specific debate skills and techniques such as refutation and adaptation.
4. To develop effective speech habits.

TEACHING MATERIALS AND AIDS

Most of the teaching materials and aids recommended to the teacher for a course or unit in discussion (see pp. 57) will likewise prove useful to the debate instructor. In selecting a textbook for debate, the teacher has a considerably wider choice than in the case of discussion, which should enable him to locate a book that approaches the subject in a way suited to his particular situation and needs. In addition, many excellent works treating both discussion and debate are available.

Among the specialized publications and collections of materials that the instructor may find useful in studying and analyzing debate propositions are *The Reference Shelf* series, *N.U.E.A Debate Handbook, Congressional Digest,* and *The Annals of the American Academy of Political and Social Science* (discussed in Chapter 4).

If at all possible, the school library should have available at least two or three reputable newspapers such as the *New York Times* and the *Washington Post* and some of the national news magazines, such as *Newsweek, Time,* and *U.S. News and World Report.* In addition, as in the case with discussion, valuable pertinent information can usually be obtained by writing to one's congressman and to interested parties such as labor unions, national organizations, professional societies, the League of Women Voters, and similar groups. Whether to invest in the purchase of debate handbooks is a question which each teacher will have to decide for himself after carefully weighing the pros and cons of such aids, as discussed in Chapter 4.

TEACHING FACILITIES AND CONDITIONS

The debate class should be arranged so that the speaker faces his listeners in the usual public speaking relationship. Two desks or tables—one for each team—large enough to accommodate all of the debaters' materials— and a chalkboard are desirable. Since no more than four to six persons normally participate in a single debate, class size should be restricted, if possible, so that every student can be heard in a debate in a short period of time. If an even number of students is enrolled in the course, the tasks of assigning debate partners and scheduling debates are simplified. (Of course, the teacher frequently has no control over this matter.)

The teacher may also wish to utilize a lectern or rostrum, an easel for displaying visual aids, and a stopwatch for timing debate speeches.

PLANNING THE UNIT OR COURSE OF STUDY

This section suggests units of study and assignments for the debate unit or course and stresses several principles of effective debate training. In view of the wide difference in conditions under which argumentation and debate are taught, the suggested units of study are intended to serve only as a guide to the teacher. Some of the units, it will be noted, duplicate those set forth for teaching discussion; and in cases where a discussion unit or course has already acquainted the student with material or methods common to both activities these, of course, should be omitted. Among the student assignments, the teacher will note several that involve the skills and techniques of discussion, thereby permitting the teacher to utilize discussion methods to teach debate.

Suggested Study Units

    I. The nature and importance of debate
        A. Definition of debate
        B. Differences among debate, discussion, and public speaking
        C. Uses of debate
        D. The role of debate in a democratic society
   II. Selecting debate propositions
        A. Types of propositions
        B. Criteria for selecting topics
        C. Phrasing debate propositions
  III. Analysis of the debate proposition
        A. Defining terms
        B. History and background
        C. Analyzing the problem
            1. What is an issue?
            2. What are the stock issues in a proposition of policy?
            3. Locating issues
        D. Finding and testing solutions
  IV. The debate case
        A. The affirmative case
            1. Responsibilities of the affirmative team
            2. The division of responsibilities among the affirmative speakers
        B. The negative case
            1. Responsibilities of the negative team
            2. The division of responsibilities among the negative speakers
   V. Gathering evidence and information for debate
        A. Sources of information
        B. Types
        C. Taking notes

   VI. Argument
       A. Types
       B. Fallacies
  VII. Evaluating evidence and argument
       A. Evaluating sources
       B. Evaluating evidence
       C. Testing argument
 VIII. The debate brief
       A. Purpose
       B. Preparation
       C. Form
       D. Parts
   IX. Refutation
       A. The rebuttal speech
       B. Preparing the rebuttal
       C. Special rebuttal techniques
    X. Delivery in debate
   XI. Special kinds of debate
       A. Cross-examination
       B. Heckling
       C. Direct clash
       D. Problem solving
       E. Legislative debate

See pp. 85–90 at the end of this chapter for examples of how course outlines and assignments can be developed around these units.

Student Assignments

 1. Listen to and evaluate a debate.
 2. Read and evaluate a debate.
 3. Select and phrase several debate propositions.
 4. Prepare a bibliography on a debate proposition.
 5. Participate in a round-table discussion of the meaning of the terms of the question.
 6. Prepare and deliver a short speech defining the terms of a debate proposition.
 7. Prepare and deliver a short speech giving the history and background of a debate proposition.
 8. Participate in a round-table discussion on the history and background of the question.
 9. Prepare an outline analyzing either the affirmative or negative on a debate proposition.
10. Participate in a round-table discussion on one phase or issue of the debate question.
11. Prepare and deliver a persuasive speech supporting either the affirmative or negative side of a debate question.
12. Prepare a scrapbook of clippings and articles on a debate proposition.
13. Participate in a debate before the class.
14. Participate in a special type of debate before the class (cross-examination, heckling, direct clash, problem solving).
15. Prepare a brief on a debate proposition.
16. Write a critique on a classroom debate.
17. Present a short refutation of a recent editorial.
18. Present a debate before another class or a club or organization.

19. Outline and discuss several types of negative cases that might be developed on a given proposition.
20. Write a first affirmative debate speech.
21. Rewrite a first affirmative debate speech for a specific audience other than the class (i.e., the PTA, a 4-H club, a civic organization, etc.) to emphasize audience adaptation and the use of persuasive techniques.
22. Prepare a list of fallacious arguments found in advertisements, editorials, articles, and (or) books with comments on the types of fallacies.
23. Prepare a short (approximately 2-minute) speech proving a single point.
24. Write two short speeches embodying the same subject matter, developing one inductively and the other deductively.
25. Convert into syllogisms two or three of the principal arguments in a classroom debate.
26. Evaluate the evidence in a printed speech.

PRINCIPLES FOR TEACHING DEBATE

In planning the course or unit in debate, the instructor should keep in mind the following principles of effective teaching: (1) Training in debate should afford the student extensive practice and experience in a variety of argumentative speaking situations; (2) effective debate teaching encourages individual thought, research, analysis, and synthesis; and (3) effective debate teaching is based on perceptive criticism. This list, by no means exhaustive, poses questions which the teacher must consider in planning instruction in debate.

Extensive Practice in Varied Situations

Since practice before audiences is essential to the development of effective speech, the instructor is faced with the problem of devising study units that provide the student with speaking experience and at the same time a thorough understanding of the principles of effective speech. As most teachers know, this raises two questions: If speeches are assigned before the student understands the fundamentals of effective speaking, how can he be expected to perform well? If, on the other hand, actual performance is postponed until the principles of good speaking have been studied, how can the teacher in the short time remaining provide each student with extensive practice?

To solve this problem, the course or unit in debate, like other speech training, should be planned so that the student is given the opportunity for several meaningful speech experiences while he is studying and preparing for later participation in complete debates.

This probably can best be accomplished by designing units of study that incorporate performances with the mastery of certain fundamentals of debate. For example, short speeches defining the terms of a debate proposition may be assigned early in the course or unit. Later, speeches covering the history and background of the question, speeches giving the pros and (or) cons related to a single issue, speeches refuting an argument, and speeches showing the practicability or impracticability of a particular proposal may be assigned. In this manner the student gains valuable speech experience, but is not faced with the frightening prospect of being expected to participate in a full-scale debate as his first speech performance. Later, needless to say, the student should be afforded as many opportunities as possible to participate in complete debates.

In planning the course or unit, the instructor has a wide choice of types of debate he may include. While the teacher of a short unit probably will find it impossible to acquaint his students with more than one or two kinds of debate, the instructor of a semester course may wish to introduce several forms, including, in addition to standard debate, the cross-examination or Oregon style of debate; the heckling debate; the direct-clash plan of debate; the open-forum, or British, system; the problem-solving debate; and the legislative debate. Most debate textbooks explain the specific procedures and regulations of each of these types of debating.[1]

In addition to presenting different kinds of debates, the teacher may wish to arrange debates before different audiences. Because all class members usually study the same question for a long period of time, the student audience frequently becomes extremely well-informed on the proposition and occasionally somewhat bored by it. The teacher may find it rewarding to confront the debaters with new and relatively uninformed listeners. The necessity of adapting complex arguments to the interests and understanding of a lay audience usually is a valuable educational experience for the debater. To locate such audiences, the teacher should investigate the possibility of presenting debates to other classes, to school clubs and organizations, and to civic and educational groups.

Individual Thought, Research, Analysis, and Synthesis

One of its principal values is that, properly conducted, debate training aids the student in developing ability to think clearly, critically, and analytically. However, to stimulate independent thought and investigation the teacher must make certain that debate propositions are challenging and that the assistance he provides in analyzing questions and in developing cases is limited.

In guiding the class in the selection of propositions, the instructor should make certain that the topics are well suited to the amount of time

[1] For a discussion of different types of debate, see David Potter (ed.), *Argumentation and Debate, Principles and Types*, New York: Holt, Rinehart and Winston, 1954, pp. 251–280; and Kenneth G. Hance, "Newer Types of Extracurricular Activities in Public Speaking," *Bulletin of the National Association of Secondary School Principals*, May, 1952, 36:132–136.

and resource materials available for study. He should plan the course or unit so that the students are not expected to become experts on more subjects than their time permits. To prevent this the instructor may ask the class to select a single topic for study and debate throughout the course or unit. A variation is to select three or four subjects, depending on class enrollment, and assign each subject to a group of four students. Teachers who conduct extracurricular forensics programs frequently adopt the national proposition for class study in order to prepare students for extracurricular debating. If a single topic is selected, the instructor should make certain that the question is sufficiently challenging to maintain interest for the duration of the unit of study.

While classroom debate propositions need not deal with ponderous international issues, neither should they be overly limited or trivial. The instructor who must teach debating in a 2- or 3-week unit unquestionably cannot demand that his students become thoroughly acquainted with a vast, complex problem; however, the teacher with more time should beware of the pitfalls of overly simple propositions. The first danger is that students will quickly exhaust the subject and lose interest. With minor problems, the teacher may also encounter difficulty in stimulating research and in teaching debate analysis. Topics that can be debated with a minimum of study and preparation seldom lead students to unfamiliar corners of the library or present them with the intricacies of analysis and case planning which make debate a challenging and exciting activity.

After a satisfactory proposition has been selected, the instructor must teach his students how to do argumentative analysis. Most high school students, and many college students, do not know how to discover the significant issues involved in a broad and complex problem. In coping with this problem, the teacher must decide how far he should go in assisting students in analyzing the question and planning debate cases? The question, of course, is one that cannot be answered precisely. With beginning debaters, the instructor undoubtedly must lend considerable assistance. With more advanced students, advice and aid are less imperative. But regardless of the level of his students, the teacher's guidance must not become a substitute for individual thought and analysis. If it does, one of the principal values of the study of debate is destroyed. The teacher should be a critic, not an architect. Rather than outlining the principal issues and arguments related to the debate proposition, the instructor should seek to direct the student to these issues and arguments through criticism, questions, and other indirect techniques. (For discussion of these approaches, see p. 276.) While this method is slower than a direct attack, it will prove more beneficial in the long run. To debate well a student must learn to think for himself; too much assistance merely delays development of the student's critical faculties.

Perceptive Criticism

To gain maximum benefit, debaters should have criticism from both the teacher and the other students. The criticism may take various forms. Certainly the teacher should prepare some kind of written critique while listening to the speaking. He may use any of several rating blanks or he may prepare one suited to his particular situation. In addition to a written evaluation for the speakers, if the entire class is to benefit from the instructor's criticism he should discuss with them the important features of the debate. The oral critique must not be devoted exclusively to faultfinding; improvement and effective utilization of debate techniques should also be noted.

If a decision is to be announced, the instructor should base his judgment on the merits of the debate rather than the merits of the question. Most debates outside the classroom seek to persuade the listeners of the superiority of a particular proposal in relation to other contentions; consequently, any vote or decision usually is based on the auditors' judgment of the merits of the conflicting points of view. However, since students engage in classroom and extracurricular debating not for the purpose of winning adherents to a cause, but rather to develop ability in argumentation, decisions should be based on the students' mastery of debate skills and techniques.

At times the teacher may find it difficult to divorce his personal convictions from his evaluation of the speeches—difficult, that is, to judge debates solely on the merits of the debating. The average listener naturally is more highly critical of arguments that contradict his personal beliefs than of contentions that reinforce his preconceived opinions. But the instructor must avoid this kind of biased listening. For suggestions regarding this aspect of criticism, see pp. 274–275.

The use of a rating blank or ballot is often helpful in obtaining greater objectivity. A well-constructed ballot is also of value to the student in indicating specific strengths and weaknesses. One type of ballot which the instructor may wish to utilize requires the critic to assign scores (for example, 1 for poor, 2 for fair, 3 for good, 4 for excellent, and 5 for superior, or some similar system) for each item on a list of debate skills and techniques that the instructor wishes to measure. A typical ballot for this purpose is shown on p. 82. The criteria included in this type of ballot should provide a satisfactory measurement of the overall effectiveness of the debating. If the rating form places undue emphasis on minor or secondary skills or unimportant aspects of the debate, use of the ballot may result in decisions in favor of the poorer of two teams. For example, with a poorly constructed rating blank the judge may find at the conclusion of the debate that team A has scored a greater number of points even though he is convinced that team B did the better debating. In using a ballot of this

SAMPLE JUDGE'S DEBATE BALLOT

Note: In the following, you are to rate each debater by a score of 1–7 on each point (1 is poor, 3–4 is average, and 7 is superior). Team scores may be obtained by adding together the totals of each speaker on the team. The team with the highest score wins the debate.

	Affirmative		Negative	
	I	II	I	II
1. Analysis, plan of case				
2. Knowledge and information				
3. Reasoning				
4. Adaptation to opposing case				
5. Skill in rebuttal				
6. Skill in speaking				
Totals				

Affirmative I _____ points
Affirmative II _____ points

Negative I _____ points
Negative II _____ points

The _____ team did the more effective debating.

_____
Judge

SAMPLE JUDGE'S DEBATE BALLOT

Contestants

Aff. _____   Neg. _____

  Name of School   *Name of School*

_____   _____

  First Affirmative   *First Negative*

_____   _____

  Second Affirmative   *Second Negative*

In my opinion the debating done by the affirmative was
  Superior
  Excellent
  Good   (*Circle correct designation.*)
  Fair
  Below Average

In my opinion the debating done by the negative was
  Superior
  Excellent
  Good   (*Circle correct designation.*)
  Fair
  Below Average

In my opinion the performances of the individual speakers were as
follows: (Superior, Excellent, Good, Fair, or Below Average)
  The performance of the first affirmative was _____
  The performance of the second affirmative was _____
  The performance of the first negative was _____
  The performance of the second negative was _____
  The better team was (affirmative or negative) _____

_____

                                              Judge

SAMPLE AUDIENCE SHIFT OF OPINION BALLOT FOR USE IN DEBATING

Before the Debate
(*Check one*)

_____ I believe in the Affirmative side of the resolution.
_____ I believe in the Negative side of the resolution.
_____ I am undecided.

After the Debate
(*Check one*)

_____ I believe in the Affirmative side of the resolution.
_____ I believe in the Negative side of the resolution.
_____ I am undecided.
_____ I believe more strongly in the Affirmative side of the resolution.
_____ I believe more strongly in the Negative side of the resolution.
_____ I have heard the entire discussion and I am still undecided.

type it is important that the sum of the parts equals the total overall effectiveness of the debating.

Some teachers prefer a rating blank that simply requires the judge to select the winning team or to assign a rating to the teams or participants, like the ballot illustrated (p. 83). The disadvantage of this approach is that, unless the ballot is accompanied by a written or oral critique, the speaker has no way of knowing why he earned the decision or rating or how he might improve his debating.

The instructor may also utilize the classroom audience in evaluating debates. One method of obtaining an audience evaluation may be to ask class members to complete a shift-of-opinion ballot above, on which they indicate their attitudes toward the proposition both before and after the debate. In using the shift-of-opinion ballot the teacher should keep in mind that such a ballot is not statistically reliable with audiences of less than 30 listeners. He also should consider the possibility, especially with younger students, that the balloting may be an indication of the popularity of the participants rather than a true expression of listener attitudes.

Class comments also may be helpful to the teacher in evaluating debates by confirming his own reactions or, conversely, in pointing out weaknesses he overlooked. Student reactions are particularly valuable in judging the

BALLOT FOR EVALUATING REBUTTAL

(For Classroom and Practice Only)

Student Name _____

      (5—superior; 4—excellent; 3—good; 2—fair; 1—poor)

Does the Student   *Comments*   *Points*

_____ Refute the central ideas?

_____ Refute each point sufficiently
to satisfy the audience?

_____ Introduce new evidence in
refutation and rebuttal?

_____ Avoid refuting points not made?

_____ Avoid crediting the other side
with arguments and evidence stated
but not developed?

_____ Use general methods of refutation?

    _____ Challenge personal observa-
tions?

    _____ Test authorities?

    _____ Evaluate statistics?

    _____ Challenge unsupported asser-
tions?

    _____ Question false assumptions?

    _____ Attack hasty generalizations?

    _____ Question attacks on personal-
ities and the use of emotional
appeals and language?

    _____ Point out circular reasoning,
begging the question?

_____ Use special methods of refutation?

    _____ Ask questions?

    _____ Reductio ad absurdum?

    _____ Method of residues?

    _____ Employ the dilemma?

    _____ Adopt opposing arguments?

    _____ Expose irrelevant arguments?

_____ Organize his rebuttal clearly?

    _____ State issues at the outset?

    _____ Clearly state argument and
evidence advanced by opponent
under the issue?

    _____ Summarize own refutation?

    _____ State what remains for the
opposition to prove?

                                  Total Points _____

speakers' adaptation to their audience. Because the teacher, ideally, is better informed on the debate proposition than any of his students, class discussion often reveals arguments that, though meaningful to the instructor, were not clear to most of the other listeners. Since effective debating aims to persuade entire audiences—not teachers and judges only—this type of evaluation is valuable. Before instituting any kind of class criticism the instructor should be careful to create the proper atmosphere and attitudes, as discussed in Chapter 12.

A ONE-SEMESTER COLLEGE COURSE IN DEBATE

The following outline for a one-semester beginning college course in debate places considerable emphasis on discussion techniques in teaching debating. The course is designed for a class of 12 to 18 college sophomores and juniors.

Course Outline

(Basic text: James H. McBurney and Glen E. Mills, *Argumentation and Debate: Techniques of a Free Society*, New York: Macmillan, 1964.)
I. Part one
  A. Introduction
    1. Explanation of general nature of the course.
    2. Discussion of debate: aims, relationships, applications.
  B. The responsibilities of the advocate
    1. Reading assignment: McBurney and Mills, Chapter 1.
  C. Debate propositions
    1. Reading assignment: McBurney and Mills, Chapter 3.
    2. Preparation: Frame eight propositions, of either policy or fact, that you would enjoy debating or discussing. Investigate international, national, regional, local, and campus events as sources for propositions.
    3. Class: Discussion of propositions and selection of a question for study and debate during the semester.
  D. Analyzing and investigating the proposition
    1. Reading assignment: McBurney and Mills, Chapters 4 and 5.
    2. Preparation: From the sources assigned below prepare 10 bibliographic listings on the debate topic. A complete bibliography, including all listings submitted by the class, will later be duplicated and distributed.
      a. *Readers' Guide*
      b. *New York Times Index*
      c. *Public Affairs Index*
      d. Card catalog
      e. Encyclopedias, almanacs, and yearbooks
    3. Class: Discussion of analyzing the proposition.

E. Discussion as preparation for debate
   1. Reading assignment: McBurney and Mills, Chapter 6.
   2. Class: Discussion of the discussion pattern and preparation of an outline for phrasing the proposition.
F. Phrasing the proposition
   1. Reading assignment: McBurney and Mills, review Chapter 3.
   2. Preparation: Assign 6 to 8 members of the class to prepare a 25-minute discussion on phrasing the selected debate topic as a satisfactory debate proposition. Follow the outline prepared in class under E.
   3. Class: Discussion by panel for 25 minutes, followed by entire class participation in final phrasing of the debate proposition.
G. Analysis and issues
   1. Reading assignment: McBurney and Mills, review Chapter 4.
   2. Preparation: Be prepared to answer the following questions:
      a. What are issues? What are main and minor issues?
      b. What principles should be followed in organizing and wording issues?
      c. What are the obligations of the speakers presenting an affirmative case on a proposition of policy? How are they usually divided?
      d. What are the alternatives that the negative can adopt in presenting a negative case on a proposition of policy?
   3. Reading assignment: Any sources that will give you background and general understanding of the debate proposition.
   4. Preparation: List the main and minor issues on the debate proposition.
   5. Class: Discussion of issues involved in the debate proposition.
H. Evidence
   1. Reading assignment: McBurney and Mills, Chapter 7. Also continue reading to gain background on the debate topic.
   2. Class: Discussion of evidence. Division of bibliography and assignment of readings for preparation of an annotated bibliography.
I. The kinds and structures of arguments
   1. Reading assignment: McBurney and Mills, Chapters 8 and 9. Also begin reading materials assigned in the bibliography. Take notes and prepare a short annotated bibliographical card for each item read. Note whether article is primarily affirmative or negative, indicate kinds of material included, and evaluate the worth of the article.
   2. Class: Discussion of McBurney and Mills, Chapters 8 and 9.
J. Argumentation
   1. Reading assignment: McBurney and Mills, Chapter 10.
   2. Preparation: Prepare a 4- to 5-minute argumentative speech for or against the debate proposition.
   3. Class: Delivery of speeches.
   4. Reading assignment: McBurney and Mills, Chapter 11.
   5. Class: Continuation of argumentative speeches.
   6. Preparation: Complete reading and annotated bibliography cards. Submit these at the end of the class period.
   7. Class: Completion of argumentative speeches.
K. Briefing
   1. Reading assignment: McBurney and Mills, Chapter 13.

2. Class: Discussion of briefing and outlining. Assignment of briefs.
L. The case
  1. Reading assignment: McBurney and Mills, Chapter 12.
  2. Class: Discussion of cases and development of broad, general outlines of possible affirmative and negative cases on the proposition chosen for debate.
M. Analysis: the "need" issue
  1. Reading assignment: McBurney and Mills, Chapter 14.
  2. Preparation: Prepare a 5-minute argumentative speech on either side of the "need" issue of the debate proposition. Your speech should answer the following questions:
    (a) Is the present policy satisfactory?
    (b) Are the alleged weaknesses inherent in the status quo?
    (c) Are there other policies that will correct the alleged weaknesses?
  3. Class: Speeches.
  4. Reading assignment: Continue reading and taking notes on the debate topic.
  5. Class: Speeches.
  6. Reading assignment: Continue reading and note-taking on proposition.
  7. Class: Speeches completed.
N. Fallacies and stratagems
  1. Reading assignment: McBurney and Mills, Chapter 16.
  2. Class: Discussion of McBurney and Mills, Chapter 16 and potential issues and arguments related to the practicability and desirability of the selected debate proposition.
O. Analysis: Practicability and desirability
  1. Preparation: Prepare a 5-minute argumentative speech on the practicability and/or desirability of the policy proposed in the debate question.
  2. Class: Speeches.
  3. Completion of speeches on practicability and desirability.
P. General
  1. Review of material covered to date.
  2. Midterm examination.
II. Part Two
A. Analysis
  1. Preparation: Class will be divided into groups of 6 to 8 persons each and each group will be assigned one of the major issues that have emerged in speeches on the proposition so far. Prepare a 30- to 40-minute panel discussion on the issue assigned. Continue reading and note-taking.
  2. Class: Panel discussion on one major issue.
  3. Preparation: Repeat preceding preparation.
  4. Class: Panel discussion on a second major issue.
  5. Preparation: Repeat preceding preparation.
  6. Class: Panel discussion on a third major issue.
B. Briefing
  1. Briefs due.
  2. Class: Organization of debate teams and scheduling debates.
C. The advocate as speaker
  1. Reading assignment: McBurney and Mills, Chapter 15.

   2. Class: Discussion of McBurney and Mills, Chapter 15.
D. Refutation and rebuttal
   1. Reading assignment: McBurney and Mills, Chapter 17.
   2. Class: Discussion of McBurney and Mills, Chapter 17.
E. Debates
   1. Preparation: Teams will prepare to present debates as scheduled under B.
   2. Class: Debates.
F. Evaluation and criticism of debates
   1. Preparation: Students not participating will each day prepare a written criticism of the debate they have just heard.
   2. Class: Discussion of most recent debate.
G. Kinds of debate
   1. Reading assignment: McBurney and Mills, Chapter 18.
   2. Class: Discussion of McBurney and Mills, Chapter 18. Explanation by the instructor of cross-examination debating, its format and rules. Assignment of cross-examination debates.
H. Cross-examination debates
   1. Preparation: Debate teams will remain the same and take the same sides as in original debates.
   2. Class: Cross-examination debates.
I. Evaluation of cross-examination debates
   1. Preparation: Each student will prepare a written evaluation of his own participation in the just-completed cross-examination debates.
   2. Class: Discussion of cross-examination debates.
J. Final debates
   1. Preparation: New partners will be assigned for the final round of debates; however, speakers will support the same side of the proposition as before. These debates will constitute part of the final examination in the course.
   2. Class: Presentation of debates (conventional style).
K. Final examination

EXERCISES

1. Plan one of the following courses:
   a. A semester course in debating.
   b. A semester course in discussion and debate.
      In your plan, include a lesson for each day, giving the assigned readings, objectives, and other classroom activities.
2. Plan a unit in debate to be presented in 4 weeks. Include (a) objectives, (b) assigned readings, (c) activities, and (d) unit examination.
3. After reading several articles in the periodicals (see references), write a 500-word paper on one of the following:
   a. Should students be required to debate both sides of a proposition?
   b. Should debating be regarded as cooperative projects in discovery of the truth?
   c. Debating makes sophists out of students.
   d. Discussion and debate are poles apart.
4. Observe a high school or college class in debate. Give attention to the following:
   a. Course objectives.

b. How are these objectives revealed?
c. How does the teacher make assignments?
d. What efforts are made to motivate the students?
e. The course plan or organization.
f. The attitudes of the students toward assignments.
g. The progress made by the group.
5. Prepare a rating blank for evaluating debate.
6. Attend a debate (presented either in class or outside). Using a prepared rating blank, evaluate the debate.
7. Prepare a list of debate topics suited to a high school or college speech class.
8. Compare several high school or college textbooks on one of the following:
   a. Debate.
   b. Argumentation (debate and discussion).
   Select the textbook you think presents the best treatment of the subject, and in a short paper justify your selection.
9. Compile a list of films that would be useful in teaching debate.

REFERENCES

BEHL, WILLIAM A., "A New Look at the Debate Brief," *Speech Teacher*, September, 1961, 10:189–193.

BROCK, BERNARD L., "The Comparative Advantages Case," *Speech Teacher*, March, 1967, 16:118.

CAPP, GLENN R., HUBER, ROBERT, AND EUBANK, WAYNE C., "Debates of Affirmative Speakers," *Speech Teacher*, March 1959, 8:139–149.

CATHCART, ROBERT S., "Adapting Debate to an Audience," *Speech Teacher*, March, 1956, 5:113–116.

CRIPE, NICHOLAS M., "Debating Both Sides in Tournaments Is Ethical," *Speech Teacher*, September, 1957, 6:209–212.

DELL, GEORGE W., "In Defense of Debating Both Sides," *Speech Teacher*, January, 1958, 7:31–34.

EHNINGER, DOUGLAS, "Decision by Debate: A Reexamination," *Quarterly Journal of Speech*, October, 1959, 45:282–287.

EHNINGER, DOUGLAS, "Debate as Method: Limitations and Values," *Speech Teacher*, September, 1966, 15:180.

GRAHAM, JOHN, "The Usefulness of Debate in a Public Speaking Course," *Speech Teacher*, March, 1966, 15:136.

KONIGSBERG, EVELYN, "What Should Be Our Objective in High School Debating?" *Quarterly Journal of Speech*, June, 1935, 21:392–396.

MURPHY, RICHARD, "The Ethics of Debating Both Sides," *Speech Teacher*, January, 1957, 6:1–9.

MURPHY, RICHARD, "The Ethics of Debating Both Sides II," *Speech Teacher*, September, 1963, 12:242–247.

REEVES, J. WALTER, "A Secondary School Course in Argumentation," *Bulletin of the National Association of Secondary School Principals*, May, 1952, 36 (187):57–78.

REUTTER, D. C., "Providing High School Students with Debate and Discussion Topics," *Speech Teacher*, September, 1963, 12:233–237.

SIKKINK, DONALD, "Evidence on the Both Sides Debate Controversy," *Speech Teacher*, January, 1962, 11:51–54.

WATKINS, LLOYD I. (ED.), "Ethical Problems in Debating—A Symposium," *Speech Teacher*, March, 1959, 8:151–156.

Textbooks on Debate

CAPP, GLENN R. AND CAPP, THELMA R., *Principles of Argumentation and Debate*, Englewood Cliffs, N.J.: Prentice-Hall, 1965.

EHNINGER, DOUGLAS AND BROCKRIEDE, WAYNE, *Decision by Debate*, New York: Dodd, Mead, 1963.

FOSTER, WILLIAM TRUFANT, *Argumentation and Debating*, Boston: Houghton Mifflin, 1932.

FREELEY, AUSTIN J., *Argumentation and Debate: Rational Decision-Making*, 2nd ed., Belmont, Calif.: Wadsworth, 1966.

MC BATH, JAMES, *Argumentation and Debate: Principles and Practices*, rev. ed., New York: Holt, Rinehart and Winston, 1963.

MC BURNEY, JAMES H. AND MILLS, GLEN E., *Argumentation and Debate*, 2nd ed., New York: Macmillan, 1964.

MOULTON, EUGENE R., *The Dynamics of Debate*, New York: Harcourt Brace Jovanovich, 1966.

MURPHY, JAMES J. AND ERICSON, JOHN M., *The Debater's Guide*, New York and Indianapolis: Bobbs-Merrill, 1961.

WINDES, RUSSEL R. AND HASTINGS, ARTHUR, *Argumentation and Advocacy*, New York: Random House, 1966.

6. Directing the Extracurricular Forensic Program

Owen Peterson

GENERAL NATURE AND SCOPE

Almost every college and university, and many high schools, today provide interested and capable students with the opportunity for extracurricular training in forensic speaking activities. Although the number and types of activities vary from school to school, most well-rounded college and high school forensic programs offer both debate and discussion training. In addition, many institutions include in their extracurricular programs oratory, extemporaneous speaking, declamation, and similar activities.

How Many Activities Should Be Included in the Program?

In planning extracurricular forensic training, one of the first decisions the director of forensics must make is to determine how extensive a program of activities should be offered. Although personal considerations, school and community demands, student interest, and finances will all influence his decision, the teacher's first concern should be for the educational values of the various possible programs. He should seek to develop a program that is neither so intensive that students develop skill in only one specialized kind of speaking nor so extensive that the activities lack depth and meaning. The program should also be sufficiently broad and varied that it will prove attractive to students of diverse interests, backgrounds, and needs.

The forensic director should next determine what kind of training best meets these criteria. Should the program be concerned primarily with debate or with discussion? Although speech educators for many years have argued the relative merits of these two activities, the perceptive teacher will see that a program organized around either activity alone fails to meet the standards of varied speech experiences and widespread appeal. A program devoted exclusively to debate, for example, may produce speakers who are well prepared to argue effectively but ill-equipped to participate in non-argumentative speech situations. Graduates of the exclusively discussion-oriented program, on the other hand, often do well so long as they remain seated, but are panic-stricken if asked to address an audience. Either program may also fail to attract many capable and talented students simply because the particular activity being stressed is of little interest to them.

Both debate and discussion, as currently practiced, have their weaknesses and both have critics to point out their flaws. But, in the opinion of the writer, the most sensible attitude toward this controversy is that of a prominent speech educator: "We can tolerate individual differences in opinion about methods of preparing discussers and debaters. These differences are probably healthy. But I am strongly of the opinion that we ought to agree here and now that we need *both* discussion *and* debate in the schools and in society."[1] The number of additional activities—oratory, extemporaneous speaking, a speaker's bureau, etc.—to be included in the extracurricular program should be determined by the teacher in light of the above criteria and considerations of time, budget, need, interest, and local conditions.

Although the forensic program can be administered in several different ways, this chapter is concerned primarily with the type of forensic program commonly found today in most high schools, colleges, and universities. Individual variations, of course, will occur from school to school. For example, in a few institutions, forensic activities are almost exclusively the concern of literary or debating societies, clubs, or fraternities; they are student directed and administered; and faculty members rarely are called on for guidance or assistance. This discussion, however, assumes that the teacher's responsibility extends to the planning, organization, and active direction of the program.

Who Should Participate in the Extracurricular Forensic Program?

Some educators believe that "the squad" should be composed of the ablest and most effective speakers in the school, with other students encouraged to participate but less extensively. The well-planned and administered program undoubtedly will attract talented speakers; however, to focus primary attention on those individuals at the expense of students in greater need of training is indefensible educationally. One of the most serious

[1] James H. McBurney, "The Role of Discussion and Debate in a Democratic Society," *Bulletin of the National Association of Secondary School Principals,* May, 1952, 36:22–26.

criticisms of extracurricular forensic programs today is that too many provide experience and training for only an extremely limited number of students and at a considerable expense to the school. If the forensic program is to serve the school effectively, it must provide training for as many students as possible. This may mean less trophies in the case, but it will also mean better education.

What Budget Is Needed?

Another important factor that will influence the nature and scope of the forensic program is the amount of money available for the conduct of this activity. Budgets for college forensic programs range from almost nothing to several thousand dollars a year, with many even small colleges appropriating more than a thousand dollars annually for this activity.[2] At the high school level, budgets also vary widely.

Among the expenses that the forensic director should include in his budget are transportation, housing, and registration costs for interscholastic conferences and tournaments; food allowances for students on out-of-town trips; expenses for events at the director's own institution; awards for contests sponsored by the school; fees and expenses for critics or judges (other than forensics directors of participating schools in a conference or tournament); postage, stationery, and materials; and reference works (although the school library usually will be able to supply these). In addition, the forensic director should anticipate any unusual expenses for special events during the year. For example, if the school is scheduled to serve as host for a state tournament or congress or if the forensic director plans to hold an international debate, to make a particularly long trip, or to undertake an activity normally not included in the program, he should plan his budget to meet these additional expenses.

A large budget is not necessary for an effective extracurricular program. Even the most modestly financed program can contribute to the speech training of the participants. Almost every community affords a variety of audiences interested in hearing student speakers. These include service and community clubs, parent-teacher organizations, business groups, women's clubs, school groups, and other organizations. By utilizing local audiences for student programs, debates, and discussions, the forensic director with a limited budget can provide his students with a rich and varied program of activities and experiences.

What Are the Types and Advantages of Interscholastic Forensic Competition?

Although the forensic director, regardless of the size of his budget, undoubtedly will wish to give his students considerable experience in

[2] Kenneth D. Frandsen, "Policies and Practices Reviewed: Report on Forensics Survey #1" (unpublished survey, 1958).

speaking before local audiences, he probably will also wish to take advantage of the valuable opportunities for practice and training afforded by interscholastic tournaments, congresses, conferences, festivals, and contests at both high school and college levels. For the beginning teacher an explanation of the general nature of the various types of competitions is offered below:

Tournament.   Usually a debate contest involving several schools represented by one or more two-member debate teams. Many tournaments have separate divisions for men and women and novice debaters. The debates usually are judged, often by the participating forensic directors, and decisions given. Several rounds of debate generally are held in one day. Some tournaments employ an elimination system in order to determine a winner; others award the championship to the school with the best record at the conclusion of the debates.

Conference.   A general term usually used to refer to a meeting in which competition in more than one event is held. Events may include debate, discussion, original oratory, interpretative reading, extemporaneous speaking, and similar contests. If discussion is included, several hours will be set aside for small groups composed of representatives of the participating schools to discuss a preannounced question. The discussion sessions, as well as other contests, usually are judged, and at the end of the conference outstanding speakers are cited.

Congress.   This name is most frequently given to meetings that culminate in a legislative session. The legislative session may be preceded by discussion, debate, or committee meetings on a preannounced topic. In the legislative assembly, students debate the merits of resolutions that have grown out of prior meetings. A typical congress might schedule several hours of discussion by small groups, to be followed by the preparation of a resolution by each group for consideration and debate by the entire congress on the legislative floor.[3]

Festivals.   Festivals commonly include a variety of activities such as oratory, interpretative reading, extemporaneous speaking, radio-television speaking, poetry reading, and declamation. Critics award ratings to participants, but usually do not select a single winner or champion. In many festivals a sweepstakes award is given to the school with the highest rating for all events.

As indicated, most of these terms lack precise meanings; consequently, the forensic director should inquire carefully into the nature of these events before he begins specific preparation of his students for participation. At the end of this chapter, programs and outlines indicating the general nature of some of these types of meetings are presented.

---

[3] For a discussion of student congresses, see Kenneth G. Hance, "Newer Types of Extracurricular Activities in Public Speaking," *Bulletin of the National Association of Secondary School Principals*, May, 1952, 36:132–157; and Carroll P. Lahman, "A One-Day Student Legislative Assembly," *The Gavel*, January, 1943, pp. 33–34, 36.

Among the benefits to be derived from participation in interscholastic forensic events are these: (1) Contests and conferences provide stimulation to the student through competition with capable students from other schools; (2) they provide extensive practice in a relatively short period of time at a modest cost; (3) they afford both student and teacher an opportunity to obtain evaluations and suggestions for improvement by disinterested and, usually, expert critics; and (4) such events often serve as a motivating factor for both students and the instructor by providing a goal or objective toward which to work.

NATIONAL TOPICS

Well-chosen, carefully worded questions are essential to good debate and discussion. While the director of forensics may face the necessity of selecting and phrasing propositions for debates and discussions to be presented before certain groups or on specific occasions, in most interscholastic contests the topic will already have been selected. In an effort to facilitate interscholastic and interstate competition in debate and discussion, methods of selecting national questions both for high schools and colleges were developed by speech educators many years ago.

High School Questions

At the high school level, the Committee on Debate and Discussion Materials of the National University Extension Association annually selects topics for the following school year at a meeting in December. Each state is invited to send representatives to this meeting. Committee members usually welcome suggestions for topics for future years from the speech teachers in their respective states. In recent years, the committee has selected a single general topic for the following year. This topic has been phrased as a general problem area question with three discussion questions and three debate propositions which fall within the problem area. Each state is encouraged to use the discussion questions as a guide to investigation and to select one or to use all three of the debate propositions during the early part of the season. Each December, at the annual meeting, a single discussion question and a single debate proposition are recommended for use during the balance of the academic year. States are free to use the recommended discussion question and debate proposition or to choose one of their own.

Under this plan no school is required to debate only the official proposition; however, if a school wishes to sponsor a debate tournament or discussion conference it can be relatively certain that several other schools in the region will be prepared to discuss or debate the national question.

Since the three debate topics are all related closely to the general discussion topic, a school wishing to participate in a contest in another state usually can develop cases without too much additional research and analysis. In discussion, of course, schools in all states usually discuss the same question.

College Questions

Among the colleges another plan has been devised. Five debate propositions and five discussion questions are selected annually by the Intercollegiate Discussion and Debate Committee, which consists of representatives of the Speech Communication Association, Delta Sigma Rho–Tau Kappa Alpha, Pi Kappa Delta, Phi Rho Pi, and the American Forensic Association. These questions are then voted on by forensic directors throughout the country. The debate and discussion topics receiving the most votes are declared the national questions for the following academic year. The committee usually asks for suggestions of possible topics for the following academic year early in the spring and sends ballots to participating forensics directors in midsummer. Each college or university in the country is entitled to one vote. Schools not affiliated with the American Forensic Association or any of the honorary forensic societies represented on the committee should contact a member of the committee from the Speech Communication Association to secure representation and ballots.

While no school is required to debate or discuss the national questions, and some conferences regularly select questions other than the national propositions in order to add variety to the forensic season, most schools—both high schools and colleges—work on the national question for a major part of the forensic year.

SCHEDULES, INVITATIONS, AND CONTRACTS

Forensic seasons vary from state to state and from region to region. Most colleges and universities begin their forensic activities soon after the start of the fall semester, engage actively in intercollegiate events throughout the winter, and conclude their programs early in the spring.

At the high school level many states follow a similar schedule. Some states, however, have specific regulations on the length of the season and prescribe the months during which interschool contests may be held. The new teacher should contact the governing body if in doubt about regulations affecting programs in his state.

Even the beginning teacher should experience little difficulty in formulating a satisfactory schedule of interscholastic contests for his students. Almost from the start of the school year, he will receive invitations to a variety of contests, tournaments, and festivals. If the school has not en-

SAMPLE DEBATE CONTRACT

Between

_____ and _____

Institution   Institution

1. Time: The debate will be held at _____ on _____

                                     Hour   Month

      _____, 19_____.

      Date

2. Place: The debate will be held at _____

3. Audience: The audience will consist of _____

4. Topic: The proposition for debate will be: _____

5. Sides: For the debate:

      The affirmative will be held by _____

      The negative will be held by _____

6. Speakers: Each school will provide _____ speakers. The speakers will be _____

         Men, Women, Mixed Team, Novice, Experienced

7. Time limits: The time limits for speeches will be:

      _____ minutes for constructive speeches.

      _____ minutes for rebuttal speeches.

8. Type of debate: _____

           Indicate Any Special Features

9. Decision: _____ Yes   _____ **No**

      If yes, the debate will be judged by _____

                Audience? Critics? Number

10. Dress: _____

11. Additional provisions (related to housing, expenses, entertainment, etc.): _____

_____   _____

Director of Forensics   *Director of Forensics*

gaged in interscholastic forensic activities previously, or for several years, the forensic director would be well advised to notify state speech association officers and speech teachers in his area of his interest in participating in such events. He may also find, particularly at the college-university level, that membership in the American Forensic Association will prove helpful in inaugurating a forensic program. Especially valuable is that organization's annual calendar of forensic events.

In some areas debates are arranged by the exchange and signing of contracts specifying time, place, proposition, and conditions for a debate. A typical contract is shown on p. 98. In most parts of the country, an invitation is sent to another school (or schools) with an entry form. In such cases the teacher can arrange to have his students participate in a tournament or conference simply by completing the entry form and returning it before the announced deadline. Once a contract has been signed or an entry blank returned, it is important that the other party or the sponsoring institution be informed as early as possible if for any reason it is necessary to alter or withdraw from the agreement.

PLANNING AND DIRECTING THE FORENSIC PROGRAM

Careful planning is essential if the forensic director wishes his program to afford the most beneficial training and experience for the participating students. Because of variations in the nature and scope of forensic programs, no attempt is made here to set forth a rigid pattern of activities. However, five general phases of the extracurricular forensic program will be discussed: (1) preliminary planning; (2) the first meeting; (3) early meetings; (4) later activities; and (5) preparing students for participation in tournaments and conferences.

Preliminary Plans

The forensic director should know before the start of the year what he hopes to achieve and, in general, how he plans to accomplish his objectives. Several factors must be considered at this preliminary stage.

First, he must determine how much time he is able and willing to devote to the activity. The direction of a debate and/or discussion program can be, and usually is, extremely time-consuming.

Next, he should devise a schedule for meeting with the group. Regular meetings are essential if real progress is to be made. After setting a date for the first meeting, the instructor should select, at least tentatively, a suitable time for subsequent meetings. If the program is to attract a sizeable proportion of those students interested in forensics he must take care not to schedule meetings to conflict with other popular student activities.

A third consideration which will affect his plans is the amount of time he can expect the student to devote to forensics. The truly interested debater or discussant probably will spend more time on these activities than on any single course; consequently, the forensic director also must make certain that his demands do not jeopardize the student's academic pursuits.

In making plans for a forensic program, the teacher will find it advantageous to investigate the resource materials available in the local libraries. Schools located in cities with good library facilities, and the larger universities, undoubtedly will find an abundance of works on the principal questions to be studied. At such institutions, the teacher's only concern will be to make certain that these materials are easily accessible. Most college and university libraries are willing to place designated books and publications on reserve so that they cannot be removed from the library, thus making them available to students at all times; some libraries will even designate special shelves for the forensic squad's materials.

If library facilities are inadequate, the director of forensics should devise other methods of securing materials. Among the possible solutions to this problem are:

1. Subscriptions to several carefully selected magazines or newspapers
2. Letters to congressmen, government departments, and interested organizations requesting literature on the debate and (or) discussion question
3. Preparation, with student assistance, of a scrapbook of pertinent clippings, articles, and speeches
4. Purchase of debate or discussion handbooks (The instructor should weigh carefully the pros and cons of utilizing handbooks before adopting this method. See the discussion of the use of handbooks in Chapter 4.)

The First Meeting

The first meeting of the forensic squad is important in determining the success of the extracurricular program. If the initial meeting has been scheduled at a convenient time and has been well publicized, the director of forensics can expect a sizeable attendance. To make certain that the initial meeting is brought to the attention of all potentially interested students, the forensic director probably will wish to employ several of the following techniques:

1. An announcement in the school paper
2. Posters giving details of the program and time and place of the meeting
3. Personal letters or post cards to all former members of the squad and to promising students in former speech classes
4. Announcement of the meeting by the teachers of all speech classes
5. Distribution of short questionnaires in all speech classes asking students to indicate whether they are interested in forensics and to give name, address, and telephone number. Letters or post cards announcing the first meeting should then be mailed to these students.

6. Interviews with members of the previous year's squad to see if they know of any prospective squad members
7. Finally, a continuous year-round publicity program will do much to arouse and maintain interest in the activity.

After a convenient date has been set and the initial meeting has been well publicized, the teacher's ability to stimulate interest in the program and to encourage beginners at the first meeting will largely determine the number of students who remain active in the program throughout the remainder of the season. The initial meeting also will greatly influence the spirit of the group for the rest of the year.

In order to create interest, the first meeting probably should be informal and social in nature. The principal objectives should be to explain the nature of the program, to acquaint new or prospective members of the squad with the director and returning members, and to obtain information about those attending the meeting. To promote an informal and relaxed atmosphere, the director may ask former squad members to present a mock debate on some humorous subject, he may arrange to have former students give brief talks, or he may plan some other kind of entertainment designed to interest newcomers in the activity. Before the meeting ends, the director should obtain from each student several items of information that will assist him in planning and conducting the program, such as the following:

Name
Address
Telephone number
Year in school
Major field of study
Former classroom training in speech (at the high school and college levels)
Former extracurricular speech training (both high school and college)
Other speech experience (such as selling, serving as an officer of a club, par-
    ticipation in radio forum, etc.)
A schedule of the student's free hours

To conclude the meeting on a friendly note, the forensic director may wish to serve light refreshments. While the group is relaxing over soft drinks, he should try to meet each person at the meeting. If former members of the squad also become acquainted with those present, most of the newcomers probably will be encouraged to attend the next meeting.

Early Meetings

At all of the early meetings the forensic director should make every effort to encourage beginners. He should avoid use of technical terminology such as *rebuttal, the second negative constructive, moderator, the goals stage, syllogism,* and *counterplan,* because these terms can easily lead the novice speaker to believe that debate and discussion are hopelessly complex and can discourage him from further participation. Early assignments should be easy for the beginner to carry out. Knowing little about the activity and uncertain of whether he has sufficient time to undertake this added responsibility, he is likely to withdraw from the squad if the first assignments are unduly time-consuming or difficult.

Because of his inexperience and his lack of knowledge of the question, the beginner needs time to become acquainted with the instructor, other members of the squad, basic terminology, and the question to be debated or discussed before he is asked to present a speech to the group. Here are some typical early assignments that are valuable and yet not highly demanding:

Student Assignments

1. Prepare a bibliography.
2. Prepare reports on assigned articles or topics.
3. Study the terms of the question.
4. Study the history and background of the question.
5. Study a specific topic, issue, or publication.
6. Attend a lecture by an expert on a problem under consideration.
7. Participate in an informal round-table discussion.
8. Attend a demonstration debate or discussion by veteran members of the squad.[4]

Informal discussion of assignments, supplemented by explanations by the teacher of the nature of debating and discussion, will serve to increase the confidence of the student, to make him feel a part of the group, and to prepare him for later participation in actual discussions and debates. The director of forensics should also try to schedule individual meetings with all new members of the squad early in the season. This will enable him to become better acquainted with each student and will provide the student with an opportunity to ask questions about procedures, techniques, and terms that he does not fully understand.

Because of the special treatment that should be accorded to beginning students, the instructor may find it necessary to divide the squad and meet separately with the different groups. Several divisions, depending on the size of the squad, the experience of the members, and the general nature of the program, are possible. The group may be divided into beginning and advanced groups, boys' and girls' squads, or a combination or variation of these two classifications. Another division may be according to student interest, i.e., discussion and debate groups.

The main advantage in dividing the squad according to experience and

[4] For suggestions on early assignments for a debate squad, see Carney Smith, "Practical Procedures in Coaching High School Debate," *Quarterly Journal of Speech*, April, 1943, 29:222–234. An outline of Smith's suggestions may also be found in Karl Robinson, *Teaching Speech in the Secondary School*, London: Longmans, Green, 1954, pp. 335–337.

abilities is that it enables the advanced students to move along at a rapid pace and permits the beginners, who for the first few weeks will be concerned with fundamentals already familiar to the experienced students, to proceed more slowly. The principal disadvantage of such a division is that the beginners are deprived of the example, assistance, and knowledge of experienced speakers.

Later Meetings

As soon as he decides that the students are adequately prepared, the forensic director should schedule actual debates and discussions. From this point on, the instructor's work will consist primarily of hearing speeches, offering criticism and suggestions for improvement, and meeting with participants individually or in small groups. In order to maintain a high level of interest, he may wish to schedule intrasquad tournaments or contests, discussions, and debates before classes, school clubs, and community organizations.

Specific Preparation for Tournaments and Conferences

Ideally, the approach of a tournament, conference, or public performance should pose no problems for the forensic director if his students have been well prepared. In practice, however, such an event usually requires the teacher to make several decisions and to take steps to insure that his students satisfactorily represent the school.

Selecting Participants. In preparation for a tournament or conference the forensic director must decide who is to participate. Some questions the instructor will wish to consider in reaching this decision are:

1. Is the student capable and well-enough prepared to represent the school satisfactorily in this contest or event? (Is he well informed? What experience does he have? Is he prepared for competition of the type or level he is likely to meet? Certainly the teacher would not want to send his beginning speakers to a meet involving only the best and most experienced representatives of other schools, nor would he want to send his most capable students to a novice tournament or conference.)

2. Will the student benefit from this experience? (Will the event provide a new, different, or unusual experience for the student? Are there other students who would benefit more from participation in this event?)

3. Is the student deserving of the chance to participate in this activity? (Has he participated loyally and regularly in the programs? Is he dependable? Has his conduct been satisfactory?)

4. Is the student's scholastic standing satisfactory? (Can he afford to spend time on this activity? Does this event conflict with important examinations or other academic activities that the student should not miss?)

The teacher must also decide how many students he wishes to send to the tournament or conference. Budget, available transportation, the type of event, and specific regulations governing entries will influence this decision.

After selecting his participants, the instructor probably will wish to schedule several additional meetings with this group to explain the nature of the meeting, to outline the events and activities in which the students will participate, and to make last-minute refinements and suggestions for improvement. He may also schedule additional practice debates or discussions.

Student Conduct. One final matter remains to be discussed: the teacher must make certain that the students know what kind of conduct is expected of them during the conference or tournament. Some teachers handle this directly by calling the students together and telling them exactly how they should behave. Others prefer to be less explicit, hoping that their example and an occasional indirect reference will make clear what kind of conduct is expected. Whatever approach the teacher takes, his own conduct must be consistent with the attitude and behavior he expects from his students. Certainly the student should be impressed with the importance of being on time. He should be able to accept criticism, comment, and defeat gracefully. He should not stoop to practices that are unethical or of questionable honesty. He should remember that as a representative of his school anything that reflects unfavorably on him will also reflect unfavorably on the school. He should be aware that practices such as scouting other debates are frowned on. He should understand that his conduct should be above question at all times—at the conference or elsewhere. Finally, he must feel that what he does and how he does it is more important than winning or a high rating.[5]

CONDUCTING TOURNAMENTS, CONFERENCES, AND FESTIVALS

The duties of the forensic director may include the sponsorship of a tournament, conference, or festival at his own school. Conducting such events demands long-range planning and attention to a multitude of details. Successful tournaments and conferences do not just happen; they are the result of many hours of preparation.

Setting a Date

The first step in planning a successful forensic tournament or conference is to select a satisfactory time for the event—a date which will not interfere

[5] For a detailed discussion of debate etiquette, see W. Charles Redding, "Presentation of the Debate Speech," in James McBath (ed.), *Argumentation and Debate*, rev. ed., New York: Holt, Rinehart & Winston, 1963, pp. 157–284.

with other school activities, is convenient for the students who will participate and assist in conducting the meeting, and will not conflict with established nearby forensic competitions.

Invitations

After a date has been selected, invitations should be sent to other schools. The number of schools to be invited will be determined by the size of meeting the director is able to accommodate. The first notice should contain the following information on the nature of the meeting: the date, location, and hours of the conference; entry fees; name and address of the conference director; events or contests to be held; the rules and regulations governing the conduct of the contest, judging and eligibility; awards; special features. Typical forms for such announcements and invitations are shown on pp. 106–108. A deadline for entering should be stated and an official entry form included. If the conference lasts more than one day, or if some participating schools will be required to stay overnight, a list of hotels, motels, and other places that can accommodate the visiting students should be included.

Securing Judges, Timekeepers, and Rooms

Well in advance of the tournament or conference date, the forensics director should begin the task of securing critics or judges and, if needed, timekeepers for the various events. In most conferences and tournaments the visiting forensic directors can be called on to serve as critic-judges; however, if each school is permitted to enter several teams or if the conference director has special reasons for not wishing to utilize the services of the visiting directors, he may need to obtain the services of others competent to criticize or judge the various contests. If the meeting is to include debating, the conference director should also provide a timekeeper for each debate. While only the most competent and well-acquainted adult critics available should be asked to judge, students can handle the job of keeping time for debates. In addition to finding critic-judges and timekeepers, suitable rooms for each event must be located and reserved. Since a large debate tournament requires many rooms, the forensics director should make certain that he has adequate space to accommodate all of the contests before he issues invitations to too many schools.

Preparation of Agenda or Outline for Discussion Conferences

If discussion is to be included in the conference activities, the host forensic director usually prepares a group discussion outline or agenda several weeks

SAMPLE CONFERENCE INVITATION

Department of Speech, Louisiana State University,
Baton Rouge, Louisiana

Dear Forensic Director:

You and your students are cordially invited to participate in the fifth annual Louisiana State University Intercollegiate Forensic Conference, Friday and Saturday, October 9 and 10, 19___. The topic for the conference will be a modification of the national intercollegiate debate proposition: that the powers of the Supreme Court should be modified.

The purposes of the conference are to provide training and promote leadership among college students through competitive experience in varied forensics activities and to act as a sounding board for the exchange and evaluation of information of current significance pertaining to the national question. To that end, the events and participants in the conference will be criticized and rated. Recognition will be given to excellent individual performances. No school or team championship will be determined.

The program is designed to provide training and experience in discussion, argumentative speaking, and parliamentary address. Since the conference convenes early in the academic year, we think it affords an excellent opportunity for forensic students to become acquainted with this year's national intercollegiate debate topic through exchange of opinions and information in an informal, nontournament atmosphere. In keeping with this objective, no limit has been set on the number of participants from any school, and beginning as well as experienced speakers are encouraged to participate. Last year more than 120 students from thirteen colleges and universities in Louisiana, Mississippi, and Alabama took part in the conference.

The conference schedule and events will include:

Friday, October 9

8:30	Registration
9:30	General assembly: announcements and orientation
10:10–11:00	Discussion: Round I—Definition of terms and goals
11:10–12:00	Discussion: Round II—Analysis of the question: problems
1:10–2:00	Discussion: Round III—Analysis of the question: causes
3:10–4:00	Advocacy speaking: Round I—Discussion groups will be subdivided into groups of approximately five each. Each speaker will give a 7-minute speech analyzing the problem and offering his solution.

After these speeches have been heard, each speaker will have 3 minutes to present a rebuttal in which he refutes the arguments of other speakers and/or reaffirms his own stand.

4:10–5:00   Advocacy speaking: Round II—Each speaker will be assigned to an entirely new group of speakers. Speakers will again present 7-minute speeches of advocacy and 3-minute rebuttal speeches.

7:15   General assembly: Announcement of places and procedures for preparing bills and planning their presentation in the legislative assembly.

7:30   Caucuses: Preparation of bills and organizing their presentation

Saturday, October 10

9:00–11:20   Legislative assembly: All participants will meet in a legislative session at which bills will be presented and debated.

11:30   Announcements of results

Housing is available in Pleasant Hall at the following rates: single room with bath, $5; double room with bath, $3.50 per person; regular room, $2.75 per person. Reservations can be made by writing directly to the Center of Continuing Education, Louisiana State University, Baton Rouge, Louisiana 70803. Baton Rouge has an abundance of hotels and motels, although none is near the campus. A few are listed below. Arrangements should be made directly with the hotel or motel.

Hotels:	*Motels:*
The Capitol House	Alamo Plaza Hotel Courts
Lafayette Street	4243 Florida Street
The Heidelberg Hotel	Bellemont Motor Hotel
Lafayette Street	7370 Airline Highway

Enclosed please find a postcard on which you may indicate your intention of attending the conference. Please note the space requesting an estimate of the number of students from your school likely to participate in the conference.

Cordially yours,

Owen Peterson
Conference Director

SAMPLE PRELIMINARY ANNOUNCEMENT OF DEBATE TOURNAMENT

(Included with invitations)

Sixth Annual Delta Sigma Rho

DePauw Debate Tournament (Greencastle, Indiana)

Date: Saturday, February 21, 19___. Entries should be mailed by February 12.

Location: Greencastle is midway between Indianapolis and Terre Haute. Railway lines are the Pennsylvania, New York Central, and the Monon. Bus lines are Greyhound and Indiana Railroad. Tournament headquarters will be in Asbury Hall on College Avenue.

Procedure and Schedule: Four rounds of decision debates on the national topic. The judges are encouraged to give critiques but should not reveal their decision to the debaters.

Registration	Asbury Hall	8:00–9:15
General Meeting	109 Asbury Hall	9:15
Round I		9:30
Round II		10:45
Luncheon	Union Bldg.	12:00
Round III		1:10
Round IV		2:00
Announcements and		
Awards	109 Asbury Hall	4:00

Eligibility: Any undergraduate man or woman student may compete. Each school may enter one affirmative team and one negative team and should provide a faculty member to serve as a critic-judge. We will be unable to provide a judge for you.

Fees: The fee of $3.50 per person attending the tournament includes the cost of the luncheon.

Housing: Hotels are: Commercial Hotel (clean, inexpensive); Old Trail Inn (6 miles north of Greencastle off Highway 40; address is Greencastle; quaint; excellent food); Heges Motel, RFD #1 Greencastle (2½ miles north of town, new last year). Write directly to any of these.

prior to the meeting and mails copies to all of the participating schools. While this step is not absolutely essential to the conduct of a discussion conference, it usually contributes to more effective preparation and, as a result, better discussion during the meeting. The outline should consist of a series of questions related to the major topics to be discussed, that is, terms to be defined, history and background of the question, possible goals, major issues in the analysis of the question, possible solutions, and similar questions—and should suggest tentatively which parts of the agenda the groups should try to cover during each round of the conference. The outline should include a statement indicating that it is intended to serve only as a guide in studying the question and that the discussants may alter or modify the agenda in any way they choose during the actual discussions.

Preparation of Instructions, Judging Forms, and Schedule of Events

The smooth operation of a forensic tournament, conference, or festival depends to a considerable extent on how well the director has anticipated difficulties that may arise and what steps he has taken to cope with these problems. The conference director can be relatively certain that the time-keepers, judges, and speakers are going to need some direction and guidance; and, since it is often inconvenient to assemble all participants and personnel in one place at the same time, much confusion can be avoided by the preparation of detailed written instructions on questions that may arise. Among the forms the director may wish to prepare in advance are the following (illustrated here and at the end of the chapter):

1. Timekeepers' instructions on their duties
2. Instructions to the judges of various events
3. Rating blanks for the judges
4. Maps of the campus or building
5. A program or schedule of events

Preparation of the schedule of events not only requires meticulous care and attention to detail, but also, unfortunately, is a job that the conference director cannot complete until the last minute. Only when all of the conference entries have been received can he begin the task of scheduling activities.

Once completed, the schedule must be regarded as tentative, for even at the last minute some school may be forced to withdraw. The withdrawal of one school or entrant creates little difficulty in discussion and individual events, but a single cancellation from a debate tournament can force the director to revise his entire schedule. Thus the forensic director should delay as long as possible the printing or duplication of the program. Even then some cautious conference directors prepare alternate schedules involving one or two fewer schools just in case bad weather, illness, or some other unforeseen development forces last-minute cancellations.

MODEL DEBATE TOURNAMENT PROGRAM

Central High School

Sixth Annual Debate Tournament

8:00   Registration, High School Lobby

9:15   General Meeting, Auditorium

9:30   Round I

Aff.	Neg.	Judge	Timekeeper	Room
1	2	9	Evans	11
2	3	1	Adsit	12
3	4	2	Ashby	13
4	5	3	Morton	9
5	6	4	Sterling	8
6	7	5	Gates	7
7	8	6	Allison	6
8	9	7	Jameson	22
9	1	8	Hales	23
		Extras:	*Extras:*	*Extras:*
		Smith	Trees	27
		Currie	Romack	24
			Murphy	26

10:45   Round II
(Pairings, judging assignments, timekeepers, and rooms for round II)

12:00   Luncheon, Cafeteria

1:45   Round III
(Pairings, judging assignments, timekeepers, and rooms for round III)

2:30   Round IV
(Pairings, judging assignments, timekeepers, and rooms for round IV)

4:00   Announcement of results, Auditorium

In preparing the schedule of events, the conference director should make sure of the following precautions:

1. That preliminary eliminations are scheduled in contests involving large numbers of competitors
2. That the same teams are not scheduled to debate each other twice if this can be avoided
3. That critic judges are not assigned to evaluate the same team or same contestant twice
4. That visiting directors are not assigned to judge their own students
5. That two events are not scheduled for the same room at the same time
6. That judges or participants are not assigned to two different events or contests at the same time
7. That sufficient time has been set aside to permit students to get from one event to another
8. That extra judges and timekeepers are available for every event in case a regularly assigned person fails to appear
9. That the schedule is prepared in such a way that there can be no question of its fairness and impartiality

Scheduling Debates

In working out a program one of the conference or tournament director's most difficult tasks is the pairing of teams for debate. This part of the schedule also is most likely to be criticized if it has not been prepared with complete impartiality. In order to allay any suspicion of discrimination in the pairings, the forensic director may prepare his schedule using numbers rather than school names. If nine schools are entered, he should prepare a schedule using the numbers 1 through 9. Just before the tournament begins, each school will draw a number at random. That number will determine who, when, and where each school debates each round. The pairing of schools thus becomes solely a matter of chance.

As soon as the tournament director decides that all entries have been received he should begin working out the pairings for debate. If not handled systematically, this task can prove to be hopelessly complicated. The three most common types of debate tournament schedules are the round-robin method, the elimination plan, and a combination of these two.

The Round-Robin Schedule. The round-robin debate schedule is a nonelimination plan. Each team is paired against a different team every round for a specified number of rounds. The principal advantage of this method is that no team is eliminated before the conclusion of the tournament. Unlike the elimination plan, under the round-robin system even the poorest team is permitted to debate every round, thereby gaining valuable practice and experience. If a champion is to be declared at the end of the tournament, the award is given to the team with the best record. In case of ties, individual team and (or) speaker ratings can be utilized to determine the winning school.

The following procedure will facilitate the scheduling of most round-robin tournaments. If carefully followed, it will prevent the same teams from debating each other twice and the critic from judging his own students. In using this method, at least seven teams must be entered for a three-round tournament and for each additional round at least two more teams must be entered.

1. Count the number of schools entered. (It will be assumed throughout that each school will enter both an affirmative and negative team, although the system can also be employed with slight modification if only one team is entered from each school, providing that every team is prepared to debate either side of the proposition.)

2. Determine the number of affirmative and negative teams. (Since each school has entered an affirmative and negative team, there will be an equal number of teams on each side.)

3. List the number of affirmative teams in a column, by numerals, on the left-hand side of a sheet of paper, as shown below (For illustrative purposes, pairings for a hypothetical nine-school tournament will be set up. If properly scheduled, each school can debate every other school once in four rounds.)

Round I

Aff.
1
2
3
4
5
6
7
8
9

4. Add a column to the right and list the negative teams, starting with team two on the first line.

Round I

Aff.	Neg.
1	2
2	3
3	4
4	5
5	6
6	7
7	8
8	9
9	1

5. Judges are assigned, next. Add a third column and list the judges beginning with judge number one on the second line.

Round I

Aff.	Neg.	Judge
1	2	9
2	3	1
3	4	2
4	5	3
5	6	4
6	7	5
7	8	6
8	9	7
9	1	8

6. At this point, pairings for the first round of debate are complete. If the tournament director wishes, he may add a fourth column and list the timekeepers for each debate. However, since there is no reason why the same person should not serve as timekeeper for the same teams or judges for several rounds, this step is omitted in the diagram.

7. The scheduling of additional rounds is extremely simple. For each successive round: (a) to arrange the team pairings, keep the affirmative column as it was in round I, and move all of the numbers in the negative column up one line, giving each team a new opponent; (b) to arrange judging assignments, move all of the numbers in the judging column downward one line. Following this procedure, the assignments for rounds II, III, and IV would be,

Round II

Aff.	Neg.	Judge
1	3	8
2	4	9
3	5	1
4	6	2
5	7	3
6	8	4
7	9	5
8	1	6
9	2	7

Round III

Aff.	Neg.	Judge
1	4	7
2	5	8
3	6	9
4	7	1
5	8	2
6	9	3
7	1	4
8	2	5
9	3	6

Round IV		
Aff.	Neg.	Judge
1	5	6
2	6	7
3	7	8
4	8	9
5	9	1
6	1	2
7	2	3
8	3	4
9	4	5

Following this procedure, at the end of four rounds each school has debated every other school in the tournament and no judge has judged his own students or has judged the same team twice, though he has in some instances judged both the affirmative and negative teams from the same school. This system works well as long as enough teams are entered in relation to the number of rounds of debate. To prevent two teams from the same school meeting each other or a judge being assigned to hear his own students there must be seven or more schools for a three-round schedule, nine or more teams for four rounds, eleven or more teams for five rounds, thirteen or more teams for six rounds, etc.

Although no attempt has been made to illustrate scheduling of tournaments in which each school sends one team prepared to debate both sides of the question on alternate rounds, with only slight variations—assigning the negative teams numbers other than those assigned to the affirmative and, after each round has been paired, reversing the side on which the teams will debate on alternate rounds—this system will work equally well for such a tournament.

The Elimination Schedule. In an elimination tournament only the winning schools in each round continue to debate in successive rounds. The principal disadvantage of this plan is that half of the schools entered are eliminated after the first debate and receive no further practice or benefit from the tournament. To avoid this shortcoming, some tournament managers schedule a loser's, or consolation, bracket. This assures every entrant of participation in at least two debates; however, it also guarantees that at the end of two rounds half of the participants will have been eliminated.

For the successful operation of this plan it is essential that all participating teams be prepared to debate either side of the question in successive rounds, since a majority of the first-round decisions might go to teams on one side of the question. Since two negative—or affirmative—teams cannot be scheduled to debate each other, one must be prepared to defend the opposite side. An elimination tournament schedule for eight teams would appear as shown in Figure 1.

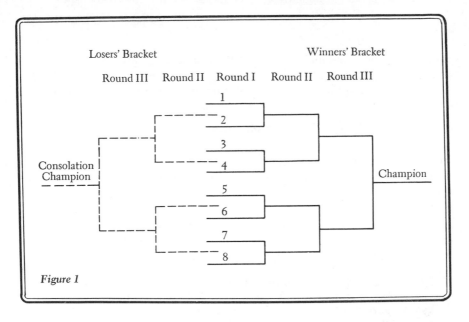

Figure 1

At the end of round I the winning teams in the debates between teams 1 and 2, 3 and 4, 5 and 6, 7 and 8 would advance to the second round of the winners bracket; the defeated teams in these debates would be paired against each other in the second round of the losers bracket. The winners of the round II debates in both brackets would then move into the third—or championship and consolation championship—rounds.

The Combination Schedule. Many tournaments combine the round-robin and elimination methods in scheduling debates. Under this arrangement, the tournament begins with several rounds of round-robin debating. At the end of a preannounced number of rounds, the best four, eight, or sixteen teams are selected—on the basis of number of debates won, individual or team ratings, or both—to participate in an elimination tournament. In this way, all teams are guaranteed a minimum number of debates and the best teams are given the opportunity to meet each other before the tournament is concluded. This plan works best in tournaments involving a large number of teams. Under this plan teams in the elimination tournament must also be prepared to debate either side of the question.

Other Plans. The tournament manager is by no means limited to a choice from among these three plans. Other methods that may be employed are the seeded-elimination plan, in which favored teams are placed in strategic positions so that, barring upsets, they will meet in the semifinal and final rounds; the double-elimination method, in which a team is not eliminated until it has lost two debates; and the matched-strength method, in which the teams with the best records are matched against each other in successive rounds and teams with poor records meet each other. (The last method has the disadvantage of forcing the tournament director to postpone the scheduling of each new round until the results of the previous round have been tabulated. Since the tournament director exercises his discretion in determining which winning teams meet each other, it also leaves him open to the criticism of partiality in the pairing of schools.)

Selecting a Method for Determining Outstanding Speakers

Before the tournament or conference begins, the director should have developed a plan for selecting the outstanding speakers in each event and should have decided the type of award or recognition to be given to these participants.

To determine the outstanding speakers, teams, or schools in each contest or activity, the director may devise a rating or scoring system designed to accomplish any of the following:

1. To determine a single winner in each event
2. To select an unspecified number of outstanding speakers in each event
3. To recognize a winning speaker or team *and* other outstanding speakers in each event

If the purpose of the contests is to select a specified number of winning speakers or teams for advancement to another contest or tournament at a higher level, the conference director should devise a scoring system that clearly indicates the rank of the participating individuals or groups. If, however, it is not necessary to arrive at a specified number of winners, he may prefer the rating system. Under this plan, all superior speakers, regardless of number, are recognized. The advantage of this method is that the true caliber of a speaker's performance often is more accurately shown by a rating than by his rank in a contest. For example, if five superior speakers of nearly equal ability are *ranked* in a contest one of the speakers *must* be placed fifth. If the *rating* system is employed, all will be rated "superior." Since the speakers' performances in this hypothetical contest are all of a consistently high level, a "superior" rating not only is more satisfying to the student than a fifth place ranking, but it also more accurately characterizes the quality of performance of the speaker than does a fifth place ranking. Some conference directors combine the two methods, both naming winning contestants and announcing all of the outstanding participants.

Each of these methods is better suited to certain kinds of activities and contests than to others. Several plans for selecting outstanding participants in different interscholastic forensic contests are suggested below.

Debate. In debate tournaments the director may determine the outstanding teams or individuals by any of the following methods:

1. An elimination tournament, or elimination rounds after a specified number of round-robin debates.

2. Selecting the team or school with the best record of wins and losses at the conclusion of a round-robin tournament. If the conference director wishes to break ties, he should include team and (or) individual ratings on the judging ballots so that he may utilize these scores to determine the winner among two or more teams or schools with the same record; or he may schedule an extra debate to determine the winning team or school.

3. Selecting the team or school with the best record of wins and losses and, in addition, announcing all "superior" and "excellent" teams or schools. Under this plan, the director would follow the procedure outlined above to determine the winning entrant. Additional "superior" or "excellent" teams would be named on the basis of their records or their ratings. For example, all teams having won eight or more of ten debates might be designated as "superior" teams and all teams that had won six or seven of ten debates might be labeled "excellent" teams. If the judges have rated the teams in each debate in addition to giving a decision, the director may average each team's ratings to determine "superior" and "excellent" teams. This can be done by giving each rating a numerical value—i.e., 5 points for "superior," 4 for "excellent," 3 for "good," 2 for "fair," and 1 for "poor"— and finding each team's average rating for the entire tournament. Under this plan, all teams with a 4.5 or above average—or any predetermined score—would be rated "superior," 3.5 to 4.4 would be "excellent," 2.5 to 3.4 would be "good," etc.

4. Selecting the outstanding individuals. In addition to determining the winning or outstanding schools and (or) teams, the director may require judges to rate each speaker in order to select the "superior" and "excellent" individual debaters. The advantage of this plan is that it gives recognition to effective individual debaters who, because of ineffective colleagues, might otherwise go unrecognized. In determining outstanding individuals, the conference director should follow the system outlined above for converting ratings into numerical scores.

Discussion. The manager of a discussion conference or contest has several methods by which he may determine outstanding participants.

1. Selecting outstanding participants on the basis of individual ratings given each round by the critic judges. At the end of the conference, these ratings are converted to numerical scores, totaled, and averaged to determine the speaker's overall rating. Some conference directors are opposed to this method because they believe it places too much emphasis on competition in a cooperative activity. See the discussion of this question on pp. 67–68.

2. Selecting outstanding discussion groups on the basis of ratings of each group by the critic judges. Under this plan the entire group is given a rating or score each round by each judge, the scores are averaged, and the outstanding groups are cited. The principal disadvantage of this method is

LOUISIANA STATE UNIVERSITY INTERCOLLEGIATE FORENSIC CONFERENCE, OCTOBER 19–20

Results

	I	II	III	Student Rating	Ave.	I	II	Ave.	Overall Ave.
	Discussion					*Advocacy Speaking*			
Louisiana State University									
Chairmen:									
Jerry Tarver	4	3	5	4.7	4.2	4	5	4.5	4.3
Sidney Fazio	5	3	4	4.7	4.2	4	5	4.5	4.3
Dorothy Freeman	4	3	3	4.1	3.5	3	4	3.5	3.5
Participants:									
Henry Green	4	4	5	4.6	4.4	5	4	4.5	4.4
James Kenner	4	4	4	3.6	3.9				3.9
George Lankford	4	3	3	4.4	3.6	2	5	3.5	3.6

Louisiana Tech
Loyola University
Memphis State University
Midwestern University
Mississippi College
University of Southern Mississippi
Northeast Louisiana State
Southeastern Louisiana College
University of Southwestern Louisiana
5—Superior; 4—Excellent; 3—Good; 2—Fair; 1—Poor

Outstanding Speakers

Superior Participants: Bill Wilson, LSU (4.8); Jim Prince, Southwestern (4.6); James Arceneaux, Loyola (4.5)

Excellent Participants: Paul McLain, Louisiana Tech (4.4); Jim Welch, LSU (4.4); Neil Folse, LSU (4.4); Henry Green, LSU (4.4); Bobby Thigpen, LSU (4.4); Dean O'Dea, Southwestern (4.3); Lane Wells, Louisiana Tech (4.3); Jerry Tarver, LSU (4.3); Sidney Fazio, LSU (4.3); Sarah Batton, Northeast Louisiana State (4.2); Allen Pierson, Southeastern (4.2); Ethel Istre, Southwestern (4.2); Wellborn Jack, LSU (4.2); John Brooks, Southeastern (4.1); Rodney Myer, Southeastern (4.1); John Gullatt, Louisiana Tech (4.1); Charis Wedgworth, Louisiana Tech (4.1); Phil Hablutzel, LSU (4.1); Bob O'Brien, LSU (4.1); Joed Price, Mississippi College (4.0).

Superior discussants:
Excellent discussants:
Superior discussion chairmen:
Excellent discussion chairmen:
Superior Advocates:
Excellent Advocates:

that superior discussants in average or below-average groups are not recognized.

3. Combining individual and group ratings by critic judges to determine a rating for each participant.

4. Combining student ratings of each other with the critic judges' ratings to determine each speaker's overall effectiveness.

Congresses and Legislative Assemblies.   Because the events and nature of student congresses and legislative groups vary greatly, methods for determining outstanding participants in these activities will be dictated by the type of program and objectives of each conference. If several different events are included, outstanding speakers in each activity and outstanding overall participants may be recognized. At the LSU Intercollegiate Forensic Conference (see p. 118), for example, students participate in discussion, advocacy speaking, and a legislative assembly. At the conclusion of the conference, recognition is given to "superior" and "excellent" discussion chairmen, "superior" and "excellent" discussion participants, "superior" and "excellent" advocates, and "superior" and "excellent" participants in all events. Although a legislative assembly is one of the important features of the LSU conference, no effort is made to evaluate student participation in this event. One of the reasons why participants are not rated in the legislative session is that some are not given the opportunity to speak; in addition, critic judges find it difficult to remember and evaluate all of the many speakers in such a meeting, the conference directors feel that ratings would discourage the free give-and-take that characterizes these sessions, and ratings would delay tabulation of results. However, many legislative assemblies do place critic judges in the hall to evaluate participants and to select outstanding speakers.

Individual Events.   For contests such as oratory, public speaking, extemporaneous speaking, oral interpretation, and others in which the students speak independently of each other, the conference director may utilize either a simple ranking or rating system.

Sweepstakes Awards.   Many conferences, festivals, and rallies provide a sweepstakes award for the school with the best record in all events. Under this plan, numerical points are awarded to each school on the basis of the rank or rating of each of its entrants in the several contests. Among the questions the director should resolve before instituting a sweepstakes award are these: (1) Should all events count equally in determining the award? (2) Should only the winning or outstanding speakers earn points toward the award?

With regard to how much weight each activity should carry in determining the sweepstakes winner, the manager will need to consider such questions as these: Should a first place or a superior rating in an individual event receive as many points as first place or superior in a four-round debate tournament? If not, what is a fair apportionment of possible points for each activity? Next, if ratings are employed, should low ratings earn points for a participating school? If so, it is possible that several poor ratings will earn as many points for a school as would a few superior ratings. Is this desirable? Would this encourage some schools to enter many unqualified participants in order to accumulate a higher total score? If all ratings are not to earn points for the school, the director must decide which ratings will be recognized in the sweepstakes tabulation and how many points each rating is to be worth.

Determining Types of Awards

Well in advance of any interscholastic contest or conference, the forensic director should determine how many entrants are to be recognized and what types of recognition or awards are to be given to outstanding participants. Most educators today agree that praise and recognition are effective motivational techniques in stimulating students to greater achievement. Thus it seems likely that the director of an interscholastic tournament or festival will wish to call attention to the efforts of a large number of outstanding participants. The citation of a single winning two- or four-man team in a tournament involving a large number of debaters—especially in view of the above-average ability of most students of forensics and the many hours of work required for effective participation in a debate—can only indicate a lack of understanding of sound educational principles on the part of the conference director. While inadequate preparation and performance should not be encouraged by too many awards, the writer is of the opinion that large numbers of participants who demonstrate unusual ability should be rewarded for the time and effort they have devoted to this worthwhile activity.

The conference director's next decision is to determine how the outstanding participants shall be recognized. Among the ways in which the director can call attention to them are these:

1. Announcement of the names of the speakers at a meeting of all conference or tournament participants
2. Stories and photographs in local and school newspapers
3. Letters to students' principals or deans
4. Publication of a booklet listing outstanding speakers and teams
5. Presentation of certificates
6. Presentation of medals, trophies, or plaques
7. Presentation of an appropriate but inexpensive gift, such as a book, fountain pen, or a subscription to a speech journal

Most forensic directors will readily endorse the first four types of recognition listed above and probably few will quarrel with the presentation of certificates to outstanding participants. However, considerable difference of opinion exists on the wisdom of awarding medals, trophies, plaques, and similar prizes to outstanding participants. The two main objections to such

awards are that too often the symbol—the trophy—becomes more important to the student than the activity—learning to debate or discuss well—
and that the money spent on trophies and medals could be better spent
elsewhere.

The second objection probably has greater validity than the first. If,
because of his eagerness to win a championship trophy, a student loses
sight of the educational nature of the activity or resorts to questionable
methods and practices, the cause of this conduct probably is the desire for
a "championship" rather than the trophy itself.

However, while the trophies may not be deterrents to sound education,
the forensic director should carefully consider whether the investment of
considerable sums in medals, plaques, and trophies is the wisest possible
expenditure of his forensic budget. Trophies probably provide some
student incentive to better performance, although how much cannot be
determined. Nevertheless, if the student is adequately rewarded and
compensated in other ways, the trophy or medal probably contributes little
to improvement or interest. On the other hand, if the purchase of trophies
or other awards will diminish by even one the number of deserving students who can participate in a public performance, debate tournament,
discussion conference, or other interscholastic forensic contest, the forensic
director is well advised to reexamine carefully the purpose and objectives of
his program.

Operation and Management of the Conference or Tournament

Although the duties of the forensic director depend on the type of conference being sponsored, in general his principal responsibilities during the
meeting will include the following:

1. Supervision of registration: In order to facilitate the smooth operation of the tournament or conference, the sponsor probably will wish to
maintain a table where the participating schools can register as they arrive,
pay fees, purchase tickets to meals, functions, or special events, and obtain
information.

2. Starting the conference on time: In order to make sure that all participants understand the regulations and, probably more important, in
order to gather together in one place all of the speakers and judges shortly
before activity begins, many conferences open with a general meeting at
which the visitors are welcomed, last-minute changes are announced, and
questions about events, procedures, and arrangements are clarified.

3. Keeping the conference running smoothly and on time: The forensic
director should obtain the services of several assistants prior to the conference. These persons, probably students, can be of help in distributing
instructions and time cards to timekeepers, passing out and collecting
judges' ballots, helping visitors find rooms and buildings in which events
are scheduled, and running errands for the director.

4. Compiling results: One of the director's most important tasks is to see that the results of contests are accurately and efficiently compiled so that he will be able to provide the participants with scores, criticisms, and similar data at the conclusion of the conference. At some meetings announcement of results of the contests is withheld until the event or the entire conference is completed. A director may wish to withhold the announcement of results because he prefers to honor all of the outstanding speakers at a single meeting at the end of the conference, or because, particularly in debate tournaments, he feels that the release of decisions may prove unduly discouraging to the losing teams in the early rounds. If the results are withheld, the director should make sure that his student assistants maintain secrecy throughout the tournament or conference. Finally, whatever procedure for announcing results is adopted, the tabulation of ratings, scores, and decisions should be accurate. No speaker or school likes to be deprived of deserved recognition because of errors in compiling the results. Because of the importance of accurate tabulation, it is essential that the conference director or another competent faculty member supervise this operation and carefully check and recheck the recording of all results.

5. Announcing results: If a general meeting is to be held at the conclusion of the conference or tournament for announcing results, the director is in charge of seeing that this is properly conducted. If trophies, medals, certificates, or other awards are to be given to outstanding speakers, teams, or schools he must make certain that these are available and ready for distribution. He should also have anticipated how he will handle such problems as unexpected ties, insufficient quantities of medals or certificates, and similar matters. If the results are to be mimeographed or duplicated in some other way for distribution to the participants, the conference director has the responsibility of arranging for tabulations to be completed and materials reproduced before the scheduled time of the concluding meeting.

6. Other responsibilities: If the conference program includes a banquet, luncheon, dramatic production, tour, athletic event, or other special entertainment, the conference director must organize and coordinate these activities. This will include seeing that tickets are sold or distributed, that conference events end on time so that the participants can take advantage of these special activities, and that arrangements for speakers, seating, and menus for meal functions are satisfactorily made.

Evaluation of the Tournament or Conference

When the conference ends, the forensic director probably will be in no frame of mind to begin planning the following year's meeting. However, this is the time, while the details and experiences are fresh in his mind, that he should seek to evaluate the conference and to plan modifications to improve future meetings. Letters to the forensic directors of the participating schools asking for recommendations for improvement for the following year usually will prove fruitful. Copies of all forms, rating blanks, and instructions, with suggested changes, should be carefully filed for future use. Only then can the teacher consider his job completed.[6]

SPECIAL FORENSIC EVENTS

In addition to regular tournaments, conferences, congresses, and festivals, the forensic director, at either the high school or college level, may wish to participate in one or more special forensic events during the season.

At the high school level most states now sponsor state debate tournaments. Many also conduct contests in discussion, original oratory, extemporaneous speaking, declamation, and similar activities. These contests usually are held at the time of the state debate tournament. Some states sponsor student congresses in conjunction with or in addition to other forensic contests. Eligibility requirements for participating in these contests vary widely. In some states speakers must win district and (or) regional contests in order to compete; in other states any school may enter the contests. Some states divide competing schools into classes according to enrollment; others make no distinction between large and small schools. Some contests are open only to members of the state debate league or the state forensic association; others have no membership requirements. Since these contests, whatever their specific nature, usually are held near the end of the forensics season, one of their principal advantages is that they serve as a goal toward which the students can work, and consequently provide considerable motivation for improvement.

In addition to state tournaments and contests, the National Forensic League annually sponsors state contests for member schools and national contests for the state winners.

Among the special forensic events at the college level are national congresses and tournaments sponsored by forensic fraternities; a "national" discussion conference; state, regional, and "national" debate tournaments; and international debates.

Some of the national forensic honorary fraternities—Delta Sigma Rho, Tau Kappa Alpha, Pi Kappa Delta—sponsor national congresses and contests either annually or biennially. These events usually are restricted to member schools and are held in the late spring. The exact nature of the meetings varies from fraternity to fraternity and sometimes changes from year to year. In the past, activities at these sessions have included legislative

[6] For a detailed checklist of duties in planning a debate tournament, see Karl Robinson, *op. cit.*, pp. 343–348.

congresses, debate tournaments, discussion, and individual speaking events. Member schools may secure information on their fraternity's national contests by writing to the organization's secretary.

In addition to national congresses, in many state or regional areas, debate tournaments and festivals are held. Several states sponsor college debate tournaments to determine the "official" state debate champion. Some include contests in other events. Still other states hold festivals open only to colleges and universities within the state. Some regional speech associations sponsor similar activities.

In addition to these events, several institutions sponsor individual debate tournaments in which schools from all parts of the country are invited to participate. Some of these tournaments have devised elaborate schemes to determine which schools will be invited. Although the label "national" is attached to some of them, none has been sanctioned or designated as an official national competition by state, regional, or national speech organizations.

A special forensic activity which is becoming increasingly popular is international debating. Begun in 1921 when a Bates College debate team argued at Oxford University, almost every year since, except during World War II, a foreign team has toured the United States debating American college students on a variety of questions. While the visiting teams usually have been British, students from other countries have also made debate tours of the country. Among the benefits of these debates, in addition to providing an unusual evening of debate, has been critical reevaluation of American debating occasioned by the different approach and techniques exhibited by the visiting debaters, particularly the British. For several years, while foreign visitors have been touring our country, the United States has also annually sent a team abroad. Tryouts for this trip are open to any college debater and usually are held in the spring. The Institute of International Education, which is in charge of both the visiting teams and the American teams sent abroad, should be queried for information on entertaining a foreign team or for details on tryouts for the trip abroad.

Still another type of speaking activity which has become increasingly popular in recent years is the campus audience-participation "debate." These exchanges usually take one of two forms: the "stump" or open-air meeting where any speaker may assume the rostrum to express his views on almost any subject and the forum-type debate on a specific question with opening speeches by prearranged speakers followed by debate between the pro and con factions of the audience.

The former activity—modeled on the speaking of Orator's Corner in Hyde Park in London—is found today on most large university campuses. A designated area and, perhaps, a specified time are set aside for students and others to discuss whatever they wish. Occasionally, discussion is restricted to particular preannounced issues. At some institutions a moderator is present to maintain order and decorum; at others the meetings are almost totally unregulated and depend on the audience's sense of justice to assure free speech and fair play.

Forum debating also derives from a British institution, the meetings of the debating unions of Oxford, Cambridge, and other universities. Forum debates are susceptible to many variations. To illustrate the basic features of this type of activity, the LSU Forum is cited as an example. The Forum meets once a month and is open to anyone. A single preannounced question is debated at each session. Upon arriving at the hall, participants find two blocs of seats facing each other. Persons favoring the proposition sit in chairs on the right side of the room; facing them on the left are those opposed. The debate, which lasts an hour, begins with two 7-minute speeches, one pro and the other con. Thereafter, the debate is taken up by the audience-participants, with a moderator alternating from one side to the other in recognizing speakers. Participants are free to change sides at any time, to interrupt for questions, and to boo, cheer, heckle, and applaud. At the end of the hour, a vote on the question is taken by having those who support the proposition file out one door and those opposed it depart by another exit. The final vote is then announced.

Any speech teacher wishing to inaugurate these activities will find that they involve little work. Probably the most important factor in setting up such debates or exchanges is to make sure that the school's administrative authorities are prepared to tolerate the freedom of expression which these confrontations engender. Beyond this, the speech instructor's main duties will consist of finding a time and place for the event, publicizing it, and, for forum debates, securing a moderator and the principal speakers.

CONTEST JUDGING

The teacher of speech generally is given the responsibility of judging various types of contest speaking: oratory, extemporaneous speaking, after-dinner speaking, and impromptu speaking. At the outset one important point should be stressed: *contest speaking, regardless of type, should be judged on the same basis as any other speaking.* When considered on any other basis, it becomes artificial and even ridiculous.

Ranking

Two general methods of determining winners of speaking contests are ranking and rating. In ranking, each judge simply places the contestants according to his preference, giving the best speaker first and other speakers successive ranks. No judge is permitted to tie two speakers. For determining a winner this method is the simplest and perhaps the best, for it usually

JUDGE'S EVALUATION FORM
OKLAHOMA SPEECH LEAGUES

By James Robinson, Director, Oklahoma Speech and Drama Services

Original Oration

Tournament _____ Site _____ Date _____
Contestant _____ School _____ Class _____

A, B, or C

Factors Considered	Evaluation	Comments
1. Suitability of subject		
2. Thought content		
3. Organization		
4. Development of ideas		
5. Use of language		
6. Voice and diction		
7. Bodily action		
8. Communication		
Total effect		

Evaluation Scale: I-Superior; II-Excellent; III-Good; IV-Fair; V-Poor
Criteria for Evaluation:

1. Suitability of Subject: Is the subject appropriate, timely, worthwhile?
2. Thought Content: Does it have depth? Is the approach fresh and challenging?
3. Organization: Is the introduction adequate? Are points apparent? Are transitions clear? Is the conclusion adequate?
4. Development of Ideas: Is there an adequate use of repetition, restatement, cumulation, example, illustration, evidence, etc., for effective oratory?
5. Use of Language: Does the wording have the simplicity, accurateness, vividness, and forcefulness essential to effective oratory?
6. Voice and Diction: Is the voice pleasant and appealing? Is there enough variety and emphasis? Is there an adequate use of climax? Is pronunciation acceptable? Is enunciation distinct without being pedantic?
7. Bodily Action: Does the speaker have unobtrusive poise and animation? Is he direct and physically communicative? Does he have distracting habits or mannerisms?
8. Communication: Does the speaker have mental as well as eye contact with his audience? Is he sincere? Naturally direct? Persuasive? Is he talking *with* rather than *at* us?

_____
Judge

gives a clear-cut winner and is easy to administer. One word of caution: Judges should not be asked to rank more than five to seven speakers.

To determine a winner, there are two methods of computation: (1) Select the speaker with lowest cumulative score; (2) Select the person who has a majority of a given rank and break ties with the cumulative score method.

These two methods are illustrated in the following example:

Contestant	Judge 1	Judge 2	Judge 3	Composite
Abel	4	1	5	10
Brown	2	2	2	6
Carr	3	4	4	11
Down	1	6	1	8
Everett	5	5	3	13
Fort	7	7	7	21
George	6	3	6	15

In this contest if the lowest score (Method one) is used, Brown wins with the low total score of six. However, Down wins by the other system, because he received two first places. This second method prevents the extreme judge (Judge No. 2, for example) from determining the final place.

Rating

Many teachers object to ranking students because they feel it is unfair to differentiate among speakers on what are sometimes extremely minor and unimportant points. They argue for the use of quality ratings: superior, excellent, good, fair, poor. Under this scheme the judge assigns one of these quality ratings to each participant, and he may give the same rating to several performers. When a panel of judges is used, the student receives the quality rating assigned to him by the most judges. Note the following case:

Student	Judge 1	Judge 2	Judge 3	Final
A	Excellent	Superior	Excellent	Excellent
B	Superior	Superior	Superior	Superior
C	Fair	Good	Fair	Fair
D	Poor	Fair	Good	Fair
E	Poor	Superior	Fair	Good

When numerical values are assigned to each quality—superior (5), excellent (4), good (3), fair (2), and poor (1)—the rating may be tabulated as follows:

Student	Judge 1	Judge 2	Judge 3	Total	Final
A	4	5	4	13	Excellent
B	5	5	5	15	Superior
C	2	3	2	7	Fair
D	1	2	3	6	Fair
E	1	5	2	8	Good

Final ratings may be calculated on the same basis as that used for determining final ranking. (See p. 127.)

The student who receives a majority of a given quality rating of course is given that rating. This procedure is illustrated above in the cases of A, B, and C. Note that Speakers D and E present a different problem because they each received three different ratings. In such cases, the final rating may be determined by averaging the numerical values and by applying a scale such as the following:

$$14-15 \quad \text{Superior}$$
$$11-13 \quad \text{Excellent}$$
$$8-10 \quad \text{Good}$$
$$5-7 \quad \text{Fair}$$
$$3-4 \quad \text{Poor[7]}$$

Number of Judges

The decision whether to use an expert judge or a panel depends largely on the goal of the contest and the availability of qualified judges. If the objective is to provide the speaker with suggestions for improvement, the expert judge is highly desirable. To qualify, a person should possess the following: (1) thorough knowledge and understanding of good speaking and the nature of the contest; (2) ability to give clear and cogent oral and written criticism; (3) respect of the contestants and teachers concerned.

In cases when the goal is to select a winner—perhaps for a prize or for the privilege of advancing to another contest—a panel is satisfactory. Anyone who has conducted contests knows how often speech judges, even those highly trained, disagree on what they consider good speaking. In an extensive study of 579 contests involving 3962 contestants judged by 1970 judges, Franklin Knower found, "The mean average deviation per judge was slightly one rank position in variation from the final average rank."[8]

How well do two persons agree in ranking student speakers? A meaning-

[7] Note that to receive a superior the student must obtain either three superiors or two superiors and an excellent. In the case of excellent he may earn his rating with any of the following combinations:
1. Superior, excellent, good
2. Superior, excellent, excellent
3. Excellent, excellent, excellent
4. Excellent, excellent, good

[8] Franklin Knower, "A Study of Rank-Order Methods of Evaluating Performances in Speech Contests," *Journal of Applied Psychology*, October, 1940, 24:637.

ful answer to this question can be expressed only in statistical terms that may seem confusing to some persons. The statistical correlations of two persons rating speakers may range from +.30 to as high as +.90 for instructors who rate together over a period of time.

In his study Knower found the "correlation of the first two judges in ranking 1201 declaimers was only +.35 and in ranking 1269 extempore speakers was +.46." These measures, which refer to consistency, are generally recognized as low. Statisticians usually suggest that a correlation of +.90 is necessary before great faith can be placed in a relationship.[9]

From these and other studies come several suggestions to be remembered in conducting a speech contest:

1. Experienced judges agree more readily than inexperienced judges; hence, a small panel of trained judges will probably produce as satisfactory a judgment as a larger panel of inexperienced judges.
2. Increasing the number of raters increases the reliability (consistency) of the judgment.
3. When they judge together over a period of time, with discussions of standards interspersed, judges are likely to increase in agreement.
4. Speakers of similar ability are more difficult to judge than speakers whose abilities are spread over a greater range.
5. As the number of contestants increases, the disagreement is likely to increase.
6. Judges are more likely to agree on the last place than on the first.
7. There is more agreement as to speakers who place at both ends of the distribution (first and last) than in the intermediate positions (third, fourth, fifth, etc.).
8. Speakers who speak first or last are more often ranked in the intermediate positions than in the higher or lower positions.[10]

EXERCISES

1. Prepare plans for a discussion conference to be held under the following conditions: (a) eighty participants, (b) four rounds, (c) one day, (d) forensic directors as judges, (e) selection of outstanding participants.
2. Prepare plans for a debate tournament to be held under the following conditions: (a) two two-man teams per school, each team debating the same side throughout, (b) round-robin, (c) two days, (d) debate directors as judges, (e) a winning school to be determined, (f) selection of superior debaters.
3. Volunteer to help conduct an extracurricular speech tournament or contest. Prepare a 500-word report on your observation.
4. Prepare plans for an extemporaneous speaking contest involving 30 speakers.

[9] .00 to .20 denotes indifferent or negligible relationship.
.20 to .40 denotes low correlation; present, but slight.
.40 to .70 denotes substantial or marked relationship.
.70 to 1.00 denotes high to very high relationship.
Henry E. Garrett, *Statistics in Psychology and Education*, London: Longmans, Green, 1953, p. 342.
[10] For data on 6, 7, and 8 see Knower, *op. cit.*

SAMPLE CONFERENCE PROGRAM
LOUISIANA STATE UNIVERSITY INTERCOLLEGIATE
FORENSIC CONFERENCE, OCTOBER 18–19

Topic: "What revision is needed in existing legislation governing the role of labor unions in determining conditions for employment?"

PROGRAM

Friday, October 18

8:30– 9:30   Registration, Lobby (all rooms in Pleasant Hall unless otherwise indicated)

9:30–10:00   General Assembly, Main Lounge. Welcome: Dr. Waldo W. Braden, Head, Department of Speech, Louisiana State University

10:10–11:00   Discussion: Round I—Definitions, background, goals

Room and Judging Assignments for Round I

Group	Room	Judge	Secretary-Timekeeper
I	Lounge, NE	Todd	Robert Burns
II	Lounge, SW	Riggs	Merryl Wright
III	131 (East)	Boyd	Patsy Dunaway
IV	131 (West)	Casey	Marilyn Richardson
V	48 (NE)	Attenhofer	Dian Theriot
VI	48 (SW)	Graham	Alvin Johnson
VII	147	Tewell	Prosper Toups
VIII	144	George	Herbie Plauche
IX	146	Murphy	Ed DeVille
X	154	Pennington	Rayford Cole
XI	54	Holland	Lynn Greig
XII	38	Everett	James Smith
XIII	179	Hamblin	Gladys Hague
XIV	Music-DA 111	Walker	Rosemary Bergin
	Extra:	*Extra:*	*Extra:*
	Music-DA 124	Evans	H. E. Landry
	Peabody 138, 206, 262	Traver Wendler	Ahmed Bahgat

Personnel of Discussion Groups for Rounds I, II, III

Group I	Group II	Group III
George Lankford, ch.	Bobby Thigpen, ch.	Allen Bierbaum, ch.
Byrd Ball	Rodney Brister	Sam Pate
Felix Collins	Shirley Watkins	Bob Winn
Mike Minchew	Jim Colvin	Caroline Vogel
Henry Sutton	Mona Champagne	Harry Smith
Wellborn Rives	Dean O'Dea	Gladys Barbee
John Tregg	Philip Carson	Melvin Turnage

(Continue list of personnel for all fourteen discussion groups.)

11:20–12:00		Discussion: Round II—Analysis of the problem	

11:20–12:00 Discussion: Round II—Analysis of the problem
Personnel of discussion groups will remain the same as for round I.
(List room, judge, and secretary-timekeeper for each group, following form used for round I.)

12:00– 1:00 Luncheon for visiting forensic directors, Faculty Club

1:10– 2:00 Discussion: Round III—Analysis of the problem concluded. Personnel of discussion groups remains the same as for rounds I and II.
(List room, judge, and secretary-timekeeper for each group, following form used for rounds I and II.)

3:10– 4:00 Advocacy speaking: Round I—Each speaker, including the chairmen, will have 7 minutes in which to present a "constructive" speech analyzing the problem and offering a solution. After everyone has spoken once, each participant will have 3 minutes to present a "rebuttal" refuting arguments advanced by other speakers and/or reaffirming his position. Participants will please STAND while speaking.

Group	Room	Judge	Chairman or Secretary-Timekeeper
I	Lounge (NE)	Heard	George Lankford, ch.
II	Lounge (SW)	Gunn	Bobby Thigpen, ch.
III	131	Melebeck	Allen Bierbaum, ch.
IV	48	Todd	Bennett Strange, ch.
V	147	Riggs	John Gunn, ch.
VI	144	Boyd	John Brooks, ch.
VII	146	Casey	Betty Clifton, ch.
VIII	154	Attenhofer	John Hey, ch.
IX	54	Graham	Glenny Castagnos, ch.
X	38	Tewell	Bill Wessel, ch.
XI	179	George	Mike Daves, ch.
XII	Music-DA 101	Murphy	Joe Perello, ch.
XIII	Music-DA 111	Pennington	Bill Wilson, ch.
XIV	Music-DA 118	Holland	James Welch, ch.
XV	Music-DA 121	Shaver	Barbara Purswell, S-T
XVI	Music-DA 124	Teague	Ed Skillman, S-T
XVII	Peabody 102	Hall	David Stone, S-T
XVIII	Peabody 119	Gravlee	Jane Babington, S-T
XIX	Peabody 130	Morvant	Dorothy Melancon, S-T
XX	Peabody 138	Tedford	Harry Daniel, S-T
XXI	Peabody 139	Parker	Mike Nance, S-T
	Extra:	*Extra:*	*Extra:*
	Peabody 142	Davis	June Young
		Traver	Miss Angelo
		Walker	
		Evans	
		Wendler	

Group Personnel for Round I of Advocacy Speaking

Group I	Group II	Group III
George Lankford, ch.	Bobby Thigpen, ch.	Allen Bierbaum, ch.
Felix Collins	Shirley Watkins	Sam Pate
Mike Minchew	Jim Colvin	Bob Winn
Henry Sutton	Mona Champagne	Caroline Vogel
Wellborn Rives	Dean O'Dea	Harry Smith

(Continue list of personnel of advocacy groups for all groups.)

4:10–5:00   Advocacy Speaking: Round II. As in the previous round, each speaker will have 7 minutes in which to present a "constructive" speech analyzing the problem and offering a solution and 3 minutes to present a "rebuttal" refuting the arguments of other speakers and/or reaffirming his position. Speakers will be assigned to new groups for this round.

                 (List groups, rooms, judging assignments, and secretary-timekeepers, list personnel of all advocacy groups for round II.)

7:00–7:15   General Assembly, Main Lounge. Announcement of rooms and temporary chairmen for caucuses and drafting of bills for the legislative assembly.

7:15 on   Caucuses: Temporary chairmen will conduct the caucuses until permanent officers can be elected. After the election of officers, participants will prepare a bill embodying their recommendations on the conference topic. As soon as the bill has been drafted, a copy should be sent to conference headquarters so that copies can be prepared for distribution at the legislative session.

Saturday, October 19

9:00–11:30   Legislative Assembly, Main Lounge. Dr. Giles Wilkeson Gray, Professor of Speech, Louisiana State University, presiding. Secretaries: Evelyn Jones, Emily Norred, Willa Wendler

11:30   Announcement of results

5. Volunteer to help prepare a group of students in a local school for one of the following: (a) debate tournament, (b) discussion conference, (c) extemporaneous speaking contest, (d) original oratory contest.
6. Listen to a radio or television discussion or debate and write an evaluation.
7. Write a 500-word paper on one of the following topics:
   a. What I gained from interscholastic debating.
   b. What I gained from participation in extracurricular discussion activities.
   c. Why I regret the time I spent on extracurricular forensic activities.
   d. The speaking contest as preparation for a public career.
   e. What famous men have said about their experience in extracurricular speech events.
8. Prepare a list of groups in your home town or a typical community who might be interested in hearing a debate or discussion.
9. After reading several articles in periodicals (see references), write a 500-word paper on one of the following:
   a. The values of tournament debating versus audience debating.
   b. Should students be required to debate both sides of a proposition?
   c. Debate versus discussion in the extracurricular forensics program.
   d. How to attract audiences to debates.
   e. How to improve extracurricular discussion activities.
10. Attend several meetings of the forensic squad in a local school. Observe the plan or organization of the program, types of activities carried on, the teacher's role in the program, frequency and length of meetings, teaching techniques employed by the director.

REFERENCES

ANDERSEN, KENNETH E. AND POLISKY, JEROME B., "The Application of the Symposium-Forum to Contest Discussion," *Speech Teacher*, March, 1960, 9:131–134.

BAREFIELD, PAUL A., "Competitive Speaking in Rhetorical Criticism," *Speech Teacher*, March, 1967, 16:109.

BOAZ, JOHN K. AND ZIEGELMUELLER, GEORGE, "An Audience Debate Tournament," *Speech Teacher*, November, 1964, 13:270–276.

BROCKRIEDE, WAYNE E. AND GIFFIN, KIM, "Discussion Contests Versus Group-Action Tournament," *Quarterly Journal of Speech*, February, 1959, 45:59–64.

CARMACK, PAUL, "State Forensic Leagues," in Potter, David (ed.), *Argumentation and Debate, Principles and Practices*, New York: Holt, Rinehart & Winston, 1954, pp. 423–453.

CATHCART, ROBERT S., "The Case for Group Discussion Contests," *Speech Teacher*, November, 1957, 6:315–318.

CRIPE, NICHOLAS M., "A Survey of Debate Programs in Two Hundred and Forty-Six American Colleges and Universities," *Speech Teacher*, March, 1959, 8:157–160.

EHNINGER, DOUGLAS, "Debating about Debating," *Quarterly Journal of Speech*, April, 1958, 44:128–136.

EHNINGER, DOUGLAS, "Six Earmarks of a Sound Forensics Program," *Speech Teacher*, November, 1952, 1:237–241.

GEHRING, MARY LOUISE, "The High School Oration: Fundamentals," *Speech Teacher*, March, 1953, 2:101–104.

GOLDEN, JAMES L., "Achieving Excellence in the College Oration," *Speech Teacher*, September, 1965, 14:184.

HUBER, ROBERT B., "Debate Tournaments," in James H. McBath (ed.), *Argumentation and Debate, Principles and Practices*, New York: Holt, Rinehart & Winston, 1963, pp. 331–350.

KELTNER, JOHN, "Discussion Contests: Sense or Nonsense?" *Speech Teacher*, March, 1952, 1:95–100.

KEMP, ROBERT, "Publicizing Forensics," *Speech Teacher*, January, 1969, 18:54.

KRUGER, ARTHUR N., "The Extempore Speakers Contest," *Speech Teacher*, September, 1956, 5:214–222.

MC BATH, JAMES H., "Debating on Television," *Quarterly Journal of Speech*, April, 1964, 50:146–152.

MILLS, GLEN E., "Audiences and Tournaments: Two Forms of Over-Emphasis," *Speech Teacher*, March, 1960, 9:95–98.

OSBORN, MICHAEL M., "A Blueprint for Diversity in Forensic Programs," *Speech Teacher*, March, 1965, 14:110.

PETERSON, OWEN, "Forum Debating," *Speech Teacher*, November, 1965, 14:286–290.

PFISTER, EMIL AND STOREY, ALFRED W., "Procedure for On-the-Spot Oral Evaluation of Performances by Students in Speech Contests," *Speech Teacher*, March, 1965, 14:132.

PHIFER, GREGG, "Organizing Forensic Programs," in James H. McBath (ed.), *Argumentation and Debate*, New York: Holt, Rinehart & Winston, 1963, pp. 304–330.

PHILLIPS, GERALD, "Imagination—The Answer to Tournament Debate," *Speech Teacher*, September, 1960, 9:207–210.

QUIMBY, BROOKS, "Is Directing Forensics a Profession?" *Speech Teacher*, January, 1963, 12:41–42.

REEVES, MARY AND OSBORN, LYNN R., "Judges of High School Debate Tournaments: Sources, Criteria, and Orientation," *Speech Teacher*, January, 1965, 14:59.

ROBERTS, MARY M., "Planning a Forensic Workshop," *Speech Teacher*, March, 1963, 12:115.

SIMPSON, JACK B., "A Speakers' Bureau for High Schools," *Speech Teacher*, November, 1952, 1:253–256.

SMITH, CARNEY C., "Practical Procedures in Coaching High School Debate," *Quarterly Journal of Speech*, April, 1943, 29:222–234.

SMITH, WILLIAM S., "Co-ordinating Classroom Instruction in Debate with Extracurricular Program," *Speech Teacher*, September, 1957, 6:213–216.

WILMINGTON, CLAY AND SWANSON, LINDA, "A Televised High School Debate Tournament," *Speech Teacher*, November, 1966, 15:299–302.

WINDES, RUSSEL R., JR., "Competitive Debating: The Speech Program, the Individual, and Society," *Speech Teacher*, March, 1960, 9:99–108.

7. Understanding and Teaching a Basic Communication Course

J. Donald Ragsdale

Meeting in New Orleans in February of 1968, the Conference on Research and Instructional Development in Speech-Communication adopted as one of its recommendations that the Speech Association of America "consider changing its name to include the word 'communication.'"[1] By July, 1970, not only had the Speech Association of America voted to change its constitution and become the Speech Communication Association, but the trend in the direction of name changing had spread to at least one of the regional professional organizations. At its annual convention in April, 1970, the Southern Speech Association voted to become the Southern Speech Communication Association. These events are but signs of a veritable communication explosion in this century. In a day of Telstar and television broadcasts from the Moon, many teachers feel that the term "communication" is both clearer and more relevant than the term "speech," which has been used alone to name their academic field since 1915. Yet, the question "What is communication?" is among the most enduring ones if recent convention programs and articles in the journals of the various professional organizations are any indication. Indeed, Frank Dance found some 95 definitions of communication in a recent survey of the professional literature.[2] Prior to any consideration of the content of a basic communication course, then, there must be some discussion of the nature of communication itself.

[1] Robert J. Kibler and Larry W. Barker (eds.), *Conceptual Frontiers in Speech-Communication*, New York: Speech Association of America, 1969, p. 21.
[2] Frank E. X. Dance, "The 'Concept' of Communication," *Journal of Communication*, June, 1970, 20:201–210.

SOME ASPECTS OF COMMUNICATION

When scholars ask "What is communication?" they are not, of course, questioning in quite the same sense as the child who asks "What is thunder?" Their purpose is not so much to know about the unknown as it is to refine the known. Often the questioner is grasping for a point of view, an answer which will tell him how one approaches the phenomenon in question or perhaps how one should approach it. The widespread use of the term "communication" makes even this kind of an answer difficult to provide, however. There are those in virtually every academic field who consider themselves to be communication specialists, to say nothing of the ministers of religion, the advertising salesmen, and the peddlers of personal influence schemes who are rife in our society. Along with the speech communication teacher, the English teacher, the journalist, the psychologist, and the sociologist, there is the electronics engineer, who may be concerned with communication between different parts of a circuit, and the computer scientist, whose interest may be in the man-machine interface. It is obvious that only the most general definition of communication would accommodate all of these interests. It is equally obvious that the term is the special possession of no single field and that few individuals could be competent in all of its aspects.

In a very general sense, "communication means that information is passed from one place to another."[3] It is comprised of "all of the procedures by which one mind may affect another. This, of course, involves not only written and oral speech, but also music, the pictorial arts, the theatre, the ballet, and in fact all human behavior. In some connections it may be desirable to . . . include the procedures by means of which one mechanism . . . affects another mechanism. . . ."[4] One of the most basic aspects of communication, therefore, is the idea of *transmission*. The notion of transferring something from one point to another is a kind of touchstone which allows persons with such diverse interests as a television service man and a psychiatrist legitimately to call themselves communication specialists. The telephone system, in fact, is one of the most popular analogies used for explaining communication. In this example, emphasis is placed on the various elements of the system and their functions.

In what must be the best-known version of the telephone system analogy, that of Claude Shannon and Warren Weaver, there are five major elements in communication. There must be an *"information source* which produces a message," a *"transmitter* which operates on the message . . .

[3] George A. Miller, *Language and Communication*, New York: McGraw-Hill, 1951, p. 6.
[4] Claude E. Shannon and Warren Weaver, *The Mathematical Theory of Communication*, Urbana, Ill.: The Univ. of Illinois Press, 1949, p. 95.

to produce a signal suitable for transmission over the channel," and a *"channel . . .* [or] medium used to transmit the signal from transmitter to receiver."[5] Although they do not include it as one of the necessary elements of communication, Shannon and Weaver note that noise may affect the signal "during transmission, or at one of the terminals."[6] Finally, there must be a *"receiver* [which] ordinarily performs the inverse operation of that done by the transmitter" and a *"destination . . .* [or] person (or thing) for whom the message is intended."[7]

Although it is widely used, the telephone system analogy with its emphasis on elements may not make the *process* aspect of communication as obvious as would be desirable. As Bernard Berelson and Gary Steiner put it, "it is the *act* or process of transmission that is usually called communication."[8] Today, it is not sufficient to speak only of the components of communication. Barnlund comments:

The contemporary scientific world has quietly replaced the two related premises of the Cartesian, or mechanistic, view of the universe—that the whole is the sum of its parts and causality the *only* unifying order—with a world view that emphasizes process. . . . To convey their discoveries biologists resort to neologisms like ecology and homeostasis; . . . rhetoricians find themselves talking about communication and meaning. All are terms that reject an atomistic or elementalistic approach in favor of a systemic or holistic one.[9]

In *human* communication, it appears to be especially necessary to emphasize the process aspect. Another one of the recommendations of the New Orleans conference in 1968 recognized that "research to date in speech-communication often has oversimplified the multidimensional, real-life communicative process by taking a static view of communicative behaviors. . . . Two [*sic*] few studies have focused on interactions, with detailed and specific examination of moment-to-moment, sequential, contingent behavior."[10]

A consideration of human communication, while less general than communication as a whole, requires that one examine some aspects which would not be especially relevant, for example, to the computer scientist. By far the most distinctively human of these aspects is symbolization. The "basic need," writes Susanne Langer, "which certainly is obvious only in man, is the *need of symbolization*. The symbol-making function is one of

5 *Ibid.*, pp. 4–5.
6 *Ibid.*, p. 5.
7 *Ibid.*, p. 6.
8 Bernard Berelson and Gary A. Steiner, *Human Behavior: An Inventory of Scientific Findings*, New York: Harcourt Brace Jovanovich, 1964, p. 254.
9 Dean C. Barnlund, "A Transactional Model of Communication," in Kenneth K. Sereno and C. David Mortensen (eds.), *Foundations of Communication Theory*, New York: Harper & Row, 1970, p. 84.
10 Kibler and Barker, *op. cit.*, p. 35.

man's primary activities. . . . It is the fundamental process of his mind, and goes on all the time."[11] Indeed, as Leslie White puts it, "the symbol is the basic unit of all human behavior and civilization. . . . It was the symbol which transformed our anthropoid ancestors into men and made them human."[12] Symbols are arbitrarily assigned entities which are used to refer to or to mean something. They are to be distinguished from signs which accompany a thing and hence may be indicators of it.

Human communication is characteristically, if not entirely, symbolic. "Like animals," says Colin Cherry, "we too have our inborn instinctive cries of alarm, pain, et cetera. . . . but such reflexes do not form part of true human language; . . . though, as signs, they can be interpreted by our fellows into the emotions they express."[13] Cherry virtually equates symbolization with the use of *language*, which is quite reasonable for most purposes. It is true that man communicates with such nonverbal symbols as flags, religious totems, rituals, and the like. Language, however, is his preeminent means. It is White again who points out that "articulate speech is the most important form of symbolic expression."[14]

It would be difficult indeed to overemphasize the importance of the language aspect of human communication. A characterization of it is nearly tantamount to a characterization of human communication. Language, for example, has the characteristic of interchangeability.[15] This means that the source and transmitter, to continue with the terms of the Shannon and Weaver model, and the receiver and destination may be one individual. Language also allows for complete feedback. The source-transmitter is able to monitor all of the aspects of the signal which he is sending. Through language, one may speak of things which are spatially and temporally displaced from the speaker's location. He may also coin novel utterances. One may even lie. It is no wonder that "spoken language is part of the 'common denominator of cultures.'"[16]

Language also occupies a central position in human *social organization*. "Without articulate speech," White notes, "we would have no human social organization. . . . Without speech we would have no political, economic, ecclesiastic, or military organization. . . . we would be all but

---

[11] Susanne K. Langer, *Philosophy in a New Key*, New York: New American Library, 1948, p. 45.
[12] Leslie A. White, *The Science of Culture*, New York: Farrar, Straus & Giroux, 1949, p. 22.
[13] Colin Cherry, *On Human Communication*, New York: Science Editions, Inc., 1961, p. 4.
[14] White, *op. cit.*, p. 33.
[15] Charles F. Hockett, "The Problem of Universals in Language," in Joseph H. Greenberg (ed.), *Universals of Language*, 2nd ed., Cambridge, Mass.: M.I.T. Press, 1966, p. 9. The ensuing discussion is based on Hockett's list of 16 design features of language. Cf. pp. 8–13.
[16] *Ibid.*, p. 14.

toolless."[17] This role of language in socialization seems to be implied in the Latin root of the term "communication," which is *communis*, meaning common. The having of things in common or sharing is, of course, one of the essential features of social organization. To some writers, language not only permits socialization but also *preserves* it. Kenneth Burke, for example, speaks of human society as a group of men *"huddling together, nervously loquacious, at the edge of an abyss."*[18] George Herbert Mead says, a bit less figuratively, that "the universe of discourse within which people can express themselves makes possible the bringing-together of those organized attitudes which represent the life of these different communities into such relationship that they can lead to a higher organization."[19]

The views of Burke and Mead are akin to those of many psychiatrists and theologians. Jurgen Ruesch, for instance, believes that "the tactics of psychotherapy revolve around . . . communicative processes."[20] Reuel Howe reasons that "every man is a potential adversary, even those whom we love. Only through dialogue are we saved from this enmity toward one another. Dialogue is to love, what blood is to the body."[21] Although the views of men such as Ruesch and Howe are popular, they are by no means universal. Further, even these men recognize that words may be used as cudgels to end human sharing. This aspect of communication, like several other ones, is arguable. There are those who would restrict communication to *verbal* behavior, some who would exclude anything which has no specific *intent*, and others who see it as a means for wielding *power*.[22] There are, finally, writers such as Barnlund who assert that communication "is not a reaction to something, nor an interaction with something, but a *transaction* in which man invents and *attributes meanings* to realize his purposes."[23] It is probably not possible at this time, then, to formulate a definition even of human communication which would satisfy every theorist. The teacher of a basic communication course will probably want to make his students aware of the many aspects of communication even if he chooses to select only a few of them for his own definition.

The reader may well ask here just how the term "communication" differs from the more traditional term "speech." The most noticeable

[17] White, *loc. cit.*
[18] Kenneth Burke, *Permanence and Change*, Los Altos, Calif.: Hermes Publications, 1954, p. 272.
[19] George Herbert Mead, "Society," in Anselm Strauss (ed.), *The Social Psychology of George Herbert Mead*, Chicago: Phoenix Books, 1956, pp. 270–271.
[20] Jurgen Ruesch, "The Role of Communication in Therapeutic Transactions," *Journal of Communication*, September, 1963, 13:135.
[21] Reuel L. Howe, *The Miracle of Dialogue*, New York: The Seabury Press, 1963, p. 3.
[22] Dance, *op. cit.*, pp. 204, 207, 208.
[23] Barnlund, *op. cit.*, p. 88.

difference between the two is surely the singular emphasis in the field of speech upon oral discourse. Indeed, the neglect and even denigration of the oral aspect of communication in academic departments of English was one of the major reasons for the split which resulted in separate departments of speech and in the founding of the organization today known as the Speech Communication Association. As Giles Gray expressed it in the first edition of this book, "the most obvious difference between speech and other common modes of communication may be observed in the simple fact that the speaker uses a medium [channel] that is quite different from those used in other modes."[24] At least partially because of this emphasis, speech as a discipline has revolved primarily around the speech producer. Traditionally, departments of speech have been subdivided into such areas as public speaking, oral interpretation, debate, and the like, whose names alone reflect the prevailing interest in the producer. Even the area of speech and hearing science has been predominantly concerned with such problems of the source and transmitter as aphasia, vocal defects, and articulatory disorders.

By comparison, the study of communication is not limited to any one medium or channel. Human communication, to be sure, occurs primarily through oral discourse, but it too is not limited to the oral mode. Men certainly communicate with gestures, through touch, and by their sense of smell to name only a few nonverbal means. They respond to such symbols as waving flags and crosses held high and, of course, to mere signs. Man has, moreover, developed technological means of surpassing the limitations of his own channels of communication. Recording equipment allows him to preserve his communicative acts and such sophisticated devices as television transmitters and receivers enable him to extend their range. In a basic communication course, there is not likely to be a main focus on any single element. As implied earlier, the process nature of communication makes any elemental or static emphasis misleading at best.

There are some teachers who would not be entirely happy with the above distinction. They would say that speech as a discipline is not limited to oral discourse and would point to traditional treatments of delivery, among other things, as evidence of an interest in nonverbal means. They might also argue, with good reason, that few speech teachers today retain the sort of speaker-oriented approach common in some earlier periods. Some of these teachers might even say that communication as a term is so general as to be ambiguous, that especially where human communication is concerned speech is a clearer term. It is undoubtedly the prevalence and the validity of these points of view which account in part for the retention

[24] Waldo W. Braden (ed.), *Speech Methods and Resources*, New York: Harper & Row, 1961, pp. 36–37.

of the term "speech" in the new names of some of the professional organizations. What is really at issue here, however, is not which of the two terms is the better but rather how the term "communication" differs from "speech" where the two are used together, especially as in departments of speech or speech communication. Under these circumstances, communication would appear logically to be the more encompassing term. It may be, therefore, that the study of communication is properly the basis for or the prerequisite to the study of speech.

In speech and speech communication departments, the term "communication" is also most commonly associated with the social and behavioral sciences and "speech" with the liberal arts or the humanities. Speech has often been concerned, for example, with the compositional and stylistic features of a public address or with the historical factors surrounding a particular speech occasion. It has further been concerned with moral issues such as the ethics of persuasion. Communication, on the other hand, has concerned itself with empirical studies principally of current examples of communicative behavior. It has been more interested in descriptions and explanations of success than in prescriptions for it. Further, communication has been more interested in theory or content than in practice or performance. These distinctions and the others as well are perhaps more matters of convenience than of necessity. Communication may be one's specialty, but that fact does not exclude an interest in other problems. The difference between communication and speech, then, is pretty much a difference of attitude or perspective rather than of substance. The New Orleans conference report expresses the communication perspective rather appropriately:

Research in speech-communication focuses on the ways in which messages link participants during interactions. Emphasis is on the behavioral antecedents and consequences of messages and their variations, as well as on the ways that messages interact with communication participants to produce behavioral outcomes.[25]

The conference report also recommends that "undergraduate programs include many of the substantive areas of study [in communication] that formerly have been identified primarily with graduate work."[26] It should similarly be added that some of these substantive areas are appropriate for study at the secondary school level. Indeed, a general plan of study at this level has very recently been formulated.[27]

[25] Kibler and Barker, op. cit., p. 33.
[26] Ibid., p. 40.
[27] William E. Buys, Charles V. Carlson, Hite Compton, and Allan D. Frank, "Speech Communication in the High School Curriculum," Speech Teacher, November, 1968, 17:297–317.

A PLAN OF STUDY

Objectives

As he considers a plan for his basic course in communication, the teacher may find it helpful to think in terms of what might be called the fundamentals of speech approach. The basic premise of this approach is that most students of the specialized areas of speech, such as public speaking or oral interpretation, benefit from prior training in what Giles Gray and Claude Wise called the bases of speech.[28] A fundamentals course might range over such topics as the cultural role of speech, the anatomy and physiology of the speaking and hearing mechanisms, the acoustic nature of speech, the role of language in speech, and the like. A unit on the phonetic alphabet or some basic training in phonetic transcription might be included. There might also be some attention given to the various forms of speech such as public speaking and discussion and, in conjunction, perhaps oral performance assignments. A practical view of the basic communication course is that it is a kind of outgrowth of the older fundamentals of speech idea. Its major objective, then, is to prepare students to pursue intelligently additional courses in communication and in speech or to provide the student who does not plan to take other courses with an informed view of communication.

The basic course in communication may also satisfy many other objectives. Some of these may be sought in conjunction with the major objective discussed above, or they may well be substituted for it completely or partially. The communication course could be conceived of as mainly preparatory for further study in communication itself. Were this the case, much emphasis would need to be placed on the terminology and concepts of the field, the research findings, and the philosophy and methodology appropriate to the social and behavioral sciences. The course might serve the purpose of providing the student with the allied knowledge necessary for being a better oral performer. For this result, the nature of the speaking mechanism, including its care and its usage, pronunciation standards, and the like could be the focus. The course might train students to do communication research. In it, the student might learn phonetic transcription, instrumentation for acoustic measurement, methods and tools for assessing such variables as personality, intelligence, attitudes, listener comprehension, and so on. Finally, the basic communication course might be expected to give the student practice in most of the forms of speech, so that in subsequent courses it might be possible to begin at a more advanced level or so that the student could experience the varieties of situations in

[28] Giles Wilkeson Gray and Claude Merton Wise, *The Bases of Speech*, 3rd ed., New York: Harper & Row, 1959.

which he might later find himself. Regardless of the particular objectives which the teacher chooses to emphasize however, there are a number of topics which would appear to be required for at least some study by the very definition of communication.

Topics for Study

Probably, the teacher will want to begin his course in much the same way that this chapter was begun with an analysis of the term "communication." A particularly useful classroom tool for this purpose is the model. Now a model is nothing more than a representation or a symbol, in this case, of communication. Communication models may be actual replicas of the elements in the process. Most often, though, they are geometric diagrams or verbal taxonomies because of the great difficulty in representing the complexity of communication with actual replicas. Through the use of a model such as that of Shannon and Weaver, discussed earlier, the teacher can summarize a large amount of information. He can represent or suggest relationships with arrows or connecting lines which would require much more time to convey were he to rely on verbal description alone. Models also afford an economical way of juxtaposing different definitions of communication for purposes of comparison. Finally, they often stimulate research by highlighting inadequacies in the state of present knowledge.

Although he should not forget that it is essentially a process, the teacher will probably need to spend some time in defining the nature of each element of communication separately. At first, he could take up those elements which are not uniquely human or those which are nonverbal. A comparison of human and animal communication would be very appropriate here. Similarly, a treatment of some of the nonverbal channels of communication would be in order. There has recently been renewed interest in cataloging various human movements and gestures and in analyzing their meanings. Kinesics, as this area of study is called, is not unrelated to the work of the elocutionists of the eighteenth and nineteenth centuries, although today it is primarily the anthropologist who is conducting the research. Proxemics is a similar area of study. It is the study of how people communicate through spatial relationships. Several sensory channels are probably involved in proxemics. Certainly, one can see the spatial relationships, but he may also differentiate them by hearing, by sensations of temperature, by touch, and by smell. The teacher and the student of public speaking, of course, recognize that audiences respond differently when the speaker walks away from his lectern toward them than when he does not do so. While they may not be part of either kinesics or proxemics, flags, banners, icons, and the like, could be discussed here with profit as nonverbal communicative means.

This may also be the best place to consider paralinguistic phenomena, for they are nonverbal even though they utilize the vocal-auditory channel of language. Paralinguistic phenomena are often referred to as the expressive aspects of speech. They are the nonfluencies, pauses, differences of voice quality, certain of the differences of pitch and loudness, and so on which accompany language. Such instances of paralinguistic phenomena as nasality, breathiness, filled pauses, and stutters may often have a significant effect on the way in which true language phenomena are received. Although it is still unclear just what individual pitch, loudness, and pause variations may mean, there is no mistaking the communicative impact of a Victor Borge reading a telephone book even in the absence of his oral and visual punctuation marks.

It will be necessary for the teacher to complete the above topics rather quickly in order that he might have sufficient time to treat the uniquely human aspects of communication. One way to begin a consideration of these would be to take up the anatomy and physiology of the speaking and hearing mechanism and the acoustic nature of speech. The teacher should keep in mind in doing this, however, that the kinds of details which might be useful in a specialized course are probably not necessary. The names of all of the muscles of respiration or of all of the cartilages of the larynx, for example, may only stifle the interest of many students. The teacher can discuss the relationships between respiration and intensity, frequency and intensity and perception, vocal fold vibration and resonation and voice quality, to name just a few, without stumbling into this trap. From this point, a logical next step is a consideration of the nature of language. The teacher may wish to begin by introducing his students to the International Phonetic Alphabet. He should also, however, give adequate attention to the syntactic component of language, perhaps trying to relate various syntactic patterns to communication situations in which they might be used. The teacher needs also to cover semantics in a general way examining the nature of meaning and its importance in communication. This material, too, should probably be covered rather rapidly in order for the more crucial process aspects of human communication to be given due consideration.

There are at least two popular ways of looking at communication as a process. The first of these centers on the kinds of elements involved in the process. When the process involves a single person it is said to be *intrapersonal* communication. It was noted earlier that, in humans, sources/transmitters and receivers/destinations are interchangeable and that language allows for complete feedback. Intrapersonal communication is involved, not when a person "talks to himself," but when he is making decisions or solving problems. Some scholars would argue that decision-making and problem-solving are nothing more than operations which a destination performs on information previously transmitted from a separate source or sources and would thereby ignore any time lag which might be involved. They would conclude that there is no such thing as intrapersonal communication.

Regardless of the name given to it, however, this process is clearly a communicative one and an important one at that. There is now a substantial body of research literature dealing with such things as the effects of personality, prior attitudes, ego-involvement, prior information, and the like on decision-making. There is also much information on plans and strategies for solving problems. Game theorists, for example, try to arrive at solutions which meet specific goals through a careful analysis of the "moves" which are available and their consequences. For most teachers, material on critical thinking would be a natural part of intrapersonal communication. Creativity is another concept which might be considered as a part of intrapersonal communication.

Writers such as Barnlund who think of communication as a transaction wherein man invents and attributes meanings would not restrict intrapersonal communication to the case of a single person both transmitting and receiving signals. As long as there is only one person they would say, the signals could be coming from either internal or external sources.[29] Similarly, intrapersonal communication in a recently proposed plan of study includes "communication to develop and maintain the integrity of self-concepts and to encourage stability of emotion and feeling."[30] What the proponents of this idea have in mind is not personality modification or mental hygiene in a strict sense but such things as self-awareness, self-criticism, personal values, and self-assurance. These characteristics would undoubtedly be developed or enhanced to some extent merely by the study of decision-making and problem-solving.

When the process of communication involves two or more persons, it is said to be *interpersonal*. Teachers of speech are, of course, most familiar with this type. In it one could include all of the familiar face-to-face forms of discourse from interviews and small group discussions to public addresses and debates. If the basic communication course is to include oral performances, then this is the section in which there should be a great variety of familiar assignments, all of which are treated in detail in other chapters of this book. A section dealing with interpersonal communication would hardly be complete, however, without some attention to the research literature on the subject. Of all the areas of communication, this is the one which has been the most extensively researched. Although many questions remain unanswered, the teacher can provide considerable understanding of such things as how evidence affects persuasiveness, how organi-

[29] Barnlund, *op. cit.*, pp. 94–98.
[30] Buys *et al.*, *op. cit.*, p. 304.

zation enhances intelligibility, and how reference groups affect the decisions of their members.[31]

Finally, when the process of communication is extended beyond its usual dimensions by such media as printing and telecasting it is called *mass communication*. The number of receivers/destinations in this situation are limited theoretically only by the size of mankind itself. Not only does mass communication allow for unlimited dissemination, but it may be readily preserved for future use. Unlike the other two forms, it does not allow for feedback between the receiver/destination and the source/transmitter except for direct monitoring in the latter. The teacher, therefore, would no doubt want to talk about the effects which this fact might have upon the source/transmitter. He would also, of course, need to consider the many different media, from film to graffiti, which his students will encounter if not use. Such intriguing topics as the effects of television viewing on behavior and the ethics of broadcasting might also be taken up.

An alternative to this way of examining communication as a process might be more suitable where the basic course emphasizes research or preparation for advanced communication courses. In a typical research study, the investigator is interested in relationships among variables. Rather than centering on the kinds of elements in the communication process, one might organize his examination around the relationships among variables in it. One could, for example, study message–receiver/destination interaction. Studies which investigate the relationships between the structure or organization of sentences or speeches and the listeners' comprehension exemplify this kind of interaction. One might examine source/transmitter–receiver/destination interactions. Studies of the effects of speaker credibility on audience attitude change are examples of such interaction. One might also look at channel-receiver/destination interactions. The impact of television on children's behavior patterns is such an interaction. Other such simple combinations of two variables or, for that matter, more complex combinations would provide units or sections for the remainder of the course. This approach might also capitalize on the primary use of research studies by dealing in detail with their methodology in order to prepare the student to do his own communication research.

The New Orleans conference recommended that the first-year graduate student in speech-communication be exposed to "(a) contemporary communication theories and research, (b) research methods, (c) philosophy of science, (d) history and development of rhetorical theory, and (e) language structure and meaning."[32] As mentioned earlier, it also recommended that much of the material presently being reserved for graduate

[31] Cf. Wayne N. Thompson, *Quantitative Research in Public Address and Communication*, New York: Random House, 1967.
[32] Kibler and Barker, *op. cit.*, p. 41.

level study be taught earlier in the curriculum. Without being so specific as is the above recommendation and with the exception of (d), the suggestions for a basic communication course in this chapter substantially embody both of these recommendations. It may be difficult to do a satisfying job of covering this material in the space of a single quarter or semester in the high school or the college. This may be especially true if oral performances are included in the course. There should be little doubt, however, that the job is eminently worth trying.

EXERCISES

1. Prepare an instructional unit on one of the following:
   a. Human communication versus animal communication.
   b. Nonverbal human communication.
   c. The place of linguistics in a study of communication.
   d. The social and economic impact of television in America.
   e. Decision-making and problem-solving.
   f. Interviewing.
   g. Measuring attitudes.
2. Draw up a list of as many communication variables as you can. Sketch a model which will account for these variables.
3. Prepare an oral performance assignment in which students assume the roles of other people and attempt to solve a hypothetical problem. Suggest roles as well as problems which will highlight educational, economic, social, cultural, age, sex, or racial differences between people.
4. Select two or more communication variables and devise an experiment to investigate their relationships. Plan a class project to carry out the experiment.
5. Compile a list of films which are appropriate for use in a basic communication course (see recent issues of *The Speech Teacher*).
6. Coordinate a class visit, depending on availability, to a television studio, an acoustics laboratory, a speech clinic, a comparative psychology laboratory, or the like.
7. Suggest a 4-year college curriculum which would give adequate preparation to the teacher of a basic communication course.

SOME ASPECTS OF COMMUNICATION: GENERAL SOURCES

Journal Articles

BARNLUND, DEAN C., "Toward a Meaning-Centered Philosophy of Communication," *Journal of Communication*, December, 1962, 12:197–211.

DANCE, FRANK E. X., "The 'Concept' of Communication," *Journal of Communication*, June, 1970, 20:201–210.

FEARING, FRANKLIN, "Toward a Psychological Theory of Human Communication," *Journal of Personality*, September, 1953, 22:71–88.

GERBNER, GEORGE, "Toward a General Model of Communication," *Audio-Visual Communication Review*, Summer, 1956, 4:171–199.

GOYER, ROBERT S., "Communication, Communicative Process, Meaning: Toward a Unified Theory," *Journal of Communication*, March, 1970, 20:4–16.

KING, WILLIAM A., "An Event-Structure Model for Communication," *Journal of Communication*, December, 1968, 18:389–403.

KNOWER, FRANKLIN H., "What Do You Mean—Communication?" *Central States Speech Journal*, Spring, 1970, 21:18–23.

MILLER, GERALD R., "On Defining Communication: Another Stab," *Journal of Communication*, June, 1966, 16:88–98.

NILSEN, THOMAS R., "On Defining Communication," *The Speech Teacher*, January, 1957, 6:10–17.

WESTLEY, BRUCE H. AND MACLEAN, MALCOLM S., JR., "A Conceptual Model for Communications Research," *Journalism Quarterly*, Winter, 1957, 34:31–38.

Books

ALLEN, R. R., ANDERSON, SHAROL, HOUGH, JERE, AND CROW, EARL S., *Speech in American Society*, Columbus, Ohio: Merrill, 1968.

BERLO, DAVID, *The Process of Communication*, New York: Holt, Rinehart & Winston, 1960.

CHERRY, COLIN, *On Human Communication: A Review, a Survey, and a Criticism*, Cambridge, Mass.: M.I.T. Press, 1957.

DANCE, FRANK E. X. (ED.), *Human Communication Theory: Original Essays*, New York: Holt, Rinehart & Winston, 1967.

DEFLEUR, MELVIN L., *Theories of Mass Communication*, 2nd ed., New York: McKay, 1970.

HOWE, REUEL L., *The Miracle of Dialogue*, New York: Seabury Press, 1963.

KIBLER, ROBERT J. AND BARKER, LARRY L. (EDS.), *Conceptual Frontiers in Speech-Communication*, New York: Speech Association of America, 1969.

LANGER, SUSANNE K., *Philosophy in a New Key*, Cambridge, Mass.: Harvard Univ. Press, 1942.

MARTIN, HOWARD H. AND ANDERSEN, KENNETH E. (EDS.), *Speech Communication: Analysis and Readings*, Boston: Allyn & Bacon, 1968.

MATSON, FLOYD W. AND MONTAGU, ASHLEY (EDS.), *The Human Dialogue: Perspectives on Communication*, New York: Free Press, 1967.

MILLER, GEORGE A., *Language and Communication*, New York: McGraw-Hill, 1951.

RICHARDSON, LEE (ED.), *Dimensions of Communication*, New York: Appleton-Century-Crofts, 1969.

RUESCH, JURGEN AND BATESON, GREGORY L., *Communication: The Social Matrix of Psychiatry*, New York: Norton, 1951.

SERENO, KENNETH K. AND MORTENSEN, C. DAVID (EDS.), *Foundations of Communication Theory*, New York: Harper & Row, 1970.

SHANNON, CLAUDE E. AND WEAVER, WARREN, *The Mathematical Theory of Communication*, Urbana, Ill.: Univ. of Illinois Press, 1949.

WHITE, LESLIE A., *The Science of Culture*, New York: Farrar, Straus & Giroux, 1949.

A PLAN OF STUDY: SPECIALIZED SOURCES

BIRDWHISTELL, RAY L., *Introduction to Kinesics: An Annotation System for Analysis of Body Motion and Gesture*, Washington, D.C.: Foreign Service Institute, 1952.

BOWERS, JOHN WAITE, *Designing the Communication Experiment*, New York: Random House, 1970.

BROWN, ROGER, *Words and Things*, New York: Free Press, 1958.

BUYS, WILLIAM E., CARLSON, CHARLES V., COMPTON, HITE, AND FRANK, ALLAN D., "Speech Communication in the High School Curriculum," *The Speech Teacher*, November, 1968, 17:297–317.

CARROLL, JOHN B., *The Study of Language*, Cambridge, Mass.: Harvard Univ. Press, 1959.

CONDON, JOHN C., JR., *Semantics and Communication*, New York: Macmillan, 1966.

DINNEEN, FRANCIS P., *An Introduction to General Linguistics*, New York: Holt, Rinehart & Winston, 1967.

EISENSON, JON, AUER, J. JEFFERY, AND IRWIN, JOHN V., *The Psychology of Communication*, New York: Appleton-Century-Crofts, 1963.

EMMERT, PHILIP AND BROOKS, WILLIAM D. (EDS.), *Methods of Research in Communication*, Boston: Houghton Mifflin, 1970.

GLEASON, HENRY A., JR., *An Introduction to Descriptive Linquistics*, rev. ed., New York: Holt, Rinehart & Winston, 1961.

GRAY, GILES WILKESON AND WISE, CLAUDE MERTON, *The Bases of Speech*, 3rd ed., New York: Harper & Row, 1959.

GREENBERG, JOSEPH H. (ED.), *Universals of Language*, 2nd ed., Cambridge, Mass.: M.I.T. Press, 1966.

HALL, EDWARD T., *The Silent Language*, Garden City, N.Y.: Doubleday, 1959.

HYMES, DELL (ED.), *Language in Culture and Society: A Reader in Linguistics and Anthropology*, New York: Harper & Row, 1964.

MC LUHAN, MARSHALL, *Understanding Media: The Extensions of Man*, New York: McGraw-Hill, 1964.

SEBEOK, THOMAS A. (ED.), *Animal Communication: Techniques of Study and Results of Research*, Bloomington, Ind.: Indiana Univ. Press, 1968.

THAYER, LEE (ED.), *Communication—Spectrum '7*, Flint, Mich.: National Society for the Study of Communication, 1968.

THOMPSON, WAYNE N., *Quantitative Research in Public Address and Communication*, New York: Random House, 1967.

8. Teaching Interpretation

Francine Merritt

Interpretation, or oral reading as it is frequently called, has an ancient and honorable history. It was closely allied historically with the beginnings of dance, song, drama, and religion. Its practice not only preserved the creations of poet and storyteller but kept them alive through human ears rather than fossilized on shards of pottery or printed pages. Today the survival of literature does not depend on oral tradition; but oral interpretation continues because people still like to hear stories, and poets still shape their works for the ears of people.

THE NATURE OF INTERPRETATION

Teachers sometimes justify the presence of oral reading among school activities by employing it as a tool. One is told that oral reading builds vocabulary, or aids in teaching sentence structure, or stimulates interest in the study of a literary selection, or is necessary to the study of delivery of a manuscript speech. All these are among the legitimate uses to which interpretation can be put, but the values inherent in the study of oral interpretation transcend all immediate utilitarian purposes. It should be the purpose of the interpretation course to realize the more subtle affective values essential to self-development and the experiencing of literature.

Among the dozen or more common definitions of the verb *to read* are the following: (1) to get the meaning of; understand; (2) to give the meaning of; interpret; (3) to speak printed or written words. The fact that the third one of these can be performed by any literate person explains the speech teacher's occasional reluctance to use the term *oral reading,* though it is suitable enough. Instead, the term *oral interpretation* or merely *interpretation* is generally used to insure the inclusion of the first two meanings in the complete description of this threefold speech activity: understanding (1) and giving the meaning (2) aloud (3). The third concept is included to indicate that the activity is normally a public one. Though the interpreter may enjoy reading aloud to himself, he assumes that an audience for whom to interpret will eventually be his.

The three foregoing definitions of reading suggest the nature of not only interpretation but also the beginning interpretation course, in which some attention is given to the following: (1) literary study: analysis and appreciation; and (2) communication of the reader's intellectual-emotional re-creations of the literature, through (3) the reader's agents of delivery: his body and his voice. An inappropriate balance among these interests will distort the interpretation course. If attention to literary analysis, for example, completely monopolizes the course, the result is likely to be mere duplication of the work of an English course. If development of vocal skill becomes the primary goal, the interpretation course will resemble a voice and diction course. Worse still, if students become preoccupied with delivery, or attempt interpretative communication without the disciplinary influence of the basic literary study that is prerequisite to reading aloud, the course will represent a reversion to the practices of the now discredited elocutionists who emphasized "external graces of delivery, especially of voice, sometimes also of gesture" before audiences who were expected to admire readers' techniques rather than to appreciate literature.

ACADEMIC INFLUENCES ON THE INTERPRETATION COURSE

It is always inadvisable to organize and teach a course in a vacuum. Before a teacher formulates the goals of the interpretation course, prepares a course outline or syllabus, chooses a textbook, or tentatively selects the type of literature for reading, he should have answers to these questions:

I. Where does this course fit into the curricula of my school?
   A. Is it an alternate or an elective substitute for an English course?
   B. Is it part of a liberal arts program?
   C. Is it expected to extend the students' general education?
II. What departmental requirements must this course meet?
   A. Is it expected to double as a voice and diction course?
   B. Is it prerequisite to courses in radio-TV, dramatics, etc.?
   C. Is it expected to provide extracurricular readers or programs?
   D. Is it expected to produce winners of contests?

III. What are the needs and expectations of the students?
   A. Do they have training in voice and diction before enrolling in inter-
      pretation? Do they have serious vocal deficiencies?
   B. Have they developed the reading habit early enough to bring an exten-
      sive reading background to the course? Do they read only what is
      assigned?
   C. Do they have a background in literature, criticism, aesthetics, art, and
      music? Must they depend on the instructor to lead them into these
      areas?

The answers to these questions must inevitably affect the objectives,
content, and teaching techniques of the course. In some schools interpretation is not taught for its own sake but exists as a service course to develop
in the students certain skills important to successful achievement in other
speech courses. This is a regrettable situation, since interpretation has its
own educational values and has no greater responsibilty toward the development of speech skills than have other speech activities. Fortunately,
interpretation is more often treated as a liberal arts course with special
emphasis on cultural goals of a high order: the appreciation of literary
masterpieces and the understanding of aesthetic principles they exemplify.
In a still different academic environment the course in interpretation
makes its contribution to the acquisition of a broad general education. In
some instances, interpretation is regarded as a professional course, the
product of which is the interpretative reading program as an art form.

How will these diverse views of the goals of interpretation and of the
place of interpretation in the curriculum be reflected in the content and
pedagogical techniques in the course itself? First, the service course is
similar to a voice and diction course. Selections for reading may be chosen
for the vocal skills that they presumably induce or exercise. The student
may read Longfellow's "The Rainy Day" to provide opportunity for a slow
rate or a low pitch or a subdued emotional tone. He may practice Poe's
"The Bells" or Lindsay's "The Congo" to improve his control of extreme
vocal variation. Unfortunately this represents much the same approach to
literature that promoted the tasteless elocutionary behavior deplored and
to some extent still feared by modern teachers. Under the circumstances it
is easy to understand why skillful vocal delivery, a desirable speech objective in itself, has been deemphasized in interpretation textbooks and
courses. Memories linger from a past in which delivery for delivery's sake
was an objective too readily adopted.

If, on the other hand, the interpretation course is taught primarily for its
humanistic values, the student will be encouraged to develop a discriminating taste in literature and an awareness of arts and letters.[1] The subject
matter of his course will include principles of literary analysis, aesthetic

[1] See Don Geiger, "Oral Interpretation in the Liberal Arts Context," *Quarterly Journal
of Speech*, April, 1954, 40:137–144.

principles, and literary criticism related to the materials he selects to interpret. He will be encouraged to choose selections of literary merit ranging from classics through standard works to the avant-garde. As a part of the development of his critical judgment, he must make his own choices and justify them. Rigid requirements and standardized assignments are not in his best interest. Flexibility of the course becomes a basic requisite for a liberal arts approach. The basic weakness of this course is likely to be a neglect of the development of speech skills to the detriment of the oral reader.[2]

The course in interpretation can be adapted to a curriculum for general education by changing the reading materials from primarily belles-lettres to include books of biography, memoirs, history, philosophy, travel, psychology, and even the sciences. By this method the course can provide the connective tissue for uniting interpretation, with its literary interests, and the nonliterary world of information and experiences. To the recurring plea for "greater intellectual commerce among disciplines, especially between the humanities and the sciences,"[3] interpretation can respond, assuming some share of the responsibility of broadening students' experiences.

All of these types of interpretation courses, representing different philosophies, are being taught successfully in response to the demands of different school and departmental curricula. There need be no serious objection to any one of them, though they are unequal in ultimate value. Nor do they represent entirely incompatible goals. A skillful and experienced teacher is often able to make one and the same course serve the student by improving his vocal and reading skills for other activities, adding to his knowledge and appreciative awareness of literary art, and widening the boundaries of his education in areas supposedly far removed from reading aloud.

TRADITIONAL METHODS OF TEACHING INTERPRETATION

In 1927 W. M. Parrish wrote: "Of the various courses commonly included in departments of Speech, it will be generally conceded that the course in Interpretative Reading is the most difficult to organize. Its content is so elusive, and the skill it aims to impart so narrowly focused, that it offers no obvious point of beginning or method of procedure."[4] The passing of

[2] See Stanley Glenn, "Echo to the Sense," *Western Speech*, Spring, 1960, 24:88–93.
[3] David Boroff, "American Colleges: What Their Catalogues Never Tell You," *Harper's Magazine*, April, 1960, 220:38.
[4] Wayland Maxfield Parrish, "Interpretative Reading," *Quarterly Journal of Speech Education*, April, 1927, 13:160.

more than four decades has served merely to confirm the truth of Parrish's observation. Lack of uniformity in courses and methods of teaching interpretation is apparent in both textbooks and professional literature. However, teachers of interpretation have not been inclined to demand uniformity, partly because they are aware that the literature they teach interpreters to read cannot be reduced to one rigid form or system, and partly because they respect the work of other teachers whose methods differ from their own but whose products are excellent. Teachers of interpretation are also sensitive to the dangers of "method," since a study of the history of their discipline reveals that promotion of and adherence to rigid schools or systems of instruction have periodically threatened the status of oral reading.[5]

An examination of contemporary interpretation textbooks reveals that interpretation is heavily indebted to the "think the thought (and feel the emotion)" school. Almost all current textbooks emphasize the necessity for studying, analyzing, understanding, and synthesizing. They insist that the student examine background, context, structure, and emotional tension of the selection. At times some of them seem to imply, by a marked avoidance of attention to techniques of delivery, that proper comprehension at intellectual and emotional levels will automatically insure effective communication to an audience. Therein lies the weakness, for interpretation, of this otherwise invaluable method. It is wishful thinking to suppose that the voice and body of the interpreter need only inner prompting to respond with perfect coordination to the subtle demands of the best in literature.[6] Perhaps the greatest danger in total reliance on this method of teaching interpretation is the possibility of the teacher's forgetting that he is teaching an oral art for communication to listeners as well as a literary art that communicates to the reader,[7] particularly since oral communication is more difficult to teach than is literary analysis.

At the time when it was most needed, the "think the thought" method was embraced as a reaction to the "mechanical" school, a reputedly pernicious system of training that seems to have developed without anyone's advocacy. The objection to this method of teaching lay in its attention to

[5] The history of interpretation is treated at length in Eugene Bahn and Margaret L. Bahn, A History of Oral Interpretation, Minneapolis: Burgess, 1970, and briefly in Charlotte I. Lee, Oral Interpretation, 3rd ed., Boston: Houghton Mifflin, 1965, pp. 449–456, and Keith Brooks, Eugene Bahn & L. LaMont Okey, The Communicative Act of Oral Interpretation, Boston: Allyn & Bacon, 1967, pp. 3–19. See also Karl R. Wallace (ed.), A History of Speech Education in America: Background Studies, New York: Appleton-Century-Crofts, 1954; and Mary Margaret Robb, Oral Interpretation of Literature in American Colleges and Universities, rev. ed., New York: Johnson Reprint, 1968.
[6] For more on strengths and weaknesses of "thinking the thought," see Martin Cobin, Theory and Technique of Interpretation, Englewood Cliffs, N.J.: Prentice-Hall, 1959, pp. 81, 82, 99, 100; and Charlotte I. Lee, Oral Interpretation, 3rd ed., Boston: Houghton Mifflin, 1965, pp. 452, 453.
[7] See Glenn, op. cit.

mechanical manipulations of voice and gesture without much relation to either the meaning of the literature or the reader's processes of thought. Students were so meticulously trained in details of delivery that they undertook to demonstrate their technical superiority in voice and movement rather than to reveal literary values. This misplaced emphasis all but destroyed reading as a serious study for some time.[8] To this day some teachers are reluctant to suggest to a student that he "lower the pitch here" or "pause there" for fear of raising the ghost of the mechanical method, and rare indeed is the teacher of interpretation who admits to requiring students to "rehearse a gesture." Yet there is nothing mechanical in teaching a specific technique, unless one requires that the technique be employed for its own sake. For obvious reasons no one appeals for a return to mechanical methods; but without some attention to the mechanics of vocal control and bodily communication, too many students find themselves, as students of the "wooden" school of delivery, incapable of expressing what they want to communicate.

Parallel to both the mechanical and the "think the thought" approaches was another teaching method or philosophy called the "natural school," based on the admirable notion that the best existing in nature should serve as the model for all. However, by degrees naturalness came to imply not merely that the reader should avoid calling attention to his own behavior, but that he should do only that which was "natural," i.e., habitual, to himself. The method has an intrinsic affinity for the area of public speaking, in which the speaker must at all costs seem to be sincerely himself. Its application to the field of interpretation oversimplifies the problems of the interpreter, as Parrish pointed out in a plea for the separation of public speaking and interpretation: "The function of the reader is interpretation of the thought of another in the language of another. The function of the speaker is communication of his own thoughts in his own language. His strongest personal asset is sincerity, genuineness. He must be himself, speak in his own person. The reader cannot in this sense be himself. . . . He must study the mood of his author and try to enter into that mood."[9]

One finds echoes of the natural school in contemporary speech textbooks that recommend natural posture or position of the hands or a natural voice or the reading of poetry "naturally" (i.e., as conversational prose?). However, for the interpreter undue emphasis on naturalness not only places a premium on the reading of literature written in a contemporary conversational style but also encourages the reader to distort the form and language of material not so written. Hence, there are misguided attempts to force

[8] For a vivid description of the extremes to which such instruction led, see Maud May Babcock, "Interpretative Presentation Versus Impersonative Presentation," in Gertrude E. Johnson (ed.), *Studies in the Art of Interpretation*, New York: Appleton-Century-Crofts, 1940, pp. 85–93.
[9] Wayland Maxfield Parrish, "Public Speaking and Reading—A Plea for Separation" (Forum), *Quarterly Journal of Speech Education*, June, 1924, 10:278.

the elevated language of classical literature, the compressed patterns of poetry, and literature's shattering revelations of private emotions into the typical behavior patterns common to normal communicative situations. The teacher of interpretation, therefore, seldom says "Be natural," but rather, "Let the reader's behavior, both vocally and bodily, be sufficiently unobtrusive to make whatever he does *seem* to be natural to the literature, to himself, and to the situation." Such a suggestion is not far from the original intention of the natural school.[10]

The fourth method of teaching interpretation, by imitation, is also eschewed by many teachers, to the point that some of them admit to refraining from reading to their own students for fear of establishing patterns for imitation. One would suppose that they must also fear the use of recorded materials and the possibility that students may imitate one another. Admittedly imitation is the least creative and beneficial method of teaching, for the student so taught cannot be expected to proceed independently beyond the immediate task. However, the imitative method is sometimes a last resort. When failure is certain without it, one prefers to risk the dangers of imitation to achieve some measure of success. Imitation, or demonstration as it perhaps should be termed, is most often used to suggest alteration of details of delivery—stubborn inflectional patterns, pronunciations, and subtleties of phrasing or pausing, for example. Conversely, teachers frequently imitate students' faults for illustration and for ear training, and some recommend that students practice the imitation of recorded reading performances or the voices of familiar entertainers and stage personalities as an exercise for developing aural sensitivity and vocal control. However, there is no doubt that these same teachers would, without exception, look with great disfavor on any imitative virtuosity that is substituted for the students' own interpretative creativity.

At this point it should be apparent that the teacher of interpretation seldom finds a solution to the problems of teaching by limiting himself to only one of the four traditional methods discussed. Each one, taken by itself and possibly subjected to oversimplification and misinterpretation, tends either to contradict the purposes of interpretation or to handicap the efforts of teacher and student to achieve their goals. Combined judiciously, the methods counteract the disadvantages of one another and complement one another to the benefit of both student and teacher.

CRITICISM AS A METHOD OF INSTRUCTION

Teachers of interpretative reading use the same methods of criticism employed by teachers of public address and are confronted by many of the same problems: Oral criticism consumes more class time than does written

[10] See Wayland Maxfield Parrish, "The Concept of 'Naturalness,'" *Quarterly Journal of Speech*, December, 1951, 37:448–454.

criticism, is more likely to be spotty or superficial, and demands constant tactfulness. Written criticism, if unreported to the class orally, reaches only one person per reading performance, is time-consuming if presented in essay form, and occasionally misinforms when a standard checklist is used. Though they deplore the disproportionate amount of time it requires, interpretation teachers usually resort to oral criticism to avoid the difficulty of writing comments about vocal nuances.

Managing Criticism Efficiently

Beginning teachers will find the following suggestions helpful for improving the handling of criticism in the interpretation class:

1. Combine oral criticism with the use of a written checklist on which can be systematically reported items irrelevant to the topics discussed orally.
2. Select one reading performance for intensive analysis and abbreviate the criticism for the remaining readers, making sure that at each successive class period a different reader is given the benefit of more thorough criticism.
3. Avoid duplication of criticism by developing the criticism topically rather than reader by reader.
4. Retain a carbon copy of written criticism for grade records and for later reference in checking improvement.
5. Use a criticism form adapted to the individual assignment rather than a single standard form. Though this procedure involves more work initially, the resulting clarification of goals will justify the extra time the instructor spends in preparing the forms.

Locating Examples of Criticism Forms

Examples of forms used for classroom criticisms or contests are readily available in textbooks, workbooks, and handbooks. The following list is intended only to suggest the variety of printed sources of evaluation forms:

BROOKS, KEITH, BAHN, EUGENE, AND OKEY, L. LAMONT, The Communicative Act of Oral Interpretation, Boston: Allyn & Bacon, 1967, pp. 401–412. Scales and checklists for evaluating effectiveness and techniques.

CROCKER, LIONEL, Interpretative Speech, Englewood Cliffs, N.J.: Prentice-Hall, 1952, pp. 262–268. Lists 45 criteria for judging reading, plus two evaluation charts.

HUNSINGER, PAUL, Communicative Interpretation, Dubuque, Ia.: William C. Brown, 1967, pp. 99, 100. A form for eliciting audience response.

YOUNG, JERRY D., "Evaluating a Readers Theatre Production," Speech Teacher, January, 1970, 19:37–42. Forms for individual and group critiques.

Other sources of evaluation forms are the interpretation contests and festivals sponsored by colleges, state high school leagues, college, state and regional conferences, regional speech associations, and forensic organizations. Many teachers acquire such forms by attending the festivals and tournaments with their students. However, copies can sometimes be obtained by addressing letters of inquiry to the director of the festival or tournament or to the sponsoring agency.

Adapting the Form to the Assignment

Eventually teachers evolve their own evaluation forms to represent the nature of their assignments and the needs of their students. Form 1 was prepared for a state interpretation contest for judges who requested a briefly phrased and relatively comprehensive list.

Form 1. Checklist for Evaluation

1. Selection: literary value, appropriateness, originality
2. Introduction and adaptation: suitability of introduction, cutting
3. Reading poise: lectern, manuscript, book; eye contact; posture
4. Visual communication: facial expression, gesture, tension
5. Communication of logical meaning: words, phrases, coherent development
6. Communication of mood and emotion
7. Basic vocal communication: articulation, quality, variety
8. Special problems: Characterization, rhythm, dialect
9. General impression of effectiveness (check on scale):
      wooden   restrained   slightly exaggerated   unrestrained
10. Comments:

For class use it is often advantageous to prepare a shorter, less comprehensive form that focuses attention on the objectives of the immediate assignment. Stating the objectives on the form is helpful to both teacher and student. A brief evaluation form for an elementary assignment is shown in Form 2.

Form 2. Achieving Conversationality

Purpose of the assignment:
1. To choose material that promotes conversational delivery
2. To make the reading SOUND as much like conversational speaking as possible
3. To make the reading LOOK as communicative as possible

Student should not write below this line

Rating

1. Is the selection well chosen:
   a. For conversationality?
   b. Otherwise?
2. What vocal characteristics are needed to improve:
   a. Conversationality?
   b. Other vocal needs?
3. What visible behavior should be altered to
   minimize the manuscript?
   Other needs?

Grade _____

An evaluation form for a subsequent lesson can be designed to reinforce the objectives of the earlier lessons, as the fourth purpose does in Form 3.

Form 3. Revealing Meaning

Purpose of the assignment:
1. To demonstrate appropriate phrasing of the selection
2. To use effective pauses
3. To reveal the selection's meaning
4. To maintain good conversational communication through visual and auditory channels

Student should not write below this line

	Rating				
1. Was the phrasing appropriate?	1	2	3	4	5
2. Did the reader take advantage of opportunities for effective pauses?	1	2	3	4	5
3. Is there evidence that the reader understands the selection? Does the audience?	1	2	3	4	5
4. Communication:	1	2	3	4	5
Visual:					
Auditory:					

Grade _____

Student Critics

The classroom audience can be involved in the evaluative process by means of the following practices:

1. Listeners can be provided with criticism sheets similar to those of the instructor. They record their observations at the same time as does the teacher. They may then (a) compare their sheets with those posted by the instructor, (b) collect all listening reports for inspection and coordination by the instructor, or (c) forward the reports to the reader.

2. The reader may prepare a report on evaluations received from his classmates, revealing both immediate and ultimate values for himself as well as inconsistencies and contradictions resulting from the failure of the audience to learn its lesson well.

Student evaluation forms, often referred to as "listening reports," should contain either leading questions about the reading performance or a statement of the purpose of the assignment. For example, the students' version of the evaluation form presented immediately above might appear as in Form 4.

Form 4. Revealing Meaning

Listener _____ Date _____
Assignment _____

Purpose of the reading assignment:
1. To phrase the selection appropriately
2. To practice effective pausing
3. To continue to demonstrate an understanding of a reading selection
4. To continue to communicate effectively through visual and auditory channels

Reader No.
   1.

   2.

   3.

IMPROVEMENT OF READING THROUGH LISTENING

Opportunities for Listening

The student in an interpretation class hears a great amount of reading. He hears readings by his classmates, his teacher, and an occasional visitor. He hears reading by professional readers on television, radio, and the lecture platform. He can acquire commercial recordings of readings by actors, authors, entertainers, and even teachers. His teacher can make available to him noncommercial disc and tape recordings of both student and professional readers. Most of these reading experiences can be repeated as often as desired by means of tape recordings.

Purposeful Listening

In spite of all these opportunities, the beginning student often seems to assume that his learning period is limited to his own five-minute periods of reading before the class. When classmates read he is not aware that he should profit from their successes or failures. Instead he succumbs to the temptation—as does an occasional experienced reader—to occupy his thoughts with his own forthcoming performance rather than attend to his classmates' reading. He needs to be guided in listening, even to be told what to listen for. His teacher tries to make listening an active experience, not only through listening reports but also by testing listening, by adding to formal examinations questions about the reading of others, and by assigning outside listening experiences.

The nonclassroom listening assignment can be interesting and profitable. A visiting actor-reader in a neighboring city, an author-reader lecturing at a local college, a television or radio reading performance by Orson Welles, Peter Ustinov, Judith Anderson, or Charlton Heston—all are raw material for oral and written reports, assignments demanding keen observation of the reader's materials and techniques. Reading hours and lecture-recitals by advanced students and guest readers may be scheduled at the discretion of the teacher to provide additional immediate nonacademic listening experiences.

The Listening Laboratory: Recordings

Disc and tape recordings are not only valuable in themselves, but represent additional listening assignments to be reported. Form 5 has been used for weekly reports of students hearing recordings in the Louisiana State University Library listening rooms.

Form 5. Listening Report for Recordings

Course _____ Name _____
Recording list no. _____ Date _____

   I. Record identification:
      A. Reader(s):
      B. Selections and authors:
  II. Source of performance (check one):
      Dramatic production __   Speech __   Discussion __
      TV performance __   Reading __   Interview __
      Other: _____
 III. Special recording effects (music, sound effects, audience response, introduction by separate speaker, etc.):
 IV. The listening situation:
      Date and time _____
      Approximate listening time __   Was record repeated?__
      Number in listening group __   Were all class members? __
      What kind of preliminary preparation would improve this assignment?
  V. Evaluation of the reading performance: (Be specific.)
 VI. Evaluation of introductory and transitional materials, if used:
VII. For what purpose(s) is this recording most useful? (check)
      Entertainment __
      Understanding of literature __
      Illustration of good reading performance __. Explain, if checked.
      Illustration of poor reading performance __. Explain, if checked.

If the teacher feels that a recording is sufficiently instructive to warrant detailed attention he may require that the listener become familiar with the material before the recording is heard and follow a copy of the selection during the listening experience. If the copy includes comments by the teacher in a column parallel to the text, it will guide the listener's attention to the techniques he should observe. Advanced students are capable of preparing materials of this kind for classroom use as part of a listening project. Note the illustrative passages included here, taken from an analysis of an early recording of "David and Goliath" read by Charles Laughton.[11]

---

8 And he stood and cried unto the armies of Israel, and said unto them,
                    Why are
ye come out to set your battle in array? Am not I a Philistine, and ye servants to Saul? Choose you a man for you, and let him come down to me.

8 Note stress: "and SAID unto them"
8 Goliath's loud call should be adjusted to the size of the room and to the occasion.
8 Note stress: "a MAN for you"

9 If he be able to fight with me, and to kill me, then will we be your servants: but if I prevail against him, and kill him, then shall ye be our servants, and serve us.

9 The reader adds a vocalized threat after the words "serve us."

10 And the Philistine said, I defy the armies of Israel this day; give me a man, that we may fight together.

10 Omitted verse

        . . .   . . .

48 And it came to pass, when the Philistine arose, and came and drew nigh to meet David, that David hasted, and ran toward the army to meet the Philistine.

48 The reader emphasizes each verb in "arose and came and drew nigh" to bring the giant nearer.

49 And David put his hand in his bag, and took thence a stone, and slang it, and smote the Philistine in his forehead, that the stone sunk into his forehead; and he fell upon his face to the earth.

49 The voice shows the cunning of David and the excitement of the situation. Reader pauses before the last clause, timing his words with the arrested forward movement, the pause, and the downward crumpling of the giant.

50 So David prevailed over the Philistine with a sling and with a stone, and smote the Philistine, and slew him; but there was no sword in the hand of David.

50 This verse runs into 51 because of continued subject matter.

51 Therefore David ran, and stood upon the Philistine, and took his sword, and drew it out of the sheath thereof, and slew him, and cut off his head therewith. And when the Philistines saw their champion was dead, they fled.

51 We hear the effort required to draw the heavy sword and use it to cut off the head.

---

[11] Laughton's Bible readings are available on a long-playing recording, "Charles Laughton, Readings from the Bible" (Decca DL8031).

PROJECTS FOR SUPERIOR AND ADVANCED STUDENTS

Like the teacher of public speaking, the interpretation teacher is caught between the Scylla of increasing class enrollments and the Charybdis of increasing demand for attention to the superior student. In the recurring round of oral assignments the advanced or superior student not only can fail to achieve his potential but also can become complacent and indolent. The problem he presents can sometimes be solved by substituting for elementary or routine assignments some special project designed to broaden his literary experiences, develop his superior talents, and at the same time enable him to contribute to the class something of his own strength. Such projects may culminate in some type of oral presentation, though it is not essential that all of them do so. The projects described below suggest the variety possible.

Projects Designed to Enlarge Literary Experiences

The Program on a Chosen Subject or Theme.   The subject- or theme-centered program is limited only by the extent of the interpreter's library resources and by his imagination. A selection the reader especially enjoys or one the class must study in an English course often provides the nucleus;[12] a date on the calendar frequently suggests an event or a person to celebrate. Occasionally an anthology can contribute a major part of the material for a subject program,[13] though complete reliance on one anthology may defeat one purpose of the project—to encourage the student to read widely. Subjects vary in scope and importance: school days, the sea, the devil, small children, the story of Noah, dramatics, reincarnation, St. Valentine's day, poems with pasts, the story of Job, elocution, music, Veterans' Day, universal brotherhood, nightmares, Indian heroes, reverence for life, the urge to communicate, etc. Subjects may be metaphorical, subjective, or concrete. The interpreter's search for selections appropriate to his subject is comparable to the development of a unit in literature.[14] However, the value of the project lies as much in the student's acquaintance with rejected selections as with those finally chosen for the program.

[12] For an account of similar program building in a high school English class see William J. Reynolds, "When Thou Doest Macbeth, Do It Quickly!" *English Journal,* February, 1958, 47:90–91.
[13] Examples of subject anthologies: A. C. Spectorsky (ed.), *The College Years,* New York: Hawthorn, 1958; Leo Deuel (ed.), *The Teacher's Treasure Chest,* Englewood Cliffs, N.J.: Prentice-Hall, 1956; Edward Wagenknecht (ed.), *The Story of Jesus in the World's Literature,* New York: Creative Age, 1946; Robert Bly (ed.), *Forty Poems Touching on Recent American History,* Boston: Beacon Press, 1970.
[14] See Virginia Alwin, "A Setting for the Interrelation of the Language Arts," *English Journal,* February, 1958, 47:77–80, 85.

The following outline for reporting preparation of a theme-centered or subject program is a useful guide for the student:

Theme-Centered Programs

I. Unifying element.
II. Selections to be used for this program (cite author, title, subtitle, and indicate approximate oral reading time and whether whole or part of the selection is used). Arrange in order of presentation.
III. Principles of program building (selection and arrangement) used for II.
IV. Bibliographical tools used in locating materials (examples: *Poetry Index, Reader's Guide*, etc.). List subject headings used for search.
V. Anthologies available as sources of selections.
VI. Critical Evaluations.
   A. Sources of critical evaluations of the selected program materials.
   B. Brief summaries of critical evaluations of the selected materials. Follow the arrangement used in II.
VII. Selections considered for this program but rejected (give reasons).

The Program from Works of One Author. The author program is probably the most common form of interpretative reading program consisting of more than one selection. A favorite author or the author of a favorite selection is likely to be the first choice of the student. The instructor should encourage a student to choose an author whose works will justify the time spent in preparing the program. To extend the student's experience into new areas, the instructor may propose a different author of the same literary school, an author whose works are frequently compared with the student's choice, or an author who uses comparable forms, themes, or moods. Controversial writers make interesting programs, since conflicting criticism can be incorporated in the program. Writers about whom other authors write are especially desirable for either an author program or a subject program. Authors who read their own works interest students if the recordings are available. A list of authors whom the student may wish to consider for either author or subject programs might include William Carlos Williams, William Shakespeare, Langston Hughes, Samuel Johnson, Clarence Day, Thomas Wolfe, 'Dylan Thomas, George Bernard Shaw, W. H. Auden, Archibald MacLeish, Gertrude Stein, Eugene O'Neill, Charles Dickens, Benjamin Franklin, Samuel Taylor Coleridge, John Keats, Ellen Glasgow, Ernest Hemingway, John Donne, Ben Jonson, Robert Graves, James Thurber, Virginia Woolf, and Bertrand Russell. The intentional diversity of this list suggests that students of many levels of maturity, taste, and insight will find the author program challenging.

The following outline is a student guide for reporting the preparation of an author program.

Author-Centered Programs

    I. Name of author
   II. Bibliography of works available to the reader for program material (Give full bibliographical information.)
 III. Critical evaluations of the author
      A. Sources
      B. Critical evaluation (summarize or quote)
 IV. Selection of program
      A. Selected works, listed in order of presentation
      B. Principles of program-building (selection and arrangement) used for IV, A above
  V. Critical evaluations of the selected program materials
      A. Sources
      B. Brief summaries, arranged as IV, A
 VI. Introductory and transitional sections of the program
      A. Plans, arranged in chronological order
      B. Sources of materials
VII. Unavailable works of the author to be considered for library purchase

The Program Unified by Literary Form. The form-centered program is less popular than the preceding types, possibly because variety in the program seems more difficult to achieve. A long program consisting solely of sonnets, for example, is extremely difficult to interpret, no matter how pleasant the period of preparation may have been. Nevertheless, it is possible to construct a varied program if the reader does not rely on the most obvious choices of materials. He may try a program of narrative poems, soliloquies, fables, letters, or personal essays, for example. The outline for author-centered programs can be adapted to this assignment.

Other Unified Programs of Reading Materials. At first glance the three types of programs already described seem to exhaust the possibilities. Yet unrelated materials can be held together by a tenuous connection. A program may be constructed of "little-known works of famous authors," or "literature of this (or any other) decade," "literature of sociological import," "favorite poems of famous people," or even, to paraphrase the title of an anthology, "this is the author's best." There is a peculiar pleasure for the interpreter in the search for "something to go with" a selection, and many interpreters discover their love of books during the process.

Projects in Adaptation of Materials for Reading Aloud

Most interpreters have experienced the disparity between the number of minutes available for reading aloud and the number of pages included in the reading selection. Once they begin cutting the selection for time they begin to find other alterations necessary to the reading situation, and the process of adaptation is under way. No doubt the fact that adaptation is important to several other speech activities motivates some students to become exceptionally proficient in altering form to fit medium.

The short story, novella, novel, and biography provide interesting experiences in adaptation.[15] Long narrative poems, even those with regular rhyme schemes, can be adapted. Following is an outline for reporting this type of project.

Adapting a Long Literary Work

I. Give complete bibliographic information for the selected work.
II. Justify the selection of this work for reading aloud.
III. Where are evaluations, criticisms, and analyses of this selection to be found? (Answer bibliographically with annotation.)
IV. What are the possible foci for construction of different adaptations? Which do you recommend?
V. What methods of adaptation will you employ for this selection?
VI. What key sections, scenes, stanzas, etc., do you consider essential to the adaptation?
VII. If techniques of characterization are required, what ones will you use? (Answer specifically in terms of the characters retained in the adaptation.)
VIII. What special reading techniques or abilities will you need to develop in order to do justice to the material?

One-act and full-length plays, radio plays, and television scripts present opportunities for adaptation. The problems involved are considerably different from those present in narrative literature, though no more difficult. An interesting variation of this assignment is the preparation of a composite adaptation from two related works in unlike forms, borrowing from one to make the adaptation of the other as close as possible to the author's intent. Pairs of plays and narratives come to mind easily: *I Remember Mama* and *Mama's Bank Account*, *The Glass Menagerie* and "Portrait of a Girl in Glass," *Life with Father* and *God and My Father*, and *A Member of the Wedding* and its narrative counterpart. All plays growing out of stories, novels, or shorter plays are potential selections for this type of program.

A strong case can be made against allowing the student to adapt his materials. Injudicious adaptation has led to amputation of the final paragraph of "The Gift of the Magi" and to subtraction of Oscar Wilde's satiric barbs from "The Happy Prince." Both student and teacher should remind themselves that they are obligated to keep intact the essence of the selection and the author's style. If that cannot be done, the selection should not be attempted at all. The fact that there exist notable examples

[15] Illustrative examples of cuttings appear in Otis J. Aggertt & Elbert R. Bowen, *Communicative Reading*, 2nd ed., New York: Macmillan, 1963, pp. 383–395, 456–462; Jean DeSales Bertram, *The Oral Experience of Literature*, San Francisco: Chandler, 1967, pp. 155–160, 202–214; and Keith Brooks, Eugene Bahn & L. LaMont Okey, *The Communicative Act of Oral Interpretation*, Boston: Allyn & Bacon, 1967, pp. 200–205.

of commercial adaptations that are devoid of the literary artistry of the originals[16] does not excuse the interpreter from his responsibility.

A Project in Criticism—The Book Review

Of all interpretation projects the book review is the most practical from the standpoint of probable future use. It is also immediately practical because it provides an opportunity for speech students to combine reading and public speaking in one unit of experience. Naturally the interpreter can be expected to seek more opportunities to read passages from the book he reviews than does the reviewer without oral reading interests. In all other respects his review will resemble the typical book review that flourishes in highly organized community life. The book review project is especially recommended for the interpreter who requires motivation for improving his skill in public speaking and the experienced speaker who needs opportunity for reading aloud materials more demanding than his own manuscript speeches.

To some extent the book review is a project in adaptation, requiring selection of passages for reading to give variety and coherence to the review. Yet the framework of the review must be a carefully prepared speech designed to acquaint the audience with the value of the book, stimulate their interest in it, or even motivate their purchasing it. As an interpretation project in criticism, the review must be grounded in educated opinion, a requirement that necessitates the interpreter's acquaintance with and consultation of sources containing critical evaluations of book and author.

Following is an outline for reporting the preparation of a book review.

Outline for Book Review

I. Complete bibliographical data (author, editor, translator; title, series; publisher; date; pages)
II. Criticism
   A. Give the location of critical evaluations or reviews found.
   B. Summarize the critical comments.
   C. Indicate the exact source of any criticism you intend to read aloud as part of the review.
III. Author
   A. Brief biographical data.
   B. Sources of A. Give exact references.
   C. Other works by the same author. Indicate the ones you are acquainted with or will read before the review is presented.
   D. Statement of the author's literary standing.
   E. Principal source of D. Give exact references.

[16] Ruth Stein, "The ABC's of Counterfeit Classics: Adapted, Bowdlerized, and Condensed," *English Journal*, December, 1966, 55:1160–1163.

IV. Passages of the work selected for reading aloud. (List in order of presentation, describing content and giving page numbers.)
 V. Arrangement or organization of the review in outline form. Show the order of quoted passages, biographical material, and criticism.
VI. Your personal evaluation of the book. Include estimate of audience appeal, audience and occasion for which review is suitable, etc.

Readers' Theater Projects

The pleasure of shared communication of literature came to be appreciated long ago. In 1806 Gilbert Austin reported a familiar playreading procedure:

Another species of dramatic reading has of late years been practised in private companies assembled for the purpose. It limits each individual to the reading of the part of a single character. In this entertainment, as on the stage, the characters of the drama are distributed among the readers according to their supposed talents; and each being furnished with a separate book, either the whole play, or certain select scenes from one or more, are read by the performers sitting round a table whilst the others of the company serve as the audience. The reading is performed by each in his best and most characteristic manner, the part allotted to each is often nearly committed to memory, and such gestures are used as can be conveniently executed in a sitting posture. Higher efforts are here required in order to keep the auditors alive to the interest of the scene, thus divided and stript of all that aids delusion, and mutilated of its complete action. On these occasions favourite scenes are often performed in a part of the room considered as a stage, by such of the party, as wish to exhibit higher dramatic powers, and temporary dresses are assumed or modified the more nearly to approach theatrical exhibition; but reading ceases here.[17]

Speech teachers and students kept this procedure alive, experimented with it, and used it in their classes, as the presence of a chapter on group play reading in a 1947 speech fundamentals textbook indicates. A fresh burst of enthusiasm for group reading followed the successful tour of Charles Laughton's First Drama Quartette in its stool-and-lectern presentation of Shaw's "Don Juan in Hell," a seldom-performed part of *Man and Superman*. Other professional groups have succeeded almost as well in encouraging experimentation with group reading of all forms of literature and all styles of presentation. The term "readers theater" is often used to cover the entire range from the stool-and-lectern reading to fully staged productions in which the only distinction marking the performance as other than conventional theater is the presence of scripts in the hands of actors (a form once called a "walking rehearsal"). A special variety of readers theater dubbed "chamber theater" takes for its domain narrative literature. Its readers—narrator and characters—shift styles of presentation as they move from straight narration to dialogue and back again, the narrator

[17] *Chironomia*, London, 1806, pp. 203, 204.

participating in the staging of the dialogue as needed. These variations in style indicate the vigor of the readers theater movement, its continuing experimental nature, and the unwillingness of readers to set artificial bounds to it.

Presently readers theater producers appear to fall into two schools, those whose productions are "theater of the mind," with the action of the scene being "offstage," and those whose productions, minus one or more of the accoutrements of theatrical staging, approach the fully staged play. Teachers of interpretation seem to lean toward the former and teachers of theater toward the latter. The former ask the audience to see *in its mind's eye* the scene and the characters of the literature and not to identify them with the place of the reading or the readers themselves. The latter provide the audience with one or more of those identifying features—stage movement, costume, properties, makeup, lighting, scenery—that spell out for the audience the specifics of the script. Teachers of interpretation have expressed certain reservations in connection with the extensively staged form, lest readers theater become poor man's theater—the substitute forced on director and actors by a short budget that does not permit full staging or a short time schedule that does not permit complete memorization. To view readers theater as deprived theater is to make it an inferior form, which it need not be. If interpreters of readers theater bring to it all the insight and skill of other interpretative reading performances, it loses nothing by the absence of features essential to the staged play. Any script that demands such features should be reserved for complete staging, with readers' theater more properly employing other literature.

Information concerning theory and techniques of readers theater is now widespread and readily available in at least eight contemporary interpretation textbooks, a handbook, an anthology of articles, and educational journals. Recordings of professional and nonprofessional readers theater performances can be added to the teacher's record collection, and scripts are now available to be used intact or to serve as a model for devising other programs. Program materials now considered classics include "Don Juan in Hell," Benet's "John Brown's Body," and Thomas's "Under Milk Wood." Less well known but ambitious and challenging are these:

The Hollow Crown. Devised by John Barton. Samuel French, 1962.
The Worlds of Shakespeare, adapted by Marchette Chute and Ernestine Perrie, New York: Dutton, 1963.
Passages from Finnegans Wake, by James Joyce. A free adaptation for the theater by Mary Manning, Cambridge, Mass.: Harvard University Press, 1957.

Projects Correlating Interpretation with Music

There was a time when mention of music in the same breath with reading brought shudders of apprehension to speech teachers still able to recall the musical reading with its saccharine strains accompanying a recitation of "That Old Sweetheart of Mine" and the radio poetry hour with its quaverings of background organ music. Fortunately today's student has no such memories, his associations being with the popular folk singer, the poet-singer-reciter, and the mingling of many arts and media. It is still true that at times music and interpretation are unhappily wed, reader and musician seeming to compete for attention.[18] Attempts to coordinate jazz and poetry still meet with mixed reactions.[19] Nevertheless, interest in correlating literature with music and other arts continues to thrive.[20] Narrators frequent all kinds of musical works, from Prokofiev's "Peter and the Wolf" to Copland's "A Lincoln Portrait" and Kubik's folk opera "A Mirror for the Sky." The literary public is not in the least surprised to find that Paul Horgan's *Great River* inspired a symphonic work complete with narration, that *Alice in Wonderland* and Eliot's *Old Possum's Book of Practical Cats* have been scored, or that Peter Ustinov joined an orchestra in concert.[21] Actors and readers are accustomed to meeting the demands of composers and musical directors.

The interpretation teacher can exploit all these opportunities to find relationships between arts and to enrich literary experience with related musical experience. Apart from any eventual cultural gain accruing to the student musically from the reading-music project, the project presents the possibility of more immediate and tangible benefits. First, it offers opportunity and motivation for searching out unfamiliar, often memorable literature. Second, it encourages the growth of insight into emotional subtleties and shadings of mood. Third, it develops the interpreter's skill in perceiving and controlling levels of emotional intensity, transitions, acceleration, and climax in oral reading. These advantages are entirely compatible with the objectives of an interpretation assignment.

The student in the interpretation class need not limit his project to those musical works using narration or to literature set to music. Instead, he can create his own opportunities by juxtaposing reading selections and musical compositions that have an inherent connection. Depending on the

---

[18] A notable example is Agnes Moorehead's recording of the Psalms of David with music composed and played by Ralph Hollander (Lyric Art Recordings).
[19] "Jazz Canto" (World Pacific Records), a jazz-poetry miscellany, is representative of the type.
[20] For comment on the use of music to enrich presentations of literature, see Mrs. H. M. Mekeel, "Say It with Music," *Library Journal*, September 15, 1953, 78:1513–1514; Martin La Forse, "Teaching a Story with Musical Interpretations," *English Journal*, January, 1957, 46:41–42; John T. Muri, "The Use of Recordings in High School English Classes," *English Journal*, January, 1957, 46:32–39. Additional items appear at the end of this chapter.
[21] "Words and Music," a "Young People's Concert" with the New York Philharmonic Orchestra, televised September 20, 1970. The program consisted of pieces for spoken voice and symphonic orchestra.

nature of the material, reading may precede music to prepare the audience for the music, it may follow the music after a mood for the reading has been established, or it may alternate with the music to tell a story, develop a mood, or illustrate an idea. Types of literature that can be coordinated with music in this manner are remarkably varied. For example, Frances Frost's narrative adaptation of *Amahl and the Night Visitors* can be interspersed with certain arias from Menotti's opera. Dialogue from *Pygmalion* can be successfully coordinated with songs from *My Fair Lady*. Richard Bales' recordings of "The Confederacy" and "The Union" can be combined with accompanying historical essays by Bruce Catton, Clifford Dowdey, and Allen Nevins. Appropriate fairy tales can be read or told alternately with musical divisions of Bernard Rogers' "Once upon a Time."

Ideas for programs of interpretation and music are necessarily limited by library resources and the availability of suitable music, live or recorded. For exploration of the contiguous borders of the music and literary worlds, examination of a current *Schwann Long Playing Record Catalog*[22] is an excellent starting point. Program music, ballet suites, overtures, operas, TV programs, musicals, plays, and movie soundtracks frequently, by their very titles, suggest related literature. The following list of authors and literary titles, compiled with the aid of a record catalog, is far from exhaustive. For easy identification of the related music, composers' names appear in the adjacent column.

Poets and Poetry	Composers
Emily Dickinson	Aaron Copland
Dylan Thomas	Igor Stravinsky
"Abraham Lincoln Walks at	
Midnight"	Roy Harris
"Dover Beach"	Samuel Barber
"Don Juan"	Richard Strauss or
	Christoph Willibald Gluck
"Childe Harold"	Hector Berlioz
"The Hollow Men"	Vincent Persichetti
"Kubla Khan"	Charles Tomlinson Griffes

Fairy Tales	
"Cinderella"	Serge Prokofiev
"Hansel and Gretel"	Englebert Humperdinck
"Bluebeard"	Jacques Offenbach or
	Béla Bartók
"Pinocchio"	Bernard Rogers
"The Sleeping Beauty"	Peter Tchaikovsky

[22] Available each month from record dealers or ordered from W. Schwann, 137 Newbury St., Boston, Mass. 02116.

Fiction

"The Red Pony"	Aaron Copland
"The Devil and Daniel Webster"	Douglas Moore
Through the Looking Glass	Deems Taylor
The Adventures of Huckleberry Finn	Jerome Kern
Pilgrim's Progress	Ralph Vaughn Williams

Drama

Hello, Out There	Jack Beeson
Medea	Samuel Barber
Oedipus Rex	Igor Stravinsky
Salomé	Richard Strauss
Faust	Hector Berlioz or Richard Wagner
Pelléas and Mélisande	Gabriel Fauré
The School for Scandal	Samuel Barber
Hamlet	Peter Tchaikovsky
Macbeth	Richard Strauss
Merchant of Venice	Gosta Nystroem
King Lear	Hector Berlioz
Much Ado About Nothing	Hector Berlioz
Romeo and Juliet	Prokofiev, Berlioz, or Tchaikovsky
Shakespeare's Songs from Plays	Igor Stravinsky
Plays by Ludvig Holberg	Edvard Grieg

The Bible

Job	Ralph Vaughn Williams
Jeremiah and *Lamentations*	Leonard Bernstein or Thomas Tallis

GUIDING THE STUDENT'S SELECTION OF READING MATERIAL

Should the teacher assume some responsibility for assisting the student in his search for reading materials? The answer is a resounding "Yes!" from all quarters.[23] In theory, all literature worthy of the name is suited to interpretative reading. Therefore, theoretically, reading materials should be as easy to find and as plentiful as the nearest library collection, public or personal. In practice, however, teachers find that these additional factors must be considered.

[23] See Jacob M. Price (ed.), *Reading for Life: Developing the College Student's Lifetime Reading Interest*, Ann Arbor, Mich.: Univ. of Michigan Press, 1959, Chap. 8, "The Broad and Narrow Paths: a Forum on the Functions of the Classroom Teacher in the Development of Reading Interest," pp. 162–179; Louis Round Wilson, Mildred H. Lowell, & Sarah R. Reed, *The Library in College Instruction, a Syllabus on the Improvement of College Instruction Through Library Use*, New York: Wilson, 1951, Unit IV, "Reading Guidance: A Function of the Entire Faculty," pp. 254–281; Mary K. Eakin (comp.), *Good Books for Children,"* Chicago: Univ. of Chicago Press, 1959, "Introduction," pp. vii–xiv.

1. Certain reading materials are more readable, and listenable, than others.
2. Many students need guidance in judging the literary value of materials.
3. The personal library does not exist in some students' homes.
4. Some school librarians cannot countenance the overnight absence of a book from the school library shelf.
5. Some large libraries are so guidance-free that their patrons are lost among the books.

Textbooks and Anthologies

The most common method of advising a student and controlling his choice of selections is the provision of an anthology, either by adoption of a textbook containing one or by adoption of a separate collection of literature. The advantages of this procedure are these:

1. The book is always available to the reader, without recharging from a library.
2. Copies of the selection are available to the reader's classmates for preclass study and classroom consultation.
3. Materials in the anthology, particularly in a textbook, are selected to exemplify and illuminate principles taught in the interpretation class.
4. Students are less handicapped by inadequate library facilities in the school and community.

The possible disadvantages in the use of a textbook or anthology are as follows:

1. Students are less encouraged to extend their knowledge of the world of literature.
2. The teacher can become habituated to the use of a limited group of selections year after year.

It should be noted that both teachers and students have a responsibility toward their own growth. Both are capable of following paths of least resistance, students by borrowing or rehashing old "readings" of questionable literary merit, teachers by continually repeating the same illustrative selections and interpretation programs.

If the anthology is discarded, the teacher can compensate for the loss of the advantages listed earlier by adopting the following suggestions:

1. Make use of the ever-increasing supply of paperback books now available at nominal cost. By encouraging students to acquire their own copies of materials the teacher is actually creating a tradition of book buying for the student, discouraging mutilation of library books by pencil-wielding adapters of materials,[24] and initiating a reading repertory collection.
2. Supply the students with titles of selections exemplifying principles to be studied for a given assignment or, preferably, provide an advance assignment sheet describing the nature of desirable literature for future assignments.

---

[24] For comment on the marked tendency of the public to abuse borrowed books and printed matter, see Jacques Barzun, *The House of Intellect*, Harper & Row, 1959, p. 176, 119 *n*.

3. Require students to announce their choices of reading selections sufficiently early to permit library copies of the selections to be examined by classmates.
4. Require students to provide the teacher with advance copies of selections to be read, to eliminate the possibility of misinformed criticism by the teacher. Copies may be marked and returned to the students or retained for the teacher's file.
5. Require all readers to provide duplicated copies of their materials for class distribution—a radical step but feasible for small groups.

Textbook Aids in Finding Materials

The fact that one is not using a given book as a class text does not eliminate it as a guide to the location of materials or as a source of materials itself. The following books are especially helpful.

AGGERTT, OTIS J. AND BOWEN, ELBERT R., Communicative Reading, 2nd ed., New York: Macmillan, 1963, chap. 2, "What Shall I Read?" contains excellent lists of books; pp. 462, 463, "A Suggested List of Playwrights for Oral Interpretation."
ARMSTRONG, CHLOE AND BRANDES, PAUL D., The Oral Interpretation of Literature, New York: McGraw-Hill, 1963. Bibliography of paperbooks, pp. 57–60.

In considering available textbooks the interpretation teacher should not overlook those used in language arts, English, and general literature courses.

Oral Reading Anthologies

Many libraries have anthologies of selections for reading and storytelling. The title usually indicates the compiler's interest in oral presentation.

BACON, WALLACE A. AND BREEN, ROBERT S., Literature for Interpretation, New York: Holt, Rinehart & Winston, 1961. English and American literature of many periods and forms. Indisputable quality.
BROOKS, KEITH, BAHN, EUGENE AND OKEY, L. LAMONT, Literature for Listening, An Oral Interpreter's Anthology, Boston: Allyn & Bacon, 1968. Selections from the past five centuries; essay, poem, story, play, and letter.
HODNETT, EDWARD (ED.), Poems to Read Aloud, New York: Norton, 1957. Variety ranging from Sir Walter Raleigh to living authors.
Poetry for Pleasure, New York: Doubleday, 1960. Plato to Pasternak. Highly readable.
VEILLEUX, JERÉ, Oral Interpretation: The Re-creation of Literature, New York: Harper & Row, 1967. Story, poem, and play, pp. 149–439, are offered in this textbook-anthology.

Bibliographies

Students should be made aware of the invaluable aid to be found in selected bibliographies, prepared most often by teachers, librarians, and book selection committees. Contrary to general supposition, the library is not the sole repository of such lists. They are to be found everywhere: in the Sunday supplements of newspapers, in popular and general magazines, and on the paperback rack at the newsstand. They appear most often during National Library Week, Children's Book Week, the Christmas season (for gifts), and the early summer (for recreational reading).

Libraries, of course, have numerous bibliographies and indexes that will guide the reader to new reading materials of good quality. Some of these are intended for parents, teachers, and the general public; others are specialized publications prepared for the use of librarians, booksellers, and scholars. The most helpful ones have subject indexes or are arranged by subjects to suggest the nature of the material cited. Thumbing through them is comparable to browsing in a large library. For example, consultation of the *Essay and General Literature Index* will suggest to the interpreter interested in prose selections or program ideas the possibility of reading a criticism of Shaw's *Candida*, an excerpt from Day's *Life with Father*, "Father Opens My Mail," or an article by Somerset Maugham called "How I Write Short Stories." Other indexes and guides to short stories, children's and young people's books, poetry, one-act plays, long plays, historical novels, and general fiction are available.[25] (Not recommended is Silk and Fanning's *Index to Dramatic Readings*, which will lead the undiscriminating user to 25 collections of "readings," more than 20 of which include highly undesirable material.) The titles below are examples of helpful bibliographies and book selection aids likely to be found in public and college libraries, as well as in the offices of librarians and bookstore managers:

COURTNEY, WINIFRED (ED.), *The Reader's Adviser, A Guide to the Best in Literature*, 2 vols., 11th ed., New York: R. R. Bowker, 1968.

DICKINSON, ASA DON, *The World's Best Books: Homer to Hemingway*, New York: Wilson, 1953.

FADIMAN, CLIFTON, *The Lifetime Reading Plan*, New York: World Publishing, 1960.

HAINES, HELEN E., *Living with Books*, 2nd ed., New York: Columbia Univ. Press, 1950.

HAINES, HELEN E., *What's in a Novel*, New York: Columbia Univ. Press, 1942.

SMITH, F. SEYMOUR, *An English Library*, 4th ed., New York: Cambridge Univ. Press, 1950.

SMITH, F. SEYMOUR, *What Shall I Read Next? A Personal Selection of Twentieth Century English Books*, New York: Cambridge Univ. Press, 1953.

For the interpreter the value of books about books lies in their combination of selectivity and catholicity. The fact that a given title is included in one of them is some assurance of the literary quality and intrinsic worth of the selection. At the same time, these books attract the interpreter to authors and titles of which he might otherwise remain unaware indefi-

25 For exact titles of these and similar aids, consult Constance M. Winchell, *Guide to Reference Books*, 8th ed., Chicago: American Library Association, 1967.

nitely. Finally, an additional value should not be overlooked: teachers of interpretation may use them to call to the attention of librarians the interpreter's special interests and peculiar needs in the world of writing.

The Student's Private Resources

Newspapers and Magazines.   The fact that the library book collection is the most obvious source of reading selections should not blind interpreters to the existence of usable materials in less likely sources: newspapers, magazines, and paperback books. The popular sport of berating the mass media for their low intellectual and literary standards tends to blind people to exceptional reading opportunities they occasionally offer to those with limited library facilities.

Is there some danger in permitting the student to use as resources for reading materials those that contain primarily writing of inferior literary quality? The answer is a positive "Yes." If the teacher permits these sources to be utilized, he must either be sure of the student's taste or maintain firm control of the student's final choice of selection. Allowing the student to waste his own and class time with material that makes no demand on his intellectual powers can seldom, if ever, be justified. On the other hand, the fact that reading selections are found in library stacks is no guarantee of their quality either. For proof one need only consult the dusty collections of "readings" published under such titles as *Choice Readings,* or *Readings for Boys and Girls,* or *Favorite Selections for Recitation,* or *America's Favorite Poems,* available in almost every library. They are likely to contain nineteenth-century selections reflecting a level of literary taste that helped to sound the death knell of elocution. To perpetuate their use is little short of treason to interpretation. The only sure and permanent solution to the problem of taste in selection of material is the raising of general standards of literary taste, a state that cannot be attained by fiat or by imposition of the teacher's taste on the student, but only by the slow steady development of the student.

Paperback Books.   The greatest boon to interpreters today is the quality paperback books. For a very small cost students can buy identical copies of collections of poetry, short stories, plays, novels, and essays for classroom use, or they can diversify their purchases and share a larger quantity of materials with one another. New paperbacks are listed periodically in the New York *Times Book Review* as well as in the *Saturday Review's* "Pick of the Paperbacks" section. They are catalogued in *Paperbound Books in Print,* published by R. R. Bowker Company and available in libraries and by subscription. Many publishers of paperbacks offer catalogues and checklists of their publications to teachers.

THE COURSE OF STUDY FOR INTERPRETATION

> Each of us is prone to teach his students
> not what they need but what he knows. (Parrish)[26]

For reasons that have been explained earlier in this chapter, considerable variety is to be found in beginning courses in interpretation. Perhaps more influential than all the logical reasons for variety in course content and method is the simple fact that, to paraphrase Parrish, each teacher is prone to teach his students not the course they need but the course he took. Being consistent, he will probably choose for his students an edition of the textbook he studied as a student, or one organized in a similar manner; and the activities his students undertake will be those he engaged in himself. This procedure would do little harm if all courses existed in like educational environments. When, however, it produces a high school interpretation course that is either a carbon copy or a diluted version of a college course,[27] for example, the result may be little short of disastrous for both students and teacher. This propensity for duplication of courses without adaptation to circumstances is an early manifestation of the pedagogical rut, the narrow confines of which can restrain the imagination and initiative of a potentially good teacher.

The Content of the Course

Below is an outline of the topics that occur most frequently in basic interpretation courses. Interpretation terminology is not standardized; nevertheless, the terms appearing in the outline, or their equivalents, are found in most treatments of interpretation. The outline is not to be regarded as a recommended course outline or syllabus. Since it is a composite of many such outlines, it contains more than the normal course should include. Neither does it imply a preferred order in which topics should be arranged, or a preferred approach. It is intended to set forth the possible subject divisions from which interpretation teachers choose the items most suited to the requirements of their courses, curricula, and students.

  I. Definition: what interpretation involves
      A. Comparison with silent reading
      B. Comparison with other speech activities
 II. Choice of selection
      A. Intrinsic values to be sought

---

[26] Wayland Maxfield Parrish, "Interpretative Reading," *Quarterly Journal of Speech Education*, April, 1927, 13:163.
[27] For a brief note on a comparable problem with English courses, see "This World of English," *English Journal*, December 1958, 47:579–580.

       1. Aesthetic principles
       2. Application of aesthetic principles to selection
   B. Adaptation to reader, audience, and occasion
       1. The reader's abilities, interests, and attitude
       2. The audience's requirements
       3. The demands of the occasion
       4. Limitations imposed by the physical environment
       5. Implications
   C. Finding materials
III. Preparation of selection
   A. Studying the selection
       1. The author's purpose: information, persuasion, amusement, emotional appeal, aesthetic appeal
       2. The thought
          a. Central idea or theme
          b. Structure: paragraphs and larger units
          c. Word groups, emphasis
          d. Words: denotations and semantic implications
       3. The feeling
          a. General mood or tone
          b. Structure: emotional development
          c. Rhythm, cadence
          d. Figures of speech
          e. Imagery
          f. Connotations
       4. The form
          a. Prose; poetry
          b. Expository; narrative; dramatic; lyric
          c. Subdivisions or interrelations of a and b
       5. Relating thought, feeling, and form
       6. Background
          a. Author: biography; related works
          b. Criticism: contemporaneous, modern
          c. Social setting
   B. Adapting the selection
       1. Planning the introduction
       2. Arranging and cutting
       3. Planning the transitions
       4. Preparation of the manuscript
   C. Learning to communicate the selection
       1. Relating meaning to delivery
          a. Thinking
          b. Imagining
          c. Empathizing
       2. Using the agents of delivery
          a. Body: eyes, facial expression, posture, movement
          b. Voice
             (1) Quality, resonance, emotional tone color
             (2) Pitch: key, range, melody, intonation, inflection
             (3) Force: intensity, loudness, projection
             (4) Time: rate, pause, rhythm
             (5) Pronunciation; dialects

      D. Planning the delivery
         1. Memorization; manuscript reading
         2. Modes of interpretation[28]
         3. Adaptation of delivery to selection, audience, occasion, and reader
  IV. Problems presented by special types of materials
      A. Poetry: regular, free
      B. Monologues
      C. Dialects
   V. Preparation of reading programs
      A. The reading hour
      B. The lecture-recital
      C. The book review
  VI. Special interpretative activities
      A. Choral reading
      B. Group reading: readers theater, chamber theater
      C. Storytelling
      D. Broadcasting programs
      E. Multimedia programs

It cannot be too strongly emphasized that a teacher should not attempt to incorporate all the topics in the outline into one course. To do so would prohibit adequate class time for development of individual abilities of the students. The beginning teacher in particular should heed this warning, because he has a marked tendency to attempt too much in too brief a span of time. The consequence of this necessarily superficial treatment of the subject is a temporary partial comprehension by the students without the attainment of any permanent results. Not unusual is the case of the practice teacher who, provided with a three-week unit in interpretation, taught it all the first day and then reported to her supervisor to ask, "Now what do I do?" She had entirely forgotten that the students should have been "doing" something besides attending a lecture.

The Organization of the Course

The high school course in oral interpretation is most likely to be some type of activities course. Instruction in interpretation may be presented in a one-semester (or, rarely, one-year) course in interpretation, a unit in interpretation in the one-semester or one-year speech or English course, or a series of assignments integrated into the high school English program. For each of these arrangements there can be found a variety of publications containing course and unit outlines, lesson plans and activities, and recommended

[28] Compare: Rollo Anson Tallcott, *The Art of Acting and Public Reading*, New York and Indianapolis: Bobbs-Merrill, 1922, pp. 216–217; Gertrude E. Johnson (ed.), *Studies in the Art of Interpretation*, New York: Appleton-Century-Crofts, 1940, pp. 77–152; Lionel Crocker & Louis M. Eich, *Oral Reading*, 2nd ed., Englewood Cliffs, N.J.: Prentice-Hall, 1955, pp. 50–59.

teaching techniques. Among the potential sources teachers should investigate are the speech and English journals, textbooks on the teaching of speech and English, high school speech textbooks, courses of study issued by curriculum divisions of state and city departments of education, publications issued by organizations of teachers of speech and English, and handbooks by individuals.

Instruction in interpretation at the college level usually begins with a one-semester basic course or a unit of interpretation in the fundamentals course. Of the four approaches to interpretation noted by Reid[29] (the types of literature approach, the principles of interpretation approach, the series of activities approach, and the special project approach), the first course in college is most likely to employ the principles of interpretation or types of literature approach. The teacher's preference for an approach will determine the organization of the course, for these "approaches" are what the word implies—pathways, not terminal points, into the common grounds of interpretation. Aids for organizing the college-level interpretation course are most often found in speech journals, textbooks on the teaching of speech, college interpretation textbooks, studies released by professional organizations, and publications of individuals. The teacher of interpretation should stay alert for new items that are constantly replacing the old. The *Education Index* (H. W. Wilson Co.) is a satisfactory aid for this purpose.

THE ORAL INTERPRETATION CONTEST

In 1946 a committee[30] of the interpretation section of the Speech Association of America was charged with the duty of defining and classifying oral reading contests. The committee report defined three types of reading contests:

Declamation: the speaking of oratorical material
Poetry Reading: the speaking of lyric and narrative verse without impersonation
Dramatic Reading: the speaking of narratives and plays containing speeches by
   one or more imaginary characters

The committee also attempted to define the modes of interpretation and to set up criteria for judging contests. In spite of this valiant effort to bring some order out of chaos, interpretation contests at local levels continue to vary in many respects. Therefore, the teacher should make every effort to assure the appropriateness of the student's material and technique rather than penalize the student by allowing him to participate with materials or

[29] Loren Reid, *Teaching Speech*, 3rd ed., Columbia, Mo.: Artcraft, 1960, pp. 197, 198.
[30] Personnel of the committee: Davis Edwards, Sara Lowrey, Argus Tresidder, Ruth Haun, and W. M. Parrish, Chairman. Information taken from a mimeographed convention report.

techniques inappropriate to the specific occasion. Though his primary purpose should not be to produce a "winner," the teacher is obligated to provide the student with the best possible opportunity for giving a creditable and unpenalized performance.

Finding Specific Information About a Contest

Since the name of the contest is not necessarily indicative of the type of activity expected from the participant, a teacher or coach preparing to enter a reader in a specific contest for the first time would do well to write to the sponsor of that contest for rules governing it. He may also find it wise to make the following inquiries concerning performances or customs:

1. Type of material preferred or forbidden: Prose or poetry? Scenes from plays? Monologues? Speeches?

2. Style of delivery: Read from manuscript? Memorized? Use of lectern preferred? Disliked?

3. Significance of special terms in the name of the contest, e.g., "dramatic": Does a "dramatic" reading refer to a reading of material in dramatic form (a scene from a play)? A dialogue (as in a short story or novel)? A monologue or character study in the first person? Does it refer to that which is opposed to comic or humorous material?

The most useful information is that designed for a specific contest. The larger and better organized state high school leagues provide their members with excellent assistance. For example, the Texas Interscholastic League has long made available to Texas teachers lists of suggested speech materials. In any state in which comparable materials are available, the teacher's inquiry addressed to the state department of education, the state university, or the state speech league should produce results. Other aids can be found in textbooks for teachers, articles in professional journals, and other speech publications. Names and addresses of declamation and recitation publishing firms are not included here, primarily because suitable material for interpretation, including the better selections found in recitation catalogs, is available without cost in libraries.

Choosing Selections for Contests

In spite of the influence of interpretation teachers, there still prevails the mistaken notion that contest selections should be a peculiar type of literature necessarily sensational, grotesque, maudlin, or ludicrous. It is high time to suppress that misconception. All that is asked of a contest reader is that he choose his selection from good literature and that he read it meaningfully. The following suggestions, if carried out, would eliminate most of the ills induced by contest materials:

1. Avoid selections known as "readings," a type of writing not repre-

sented in textbooks in literature and English. Examples: "His Sister's First Date," "The Poor Little Orphan," "Death-Row," and "The Yellow Button." (Titles are fictitious, but apt.)

2. Avoid selections historically famous as elocutionary selections. Examples: "Spartacus to the Gladiators" and "Curfew Shall Not Ring Tonight."

3. Avoid selections that a critic-judge would regard as being trite because of their repeated use. Examples: Amy Lowell's "Patterns," James Weldon Johnson's "The Creation," Poe's "The Tell-Tale Heart." Note: Titles in this category vary with geographical region, academic level of the student, and vagaries of taste.

AIDS FOR THE TEACHER

Audio Aids

Thanks to the tape recorder and the television set, no teacher need lack for recorded materials to use in interpretation classes. The recorder can provide a permanent collection of recordings of "live" readings, readings recorded from television programs or radio, and readings reproduced from borrowed tapes and recordings. Nevertheless, the number of commercial recordings of readings has increased so rapidly in recent years that interpreters can now build both school and personal collections, not only for enjoyment but also for comparison of reading styles and techniques. There should be no hesitancy in buying the same literature read by different readers. Teachers of speech do not regard such purchases as duplications, since they offer opportunities for comparing approaches to literature. At times the recordings are disillusioning, particularly when certain authors read their own works; but even the recordings of poor readings have their uses.

The Core Record Collection.   Teachers should be warned that recordings are a less stable item than books: records do not remain available over long periods. One disadvantage in adopting a textbook that bases instructional materials on recordings is that the recordings are likely to become unavailable before the book is revised. Similarly, any basic purchase list will remain a purely tentative suggestion until there exist standard recordings comparable to standard editions of literature.

If the teacher is starting a collection, a selection should be made to represent as many types of literature and varieties of readers as the record budget will permit. The collection might consist of recordings of outstanding professional reading programs, children's literature, and traditional literature; individual and group reading; and serious and playful reading.

The following items suggest the wealth of materials from which to choose:

Reading Programs by Single Artists

"The Importance of Being Oscar, An Entertainment on the Life and Works of Oscar Wilde," with Micheál MacLiammóir (Columbia)
"The Story-Teller—A Session with Charles Laughton" (Capitol)
"An Evening with Dylan Thomas, Reading His Own and Other Poems" (Caedmon)
"More Mark Twain Tonight!" with Hal Holbrook (Columbia)
"Shakespeare's Women," a concert reading by Claire Luce (Folkways)
"The Brontës, a Dramatic Reading" by Margaret Webster (Vanguard)

Anthologies

"The Caedmon Treasury of Modern Poets Reading," 20 poets reading their own works (Caedmon)
"Conversation Pieces," duologue poems read by 12 artists (Folkways)
"Golden Treasury of Contemporary Catholic Verse" (Spoken Arts)
"The Jupiter Book of Ballads," 17 ballads performed by 6 artists (Folkways)
"Palgrave's Golden Treasury," read by three artists (Caedmon)

Works of One Author

"The Golden Treasury of John Betjeman" (Spoken Arts)
"The Poems of William Butler Yeats," with Yeats, McKenna, and MacLiammóir (Spoken Arts)
"The Poetry of Blake," read by Sir Ralph Richardson (Caedmon)
"Poetry of Browning Read by James Mason" (Caedmon)
"Poitier Meets Plato" (Warner Brothers)
"Vachel Lindsay Reading 'The Congo,' 'Chinese Nightingale,' and Other Poems" (Caedmon)

Reading with Music

"The Ballad of Robin Hood," read and sung by Anthony Quayle (Caedmon)
"Façade" with Dame Edith Sitwell (Columbia)
"Mother Goose," read by Cyril Ritchard, Boris Karloff, and Celeste Holm (Caedmon)
"Poetry and Jazz in Concert" (Argo)

Readers Theater

"Don Juan in Hell," with the First Drama Quartette (Columbia)
"The Hollow Crown," with Adrian, Barton, Johnson, and Tutin (London)
"John Brown's Body" (Columbia)
"Now, What Is Love?" with Adrian, Barton, and Tutin (Argo)
"The Shaw-Terry Letters," read by Dame Peggy Ashcroft and Cyril Cusack (Caedmon)
"Under Milk Wood," three versions available

Educational

"The Forms of Poetry" (Lexington)
"How to Read and Understand Poetry," correlated with filmstrip (Lexington)
"The Nature of Poetry," with Frank C. Baxter (Spoken Arts)

Since they are fugitive items requiring prompt purchase, it is highly desirable to keep abreast of the new releases in spoken records. Unfortunately, they are not as systematically reviewed as are musical items, nor do all reviewers have a point of view sympathetic with that of specialists in speech. One who does is poet John Ciardi, whose comments appear in the

Saturday Review.[31] Periodically teachers recommend recordings they find helpful.[32]

Bibliographies of recordings appear at irregular intervals but as purchase lists they are soon outdated. Those most useful to interpreters appear in speech, English, and library publications. The best single up-to-date catalog is the *Schwann Supplementary Catalog,* available in record shops. Some recording companies and record clubs send checklists and catalogs to select mailing lists. Inquiries about this service should be addressed to the educational departments of the recording firms or their retail outlets.

An annotated bibliography by Helen Roach, *Spoken Records,* should be made available to every teacher who purchases or uses recordings.[33]

Textbooks

One of the most neglected aids for teachers is the unadopted textbook. Such a textbook, perhaps undergoing the preparation of a new edition, or waiting its turn for adoption, or merely unsuited to the peculiar demands of a given class, should not be forgotten by the teacher. In it may be found an unfamiliar pedagogical technique, a helpful bibliography, an apt quotation, or a new illustration for the teacher to use. Nor are such aids limited to interpretation textbooks. College teachers of units or short courses and high school teachers of interpretation may find the brief treatent of oral reading in a fundamentals or public speaking textbook more helpful than the comprehensive treatments designed for a concentrated semester or year of interpretation. Similarly, the high school speech textbook can be useful to teachers at all academic levels.

A teacher is unlikely to overlook a book on the teaching of speech, but two other types of materials should come to his attention. The first is the textbook, or section of the textbook, on voice and diction.[34] Since selections for reading aloud are standard practice material for most books of this type, interpreters will almost always find the books useful for reading material and vocal drills. Second, the teacher should not forget books on the teaching of English, many of which contain chapters on oral reading, play reading, and reading guidance for students.[35]

[31] Beverly Whitaker, "John Ciardi on Poets' Recorded Readings," *Southern Speech Journal,* Spring, 1964, 29:209–213.
[32] John R. Searles, "Selected Filmstrips and Recordings for the English Classroom," *English Journal,* December, 1966, 55:1216–1220.
[33] Metuchen, N.J.: Scarecrow Press, 1st ed., 1963, 3rd ed., 1970.
[34] See Virgil A. Anderson, *Training the Speaking Voice,* 2nd ed., New York: Oxford Univ. Press, 1961.
[35] See Ethan Allen Cross and Elizabeth Carney, *Teaching English in High Schools,* rev. ed., New York: Macmillan, 1950; John James DeBoer, Walter V. Kaulfers and Helen Rand Miller, *Teaching Secondary English,* New York: McGraw-Hill, 1951; Walter Loban, Margaret Ryan and James R. Squire, *Teaching Language and Literature,* Harcourt, Brace Jovanovich, 1961; Mildred A. Dawson, *Teaching Language in the Grades,* Harcourt Brace Jovanovich, 1951.

New textbooks appear frequently in the speech field. An up-to-date brief checklist of available books is published annually in the Speech Communication Association *Directory*. Reviews of textbooks appear in book sections of professional speech journals.

Professional Journals

The teacher of interpretation cannot afford to limit his reading to pedagogy but must read more extensively than most of his colleagues because of the peculiar relationship of interpretation to literature, cultural history, aesthetics, and still more distant areas of learning. Therefore, the interpreter who reads widely probably relies on professional journals less than do other speech teachers. Nevertheless, he will find useful articles and reviews in the *Quarterly Journal of Speech*, the *Speech Teacher*,[36] *Western Speech*, the *Central States Speech Journal*, the *Southern Speech Journal*, and *Today's Speech* (the Eastern regional journal). To these he should add the *English Journal, College English*, the *Library Journal,* and other professional publications that are in some way related to literature. Occasionally he will find it necessary to examine publications in psychology, philosophy, history, and education, but always literature remains his chief concern. The "little" magazines and the numerous journals of literary criticism are basic reading materials for him.

Professional Associations

The interpreter is fortunate in having two national professional organizations interested in serving him. The first is the National Council of Teachers of English, the second the Speech Communication Association with its Interpretation Division.

The National Council of Teachers of English. The following services are provided by the NCTE for its members and other teachers who may purchase its aids.

It publishes the *English Journal* and *College English*, an English curriculum series, literary maps, books, pamphlets, and reprints from its own publications and those of other organizations. Through it can be ordered tape recordings, filmstrips, recordings of literature prepared by NCTE and commercial firms, and linguistic recordings. A catalog of its offerings is available on request. Members of NCTE are entitled to discounts on purchases, including the commercial recordings it makes available.

The National Council of Teachers of English also shows a sincere interest in oral interpretation by including on its convention programs sections and symposia on the oral reading of literature.

The Interpretation Division of SCA. Teachers of interpretation have

---

[36] Indexed in the *Education Index*.

a strong Division in the Speech Communication Association. This unit of the association, reasonably autonomous, meets annually to select its own officers and advisory group, choose projects of benefit to its membership, and hear reports and papers. In a very short span of years the group has authorized and sponsored a variety of projects. Any teacher of interpretation would do well to affiliate with the Interest Division through SCA in order to be eligible for whatever services the group is currently sponsoring.

EXERCISES

1. Write a paper analyzing definitions of interpretation found in six interpretation textbooks; in six fundamental textbooks.
2. Examine a speech textbook written before 1900 and compare the reading selections and methods of instruction with those of a current textbook.
3. Prepare a unit in interpretation, emphasizing one form of literature, for a beginning college speech course; for a high school course.
4. Prepare a course outline in interpretation with a principles-of-interpretation approach for a one-semester high school course; for a college course.
5. Construct an evaluative outline for a specific assignment in interpretation. Test the phraseology, form, and purpose of the outline by using it for a reading assignment in class.
6. Construct a listener's guide to accompany a recorded selection.
7. Record a reader on a television program and make two critical evaluations of his performance, one as the program is being televised, one a week later from the recording. Compare reactions with a classmate who did not view the reading. Does the listener gain or lose through the absence of visual stimuli?
8. List the articles on oral reading indexed in *Readers' Guide* during the past 5 years. Read those that are available and prepare a paper summarizing their content.
9. Make a bibliography of all the articles and book reviews of interest to interpreters published during the past year in one of the following: *The Saturday Review, Harper's Magazine, Atlantic Monthly, American Literature, College English, The Sewanee Review, Yale Review,* or *Commonweal*.
10. Obtain from your librarian a listing of "books for young adults" and prepare a recommended reading list for a high school interpretation class.
11. Write for catalogs to five publishers of paperback books, or obtain them from your your bookseller. From the catalogs compile titles of books of interest to interpreters, listing them in the following categories: books for reading aloud (subdivide into the forms of literature), books of literary criticism, books of literary history, and reference books and bibliographies.
12. Survey the local newsstand for magazines and paperback books containing material suitable for classroom or family reading. Report your findings to the class.
13. Using book review publications and the *Book Review Digest*, evaluate 15 currently popular books as to their suitability for oral reading. Examine actual copies of as many of the 15 as are available and note necessary modifications in your list.
14. Prepare a bibliography of all library resources available for *locating* selections for an author program; a subject program.
15. Prepare a list of 25 authors who are sufficiently well represented in the school library to permit their use as subject programs.
16. Using a bibliography in an interpretation textbook as a checklist, survey the hold-

ings of the nearest library. Prepare a bibliography of reading resources available in the library.

17. Make a bibliography of textbook references on adaptation of materials for reading aloud.
18. Adapt for oral reading: a short story, a long novel, a short play, a full-length play, a biography or diary, a narrative poem.
19. Prepare a reading program coordinating scenes from a musical play and songs from the production.
20. Prepare an oral review of a book of modern poetry, a humor anthology, a play, or a currently popular work on history or sociology.
21. Locate an author's account of the writing of a poem and read it to the audience in connection with the reading of the poem.
22. Find similar materials prepared by a writer in two different forms and present each form orally to reveal differences in reading techniques required by differences in form.
23. Prepare a dramatistic analysis of a selection.
24. Make a survey of your community and report the opportunities for oral reading.
25. List library sources available for tracing allusions, identifying proper names, and determining pronunciation of proper names appearing in literature.
26. List library anthologies containing introductions to literary selections that could serve as models for students' introductions. Read five introductions from the anthologies to your classmates for evaluation.
27. Find brief poems or extracts, prose passages, and dialogue from plays to serve as practice selections for interpreters studying the following topics: phrasing, pause, rising inflections, subordination, climax, change of tempo, contrasts in loudness, and contrasting emotions. Find at least half of your material in nonspeech books.
28. Using a nineteenth or twentieth century poem, draw up a review lesson of basic principles of interpretation.
29. Using all available library resources, prepare a historical and critical study of a short poem, including information on the genesis of the poem, the circumstances of its writing, its publishing history, critical reactions contemporaneous with it, and contemporary critical comment. If the author recorded it, add an evaluation of his presentation.
30. In books appearing on the reading list prepared for Exercise 10, find five examples of new, i.e., unused, material suitable for an interpretation contest or festival.
31. Prepare an examination over a unit of material in a standard interpretation chapter or textbook, take the test, and grade your paper. Ask a classmate to take the test and criticize it.
32. Discuss the following questions:
    a. What are the advantages of beginning a reading class with "cold prose"?
    b. What are the advantages of beginning with poetry?
    c. What means can a teacher use to develop reading skills at the beginning of a course if the syllabus prescribes beginning with methods of studying a selection?
    d. What objections are sometimes made to beginning a course with attention to vocal skills? Are they valid?
    e. How can the teacher encourage total bodily participation without emphasizing the need for gesture? Can gesture be planned?
    f. What is the danger in emphasizing bodily action and gesture?
    g. What dangers are inherent in staged readings? In choral speaking?
    h. What advantages do staged readings present? Choral speaking?
    i. Is storytelling interpretation? Explain your answer.
    j. Is the presentation of a memorized selection interpretation? Why?

  k. Is the creator of a Charles Dickens or Mark Twain in a reading performance an actor? A reader? Both?
  l. In what different phases of interpretative reading is correctness not an absolute but a matter of taste?
  m. How can the taste of readers and audiences be improved?

REFERENCES

General

"Approaches to Oral Interpretation: A Symposium," *Speech Teacher*, September, 1969, 18:187–203.

ARNEZ, NANCY L., "Racial Understanding Through Literature," *English Journal*, January, 1969, 58:56–61.

BOOTH, WAYNE, "The Use of Criticism in the Teaching of Literature," *College English*, October, 1965, 27:1–13.

BROWER, REUBEN ARTHUR, "The Speaking Voice," in Barnet, Sylvan, Berman, Morton and Burto, William (eds.), *The Study of Literature: A Handbook of Critical Essays and Terms*, Boston: Little, Brown, 1960.

GEIGER, DON, *The Dramatic Impulse in Modern Poetics*, Baton Rouge: Louisiana State University Press, 1967.

GEIGER, DON, *Sound, Sense, and Performance of Literature*, Glenview, Ill.: Scott, Foresman, 1963.

GLEASON, H. A., JR., *Linguistics and English Grammar*, New York: Holt, Rinehart & Winston, 1965, chap. 18, "Literary Form and Style."

KINNAMON, KENETH, "Afro-American Literature, the Black Revolution, and Ghetto High Schools," *English Journal*, February, 1970, 59:189–194.

LAMBERT, ROBERT C., "Pitfalls in Reading Drama," *English Journal*, November, 1964, 53:592–594, 602.

LOESCH, KATHARINE T., "Literary Ambiguity and Oral Performance," *Quarterly Journal of Speech*, October, 1965, 51:258–267.

MACKSOUD, S. JOHN, "Anyone's How Town: Interpretation as Rhetorical Discipline," *Speech Monographs*, March, 1968, 35:70–76.

NATHAN, LEONARD E., "Reading 'To a Friend Whose Work Has Come to Nothing,'" *Western Speech*, Fall, 1962, 26:205–210.

OSTROFF, ANTHONY (ED.), *The Contemporary Poet as Artist and Critic*, Boston: Little, Brown, 1964. Eight symposia.

POST, ROBERT M., "Achievement of Empathic Response in Oral Reading," *Southern Speech Journal*, Spring, 1963, 28:236–240.

REYNOLDS, WILLIAM J., "Let's Talk Speech," *English Journal*, January, 1968, 57:105–110.

ROSENBLATT, LOUISE M., "A Performing Art," *English Journal*, November, 1966, 55:999–1005.

SLOAN, THOMAS O. (ED.), *The Oral Study of Literature*, New York: Random House, 1966. Five essays.

STRANG, RUTH AND ROGERS, CHARLOTTE, "How Do Students Read a Short Story?" *English Journal*, December, 1965, 54:819–823, 829.

VEILLEUX, JERÉ, "The Interpreter: His Role, Language and Audience," *Speech Teacher*, March, 1967, 16:124–133.

VEILLEUX, JERÉ, "Toward a Theory of Interpretation," *Quarterly Journal of Speech*, April, 1969, 55:105–115.

Pedagogy

CROCKER, LIONEL G., "How to Multiply the Side Values of Oral Interpretation," *Speech Teacher*, January, 1961, 10:63–64.

FERNANDEZ, THOMAS (ED.), *Oral Interpretation and the Teaching of English*, Champaign, Ill.: National Council of Teachers of English, 1969.

HEZEL, PAUL, "Teaching Freshman English in Middle Earth," *English Journal*, March, 1970, 59:387–392.

HOOPES, NED E., "What Literature Should Be Used in Oral Interpretation?" *Speech Teacher*, September, 1961, 10:206–210.

JARVIS, BOYER, "A Note on Oral Interpretation," *Western Speech*, Winter, 1960, 24:29–32.

MOHRMANN, G. P., "Children's Literature and the Beginning Class in Oral Interpretation," *Speech Teacher*, March, 1964, 13:128–132.

"Poetry in the Classroom," *English Journal*. Explicative articles appear irregularly.

POST, ROBERT M., "The Oral Approach to the Teaching of High School Literature," *Speech Teacher*, March, 1968, 17:156–159.

Speech in the Junior High School, Michigan Speech Association Curriculum Guide Series, Chicago: National Textbook Corporation, 1968.

"Teaching Interpretation: Students Recall Methods of Early Leaders," *Speech Teacher*, November, 1962, 11:290–310. Eight articles.

WAMBOLDT, HELEN JANE, "Haiku as a Tool in Teaching Oral Interpretation," *Speech Teacher*, September, 1964, 13:171–175.

Textbooks

BACON, WALLACE A., *The Art of Interpretation*, New York: Holt, Rinehart & Winston, 1966.

BELOOF, ROBERT, *The Performing Voice in Literature*, Boston: Little, Brown, 1966.

CAMPBELL, PAUL, *The Speaking and the SPEAKERS of Literature*, Belmont, Calif.: Dickenson, 1967.

GEETING, BAXTER M., *Interpretation for Our Time*, Dubuque, Ia.: William C. Brown, 1966.

HOLLAND, JACK B. AND SESSIONS, VIRGIL D., *Oral Interpretation Drill Book*, Boston: Holbrook, 1968.

MATTINGLY, ALETHEA SMITH AND GRIMES, WILMA H., *Interpretation: Writer, Reader, Audience*, Belmont, Calif.: Wadsworth, 1970.

MOUAT, LAWRENCE H., *Reading Literature Aloud*, New York: Oxford Univ. Press, 1962.

SCRIVNER, LOUISE M., *A Guide to Oral Interpretation*, New York: Odyssey, 1968.

SESSIONS, VIRGIL D. AND HOLLAND, JACK B., *Your Role in Oral Interpretation*, Boston: Holbrook, 1968.

THOMPSON, DAVID W. AND FREDRICKS, VIRGINIA, *Oral Interpretation of Fiction*, A *Dramatistic Approach*, 2nd ed., Minneapolis: Burgess, 1967.

WALTERS, DONALD N., *The Reader, An Introduction to Oral Interpretation*, New York: Odyssey, 1966.

WOOLBERT, CHARLES HENRY AND NELSON, SEVERINA E., *The Art of Interpretative Speech*, *Principles & Practices*, 5th ed., New York: Appleton-Century-Crofts, 1968.

Book Reviewing

DREWRY, JOHN ELDRIDGE, *Writing Book Reviews*, Boston: Writer, 1966.

OPPENHEIMER, EVELYN, *Book Reviewing for an Audience: A Practical Guide in Technique for Lecture and Broadcast*, Philadelphia: Chilton, 1962.

ROBB, MARY MARGARET, "Oral Intepretation and the Book Review," *Speech Teacher*, November, 1956, 5:285–289.

Choral Interpretation

ARBUTHNOT, MAY HILL, *Children and Books*, 3rd. ed., Glenview, Ill.: Scott, Foresman, 1964, "Verse Choirs" and "How to Read Poetry Aloud."

CULLEN, WILLIAM H., "The First Thirty Minutes of Choral Reading," *English Journal*, March, 1968, 57:395–399, 419.

HAMM, AGNES CURREN, "Why the Professional Cold Shoulder?" (Forum), *Quarterly Journal of Speech*, February, 1960, 46:80, 81. Response to Hamm: Sanson, Clive, "Choral Speaking" (Forum), *Quarterly Journal of Speech*, October, 1960, 46:306–307.

PALLER, RUTH, "Choral Reading in Junior High School," *English Journal*, February, 1965, 54:121–123.

RECLAM, HERTA, "Choric-Speaking in Greek Tragedies, Performed by Students," *Speech Teacher*, November, 1962, 11:283–289.

STASSEN, MARILYN E., "Choral Reading and the English Teacher," *English Journal*, March, 1969, 58:436–439.

Readers Theater

BENSON, ALAN W., "The Dramatic Director and Reader's Theatre: Blessing or Curse?," *Speech Teacher*, November, 1968, 17:328–330.

BROOKS, KEITH AND BIELENBERG, JOHN E., "Readers Theatre as Defined by New York Critics," *Southern Speech Journal*, Summer, 1964, 29:288–302.

COGER, LESLIE IRENE AND WHITE, MELVIN R., *Readers Theatre Handbook: A Dramatic Approach to Literature*, Glenview, Ill.: Scott, Foresman, 1967.

COGER, LESLIE IRENE AND WHITE, MELVIN R. (EDS.), *Studies in Readers' Theatre*, Brooklyn, N.Y.: S and F Press, 1963.

MACARTHUR, DAVID E., "Reader's Theatre: Variations on a Theme," *Speech Teacher*, January, 1964, 13:47–51.

ROBERTSON, RODERICK, "Producing Playreadings," *Educational Theatre Journal*, March, 1960, 12:20–23.

Storytelling

SEABERG, DOROTHY I., "Can the Ancient Art of Storytelling Be Revived?" *Speech Teacher*, September, 1968, 17:246–249.

SHEDLOCK, MARIE L., *The Art of the Story-Teller*, 3rd ed., New York: Dover, 1951.

TOOZE, RUTH, *Storytelling*, Englewood Cliffs, N.J.: Prentice-Hall, 1959.

Interpretation of the Bible

ARMSTRONG, CHLOE, *Oral Interpretation of Biblical Literature*, Minneapolis: Burgess, 1968.

CURRY, SAMUEL SILAS, *Vocal and Literary Interpretation of the Bible*, Magnolia, Mass.: Expression, 1923.

LANTZ, J. EDWARD, *Reading the Bible Aloud*, New York: Macmillan, 1959.

Interpretation of Poetry

BESSINGER, J. B., "The Oral Text of Ezra Pound's 'The Seafarer,' " *Quarterly Journal of Speech*, April, 1961, 47:173–177.

CAMPBELL, PAUL N., *Oral Interpretation*, New York: Macmillan, 1966.

CIARDI, JOHN, *How Does a Poem Mean?* Part III, in Herbert Barrows, Hubert Heffner, John Ciardi, and Wallace Douglas (eds.), *An Introduction to Literature*, Boston: Houghton Mifflin, 1959.

DOLMAN, JOHN JR., *The Art of Reading Aloud*, New York: Harper & Row, 1956.

ELIOT, THOMAS STEARNES, "Three Voices of Poetry," *Atlantic Monthly*, April, 1954, 193:38–44.

HILLYER, ROBERT, "On Reading Verse Aloud," *Atlantic Monthly*, July, 1939, 164:91–95.

LIGHTFOOT, MARJORIE J., "Prosody and Performance," *Quarterly Journal of Speech*, February, 1967, 53:61–66.

MERRITT, FRANCINE, "Concrete Poetry—Verbivocovisual," *Speech Teacher*, March, 1969, 18:109–114.

ROBB, MARY MARGARET, "Growing a Taste for Poetry," *Speech Teacher*, November, 1963, 12:317–321.

SHELTON, RICHARD, "The Poem in Context: Aiken's 'Morning Song,' " *Speech Teacher*, January, 1967, 16:28–32.

THOMPSON, PHYLLIS ROSE, "The 'Haiku Question' and the Reading of Images," *English Journal*, April, 1967, 56:547–551.

Multimedia

CLIFTON, LINDA J., "The Two Corys: A Sample of Inductive Teaching," *English Journal*, March, 1969, 58:414–415.

DAIGON, ARTHUR, "Pictures, Punchcards, and Poetry," *English Journal*, October, 1969, 58:1033–1037.

MAY, STEVE, "Man's World: An Electronic Experience in the Humanities," *English Journal*, March, 1970, 59:413–415.

MORGAN, ROBERT E., "More Avant-Rock in the Classroom," *English Journal*, November, 1969, 58:1238–1240.

MORSE, DAVID E., "Avant-Rock in the Classroom," *English Journal*, February, 1969, 58:196–200.

MURPHY, GERALDINE, "Teaching Fiction Through Visual and Verbal Art," *English Journal*, April, 1970, 59:502–508.

RAHLF, ARLAN W., "Let's Sing—Read," *Speech Teacher*, September, 1966, 15:229–231.

STOWE, RICHARD A. AND MAGGIO, ANDREW J., "Language and Poetry in Sight and Sound," *English Journal*, May, 1965, 54:410–413.

9. Teaching Drama

Claude L. Shaver

AIMS AND PURPOSES

A majority of schools engage in some kind of dramatic activity, even if it is nothing more than the traditional class play. School plays are put on for a variety of purposes—to raise money for various school projects, because "it has always been done," and to satisfy the desire of some of the students to appear before a public. But it is safe to say that the purpose of dramatic activity in a school situation ought to be educational; that is, it should have some relationship to the educational purposes of the institution. What are some of these educational purposes?

Let us begin by saying that theatrical activity is an art. It is a literary art in the manuscript; a visual art in setting, costume, and the movement of the players; an expressive art on the part of the actors; an interpretative art on the part of the director—in short, a synthesis of many arts brought together and culminating in the act of stage presentation. The teaching of the arts has been clearly established as a part of the educational system. In general, the teaching of the arts has followed along two major paths: the development of appreciation in the participants and the spectators, and the development of skills in the various artists. The drama has followed this pattern, but for the most part emphasis has been put on the second of these, with the general idea that appreciation will naturally follow. This latter idea is not basically established and certainly more attention needs to be given to this aspect. Both of these directions may be considered in both the teaching of drama in the classroom and in public performances.

192

In recent years there has been a widespread development of children's theater production in the United States. This emphasis differs from the older practice of creative dramatics in that currently the plays produced are for audiences of children but with adult performers. The purpose of such performances is to give children plays on their own level, to develop a liking for live theater, and thus to build potential theater audiences.

Basically, a drama teacher must realize that the majority of his students, if they maintain any contact with theater in adult life, will eventually become audience members for the live drama; a considerable number will become participators in community theater enterprises, either as actors, board members, or patrons; a few may become teachers in the fields of speech and drama; a very few may become civic theater directors working in little theaters or in city- or county-sponsored recreational programs; a rare student will find a place in the professional theater. The major job of the drama teacher is thus to build an appreciation of theater art, to inculcate a love for live theater, to establish aesthetic values that may be applied to motion pictures and television as well as to live theater, and to build a respect for the tradition of theater as a major part of a civilized society.

Literature in various forms has existed in every civilization. Before writing was invented and printing had promoted widespread literacy, literature was in the oral tradition—storytellers, reciters, actors. In Greece the art of the rhapsody and the art of the actor reached a high point in the cultural life of the society. Many attempts have been made, both among the Greeks and later, to explain the significance and value of poetic and dramatic literature. Basically, drama organizes and compresses life processes into capsule form that may be seen, comprehended, and understood. The observation of men "like ourselves" in travail in situations where the motivations, emotions, and resulting actions may be clearly set forth brings a greater understanding of and compassion for humanity.

The development of appreciation and of understanding may be achieved both through audience attendance at dramatic productions and through participation as an actor or stage worker. But those who actually participate in dramatic production acquire other abilities, equally important, of two kinds: (1) an ability largely limited to actors, control of the expressive mechanism, improvement of voice and speech, development of body control and poise, satisfaction of self-mastery in the creation of a role, and (2) for all participators, an understanding of the democratic processes and responsibilities of group activities, with the concomitant development of community activity skills and leadership.

It should be obvious that there are real values in a well-developed school drama program, both for the students who participate and for those who attend the performances. That there are values for the school as a whole in providing cultural outlets for its students and in the public-relations aspects of the drama is perhaps less obvious, but the values are nonetheless real.

That there are values to the community is equally true. In many towns the school provides the only live theater activity. In some cases school and community combine in a Town-and-Gown program of theater. In other situations the school drama program serves as a support and resource for a local little theater organization, training future actors, backstage workers, and audiences. Schools often serve the community in providing club and organization programs and in assisting with community activities. Thus the drama program helps to preserve the tradition of live theater and provides the community a cultural service. Additionally, such activities as role-playing, improvisation, creation of original dialogues and playlets, should help both participator and spectator to better understanding of current issues and problems of personal relationships.

The educational aims of drama teaching and activities may then be listed as follows:

1. The appreciation of the drama as literature and of acting and production as fine arts
2. A better understanding of people and their problems and their successes and failures in meeting them
3. Control over expressive mechanisms
4. The development of leadership and responsibility in cooperative activity

The first two of these may be developed among both audience members and participators, the last two only through direct participation in dramatic activities.

ORGANIZATION

Organizing a Program

The achievement of the aims outlined in the preceding section calls for a drama program that will provide plays both for the enjoyment of audiences and for the active participation of actors and stage workers. In many schools play production is looked on simply as a means of raising money to support other activities in the school. This attitude should be discouraged. Dramatic production should be undertaken for its educational values. However, a joint program in partial support of other activities sometimes secures better cooperation from students and administrators and serves as excellent motivation for the improvement of the drama program. An effective program generally is developed through a combination of classes in drama and a program of public performances. Obviously the program must be worked out in individual cases to meet and satisfy local needs. The numer of plays and the type of play, the size of the school and of the group interested in drama, rehearsal conditions, and physical equipment are examples of local situations that may affect the nature of the program.

Certain general ideas, however, may serve as useful guides in planning a program. First, there should be some kind of producing group. This may be a drama class, drama club, a school class (junior or senior, for example), or an organization other than a dramatic club. The program may be purely curricular, that is, limited to classes in drama; it may be purely extracurricular, in which there are no classes but the program is developed through clubs or class organizations; or the program may be cocurricular, in which the program may be centered in classes but supported by outside activities. A program limited to junior and senior class plays may be useful if there is no other possible outlet, but obviously it is restrictive in nature since only members of the specific class would be permitted to participate. A program limited to drama classes also seems unnecessarily restrictive in that participation is permitted only to those able to schedule the drama class or classes. This leaves a cocurricular situation as probably the best solution, with a concentrated program in classes and a wide participation generally through a dramatic club or workshop group of some sort.

Organizing the Drama Class

Many states have state courses of study in speech that often include one or more units in drama. In other cases the teaching of drama must proceed without the aid of such a course outline. State courses of study are generally helpful in planning what to include in a course. In a well-developed program there may be three courses in drama: a general introductory course, a specific course in acting and directing, and a course in stagecraft and play production. It is not the purpose of this chapter to outline a complete course of study; rather it suggests major divisions in the areas suggested above that may be treated in each. If only one course is taught, material from all three areas may be judiciously selected to fill out the single course.

    I. Introduction to drama
        A. A unit on dramatic literature
           This would include the reading and discussion of a number of plays from the different periods of dramatic history such as the following:
           1. A Greek tragedy
           2. A Greek comedy
           3. A Roman comedy
           4. A medieval mystery play
           5. A medieval farce, such as *The Farce of the Worthy Master Pierre Patelin*
           6. A pre-Shakespearian farce, such as *Gammer Gurton's Needle*
           7. A Shakespearian play
           8. A Molière play
           9. A Restoration play
          10. A play by Sheridan or Goldsmith

11. A play by Ibsen
12. Plays from the modern theater as time will permit, including social thesis plays and plays dealing with current issues and dramatic styles. This list is merely suggestive. It is not intended that students would necessarily read all the plays listed.

B. A unit on theater history

This unit would attempt to survey the kinds of theaters, methods of production, styles of acting, styles of playwriting, and important persons in various periods of theater history such as the following:

1. The Greek theater
2. The Roman theater
3. The medieval religious theater
4. The commedia dell' arte
4. The Spanish theater of Lope de Vega
6. The Elizabethan theater
7. The theater of Molière
8. The eighteenth-century theater
9. The realistic theater of Ibsen and Belasco
10. The contemporary theater

II. Acting and directing

A. A unit on play directing

This unit would consider the major problems of a director, such as the following:

1. Interpreting the script
2. Working with the actors
3. The process of production, such as:
   a. Blocking the action
   b. Developing the movement
   c. Creating the picture
   d. Conducting the rehearsals
   e. The rehearsal schedule
      (1) Blocking period
      (2) Memorization period
      (3) Polishing period
      (4) Technical rehearsal period
   f. The performance

B. A unit on acting

1. The actor's media
2. Emotion and technique
3. Voice and speech
4. Bodily action
5. Characterization
6. Styles of acting
7. Improvisation
8. Varying relation of actor to audience.

III. Play production

A. A unit on staging and costume

This unit would survey scenery and costume practices, such as:

1. A consideration of kinds of theaters, such as:
   a. Proscenium theater
   b. Arena theater
   c. Platform stage

2. A consideration of kinds of scenery, such as:
    a. Complete realism
    b. Simplified realism
    c. Stylistic scenery
3. A consideration of costuming
    a. Costume periods
    b. Stage costumes versus street clothes
    c. Costume problems in modern plays
4. A consideration of lighting
    a. Lighting units
    b. Control units
    c. General practices in lighting

Advanced courses could develop in detail the general suggestions given here for the beginning course and could, of course, add other courses as needed.

It should also be clear that these units may be interlaced; that is, the unit on dramatic literature may be easily combined with the unit on theater history, so that as plays are read the historical material could also be included in the reading and discussion. Acting, directing, and staging units can center about specific plays, periods, and styles. Ultimately all units may culminate in one or more productions of scenes from plays, one-act plays, or a long play.

A course or courses that culminate in one or more productions that combine participation of class members and drama club members constitutes what may be called a cocurricular program. This is probably the soundest approach for most schools.

Operation of a Dramatic Club

The dramatic club can be the most important support for the drama teacher in both classwork and in public performances. The club should be organized so that participation is open to everyone. Participation may be arranged so that a student earns a number of points for each type of work—acting, directing, scene painting, or ushering. When he has earned a certain number of points he may be eligible for a smaller, more exclusive club, within the framework of the larger one. Such an arrangement allows for wide participation—and thus interest—on whatever level the individual can best make a contribution. The club can serve as an agent of publicity, business management, ticket selling, and house management, as well as providing actors and backstage workers. Enthusiastic club members usually turn up in drama classes.

There should be some sort of regular activity for the club. While some of the events may be purely social, there should be drama programs of some sort in which members may participate. Major public performances provide part of the answer. However, in these public programs there is a tendency, generally a proper one, to use the best actors of the group. This provides little opportunity for the beginner and little opportunity for experiment with a variety of roles by the established members of the group; for if a student actor has been successful in one type of role, there is a tendency to cast him thereafter in the same sort of role. All of this indicates some form of workshop activity in which new members may gain some experience and the older ones may experiment with various types of plays and roles. Students are often interested in playwriting, and some outlet should be provided for them to see their plays in performance.

Workshop productions may be given at club meetings, at various special occasions, or at assembly or auditorium programs.

Since a full program of plays for club meetings may strain the resources of the school and the director, other types of activities may well be used. Among these can be demonstrations of acting techniques, scene construction, and makeup; group play-reading; films and filmstrips; occasional lectures by visitors; field trips to professional productions, and to neighboring school and little theater productions; and movie or TV nights for special productions.

A useful form of activity in current use is readers theater. In this activity, which is closely related to interpretation, the performers read the lines from the manuscript (although in some cases the lines are learned) and a minimum of activity or rather stage movement is used. Such programs are often given as public performances, and provide an additional outlet for student participation.

The general organization of the club may follow the pattern of club organizations as established in the particular school, but students should be given as much responsibility as possible for the operation of the organization, consistent with satisfying the needs of the club in relation to the drama program as a whole. On the other hand, be careful of assigning students tasks beyond their abilities. Such assignments generally result in failures that reflect no credit on the drama program.

PHYSICAL FACILITIES

Most schools provide some sort of auditorium that may be used for public performances. In many cases, however, the auditorium is combined with a gymnasium or some other feature that makes it less useful in arrangement, equipment, and scheduling than an auditorium devoted solely to assembly purposes. While a director may have to exercise considerable ingenuity in overcoming difficulties in production because of faulty auditorium and stage construction, in general it is possible to use the school auditorium for public programs. The current trend in the modern theater toward the apron or platform stage makes some of the older auditorium stages, with their extensive aprons which seemed impossible to use in a period of complete realism, more nearly usable in a modern style.

A few observations about the auditorium may be in order. Often the seating area is much wider than the stage opening, which means that persons sitting on the side do not have a full view of the stage. See to it that everyone does have a full view. This may be done by arranging the action to play within view of all spectators or by blocking off some of the side seats and not seating spectators there. Determine the sight lines in advance and arrange the action or seating accordingly.

Most auditoriums will have a curtain that can be used to open and close acts. In many cases, however, the apron projects a considerable distance beyond the curtain line. Acts may be closed by moving the final action upstage behind the curtain or by blackouts with the actors clearing the stage in the dark. The method used will depend on the play. Current practice often places furniture and other properties on the apron in front of the curtain. This allows actors to play on the apron nearer to the audience, which generally is desirable. Often the curtain is not used at all, the beginning and ending of acts or scenes being marked by light changes.

Lighting must also be considered. If there is no lighting except the traditional footlights and border lights, plans should be made for the purchase from time to time of units to light the acting area, particularly the stage apron. Such units may be conveniently hung from the balcony railing or from some other advantageous spot in the house.

Consider also the acoustics of the auditorium. In very large houses— those in which the stage is also the basketball court, for example—it may be advisable to concentrate the audience in a smaller area down front and not sell seats in the rear of the house. In other cases the balcony should not be used. Work with the actors so they will be able to project voice and speech over the necessary spectator area without undue strain.

A second item of considerable importance is a small practice or workshop theater for class use, rehearsal of small shows, early rehearsals of long shows, storage of properties, drama library, and clubroom. A platform can often be placed in the classroom, with simple draw drapes to serve as a front curtain. If a few pieces of lighting equipment and some curtains and properties are added, a practicable workshop theater may be achieved. Such an arrangement is invaluable in teaching acting, directing, and stagecraft. It will also serve as a practice theater for the drama club in its experimental program for beginners and for experienced actors trying new roles.

In case there is neither an auditorium nor a workshop stage, the director may turn to arena staging to solve his problems. Indeed, a director who has available both an auditorium and a workshop stage may also wish to work with an arena stage. Theaters-in-the-round are increasingly popular, and students should be given some opportunity to experiment with this mode of operation. For experimental purposes any large room may serve as an arena. For public performances, however, the room should meet certain requirements. The acting area should be at least 20 feet by 20 feet, larger if possible. There should be room for two or three rows of chairs on each side of the playing area, though the arrangement of seating may vary considerably. There must be entrances and exits to the playing area; generally these are at the four corners. Exits may be made behind screens placed in the corners; but at least one and preferably two exits should be through doors that open out of the room and thus give some sort of access to dressing and makeup rooms. A variation of arena staging is the thrust stage with the audience seated on three sides of the playing area. This allows for some scenery at the back of the thrust stage and entrances are generally placed at the back. Some entrances and exits may be made through the audience as in arena staging. The playing area must be lighted separately from the general lighting used for the audience.

THE ONE-ACT PLAY

The one-act play is frequently used in school productions, both for experimental and for public performances. It has certain advantages and certain disadvantages. Among the advantages are: production is generally simpler than production of a long play. It is easier for beginners to understand the characters, to memorize the lines, to master the techniques involved. If plays are to be student directed, experience with several one-act plays is indicated before the student attempts the directing of a long play. Furthermore, the one-act play allows more varied experience with a number of types of roles and more students may participate more often. The one-act play is also well adapted to workshop production.

On the other hand, there are disadvantages in the one-act form. The student actor does not face the problem of sustaining a character over three acts; he receives no experience in making a character grow over a period of time; he has no opportunity to build to a climax. He may also, after working in a number of one-act plays, underestimate the amount of work and effort needed to do a satisfactory job in a longer play.

In general, however, the advantages of the one-act play indicate its value in workshop situations and in occasional public performances, while the three-act play, with its greater magnitude, is generally used for public performances.

PLAY FESTIVALS

An important use of the one-act play is in play festivals. Many states have such festivals or contests. When properly treated these occasions may have real value. Production of a play for a festival constitutes a special problem.

Generally it is presented on a stage with which the director and cast are unacquainted. Scenery, properties, and lighting are usually furnished by a local crew, and elaborate effects generally cannot be rehearsed properly. It is better to plan the play to call for a minimum of effects, scenery, and furniture. Arrange to take with you the necessary props, costumes, and makeup. Concentrate on the actors and their performance rather than on stage effects. It goes without saying that a good play should be selected.

Often such contests or festivals are arranged so that the director and cast may meet with the judges to receive criticism of the performance. Learn to take criticisms in good part and try to profit from them. Student actors will often feel that they have performed better than the judges rating indicates. Part of the director's job is to help them understand the criticism and to use it for improvement. The director must also realize that much of the criticism should rightly fall on him, not the actors.

If too much emphasis is placed on winning, the contest generally fails in educational value. Most directors prefer a festival rather than a contest.

The director should acquaint himself thoroughly with the rules and regulations of the particular contest or festival he is entering. He may save himself and the cast considerable unhappiness by knowing the rules in advance and preparing the production in line with them.

PLAY SELECTION

In selecting a play for production the director must keep clearly in mind his educational purposes. Quite often he is under pressure to present a play that will be "popular" and make money for some school project. Such pressure should be resisted and the director should insist that the play selected should embody some educational values. It is sometimes possible to find a "popular" play that is educational also; sometimes it is not.

In general, the play selected should have good literary quality. This is hard to define, but certain observations may be made. First, the play should have a satisfactory plot structure. It should be credible—though a farce may properly have an incredible plot, as in *The Importance of Being Earnest*. In other cases, however, the plot structure should be reasonable and logical. Second, the characters should also be credible, and of a type and quality that student actors may comprehend and thus better portray. Third, the play should have an appropriate theme; that is, it should be meaningful.

A number of years ago Ernest Bavely prepared a list of standards of play selection, based on an extensive questionnaire circulated to a large number of school directors. The list is worth including here:

1. The high school play should have a worthwhile theme, be sincere and true in its interpretation of life, and accurate in its reflection of customs and manners.

2. It should have literary value. That is, it should be written in acceptable language and in accordance with accepted standards of playwriting. As such it should be emotionally and intellectually stimulating.
3. It should be within the capacities of the high school student to understand and appreciate, taking into consideration the influence of vicarious experience and the student's natural interests.
4. It should challenge the highest creative and artistic abilities of all who are associated with its production, thereby affording rich opportunities for study, analysis, and experimentation.
5. It should be good theater, affording opportunities for sincere acting, and be satisfying as entertainment. It should lead rather than follow the community standards of entertainment and appreciation.
6. It should be free of highly sophisticated or advanced roles, vulgarity or profanity, objectionable subject matter, and sordid and unwholesome presentations of characters and scenes.

Other factors that should be taken into consideration in selecting the high school play include the following:

1. Is the play adaptable to the physical equipment of the school in which it will be produced?
2. Does it make unreasonable demands on the production budget? On the other hand, does it take its proportionate share of the budget, thereby giving the school the highest type of play it can afford?
3. Does it fit in with the plays that have preceded it and those that will follow it, giving variety to the year's production schedule?
4. As a dramatic project, does it afford opportunities for the participation of many students?
5. Does it come within the interests and qualifications of the teacher on whom the responsibility for producing it is placed?[1]

While this list was intended primarily for high schools, it applies in many ways to colleges as well. A few general observations are in order. Plays should always be selected in relation to the plays preceding and following. If a particular play has been especially successful, avoid the temptation of following it with another just like it. Variety is essential in the program. It is better to choose a program of plays for the season rather than to select one at a time on a hit-or-miss basis. A proper program will include an occasional classic and a balance of comedy and serious drama. If you are uncertain, stick to standard authors and standard publishers.

Much has been written about profanity, obscenity, drinking, kissing, etc., on the school stage. Often a school or a community has a strong bias about these things. Generally, a director must work within the mores of his community. Student actors often find it embarrassing to perform such actions before a local audience. The result more often than not is that the

[1] Ernest Bavely, "Play Standards at the High School Level," *Quarterly Journal of Speech*, February, 1940, 26:89. Reprinted by permission.

actor drops out of character and shows his embarrassment, thus breaking the dramatic illusion for the audience. Work carefully with such situations to fit them naturally into the play. If you cannot, either cut them or choose another play. It should be noted that what is acceptable is subject to change and that communities vary in permissiveness.

Another problem to be considered is that of royalties. It is not true that all royalty plays are good ones and that all nonroyalty plays are bad ones. There are many good nonroyalty plays. To insist on producing only non-royalty plays in order to make money, however, generally results in the selection of a considerable number of poor plays. Plan to include royalty plays in the budget.

CASTING

After the play has been selected the next step is the selection of actors to fill the particular roles. There is no easy solution to this problem. The director must first decide on the purpose of the particular production. Is this a public performance or is it an experimental one? If the former, generally, he uses experienced actors and casts them in the kind of roles in which they have been successful previously. This is probably sound, though it denies the use of newcomers who may be better than established actors. If the production is an experimental or workshop one, obviously the director should cast new people and experiment with older ones.

Type Casting

Type casting means selecting an actor to play a role because he "looks the part" as described in the text or created in the director's mind or, often, because he looks like the actor who played the role in the motion picture. Physical type has certain significance—generally the heroine should be pretty and the hero taller than the heroine—but the director should look for acting ability first and type second.

Tryouts

The usual procedure in casting is to announce a tryout at which any interested student may appear. Usually the students are asked to read from the script of the play. Some directors make the play available to the actors ahead of time so that they may be familiar with it at tryouts. This certainly has advantages. On the other hand, it sometimes results in an actor trying out for a part for which he is obviously not suited and suffering a real disappointment when not given the role. He may then refuse a role for which he *is* well suited. Also, actors may establish an interpretation from undirected reading that may be at variance with the director's interpretation, and thus make for difficulties in rehearsal. On the other hand, reading cold often does not give much of an idea of an actor's real ability. The more usual practice is to make scripts available.

From the reading tryout the director may determine certain things, such as the actor's physical qualifications for the role, his skill in voice and articulation, flexibility of voice and body, projection of vocal and physical effects, and sometimes emotional tone or comic sense. Other tryout activities may be used, such as improvisation, pantomime, or interviews.

Each individual should be considered in relation to the other characters.

Other qualities—willingness to work, ability to memorize, ability to get along with others, and a sense of responsibility—are also important in casting.

Double Casts

In some cases where many students try out for a particular play it may be advisable to double cast some or all of the roles. This doubles the work of the director, but it also provides opportunity for more student actors. At the same time, it provides a bulwark against illness in the cast. However, double casting creates a number of problems: Each cast must be allowed to play an equal number of performances; ill feeling may be engendered over the question of which cast plays opening night; too strong a spirit of competition may develop. All of these problems, however, can be solved by a skillful director.

REHEARSING

It is not possible to outline a rehearsal schedule that will fit all situations. In general, however, a three-act play is in rehearsal from 4 to 6 weeks, with five 2-hour rehearsals per week.

A rehearsal schedule is ordinarily divided into five major units: (1) the reading or interpretation rehearsals, in which the basic interpretation of lines and characters is established; (2) the blocking rehearsals, in which the plan of the major action is established; (3) the memorization period, in which the emphasis is on memorization of lines; (4) the polishing period, in which the fine details of interpretation and action are developed; and (5) the technical rehearsals, in which the play is fitted to the stage, the scenery, lighting, costumes, etc. Roughly, one week may be allotted to each of these major periods, though they may overlap a great deal.

The director should so plan his rehearsals in advance that each rehearsal has a particular purpose, and the actors should be acquainted with the schedule.

THE PRODUCTION

During the final rehearsals the director should organize his staff and assign and rehearse delegated duties. The staff should include a stage manager, who is in charge of the performance; crew heads in charge of scenery, properties, and lights; and a makeup and costume head. There should be a house manager and ushers, of course. Other assignments are made as needed. During the performance the director should allow his staff to run the show. His duty at the performance is primarily to serve as a critic to evaluate his own work as director and the work of the individual actors.

EXERCISES

1. Analyze a number of course outlines in drama in state courses of study and speech and drama journals. What similarities do you find? What differences?
2. Read a number of one-act plays. Comment critically on their usability in a school situation.
3. Read several three-act plays. Report to the class on your reading. Suggest reasons why these plays would or would not be suitable for school use.
4. Select a long play. Prepare a plan for production including tryouts, casting, rehearsal schedule, scenery, lighting, and property lists.
5. Make a report to the class on arena staging. Discuss the advantages and disadvantages of this method of production.
6. Prepare a unit of drama for a high school class. Plan it for no more than 4 weeks.
7. Prepare a plan for organizing a theater party. Include in your plan specific directions to be given to the students who participate.
8. Work out an activity point system for a high school (or college) drama club. Write a 200-word justification of the point allotments.
9. Attend several rehearsals of plays. Observe how the director organizes his work and keeps the cast working.

REFERENCES

General

ALBRIGHT, H. D., HALSTEAD, WILLIAM P. AND MITCHELL, LEE, *Principles of Theatre Art*, 2nd ed., Boston: Houghton Mifflin, 1968.

BROCKETT, OSCAR G., *The Theatre: An Introduction*, New York: Holt, Rinehart & Winston, 1964.

CAMERON, KENNETH E. AND HOFFMAN, THEODORE J. C., *The Theatrical Response*, New York: Macmillan, 1969.

CHILVER, PETER, *Staging a School Play*, New York: Harper & Row, 1968.

HATLEN, THEODORE, *Orientation to the Theater*, New York: Appleton-Century-Crofts, 1962.

KERNODLE, GEORGE R., *Invitation to the Theatre*, New York: Harcourt Brace Jovanvich, 1967.

MOTTER, CHARLOTTE KAY, *Theatre in High School: Planning, Teaching, Directing*, Englewood Cliffs, N.J.: Prentice-Hall, 1970.

TENNYSON, GEORGE B., *An Introduction to Theatre*, New York: Holt, Rinehart & Winston, 1967.

WHITING, FRANK, *An Introduction to the Theatre*, rev. ed., New York: Harper & Row, 1961.

Acting and Directing

BLUNT, JERRY, *The Composite Art of Acting*, New York: Macmillan, 1966.

CANFIELD, CURTIS, *The Craft of Play Directing*, New York: Holt, Rinehart & Winston, 1963.

COLLIER, GAYLAN JANE, *Assignments in Acting*, New York: Harper & Row, 1966.

DEAN, ALEXANDER, *Fundamentals of Play Directing*, rev. by Lawrence Carra, New York: Holt, Rinehart & Winston, 1965.

FRANKLIN, MIRIAM A., *Rehearsal*, 4th ed., Englewood Cliffs, N.J.: Prentice-Hall, 1963.

KAHAN, STANLEY, *An Actor's Workshop*, New York: Harcourt Brace Jovanovich, 1967.

KAHAN, STANLEY, *Introduction to Acting*, New York: Harcourt Brace Jovanovich, 1962.

MC GAW, CHARLES, *Acting Is Believing*, 2nd ed., New York: Holt, Rinehart & Winston, 1966.

MC MULLAN, FRANK, *The Director's Handbook: An Outline for the Teacher and the Student of Play Production and Direction*, Hamden, Conn.: The Shoe String Press, 1964.

SPOLIN, VIOLA, *Improvisation for the Theatre: A Handbook of Teaching and Directing Techniques*, Evanston, Ill.: Northwestern University Press, 1963.

Technical

BELLMAN, WILLARD F., *Lighting the Stage: Art and Practice*, San Francisco: Chandler, 1967.

CORSON, RICHARD, *Stage Make-Up*, 4th ed., New York: Appleton-Century-Crofts, 1967.

GILLETTE, A. S., *An Introduction to Scene Design*, New York: Harper & Row, 1967.

GILLETTE, A. S., *Stage Scenery: Its Construction and Rigging*, New York: Harper & Row, 1959.

LOUNSBERRY, WARREN C., *Theatre Backstage: A Dictionary of Technical Terms and Methods with a Survey of American Stage Practices*, Seattle: Univ. of Washington Press, 1967.

PRISK, BERNEICE, *Stage Costume Handbook*, New York: Harper & Row, 1966.

Journals

Educational Theatre Journal, published by American Educational Theatre Association, Executive Office, John F. Kennedy Center, Suite 500, 1701 Pennsylvania Ave. N.W., Washington, D.C. 20006.

Speech Teacher, published by Speech Communication Association, Statler Hilton Hotel, New York 10001.

Players Magazine, published by National Collegiate Players.

The Cue: Official Magazine of Theta Alpha Phi.

Dramatics, published by National Thespian Society.

Theatre Crafts, 33 East Minor Street, Emmaus, Pennsylvania 18049.

Other Materials

Play Selection Aids for the Secondary Schools, American Educational Theatre Association, Washington, D.C.

RATLIFFE, SHARON AND HANCE, KENNETH C., *Dramatic Arts in the Secondary School*, Skokie, Ill.: National Textbook Co., 1968.

A *Suggested Outline for a Course of Study in Theatre Arts: Secondary School Level,* American Educational Theatre Association, Washington, D.C., 1963.

Play Publishers and Distributors

Baker's Plays, 100 Summer Street, Boston, Mass. 02110.
Children's Theatre Press: Cloverlot; Anchorage, Ky. 40223.
David McKay Company, Inc., 750 Third Avenue, New York 10017.
T. S. Denison & Co., 315 5 Ave South, Minneapolis, Minn. 55415.
Dramatic Publishing Co., 86 E. Randolph, Chicago, Ill. 60601.
Dramatist Play Service, 440 Park Avenue, South, New York 10016.
Eldridge Publishing Company, Franklin, Ohio 45005.
Samuel French, 25 W. 45th Street, New York 10036.
Music Theatre International, 119 West 57th Street, New York 10019.
Plays, Inc., 8 Arlington Street, Boston, Mass. 02116.
Tams-Witmark, Music Library, Inc., 757 Third Avenue, New York 10017.
Theatre Arts Books, 33 Sixth Avenue, New York 10014.

Costumes

Bob Kelly, Wig Creations, Inc., 151 West 46th St., New York 10036.
Brooks-Vanhorn, 117 West 17th St., New York 10011.
Costume Armour, Inc., 381 Canal Place, Bronx, N.Y. 10451.
Eaves Costume Co., 151 W. 46th St., New York 10036.
Norcostco, Inc., 2409 Piedmont Road, N.E., Atlanta, Ga. 30324.
Tobins Lake Studios, 2650 Seven Mile Road, South Lyon, Mich. 48178.
Western Costume Co., 5335 Melrose Ave., Hollywood, Calif. 90038.

Theater Equipment and Supplies

American Stage Lighting Company, 1331c North Avenue, New Rochelle, N.Y. 10804.
The Astrup Co., Inc., 39 Walker St., New York 10013.
ATS Administrative Ticket Service, 131 Mineola Boulevard, Mineola, N.Y. 11501.
Berkey-Colortran, Inc., 1015 Chestnut St., Burbank, Calif. 91502.
Brigham Gelatine, 16–19 Weston St., Randolph, Vt. 05060.
Capitol Stage Lighting, 509 W. 56th St., New York 10019.
Castle Lighting, 1014 N. La Brea Avenue, Los Angeles, Calif. 90038.
Century Strand Inc., 3 Entin Road, Clifton, N.J. 07014.
Costume Armour, Inc., 381 Canal Place, Bronx, N.Y. 10451.
E and H Theatrical Imports, 318 North 4th, Reading, Pa. 19601.
Electro Controls, 2975 South Second West, Salt Lake City, Ut. 84115.
Electronics Diversified Inc., 0625 S.W. Florida St., Portland, Oreg. 97219.
Gothic Color Co., 127 Washington St., Newark, N.Y., 10014.
Joseph C. Hansen, Co., 423 W. 43rd St., New York 10036.
Kliegel Brothers Lighting, 32–32 48th Ave., Long Island City, N.Y. 11101.
L & M Sales & Rentals, 1740 East 17th St., Cleveland, Oh. 44114.
Lighting Associates, 601 E. 32nd St., Suite 604, Chicago, Ill. 60616.
Little Stage Lighting, Box 20211, Dallas, Tex. 75220.
Major Records, Thomas J. Valentino, Dist., 150 W. 46th St., New York 10036.
Mole-Richardson, 937 North Sycamore Ave., Hollywood, Calif. 90038.
Mutual Hardware Corp., 5–45 49th Ave., Long Island, N.Y. 11101.
Northwestern Theatre Associates, 1615 Maple Ave., Evanston, Ill. 62201.
Olesen Company, 1535 Ivar Ave., Hollywood, Calif. 90028.
Package Publicity Service, 1564 Broadway, New York 10036.
Paramount Theatrical Supplies, 32 W. 20th St., New York 10011.

Playhouse Colors, 771 9th Ave., New York 10019.
Premier Studios, Inc., 414 West 45th St., New York 10036.
Roscoe, 36 Bush Ave., Port Chester, N.Y. 10573.
Rose Brand Textile Fabrics, 138 Grand St., New York 10013.
Strobe Optics, Box 881, Miami, Fla. 33156.
Theatre Sound, Inc., Post Office Drawer AQ, New Haven, Conn. 06525.
Skirpan Lighting Control Corp., 41–43 24th St., Long Island City, N.Y. 11101.
Strong Electric Corp., 522 City Park Ave., Toledo, Oh. 43601.
Theatre Production Service, 59 Fourth Ave., New York 10002.
Tobins Lake Studios, 2650 Seven Mile Road, South Lyon, Mich. 48178.
Wenger, 48P Wenger Building, Owatonna, Minn. 55060.

10. Teaching Students to Understand Broadcast Media

John H. Pennybacker

No one can deny that radio and television occupy a central place in the structure of American society today. Every day, the average American over 18 watches television for 6 hours and 9 minutes.[1] He listens to radio for an average of almost 2½ hours a day.[2] In 1968, 59 percent of the people got most of their news from television and 25 percent chose radio as their primary source (according to one survey in which multiple answers were permitted).[3] It is clear that broadcasting is an important part of our culture and will continue to be so for many years to come.

This chapter provides a minimal core of material that can be used to prepare a unit of instruction in broadcast media, and supplemental references that can be used to expand the unit. No production or skills elements are included and no equipment is needed. Chapter 11 builds on this base, adding the production elements necessary to teach students how to use the media effectively.

HISTORY OF RADIO

The most dramatic—and probably the most interesting—starting point for the history of broadcasting would be the career of Gugliemo Marconi. Through the work of Marconi, with a few backward glances toward Hein-

---

[1] *Broadcasting Yearbook*, 1970, p. A126.
[2] *Ibid.*
[3] Burns W. Roper, *A Ten Year View of Public Attitudes Towards Television and Other Mass Media, 1959–68*, New York: Television Information Office, 1969, p. 2.

rich Hertz to set the stage, the teacher can trace the development of wireless telegraphy from theory to practical application. Beginning with Marconi, the early history of wireless transmission can be traced through the lives and contributions of a series of pioneering men as follows:

Gugliemo Marconi develops wireless telegraphy with British cooperation between 1896 and 1900.

Reginald Fessenden takes the first step toward voice transmission by developing the "electrolytic detector" in 1903.

Dr. Ernst Alexanderson develops a more efficient transmitter called the "alternator" in 1906—voice transmission is now possible.

Dr. J. Ambrose Fleming and *Lee DeForest* produce the three-element "vacuum tube" that makes amplification possible in 1904 and 1906 respectively.

The Navy Department blocks the sale of *Alexanderson* patents to British Marconi and asks *Owen Young* to form the Radio Corporation of America (RCA) as a patent pool in 1919.

Dr. Frank Conrad of Westinghouse starts experimental broadcasting of music in Pittsburgh and demonstrates the ability of radio to sell sets in 1920.

By 1920, then, the technical problems surrounding the efficient transmission of voice and music had been solved and some system of broadcasting as we know it was possible.[4] In the period from 1920 to 1927 major forces in our society—large corporations and the federal government—worked out three basic questions concerning radio. The three questions form the basis of the following outline of the period between the formation of the Radio Corporation of America in 1919 and the formation of the National Broadcasting Company in 1926.

   I. Who will pay the bills?
      A. Initial organization of RCA
         1. "Radio group" (GE and Westinghouse) to manufacture and sell sets
         2. "Telephone group" (AT&T and Western Electric) to
            a. Sell and (or) lease transmitters
            b. Control all telephone lines used for any purpose
      B. Income philosophies differ and groups seek a balance.
         1. Initial set sales give the radio group an early advantage.
         2. Telephone group sells commercials and forges ahead in income.
      C. AT&T "quits while ahead" and reverts to telephone business.
      D. Radio group uses commercial sales as primary source of income.
  II. How can a quality service be provided?

[4] At about this time, first in 1916 and then in 1920, David Sarnoff, a young engineer working for American Marconi and later for RCA, made a remarkable series of predictions concerning the development of this new service. These can be found in *History of Radio to 1926*, by Gleason Archer (New York: The American Historical Society, 1938), pp. 112–113 and 189, and in the more recent *A Tower in Babel*, by Erik Barnouw, New York: Oxford University Press, 1966, pp. 78 and 79.

    A. Telephone group develops the principle of "networking."
    B. Radio group tries to counter with inferior telegraph lines.
    C. AT&T withdraws and radio group has access to telephone lines.
    D. NBC begins on November 15, 1926.
       1. NBC Red—based on the telephone group network
       2. NBC Blue—based on the radio group network
    E. The concept of a centralized network service, with costs spread among many stations, is adopted as the best means of providing a quality service.
III. What shall be the Federal relationship to broadcasting?
    A. 1910 Wireless Ship Act
    B. 1912 Act to license stations and operators
    C. Secretary of Commerce Hoover opens two "limited commercial" frequencies in 1921.
    D. Another frequency authorized in 1922 as number of stations rises to 564.
    E. The breakdown of regulation:
       1. The Court of Appeals in the District of Columbia rules that the Secretary of Commerce must grant a license to all applicants (1923).
       2. A District Court in Illinois rules that the Secretary has no right to assign wavelengths (1926).
       3. The U.S. Attorney General rules that the act of 1912 is completely inadequate to regulate the broadcasting service.
    F. The Radio Act of 1927 and the Federal Radio Commission
    G. The Communications Act of 1934 and the Federal Communications Commission

By 1927, then, the basic structure of a broadcasting service in the United States had evolved. The system would support itself through the sale of time; a strong backbone of programming would be provided by the networks; and the entire system would be regulated by the federal government through the Federal Radio Commission (later the Federal Communications Commission). With stability and income assured, radio developed rapidly and for more than 20 years was the king of the electronic media.

The only practical way of recapturing the spirit of the early days of radio is to use recorded highlights of actual programs. Probably the best known and most easily available of these collections is that distributed by Longines and hosted by Jack Benny and Frank Knight. Another source of recorded radio programs is Radio Yesteryear, Box H, Croton-on-Hudson, New York 10520. For $1.00 this organization offers an excellent catalog of over 100 pages offering programs at $10.00 an hour. The library under development at the headquarters of the National Association of Broadcasters, 1771 N St. N.W., Washington, D.C. 20036 will also be a rich source of such material.

The period between 1927 and 1948 was interesting historically, of course, and included the evolution of an industry structure that was changed very little by the advent of television. This aspect of history is better considered as a part of the present structure of the industry, however, and will be included in the next section.

An instructor can cover the highlights of this period by focusing on four important trends or events: (1) the growth of the networks, (2) the press-radio conflict, (3) the conflicts with the American Society of Composers, Authors and Publishers (ASCAP) and the American Federation of Musicians (AFM), and (4) the growth of advertiser control.

After 1948, network radio began to feel the effect of television and the decline of a national service began. National radio network sales dropped from a peak of $133,671,834 in 1948 to a low of $35,026,000 in 1960.[5] This has climbed back to an estimated $52 million in 1970, but network radio still lags far behind network television in total sales.

In 1948 some were predicting that radio would be swamped by television and eliminated as a service. While network sales fell, however, the slack was more than taken up by national nonnetwork and local sales and total radio time sales rose steadily from $416,720,279 to over an estimated $1 billion in 1969.

At the same time, the number of stations on the air jumped from 866 in 1945 to 4276 (including 2070 FM stations) in 1970. In other words, an explosive growth in the number and strength of local radio stations has made it possible for radio to remain as a strong service and grow with the economy. Radio has evolved with the times to become an essentially background service that moves quickly to the foreground in times of emergency.

HISTORY OF TELEVISION

Just as the development of radio can be said to have begun with the work of Gugliemo Marconi, the beginnings of the growth of television as we know it can be traced to the work of Vladimir Zworykin. This brilliant RCA engineer developed the first all-electronic scanning tube in 1923 and thus opened the door to the development of a national service. This door, however, opened very slowly and the first really significant progress toward a commercial television system was not made until 1940. Accordingly, this outline of the history of television begins in that year.

I. The FCC hearings on television standards of 1940
  A. Lines per picture—525
  B. Frames per second—30 complete frames
  C. Number and frequency of channels—13 in "Very High Frequency" (VHF)
  D. Color or black and white—black and white first
II. The FCC and channel allocations
  A. Primary goals of the Commission in allocating channels to communities

[5] All figures are drawn from *Broadcasting*, January 26, 1970, 78 (4):29.

        1. All areas should have at least one service.
        2. The largest possible number of communities should have a local
           television station.
        3. Multiple service should be available to as many areas as possible.
     B. Conflicts between VHF and UHF interests
     C. The 1945 allocations open the way for a commercial service
     D. The "Freeze" (September 1948 to June 1952) imposed by the FCC
     E. The 1952 allocations (The Fifth Report and Order) and UHF
 III. Color television development through CBS and RCA
 IV. Cable television (discussed in detail in the next section; see p. 228)

Television grew even more rapidly than had radio because it adopted the basic structure and business procedures developed by radio networks; because many program formats and programs themselves transferred directly to television; and because the energies of most of those who had been working with radio shifted to television. In the next section we consider the structure of the broadcasting industry as it has evolved.

The best single source for the history of broadcasting from its beginnings to the present is a three-volume series written by Erik Barnouw.

BARNOUW, ERIK, A Tower in Babel, New York: Oxford Univ. Press, 1966.
BARNOUW, ERIK, The Golden Web, New York: Oxford Univ. Press, 1968.
BARNOUW, ERIK, The Image Empire, New York: Oxford Univ. Press, 1970.

Many other publications present a part of this history in great detail. Some of the most valuable of these are

ARCHER, GLEASON L., Big Business and Radio, New York: American Historical Society, 1939.
ARCHER, GLEASON L., History of Radio: to 1926, New York: American Historical Society, 1938.
BANNING, WILLIAM PECK, Commercial Broadcasting Pioneer: The WEAF Experiment, 1922–1926, Cambridge, Mass.: Harvard University Press, 1946.
BLUM, DANIEL C., A Pictorial History of Television, Philadelphia: Chilton, 1959.
BUXTON, FRANK AND OWEN, BILL, Radio's Golden Age: The Programs and the Personalities, New York: Easton Valley Press, 1966.
GROSS, BEN, I Looked and Listened, New York: Random House, 1954.
HARMON, JIM, The Great Radio Heroes, Garden City, N.Y.: Doubleday, 1967.
SCHMECKEBIER, LAURENCE F., The Federal Radio Commission, Washington, D.C.: Brookings Institution, 1932.
STEELE, IRVING, A Pictorial History of Radio, New York: Citadel, 1960.
United States House of Representatives, Committee on Interstate and Foreign Commerce, Regulation of Broadcasting, 85th Congress, 2nd session, 1958. This is often referred to as "The McMahon Report."

Certain other publications include a summary of the history of broadcasting as a part of an overview of the industry or an attempt to make a point. Some of these books that make good basic texts are starred.

BARNOUW, ERIK, *Mass Communication*, New York: Holt, Rinehart & Winston, 1956.

CHESTER, GIRAUD, GARRISON, GARNETT R., AND WILLIS, EDGAR E., *Television and Radio*, New York: Appleton-Century-Crofts, 1963.*

HEAD, SYDNEY W., *Broadcasting in America*, Boston: Houghton Mifflin, 1971.*

SIEPMANN, CHARLES A., *Radio, Television and Society*, New York: Oxford Univ. Press, 1950.

SKORNIA, HARRY T., *Television and Society*, New York: McGraw-Hill, 1965.

SUMMERS, HARRISON B. AND SUMMERS, ROBERT E., *Broadcasting and the Public*, Belmont, Calif.: Wadsworth, 1966.*

United States House of Representatives, Committee on Interstate and Foreign Commerce, *Network Broadcasting*, 85th Congress, 2nd session, 1958. This is often referred to as "The Barrow Report."

WHITE, LLEWELLYN, *The American Radio*, Chicago: Univ. of Chicago Press, 1947.

Student Assignments

1. Study the influence of an important man in the early history of broadcasting and prepare a report to be read to the class. Some possibilities are Gugliemo Marconi, Heinrich Hertz, Dr. Ernst Alexanderson, J. Ambrose Fleming, Lee DeForest, Owen Young, David Sarnoff, Dr. Frank Conrad, Herbert Hoover (as related to radio), Vladimir Zworykin, Dr. John Brinkley, Dr. Edwin Armstrong, Father Charles Coughlin, H. V. Kaltenbourne, George Washington Hill, and William Paley.

2. Prepare a report on one of the following historical events:
   a. The sinking of the "Titanic."
   b. The conflicts between the "radio" and "telephone" groups over the sale of advertising time and networking.
   c. The details of the settlement which led to the formation of NBC.
   d. The formation of CBS, the Mutual Broadcasting Co., ABC, or the Dumont net.
   e. The 1910 Wireless Ship Act and the 1912 act relating to licensing.
   f. The breakdown of regulation under the 1912 act.
   g. The formation and activities of the Federal Radio Commission.
   h. The formation of the Federal Communications Commission.
   i. The "press-radio" battle.
   j. Radio's struggles with ASCAP.
   k. Radio's struggles with the AFM.
   l. The growth of advertiser control over network radio programming.
   m. The impact of television on radio in the late 1940s and early 1950s.
   n. The FCC "freeze" of 1948–1952.
   o. The "UHF problem."

THE STRUCTURE OF THE BROADCASTING INDUSTRY

Strictly speaking, the broadcasting "industry" can be divided into six basic components:[6] (1) the advertiser and advertising agency, (2) the networks, (3) the local stations, (4) independent program producers, (5) national station representatives, and (6) interconnection and the telephone company.

[6] This system of classification of "the component operations of the broadcasting service" is drawn from "The Barrow Report," mentioned on p. 214 above, pp. 37–53.

It is difficult to discuss the structure of broadcasting without reference to the Federal Communications Commission. Thus, even though the Commission cannot be considered a part of the broadcasting industry *per se*, it will be considered here. This makes a seventh component: (7) the Federal Communications Commission.

In recent years two additional entities of significance have developed in, or on the edges, of the industry. These must be added to the list if students are to understand the business of broadcasting. They are (8) community antenna systems (CATV) and (9) public broadcasting.

Some notes on each of these nine broad areas follow, with references and assignments.

The Advertiser and the Agency

Most beginning students are unaware of the complex relationships between the advertiser, his agency, and the station and (or) network. Starting with the advertiser and agency helps clear this up and leads naturally to a discussion of networks and stations. Major points which should be covered are

I. Advertiser-agency relationships
   A. Agency services
   B. Method of payment
   C. Research functions
   D. Media buying services
II. Types of program sponsorship (How the message is connected with a *program.*)
   A. Full sponsorship
   B. Partial sponsorship
   C. Participating sponsorship
   D. Adjacencies
III. Types of advertising (How the message is placed in a *market.*)
   A. Network
   B. National spot
   C. Local

The most widely used text on advertising still seems to be *Successful Television and Radio Advertising*, by Seehafer and Laemmar (see the references below), in spite of its 1959 publication date. A good, basic bibliography would also include the following:

BELLAIRE, ARTHUR, *Television Advertising*, New York: Harper & Row, 1959.
PECK, WILLIAM A., *The Anatomy of Local Radio-TV Copy*, Blue Ridge Summit, Pa.: TAB Books, 1965.
SEEHAFER, E. F. AND LAEMMAR, J. W., *Successful Television and Radio Advertising*, New York: McGraw-Hill, 1959.
WAINWRIGHT, CHARLES A., *The Television Copywriter*, New York: Hastings House, 1966.

ZACHER, ROBERT V., *Advertising Techniques and Management*, Homewood, Ill.: Irwin Press, 1961.

Section I in the outline above, obviously, is most amenable to expansion or contraction. Some instructors may wish simply to devote a lecture or two to the nature of the agency and its relationship to clients and stations. Others may wish to contact a local agency and invite a speaker to cover the topic.[7] Still others may wish to dig more deeply and assign projects to their students.

Student Assignments

1. Select a local store that advertises heavily in local newspapers. Instruct students to study the newspaper ads over a period of a week or two and try to determine immediate and long-range goals of the advertiser. (If possible, try to check conclusions by talking with the individual in the store who is responsible for the advertising.) With these goals in mind, ask students to develop a radio and (or) television campaign for the client. They should develop a theme—or adapt the current theme to the media in use—and write some sample copy.
2. Invite a representative of a local advertising agency to class and ask him to outline an actual problem his organization is facing, together with a 1-year budget for radio and television. With this budget, the data supplied about the product, the objective, and the prospects, ask the class to (a) recommend a radio-television time sale purchase plan for the client and (b) prepare sample 1-minute radio and (or) television commercials. In developing such a project, it is convenient to divide the class into committees which include: account executive (with overall responsibility, integration, and formal presentation to the agency), time buying—radio; time buying—TV; radio writing; and television writing.
3. Choose a product in which there is little real difference between brands (that is, milk, gasoline, bread, etc.) and ask each member of the class to rough out an idea for a radio and television campaign designed to introduce a new brand of this product, complete with at least one 30-second and one 60-second radio and (or) television commercial.

The Networks

As they did with radio, networks have become the backbone of television programming. Although local stations make most of their money from local and national spot advertising, the network programs provide the prestige offerings needed to build an audience.

The relationships between local stations and networks have changed a great deal since the early days of radio. The most comprehensive survey of

[7] The American Association of Advertising Agencies maintains an Agency-Educator Committee. The activities of this group vary according to its membership from year to year, but they usually include the distribution of papers of interest, the dispatch of "task-forces" of agency personnel to interested colleges or universities for intensive educational sessions, and, at least in the central division, provision of opportunities for faculty internships during the summer. For up-to-date information, contact the AAAA at 200 Park Avenue, New York, 10017.

the evolution of this relationship from the beginnings of networks to 1958 is found in the "Barrow Report."[8] This evolution has continued since 1958, however. Since this time FCC rulings and proposed rulings relating to option time, affiliation practices, network ownership and syndication of programs, and the hours of time available for network programming have continued to weaken the relative degree of network influence and control over affiliates. Unfortunately, the history of this further evolution has yet to be written. Interested teachers and students must trace it through reports in the trade press.

Some basics have remained constant:

I. Network functions
   A. Sale of affiliate time to network advertisers
   B. Production and (or) supply of a program service
   C. Provision of interconnection facilities through AT&T
II. Network operations
   A. Owned and operated stations
   B. Affiliate relationships
     1. Amount and method of payment to stations
     2. Other contract provisions
     3. Program selection by affiliates
       a. Right of first call
       b. Delayed broadcasts
       c. Network alternatives to delayed broadcasts
   C. The evolution of network-advertiser relationships
   D. Network program planning and scheduling procedures
   E. Program production by networks
   F. Program syndication by networks
   G. Revenues and expenses

No single book dealing exclusively with the area is available. Among those covered in the previous bibliography[9] *The Golden Web*, the second volume of the Erik Barnouw trilogy, covers the development of the networks from 1933 to 1953 with a slight antibusiness bias the instructor may wish to balance. *Television and Radio* by Chester, Garrison, and Willis, *Broadcasting in America* by Head, and *Broadcasting and the Public* by Summers and Summers each contain some information about the networks and their relationship with affiliates. *Broadcast Management* by Ward Quall and Leo Martin (Hastings House, 1968) also includes a brief discussion of network television from the point of view of the station manager.

Student Assignments

1. Using either the "Barrow Report" or *The Golden Web* as a baseline, dig through the trade press and update network practices in one of the following areas:
   a. Affiliation contracts

[8] See p. 214 above.
[9] See pp. 213 to 214 above.

   b. Option time
   c. The "Right of First Call" and territorial exclusivity
   d. Network rates
   e. Network compensation patterns
   f. The "must buy" pattern
   g. Network representation of stations in national spot sales
   h. Network production and ownership of programs
   i. Network syndication of "off-net" programs
   j. Time available to stations for network programming
   k. Specific affiliation problems relating to radio
   l. Network ownership of local stations
2. Prepare a report on the history of regional and special purpose networks.
3. Prepare a report on the unsuccessful "Overmeyer" network (or Dumont).
4. Prepare a report on educational networks—national, state, and (or) regional.

The Local Station

Although it is not difficult to locate information on the organization, policies, programming, and so on of local stations, the fact that these stations are local provides another opportunity to bring in a speaker from the business itself. Almost every market has at least one station whose management would be happy to send a representative to speak to broadcasting classes. In large markets (the top 50) a call to the station public relations department should produce a speaker. In smaller markets a call and (or) a visit to the station manager should do the job.[10]

These visits work to the benefit of the student, the teacher, and the stations themselves, but they require preparation to make them effective. Students should have enough background to understand the speaker, the instructor should have a clear idea of what he wishes to accomplish, and the broadcaster must know what is expected of him.

Student preparation includes some of the basics of station organization.

   I. Basic station organization
      A. Programming
      B. Sales
      C. Engineering
      D. Management
  II. Station-audience relationships
      A. Radio
         1. Target audiences
         2. Feedback (surveys, letters, talk programs, etc.)
         3. Station formats

[10] The Association for Professional Broadcasting Education maintains a standing committee called the State Association Liaison Committee which has been established to help open the channels of communication between broadcast educators, state associations of commercial broadcasters, and local stations. For information about this committee, contact Dr. Harold Niven, Executive Secretary, APBE, 1771 N St. N.W., Washington, D.C. 20036.

      B. Television
         1. Audience flow
         2. Network and local programming decisions
         3. Feedback
         4. Community "image"
III. Station-advertiser relationships
    (Review material on pp. 215 and 216.)
IV. Station-network relationships
    (Review material on pp. 216 and 218.)
 V. Station-FCC relationships
      A. License renewal requirements
      B. FCC influences on programming
      C. Section 315 of the Communications Act of 1934 and politics
      D. The Fairness Doctrine
      E. Ownership restrictions, reports, etc.
      F. Punishment and fines

The goals of the instructor in planning a visit will be influenced by the specialty of the person designated by the station as well as by weaknesses in the instructor's own background. In many cases, the visitor will ask what should be discussed. Be prepared to be as specific as possible ("How does your radio station arrive at and control its music policy?" "How does the program director at your TV station put together his program schedule each year?"). The absence of such questions can lead to little more than a promotional speech on the glories of WXXX.

It is implied, of course, that the instructor and the visitor should communicate with each other in some way before the class meeting. Many professional broadcasters are interested in the texts used, and it is often helpful to send a copy along well in advance of the visit—complete with some indication of the chapters the students will have covered. If this is impossible, meet the guest for lunch, drop by his office, or, at least, call him to discuss what he is going to present.

In many cases it is also possible to arrange for a visit to a local station. Experience indicates that students find these interesting and a welcome break from routine. It also indicates that their educational value is limited unless the class is very small and (or) the station is willing to disrupt operations enough to allow for adequate explanation of what is going on.

A well-prepared visit can be of some value, however, especially at the end of a semester or unit. If the visit can be scheduled when live production is going on, a visit to a television station is usually of great interest. A visit to the favorite radio station of a large portion of the class can also be helpful—particularly so if one of the local personalities is willing to meet with the class, discuss his work and, if he is skilled, demonstrate some of his production work.

The best known books in the field are probably

LAWTON, SHERMAN P., *The Modern Broadcaster*, New York: Harper & Row, 1961.
QUALL, WARD L. AND MARTIN, LEO, *Broadcast Management*, New York: Hastings House, 1968.
REINSCH, J. LEONARD AND ELLIS, ELMO I., *Radio Station Management*, New York: Harper & Row, 1960.
ROE, YALE (ED.), *Television Station Management*, New York: Hastings House, 1964.

TAB Books, a publisher located in Blue Ridge Summit, Pa. 17214, is publishing a series of books on all aspects of broadcasting. These are generally "how-to" books written for professional broadcasters by other broadcasters. Their organization and style sometimes leave something to be desired and most of them are quite expensive. On the other hand, they are often more practical and directly applicable than more "academic" books. Some appropriate titles are

CODDINGTON, ROBERT H., *Modern Radio Broadcasting*, 1970.
ETKIN, HARRY A., *AM/FM Broadcast Station Planning Guide*, 1970.
HOFFER, JAY, *Managing Today's Radio Station*, 1968.
ROBINSON, SOL, *Broadcast Station Operating Guide*, 1968.

Broadcast journalism is an important area of consideration, and many colleges and universities offer one or more courses in the area. One of the limitations of this chapter is the caveat that "no production skills or elements are included and no equipment is needed." Under these restrictions, the instructor's major responsibility is to update his students as to the status of broadcast journalism since the "press-radio war," show its importance to present day broadcasting, and touch on news operation and organization on both the local and network levels.
Some of the best texts in the field are

ATKINS, JIM, JR. AND WILLETTE, LEO, *Filming TV News and Documentaries*, Philadelphia: Chilton, 1965.
BLEUM, A. WILLIAM, *Documentary in American Television*, New York: Hastings House, 1964.
DARY, DAVID, *Radio News Handbook*, Blue Ridge Summit, Pa.: TAB Books, 1967.
GREEN, MAURY, *Television News*, Belmont, Calif.: Wadsworth, 1969.
WOOD, A. WILLIAM, *Electronic Journalism*, New York: Columbia Univ. Press, 1967.

Student Assignments

1. Break the class into groups and require each group to make an intensive study of the programming of a local radio station, to include as a minimum:
   a. An evaluation of the target audience in the morning, afternoon, and evening hours.
   b. The basic format of the station (for example, contemporary, MOR, all-news).

c. An analysis of the balance between music and other programming.[11]
d. An evaluation of the job the station is doing in serving its public.
2. Assign similar studies of television stations in the area. The questions of target audience and format are less important here, while program balance is of greater importance.
3. During a local, statewide, or national election campaign, ask students to study the use of radio and television by key candidates, trying to determine how much emphasis each places on radio and television as distinct from other media and exploring their techniques (i.e., the length and frequency of programs and[or] spots, types of programming used, etc.).
4. Ask students to study the Fairness Doctrine and report on the rights of the public and stations under the requirements of this Doctrine.

Independent Program Producers

Since 1958, when the writers of the "Barrow Report"[12] found independent program producers to be "a major component of the television broadcast industry," these producers have experienced some lean years as the television networks grew to dominate the production of programs. Action by the FCC in 1970, however, may put new life into this aspect of the business. Briefly, independent program activities in television break into three headings (radio is considered later):

1. The production and (or) distribution of programs, on film or videotape, to advertisers or local stations for nonnetwork programming. This category includes both the distribution of programs made exclusively for syndication and off-network programs that are put into syndication after their network run. It does *not* include the distribution of feature films made originally for theatrical use and sold to television.

During the 1960s, off-network programs came to dominate the syndication market and the production of "first-run" syndicated products fell off sharply.

In 1970, however, the FCC ruled that networks would be restricted to three hours of programming an evening between the prime-time hours of 7 P.M. to 11 P.M., EST, effective October 1, 1971. As of October 1, 1972, stations will be prohibited from filling this time with off-network productions or movies previously shown by networks in the market. This will open 30 minutes an evening for programming by independents and the syndication market should loosen up somewhat.

2. The television networks themselves dominate the production of the programs they use, either through their own production companies or by

[11] Any discussion of program balance is aided by reference to an FCC policy statement dated August 3, 1960 which includes a statement of "the major elements [of programming] usually necessary to meet the public interest, needs and desires." The complete text of this important policy statement is included as Appendix VII of *Broadcasting and Government* by Walter B. Emery, E. Lansing, Mich.: Michigan State University Press, 1971, pp. 505–517, or in *Documents of American Broadcasting*, Frank J. Kahn (ed.), New York: Appleton-Century-Crofts, 1968, pp. 207–223.
[12] See p. 214 above.

controlling the production of others. Some of the major "independent" producers in this category—most of whom receive the bulk of their financing from the networks—are Sheldon Leonard Enterprises, Paramount Television, Screen Gems, Inc., and Twentieth-Century Fox. These and other producers will continue to produce for the networks, and, with more local time possibly opening up, may also turn to the production of first run material for local syndication.

3. In the mid-fifties, many major motion picture studios dropped their restrictions on the release of their features to television and large numbers of these films were made available for sale or lease to local stations. For many years these films were a programming bonanza as the stations worked their way through an enormous backlog of films from the 1930s, 1940s, and 1950s. The number of features available was finite, however, and the number of hours devoted to "old movies" has declined on local stations in recent years.

Another factor contributing to the decline of local use of feature films is the increasing use of these films by networks. Since the advent of NBC's "Saturday Night at the Movies" in 1961–1962, the floodgate has been opened and the night without a network movie is now rare. With the nets siphoning off the best and most recent features, and showing them several times before releasing them for syndication, the supply of salable features for local use has continued to shrink.

An examination of the advertisements in any recent issue of *Broadcasting* will demonstrate that packages of feature films are still being sold, however. These, plus older packages, will continue to hold a place in local television schedules, but the heyday of "Million-Dollar Movies" seems to be over.

Radio also has its independent program producers, but the variety is not so great as in television. Record companies are, of course, the most important such producers, but they look upon radio more as a promoter than a buyer of their product. Indeed, most companies supply records free or at greatly reduced prices.

Other production sources do exist. Automated stations can now purchase complete packages of taped music to fill their broadcast day—with provision made for the insertion of commercials, local and (or) network news, and live segments. Also available is a broad spectrum of short (1- to 5-minute) feature series which can be purchased and dropped into the schedule where the program director wishes. These include comedy, news, and information, opinion and analysis, items of interest to women, educational features and many other varieties.

With one exception, longer features have met with little success in recent years, in spite of occasional efforts to revive an interest in radio drama and the like. The exception has been a few longer radio "talk" programs like "The Manion Forum" and "Life-Line." These longer programs have become an exception, however, and those involved in radio programming think primarily in terms of 3- to 5-minute units of programming for a fluid and constantly changing radio audience.

It is almost impossible to present a bibliography for this aspect of broadcasting. Most of the basic texts already mentioned summarize the activities of independent program producers, and of these the Summers and Summers book seems to devote the most attention to programming and program sources. The instructor must update, however, by paying constant attention to the trade press.

The projects that seem to do the best job of making students aware of the varied sources of program material are those in which the students are asked to make a detailed study of a programming day, or of portions of a day spread across a week.

Student Assignments

1. Select a local television station and assign various portions of a day or week to members of the class—taking care that no one is fortunate enough to receive a solid block of network time. Ask each student to record each program in his time period and identify the source.

SAMPLE REPORT FORM

Name: _____ Station: _____

Time Period: _____ Date: _____

Start Time   Name of Program   Source   Produced By

(A major difficulty here, of course, is the problem of teaching how to identify the sources of programming. Start with the basic network schedule, printed periodically in *Broadcasting*. The students can spot preemptions and delays on their local stations. Local programming of theatrical films can be identified by reference to the network schedule and the fact that the networks identify their features carefully and constantly. Local productions, either live or on tape, will be obvious. What is left on the schedule should be syndicated material. Many students will be able to identify off-network syndication by memory, but warn them to check programs thus identified against daytime feeds of re-runs by the nets themselves. Other sources of syndication will be identified by the closing credits.)

2. Select a local radio station and assign portions of the day or week to students as above. Ask each student to keep a record of each program unit in his time period and identify the source.

(Because of the absence of visual cues, the identification of the source of many radio programs may be more difficult than is the case in television. Generally speaking, though, a "programming unit" will consist of either recorded music, local-live, local-recorded—often difficult to identify without a log—network as scheduled, network delays—also difficult to identify without a log—or syndicated programs.)

National Station Representatives

In explaining the role of the station "rep" the instructor should consider:

I. The nature of national spot advertising (a review)
II. The relationship between local stations and station representatives
    A. Territorial agreements
    B. Exclusivity within markets
    C. Information to be supplied by the station
    D. Services expected from the representative firm
    E. Payment procedures
III. The relationship between national and regional agencies and rep firms
IV. Types of advertising placed on local stations
    A. Adjacencies
    B. Sponsorship of syndicated programs
    C. Participating spots

The "Barrow Report"[13] includes an excellent summary of this phase of broadcasting and the presentation in the Seehafer and Laemmar book on radio and television advertising[14] is equally good. Any basic text in the field will also include some information.

Few survey courses include the time necessary for a significant project in this area. For those who do have the time, however, student progress to this point will have prepared the class for a project in which: (1) The class is divided into groups representing an advertising agency, at least two stations, and a rep firm for each station. (2) The agency studies the needs of an advertiser and prepares a tentative campaign with budgeting percentages applied to various media. (3) The stations prepare the material needed by a rep firm to sell their time to the agency. (4) The rep firms prepare a presentation in an effort to sell their client's time to the agency.

Interconnection and AT&T

From the day in 1926 when the American Telephone and Telegraph Company withdrew from active participation in broadcasting to the present, network interconnection has meant AT&T. It provided the lines that made network radio possible and it constructed the microwave and coaxial

[13] See p. 214 above.
[14] See p. 215 above.

networks necessary for television networks. This monopoly has been supervised by the FCC, which has the authority to regulate rates.

Assuming that much of the material relating to AT&T and radio has already been covered in a review of broadcasting history, here are some additional points that should be covered.

I. The nature of network—AT&T contracts
   A. Payment schedules
   B. AT&T responsibilities for service
II. Implications of the AT&T monopoly
   A. The effects of TV net expansion on line charges
   B. The effects of AT&T charges on network service
   C. The effects of AT&T charges on small and(or) remote stations
III. The relationship between AT&T and CATV
IV. Proposals for satellite interconnection

Although most of the material needed here is in the public record, locating it may be difficult. The "Barrow Report"[15] gives some historical information and outlines the situation as of 1958. Rate increases since then have changed the picture somewhat and new proposals before the FCC may change it even further. Instructors with access to a reasonably complete library of Government documents should check

Annual Reports of the Federal Communications Commission, Washington, D.C.: U.S. Government Printing Office.
Decisions and Reports of the Federal Communications Commission of the United States, Washington, D.C.: U.S. Government Printing Office.
Statistics of Communications Common Carriers, Washington, D.C.: U.S. Government Printing Office.

The only feasible student projects in this subject area would be individual reports on topics noted in the outline above.

The Federal Communications Commission

As noted in the introduction to this section, the FCC cannot really be considered a part of the broadcasting industry. As the regulatory agency designated watchdog of the industry by Congress, however, it is impossible to ignore.

A full study of the FCC and its organization, goals, accomplishments, and failures can take almost as much time as the instructor wishes to devote. Some basic points are:

I. The creation of the Federal Communications Commission
   A. The demise of the Federal Radio Commission
   B. The rationale behind the creation of the new commission

[15] See p. 214 above.

C. The organization and responsibilities of the commission today
II. The Communications Act of 1934
   A. Stated purposes of the act
   B. Public interest standard to be applied to the broadcast service
   C. Fundamental premise of the Act (drawn from the "Barrow Report"):[16]
      "The right of the public to service is superior to the right of any licensee
      to make use of any frequency or channel for his own private purposes."
III. The FCC in operation
   A. Scope and limits of its power
   B. General powers relating to broadcasting
   C. Extent and nature of the licensing power
   D. General areas of commission concern
      1. Keeping the industry competitive
      2. Diversification of ownership and control
      3. Affirmation of the ultimate responsibility of the licensee for programming
   E. Recent commission actions and proposals
      1. Changes in the "duopoly" rules
      2. Increased fee schedule
      3. Fair employment obligations of licensees
      4. Restrictions in prime-time access by networks
      5. Changes in multiple ownership rules leading to divestiture
      6. Domestic satellite ownership policies
      7. Regulation of CATV
      8. Increased fining authority

The best single book available in this area is *Broadcasting and Government* by Walter B. Emery (E. Lansing, Mich.: Michigan State Univ. Press, 1971). Other books of interest include:

CHAFEE, ZECHARIAH, JR., *Government and Mass Communications*, Chicago: Univ. of Chicago Press, 1947.

COONS, JOHN E., *Freedom and Responsibility in Broadcasting*, Evanston, Ill.: Northwestern Univ. Press, 1961.

EDELMAN, MURRAY, *Licensing of Radio Services in the United States, 1927–1947*, Urbana, Ill.: Univ. of Illinois Press, 1950.

Federal Communications Commission, *Annual Reports*, Washington, D.C.: U.S. Government Printing Office.

Federal Communications Commission, *Federal Communications Commission Reports*, Washington, D.C.: U.S. Government Printing Office.

Federal Communications Commission, *How to Apply for a Broadcast Station* (Information Bulletin No. 1-B), Washington, D.C.: U.S. Government Printing Office, 1970.

Federal Communications Commission, *Rules and Regulations*, Washington, D.C.: U.S. Government Printing Office, 1968.

GILMOR, DONALD M. AND BARRON, JEROME A., *Mass Communication Law: Cases and Comment*, St. Paul, Minn.: Western Publishing Company, 1969.

KAHN, FRANK J., *Documents of American Broadcasting*, New York: Appleton-Century-Crofts, 1969.

[16] See p. 214 above.

KITTROSS, JOHN M. AND HARWOOD, KENNETH, *Free and Fair: Courtroom Access and the Fairness Doctrine*, Philadelphia: The Association for Professional Broadcasting Education, 1970.

LANDIS, JAMES M., *Report on Regulatory Agencies to the President-Elect*, Washington, D.C.: U.S. Government Printing Office, 1960.

SMEAD, ELMER A., *Freedom of Speech by Radio and Television*, Washington, D.C.: Public Affairs Press, 1959.

See also the "McMahon Report" referred to on p. 213 and the "Barrow Report" referred to on p. 232.

Special Sources. 1. Pike and Fischer, *Radio Regulations* (1945—) is the standard, comprehensive reference work, maintained to date with weekly reports on all phases of the regulation of radio and television by federal administrative agencies and the courts. The service is expensive, but valuable, and should be in the library of any college or university with a broadcasting sequence. Be sure to check the Law Library before determining that the series is not available. For further information contact Pike and Fischer, Inc., 1726 M St. N.W., Washington, D.C. 20036.

2. Each annual issue of the *Broadcasting Yearbook* (see the bibliography of periodicals on p. 232) includes a section called "Broadcast Primer." Usually written by someone with a prior connection with the FCC, this primer is a summary of the evolution of broadcasting from the point of view of the FCC. It can be a valuable source of information.

3. Each issue of the *Yearbook* also includes selected sections of the "FCC Rules Regulating Radio-Television," amended to September of the year prior to publication with the cooperation of Pike and Fischer, Inc.

4. Those interested can contact the Office of Reports and Information, FCC, 1919 M St. N.W., Washington, D.C. 20554 and ask to be included on the mailing list for Public Notices and News Reports. These include summaries of many Commission actions of general interest.

Student Assignments

1. Report on the influence of the FCC on radio and television programming.
2. Report on the evolution of the Fairness Doctrine.
3. Report on provisions and applications of Section 315 of the FCA of 1934.
4. Report on Commission use of its punative powers.
5. Report on definitions and applications of the "public interest, convenience and necessity," and "public service" standards.
6. Report on the evolution of the Commission attitude toward editorializing.
7. Prepare a summary of FCC efforts to keep the industry competitive.
8. Prepare a summary of FCC efforts to diversify ownership and control.
9. Prepare a summary of FCC efforts to affirm licensee responsibility.
10. Report on the Commission and UHF.
11. Report on the Commission and color television.
12. Report on the Commission and pay-television.
13. Report on the Commission and FM broadcasting.
14. Report on the Commission and CATV.

15. Report on the Commission and its critics.
16. How to get a license or a renewal from the commission.
17. Report on the Commission and the "local institution" concept.

Community Antenna Television[17]

The CATV situation is so fluid at this writing that it is impossible to predict what form the industry will have taken by the time this book appears. Community Antenna Television originated in 1950 primarily as a "master antenna" service for communities not served by an adequate television signal. The first systems simply erected large, high-gain antennas, installed equipment to clean up and amplify the signals received, and distributed these signals by cable to those willing to pay a small monthly fee. In the 20 years since that time, the number of such systems has grown to over 2000, serving more than 3-million homes.

In addition to this numerical growth, many systems have broadened their services by importing the signals of educational and independent stations from one or two thousand miles away; importing signals from distant A.M. and F.M. stations for background to "news and weather" channels which do nothing but scan weather dials, printed forecasts, and news summaries; originating local programming of their own; and selling commercial time. CATV interests also began to seek franchises in major markets like New York and Philadelphia, arguing that they can provide more stations and a clearer picture.

By 1966 the FCC had decided that it had the right to regulate all CATV systems, and this decision was upheld by the Supreme Court in 1968. Since that time the commission has wrestled with a series of proposals concerning the ground rules it should impose on CATV, but at this writing, no decision had been reached. Thus it is impossible to speak with any authority about the form or growth potential of CATV.

The question of pay-television is also a consideration here. Whereas CATV systems charge subscribers a blanket monthly fee for access to everything on the system, pay-TV systems charge on a per-program basis. Signals, either over the air or on cable, are scrambled in some manner and the subscriber pays for the operation of an "unscrambler" for those programs he wishes to see.

After years of experimentation, the commission authorized pay-television in December of 1968. Several restrictions were imposed: (1)Pay-TV was allowed only in communities presently served (within the Grade-A con-

---

[17] Much of the historical information in this section is drawn from Report 219 of the Freedom of Information Center, School of Journalism, University of Missouri, Columbia, Mo., entitled "CATV: Enter the FCC," and dated April, 1969. These reports are mailed regularly to members of the Freedom of Information Center and are often of great value to the broadcast educator. For further information, contact Dr. Paul Fisher, Director of the Center, at the above address.

tours) of five commercial stations, four of which must be in operation. (2) Pay-TV stations are required to broadcast a minimum number of nonsubscription hours each day. (3) They cannot show feature films which have been run in the market on a first-run basis more than 2 years previously. (4) Commercials, series-type programs with interconnected plots, and sports events carried regularly on a free basis during the past 2 years would also be forbidden.

As was the case with CATV, the feature of pay-television is so clouded at this time that no prediction is possible. The interested instructor will have to depend on the trade press for a reasonable updating.

No real bibliography on these two subjects is possible, but the National Cable Television Association, Inc. (NCTA) distributes a membership bulletin regularly, and this is available to interested instructors in the broadcast field. Contact NCTA at One Farragut Square South, 1634 Eye St. N.W., Washington, D.C. for further information. Also of interest is *Television and the Wired City,* Herbert W. Land Associates, Inc., Washington, D.C.: National Association of Broadcasters, 1968.

The best project for this subject would be a visit to a local CATV or pay-television system, if one is available. All the recommendations and admonitions concerning a visit to a local station (see pp. 218–219) apply here.

Public Broadcasting

Public broadcasting, as a concept, and the Corporation for Public Broadcasting, are lineal descendants of what were known for years as Educational Radio and Educational Television. The history of educational broadcasting from its early days to 1960 is nicely summarized in *Channels of Learning*, by John Walker Powell. Briefly, this history is as follows:

I. Educational Radio
    A. 1917—the University of Wisconsin and 9XM (later WHA)
    B. 1927—202 "educational" stations on the air, mostly experimental
    C. 1935—this number reduced to 35
    D. Efforts toward the reservation of A.M. channels for educational radio
    E. Growth of the NAEB during the 1940s
    F. Successful reservation of F.M. channels
II. Educational Television
    A. Allerton House seminars in 1949
    B. NAEB efforts toward ETV reservations by the FCC
    C. Joint Council on Educational Television (JCET) formed in 1950
    D. Reservation by FCC of channels for ETV in 1951
    F. Ford Foundation assistance through the Fund for Adult Education

During the 1950s and early 1960s educational broadcasting developed slowly, leaning primarily on local support and funds from the Ford Foundation. Federal money became available in significant quantities with the

Educational Television Facilities Act of 1962. Then came the Carnegie Commission on Educational Television, its report, the Public Broadcasting Act of 1967, the Corporation for Public Broadcasting, and the concept of "public broadcasting."[18]

The report of the Carnegie Commission, published in 1967, divided educational television programming into two parts:

1. Instructional television, "directed at students in the classroom or otherwise in the general context of formal education."
2. Public television, presenting "all that is of human interest and importance which is not at the moment appropriate or available for support by advertising, and which is not arranged for formal instruction."[19]

Since this report, these concepts have been amended by the inclusion of educational radio and the idea of continuing public education broadcasting, the latter falling roughly between types 1 and 2 above.

Acting on the impetus provided by the release of the Carnegie Report, Congress passed the Public Broadcasting Act of 1967—actually an amendment of the Federal Communications Act of 1934. The act does the following:[20]

   I. Establishes the Corporation for Public Broadcasting to
      A. Facilitate the full development of educational broadcasting.
      B. Facilitate the development of high-quality program sources.
      C. Assist in problems of interconnection.
  II. The Corporation may
      A. "Obtain grants from and make contacts with individuals and with private, state, and federal agencies, organizations and institutions."
      B. Make grants to "noncommercial educational broadcast stations."
 III. The Corporation may not
      A. Produce programs.
      B. Operate any broadcast facility.

Since its formation, the CPB has found financing to be its greatest difficulty. Congress authorized appropriations of $10.5 million for fiscal 1968, $12.5 million for 1969, and $15 million for 1970. No appropriations were forthcoming in 1968, although grants from outside sources were received. Only $6 million was appropriated for 1969. The CPB got its $15 million for 1970 and at this writing still another congressional debate over long-term financing is in progress.

[18] Refer to *Public Television: A Program for Action*, The Report and Recommendations of the Carnegie Commission on Educational Television, New York: Harper & Row, 1967.
[19] *Ibid.*, p. 1.
[20] This analysis is based on portions of "Is There a Constitutional Flaw in Portions of the Public Broadcasting Act of 1967?" by Walter Emery, *Educational Broadcasting Review*, February, 1968, 2 (1):17–21.

A major factor in the debate over long-term financing is the desire to insulate the corporation from "the ordinary budgeting and appropriations procedure followed by the government." The Carnegie Commission felt the CPB should be free from "governmental procedural and administrative regulations that are incompatible with its purposes" and should avoid "the overseeing of its day-to-day operations" that could be the result of annual funding.[21] The procedures for assuring this insulation have yet to be worked out and, as a result, the futures of public broadcasting, instructional television, etc. are not yet clear. Financing may yet come through satellite transmission plans, the CATV proposals of the commission, or through the excise tax on receivers recommended by the Carnegie Commission.

ADAMS, J. C., CARPENTER, C. R., AND SMITH, D. R., *College Teaching by Television*, Washington, D.C.: American Council on Education, 1958.

Carnegie Commission on Educational Television, *Public Television*, New York: Harper & Row, 1967.

COSTELLO, LAWRENCE F. AND GORDON, GEORGE N., *Teach with Television*, New York: Hastings House, 1965.

EVANS, RICHARD I., *Resistance to Innovation in Higher Education*, San Francisco: Jossey-Bass, 1968.

GRIFFITH, BARTON L. AND MAC LENNAN, DONALD W. (EDS.), *Improvement of Teaching by Television*, Columbia, Mo.: Univ. of Missouri Press, 1964.

POWELL, JOHN WALKER, *Channels of Learning*, Washington, D.C.: Public Affairs Press, 1962.

WITHERSPOON, JOHN P. AND KESSLER, WILLIAM J., *Instructional Television Facilities*, Washington, D.C.: U.S. Government Printing Office, 1969.

Student Assignments

1. Report on the failure to secure A.M. reservations for education.
2. Report on the successful reservation of F.M. channels.
3. Report on the Allerton House seminars and their influence.
4. Report on JCET and the reservation of ETV channels.
5. Report on the influence of the Ford Foundation on educational broadcasting.
6. Report on educational radio in an age of television.
7. Report on the satellite-funding proposals of the Ford Foundation.
8. Report on the Carnegie Commission and the influence of its report.
9. Report on FCC proposals for the financing of ETV by CATV.

SOURCES OF INFORMATION

This completes a summary of the broadcasting industry as it exists today. Bibliographies have been scattered throughout this chapter, but other sources of information are available. The trade press is helpful; several

[21] Carnegie Commission, *op. cit.*, p. 69.

academic journals are published regularly; many organizations are willing to supply the teacher with information; and three professional organizations exist. These additional sources of information are listed in references.

Reference has been made many times in the preceding pages to the "trade press." Many publications can be thus characterized and each has its own niche in the publications spectrum. *Broadcasting* is probably the best known of all these publications and a subscription to this weekly is a minimum essential to the student of the industry. The radio-television section of *Variety* provides some balance to the relentless industry orientation of *Broadcasting,* and *Billboard* will be helpful to the instructor who is trying to stay abreast of the bewildering world of teen-age "contemporary" music.

The major trade publications in the broadcasting and advertising area are indexed monthly by a service calling itself "Topicator." It is published by the Thompson Bureau, 5395 S. Miller St., Littleton, Colorado 80120, and is well worth its expense, since few trade magazines are indexed in conventional guides. Publications starred in the references are indexed in "Topicator."

The Trade Press

Advertising Age, 740 Rush St., Chicago, Ill. 60611.*
Billboard, 165 W. 46th St., New York, N.Y. 10036.
Broadcasting, 1735 DeSales St. N.W., Washington, D.C. 20036.*
Direct Marketing, 224 Seventh St., Garden City, N.Y. 11530.*
Telecommunications Report, 1208–1216 National Press Bldg., Wash., D.C. 20004.
Television Digest, 2025 Eye St., N.W., Washington, D.C. 20006.*
TV Guide, Radnor, Penn. 19088.*
Variety, 154 W. 46th St., New York, N.Y. 10036.*

Academic Journals

AV Communication Review, published by the Department of Audio-Visual Instruction of the National Education Association, 1201 16th St. N.W., Washington, D.C. 20036.*
College Radio Magazine, published by the Intercollegiate Broadcasting System, Box 269, Middletown, Conn. 06457.
E.B.U. Review published by the European Broadcasting Union, Administrative Office, 1 rue de Varembe, CH-1211, Geneva 20, Switzerland.
Educational Broadcasting Review, published by the National Association of Educational Broadcasters, 1346 Connecticut Ave. N.W., Washington, D.C. 20036.*
Educational/Instructional Broadcasting, published by Acolyte Publications, Inc., 647 N. Sepulveda Blvd., Los Angeles, Calif. 90049.*
Educational Television, 140 Main Street, Ridgefield, Conn. 06877.*
Journal of Broadcasting, published by the Association for Professional Broadcasting Education, Temple University, Philadelphia, Pa. 19122.*

Miscellaneous Sources

Advertising Council, 825 Third Ave., New York, 10022.
American Advertising Federation, 1225 Connecticut Ave. N.W., Washington, D.C. 20036.

American Association of Advertising Agencies, 200 Park Ave., New York, 10017.
American Women in Radio and Television, 1321 Connecticut Ave. N.W., Washington,
D.C. 20036.
Broadcast Rating Council, Inc., 420 Lexington Ave., Room 2347, New York, 10017.
Corporation for Public Broadcasting, 888 16th St. N.W., Washington, D.C. 20006.
Joint Council on Educational Telecommunications, 1126 16th St., Washington, D.C.
20036.
National Educational Television, 10 Columbus Circle, New York, 10019.
Radio Advertising Bureau, 116 55th St., New York, 10022, provides associate member-
ships for colleges and universities.
Television Bureau of Advertising, 1 Rockefeller Plaza, New York, 10020, also provides
associate memberships.
Television Information Office, 745 Fifth Ave., New York 10022.
U.S. Office of Education, Media Dissemination Branch, 400 Maryland Ave. S.W.,
Washington, D.C. 20202.

Professional Associations

The Association for Professional Broadcasting Information, 1771 N St. N.W., Washington, D.C. 20036.
The National Association of Educational Broadcasters, 1346 Connecticut Ave., Washington, D.C. 20036.
The Speech Communication Association, Statler Hilton Hotel, New York 10001.

The Intercollegiate Broadcasting System, Box 269, Middletown, Conn.
06457 also exists as a service organization for "wired-wireless" and other
forms of campus broadcasting. Various regional and state associations in
the areas of speech, broadcast education, and educational broadcasting also
exist.

SOCIAL IMPACT OF BROADCAST MEDIA

The instructor who has led his students through the material already
included in this chapter will, of necessity, have dealt with the impact of
the electronic media on our society. It is the intent of this section to pull
together a bibliography of books with primary emphasis on this aspect of
media study. A brief comment and evaluation follows each entry.

REFERENCES

Collections of Readings

BERELSON, BERNARD AND JANOWITZ, MARRIS (EDS.), *Reader in Public Opinion and
Communication*, New York: Free Press, 1963. General scholarly readings in the
field. Some focus on electronic media.
CASTY, ALAN (ED.), *Mass Media and Mass Man*, New York: Holt, Rinehart & Winston,
1968. Articles and essays on the impact of mass media on society.
COONS, JOHN E. (ED.), *Freedom and Responsibility in Broadcasting*, Evanston, Ill.:
Northwestern Univ. Press, 1961. Report of a conference attended by LeRoy Collins,
then president of the NAB, Warren K. Agee, and others.

DEXTER, LEWIS A. AND WHITE, DAVID MANNING (EDS.), *People, Society and Mass Communications*, New York: Free Press, 1964. Articles and essays with interpretive introductions and an analytical conclusion by the authors.

DONNER, STANLEY T. (ED.), *The Meaning of Commercial Television*, Austin: Univ. of Texas Press, 1967. A report on the Texas-Stanford Seminar in 1966.

HACHTEN, WILLIAM A. (ED.), *The Supreme Court on Freedom of the Press*, Ames, Ia.: Iowa State Univ. Press, 1968. A reader of significant cases, with commentaries.

International Encyclopedia of the Social Sciences, Communication, New York: Academic, 1968. A series of articles on structure, control, audiences, and effects of both mass and interpersonal communication.

LARSEN, OTTO (ED.), *Violence and the Mass Media*, New York: Harper & Row, 1969. Essays and articles on media violence and its regulation in America.

LINDZEY, GARDNER (ED.), *Handbook of Social Psychology*, Reading, Mass.: Addison-Wesley, 1969. "Effects of Mass Media" by Walter Weiss and "Attitude Change" by William J. McGuire are excellent articles on these two subjects.

PENNYBACKER, JOHN H. AND BRADEN, WALDO W. (EDS.), *Broadcasting and the Public Interest*, New York: Random House, 1969. Includes several readings dealing with social impact.

STEINBERG, CHARLES S. (ED.), *Mass Media and Communications*, New York: Hastings House, 1966. Includes several early "classic" articles in the field.

YU, FREDERICK T. C. (ED.), *Behavioral Sciences and the Mass Media*, New York: Russell Sage Foundation, 1968. General readings from the point of view of the behaviorists.

Books

ARLEN, MICHAEL J., *Living Room War*, New York: Viking, 1969. A collection of articles on television by the TV critic of the *New Yorker*.

GILLMOR, DONALD M., *Free Press and Fair Trial*, Washington, D.C.: Public Affairs Press, 1966. An excellent treatment of a subject of great interest and concern to broadcasters today.

HALL, STUART AND WHANNEL, PADDY, *The Popular Arts*, Boston: Beacon Press, 1967. Largely based on experiences in Great Britain, this is an excellent discussion of the nature of the media and the nature of modern life.

Institute for Policy Studies, *Television Today: The End of Communication and the Death of Community*, Washington, D.C.: Institute for Policy Studies, 1969. An analysis of television today and how well it is serving a society in the throes of upheaval and social change. Generally critical.

NICHOLAS JOHNSON, *How to Talk Back to Your Television Set*, Boston: Little, Brown, 1970. An expression of the views, often critical, of an FCC commissioner.

MAC NEIL, ROBERT, *The People Machine*, New York: Harper & Row, 1968. A discussion of the use of television by politicians by a former NBC newsman now with the BBC.

MENDELSOHN, HAROLD, *Mass Entertainment*, New Haven, Conn.: College and Univ. Press, 1966. A social psychologist looks at entertainment and our attitudes toward it.

SCHRAMM, WILBUR, *Mass Media and National Development*, Stanford, Calif.: Stanford Univ. Press, 1967. A discussion of the effects of the media on emerging nations.

SCHRAMM, WILBUR, *The Processes and Effects of Mass Communication*, Urbana, Ill.: Univ. of Illinois Press, 1954. A summary of research and theories in this area to the early 1950s.

SCHRAMM, WILBUR, *The Science of Human Communication*, New York: Basic Books, 1963. A series of lectures first broadcast on the Voice of America in 1962.

SCHRAMM, WILBUR AND RIVERS, WILLIAM L., *Responsibility in Mass Communication*,

New York: Harper & Row, 1969. A revised edition of a classic in the field. Includes a new and interesting case study of "The Negro and the News."

SEPKIN, CHARLES, *Seven Glorious Days, Seven Fun-Filled Nights*, New York: Simon & Schuster, 1968. A perceptive and amusing report by a man who spent a week monitoring six commercial television channels in New York.

SIEBERT, FRED S., PETERSON, THEODORE B., AND SCHRAMM, WILBUR, *Four Theories of the Press*, Urbana, Ill.: Univ. of Illinois Press, 1956. An excellent starting point for the study of foreign media systems. Includes a development of the "social responsibility" theory.

SKORNIA, HARRY J., *Television and Society*, New York: McGraw-Hill, 1965. An attack on U.S. television. Some good points, but needs balance.

WHITE, LLEWELLYN, *The American Radio*, Chicago: Univ. of Chicago Press, 1946. Includes interesting material on the early days of radio and the impact of radio on our society in the 1930s and 1940s.

Research Reports

CANTRIL, HADLEY, *The Invasion from Mars: A Study in Panic*, Princeton, N. J.: Princeton Univ. Press, 1939. A classic study of the reaction to the 1938 Orson Welles broadcast of "The Invasion from Mars." Includes a script of the program.

COGLEY, JOHN, *Report on Blacklisting: II Radio and Television*, Fund for the Republic, Inc., 1956. A study and analysis of the effects of society on the media.

DE FLEUR, MELVIN L., *Theories of Mass Communication*, New York: McKay, 1966. An attempt to pull together theories, findings, etc. of mass media research into an organized framework.

KATZ, ELIHU AND PAUL LAZERSFELD, *Personal Influence*, New York: Free Press, 1955. A landmark study of the dissemination of information through the media. Introduced the "two-step" theory of information flow.

KRAUS, SIDNEY, *The Great Debates*, Bloomington, Ind.: Indiana Univ. Press, 1962. Analysis of the Kennedy-Nixon debates of 1960.

LAZERSFELD, PAUL F., *The People Look at Radio*, New York: Prentice-Hall, 1946. Early research into radio listening habits and attitudes.

SCHRAMM, WILBUR (ED.), *The Impact of Educational Television*, Urbana, Ill.: Univ. of Illinois Press, 1960. Selected studies on educational television in the 1950s.

SCHRAMM, WILBUR, *The People Look at Educational Television*, Stanford, Calif.: Stanford Univ. Press, 1963. A report of research on nine representative ETV stations.

SCHRAMM, WILBUR, LYLE, JACK, AND PARKER, EDWIN B., *Television in the Lives of Our Children*, Stanford, Calif.: Stanford Univ. Press, 1961. A major American study of the effects of television on children.

STEINER, GARY A., *The People Look at Television*, New York: Knopf, 1963. A generous reference volume with masses of figures on audience attitudes and tastes.

STEPHENSON, WILLIAM, *The Play Theory of Mass Communication*, Chicago: Univ. of Chicago Press, 1967. Interesting exposition of a controversial theory.

By and About Marshall McLuhan

FINKELSTEIN, STANLEY WALTER, *Sense and Nonsense of McLuhan*, New York: International Publishers, 1968.

MC LUHAN, HERBERT M., *The Gutenberg Galaxy*, Toronto: Univ. of Toronto Press, 1962.

MC LUHAN, HERBERT M., *Understanding Media*, New York: McGraw-Hill, 1964.

MC LUHAN, HERBERT M. AND CARPENTER, EDWARD S. (EDS.) *Explorations in Communication*, Boston: Beacon Press, 1960.

ROSENTHAL, RAYMOND B. (ED.), *McLuhan Pro and Con*, New York: Funk & Wagnalls, 1968.

STEARN, GERALD E. (ED.), *McLuhan, Hot and Cool*, New York: Dial Press, 1967.

11. Teaching Students to Use Broadcast Media

John H. Pennybacker

Production represents the glamorous side of the broadcasting business to most young students, and they are usually eager to lay hands on equipment and develop their skills. The media instructor must use this enthusiasm, of course, and give his students the best instruction he can, but he should not let student attitudes deter him from heavy concentration on the areas discussed in the previous chapter. Production techniques vary widely and change rapidly and jobs in production or on the air represent only a small portion of the opportunities available in broadcasting. If a student is to realize his full potential in broadcasting, or is to reach a full understanding of the nature of the media, his instruction in production must be subordinate to that in the history, structure, and impact of the media.

RADIO PRODUCTION

Some elements of radio may be taught with no specialized equipment at all, especially in a secondary school. Two major routes are suggested, and the imaginative instructor can find many variations on these suggestions.

Local Station Facilities

In many communities local stations are willing to help interested high school students produce a series of school news programs, aired as a public service and logged as such by the stations. Depending on the station format, these may be weekly 15-minute programs, or prerecorded 5-minute segments scheduled regularly, or 1- to 2-minute features produced continually as news occurs and scattered throughout the program day.

Planning the type of program involves five steps:

1. Locate those students who are genuinely interested in learning about broadcasting in general and radio in particular. Radio enthusiasts can be found in "ham" clubs, in speech classes, and through guidance counselors.

2. Be sure that the students are genuinely interested, understand the amount of work involved, and promise to work through the entire school year. A local broadcaster disappointed by a nonproductive group is not likely to be receptive to future proposals.

3. It is always a good idea to approach a station manager with a sample of the kind of program you are proposing. Use a school tape recorder and prop the microphone up in front of a record player, if necessary, but try to put something together to demonstrate the program idea. Station personnel can spot flaws and errors that are due to equipment and will make allowances.

In preparing a sample program (or in preparing the first program after acceptance by the station), follow these steps: (a) Determine which station is to be approached and have the students analyze its format at the times the program would be most effectively scheduled. (b) Begin the selection of a format which best fits the station format. Will the station manager be willing to set aside large blocks of time for single concept "programs" (these days, 15 minutes is a "large block of time" and many station managers would be afraid of the audience they would lose in this period). Decide what length program would be best for the students and for the station and be prepared to recommend an air time. (c) Determine how the program best fits into the format of the station. A "sandwich" of music suitable to the station surrounding one or more news items is a basic format. If at all possible, let the students take the lead in all aspects of this project. (d) Produce one or two samples of the program. Discard "takes" until the group has put together the best possible production within the local limitations.

4. Approach a manager and "sell" the material or the idea. In smaller communities a group should find little difficulty reaching the program director or even the station manager. In larger communities the most appropriate route is through the public relations director or his equivalent.

5. If the station commits itself, produce the program regularly, keep within the format, and deliver tapes faithfully. Organize the group according to the talent, skills, interests, and time available to the students, but have one individual always responsible for and in charge of each program unit to be delivered—recognizing, of course, that in the eyes of the station manager the instructor has the ultimate responsibility for delivering what was promised.

School Facilities

In many secondary schools the classrooms are interconnected by a public address system that may serve as an outlet for students interested in broadcasting. The basic idea is to gain permission from school administrators to allow a student group to "program" over the PA system a morning show piped regularly into the classrooms, perhaps for 30 to 45 minutes prior to the start of the school day. The program may have a basic music and news format with student-oriented music and news and announcements of interest to students and teachers.

In pursuing the plan, follow these steps:

1. Find students who are eager and able to work on the project throughout the term.

2. Determine just what kind of equipment is available at the originating end of the public address system. If there is no turntable for playing records, installation of this equipment should be requested. If the system has only one turntable ask for a second to make the job of the DJ easier and more realistic. Check on how many microphones are available and whether a tape recorder is part of the system.

3. Within the limitations of equipment plan the program format. Have the students take the lead here. Guide them to consider audience flow and tastes (Who usually gets to school earliest? Freshmen? Seniors? Is there a difference in taste among significant groups in the school? Which local stations are most popular? How can the group improve on the programming of this station with a much narrower audience to focus on?), but let *them* decide on music format, news and announcement balance, scheduling of air time for DJs, assistants, news gatherers, and writers. Prepare to back their decisions, especially relating to music, for the chances are that neither teachers nor administrators will be enthusiastic about the music they select.

4. Try to put together a 15–30-minute sample for use when asking for permission to broadcast.

5. Sell the program, organize the students into teams to produce it each day, and go "on the air." Encourage the students to stay in touch with their audience and be prepared to change or shift format when needed. If possible, have the students organize a regular series of audience polls.

Teaching Radio Production with Appropriate Equipment

Although the exercises just described give the students insight into the nature of radio production and programming, probably the productions will be limited by inferior or nonbroadcast equipment, severe time limitations, and restrictions on equipment available at local stations. An answer of course is to plan a radio studio in which to teach a regularly scheduled radio production course.

Minimum essentials of equipment for teaching radio production are the following:

One audio mixer console with at least four microphone inputs, mixers for turntables and tape recorders with some sort of "cue" arrangement, and one or more mixers for remote inputs of various types
Two turntables
Two reel-to-reel tape recorders, at least one preferably rack-mounted
One cartridge tape recorder (record and play)
A patch panel
A monitor system into all studios, control rooms, announce booths, etc.
At least one headset for the control board operator
A bulk tape eraser
A tape splicer
Microphones

The studio itself should consist of at least (1) a control room, housing most of the equipment and including space for some student observation, and (2) a production studio. In addition, the following are desirable:

An additional production control room
Announce and (or) audition booths
A portable tape recorder
A teletype news service
A campus broadcast facility
Portable turntables, remote mixer consoles, sound amplifier, speakers, for remote operations

Materials necessary for operation are

Recording tapes (reel-to-reel) of various sizes
Empty tape reels for take-up
Cartridge tapes of various lengths
Splicing tape
Tools (scissors, small adjustable wrench, long-nosed pliers, solder gun, solder, electronic tape, screw drivers, trouble light, hammer, voltage tester, head cleaner, strobe disc, etc.)
Records in various categories (jazz, contemporary, classical, country and western, easy listening, middle-of-the-road, "golden oldies," etc.)
A basic sound effect library
Station forms (logs, etc.)

With this equipment, facilities, and materials at hand, a teacher can offer effective instruction in radio production. In the three suggested curricula, the instructor may supplement these exercises with lecture and reading material best adapted to the time available, the level of the students, and other broadcast-related courses.

The third curriculum is adapted from an "APBE Composite Outline— *Radio Production*" which is part of a 1970 publication by the Association for Professional Broadcasting Education called *Radio-Television-Film*

Composite Course Outlines, Volume II. The two volumes of this publication include composite outlines of broadcasting and broadcast-related courses taught at many of the leading colleges and universities in the United States.[1]

Fundamental Radio Production Curriculum

Project One. Students are divided into laboratory groups of no more than 15 and each group is given a radio script for a brief music program consisting of a theme to be used for opening and closing and two records. The program also includes two brief commercials and these, scripted on a separate sheet, are given to each student.

A basic production "crew" is as follows:

In the studio Announcer One reads the program introduction, scripted introductions to each record, and the program close. His goal is to be as natural in his delivery as possible and he is encouraged to work over the script and make word and phrase changes which better suit his style.

In the studio Announcer Two reads the commercials. His goal is a natural, friendly, direct delivery and he also is encouraged to adapt the script to his style, although he is not permitted to change any basic selling points in the commercial.

In the control room, the control board operator opens and closes proper microphones at the proper time, cues up records, and brings them in as soon as the announcers have finished. The control board operator strives throughout the course to run as "tight" a board as possible with no observable mistakes and no pauses between announcers, records, and so on.

In the control room, the tape recorder operator, turns the recorder on and off, as all exercises are taped for later grading by the instructor. Obviously this task is not challenging and could be done by the instructor, but the position is included to allow at least one person at a time in the control room to observe the control board operator. At this stage few students are well enough adapted to operate effectively with several fellow students hovering over their shoulders, but the tape operator seldom bothers them. It is most effective to have this crew member move directly to control board operator when the students shift.

A schedule is then set up whereby each student rotates through each position and programs are recorded as follows:

	Announcer 1	*Announcer 2*	*Control Bd.*	*Tape*
Recording 1	Student A	B	C	D
Recording 2	Student B	C	D	E
Recording 3	Student C	D	E	F

[1] Availability of this publication is limited, however, and permission has been received from the APBE and the National Association of Broadcasters to include whatever material is needed for this methods book.

It is important that the students understand they are not duplicating station operation at most commercial stations. Few stations use two announcers and a control board operator for a simple music program and even fewer fully script their programs. The student should understand that this introductory exercise tries to isolate the major components of music programming in order to allow the student to concentrate on one job at a time. Scripts may be discarded and tasks combined as students gain experience.

Grading of this project is left to the discretion of the instructor. Many use it as a breaking-in exercise for nervous students and use the tapes simply as a basis for comments. When possible, it is also helpful to allow the students to hear their tapes.

Project Two. Each student is given a simple "run-down" sheet of a music program similar to that in Project One. In this case, however, program and record introductions are not included and the announcers are expected to ad-lib or pre-script this material. Students are to provide their own records for this exercise and give them to the control board operator when they move into the Announcer One slot. Goals in this exercise are also an easy, natural delivery, but students should start thinking about adapting delivery to fit the music they select. During the discussion of this project the instructor discusses the questions of music balance, station formats, program themes.

Commercial copy should be scripted and given to Announcer Two who has the same options as in Project One.

The same basic production crew as in Project One is established and each student moves through all positions. Students not occupied with the project may listen to the tapes of Project One.

Project Three. In this project each student puts it all together and performs a "combo" operation in the control room. Working from a run-down sheet calling for an opening and closing theme and two records and a second sheet with commercials fully scripted, the student performs all operations in the control room. He introduces the program and the records; he gets everything on in the proper order and on time. The next student on the schedule operates the tape recorder.

Project Four. In the fourth project the students come to grips with two new problems: timing a show and preparing a brief newscast. The production unit for this assignment consists of three positions:

A control board operator is responsible for preparing a 10-minute music program similar to that in Project Three. For this assignment he has the option of putting together a brief music unit with opening and closing theme or assuming that he is working the last 10 minutes of a longer music program which precedes a news summary. His unit must run *exactly* 10 minutes and he is assigned a starting time.

A newscaster is responsible for the preparation of a 3-minute newscast suitable for a student audience on a campus radio station. The latter provision forces the students to work on campus news and local news of interest to students and makes it difficult to use wire service material. The newscast follows the music program immediately and should run exactly 3 minutes, no matter when the music program ends. Some instructors may wish to alter the last provision and insist that the news broadcast and exactly 13 minutes after the beginning of the music segment, but at this stage of their development few beginning students are able to handle the responsibility of possible variations in the time they are allowed.

A tape recorder operator is the next assigned control board operator.

All students rotate through these positions and are graded on their work as announcer and control board operator, their music selection and balance, news selection and arrangement, and news reading. The following is a typical schedule:

Time	Music	News	Tape Recorder
1:45	Student A	B	C
2:05	Student B	C	D
2:25	Student C	D	E
2:45	Student D	E	A
3:05	Student E	A	B

Project Five.   Because of the length of Project Four it normally takes 3 weeks to get through a group of 15 (assuming 2-hour lab sections) and two-thirds of the class are unoccupied at any given time. This problem is solved by assigning Project Five at the same time as Project Four.

The project follows a discussion of radio commercial writing and production and calls for each student to write two 60-second commercials for a real or believable product or service of his choice. Students are then assigned to production groups of five each in such a way that all the students assigned to produce Project Four on a given day are in the same group. (See the sample schedule for Project Four. Students A, B, C, D, and E are in the same production group. Students F, G, H, I, and J produce Project Four the following week and are in the same production group. The remaining five students are in the last production group and produce Project Four in the final week.)

During the two laboratory sessions in which they are not involved in Project Four each of these production groups meets and each member of the group reads his two commercials. The groups select the two best commercials (considering both the quality of the commercial and their ability to produce it) and produce them at the time assigned them in the week or weeks following Project Four. Commercials not used by the groups are retained for possible use in Project Six or to be turned in at the end of the semester.

Project Six. This final project occupies approximately the last third of the semester. The production groups established for Project Five are instructed to put together 1 hour of programming suitable for a time and audience which they must select and identify beforehand. The program must include the following elements as a minimum.

1. News: At least 5 minutes and no more than 10 minutes of news suitable for the selected audience.

2. Spot announcements: At least 4 and no more than 8 minutes of spot announcements in the hour. There must be at least one spot in every 15-minute segment of the program. Two of these announcements are those prepared by the group for Project Five and transferred to cartridges. The remaining spots may be PSAs, commercials, or a mixture of both. Internal promotions of features which are coming up in the show are *not* counted in this time.

3. Prerecorded material: At least 5 minutes and no more than 10 minutes of the program must be devoted to prerecorded "special feature" material. The spot announcements are not to be counted in this time. These features usually take the form of prerecorded interviews with someone of interest, either real or simulated, but other ideas are welcomed.

4. Music: Most of these programs are devoted primarily to recorded music. Students are instructed to select an overall theme or format and identify it when the program is introduced. Within this format a well-balanced variety of music is required.

The amount of paperwork to be handed in is up to the instructor, but students are expected to work from logs and have news, and editorials fully scripted. It is helpful if the instructor can arrange his schedule to allow the radio studio to be open in times other than regularly scheduled class periods. Much preliminary planning is required for this project, and the students appreciate extra time in the studio for production, planning, and so on.

The grades for Projects Five and Six are group grades, but it is a good idea to reserve the right beforehand—and state it clearly—to raise or lower the grades of those in the group who do extraordinary work or fail to pull their weight.

Advanced Radio Production Curriculum

Project One. Even though this is a course in advanced production, it is helpful to assign a relatively simple project at first. This gives the instructor an opportunity to assess the relative abilities of the students, locate those who seem most advanced, and help those who have a lower level of skill. Project Two in the fundamental course is a convenient way to accomplish this task and it may be used with little or no change. Grading of the project, of course, is more rigorous than in the fundamental course.

Projects Two and Three.   Following a discussion of the preparation and production of radio commercials, each student is instructed to write a series of three 60-second commercials for a real or believable product or service. The commercials are planned as part of a single campaign for the product or service and are to be built around the same basic theme idea. Each should be written for at least two voices.

A production staff is put together as follows:

1. The producer-director is responsible for casting the commercial from the talent in his group and molding all the elements of the commercial into a unified selling message. During the planning and production he is in complete charge and may make whatever changes in the commercials he wishes—except basic selling points. He is responsible for giving all cues to talent and the control board operator, keeping time, and, in general, co-ordinating the entire production. He should not ignore advice from any member of the group, but he must make the final decision in all cases.

2. The control board operator works essentially as an engineer under the supervision of the producer-director.

3. Talent is to be used as talent for the commercial chosen.

Each production group is assigned a time to produce its commercials and a time in which they are evaluated and criticized by the other members of the class, the instructor, and, if possible, a commercial broadcaster or advertising man.

Following this critique, the groups are reshuffled, new commercials are chosen and produced, and another round of critiques is scheduled.

All projects following the first are group projects with an assigned producer-director. Everyone in the class should have the opportunity to be a producer-director at least once, with second rounds possibly assigned to graduate students. Each student should get at least one assignment to the control board.

Project Four.   Production groups are reshuffled and each is instructed to prepare and record a "typical" 30-minute segment drawn from a radio station whose format is to be determined by the group. This station will be a music station, primarily, but the segments should also include at least 3 minutes of commercial time and at least 2 minutes of news headlines. Commercials used may be selected from those produced in Projects Two and Three.

The station chosen must be a hypothetical radio station, commercial and A.M. of the type located in large, medium, or small cities. The problem is selecting a music format, choosing records and commercials to fit it, and matching available talent to the format. The final program is expected to be professional, well paced, and unified within the format selected.

The production group consists of (1) the producer-director; (2) the control board operator; (3) the commercial director, who selects the commercials to be used and, if necessary, supervises the production of new commercials; (4) the news director, who is responsible for preparation of the news segment of the project (the PD will determine whether or not this individual actually reads the news on the air); and (5) talent.

Project Five. Each group is responsible for the preparation of a 15-minute newscast of campus and local news of interest to the college or university campus community. This should be a weekend review type of newscast in which the high points of the previous week are summarized. Groups are responsible for covering the Monday through Friday period of the week before the assigned production date. The program must contain at least one interview, and may contain more. The production group consists of five positions.

1. The project editor (producer-director) is responsible for selecting stories to be covered and assigning the reporting staff. He approves all rewrites, supervises editing of all interview tapes, and determines the order of presentation and time allotted to each story.

2. The reporting staff is responsible for covering stories assigned by the project editor and, if assigned to do so, handling interviews for the stories. All assignments are to be written up as complete stories and given to the project editor for his approval. These original stories will be attached to the rewritten stories used on the air when the project copy is handed in.

3. For consistency of style, all stories are rewritten by a rewrite man, who may also double as the on-the-air reporter. Under the supervision of the project editor he assembles all material gathered and written by the reporting staff and rewrites the stories to fit time allottments as determined by the project editor.

4. The board operator works under the supervision of the project editor.

5. The on-the-air reporter actually reads the prepared newscast on the air. He should attempt to do this as professionally as possible, introducing variety and enthusiasm and, as far as possible, fitting his manner to the story.

Project Six. Each group is responsible for the preparation of 15 minutes of special feature broadcasts which would be of interest to a college or university audience. These may be panel discussions, interviews or a series of interviews, women's features, farm features, analyses of important issues, or any other type of special program that occurs to the group. They cannot be news roundups or programs of recorded music.

The group goal is the preparation of special feature programs that will hold the attention of a college or university audience. To accomplish this it may bring in as many guests as it wishes or use taped interviews. If it wishes, the group can draw on its own talent and create fictional personalities and interviews (which must, of course, be believable).

The timing of each feature is flexible, with a minimum time of 3 minutes and a maximum time of 7 minutes. The total time should be 15 minutes.

The production crew consists simply of a production director, an Assistant PD, a control board operator, and talent.

Project Seven. This is the final project and, as such, is similar to the final project in the fundamental course. Each group is responsible for 60 minutes of balanced programming but in the advanced course the emphasis cannot be primarily on music.

The hour must include the following as a minimum:

1. News: At least 5 minutes, with no maximum amount of time.
2. Spot announcements: Six spot announcements are included. Three are drawn from those prepared for Projects Two and Three and 3 additional minutes are produced.
3. Interview: At least one will be included and it should be no shorter than 2½ minutes. More can be added.
4. Special features: No maximums or minimums here, but the more variety the better.
5. Music: No more than 25 minutes can be devoted to music. An interview with an artist which includes some of his music will not be counted against this time, but the emphasis must be on the interview.

Students are encouraged to pattern this hour after the NBC monitor format and to listen to the program for ideas. The program must be directed toward a college or university audience with all segments put together to capture and hold this audience.

The basic production crew consists of a production director and assistant, a commercial director, a special features director, a news editor, a control board operator, and talent.

An Alternative Radio Production Curriculum Outline

Course Objectives. (1) Present a historical overview of radio operation up to the present moment. (2) Provide learning experiences in all production and operating practices. (3) Show relation of production and operation formats to demands of commercial, legal, and esthetic requirements.

Outside Projects

1. Production of commercials: 60 seconds, 30 seconds, 10 seconds; national spots, local spots; adult audiences, teen audiences.
2. Production of newscasts: headline news, in-depth commentary, editorial, weather, sports.
3. Production of continuity: introductions (variety shows, classical music, programs, discussion, political speech, religious program); tags; sign ons and sign offs; station IDs.
4. Interviews (actual or simulated): sports, celebrities (visiting), news events, man-on-the-street, local officials.
5. Sports play-by-play.
6. On-the-scene remote.

7. Weather report.
8. Music formats: rock (acid, hard, contemporary, folk), middle-of-the-road, easy listening, country and western, religious, classical (traditional, romantic), oldie, novelty.

Course Outline

I. First week
    A. Historical overview of radio production
    B. Early studios (improvised, no acoustics)
    C. Components (Console mixer, microphones, turntables, tape recorders, remote equipment, cartridge tape recorders, speakers, phone patch)
II. Second week
    A. Early programs (live)
    B. Early artists (from other arts)
    C. Early announcers
III. Third week
    A. Use and operation of console (inputs, output, channels, switching, fading, remotes, auditioning, monitoring, monaural-stereo, radio relay)
    B. Microphone (directional, bidirectional, nondirectional, carbon, ribbon, dynamic, magnetic, high Z, low Z, cables, wireless, frequency response, selective impedance, rejection characteristics, feedback, limiting types, costs, sensitivity, boom, blasting, sibilance, smacking, script, noise, brands)
IV. Fourth week
    A. Use of turntables (sizes, speeds, rumble, acceleration, remote operation, makes, costs, compensators)
    B. Tone arms (makes, costs, stylus pressures, monaural, stereo, damping, handling and care, response, manipulative characteristics)
    C. Demonstration of console, microphone, and turntable operation
    D. Assignment in operation of console, microphone, turntables.
V. Fifth week
    A. Tape recorders (makes, speeds, sizes, inputs, outputs, threading, cueing, operation, quality characteristics, maintenance and care, tape splicing and editing, types of tape, tape blanking, costs)
    B. Cartridge tape recorders (makes, costs, tape lengths, speeds, operation)
    C. Demonstration of complete operation (including mixer console, turntables, microphones, tape recorders, cartridge tapes, phone patch, relay, remotes)
VI. Sixth week
    A. Review and test over history and components, nomenclature, operation, care, functions
    B. Assign project involving use of all components (see list of projects).
VII. Seventh week
    A. Study of operational problems
        1. Licenses (operator, station)
        2. Logs (program, operating, maintenance)
    B. Assignment
        1. Study for third-class license with broadcast endorsement
        2. Practice making up and filling in program logs
VIII. Eighth week: Operational problems (cont.)

      A. Emergency broadcast system
      B. Music storage
      C. Tape handling
      D. Remote program production
      E. Monitor practices
      F. Program level
      G. FCC operating requirements
  IX. Ninth week
      A. Examination on operation problems
      B. Begin "program problems"
          1. Formats (R & R, C & W, MOR, talk, educational public service, classical, background music, religious, news and commentary, driving time)
          2. Pacing, cueing, program content, intended audience (age, time of day, day of week, time of year, geographical location)
      C. Assign practice projects (formats)
  X. Tenth week
      A. Program problems (cont.)
          1. Station policies
          2. NAB Programming and Advertising Code
          3. Script writing
          4. News sources
      B. Assign practice projects
  XI. Eleventh week
      A. Examination on program problems
      B. Management problems
      C. Assign final projects
      D. Management problems
          1. Staff organization
          2. Traffic
          3. Program scheduling
          4. Sales
          5. Promotions
          6. Announcing staff
 XII. Twelfth week
      A. Engineering and Maintenance
      B. Work schedules
      C. Music licensing agencies (BMI, ASCAP, SESAC)
      D. Unions (ADTRA)
      E. Copyrights
      F. Budget
      G. Responsibilities to FCC
      H. Community rapport
XIII. Thirteenth week
      A. License renewals
      B. Political broadcasts
      C. Fairness doctrine
      D. Equal time provision
      E. Editorializing
      F. Program evaluation criteria
      G. Clerical
      H. Music library

XIV. Fourteenth–sixteenth weeks
A. Projects
B. Final examination

TELEVISION PRODUCTION

The nature of the medium makes teaching even the rudiments of television production on the secondary level next to impossible for most instructors. Few stations will do more than allow tours of their facilities and even fewer schools themselves have more than the most basic closed-circuit television equipment for instructional television.

In some communities, however, it has been possible to arrange a junior achievement program in cooperation with a local television station. If a group of dependable youngsters interested in the idea can be located, this may be attempted in your area.

Two suggested television production curricula are included. Each is adapted from the Association for Professional Broadcasting Education publication mentioned on p. 241 and each is flexible enough to meet individual needs.

Beginning Television Production

Course Objectives. (1) To study the communication assets and liabilities of television in comparison and in contrast to other information-entertainment media: radio, cinema, theater, newspapers, books, magazines. (2) To understand the function of television production equipment and facilities: cameras, microphones, switchers, special effects machines, audio boards, tape recorders, lighting equipment, etc. (3) To learn the basic principles, procedures, and techniques of television production. (4) To develop skill and creativity in the various production posts: director, assistant director, floor manager, cameraman, audio man, boom operator, projectionist.

Facilities. A television studio and control room are required, with two-camera chain, film chain, video-tape recorder, audio board, turntables and (or) tape cartridge machines, microphones, studio monitors, lighting instruments, scenery, and miscellaneous props.

Special Required Reading and Viewing. Program reviews by television critics and staff writers in current trade and professional publications are assigned. The student is asked to view and evaluate selected current broadcasts. The following general directives should prove helpful:

1. In addition to your name and course number include the following information at the top of your paper of program-production evaluation: (a) the type of program you are viewing; (b) the program title; (c) the date and time of broadcast and the station or network.

2. In your critique evaluate the program with respect to points given in lectures, handouts, and (or) collateral readings.
3. Assess the program with respect to its effectiveness or ineffectiveness. You may want to comment on the content of the program, the various production techniques, and the value or effectiveness of the program in light of its patent objectives.
4. Back up your generalizations with specific examples from the program.
5. You may find it helpful to assume that you are writing for a foreigner who is unfamiliar with American television programs.
6. You may find it helpful to use the accompanying checklist as an aid in your viewing and evaluation. Of course, not all sections of the checklist are germane for all program types.

Outside Projects.   The student is expected to visit at least two commercial and (or) educational stations and write an essay concerning his stay and what he observed. The accompanying checklist may be of help to him during his visit.

The following outline presents a framework for a series of lectures on television production which the instructor can expand or contract as time allows.

Outline for a Series of Lectures

    I. Television as a medium of communication
       A. Characteristics of mass media
       B. Assets and liabilities of television
       C. Television compared to other media
       D. Limitations
       E. Psychological impact of audio and video stimuli via television
    II. Television cameras—characteristics, uses, assets, liabilities
       A. Types (vidicon, image-orthicon, color; studio, remote, film chain)
       B. Mounting equipment (pan heads; tripods, pedestals, dollies, cranes)
       C. Lenses (function, parts, characteristics of long and short lenses; zooms compared to dollies; special lenses focal length, f-stops, depth of field)
   III. The television cameraman—duties, skills, procedures
       A. Focus, lens racking, zooming
       B. Camera movements (panning and tilting; dollying, trucking and arcing; pedestaling and booming)
       C. Composition and framing
       D. Duties and responsibilities
    IV. Audio
       A. Microphone characteristics (frequency response, pick-up pattern, quality)
       B. Types of microphones (assets and liabilities, uses)
       C. Factors affecting audio pick-up (studio, set, microphone)
       D. Microphone selection and location for television program types
       E. The audio console (function, basic similarities of all)
       F. Use of turntables and (or) tape cartridge machines
       G. Audio patching and use of sound distortion (echo, filter)
       H. Use of recorded sound and music; use of live sound effects

Checklist for Evaluating a Television Program[a]

I. Production values—artistic-esthetic
- A. Theme, thesis, message, or idea   0 1 2 3 4 5
- B. Plot, structure, or organization   0 1 2 3 4 5
- C. Script   0 1 2 3 4 5
- D. Performance   0 1 2 3 4 5
- E. Settings   0 1 2 3 4 5
- F. Costumes   0 1 2 3 4 5
- G. Makeup   0 1 2 3 4 5
- H. Sound   0 1 2 3 4 5
- I. Camera   0 1 2 3 4 5
- J. Direction   0 1 2 3 4 5
- K. Switching or editing   0 1 2 3 4 5
- L. Lighting   0 1 2 3 4 5
- M. Color—balance, design, fidelity, credibility   0 1 2 3 4 5

II. Entertainment values
- A. Believable characters[b]   0 1 2 3 4 5
- B. Believable situations[b]   0 1 2 3 4 5
- C. Comedy rating   0 1 2 3 4 5
- D. Conflict rating[b]   0 1 2 3 4 5
- E. Participation rating[b]   0 1 2 3 4 5
- F. Human interest rating   0 1 2 3 4 5
- G. Sex appeal rating   0 1 2 3 4 5
- H. Emotional appeals rating[b]   0 1 2 3 4 5
- I. Novelty rating   0 1 2 3 4 5
- J. Others   0 1 2 3 4 5

III. Instructional Values
- A. Is new information presented on places, processes, methods, techniques, events, or people?   0 1 2 3 4 5
- B. Are social, psychological, and(or) emotional problems presented with new insight?   0 1 2 3 4 5
- C. Are new and fresh insights on character and personality presented?   0 1 2 3 4 5
- D. Are new ideas or concepts presented?   0 1 2 3 4 5
- E. Are old ideas presented with a new, novel, or different interpretation?   0 1 2 3 4 5

IV. Social Values
- A. Does it further the democratic process?   0 1 2 3 4 5
- B. Are desirable mores, and(or) customs reinforced?   0 1 2 3 4 5
- C. To what extent does the program point out, dramatize, or highlight social problems that need solving?   0 1 2 3 4 5
- D. To what extent does the film/program suggest ways to improve a social problem or situation?   0 1 2 3 4 5

V. Ethical values (dependent on treatment or subject)
- A. Is the interpretation accurate? Or distorted, false, one-sided?   0 1 2 3 4 5
- B. Does the interpretation illuminate and inspire human destiny?   0 1 2 3 4 5
- C. To what degree is the interpretation timeless? Timely? Universal? Applicable to other cultures and people?   0 1 2 3 4 5

[a] 0 to 5: Absent to high; 0 = absent; 5 = very high   [b] Dramatic program

OBSERVATION REPORT FOR TELEVISION REHEARSAL AND(OR) PRODUCTION

Date _____ Your name _____

Station _____ Check-in/-out times _____

Program title _____ Program length _____

Program type _____

Vantage point: Control room _____ Studio _____

Announce booth _____ Other _____

Signature of Director _____

Your primary focus of attention was on:

1. Direction _____

2. Production _____

3. Performance _____

4. Lighting _____

5. Setting _____

6. Other _____

Partial Checklist:

Control Room
  Switching
  Audio
  Director's commands
  Use of camera:
    movement
    angle
    shots

Studio
  Lighting
  Floor direction
  Scenery
  Props
  Cameramen
  Talent

Detailed evaluation attached
(What did you learn? Of what—if any—value was your visit? Compare the production-direction techniques you observed in practice with those recommended by your text and instructor. What generalizations can you make concerning the effectiveness of the men you observed. Document with specific examples.)

V. The audio engineer
   A. Levels
   B. Cueing procedures
   C. Mixing
   D. Techniques in editing audio tape
   E. Script marking and timing
VI. Television lighting
   A. Television lighting compared and contrasted to lighting for cinema, still photography, and stage
   B. Functions and objectives of television lighting
   C. Lighting instruments (characteristics, assets, and liabilities)
   D. Lighting control equipment
   E. Definitions of lighting terms
   F. Lighting for color (cf. monochrome)
VII. The television lighting director—techniques and procedures
   A. Keeping the kind and amount of light compatible with the intent of the program
   B. Selection, location, angle, distance of instruments
   C. Use of cue sheets
   D. Use of manual, present, and automated control systems
VIII. Scenery and properties
   A. Psychology of line, mass, form, color
   B. Relationship between director and designer
   C. Styles of scenic design
   D. Scenery construction (theatrical flats; plywood, hardboard, cardboard, plastic)
   E. Bracing, joining, and mounting sets
   F. Painting scenery for monochrome and color
   G. Utilizing the studio floor as part of the set
   H. Set pieces
   I. Selection and location of properties
IX. Graphics
   A. Types of graphics
   B. Television requirements for graphics (aspect ratio, contrast values, detail, and amount of information)
   C. Advantages and disadvantages of live graphics over film graphics
   D. Scanning and essential areas
   E. Preparation of studio visuals (maps, diagrams, and charts; title cards)
   F. Use of lettering devices
   G. Use of photographs
   H. Use of credit devices (crawls, drop-ins, pulls, slides)
   I. Special effects with graphics
X. Telecine
   A. Use of 2 × 2 slide projectors, 16-mm. film projectors, balops, telops, multiplexers
   B. Silent and sound film
   C. Techniques of film splicing
   D. Steps in preparing film for broadcast (checking, timing, cleaning, splicing, adding academy leader and cue marks)
XI. Producing and directing
   A. The producer's duties
   B. The director's duties

C. Production procedures (planning, integration of crew efforts; re-
   hearsals)
D. Thinking in pictures (manipulation of talent and cameras)
E. The script (revising, marking, using)
F. Directing talent
G. On-the-air procedures

Laboratory Assignments.   Laboratory projects are videotaped and played
back with instructor-class evaluation. The instructor divides the class into
production crews, or groups. The crew assignments change several times
during the semester to give each student the experience of working with as
many different crew members as possible. Students are usually rotated in
the various production posts, using the same script or production vehicle,
until each is thoroughly familiar with the operation of the equipment involved, and the execution of the duties of the various production posts.

Project One.   Presentation of a prepared television newscast. This exercise gives the student experience as a director in (1) cutting from performer to studio graphic and back to performer; (2) cutting from the
performer to the film projection room and back to the performer; (3)
following a moving performer; (4) dollying in for a close-up· shot; (5)
utilizing a short commercial (voice-over graphic); and (6) using a PSA on
film at the close of program. Time: 5 minutes. The instructor gives out
prepared scripts.

Project Two.   Visualization for television; 5-minute program using still
photographs:

I. Objectives
   A. To communicate interestingly and effectively to the viewer through a
      series of related still photos and (or) pictures. The exercise demands
      that the student director creatively interpret for the viewer, selecting
      only those pictures which reinforce the text of the script.
   B. To select, edit, rearrange, and delete material from a photo essay to
      make it more meaningful for the viewer.
   C. To give each director an opportunity to perfect his skill in giving the
      proper verbal cues and directions to his production crew at the right
      time, obtaining from his production crew a high degree of integrated
      effort and immediate response.
   D. To give the members of the production team—switcher, cameraman,
      audioman, floor director—an opportunity to improve their skills in the
      reflexive manipulation of their equipment, and to receive commands
      from the director and to execute them promptly and efficiently.
II. Sources and materials
   A. The student may write his own original material if he prefers.
   B. Articles and pictures may be drawn from any of the mass media maga-
      zines, such as *Life, Time, Saturday Evening Post, National Geographic,*
      etc. A number of sources are desirable, especially with respect to the
      photographs, drawings, or pictures.
   C. Three credit cards should be prepared, one of which will be used for
      the opening and the closing.

  D. The text of the article must be edited, condensing, and omitting much of the original to make it fit the 5-minute format. It may be rewritten to make the style more conversational and informal.

III. Production techniques

  A. Two flip stands, or pods, should be used for photos, visuals, and credits.

  B. On-camera talent should not be used without clearance from the instructor. This requirement avoids using the on-camera talent as a crutch when the student is unable to find the proper visual reinforcement in his preliminary search for visuals.

  C. The instructor should approve the visualization project before extensive work is done. There should be two conferences with the instructor before the laboratory production session. After each conference changes in both script and visualization should be made along the lines suggested during the conference. At the first conference the student will need a complete rough draft of his script and all of the visuals that he is considering using. A final typed script should be brought to the second meeting, along with all of the visuals, appropriately mounted for on-camera presentation.

Project Three. This production utilizes two people—interviewer and interviewee. They will be seated comfortably together, with the cameras changing the visual picture through cutting, panning, and dollying in or back. The most important thing for the director to remember is that, from the video point of view, the guest is the star of the show. It is often far better to hear the interviewer's question from off-screen and keep the camera on the guest, whose immediate reaction may prove to be much more interesting. Good picture composition is a "must." Whether the hand-out exercise provided by the instructor or original material is used, the interview should appear natural and spontaneous. The interview time is 5 minutes. Title cards, the dissolve, the dolly, back-timing, etc. should be employed. The interviewer should back-time his closing remarks so that at the 1-minute or 30-second sign from the floor manager he can adjust his questions, signal his guest, and have a comfortable margin of time in which to conclude. The interviewer should realize that the best way to put himself at ease is to have a well-prepared introduction and closing.

Project Four. Have the student write a 1-minute commercial for production by his crew. The commercial will include a short, simple station break. The production will simulate the broadcast situation, moving from a network film to station break, to the commercial, and back to network film. Film length will be 60 seconds; SB, 10 seconds; and the commercial, 60 seconds.

Project Five. Example of residue directing. The student selects for production a 2-minute segment. This may consist of two back-to-back commercials, two public service announcements, other short productions that may take a form similar to that of "Dimension" on the CBS radio network, etc., or a combination of the above. First, a 60-second commercial, 10-second ID (graphic or slide), a 60-second PSA on film, and close with a 10-second ID with sound.

Project Six. ITV or ETV lecture. This production consists of a segment of an instructional television program. The emphasis will be ability to help the viewer visualize the course material. Encourage the student to use a multiplicity of visual aids—if they reinforce content. Time limit: 7 to 10 minutes.

Project Seven. Final production. The concluding production should be the most complex and carefully done of the semester. The program format and subject matter should be selected with approval of the instructor. This production will carry important weight in deciding the final course grade. Professional quality is expected in every production detail. Possible subjects: a dance sequence; dramatic scene; variety act; demonstration; skit. Encourage the student to seek outside-of-class talent for this project.

Advanced Television Production

Course Objectives. (1) To develop imagination, creativity, and esthetic judgment of different types of television programs. (2) To offer opportunities for the exercise of direction and leadership—in assuming command, in delegating responsibilities to others, in supervising their efforts, and in evaluating their performances. (3) To provide opportunities for the application of television broadcast techniques to specialized programs of an educational, informational, and cultural nature. (4) To develop and perfect skills involved in television production, and in a variety of production posts.

Facilities. A television studio and control room are required, with two-camera chains, film chain, video tape recorder, audio console, turntables and (or) tape cartridge machines, microphones, studio monitors, lighting instruments and board, scenery, miscellaneous props.

Course outline. Course content and procedures vary considerably among institutions, running the gamut from "canned" scripts distributed by the instructor to courses in which the students conceive, write, and produce all programs. A wide variety of program types are studied and two to three are produced: interview, news, musical, variety, quiz and audience participation, educational-instructional, documentary, dramatic, demonstration, sports, and remotes. Occasionally the class is divided into crews, or groups (of three to six), and each group produces two to three half-hour programs (universities with large class enrollment cut the program time to 14 minutes) during the course, or the equivalent in shorter programs, program segments, or spot announcements. Occasionally only one production is attempted, but it is an unusually complex and demanding one. All productions are videotaped and most are intended for broadcast on local educational or commercial outlets.

Role of the Instructor.   The instructor sees that the student acquires a variety of production-direction experience by assigning him a different production post in each program. The instructor serves as an advisor, guide, and counselor, approving program topics, suggesting methods of treatment, and serving as an at-elbow mentor as he circulates through the studio and control room. The instructor apprises each student periodically of his progress, or lack of it, in various phases of production, and of the effectiveness of his interpersonal relations with program participants and members of the production crew. This evaluation may take a number of forms: oral critiques during dry runs, immediately after a production, or in class, or conferences at a later date.

Program Ideas.   Each student is expected to report to the first class meeting with a written synopsis for two programs. Using the written synopsis as a "pony" each student makes an oral presentation to his instructor and the members of the class. The two or three productions for the quarter are chosen by the instructor and the members of the class. The members of this group role-play as members of a station staff, network, or sponsor organization, hearing a program presentation by a member of an agency, package producer, or entrepreneur. A superior written synopsis, oral presentation, and defense and argument in cross examination are often persuasive in the selection of the three best program ideas. In the event that no program ideas are deemed worthy of production the instructor supplies program ideas or scripts for the laboratory work.

Scripts.   Students are urged to submit scripts and projects conceived prior to enrolling in the course. Scripts written in writing courses, or independently over the summer, are likely to have more polish than those written in haste in the production class. Time does not permit the leisurely contemplation of program ideas, the writing of scripts, and the careful and detailed production of two or three meritorious programs all in one semester.

Production Procedures.   The purpose of the eight following required projects and reports is to assist the student in getting organized, in making up his mind. It is to enable him to fulfil his function as producer-director; to interpret the content of a program, to translate the ideas of his program into visual and aural images which communicate meaning.

1. The first step in preparing a program for production is the program outline, indicating what the program is, why it is, and how it is to be produced. The outline should consist of four main parts:

I. Purpose
   A. What is the general purpose of the program? To inform, to entertain, to persuade, or what? To what degree? In what combination? Include a general statement of general purpose.

    B. What is the specific purpose of the program? State it in a concise sentence, including the response you want from your audience.

    C. What value will the program have, if any, for the viewer? What will he get out of it? How will he profit?

      1. Will he be entertained? To what degree?

      2. Will his artistic-esthetic senses be appealed to?

      3. Will he receive information that will be of value to him?

      4. Are social or ethical problems presented and clarified?

II. Methods: This part of the Program Outline indicates how you anticipate fulfilling your purpose. You will want to include a discussion of the

    A. Content—The body of information that you want to communicate, the ideas you want to express, or the material or talent that you will use to provide entertainment, if it is a musical or dramatic program. How many units do you think you will have at this time? How long do you think each will run? What transitional devices do you plan to use to move from one major segment of the program to another?

    B. Form—Interview, panel discussion, voice-over narrator for film, still pictures, or pantomime, musical selections, scenes from plays, readings of literary works? Or what combination of these and other forms?

    C. Production—Will you use live talent, visuals (kind and number), film, recorded background music? Can you produce this program, and another one, during the course of this semester? (Avoid getting yourself into a "bind" with promises of film footage, talent, visuals, and so on, that are located away from your university or college, and which may not arrive in time to meet your deadlines). What devices can you use to give the program movement, pace, variety, unity, and climax?

    D. What is your working title at this time? Short enough for the television screen? Does it titillate, excite curiosity, or have mnemonic value?

    E. What are your preliminary estimates on cost? Can you produce the program for the amount currently allocated for each production?

III. Sources—This part of the program outline discusses the sources of information and (or) talent available to you. If you plan on using written sources for information you should include a list of books, periodicals, or articles. If you plan on using an expert, or talent of any kind, you should obtain a tentative commitment on his availability, and in your discussion you should make value judgments on his probable degree of interest, availability, and competence.

IV. Audience—Here you should discuss your analysis of the viewing audience. What is its nature? Composition? Number? Probable attitude toward your program topic? Probable response toward your program? You may want to consider the following:

    A. What interest-appeal factors are there inherent in the program content? Is it timely? Novel? Unique? Are there any emotional appeals inherent in the program content? Community pride, conflict, sympathy? Are there segments of the program that might appeal to basic human motives? To save money, preserve health, obtain group approval, and so on?

    B. Are there interest-appeal factors inherent in the talent or performers? Sex appeal, warmth, human interest, notoriety, humor, and so on?

    C. Do you think that viewer interest would be sustained during the program? Do you think it would have to be stimulated?

D. On what do you base your expectations of audience response? Have polls been conducted? Has the audience been analyzed or researched in any way? What is the makeup of the audience? Have you studied programs with similar content to judge their success or failure?

Each student must present a program outline at the first meeting of the class. No idea or program will be considered for production if a seriously thought-out and correctly prepared program outline is not submitted at the first meeting.

Once the program outline has been accepted by the class and the instructor, who reserves the right to final judgment, the producer-director can begin to formulate his program in detail. A series of additional reports and projects are to be completed during the formulative phase. Their completion, during the next several class meetings, will insure the creative development of the program.

Each report and project must be submitted to the instructor and other members of the crew *prior* to their discussion in class. Any report or project not submitted in advance will not receive consideration.

2. The content outline represents the producer-director's analysis of his program. The information to be presented during the program is arranged and organized in the content outline: the information should be classified into main topics and subtopics, arranged in some definite order; the place of each topic in the program should be clearly indicated. If the ideas or topics of the program are to be augmented by interview, by musical performance, or dramatic performance, the outline should indicate where each method of augmentation will occur. Approximately how long is each unit or segment expected to run?

Organized content and content arranged in outline form are discussed in *Speech: Its Techniques and Disciplines in a Free Society,* by William N. Brigance, New York: Appleton-Century-Crofts, 1952, Chapter 2, pp. 215–232 and Chapter 14, pp. 272–297.

3. Once the content of the program has been determined and organized, the producer-director can prepare the production treatment report.

When we televise or film an event, we do much more than just show what is going on. The camera and the microphone are essentially selective tools. We cannot use them without some degree of selectivity. How the subject is arranged, and how we look at it, may seem fortuitous, but our tools have selected their material from what is there.

The production treatment report should discuss the mood and atmosphere of the whole program and parts of the program; the idea or concept underlying the whole program and parts of the program; the visual-aural images which will embody and communicate mood, atmosphere, idea, and concept. It is concerned with the methods of communicating the intellectual and emotional meanings of the program.

The production treatment report, then, should discuss what is being communicated and how it can be communicated. The style of the production; the rhythm and tempo of the program; the overall shot pattern; the quality of music and sound effects; the symbols of meaning—these factors are to be discussed in the report.

It is concerned with the general treatment. You are not formulating specific shots or sounds; you are dealing with concepts.

4. The Script should be laid out in correct form. In the case of the semiscripted program, each discussant's remarks should be topically outlined. If the producer-director or writer is uncertain of the correct form and layout of the television script, he should refer to Herbert Zettl, *Television Production Handbook*, Belmont, Calif.: Wadsworth, 1968, pp. 443–451.

5. In his report on the selection of shots and sounds, the producer-director should organize his shots and visual images, the physical movement of the talent or performers and the specific sound effects and music. The positions of the microphone and cameras, the lighting, and the set should also be determined. The arrangement and organization of visual and aural images should be based on the production treatment report. Specificity is the key word in the selection of shots and sounds: The exact shot, the exact subject of each visual or film sequence, should be determined in this report.

6. The detailed shooting script is what you take into the control room with you. It represents the planning, writing, and creating that went into the preceding projects and reports. Three copies of the shooting script should be made. The first is for the beginning rehearsals; the second for the dress rehearsals; the third for performance. Not only should each shot, visual or film sequence, sound effect, music cue, lighting change be noted in the script, but their exact occurrence should also be scripted. The method of transition from shot to shot should be scripted: Are you cutting, dissolving, fading, etc.? Warnings for difficult shooting spots or special effects should be noted in the script.

7. About midway in the preparation of a program for production, a rehearsal schedule should be developed and submitted. The rehearsal schedule should include (1) the time and place of each rehearsal; (2) what you wish to accomplish during the whole rehearsal and at specific parts of the rehearsal; (3) who is involved at each rehearsal—talent and crew. The director must know what he wants to achieve during the whole rehearsal period, each specific rehearsal, and specific parts of each rehearsal. Rehearsals are not accidental. Everything that is to occur should be well planned in advance.

Copies of the rehearsal report will be distributed to the performers and talent when they are submitted to the class.

8. A production report is the permanent record of a program. As such, it

remains on file, open for study by faculty members, students, prospective employers, and (or) any other interested party.

When a program has been broadcast only fleeting memories remain. The production report provides concrete testament to the work, effort, and talent that was exerted to produce the program. In this respect, it is a significant document. In the highly competitive world of professional broadcasting, the student who can present a record of his past endeavors, indicating his ability to develop a program idea, to conceive of a production treatment, to work with performers and crew personnel, to evaluate his intellectual and creative efforts—this student, equipped with such a record, should certainly be able to hold his own against stiff competition, armed with the confidence which comes from a job well done.

It is important for the director to be able to evaluate his work and the work of his crew. Through critical evaluation the student director demonstrates his knowledge of the principles of production, direction, writing, and performance. Critical evaluation allows him to gain insights into his strength and weakness; it enables him to lay the foundation for future growth and development. Above all, critical evaluation permits the student director to establish professional standards which will serve as guidelines for excellence throughout his career in broadcasting.

Evaluations should be complete and thorough; specific and concrete. They should point out problems in detail and suggest their causes and methods of solution.

Evaluations should be positive; that is, they should be viewed as helping the director improve upon his performance and aiding in growth and development. In positive evaluations, criteria need to be established so that each point being evaluated may be measured against these criteria. Then a judgment must be rendered.

Subjective evaluation and unsupported evaluations should be avoided. To say that a particular production element was "good," or that something went "smooth," or was "OK," is not solid evaluation. To say, "I enjoyed directing," or "The cameraman did a terrific job," does not pinpoint the principles upon which the elements of production are based. For example, it is inadequate to say that someone was a good host. You need to ask why. What is the function of the host? What is his relationship to the guests? How should he act? What is he trying to accomplish? The answers to such questions will provide sound, critical, objective judgments.

Finally, all evaluations should be supported. Assertions and value judgments should be proved and developed with specific references and examples.

In essence, a production report is a textbook from which the student learns, enabling him to constantly improve, aiding him in his search for professional excellence.

The production report is the responsibility of the director of the program. The first draft of the Report is to be submitted to the faculty director *at least 2 weeks after the program has been produced.* The final draft must be approved by the third week following the production. It should include

A title sheet, including the name of the program, all crew and production personnel and their assignments, the quarter the program was produced, the date it was produced, the crew number, and the date the Report is submitted.
A detailed table of contents.
A title page for each major section.
A title affixed to each outline, report, script, or miscellaneous written material and project.
A method of pagination, with page numbers indicated in the table of contents.

The production report consists of four major sections, detailed in the following outline.

I. The Production Diary. This enables the reader to follow the step-by-step development of the program, from its inception to its fulfillment. It should contain final drafts, arranged in chronological order, of the following items:
   A. Program idea
   B. Content outline
   C. Program outline
   D. Production treatment report
   E. Content script
   F. Selection of shots and visuals
   G. Selection of sound and music
   H. Shooting script
II. The Production Aids. This record should contain the *final* plans, drafts, or designs of the following items:
   A. Floor plan
   B. Set design
   C. Light design
   D. Microphone placement design
   E. Cameramen's log
   F. Visual, slide, and (or) film cue sheets
   G. Audio cue sheets
   H. Lighting cue sheets
   I. Rehearsal schedule
   J. Crew assignments
III. The Production Evaluation
   A. Development of the program idea
      1. Program content
         a. Program idea or specific purpose
         b. Organization of the content of the program
         c. Writing of the program
         d. Communication of the program idea
      2. Production treatment. This evaluation should be concerned with how production treatment and methods contributed to the communication of the content (2a), and how the treatment and methods contributed to the interest and appeal of the program (2b).
         a. Interpretive value of the production treatment: shot composition,

shot variety, editing (shots in sequence), transitional devices, visualization, sound and music, lighting and set design, rhythm and tempo, style

   b. Aesthetic value of the production treatment: shot composition, shot variety, editing (shots in sequence), transitional devices, visualization, sound and music, lighting and set design, rhythm and tempo, style

B. Mechanics of Production. This evaluation should be concerned with the *quality* of the elements of production—the craftsmanship of the crew. It should emphasize technical considerations.
   1. Video: camera work, switching, picture quality
   2. Audio: sound and music, microphone quality, tape editing

C. The Performers. This evaluation is concerned with anyone who is seen on-camera or heard off-camera. It includes actors, musicians, guest experts, host, narrator, announcer, and so on. Critical emphasis should be on the director's work with the performer, as well as the performance itself.
   1. Planning the program idea with the performer
   2. Developing and planning the program with the performer
   3. Directing the performer
   4. The performance
   5. Human relations

D. Critiques by other members of the production crew, producer, writer, technical director, production secretary, and audio man, for example. Each major member of the crew should evaluate
   1. His own performance in the production
   2. The performances of other crew members
   3. The effectiveness of the completed program, covering as many of the above points given for the director as he feels are important and germane

E. The Director. This evaluation is supplied by the faculty director. Students working on the production should read the entire production report, but especially this section, and they should sign and date it on the last page.
   1. Planning the production
   2. Developing the production
   3. Coordinating the production
   4. Human relations
   5. Studio and control room procedure
   6. The performance

IV. The Appendix
A. Rewrites and revisions of outlines, reports, scripts, and miscellaneous written material and projects
B. Itemized budget
   1. Proposed budget
   2. Actual budget
C. Miscellaneous materials
   1. Publicity information prepared and issued by the crew
   2. Publicity information issued by outside sources (news clippings, *TV Guide*, synopsis, photos)
   3. Performers' release slips
   4. Thank-you letters

If the form and content of the production report meet the requirements set forth, each student director will have taken a step forward in preparing himself for entrance into the highly competitive world of professional broadcasting. He will have proven his ability to analyze, criticize, and remedy. He will have proven his competence as an organizer and coordinator. He will have proven his sincerity toward his profession. In short, he will have something of which he can be proud.

REFERENCES

Television Production

BRETZ, RUDY, *Techniques of Television Production*, New York: McGraw-Hill, 1962.

DAVIS, DESMOND, *The Grammar of Television Production*, New York: Macmillan, 1960.

JONES, PETER, *The Technique of the Television Cameraman*, New York: Hastings House, 1965.

LEWIS, COLBY, *The TV Director-Interpreter*, New York: Hastings House, 1968.

MC MAHAN, HARRY W., *TV Tape Commercials*, New York: Hastings House, 1960.

MILLERSON, GERALD, *Technique of Television Production*, New York: Hastings House, 1968.

STASHEFF, EDWARD AND BRETZ, RUDY, *The Television Program: Its Production and Direction*, New York: Hill & Wang, 1962.

WILLIS, EDGAR E., *Writing Television and Radio Programs*, New York: Holt, Rinehart & Winston, 1967.

ZETTL, HERBERT, *Television Production Handbook*, Belmont, Calif.: Wadsworth, 1968.

ZETTL, HERBERT, *Television Production Workbook*, Belmont, Calif.: Wadsworth, 1968.

Radio Production

GIRAUD, CHESTER, GARRISON, GARNET AND WILLIS, EDGAR, *Television and Radio*, New York: Appleton-Century-Crofts, 1963.

HILLIARD, ROBERT L., *Radio Broadcasting*, New York: Hastings House, 1967.

HYDE, STUART, *Television and Radio Announcing*, Boston: Houghton Mifflin, 1959.

LAWTON, SHERMAN, *The Modern Broadcaster*, New York: Harper & Row, 1961.

NISBETT, ALEC, *The Techniques of the Sound Studio*, New York: Hastings House, 1962.

ORINGEL, ROBERT, *Audio Control Handbook*, New York: Hastings House, 1962.

WILLIS, EDGAR, *A Radio Director's Manual*, Ann Arbor, Mich.: Ann Arbor Publishers, 1961.

12. Teaching Speech Content

Owen Peterson

The first and most essential requirement of effective speech is that the speaker have ideas worthy of communication. All other elements essential to effective speaking serve to enhance and to clarify the speaker's premises. If content is not substantial, the other elements—style, organization, and delivery—become useless trappings, and even the most skilled speaker cannot hope to achieve eloquence. Thus, one of the instructor's most important duties is to teach the student how to find, to analyze, and to use effective speech materials.

Speech content, or the speaker's invention, includes his choice of subject, his arguments, and his methods of developing and supporting his ideas; it embraces the adaptation of his thoughts and evidence to his listeners, to the occasion, and to the speaker himself; it involves the speaker's attempts to utilize ideas and materials in achieving his purpose in speaking.

SCOPE OF THE UNIT IN SPEECH CONTENT

The instructor should regard every classroom speech as an assignment in speech content; thus, speaking activities designed primarily to teach students specific skills, principles, or types of speech also afford an opportunity to stress the importance of subject matter.

Although the instructor teaches speech content throughout the course, he also should focus specific attention on this important aspect through

266

systematic study, exercises, and speaking assignments. The following outline can be adapted to fit a variety of assignments.

    I. The nature and importance of content
       A. Definition of speech content
       B. How content differs from other aspects of speaking
       C. Importance of speech content
   II. Selection of speech topics
       A. Sources
       B. Criteria
       C. Narrowing the topic
  III. The purposive nature of speech
       A. Types of speeches according to purpose
          1. Speeches to inform
          2. Speeches to entertain
          3. Speeches to convince
          4. Speeches to persuade or actuate
          5. Speeches to stimulate or impress
       B. Influence of the speaker's purpose on his selection of a topic and his formulation of a central thought
          1. How to determine the purpose
          2. How to select a speech topic suitable to the speaker's purpose
          3. How to frame the central thought or thesis
       C. Influence of the speaker's purpose on his selection of supporting materials
   IV. Sources of information and supporting materials
       A. Personal observations and experiences
       B. Interviews, broadcasts, telecasts, speeches
       C. The library
          1. General reference works
          2. Books
          3. Periodicals
          4. Newspapers
          5. Pamphlets and brochures
          6. Government documents
       D. Other sources
          1. Special interest groups and organizations
          2. Members of Congress and other government officials
    V. Collecting supporting materials
       A. Reading with a purpose
       B. Note taking
   VI. Analysis of the topic
       A. How to divide or partition a subject
       B. How to find issues
       C. Definition of an issue
       D. Selection of issues
  VII. Developing an idea by exposition
       A. Types of supporting materials (details, examples, statistics, etc.)
       B. Uses of supporting materials (narration, exposition, definition)
 VIII. Developing an idea by argument
       A. Definition of some terms

1. What is a fact?
2. What is evidence?
3. What is argument?
   a. What is a syllogism?
   b. What is an enthymeme?
  B. Kinds of proof
   1. Logical proof
   2. Emotional proof
   3. Ethical proof
  C. Types of argumentative supporting materials
IX. Testing argument and evidence
  A. The tests of argument and reasoning
  B. The tests of evidence
X. The presentation of supporting materials
  A. Use of notes
  B. Use of visual aids
  C. Clarifying statistics
  D. Inductive versus deductive presentation

AN APPROACH TO THE TEACHING OF SPEECH CONTENT

Teaching speech content presents several problems that the instructor is unlikely to encounter in the study of the other elements of effective speech. Unlike language, organization, pronunciation, and some of the other elements of speech in which there is a fairly clear-cut distinction between correct and incorrect, clear and unclear, proper and improper, good speech content is largely a matter of point of view. In addition to his own judgment of the content of a speech, the teacher must always consider the attitudes and interests of the speaker himself and his listeners.

An awareness of speaker and audience attitudes and interests is particularly important in teaching audience adaptation, the choice of subjects and materials, and the importance of reliable supporting material and in checking on the instructor's own objectivity. Teaching speech content may be approached in several ways. One possible method is suggested below and then applied to the problems mentioned.

In the opinion of the writer, speech content can best be taught in a democratic and permissive classroom situation which encourages student freedom of expression and choice wherever possible. To remind a speech teacher of the importance of free speech may seem unnecessary. Regrettably, it is not. Some speech classes are among the most undemocratic in the school: the teacher dictates the subjects for student speeches, serves as the sole judge of the effectiveness of the speech, and, indirectly but nonetheless firmly, determines what the student should say. This approach not only is questionable pedagogically, but also makes the teacher's task more difficult than it need be. If the instructor assigns topics for speeches, the student is deprived of practice in selecting subjects suitable to his audience.

If the teacher serves as the sole judge of the effectiveness of classroom speeches, the student is deprived of the opportunity to develop skill in audience adaptation; for, instead of learning to adapt to listeners of varied interests and background, he speaks to please only one person. Finally, if the instructor is overly critical of ideas that conflict with his own, the student is deprived of valuable training in analysis and argumentation, for he will quickly learn to accommodate his remarks to the prejudices of that all-important listener, the instructor.

While the greatest disadvantage of the authoritarian approach undoubtedly lies in the restrictions and limitation that it places on the nature of the students' speech training, this method also imposes unnecessary burdens on the teacher. If a truly democratic and open atmosphere prevails in the classroom, the students can and will do much of the instructor's work—and often more effectively than he—in evaluating speech content.

Three aspects of teaching speech content in which this approach is helpful are (1) teaching audience adaptation, (2) teaching choice of subjects and materials, and (3) teaching the importance of reliable content.

Teaching Audience Adaptation

If he wishes his students to develop skill in audience analysis and adaptation, the instructor must provide a speaking situation that requires the speaker to take into account and to adjust to differences in the background, understanding, interests, and attitudes of his listeners. Since the audience consisting of both the instructor and the class provides a more heterogeneous group of hearers and a more challenging and realistic speaking situation than does a single listener, the teacher will wish to discover and consider the reactions of the entire class.

In evaluating the content of a student speech an instructor often finds it difficult to gauge its suitability to the audience. Most students are reluctant, especially early in the course, to admit that they were confused by a fellow student's speech. When the instructor asks the class members if they understood the speech, he probably will get an affirmative response from all. However, if the class is to play a significant role in evaluation, it must be more than a mutual admiration society.

The teacher can employ several approaches to secure a candid reaction from the students. First, if the teacher himself did not understand the speech, the chances are good that others also were confused. To test their comprehension, the instructor may begin by inviting the class to question the speaker on points that they did not understand. If this evokes several questions, it is justifiable to point out that the speaker apparently failed to make his ideas completely clear. If the invitation to question the speaker brings no response and if the instructor still suspects that the speech was not understood, he may ask members to volunteer to present 2-minute summaries of the speech. The number of students who are willing to attempt short summaries usually reveals the general response to the speech. Questioning those who were unwilling to present a summary on what they did not understand usually will evoke valuable criticism.

The teacher may also assess audience understanding of a speech by asking questions concerning specific concepts developed by the speaker. For example, the instructor may reasonably expect girls to have some trouble grasping all of the details in speeches on offensive football plays, how to build a hot rod, and the basic principles of jet propulsion. On the other hand, he may expect boys to experience difficulty in understanding terminology concerning how to make Danish pastry, the application of cosmetics, and similar topics. In each of these examples, the instructor probably should probe the suitability and the appropriateness of the subject matter to the audience. A few specific questions directed to persons the instructor suspects did not understand the speech will often reveal to the teacher and the student the speaker's weaknesses. This approach is particularly effective in college classes in which students in one section come from several different colleges or fields of study—engineers, premedical and prelaw students, musicians, art majors. The discovery by the student that the basic terms and fundamental concepts that he uses every day in his major area of study mean little to persons in other fields provides a valuable lesson in audience adaptation.

In testing the appropriateness of subject and supporting materials, the instructor should insist that the audience is always right. If listeners are bored, he should stress that the topic or its development was ill-suited to the audience; if classmates did not understand the speech, he should insist the material was unclear or too technical. For a speaker to argue that his audience *should* have been interested or *should* have understood does not alter the fact that speakers cannot choose their listeners, but must take them as they find them.

Another approach to teaching speech content is the hypothetical situation. In an effort to provide students with a variety of audiences, some instructors let their students deliver speeches to imaginary audiences on hypothetical occasions. This approach poses several questions. As soon as the student begins to speak, the instructor is faced with the impossible task of determining how the imaginary listeners would react to the speech. Would they be interested in this topic? Would they understand these terms? Would they be impressed by this argument? Would they be motivated by this appeal? These and dozens of similar questions arise in the mind of the discerning teacher.

How can these questions be answered? Unless the instructor is presumptuous enough to assume that he can accurately foretell how a Ubangi tribe would react to a missionary's plea, how wildcat strikers would respond to a union leader, or how the Daughters of the American Revolution would react to Stokely Carmichael, there is no way of accurately evaluating speech content in hypothetical situations. At best, the teacher must rely on an educated guess; but he has no assurance that his guess is either right or any better than the student's guess. If the instructor assigns imaginary speeches to imaginary audiences by imaginary speakers, the best evaluation he can provide the speaker is a judgment based on imagination. For this reason, the teacher probably should avoid assignments of this type. Since the classroom provides an audience and a situation in which the speaker's efforts can be judged in the light of actual responses, opinions, and attitudes, there seems to be little point in constructing a wholly unrealistic and hypothetical situation in which nothing can be measured with certainty or accuracy.

Teaching Choice of Subjects and Materials

Effective speaking is based on the selection of subjects and materials that are familiar and interesting to the speaker. Thus, another task of the instructor in teaching speech content is to determine the suitability of the speaker's choice of topics and his supporting details.

Since the subject matter of most speeches outside the classroom is based on the speakers' interests and experiences, if practice in speaking in the classroom is to be realistic, the student should draw on his own interests and knowledge for his speeches. He, of course, should then supplement his ideas with the observations and opinions of others. As a critic, the instructor sometimes finds it difficult to determine the degree of understanding and interest of the speaker in relation to his subject. Specifically, he may wonder: (1) Is the subject matter accurate? (2) Is the subject matter original?

The first of these questions is the easier to answer. The teacher's own knowledge of a subject often enables him to detect inaccuracies, omissions, and other errors indicating the speaker's inadequate understanding of his material. If the instructor is not familiar with the subject, he may invite the class to question the speaker about his topic. If the proper atmosphere has been created, members should not hesitate to inquire about aspects they failed to understand. The speaker's handling of questions often reveals much about his familiarity with the subject. Furthermore, the knowledge that he may be expected to answer questions may discourage him from speaking on subjects with which he is unfamiliar.

The question of originality undoubtedly is the more serious of the two, for plagiarism is no less reprehensible in speaking than in writing. To take another's ideas and to pass them off as one's own, whether in written or oral discourse, is both unethical and dishonest. This, of course, is not to suggest that the opinions and statements of others are to be excluded from public speeches. The student should be encouraged to investigate a variety of sources on his topic and to utilize data from several different ones. However, he should be taught to give credit to the source supplying his information.

What are the clues that distinguish plagiarized speech from original discourse, and how can the instructor detect and discourage plagiarism? There is no foolproof formula for detecting plagiarism; however, speeches that are not original often display at least some of the following characteristics:

1. The speaker shows little interest in the subject.
2. The speaker seems to lack familiarity with his material; he relies heavily on notes and seems uncertain of himself.
3. The speaker has difficulty in correctly pronouncing proper names and technical terms.
4. The speaker's language does not seem to be his own; it sounds written rather than oral, with long and complex sentences and phrases; it uses the third person almost exclusively; and it possesses a "literary" tone and other characteristics of written composition. The speech may even include phrases such as "the above paragraph" or "the above reasons."
5. The speech includes no personal observations, experiences, or conclusions.
6. The speech seems to have no relation to the known interests and experiences of the speaker; the teacher cannot understand why the speaker selected this subject or how he obtained his information.
7. Finally, the teacher remembers having read the same material in a recent Sunday newspaper supplement or *Reader's Digest*.

What should the instructor do if he suspects that a student's speech is not original? First, he should be cautious about accusing the student of plagiarism on the basis of most of the above characteristics. Except for the last criterion, each of these characteristics may result from some other cause. Although the student's material was original he may have written the entire speech; consequently the style sounded written rather than oral. He may have prepared insufficiently or have failed to consult a dictionary to learn the correct pronunciation of some terms. He may simply have neglected to include personal observations and experiences or to show how and why he became interested in such an unusual topic. All of these are weaknesses of the speech and should be pointed out to the student, but they do not constitute plagiarism.

To discover the source of the speaker's material when the teacher is in doubt, the best approach probably is to ask the student directly where he obtained his information. If the instructor recalls having read the same material, he should mention this fact. In either case, if the speech was not original, the teacher should stress the seriousness of plagiarism, and he should penalize the student accordingly.

How can a teacher encourage students to select subjects and supporting material based on personal interest and knowledge? Early in the course, he should emphasize the following:

1. That the speaker usually is more enthusiastic, natural, and direct if his subject matter is drawn from his personal experiences.
2. That the speaker usually is more confident, fluent, and sure of his material when his materials come from his own knowledge and wide reading.
3. That the speaker's task actually is easier if he is already interested in and familiar with his subject.
4. That, throughout his life, the student will speak on topics related to his own activities.
5. That the speaker who repeats or summarizes materials appearing in popular journals or newspapers runs the risk of boring listeners who have read the article or report.

Teaching the Importance of Reliable Content

The unit devoted to speech content should develop in the student a healthy skepticism for the printed word. If he is to be a well-informed speaker, the student must supplement his own ideas and observations with information drawn from a variety of sources. If he is to be a persuasive speaker, he must reinforce his arguments with expert testimony, reliable statistics, and unbiased evidence. Unfortunately, many students possess neither the faintest inclination to question the reliability of sources nor the vaguest idea of how to evaluate ideas were they so inclined. This is due partly to the fact that many have not read widely. At both the high school and college levels, many students read little other than required textbook assignments, a few popular magazines, and perhaps parts of the daily newspaper. To add to the teacher's difficulties, many students regard the printed word as law. Because at some earlier stage in his education the textbook was the final adjudicator between "right" and "wrong," the student too often considers anything and everything printed as inviolate.

The speech teacher first must teach the student that the printed word is the product of human, fallible hands and that often the only requirement for breaking into print is sufficient money to pay the printer. But, having planted the first seed of doubt, how is the instructor to teach the student the biases, prejudices, political leanings, pet projects, peeves, and personal foibles of the thousands of authors, editors, and publishers of newspapers, magazines, and books? Obviously he cannot. At best, he may point out the biases of some prominent publications and may suggest the subjects on which they would probably be regarded as poor sources by the well-informed reader and other matters about which they may be acceptable to most people. He must emphasize that the student should consult many sources to gain an understanding of a problem. He must assist his students in setting up criteria to measure and to evaluate the sources of evidence.

Having done this, the instructor still needs to reinforce and to re-emphasize the importance of reputable and reliable sources. First, as a critic he should be well informed himself. Second, he should be objective, taking care that his own biases do not unduly influence him. Third, he should be tactful and tolerant in evaluating materials. An expression of disgust or utter contempt for a particular source is far less effective than a calm and thorough explanation of why a source probably will not prove acceptable to most well-informed auditors.

Objectivity in Teaching Speech Content

Perhaps the single most important attribute of effective speech criticism is objectivity. Every teacher of speech strives to be impartial in his evaluation of the content of student performances; yet no matter how diligently he cultivates this virtue almost every teacher at times wonders whether he has been entirely fair in his judgment of a particular speech. The problem becomes particularly acute in argumentative speeches, debates, and discussions. The teacher, possessing his full share of both conscious and subconscious instincts, emotions, feelings, drive, desires, motivations, and experiences has a natural tendency to be overly critical when someone contradicts a deep-seated conviction or long-held belief. If he believes in racial equality, can he consider objectively a speech in favor of segregated schools? If he comes from a family or community heavily indebted to organized labor for improved wages, hours, and working conditions, can he regard impartially an attack on unionism? And how open-minded and receptive will he be toward a speech whose central thought is, "The low caliber of teaching at this school must be improved." Conversely, if the speaker endorses beliefs shared by the instructor, is the teacher not likely to be less critical and exacting than otherwise in his demands? Will the arguments and evidence of the student who contends that teachers are underpaid or that every student should be required to take a course in speech be subjected to the same rigorous scrutiny as the content of a speech that contradicts a personal predilection of the teacher?

How can the teacher prevent biased listening of this type? Should he seek to find the correct answer to every question and undertake to settle once and for all time the "rightness" or "wrongness" of each point of view presented in his classes? Or should he pretend that there is no right or wrong answer to any question?

The first solution obviously is unsatisfactory. If he adopts this approach the teacher not only proscribes all freedom of speech in the classroom, but he places himself in the untenable position of an infallible judge of all about him. Should he then adopt the position that every question has two sides and it is not his job to distinguish between the alternatives? If this approach is construed to mean that every question has two *equally* valid sides and that the only requirement for satisfactory content is that the speaker present *some* arguments and evidence to support his contention, this position is hardly more tenable than is the former. If he adopts this attitude, he can say little in criticism of a speech in which the speaker contends that polio is a blessing because it teaches the victim to appreciate the blessed gift of good health, it permits him abundant leisure in which to contemplate the universe and to improve his mind, it helps him develop compassion for all of the handicapped. While these are valid arguments for which any enterprising student could find ample supporting evidence, they simply do not prove the main contention. To permit the student to indulge in this kind of reasoning without critical comment is a disservice. Thus, the teacher cannot avoid the evaluative process.

If students are to feel free to speak on either side of any proposition without fear of penalty, the speech teacher must seek to cultivate his own objectivity. To accomplish this he must do the following:

1. Refrain from regarding himself as the final authority on all subjects.
2. Try to curb the tendency to be overly critical of unpopular viewpoints.
3. Develop a more critical attitude toward his own beliefs and convictions.
4. Encourage class discussion of student speeches and take cognizance of the response of the *entire* audience.
5. Most important, he should withhold judgment on the main contention until he has considered the speaker's content from the point of view of the acceptability of his basic premises, the validity of his reasoning, and the adequacy of his supporting material. The teacher need not determine whether the speaker has taken the "right" stand on the question; but rather he should discover whether the student's reasoning and evidence support the conclusion he has drawn. The teacher's criticism should concern the adequacy of the supporting materials and the validity of the speaker's reasoning. One method of revealing weaknesses in speech content is through questions concerning the speaker's argument and evidence. If the teacher can lead the student, by questions, to see the fallacy of his argument or the inadequacy of his evidence, the student probably will be less inclined to attribute criticism to personal differences of opinion and more inclined to accept the instructor's suggestions for improvement. The accompanying table on p. 276 contrasts the types of questions that are likely to lead to penetrating self-analysis by the student with questions that often provoke disagreement and incur ill will.

The indirect approaches suggested can also be turned to the audience to direct them to evaluate speeches on the basis of the reasoning and evidence. By repeatedly emphasizing the importance of ample supporting facts and carefully constructed arguments, the instructor can greatly improve the critical insight of the students.

METHODS OF TEACHING SPEECH CONTENT

Speech content probably is best taught through the evaluation of student speeches. However, if the student is to derive maximum benefit from critical analysis of his speeches, he must first know what constitutes good speech content. For this reason, the instructor probably will wish to sched-

Direct vs. Indirect Approaches to Evaluating Evidence and Argument

Type of Weakness in the Speech	Direct Approach by the Instructor (Undesirable)	Indirect Approach by the Instructor (Preferable)
Argument developed around minor or secondary issues	Tell speaker that these arguments are unimportant; issues which he should have discussed are A, B, C.	Ask questions that will lead the speaker to see relative importance of various issues; then suggest that speech would have been more effective if major issues had been discussed.
Argument revealed poor understanding of part or all of the subject	Tell speaker that he doesn't know what he's talking about; and that he should have said D, E, F.	Ask questions that will lead speaker to see his lack of understanding. Suggest sources he might investigate to clear up confusion.
Inadequate supporting evidence	Instruct the speaker to add quotation by G or example of H.	Ask whether the speaker's single piece of evidence is enough to warrant his conclusion.
Biased authority or source	Tell speaker that J is prejudiced and that he should substitute statement by K or L.	Ask speaker whether he thinks J is completely unbiased. If not, ask speaker if he has any evidence that is more objective.
Fallacious argument	Tell speaker argument was fallacious because M, N, O.	Through questions, get speaker to reconstruct argument in form of a syllogism and test validity of his own reasoning.
Out-of-date evidence	Tell speaker that his evidence is out-of-date, that the situation has changed in these ways, and that he should have cited P, Q, R.	Ask speaker if he can think of any changes since date of the evidence that might have altered condition under discussion. Then ask speaker where he might have obtained more recent data.

ule a unit on this aspect early in the course. The unit need not include all of the material suggested in the outline on pp. 267–268, but it probably should embrace those aspects essential to early speaking assignments. In presenting material, the teacher may employ lectures, class discussions, reading assignments, and written and oral exercises designed to give the student practice in applying the principles of effective subject matter.

Written Exercises

In the following exercises, which are designed to suggest possible approaches to the study of content, the teacher probably should assign one or two of the written assignments before each speaking assignment.

Student Assignments

1. Have each student prepare an inventory of possible speech topics for future use in the class. Suggest that students make a list of sources of speech topics (personal experiences, reading, sports, extracurricular activities, radio and television, etc.). Under each heading he will then attempt to list several topics in which he is interested.
2. Require each student to select four or five topics from his speech subjects inventory (or, if this exercise has not been assigned, to select four or five topics in which he is interested) and apply the tests of a good speech subject to each.
3. Ask each student to select four or five topics from his speech subject inventory and to evaluate the suitability of each topic for several hypothetical audiences or occasions which the teacher has devised (i.e., meetings of the Boy Scouts, PTA, Kiwanis Club, Sunday school class, Catholic Youth Organization, or the Golden Age Club; a school banquet; dedication of a new library; etc.).
4. Assign a general subject with which the entire class is familiar (i.e., sports, clothing, books) and ask each student to narrow the subject by progressive steps. (See Figure 2. In this case, a specific purpose might be: "to show the prospects of the DePauw University basketball team for the coming season.")
5. Ask each student to select a subject and frame a central thought suitable for a speech (1) to inform, (2) to entertain, (3) to convince, (4) to persuade or actuate, and (5) to stimulate or impress.
6. Ask each student to prepare a bibliography on some subject taken from his speech subjects inventory (other than a topic based on personal experience). The teacher may specify the number and kinds of sources to be included or may leave this to the discretion of the student.
7. Have each student prepare five note cards on his reading in preparation for a speech to convince or persuade. Check the note cards for correctness of form, identification of sources, and usefulness in speech preparation.
8. Have each student find and bring to class three one-sentence items from newspapers, magazines, or books that appear to be statements of fact and three that clearly are theories, hypotheses, or opinions.
9. Exercise 8 may be followed by an assignment to verify two of the three statements of fact. If this exercise is used, the instructor should not indicate in advance that the students will later be asked to verify the statements of fact. He probably should suggest, however, that the students try to find statements of fact concerning local events or conditions.

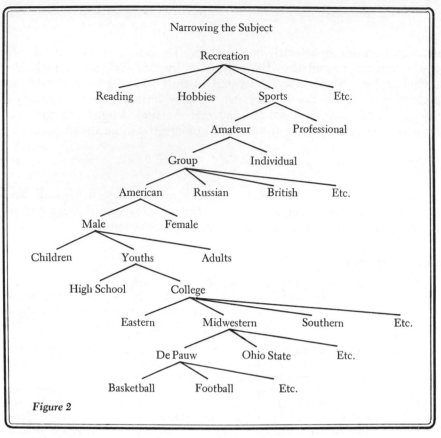

Narrowing the Subject

Recreation

Reading   Hobbies   Sports   Etc.

Amateur   Professional

Group   Individual

American   Russian   British   Etc.

Male   Female

Children   Youths   Adults

High School   College

Eastern   Midwestern   Southern   Etc.

De Pauw   Ohio State   Etc.

Basketball   Football   Etc.

Figure 2

10. Prepare a list of enthymemes and provide each member of the class with a copy. Ask the class members to construct a syllogism from each by supplying the missing premises and to identify each type of syllogism as to kind.
11. Prepare a list of syllogisms. Ask class members to (1) identify each as to kind, (2) test the validity of each, and (3) indicate why each syllogism is valid or invalid.
12. Ask each student to find in a newspaper, magazine, speech, or book an example of of each of several types of argument, i.e., argument by authority, argument from specific instances, argument by analogy.
13. Ask each student to find in a newspaper, magazine, book or other publication an example of each of several kinds of supporting material.
14. Assignment 12 may be followed or supplemented by requiring students to evaluate the supporting material used in each of the arguments cited.
15. Prepare a list of well-known publications (i.e., *Time*, Chicago *Tribune*, *Democratic Digest*, *New Republic*) and ask each student to attempt to determine possible biases and prejudices that he might expect to discover in each publication.
16. Assign a study of the reporting of a given event by several different newspapers, if possible from different areas (i.e., the *New York Times*, New Orleans *Times-Picayune*, Denver *Post*, the Chicago *Tribune*).
17. Have the class compare the reports of a Congressional speech as presented in a newspaper or magazine and in the *Congressional Record*.
18. Assign a written analysis of the supporting material in a printed speech in the *New York Times*, *Vital Speeches of the Day*, or *Representative American Speeches*.

19. Distribute copies of an editorial that utilizes several types of supporting material. Have class members identify types of supporting materials used in the editorial. The teacher may also, if he wishes, require the students to evaluate the supporting evidence.
20. Prepare a series of arguments—some valid and some invalid. Ask class to evaluate each.
21. Classify and evaluate the arguments and evidence in several magazine advertisements.
22. Ask each student to find at least one reputable and acceptable authority or expert on each of several diverse subjects (such as Arab nationalism, opera, atomic submarines, narcotics addiction, overpopulation, prison riots, etc.). Each student should cite qualifications of the authority and indicate why he would be acceptable to most audiences.
23. Ask students to find in newspapers, magazines, speeches, or books examples of several different kinds of illogical or faulty argument (i.e., unsupported assertions, arguing in a circle, ignoring the question, slanted or emotionalized language, substitution of questions for argument, name calling, etc.).

Speaking Exercises

It is impossible to suggest even a small percentage of different speaking assignments that the teacher may utilize in teaching speech content. The exercises below are designed for a special unit and are included because they focus attention on the speaker's subject matter and require him to demonstrate understanding and mastery.

Student Assignments

1. Assign a speech to inform in which the student develops his ideas primarily through the use of one or two specified types of supporting details (i.e., examples or illustration, comparison or contrast, narration, definition, etc.)
2. In order to acquaint the students with the library and research methods, assign a speech on a topic with which the student is unfamiliar.

100 Unfamiliar Subjects Designed to Acquaint Students with Library and Research Methods

1. Why we bury the dead
2. The origin of the Academy Awards
3. Chief principles of Fascism
4. How to score points in pinochle
5. Personality—what it is
6. Chief tenets of Moslem religion
7. Rationalization
8. Causes of earthquakes
9. How a warm front develops
10. Ethnocentrism
11. The antiquity of insects
12. Methods of gate crashing
13. Why the Great Lakes tilt
14. Training dogs for the blind
15. Positions in fencing
16. How a newspaper is printed
17. How to tie a bowline knot
18. Esperanto
19. What makes clothes "dramatic"
20. Training dogs for hunting
21. Hunting to hounds
22. Hazards of the home
23. What makes people buy
24. What goes on in a beehive
25. How records are pressed
26. Why we have social strata
27. Why the tower of Pisa leans
28. The Fabian Society
29. Modern etiquette
30. What determines our hobbies

31. How weather is forecast
32. Why we sleep
33. How to clean a rabbit
34. How to bind a book
35. How a cold front develops
36. Mardi Gras
37. The four thermometer scales
38. How hail is produced
39. How to apply an arm splint
40. The sine curve
41. Causes of drought
42. How to convert time in time zones
43. What constitutes literature
44. Powers of the Federal Communications Commission
45. Interpretation of dreams
46. The essence of jazz
47. How a television commercial is made
48. Sources of superstition
49. Wirephoto
50. Palmistry
51. Chief causes of suicide
52. The photoelectric cell
53. Mercy killing
54. The Davis Cup in tennis
55. Delusion and illusion
56. The scientific lie detector
57. Making an etching
58. How to select a good steak
59. How to improve your memory
60. Why birds sing
61. Balance and emphasis in pictures
62. Products from waste wood
63. Habits of salmon
64. Antiquity of wedding customs
65. Plastic surgery
66. Economic value of cheese
67. Methods of trick photography
68. How to ski jump
69. How fish see
70. Taxidermy
71. Handling and classification of telegrams
72. The art of cockfighting
73. The bunt in baseball
74. How sound is recorded on tape
75. Jefferson's idea of liberty
76. How an igloo is built
77. Caring for indoor plants
78. Writing good letters
79. Honor system
80. Setting stones in rings
81. How income tax money is used
82. The Astrodome
83. The fingerprint system
84. Air traffic control
85. How to play the bagpipe
86. City manager form of government
87. Mayor-council form of government
88. Soy beans as a crop
89. Control of soil erosion
90. Causes of inflation
91. Paul Bunyan
92. The Nobel prize
93. The sculpting of Mt. Rushmore
94. Balanced diet
95. Buying a car
96. Planning a garden
97. Types of advertising
98. Filling a silo
99. How to play soccer
100. The great Chicago fire

3. Assign an expository speech in which the student explains or defines some abstract, philosophical, and (or) theoretical concept. Suggest terms such as the following:

agnosticism	democracy	highbrow	progressive
anarchy	discrimination	ignorance	race
art	empathy	illiteracy	rationalism
atheism	equal rights	libel	rationalization
capitalism	equality	liberal	reactionary
charisma	ethical	moral	romanticism
classicism	ethnocentrism	nationality	slander
communism	faith	nihilism	sympathy
culture	fanaticism	prejudice	

To prevent several speeches on the same subject, assign topics or let students choose topics with the provision that each student must secure the teacher's approval; and allow no more than two students to speak on any one topic.

4. Assign a short speech to convince or to persuade in which the student is instructed to depend primarily on one or two specified types of supporting evidence (i.e., testimony, analogy, specific instances or examples, statistics).

5. Assign a 2-minute speech in which the student is asked to prove a single point. Stress the necessity of limiting the subject to a topic sufficiently narrow that it can be proved in this short time. Emphasize, too, the difference between proving a contention and simply elaborating on a fact. Indicate that the student should (1) state in a single declarative sentence the point he plans to prove, (2) present his supporting evidence, and (3) restate his point.

6. Assign a speech in which the student either agrees or disagrees with an opinion expressed in an editorial. The student must present supporting material in addition to that found in the editorial to reinforce his stand.

7. Assign a speech to persuade in which the speaker asks for an immediate (within two or three days) overt response. When the assignment is made, warn the speakers that one week later they will be asked to report orally on how successful they were in obtaining the desired response from their classmates and to explain the reasons for their success or failure. It is important that the speakers know in advance that they will be expected to measure the response to their speeches so that they will propose specific overt actions and can devise a method of measuring (self-addressed postcards, interviews, telephone calls, questionnaires, etc.) the response. To motivate students, announce that their grade on the assignment will depend in part on their success in persuading their classmates.

8. Assign a speech to actuate in which the speaker urges an unpopular course of action. Be sure to define carefully *unpopular*. One definition of the phrase "an unpopular course of action" might be an action that the speaker judges a majority of his listeners will not want to perform—they not only are apathetic, but are actually opposed to this course of action. This assignment, which should come late in the unit or semester, not only challenges the student to utilize the strongest and most persuasive forms of support at his command, but also serves to test his ability to analyze his audience.

9. Assign an argumentative speech on some local, state, national, or international problem of current interest. The speaker's purpose may be either to convince or to actuate.

10. Assign a speech on how some speaker heard by the student succeeded or failed because of good or poor adaptation to the audience or occasion. Suggest that the student consider the speaker's choice of subject, purpose or central thought, and supporting material in relation to his listeners and occasion.

11. Assign a speech in which the student is required to simplify or clarify complex statistical data, a relationship, an analogy, or other supporting material through the use of a visual aid. You may wish to designate the type of visual aid to be utilized.

EXERCISES

1. Prepare a four-week unit on speech content for a high school or college speech class. Include the following: (a) objectives, (b) assigned readings, (c) activities, and (d) examination.

2. Begin a collection of examples of fallacious reasoning found in advertisements, editorials, and newspaper and magazine articles and columns.

3. Prepare a test on the syllogism for a high school or college speech class. Include at least 10 syllogisms, some valid and some invalid. Ask students to classify and evaluate the syllogisms.

4. Begin a collection of examples of inadequate supporting evidence found in advertisements, editorials, and newspaper and magazine articles and columns.
5. Prepare a test on supporting materials for a high school or college speech class. Include several examples of both good and poor supporting materials. Ask students to classify types of supporting materials used and to evaluate the supporting material.
6. Prepare a self-inventory of topics toward which you are likely to be biased in your listening. List both those topics toward which you would be inclined to react favorably and those toward which you would be inclined to react unfavorably.
7. Prepare a rating blank for evaluating speech content.
8. Visit a speech class on a day when students are assigned to present speeches. Using a prepared rating blank, evaluate the content of the speeches you hear. Also note how the instructor handles the evaluation of speeches.
9. Aftr careful thought, write a paragraph on "How I would handle plagiarism in speech classes."
10. Compare the chapters on speech content in several high school or college speech textbooks, select the three books you think present the best treatment of the subject, and, in a short paper, justify your choices.

REFERENCES

BRYANT, DONALD C., "The Role of Rigor in the Teaching of Speech," *Speech Teacher*, January, 1952, 1:20–21.
CHASE, STUART, *Guides to Straight Thinking*, New York: Harper & Row, 1956.
GUNDERSON, ROBERT, "Teaching Critical Thinking," *Speech Teacher*, March 1961, 10:100–104.
HOWELL, WILLIAM S., "Training the Speaker: Deductive Logic," *Speech Teacher*, March, 1957, 6:106–108.
KERR, HARRY P., "Using *Opinion and Evidence*: The Case Method," *Speech Teacher*, January, 1967, 16:19.
LUSTY, BEVERLY L., "Speech Content in Language Arts Textbooks," *Speech Teacher*, November, 1967, 16:289–294.
MC EDWARDS, MARY G., "The Student and His Logic," *Speech Teacher*, January, 1965, 14:35–37.
RUBY, LIONEL, *The Art of Making Sense*, Philadelphia: Lippincott, 1954.
SARETT, LEW, FOSTER, WILLIAM TRUFANT, AND MCBURNEY, JAMES H., *Speech: A High School Course*, Boston: Houghton Mifflin, 1956, chap. 13, "How to Develop Ideas in Speech," and chap. 14, "How to Develop Ideas in Speech-Argumentation."
THOULESS, ROBERT, *How to Think Straight*, New York: Simon & Schuster, 1950.
WALLACE, KARL R., "More Than We Can Teach," *Speech Teacher*, March, 1957, 6:95–102.

13. Teaching Voice and Diction

Francine Merritt and Claude L. Shaver

At the outset some simple definitions may be in order. *Voice* refers to the vibrated tone produced by the vocal mechanism. It is conventionally analyzed into elements of quality, force or loudness, pitch or melody, and tempo. *Diction* in the field of speech refers to the production of sounds and their combination into words. It is a general term that includes articulation, enunciation, and pronunciation. Obviously, in an utterance all of these elements appear simultaneously. However, for convenience in discussion and practice the work may be divided into separate parts dealing with voice, articulation, and pronunciation.

Voice and diction may be presented to students in three different contexts:

1. A separate beginning course, usually titled "Voice and Diction," "Voice and Articulation," "Speech Improvement," or occasionally "Speech Fundamentals."
2. One or more units in a course devoted primarily to some speech activity—public speaking, oral interpretation, debate, acting, or "general speech."
3. Individual training for speech improvement.

CHOOSING OBJECTIVES AND CONTENT

Plans for teaching voice and diction vary with conditions reflected in the following questions:

A. Who is to be enrolled in the course? Students who fail a screening test? Speech majors? All students?

283

B. Is the course required? Elective? Required for some and elective for others?
C. What is the principal objective of the course? To impart knowledge? To improve skills? Both?
   1. If the objective is to impart knowledge, is the course prerequisite to other speech courses?
   2. If the objective is to improve skills, is improvement required for successful completion of the course regardless of the student's achievement at the time of enrollment?

The answers to these questions will in some measure determine the content and the direction of the course and the standards set up as goals for student achievement. The answers reveal whether the work is intended to be primarily remedial or designed to assist even the superior student to develop his abilities.

The Voice and Diction Course

The full-length separate course in voice and diction is designed to achieve one and sometimes both of the following goals:

1. To improve the skills of the speaking voice
2. To provide basic information concerning voice and diction as a prerequisite to further speech study or as a terminal course

These two goals are not as compatible as speech teachers sometimes lead themselves to believe, since improvement in skills flourishes with drill and individual attention, whereas the study of basic information lends itself to group methods of lecture and discussion. Many a realistic teacher, unhappy with the dichotomy and pressed for time, feels compelled to resign himself to either a "content" course or a "skills" course, to the dismay of colleagues who expect his products to display vocal mastery plus a knowledge of basic phonetics, elementary physics of sound, physiology of the vocal mechanism, and anatomy of the ear.

To achieve the combined objectives of both informational and skills courses requires a course of conventional length supplemented by work under supervision in a language laboratory. When these optimum conditions are lacking, as is more often than not the case, particularly in high school, the instructor will find it necessary to evaluate the possible objectives and frame the work in voice and diction accordingly.

When determining the direction that voice and diction training is to take, the teacher sometimes unintentionally misdirects the course into one that devotes the major share of the time to his specialty—phonetics, voice science, interpretation, or dramatics. Beginning teachers, fresh out of intensive courses in these subjects, have often been known to fall into this unfortunate shift. This error is especially easy to make because speech sciences and speech activities offer opportunities for oral practice and methods of approach to the improvement of voice and diction. For that reason alert teachers must continually scrutinize daily objectives and activities of their course plans.

The Unit on Voice and Diction

If a course primarily devoted to some other phase of speech contains some assignments on voice and diction, the work is usually designed to provide general information on standards and methods of improvement, to analyze student needs, and possibly to motivate either a private regimen administered by the student or else enrollment in a voice and diction course. When the work of the unit is limited to reading a chapter in a textbook, a few days of class discussion, and self-analysis, it cannot be expected that the unit will contribute significantly to improvement. Improvement must be made habitual by conscious practice at times other than those devoted to presentation of the major speech activity in which the student is engaged. Both teacher and student must remember that, though many factors of voice and diction such as tempo, pitch, pronunciation, and so on, are subject to conscious control, the successful speaker, interpreter, or actor usually cannot simultaneously attend to delivery and to his other goals at the time of performance without losing to some degree his control over his material and his audience. Therefore, any unit in voice and diction that has personal improvement for its goal must provide sufficient opportunity and motivation for oral practice. Furthermore, some portion of the oral practice must be supervised and the student's progress measured.

ANALYZING NEEDS AND ABILITIES

At some time fairly early in the course the teacher should analyze each student's voice, articulation, and pronunciation. This testing procedure should be of sufficient length to demonstrate the voice quality and the student's use of his voice. The analysis may involve testing in the form of a short speech, a short reading, a brief conversation, a list of loaded sentences containing, in various positions, the various sounds of English, or simply a word list. All of these are useful and each has its particular value. The use of loaded words and sentences, designed to require the utterance of each of the sounds of English, gives the most direct results. On the other hand, conversation probably gives a better understanding of the student's sound production in normal utterance. It is probably best to combine several test procedures in order to determine the student's problems. Each student may read a word list or series of sentences; the results may be checked in a short speech and rechecked in a brief conversation.[1] If equipment is available, the test materials may be recorded for more careful analysis.

While planning the test, the teacher should also prepare a chart on which to note significant items.[2] Loaded material lends itself most easily to this preliminary checking, the results of which can then be verified in speech and conversation. Most voice and articulation textbooks or workbooks contain a checklist or chart of this sort.

IMPROVING THE VOICE

After the preliminary analysis, improvement procedures can begin, with frequent retesting to determine progress. Procedures will vary, of course, with the specific problems. Most students, even those without serious vocal deficiencies, can benefit from training to increase vocal variety in pitch and tempo. Voice qualities subject to improvement range from common nasality to shrill, tense, and muffled tones. Inappropriate pitch levels can be adjusted to those more nearly approaching the students' optimum pitches. Improvement is possible in projection and in adjustment of loudness levels to speaking situations and varying auditoriums. Failure to maintain sufficient breath control for ease in speaking can be analyzed for possible causes and remedial steps taken. Above all, the student can be taught to protect his voice, to keep it in good health, and to observe danger signals deserving of medical attention and advice.

Instruction in voice should not be limited to remedial work for gross deficiencies. To assume that the student free of major vocal defects is not properly enrolled in the voice and diction class is to depreciate the potentialities of the course and to deny to the student the opportunity to raise his proved abilities to superior levels. Work in voice is not necessarily remedial. Any person, including the teacher himself, can effect an improvement in his vocal habits by conscious attention to beneficial techniques. Descriptions of these techniques and procedures by which these improvements are accomplished can be found in any good textbook on voice and diction and will not be delineated here.

A word of caution is possibly in order here. Any vocal change that produces strain is unwise and should never be required of the student by his teacher. Insistence on a radical shift of pitch, for example, opens the door to possible harm to the vocal instrument. Vocal exercises performed while the vocal mechanism is inflamed and infected are unwise. Since the

---

[1] See Grant Fairbanks, *Voice and Articulation Drillbook*, 2nd ed., New York: Harper & Row, 1960, pp. x–xix.
[2] See Virgil Anderson, *Training the Speaking Voice*, New York: Oxford Univ. Press, 2nd ed., 1961, pp. 14–16.

student can hardly be aware of the long-term consequences of mismanagement of his voice, it is the responsibility of the teacher both to inform him and to avoid offering him opportunities to abuse the mechanism.

TEACHING PRONUNCIATION AND ARTICULATION

The major purpose of training in pronunciation and articulation is improved intelligibility. Beauty of sound and sharpness of articulation certainly need not be discouraged, but the basic reason for improving speech is to make the speaker more easily and quickly understood by the hearer.

What is the difference between pronunciation and articulation? Generally, *pronunciation* is understood to refer to the speaking of the whole word—the placement of stress or accent on certain syllables, the unstressing of certain others, and the morpho-phonemic changes that take place when words are put together into connected utterance. *Articulation* is usually understood as the production of the individual sounds that make up the word or utterance. Pronunciation and articulation may also be differentiated by the speaker's ability or inability to exercise choice: if the speaker cannot produce an appropriate sound in a given phonetic context, his problem is articulatory; if he can produce the appropriate sound but chooses an inappropriate one, his pronunciation is faulty. Hence, if the student says "rethieve" for *receive*, his problem is misarticulation of the [s] sound, especially if he has similar difficulty with other words containing a medial [s]. But if he customarily produces "champeen" for *champion* or "mischeevious" for *mischievous* although he can produce the preferred forms on request, he mispronounces. The teacher should not determine which problem exists on the basis of difficulty of production of sound sequences, since what is not habitual for the student is usually more difficult to produce than the familiar. Both pronunciation and articulation are important, and both demand a certain share of attention on the part of the student and teacher in a beginning course.

Regional Differences in Pronunciation

Many words are pronounced alike in all parts of the country. This uniformity is promoted by the influence of radio, movies, television, and mobility of population. However, regional differences in pronunciation, called *dialects*, still exist; a westerner speaks somewhat differently from a southerner or a New Englander.[3] These differences are not dependent upon differ-

---

[3] For extended discussion, see Giles W. Gray and Claude M. Wise, *The Bases of Speech*, 3rd ed., New York: Harper & Row, 1959, pp. 253–320.

ences in education and social standing, nor are they peculiar to backward regions or culturally deprived groups.

Is the speech of one region any more "correct" than the speech of other regions? It is the point of view of this chapter, and of lexicographers and linguists generally, that regional speech forms are equally correct, provided that the individual speaks a regional form that is approved within his region.[4] But who "approves" of this regional pattern? How are regional standards determined? There is no simple answer to these questions; but it may be reasoned that, while there is much variation within a region or in a particular locality, the accepted speech is that spoken by the more cultured, better educated speakers of the region. Thus, the attitude expressed here is that the correct speech for a student to learn is that used by the better educated people of his community and region. A student may learn dialects for a variety of purposes, such as presenting plays or giving dialect readings, but he should be capable of producing the best speech of his own region with ease.

Standard and Nonstandard Pronunciations

It is sometimes assumed that there is a "standard" English pronunciation which is "right" or "correct," that all other pronunciations are "wrong" or "incorrect," and that the "correct" pronunciation should be taught to students. This view overlooks a well-known fact: Everyone has different standards of pronunciation for different occasions, corresponding to different levels of social behavior appropriate to circumstances. One is not and need not be on his best behavior at all times; he relaxes with family and close friends who will ignore or forgive carelessness, but he raises his level of achievement in more formal surroundings. The point to make with students in the voice and articulation classroom is that the speaker, who already has at his command nonstandard speech forms, should also be able to produce speech that will fit more demanding occasions and represent him well enough to meet requirements of vocation or social situation. It is not that he needs to eradicate nonstandard speech but rather that he also needs to be able to use widely acceptable speech when the occasion requires it.

Viewed as communication, standard speech is highly desirable in that it is intelligible to the largest number of people over the widest geographical area. Nonstandard varieties are more restricted and make communication difficult. By the same token, their variations are more interesting than the dullness of uniform speech would be, if it were attainable. Like ethnic humor, speech varieties make people individual. Their availability for use, especially on the stage, is an asset.

4 See the introductory pages on pronunciation in any recent dictionary.

Problems in Producing Speech Sounds

The problems to be dealt with here are not the abnormalities commonly known as speech defects. The student with a speech defect should have instruction under clinical supervision. The student in a voice and articulation course has speech habits in need of improvement. No matter how well he speaks, almost anyone can make continued improvement.

Misarticulation of consonant clusters is a common problem. Failure to pronounce all the consonants in a cluster may result in the confusion of words, such as *track* and *tract, ax* and *acts, Hans* and *hands.* Furthermore, the extra *s* in the forming of plurals, the *ed* ending of the past tense and past participle, pronounced as *t* or *d* or *id* depending on the previous sounds, constitutes a special problem in that, if these sounds are omitted, the resulting pronunciation is ungrammatical; that is, *post* and *posts, ask* and *asked,* etc., may erroneously be pronounced alike with no distinction between them. If one says "two post," instead of the proper plural form of "two posts," or "yesterday I ask," instead of "yesterday I asked," he is clearly in error in number in the first example and in tense in the second example. Improvement in the production of consonant clusters reduces the possibility of ambiguity and thus improves communication.

Problems in vowel production usually involve placement of the tongue, less frequently the jaw and lips. A knowledge of the articulatory mechanism will assist the student in making required adjustments. A vocabulary for referring to positions is helpful: *front, center, back* refer to the location of the hump of the tongue in the horizontal dimension; *high, mid, low* refer to the vertical dimension; and *round* or *unround* refer to the shape of the lips. Students should be encouraged to use both the kinesthetic sense and mirrors to discover their own habits of vowel production.

Common faults in vowel production include centralization of vowels, failure to open the mouth sufficiently for low vowels, and failure to round the lips for back vowels. *Centralization* means forming the front and back vowels too near the center of the mouth, resulting in production of a series of obscure sounds rather than clearly distinguished front and back vowels. Failure to open the mouth enough for low vowels or to round the lips for back vowels also produces indistinct vowels not easily understood.[5] Since improvement in vowels comes only with replacement of old habits or modification of them, drill is in order if the student is to overcome these difficulties.

Nasality is a problem of vocal resonance, the amount of nasal resonance being excessive. It is often perceived as a problem in vowel production, and

[5] For more complete discussion see C. M. Wise, *Applied Phonetics,* Englewood Cliffs, N.J.: Prentice-Hall, 1957, or *Introduction to Phonetics,* Englewood Cliffs, N.J.: Prentice-Hall, 1958; Giles W. Gray and Claude M. Wise, *The Bases of Speech,* 3rd ed., New York: Harper & Row, 1959; Virgil A. Anderson, *Training the Speaking Voice,* New York: Oxford University Press, 2nd ed., 1961; or any good phonetics book.

reduction in nasality sometimes comes with improved vowels, particularly when the student has not been opening his mouth fully for low vowels. Decided improvement can be attained by lowering the tongue and opening the mouth more, thereby adding oral resonance and counterbalancing the nasal resonance. A tense, tight jaw, a narrow aperture between the teeth, or an unnecessarily raised tongue reduces the amount of oral resonance and makes a listener perceive the voice as nasal. In cases of doubt, students can be convinced of their own nasality by use of a piece of rubber tubing leading from a nostril to the ear as a conductor of nasal sounds. Initially practice to overcome nasality should involve only nonnasal selections—language without *m* or *n*.

Numerous problems are related to the production of diphthongs, one of the major factors in differentiating standard and nonstandard speech patterns. Errors of opposite types may occur in the speech of the same student. He may make diphthongs of single vowels and conversely reduce diphthongs to single vowels. Since a diphthong always involves two different vowel positions, he can determine for himself whether he produces a single vowel or a diphthong in isolation by repeating the questionable sound several times and observing, in a mirror if necessary, whether there is required movement of lips, tongue, or jaw. A diphthong repeated in isolation resembles a chewing motion. For a single vowel repeated in isolation the articulators can be immobilized. This feature of movement or nonmovement can also be used as a teaching device in the phonetics class: A student who has difficulty producing [a] in isolation can bring it about, if he has the same sound in his pronunciation of *I*, by being told to pronounce *I, I, I* while holding lips, tongue, and jaw immobile. He will then produce the first element only. On the other hand, the student who has no diphthong is told to "chew" the sound. Triphthongs and double diphthongs are extensions of the diphthongizing problem and require comparable treatment.

Anyone who writes of mispronunciations and gives specific examples runs the risk of discovering his examples have entered the dictionaries as permissible by the time he has them in print. Nevertheless, a number of words widely recognized as nonstandard and inadvisable are commonly heard—*git* for *get*, *runnin'* and *jumpin'* for *running* and *jumping*, for example. Substitution of one vowel for another, as in the case of *pin* for *pen*, *tin* for *ten*, and *since* for *sense* and *cents*, can create homonyms and introduce ambiguity into communication.[6] Some vowel substitutions simply call attention to themselves, as *aig* for *egg* and *laig* for *leg*. A different type of mispronunciation involves reversal or misplacement of sounds, as in

[6] See Giles W. Gray and Claude M. Wise, *The Bases of Speech*, 3rd ed., New York: Harper & Row, 1959, pp. 296–297 for a list of words of this type.

modren for *modern, prespiration* for *perspiration, hunderd* for *hundred,* and *nucular* for *nuclear.*[7]

Still another problem of pronunciation is the location of accent or stress and the removal of stress. English characteristically has primary stress, secondary stress, and weak stress in the pronunciation of single words. Examples are 'lo·cate, ·in ter 'lace, 'gov ern ment, etc. To these, modern linguists have added a fourth form, called *tertiary stress,* which appears when words are combined into utterances. Stress is made up chiefly of loudness, but pitch and time factors may enter in. Dictionaries give the location of primary stress and generally secondary stress. All other syllables are considered to have weak stress, often called *unstressed.* In these weakly stressed syllables, the vowel usually changes to one of three forms: it may become a very short form of itself; it may become the vowel of *bit;* or it may become a very short *uh.*

It should be understood that these forms are proper. Furthermore, in a sentence many of the words—the articles, the auxiliary verbs, and many of the prepositions, for example—are unstressed. Any insistence that *a* must always be pronounced as in *play* violates the natural patterns of English and creates a highly artificial speech pattern. Properly one should say "uh boy and uh girl," not "ay boy and ay girl." The student who has been taught to use stressed pronunciations of articles (*a, an, the*), prepositions (*of, from, for*), conjunctions (*and, or*), and auxiliaries (*have, had*) at all times, whether the sense calls for stress or not, should unlearn the practice, for it is both mispronunciation and an impediment to good speech rhythm.

THE SUBJECT MATTER OF THE COURSE

The study of voice and articulation is grounded in sciences related to speech. To the extent that time permits, the course may include the anatomy and physiology of the vocal mechanism, the physics of sound, phonetics, the development of language, dialectal varieties, social influences on speech patterns, and communication theory, all or some combination of which regularly appear in voice and articulation textbooks. Since time seldom permits full treatment of all these topics, the teacher must eliminate those least likely to contribute to the specific needs of the students. The teacher may elect to omit the physiology of the ear, for example, in order to retain the anatomy of the vocal tract, if the latter information is more functional. Or the teacher may refrain from detailed information about dialects unlike the students' own. Such omissions, though regrettable, often become necessary. Ultimately the teacher must

[7] See Giles W. Gray and Claude M. Wise, *The Bases of Speech,* 3rd ed., New York: Harper & Row, 1959, pp. 274 and 372, for additional words.

justify inclusion of whatever content is retained on the basis of (1) its utility in motivating and promoting speech improvement, (2) its provision of a groundwork for future speech courses, and (3) its contribution to the student's understanding of himself and the world in which he communicates.

Use of Phonetics

Should phonetics be used in the beginning course as an aid to understanding the nature of English sounds and identifying them? The answer may depend on the amount of time available, the preparation of the teacher, and the use both teacher and student make of phonetics as a tool in and out of the classroom. Most treatments of diction in textbooks use phonetic symbolization. Dictionaries are increasing their use of phonetic symbols to replace traditional diacritical marking, and phonetic dictionaries exist. Moreover, reading of sophisticated treatments of language requires some acquaintance with phonetic symbols. The case for teaching concepts of phonetics and phonetic symbols to the student studying voice and diction is a strong one.

On the other hand, whether phonetics should be taught may depend on the amount of time available, the preparation of the teacher, and the way in which it is put to use as a tool in and out of the classroom. A smattering of phonetics as time permits may be worse than useless. In the event time is short, perhaps all that can be done is to alert the class to (1) the nonphonetic character of the English alphabet and English spelling, (2) the existence of a linguistic discipline with an accurate symbolic system for sounds based on observable anatomical positions and physiological procedures, and (3) the introduction of those symbols now appearing in newer dictionaries. The teacher who has not received sufficient aural training should not attempt to introduce phonetics into the voice and diction class, for mere memorization of a list of symbols or transcription without accompanying oral activity is not truly phonetic study at all. When there is adequate time for acquisition of phonetic skills, those skills are, in order of importance, first, the ability to produce appropriate sounds; second, the ability to associate received sounds with phonetic symbols; third, the ability to associate a written symbol with its oral counterpart; and last of all, the ability to transcribe discourse in phonetics. The student's needs relate to oral performance, not to graphic reproduction. Least defensible is the introduction of phonetics in the course merely for the sake of learning phonetics and so diverting the voice and diction course from its appropriate goals.

If phonetics is made a part of the voice and diction course, it is not at all necessary to delay introduction of all phonetic concepts and symbols until a phonetic unit is reached. The three nasal sounds, their symbols, and the positions of the articulators can be introduced when nasal resonance first comes to the attention of the class, or when the undesirability of nasalized vowels is pointed out, or when the possible exits of the vocalized breath stream are noted; [m, n, ŋ] are thus put to good use when vocal anatomy and physiology, or resonance, or mispronunciations are the focus of attention. The plosive sounds appropriately fit into experiments with the ways in which the breath stream can be stopped. There are comparable ways of inserting some of the remaining consonants, and even vowels, into discussions preceding a phonetic unit. One consequence of this early and gradual introduction of the student to the phonetic alphabet is that the multiplicity of strange symbols with which he might otherwise be confronted is considerably reduced and so is some of the shock inherent in learning any new symbolic system.

Phonetics probably should be consciously related to the conventional diacritical systems of most dictionaries in such a way that the student can afterwards bring his phonetic skills to bear on the use of his dictionary. Most English classes teach use of the dictionary, but students sometimes remain unable to translate a diacritically marked pronunciation into an appropriate oral form. The speech teacher can help by teaching students to understand and to use the diacritical system of indicating pronunciation and the accent marking system for indicating the stress pattern. As dictionaries continue to incorporate phonetic or phonemic symbols into their diacritical systems, the role of the speech teacher as an interpreter will become increasingly important, until that time when the diacritical systems are abandoned.

MOTIVATION OF THE STUDENT

One of the major problems in the teaching of voice and diction is the motivating of each student. Often students are fiercely defensive about their voices and their way of speaking. They may insist that they speak like everyone else and that any attempt to change their pronunciation will only result in artificiality and hence in laughter and social disapproval. The student must be persuaded that his voice and articulation need improvement and that the improvement will not sound artificial. The first of these may best be established through demonstration by recording and playing back each student's voice. Often a student will insist that a recording does not sound like him. The other students in his class can help here, for they can assure him that he does sound like the recording. Intelligibility tests often provide the student with convincing proof that he is not making himself understood. A little practice may persuade the student that the change will not produce artificiality. In any case, the student must be motivated to the point of wanting to improve and to incorporate the improvements into his daily speech. Other students may respond to critical comment on their voices with the statement that they know their speech is "just awful." This judgment may be as unsound as the one the defensive student has made.

In either case the teacher should encourage the student to adopt a more objective attitude toward his problems. Entering a voice and diction course, one might say, is comparable to taking a physical fitness course, or a health examination, or even to standing in front of a mirror, and quite as purposive—one expects to try to improve whatever is perfectible. A tape recorder is a voice mirror with which the student checks how he sounds to others. Viewed in that light, the voice and diction class is his golden opportunity.

Some students are self-motivating because of their participation in speech activities or their hopes for professional careers in theater, broadcasting, and the like. They should be encouraged not only to develop superior personal speech but also to acquire a variety of vocal skills unnecessary to the average student. Theirs is the task of acquiring dialects, regional and nonstandard, unlike their own. They should work for greater mastery of breath control, superior projection, great clarity of diction, and a variety of voices matching that of vocal artists who deliver dialogue for broadcasting commercials. The fact that a professional actress says, "Every actress ought to have an assortment of voices, from age to youth, from tough to elegant," or that a play script calls for an actor to produce more than one voice—"a voice that is larger and more resonant than his usual one"[8]—should be cause sufficient to motivate young aspirants to make the most of opportunities the course offers.

It is a common occurrence to have students report at the end of a semester that they are only beginning to become aware of their vocal deficiencies and to make improvement. "If only there were another semester!" is a common cry. To some extent such statements are exaggeration, but there is some truth in the claim that inexperienced students who work as a classroom group rather than individually require almost a semester to develop their critical faculties for self-evaluation. Almost every student hearing a recording of his voice for the first time expresses dissatisfaction with the results. The problem lies in the student's inability to make a more specific analysis, to isolate the less satisfactory characteristic, before attempting techniques for improvement. Yet until the student hears, recognizes, and knows the undesirable characteristic for which he must find a substitute, any improvement he makes by his own effort will be accidental. This fact alone justifies the inclusion of subject matter in voice and diction training that might otherwise be sacrificed to provide additional time for routine drill.

[8] Jean-Claude van Itallie, *The Serpent*, New York: Atheneum, 1969, p. 36.

The teacher and student of voice and diction find yet another problem in the naive assumption that knowing and doing are synonymous. The physiological act of speaking is the product of nerves and muscles, neither of which readily depart from habitual modes of behavior. It is unreasonable to expect that 15 minutes of vocal exercise during each of 3 to 5 weekly class periods (a liberal estimate) will noticeably affect the vocal behavior of a high school or college student who has been talking for years and who spends several hours each day reinforcing his habitual patterns. In some way the student must be made aware that speech improvement is not comparable to an embossing or engraving process, requiring only the passive presence of the inert object, but instead demands the conscious effort and consumes the time of the person seeking improvement, as does any art, skill, or game requiring physical agility.

The business of the voice and diction skills unit or course, then, is (1) to alert the student to his own needs, (2) to acquaint him with methods for improving his vocal effectiveness, (3) to motivate him, and (4) to measure his progress.

SPEECH ACTIVITIES FOR TEACHING VOICE AND DICTION

Generally speaking, any speech activity is compatible with work for improvement of voice and diction. However, it is obvious that an activity that permits exact repetition while encouraging direct attention to delivery accomplishes habituation most readily. Conversely, an activity that consumes time in preparation or that is only distantly connected with vocal delivery will be uneconomical. Measured by these standards, speech activities used for training in voice and diction should probably rank in the order of efficiency as follows: (1) drill on sounds, words, and sentences by rote (most efficient); (2) choral speaking, (3) oral reading, (4) recitation from memory, (5) public speaking, (6) conversation and discussion, (7) debate, and (8) dramatics.

If efficiency alone were the determining factor, repetitious drill would suffice as an activity for the development of voice and diction. But because human beings quickly tire of drill that does not command and occupy the mind, teachers should resort to activities that are theoretically less efficient yet hold the student to the practice period by maintaining his interest. When the material is carefully chosen and varied, choral speaking is thought by many to be an ideal tool for improving vocal techniques. Recitation and oral readings are also frequently employed for this purpose. Most textbooks and workbooks on voice and diction include selections for oral reading as the major type of practice material other than drill material. The remaining activities on the list are somewhat less valuable for training in voice and diction. Dramatics, if pursued beyond the line-reading stage, is most uneconomical of time. Debate requires specialized training that is unrelated to delivery and properly belongs in its own course. Public speaking, conversation, and discussion present two handicaps: (1) exact repetition so useful in training vocal skills is almost never possible, and (2) the necessity for simultaneously composing and delivering one's thought discourages attention to vocal techniques. In summary, a speech activity is useful in voice and diction training if it fosters attention to vocal delivery, permits exact repetition, interests the student, and borrows little or no classroom time for techniques or training unrelated to vocal delivery.

USE OF RECORDING EQUIPMENT

Some type of recording equipment is almost a must for teaching voice and diction. Laboratories available in some schools for teaching foreign languages by the aural-oral method are sometimes adapted to and available for use by the speech students. However, in most cases the tape recorder is the most convenient recording equipment. But equipment alone will not teach the course; the teacher must know how to use it and how to direct student use of it. Recording is an adjunct to class work, not a substitute for it. The recording session must be planned to avoid lost time, and the student must know what he is listening for. He needs time to practice and rerecord, and an opportunity to determine his progress. "Before and after" tapes made at the beginning and end of the course are useful for final assessment.

Students should be encouraged to listen to the speaking of others and to analyze the voice, pronunciation, and articulation. They may listen to classmates in pairs or in groups, and may listen to recordings of various kinds. Listening reports of radio and television programs may be made.

OTHER TEACHING AIDS

Both the content and the objectives of a unit or a course on voice and diction demand the use of more auxiliary teaching devices than are customarily used in other speech activities. The content is rooted in sciences—physics, anatomy, physiology, neurology, phonetics, etc.—all of which are illustrated by models, demonstrations, and audiovisual devices. The practical objective of improvement in voice and diction likewise demands the use of every sensory avenue to the student's awareness of his speech processes and their auditory effect if he is to alter long-established behavior patterns. Not only should the student attempting speech improvement use his ears but his eyes, touch, and motor-kinesthetic sense as well.

Types of visual aids available are as diversified as the following: films and filmstrips of vocal processes; models of anatomical structures; plates, charts, and diagrams, separate or collected in encyclopedias and textbooks; laryngeal and breathing mechanisms of livestock (acquired through the butcher or abattoir); blackboard drawings; practical anatomical models constructed by students; mirrors (collected from purses) for self-examination of the articulatory mechanism; and a variety of electronic instruments borrowed from science laboratories for demonstration.

Audio aids are equally important and varied: films and filmstrips demonstrating principles of sound; commercial recordings of speech and sound; tape and disc recordings prepared and analyzed by the class; an audiometer; radio, television, and sound tracks of movies; practical models of musical and sound instruments constructed by students; tuning forks and resonance boxes; sticks of molding cut to appropriate lengths to sound a scale; water glasses, bottles, and other improvised "musical instruments"; discarded organ pipes and broken strings from violins; all varieties of musical instruments including toy xylophones and pianos; a collection of rubber bands of varying lengths and thicknesses; and, again, expensive electronic equipment borrowed from the laboratory.

A teacher with imagination and a small collection of objects from school and household is not severely handicapped by the lack of a budget for expensive equipment. Though one might wish for a spectrograph and a video tape recorder in every classroom, their possession neither guarantees nor is required for successful teaching of voice and diction. Far more important is the teacher's ability to find analogies and to be inventive.

The teacher will find it useful to build a collection of exercises and supplementary illustrative materials to reinforce the textbook materials and provide variety.[9] A useful collection may include: paragraphs of reading material containing no nasal consonants; lists of phonetic transcriptions of mispronunciations; loaded paragraphs and sentences for testing pronunciation and articulation; nonsense limericks written in phonetics; phonetic crossword puzzles; anecdotes typed in phonetic script; paragraphs loaded with words difficult to pronounce; lists of misspelled words reflecting common mispronunciations; reading selections requiring controlled breathing; materials written in dialect; verses that offer contrasts in rhythm and tempo; quoted conversations that demand different voice qualities; anecdotes that present radical changes in mood; tongue twisters; scripts of recorded speeches and readings for imitation and comparison; syndicated magazine and newspaper columns containing human-interest stories for

[9] For example, the writer frequently introduces the subject of denasality by copying on the blackboard a brief verse from a popular magazine. Students read it aloud to accompanying laughter. The title: "Abril Sog" (April Song). Opening line: "Sprig is cub."

reading aloud. All these and others are grist for the voice and diction mill.

No discussion of teaching aids should neglect to mention printed resources available to the teacher and his students. The group of selected titles at the end of this chapter is at best only a sampling and may inaccurately reflect the wealth of reading materials and teaching aids touching the area of voice and diction. The basic teaching materials are of course textbooks and workbooks in voice and diction, dictionaries, and books on vocal health and relaxation. In addition, the teacher should consult books on voice science, speech pedagogy, and speech correction, chapters on voice and diction in textbooks on public speaking, interpretation, radio, and television, workbooks in the same areas, units on oral English in high school and junior high English textbooks, and books on English pedagogy. Helpful suggestions can be found in encyclopedias, physiology textbooks, and books on general science and laboratory experimentation. Relevant periodical material appears in journals published by the Speech Communication Association, the American Speech and Hearing Association, and the regional speech organizations, in the *English Journal,* in medical journals and health magazines, in linguistics and language journals, and in articles in popular magazines and newspapers.

ADAPTING INSTRUCTION TO CHANGING CONDITIONS

Like the instructor of any other subject, the teacher of voice and diction must be prepared to adapt his material to changing conditions. The most frequently required change arises from the necessity of condensing the course or units because of a reduction in number of scheduled classroom hours or because of increased class enrollment. Either factor can reduce critically the optimum time allotted for discussion of subject matter and practice for vocal improvement.

What choices are open to the teacher facing this situation? His first thought may be to abandon oral practice, which is time-consuming for the large class and relatively unsusceptible of objective testing for results, in favor of content. A second possibility is the elimination of traditional subject matter, the practical value of which is vigorously challenged in some quarters, in favor of skills and activities. A teacher unreconciled to either of these extremes may attempt a compromise by constructing an abridged course containing the most practical and most immediately valuable content and practice for the class at hand.

For a teacher who elects to teach voice and diction in fewer units, the following suggestions may prove helpful:

1. From the subject matter of the normal offering, eliminate topics that contribute least to speech improvement. For example, a knowledge of the

anatomy of the ear or even the larynx is of little practical value to the student as compared to knowledge of the physiology of the articulatory mechanism.

2. From the list of possible skills to be developed in the normal course, retain in the abridged course (a) skills in which tests prove the class to be deficient, (b) skills that can best be developed in the shortened period of time, and (c) skills needed by the largest number of students. For example, practice designed to eliminate a single basic pronunciation problem of the students' geographical area should rank higher than reduction of nasality since, first, the pronunciation problem is probably common to more students than is objectionable nasality and, second, the pronunciation problem is more readily overcome. However, both of these needs should rank higher as goals than the development of projection suitable to an audience of five hundred, since, unless the class consists of prospective actors, the need for that amount of projection will probably never arise as long as public address systems remain popular.

3. Find ways to coordinate the teaching of voice and diction and of content and skills. To illustrate, the subjects of nasal resonance and denasality, the articulation of nasal consonants, and common mispronunciations involving nasal sounds and substitutions are sufficiently related to justify their being studied together to save time. This step in organization will tend to break down the conventional dichotomy of voice and diction revealed by most textbooks and courses of study and eliminate the necessity of giving either voice or diction the preferred first place in the course.

4. When choices in arrangement are possible, plan to introduce earlier those skills that develop more slowly and reserve to the last weeks or lessons those that are more speedily acquired.

5. Revise the syllabus to meet needs revealed by testing the students and continue to revise it to meet unanticipated problems and the needs of atypical class members. Only by careful adaptation to each class can maximum improvement be attained in minimum time. Where multiple sections, standardized syllabi, and uniform group examinations make adaptation difficult, the teacher may be obliged to conduct his work below maximum efficiency and productivity for individual students.

6. Use group activities for oral practice whenever possible. Many instructors find that choral reading produces excellent results. Others recommend reading, discussion, and conversation in small groups in which students themselves serve as critics and assistants. Some portion of this activity may be delegated to out-of-class hours. However, the teacher cannot be expected to add to a teaching load already increased by enlarged enrollments the additional supervision of impromptu laboratory sessions.

There is immense personal satisfaction to be found in teaching voice and diction, particularly when the students give evidence that the instruction is meeting their needs, whether they be present practical or future theoretical ones. The subject challenges the high school or college teacher to bring all his personal resources to bear on its problems. Whatever he knows of speech pathology, voice science, education, public speaking, psychology, and a host of other areas, and whatever skills he has acquired, he may be called on one day to use in teaching a difficult basic subject, voice and diction.

EXERCISES

1. Questions for discussion:
   a. Must vocal drills be supervised for effective reeducation of the student's vocal habits?
   b. Why are vocal drills often preceded by relaxation exercises?
   c. What problems are involved in the teaching of breath control?
   d. Is there a best method of breathing? Find documentary proof of your answer.
   e. Can the voice be "placed"?
   f. Why do textbooks frequently employ terms and recommend exercises that are without scientific foundation? Is this practice justified?
   g. Can skill in the use of a vocal characteristic (quality, loudness, melody, tempo) be developed in isolation—that is, without affecting other vocal characteristics? Why or why not?
   h. Which vocal problems can be directly attributed to stage fright? Explain the physiological basis of their occurrence.
   i. Which vocal problems can result from personality problems or emotional difficulties? Can work in voice and diction remedy these vocal faults?
   j. Under what circumstances must the voice and diction teacher carefully refrain from acting as a clinician or physician?
   k. Is the first pronunciation listed in a dictionary the "best" pronunciation? Prove your answer by quoting directly from the introductory sections of several dictionaries.
   l. What is the relation of *phonetics* to *phonics*?
   m. Can improvement in habits of pronunciation be expected to affect spelling ability? Is the reverse possible?
   n. What methods of determining the optimum pitch of the speaking voice can be recommended?
2. Collect from various sources speech tests and loaded sentences. What are the values of each? Comment on the uses of the various kinds of materials. Which would be most useful?
3. Collect examples of possible word confusions resulting from failure to pronounce all the consonants in a cluster. Which ones are ungrammatical?
4. Compare and contrast the diacritic systems used in several dictionaries. Are they sometimes confusing? Misleading?
5. Work out a form chart for student use in recording. Make up some sample sentences for use.
6. Compile a list of mispronunciations that cannot be accurately indicated by diacritical markings or respellings.
7. Draw from at least five different sources a collection of exercises and brief selections for practice to improve each of the following vocal problems:

a. Tempo too fast or slow
b. Tempo lacking variety
c. Pitch too high or low
d. Objectionable pitch pattern
e. Lack of projection
f. Inflexibility of loudness
g. Excessive nasal resonance
h. Shrill vocal quality
i. Muffled voice
j. Lack of breath control

8. From textbooks of different dates make a list of topics or questions about which conflicting opinions have been expressed. Give particular attention to the following: functioning of the larynx, purpose of the epiglottis, methods of improving breathing, causes of nasality, preferred pronunciations.

9. Read an account of the treatment of emphysema and relate the breathing exercises described to those suggested for improving vocal control.

10. Collect examples of misspellings in newspapers, advertisements, and student papers. Which ones suggest the possibility that the speller also mispronounces the word?

11. Find a discussion and table of the Initial Teaching Alphabet and compare it with the International Phonetic Alphabet. Is it a phonetic system?

REFERENCES

Textbooks and Manuals on Voice and Diction

AKIN, JOHNNYE, *And So We Speak*, Englewood Cliffs, N.J.: Prentice-Hall, 1958.

ANDERSON, VIRGIL A., *Training the Speaking Voice*, 2nd ed., New York: Oxford Univ. Press, 1961.

BLACK, JOHN W. AND IRWIN, RUTH B., *Voice and Diction: Phonation and Phonology*, Columbus, O.: Charles E. Merrill, 1969.

BRONSTEIN, ARTHUR J. AND JACOBY, BEATRICE F., *Your Speech and Voice*, New York: Random House, 1967.

ECROYD, DONALD H., HALFOND, MURRAY M., AND TOWNE, CAROL CHWOROWSKY, *Voice and Articulation: A Handbook*, Glenview, Ill.: Scott, Foresman, 1966.

ECROYD, DONALD H., HALFOND, MURRAY M., AND TOWNE, CAROL CHWOROWSKY, *Voice and Articulation: Programed Instruction*, Glenview, Ill.: Scott, Foresman, 1966.

EISENSON, JON, *The Improvement of Voice and Diction*, 3rd ed., New York: Macmillan, 1965.

FAIRBANKS, GRANT, *Voice and Articulation Drillbook*, 2nd ed., New York: Harper & Row, 1960.

FISHER, HILDA, *Improving Voice and Articulation*, Boston: Houghton Mifflin, 1966.

GORDON, MORTON J. AND WONG, HELENE H., *A Manual for Speech Improvement*, Englewood Cliffs, N.J.: Prentice-Hall, 1961.

GRASHAM, JOHN A. AND GOODER, GLENN G., *Improving Your Speech*, New York: Harcourt Brace Jovanovich, 1960.

HAHN, ELISE, LOMAS, CHARLES W., HARGIS, DONALD E., AND VANDRAEGEN, DANIEL, *Basic Voice Training for Speech*, 2nd ed., New York: McGraw-Hill, 1957

HANLEY, THEODORE AND THURMAN, WAYNE L., *Developing Vocal Skills*, 2nd ed., New York: Holt, Rinehart & Winston, 1970.

HICKS, HELEN GERTRUDE, *Voice and Speech for Effective Communication*, Dubuque, Ia.: William C. Brown, 1963.

KING, ROBERT G. AND DIMICHAEL, ELEANOR M., *Improving Articulation and Voice*, New York: Macmillan, 1966.

MAYER, LYLE V., *Fundamentals of Voice and Diction*, 3rd ed., Dubuque, Ia.: William C. Brown, 1968.

RIZZO, RAYMOND, *The Voice as an Instrument*, New York: Odyssey, 1969.

Books on Speech and Dictionaries

ANDERSCH, ELIZABETH G., STAATS, LORIN C., AND BOSTROM, ROBERT N., *Communication in Everyday Use*, 3rd ed., New York: Holt, Rinehart & Winston, 1969.

CARRELL, JAMES AND TIFFANY, WILLIAM R., *Phonetics: Theory and Application to Speech Improvement*, New York: McGraw-Hill, 1960.

GRAY, GILES WILKESON AND WISE, CLAUDE M., *The Bases of Speech*, 3rd ed., New York: Harper & Row, 1959.

HIBBETT, GEORGE W., *Fundamentals of Speech*, Garden City, N.Y.: Doubleday, 1962.

JONES, DANIEL, *The Pronunciation of English*, 4th ed., New York: Cambridge Univ. Press, 1966.

JUDSON, LYMAN S. AND WEAVER, ANDREW T., *Voice Science*, 2nd ed., New York: Appleton-Century-Crofts, 1965.

KANTNER, CLAUDE E. AND WEST, ROBERT, *Phonetics*, 2nd ed., New York: Harper & Row, 1960.

KENYON, JOHN S. AND KNOTT, THOMAS A., *A Pronouncing Dictionary of American English*, Springfield, Mass.: Merriam, 1953.

LEUTENEGGER, RALPH R., *The Sounds of American English*, Glenview, Ill.: Scott, Foresman, 1963.

MALSTROM, JEAN AND ASHLEY, ANNABEL, *Dialects—U.S.A.*, Champaign, Ill.: National Council of Teachers of English, 1963.

WISE, CLAUDE M., *Applied Phonetics*, Englewood Cliffs, N.J.: Prentice-Hall, 1957.

WISE, CLAUDE M., *Introduction to Phonetics*, Englewood Cliffs, N.J.: Prentice-Hall, 1958.

ZIMLIN, WILLARD R., *Speech and Hearing Science: Anatomy and Physiology*, Englewood Cliffs, N.J.: Prentice-Hall, 1968.

Articles

ALGEO, JOHN, "Why Johnny Can't Spell," *English Teacher*, March, 1965, 54:209–213.

AURBACH, JOSEPH AND KAPLAN, ROBERT B., "Teaching Language Rhythm: Unstressed Function Words," *Speech Teacher*, January, 1966, 15:77–81.

BLACK, JOHN W., REITZEL, JOYCE A., AND TAKEFUTA, YUKIO, "A Study of Production of Five Basic Patterns of Speech Melody," *Speech Teacher*, September, 1966, 15:175–179.

BRODNITZ, FRIEDRICH S., "The Holistic Study of the Voice," *Quarterly Journal of Speech*, October, 1962, 48.280–284.

BRONSTEIN, ARTHUR J., "Some Unresolved Phonetic-Phonemic Symbolization Problems," *Quarterly Journal of Speech*, February, 1961, 47:54–59.

BRONSTEIN, ARTHUR J. AND BRONSTEIN, ELSA M., "A Phonetic-Linguistic View of the Reading Controversy," *Speech Monographs*, March, 1965, 32:25–35.

BUCK, JOYCE F., "The Effects of Negro and White Dialectal Variations upon Attitudes of College Students," *Speech Monographs*, June, 1968, 35:181–186.

BYERS, BURTON H., "Speech and the Principles of Learning," *Speech Teacher*, March, 1963, 12:136–140.

CANFIELD, WILLIAM H., "A Phonetic Approach to Voice and Speech Improvement," *Speech Teacher*, January, 1964, 13:42–46.

COHEN, SAVIN, "Speech Improvement for Adults: A Review of Literature and Audio-Visual Materials," *Speech Teacher*, September, 1964, 13:208–215.

COOPER, JUNE M., "Training of Teachers of Speech for the Economically Disadvantaged Black American Student," *Western Speech*, Spring, 1970, 34:139–143.

FRANKS, J. RICHARD, "Determining Habitual Pitch by Means of Increased Reading Rate," *Western Speech*, Fall, 1967, 31:281–287.

GRIFFIN, DOROTHY M., "Dialects and Democracy," *English Teacher*, April, 1970, 59:551–558.

HARGIS, DONALD E., "Some Basic Considerations in Teaching Voice," *Speech Teacher*, September, 1963, 12:214–218.

HAUTH, LUSTER, "Voice Improvement: The Speech Teacher's Responsibility," *Speech Teacher*, January, 1961, 10:48–52.

HAWKINS, ROBERT B., "A Speech Program in an Experimental College for the Disadvantaged," *Speech Teacher*, March, 1969, 18:115–119.

HOLT, GRACE S., "The Ethno-Linguistic Approach to Speech-Language Learning," *Speech Teacher*, March, 1970, 19:98–100.

IRWIN, RAY, "A Problem of Assimilation," *Quarterly Journal of Speech*, October, 1960, 46:302–303.

MC DAVID, RAVEN I., JR., "American Social Dialects," *College English*, January, 1965, 26:254–260.

MC DAVID, RAVEN I., JR., "Sense and Nonsense about American Dialects," *PMLA*, May, 1966, 81:7–17.

NASH, ROSA LEE, "Teaching Speech Improvement to the Disadvantaged," *Speech Teacher*, January, 1967, 16:69–73.

NEEDLER, GEOFFREY D., "On the Origin of New York City's Pathognomic Diphthong: A New Hypothesis," *Speech Monographs*, November, 1968, 35:462–469.

PANAGOS, JOHN M., "Helping a Boy Pronounce /r/," *Western Speech*, Winter, 1970, 34:33–37.

PARRISH, WAYLAND MAXFIELD, "As in *Hear, Yea, Hearken, Learn, Sweat, Speak*," *Quarterly Journal of Speech*, December, 1962, 48:359–365.

PEINS, MARYANN AND PETTAS, MARY, "A College Speech Improvement Course," *Speech Teacher*, January, 1963, 12:37–40.

PICKLER, JANET WIRTH AND LEUTENEGGER, RALPH R., "The Prediction of Phonetic Transcription Ability," *Speech Monographs*, November, 1962, 29:288–297.

REES, NORMA SCHNEIDERMAN, "Measuring and Training Pitch Discrimination Ability in Voice Improvement," *Speech Teacher*, January, 1962, 11:44–47.

SCHOLL, HAROLD M., "A Holistic Approach to the Teaching of Voice Improvement," *Speech Teacher*, September, 1961, 10:200–205.

SCHUELER, HERBERT, "Audio-Lingual Aids to Language Training—Uses and Limitations," *Quarterly Journal of Speech*, October, 1961, 47:288–292.

SLAGER, WILLIAM R., "Effecting Dialect Change Through Oral Drill," *English Journal*, November, 1967, 56:1166–1176.

STAMBUSKY, ALAN, "Speech in the Theatre: The Importance of Voice Science to Director and Actor," *Speech Teacher*, November, 1963, 12:289–298.

STEGMAIER, NORMA K. AND STEVENS, C J, "Word Lists, Loaded Passages, and Possible Distant Vowel Assimilations," *Speech Monographs*, June, 1969, 36:152–154.

"A Symposium on Speech for Elementary Schools," *Speech Teacher*, November, 1960, 9:267–303 (ten articles).

THOMAS, STAFFORD H., "Effects of Monotonous Delivery on Intelligibility," *Speech Monographs*, June, 1969, 36:110–113.

TIFFANY, WILLIAM R., "Slurvian Translation as a Speech Research Tool," *Speech Monographs*, March, 1963, 30:23–30.

TIFFANY, WILLIAM R., "Sound Mindedness: Studies in the Measurement of 'Phonetic Ability,'" *Western Speech*, Winter, 1963, 27:5–15.

TWOMEY, MARK, "Attitudes of Americans Toward Pronunciation," *Speech Teacher*, September, 1963, *12*:204–213.

WHITE, HARVEY, "Some Techniques for Teaching Anatomy and Physiology," *Speech Teacher*, March, 1963, *12*:122–124.

WOLFRAM, WALT, "Sociolinguistic Premises and the Nature of Nonstandard Dialects," *Speech Teacher*, September, 1970, *19*:177–184.

14. Teaching Delivery

Waldo W. Braden

Few will deny that "a speech to be a speech must be delivered to an audience." Although it shares invention, arrangement, and style with written discourse, a speech gains its distinctiveness from delivery—that is, from its oral and visible aspects. The communicator must be seen and heard to transmit fully his message. One authority says, "The golden thread of common essence" which runs through the discipline of speech in its various forms is "social adaptation through reciprocal stimulation by voice and visible action."[1] G. W. Gray has observed that "a speech consists not of language *and* delivery, but of delivered language" (first edition of *Speech Methods and Resources*, p. 37).

The present chapter considers how to teach visible action or what is called *control of bodily activity*. (Chapter 13 has considered the teaching of vocal delivery.) Within the scope of the subject are the following: facial expression, gesture, movement, and posture.

FIVE QUALITIES OF GOOD DELIVERY

Good Delivery Is Natural and Unaffected

As a starting point, the teacher of speech must have an understanding of what is good delivery and must have a standard of excellence by which to measure the student's efforts. As a general rule, most authorities agree with

[1] Andrew Thomas Weaver, "The Case for Speech," *Quarterly Journal of Speech*, April, 1939, 25:185.

Quintilian that "the perfection of art is to conceal art." In other words, effective delivery facilitates the communicative process without drawing attention to itself. "When the delivery is *really* good," Richard Whately said, "the hearers . . . *never think about it,* but are exclusively occupied with the sense it conveys and the feelings it excites."[2] If the listeners react, "Weren't his gestures and posture superb," the speaker may have failed in his primary purpose, to put over his idea; but when the listeners are moved to act without being aware of what the speaker did, the delivery may qualify in Quintilian's terms as a "concealed art."

An important point to remember is that good delivery conforms to what the listeners, not the speaker, consider normal and acceptable. In other words, what may seem or feel natural to the speaker may appear awkward, inappropriate, or even uncouth to the listeners. W. M. Parrish observes, "Even when expression feels right to the speaker, it may not be adequate as communication, may not deliver to the hearers what he wishes and intends to deliver and may not seem natural to them."[3]

Good Delivery Is Varied

The polished speaker or reader makes full use of the principles of variety. An expressionless face, stereotyped gesture, stilted posture, monotonous swaying, or pacing encourage inattention and boredom. The alert communicator attempts to make his presentation vital and stimulating by moving freely about the platform, by changes in facial expression and gesture, and by shifting his position, in order to hold attentiveness, to emphasize an idea, to manipulate an apparatus, or to drive home a point. He strives to keep the listener expectant and eager to hear what is coming.

Good Delivery Is Animated

The forceful speaker reflects vigor and eagerness to communicate his message. He makes his listeners aware of his urge to share his thoughts and aspirations with them. He knows that enthusiasm is contagious. Using subliminal stimuli—that is, those below the threshold of perception—he stirs the listeners through his animation to accept what he says. Woolbert said, "The world likes the animated person."[4]

[2] Richard Whately, in Douglas Ehninger (ed.), *Elements of Rhetoric*, Southern Illinois University Press, 1963, p. 355.
[3] W. M. Parrish, "The Concept of 'Naturalness,'" *Quarterly Journal of Speech*, December, 1951, 37:450.
[4] Charles Henry Woolbert, *The Fundamentals of Speech*, rev. ed., New York: Harper & Row, 1927, p. 72.

Good Delivery Is Purposeful

The speaker consciously uses action to make more impelling what he says. He is attuned to the peculiar requirements imposed by the time, the place, and the prevailing customs. In a large auditorium, he selects broad gestures and decisive action, while in the drawing room he moves with restraint. He recognizes that a place such as a church or a lodge imposes restrictions not present at a student assembly or a pep rally. He knows that different types of activity demand different approaches. For example, the alert interpreter with a book in hand does not attempt impersonation. When the speaker or reader shifts his weight or moves across the platform, he does so, not haphazardly, but as a part of a plan to achieve his goal.

Good Delivery Is Pleasing

Weaver suggests that, "If a speaker's action is to be pleasant to contemplate it must be graceful, smooth, and economical, rather than awkward, jerky, and wasteful."[5] Of course, through his appearance and manner, the speaker does much to establish rapport, or what Robert Oliver has referred to as a "bond of sympathy" and "a current of warm and cordial understanding between listener and speaker."[6] The listeners size up the speaker by what he does, his posture, his gesture, and his facial expression. They are quick to notice timidness, inappropriate dress, or distracting mannerisms, and they are inclined to listen with greater eagerness and to react more favorably to persons they like.

A Cardinal Principle

Good delivery reinforces the speaker's message. As long as the listeners are concentrating upon what is said, the delivery is probably effective, but when the listeners commence to watch what the speaker does instead of what he says, it is ineffective.

APPROACHES TO THE TEACHING OF DELIVERY

Through the centuries there has probably been more disagreement on how to teach delivery than on any other phase of speaking. Let us review three systems that have had wide followings in the past: imitation, the mechanical school, and "think-the-thought" school.

[5] Andrew Thomas Weaver, *Speech, Forms and Principles*, London: Longmans, Green, 1942, p. 169.
[6] Robert T. Oliver, "Wilson's Rapport with His Audience," *Quarterly Journal of Speech*, February, 1941, 27:79–90.

Imitation

Quintilian has said, "Indeed the whole conduct of life is based on the desire of doing ourselves what we approve in others."[7] This quotation, of course, suggests imitation, a method of teaching long respected and widely used even today. Under this system the teacher directs the students to follow a model—that is, to imitate, to mimic, or to copy the actions of another person—the teacher himself, a famous speaker, a classmate, or a hypothetical or idealized person.[8] The student is directed to "Watch how I gesture. . . . Now let me see you do it." Or perhaps he is told, "Notice how John approaches the platform. You should follow his example."

The method, used since the time of the Greeks and Romans, is employed on occasion by almost every teacher of speech. Its effectiveness depends on (1) directing the student to a good model, (2) getting him to imitate the model, and then (3) attempting to get him to improve on his model, thus developing techniques that are distinctly his own. Often of course the student may learn much through the study and imitation of good models. But under poor direction the novice is likely to mimic external or surface characteristics without analyzing the motivation for the movement; he copies mannerisms and idiosyncrasies as well as good points. In the end, he may act very much like his model; but he fails to develop an approach that is distinctly his own.

The Mechanical Approach

The next approach is one that English elocutionists of the eighteenth and nineteenth centuries popularized and put into wide use. Although it has completely lost favor with most educators, it still has a few proponents. The purpose in explaining it here is purely for information, hoping that it may provide the teacher with a better perspective of the problems of teaching delivery. Indeed it is doubtful that anyone will attempt to make use of its techniques in a present-day speech course.

In the mechanical approach, the teacher attempts to formulate principles, rules, systems of notations to govern delivery in reading and in speaking. Action is rigidly prescribed so that the student follows directions the way a musician reads notes. For example, a fixed gesture or body pose is suggested to portray a fixed idea or a certain emotion.[9] The teacher or critic may read and analyze the material and mark it with appropriate symbols. In turn the student, understanding the symbols, goes through the

[7] Quintilian's *Institutes of Oratory*, trans. by John Selby Watson, Bohn, 1856, X, ii, 2.
[8] For discussion of the method of the ancient rhetoricians, see Donald Lemen Clark, *Rhetoric in Greco-Roman Education*, New York: Columbia University Press, 1957, pp. 144–176.
[9] Frederick Haberman, "English Sources of American Elocution," in Karl R. Wallace (ed.), *History of Speech Education in America*, New York: Appleton-Century-Crofts, 1954, pp. 105–126.

motions, sometimes without any direct concern for communicating ideas to listeners. In this event he may be dull, stereotyped, and even ridiculous in his performance.

Schooled in present-day speech pedagogy, the speech communication teacher has difficulty even imagining how an elocutionist would pursue the teaching of delivery. For illustrative purposes only, two exercises found in elocution books are given below:

Exercises in Facial Expression

By means of the eyes indicate:
Courage, Determination: Look straight forward.
Joy, Hope, Delight: Raise the eyes slightly upward.
Shame, Modesty, Humility: Look downward.
Disgust, Aversion: Turn the eyes to either side.
Madness: A steady glare, seeing nothing.
Sudden Anger: Let the eyes flash.
Consternation: Open the eyes wide with a fixed stare.
Rage: Roll the eyes well open.
Despair: A vacant stare.
Laughing: Eyes partially closed.
Supplication: Eyes elevated.
Flirt: To the side with a twinkle.[10]

Exercises in Gesture

Practice on the following exercises cannot fail to give ease and grace to the movement of the arm and hand. The letters refer to the direction of the gesture, which should be made upon the word or syllable underlined.

Right hand supine:
D.F.   This sentiment I will maintain with the last breath of *life*.
H.F.   I appeal to *you*, sir, for your decision.
A.F.   I appeal to the great searcher of *hearts* for the truth of what utter.
D.O.   Of all mistakes, *none* are so fatal as those which we incur through prejudice.
H.F.   Truth, honor, *justice* were his motives.
A.F.   Fix your eye on the prize of a truly *noble* ambition.
D.L.   *Away* with an idea so absurd.
H.L.   The breeze of morning waited *incense* on the air.
A.L.   In dreams thro' camp and court he bore the trophies of a *conqueror*.
D.F.   *Away* with an idea so abhorrent to humanity.
H.F.   Search the records of the remotest *antiquity* for a parallel to this.
A.F.   Then rang their proud *hurrah*.[11]

[10] I. H. Brown, *Brown's Standard Elocution and Speaker*, Land and Lee, 1911, pp. 45–47.
[11] Note concerning symbols: D.F. means descending front; H.F., horizontal front; A.F., ascending front; D.O., down oblique; D.L., down lateral, etc. Frank H. Fenno, *The Science and Art of Elocution or How to Read and Speak*, New York: Potter, 1878, pp. 45–46.

Teaching delivery by this method becomes a matter of: (1) mastery of rules, (2) drilling the student in application of rules, and (3) developing insight into when to apply rules.

"Think-the-Thought" Approach

A revolt against the mechanical method brought forward what has been called the "think-the-thought" approach, or natural delivery. This system is based on the view that action is a matter of impulse, and that natural inclinations are therefore regarded as reliable guides to delivery. The speaker is directed to gesture and to move when his thoughts seem to demand action. The teacher is likely to say, "Just move and gesture when you have the urge to do so."

The method was advocated by Richard Whately in his famous *Elements of Rhetoric* published in 1828. Whately explained that the speaker following this system will "withdraw" his thoughts from delivery and will "dwell as intently as possible on the Sense, trusting to nature to suggest spontaneously the proper emphases and tones."[12] Further:

Practice also (i.e., private practice for the sake of learning) is much more difficult in the proposed method; because, the rule being, to use such a delivery as is suited, not only to the *matter* of what is said, but also, of course, to the *place* and *occasion*, and this, not by any studied modulations, but according to the spontaneous suggestions of the matter, place, and occasion, to one whose mind is fully and exclusively occupied with these, it follows, that he who would practice this method in *private*, must, by a strong effort of a vivid imagination, figure to himself a place and an occasion which are *not* present; otherwise, he will either be *thinking of his delivery*, (which is fatal to his proposed object,) or else will use a delivery suited to the situation in which he actually *is*, and not, to that for which he would prepare himself.[13]

At the outset the teacher should recognize that the Whately analysis has much merit. In fact, there is general agreement among teachers of speech communication that the conversational mode and natural, unaffected, visible action are the bases of effective communication. Under ideal conditions the student who concentrates on his thought and trusts to nature will probably comply with the qualities discussed in the previous section. But, as every teacher knows, *ideal* students seldom enroll in speech classes; and teaching conditions are usually far from ideal. Before arriving in class many students acquire unwholesome attitudes and develop undesirable habits which interfere with direct and effective communicating.

It is true that some students need little instruction in gesture, move-

[12] Whately, *op. cit.*, p. 352.
[13] *Ibid.*, p. 355.

ment, and platform deportment. For these the teacher may be thankful, but often they are few in number. Below are some examples of types who, because of previous conditioning, will need instruction in control of bodily activity.

1. The timid student who thinks more about himself than his subject.
2. The student who copies a poor or inappropriate model.
3. The student who is misinformed about what is good delivery (many ministerial students fall into this category).
4. The student who has developed bad habits in previous speech activities (declamation, oratory, or debate).
5. The exhibitionist who craves attention.
6. The student who confuses acting, interpretative reading, and speaking.
7. The student who has a distracting mannerism: hands in pockets, folded arms, military posture, lip licking, casual slouch, unpleasant grimace, etc.
8. The student whose natural or habitual manner seems repulsive to listeners.
9. The student who does not know how to use visible action to reinforce his meaning.
10. The student who is subject centered and who lacks an urge to communicate.
11. The student who uses no gestures and sees no need for them.

Integration of the Teaching of Delivery with Other Units

The thoughtful person will recognize useful elements in each of the three previous ways of teaching delivery. In his experience the author has found it necessary to resort to all of them on occasion. Different students and different problems require a variety of approaches.

Today, however, teachers of speech communication generally have abandoned the practice of devoting a specific unit of instruction to visible action; they are more likely to attempt to develop it in connection with other units. In contrast to the teaching of speech organization, for example, which may occupy a unit of two or three weeks, delivery is a concern in every assignment—no matter what other phase is under consideration.

Whenever the student appears before the class he cannot avoid visible action. This fact gives the teacher a starting point or an avenue through which to motivate him to use purposeful movement. For example, at the opening of the semester the student is encouraged to speak on subjects in which he is intensely interested and about which he has a great urge to communicate; consequently, he is likely to use purposeful action with a minimum of self-consciousness. Likewise, early assignments may include how-to-do-it speeches, demonstrations, and visual-aid talks. Later speeches demand more subtle movement and more restraint. But always during the criticism of the talk the teacher keeps working for refinement. He integrates instruction in delivery with other units.

A PROGRAM FOR TEACHING DELIVERY

The teaching of the control of bodily activity may be planned on a continuum or progression of phases through which the student passes in his development:

1. Recognition of what is good delivery and its importance in the communicative process
2. Development within the student of the desire to improve
3. Realization by the student of how he fails to measure up to standards
4. Releasing the student from his inhibitions
5. Elimination of gross faults
6. Refinement of skill
7. Development of artistry

As an introduction to the presentation of these phases, three observations are in order. First, not all students develop in the sequence in which these are listed. Second, some students may actually achieve several of these objectives together. And third, seldom does a single class within a quarter or semester attempt to consider all of them. They are achieved more properly in a sequence of courses. Now consider each phase.

1. *Recognition of what is good delivery and its importance in the communication process.* This phase involves building in a student a picture or image of what he is attempting to achieve. Before self-improvement he must know what is expected of him or what is considered satisfactory delivery. This phase may be achieved by one of a number of methods. (a) The viewing of films or videotapes is a way to develop awareness of standards. (b) On-the-spot observations by the teacher of each performance are also important in establishing what is acceptable and attractive. The student becomes more analytical and thoughtful about standards when he observes what the teacher finds to compliment in the performance of others. He compares his own gestures, stance, and posture with those of his colleagues. Such self-analysis is fruitful and stimulating. (c) Often a chapter on delivery in the textbook is to give the student an understanding of what good delivery is. (d) Equally important is direct observation and study of the performances of others, whether classmates or public figures. The instructor may use assignments such as the following:

Student Assignments

1. Make a list of five celebrities or people you know whose delivery is underplayed. In what ways does the delivery of each of these people differ from the others?
2. Compare your delivery in conversation with your delivery in formal speaking situations. Do you demonstrate a sense of communication in either, neither, or both situations?
3. Recall five good speakers whom you have heard recently. Did they speak from the moment, notes, manuscript, or memory? If you don't know which method they used, why don't you know?

4. Describe the delivery which you would expect from the following people in the following speech situations:
   a. a high school senior interviewing with an admissions officer from the college he wishes to attend.
   b. a waitress addressing a customer at a very "swank" supper club.
   c. the student council president addressing the school board.
   d. a speeder speaking to a traffic-court judge.
   e. a young man saying good bye to his fiancée at the airport as he prepares to go overseas on a 2-year tour of military duty.[14]
5. For developing awareness of effective bodily action
   a. Observe a speaker in an assembly, a church meeting, or on television. Note the phrases he supports by gestures, movement, or facial expression. On the left side of a sheet of paper list the action employed, and on the right side list the corresponding words or phrases. Note the actions which were especially effective.
   b. From some picture magazine select pictures showing good or poor bodily action. In your own speaking try to use the types of action you consider best.
   c. Watch several television news commentators for a period of 2 or 3 weeks. Note the ways in which they use facial expressions to enhance meanings or heighten the emotional effect of their news.
   d. Make a collection of 15 to 20 newspaper pictures of speakers in action. If you can get a number of shots of the same speaker, that is even better. Now try to determine how effective his bodily action has been. Do you note that a speaker acts differently in formal and informal situations? How? With what effect?[15]

2. Development within the student of the desire to improve. Learning cannot take place until the student is ready to learn. Fortunately, creating a desire to improve is not ordinarily a problem with many students, for they want to do what is considered acceptable and are not eager to be considered peculiar or different. The teacher here has an excellent point of departure; that is, he shows that good delivery is a matter of making oneself attractive. However, on those occasions when the teacher demands bodily activity markedly different from group norms, he is most likely to meet resistance to his suggestions.

Problems sometimes arise with those who refuse to give up some preconceived notion or to break a firmly entrenched habit pattern. In an attempt to appear shorter the tall girl may not stand up straight. The football player may think it looks manly to stand with his feet wide apart. The person who attempts to mimic a country politician or a hell-fire-and-damnation preacher, or who has developed certain stereotyped gestures in high school debating or declamatory work, may resist change or even refuse to listen seriously to suggestions. Under these circumstances the teacher must blast indifference by specific and even sharp criticism.

3. Realization by the student of how he fails to measure up to standards. The individual can seldom see himself as others see him. He is likely to be

[14] R. R. Allen, Sharol Andersen, and Jere Hough, *Speech in American Society*, Columbus, Oh.: Charles B. Merrill, 1968, p. 133.
[15] L. Day Hanks and Martin P. Andersen, *From Thought to Speech*, Lexington, Mass.: Ratheon/Heath, 1969, p. 233.

completely unaware of an awkward stance, a facial tic, a silly laugh, a nervous gesture, or a shifting from foot to foot. He may continue to follow an undesirable habit even when it has been called to his attention several times. He may argue that these habitual movements feel or seem natural to him even though they may be annoying or unattractive to the listeners.

Classes fortunate enough to have available a motion-picture camera can let the student see exactly what he does. But in most classes the teacher and fellow classmates must take the place of the camera in helping the novice see himself. Indeed a teacher is fortunate to have available a video-tape recorder or motion picture camera to use in teaching delivery. The teacher may demonstrate what he does, and then explain why the gesture is ineffective. Or he may ask a classmate to explain why the gesture is annoying.

4. *Releasing the student from his inhibitions.* Self-conscious students often become rigid and unresponsive when they stand before an audience. Their movements are forced and awkward. Gestures stop with a feeble move of the hand. Facial expressions are often dead-pan. Early assignments must be planned to break down this rigidity, to relieve these first fears, to release the student, thus making him want to express himself. Below is a typical assignment for this purpose:

Student Assignments

1. "Throw" each of the following objects as would be appropriate. Do this in random order. See if your classmates can identify what you are throwing:
   a. a football from the quarterback to the end
   b. a baseball from the center fielder to the catcher
   c. a tennis ball to a player across the net as you begin a new set
   d. a rubber ball to a year-old baby
   e. a horseshoe in a tight match
   f. a light bulb to your father across the table
   g. a toy balloon to a three-year-old girl
   h. a basketball from the free throw line[16]

The teacher may direct the student speaker to subjects about which he is enthusiastic—his hobby, a favorite pastime, a pet peeve, an unusual experience. Many teachers open the semester with a speech of introduction. If the subject is a vital one, the student is likely to move and to gesture with little fear; he talks enthusiastically about his subject, forgetting inhibitions. These first efforts must let him gain confidence in himself and assurance that he will not be ridiculed when he stands before the audience. Notice how the following series of exercises is designed to stir the student to use bodily action through animated narration.

[16] Paul Hibbs, Seth A. Fessenden, P. Merville Larson, and Joseph A. Wagner, *Speech for Today*, New York: McGraw-Hill, 1965, p. 240.

Student Assignments

1. Prepare an extemporaneous speech which calls for swift-moving narration; if possible, one that is an animated narrative from first to last.
2. Choose a story so full of excitement that the action impels you to respond with abundant action; if possible, tell about something which so moved you that you could hardly wait to get home to tell it.
3. In one type of story, the chief interest is in characters. In another type, the chief interest is in what the characters do; in dramatic crises, conflicts, races, fights, escapes, victories, and catastrophes. For this exercise, choose an action story.
4. Draw on your own adventures, or on a play you have seen or heard over the air, or a novel or short story you have read.
5. Tell the incidents in the story either in the order in which they occurred, or in an order better suited to secure suspense.
6. After preparing a careful outline, memorize it.
7. In the privacy of your room, practice delivering the speech with abundant, spontaneous action. Let the pressure exerted upon you by the ideas and feelings govern your action. Let yourself go. If your action is too rough, never mind; later on, you can take care of that.
8. Deliver the speech in class, using all the gestures and bodily movements that seem natural.[17]

5. *Elimination of Gross Faults.* The beginning teacher sometimes feels that he must comment on and personally supervise the elimination of all the faults of each student. Experience shows how unnecessary—and impossible—such an approach is. With the right type of assignment, the student may eliminate gross faults without conscious effort or without comment from the instructor. Good teaching helps him to recognize what is effective and what is ineffective. This natural development comes when the teacher carefully plans the progression of assignments starting with those that demand broad action and movement. These early ones should take into account that probably 75 percent of the students feel that their greatest initial problem is stage fright. Therefore, first appearances before the class should be simple enough so that the beginner experiences some pleasure in speaking and some feeling of success. Early assignments that demand broad overt action focus the student's attention on the subject and not on himself. The teacher may wish to resort to assignments such as the following:

1. Pantomime
2. Impromptu skits in which the student must play a character different from his own
3. The demonstration talk in which the student must manipulate an object or model
4. The talk in which the student must use a chart or chalkboard sketch
5. The direction-giving speech in which the speaker tells how to reach a certain place
6. The speech in which the speaker mimics some famous personality

[17] Lew Sarett, William Trufant Foster, and James H. McBurney, *Speech: A High School Course,* Boston: Houghton Mifflin, 1951, pp. 63, 64. Reprinted by permission.

Below are several exercises that may aid in eliminating gross faults:

Student Assignments

1. Select a chapter from a favorite novel and act out the main character.
2. Impersonate the carriage and actions of a cheerleader, an old lady, a fruit vendor, a newsboy, a hunter, a fat man, and a miser.
3. Perform the following individual pantomimes:

cooking	washing a dog
mending	cleaning a house
ironing	repairing a flat tire
directing traffic	conducting an orchestra
doing setting-up exercises	rowing a boat[18]

6. *Refinement of skill.* It is a mistake to assume that all faults in the use of bodily action may be eliminated indirectly. Even the good Bishop Richard Whately, who so fervently preached natural delivery (which we discussed earlier), recognized that "If anyone spontaneously falls into any gestures that are unbecoming care should *then* be taken to break the habit. . . . It is in these points, principally, if not exclusively, that the remarks of an intelligent friend will be beneficial."[19] It is hoped that the teacher may qualify in the role of the "intelligent friend," or at least as effective critic.

The experience and testimony of large numbers of prominent speakers suggest that the student should be encouraged to spend considerable time in experimentation and self-analysis of gestures, stance, facial expression, and movement. Much of this practice perhaps may be carried on in private after the student is made fully aware of what is good delivery and wherein he fails to meet acceptable standards.

Below are 25 distracting habits that the teacher is likely to encounter with beginning speakers.

1. Wringing hands
2. Rolling or playing with notes
3. Jingling money or keys
4. Buttoning and unbuttoning coat
5. Pulling an ear or a nose
6. Fumbling with a pencil
7. Putting thumbs under belt
8. Standing with hands on hips
9. Scratching
10. Fussing with ring, watch, or beads
11. Fixing tie or pin
12. Clutching or straightening clothing
13. Cracking knuckles
14. Looking at the ceiling or out the window
15. Shifting eyes constantly from place to place
16. Folding and unfolding arms
17. Giving nervous or silly laugh
18. Standing with feet too wide apart or close together

[18] Wilhelmina G. Hedde, William Norwood Brigance, and Victor M. Powell, *The New American Speech*, 3rd ed., Philadelphia: Lippincott, 1968, pp. 53, 54.
[19] Whately, *op. cit.*, p. 389.

19. Rocking backward and forward from heels to toes
20. Standing cross-legged
21. Shifting constantly from one foot to the other
22. Placing foot on a chair or table
23. Leaning heavily on a lectern or reading stand
24. Wetting lips frequently
25. Smoothing repeatedly or replacing stray wisps of hair

How should the teacher handle the student who persists in using such a distracting mannerism or ineffective action? He must do at least four things:

1. Isolate and identify the fault for the student.
2. Make sure that the student understands *why* what he does is ineffective or unattractive.
3. Give the student constructive suggestions as to how to improve.
4. Check later performances to see that the student eliminates the fault and substitutes effective action.

When he encounters a persistent awkward mannerism, the teacher may find it quite difficult to make the student understand how and why it is ineffective or undesirable. If the teacher comments casually or generally, the student may miss the significance of the comment or ignore it entirely. Or he may conclude that he has eliminated his fault when in reality he has modified it very little. Habitual faults require persistence and expert criticism on the part of the teacher.

To illustrate, the teacher may observe, "There is a sameness in your gesturing. You should work for variety." This comment is too general; it will probably leave the student confused or frustrated. To break through the student's lack of awareness or unwillingness to listen, the teacher may be more effective by rephrasing his criticism as follows: "Do you know that in your 5-minute speech, you used the same up-and-down gesture with your right hand nine times?" After the next performance, the teacher may clinch his point by saying, "In contrast to the nine times you used the up-and-down gesture in your last speech, today you used it only four times. But that is still too many." Then the teacher may ask the student to show him several alternate gestures or movements that may be substituted for the so-called "pump handle" motion. In this way he makes sure that the student understands both what is faulty and how to improve his communicative effort. At moments like these the teacher may recommend broad action and sweeping gestures as a means to help the student develop a "feel," or muscle alertness, for the new gesture.

Below are some suggestions that may help in refining visible action:

Student Assignments

1. Rehearsal of bodily action before a mirror. This is an excellent way to encourage the student to experiment with different approaches. However, there is danger that in the process the student may lose sight of the real objective of speaking—the communication of ideas.

2. Planning and rehearsing the action for a memorized selection. With the content fixed, the student has an opportunity for experimentation. After a formal presentation in class, the student may gain much from class discussion of his performance and ways in which he could have improved his presentation. Selections such as Patrick Henry's "Give Me Liberty or Give Me Death" are frequently used for this type of exercise.
3. Rehearsal of an original speech with planned movement and gesture. This type of assignment differs from the previous one only in that the substance is the speaker's own. Following the speech, the student may be asked to justify his visible action.
4. Participation in related speech activities such as acting or impersonation. In play acting the student often forgets his inhibitions and enjoys movement about the stage. Because he must refine his action, particularly his stage business, he is often able to perfect his action.

One speech textbook for high school students introduces a series of exercises designed to encourage the refinement of the students' control of bodily activity. Several of these illustrate the points just listed.

Student Assignments

1. Walk properly to a "speaker's position" before the class, pause, take a deep breath, and look over your audience as you assume proper speaking posture. Then move backward and forward, right and left, as you might while giving a speech. Return to your seat as though you were leaving the platform after a speech.
2. Speak impromptu on any topic you choose long enough to practice movement backward and forward and to the sides. For this talk, your movements will be more important than your ideas.
3. Plan a two-minute talk on some school subject. Determine beforehand, preferably before a mirror, when you will move about. Give the talk in class. Have your classmates discuss with you whether your movements were well planned. Was the class too aware of them, or were they helped by them to follow your speech?
4. Practice before a mirror a 2-minute talk which you have previously given. Enliven it with gestures, but make them natural. Deliver the talk to the class again, and discuss whether it "went over" better.[20]

7. Development of artistry. The great actor, the polished reader, or the eloquent speaker does not learn his art in a semester course. On the contrary, he usually develops artistry through careful observations, long and patient practice, and hard work. Throughout his career he may continue to strive to improve. Sometimes he may seek out a skilled critic to observe and to counsel him. But always he eagerly studies the reactions of his listeners, hoping to find a better approach.

EXERCISES

1. Prepare a lesson plan for teaching a unit on visible action. You may develop it for a high school, college, or adult class.

[20] Harlen Martin Adams and Thomas Clark Pollock, *Speak Up!* New York: MacMillan, 1956, p. 441.

2. Observe a high school or college class in speech fundamentals, public speaking, or oral interpretation. Prepare a written analysis of the problems in bodily action that students encountered. In your report describe how the teacher handled these problems.
3. Study carefully the bodily action of one student in the class you observe. Prepare a careful description of your observations, and then write a statement of what you would advise the student concerning his problems. In your method class you will be asked to read this statement. Your colleagues will discuss how you handled the problem.
4. Study carefully the exercises on bodily action given in one of the leading high school or college textbooks. Determine the purpose of each exercise and classify it according to seven steps found on p. 312.
5. Discuss the following problems:
    a. Should the teacher tell the student how and when to move and gesture? Why or why not?
    b. Should the mechanical approach to teaching bodily movement ever be used?
    c. Should the teacher insist that every student stand up straight and keep his hands at his sides?
    d. Should the teacher call a student's attention to a facial tic? In class? In a private conference?
    e. How should the teacher handle the spastic or cripple who enrolls in a public speaking class?
    f. How should the teacher handle the novice speaker who is attempting to imitate a famous actor or well-known politician?
    g. Should the speaker and the reader follow the same principles of bodily action? The same approach?
    h. What limitations does television impose on bodily action?
    i. How should the teacher handle the adult student who has developed some extreme mannerisms? (The country preacher, the housewife, or the salesman, for example.)
    j. How can bodily action contribute to speakers or readers effectiveness?

REFERENCES

BOLTON, JANET, "The Garnishing of the Manner of Utterance," *Western Speech*, Spring, 1964, 38:83–91.

BOWEN, HARRY W., "A Reassessment of Speech Delivery," *Today's Speech*, November, 1966, 14:21–24.

BROOKS, WILLIAM D., "Investigation of Improvement in Bodily Action as a Result of the Basic Course in Speech," *Southern Speech Journal*, Fall, 1969, 35:9–15.

DENSMORE, G. E., "The Teaching of Speech Delivery," *Quaterly Journal of Speech*, February, 1946, 32:67–71.

FESSENDEN, SETH A., *et al.*, *Speech for the Creative Teacher*, Dubuque, Ia.: William C. Brown, 1968, chap. 6, "Visible Communication."

GORDEN, WILLIAM I., "A Comparison of Two Types of Delivery of a Persuasive Speech," *Southern Speech Journal*, Fall, 1961, 27:74–79.

PARRISH, WAYLAND MAXFIELD, "The Concept of 'Naturalness,' " *Quarterly Journal of Speech*, December, 1951, 37:448–454.

PARRISH, WAYLAND MAXFIELD, "Elocution: A Definition and a Challenge," *Quarterly Journal of Speech*, February, 1957, 43:1–11.

THONSSEN, LESTER, BAIRD, A. CRAIG, AND BRADEN, WALDO W., *Speech Criticism*, 2nd ed., New York: Ronald Press, 1970, chap. 17, "The Delivery of the Speech."

WALLACE, KARL R., "A Modern View of Delivery," in Bronstein, Arthur J., *et al.* (eds.), *Essays in Honor of C. M. Wise*, Hannibal, Mo.: Standard Printing Co., 1970, pp. 153–166.

15. Teaching Through Criticism

Waldo W. Braden

Too often after hearing four or five halting classroom efforts, a teacher becomes weary or even numb. He may be tempted to take the easy way and dismiss a speech with a vague, noncommittal, seemingly complimentary remark or some small talk, and then hurry on to the next student. When the class is large, there is pressure to hold comments about speeches to a minimum in order to work in as many speeches as possible in the class period. Under these conditions, speech criticism becomes difficult. Occasionally a student is brave enough to attempt to slow down the teacher by asking, "How can I improve?" "What was wrong with my speech?" or more likely, "Tell me how I can make a better grade." But unfortunately too few students demand constructive suggestions. Often they give a sigh of relief when the instructor passes them by without comment.

Criticism is synonymous with teaching. *The teacher has a solemn obligation to tell each student speaker after each performance how he can improve.* Furthermore, he has a solemn obligation never to tell a student about a fault without telling him what he can do about it. To say to the student, "You have a nasal voice," or "You can't put over your speeches," is likely to result in frustration unless a concrete suggestion follows. Fault finding is easy, but constructive suggestions are difficult—and valuable.

Hargis has reported that about 15 percent of the class time of the average college public speaking class is devoted to criticism.[1] It is a goal of

[1] Donald Hargis, "The First Course in Speech," *Speech Teacher*, January, 1956, 5:26–33.

this chapter to discuss how this time can be used profitably. It deals with the critique as it is handled in the beginning class; it makes no attempt to present a discussion of rhetorical criticism as applied to important speakers.[2]

CHARACTERISTICS OF GOOD CRITICISM

Good Criticism Is Objective

The critic who is a trained observer evaluates student performance in terms of a clearly defined yardstick or criterion. He must see all, be aware of what actually happens, refusing to let personal likes or dislikes color his conclusions. He must guard against assigning undue weight to a given characteristic, such as delivery or directness, or grammar at the expense of another aspect of the speaking process.

Good Criticism Is Clear and Understandable

The teacher should express his observations in language that is meaningful to the student. He must speak in concrete words, avoiding abstractions and jargon. To say, "you need more ethical appeal" is likely to be misunderstood unless the student is aware of the peculiar usage of the term *ethical*. By rephrasing this remark the teacher may communicate more effectively with: "You need to tell your listeners where you found your facts" or "You need to emphasize that you had direct experience with your subject."

What does it mean to the student when the teacher comments, "You are not putting your subject over" or "You are not getting through to your listeners?" Perhaps the teacher means, "You should illustrate the third point with actual incident or experience" or "You should be more animated in your delivery." Good criticism is meaningful to the student.

Good Criticism Is Definite

The characteristic of definiteness is closely related to the criterion of clearness, just discussed. The act of speaking is so complex that it is likely to impress the unskilled observer without his understanding why he is influenced. In making a judgment he may respond, "I liked the speaker," or "It was an interesting talk," or "I found the speaker was dull," or "I disagreed with everything he said." But none of these remarks expresses any more than a superficial reaction that gives no indication of why the speaker did or did not make his point. In direct contrast, the teacher must give specific reasons for the success or failure of the utterance.

[2] For persons interested in an extensive treatment of this subject, see Lester Thonssen, A. Craig Baird, and Waldo W. Braden, *Speech Criticism*, 2nd ed., New York: Ronald Press, 1970.

Good criticism is centered on select aspects or elements understood by both student and teacher. This requirement demands that the critic isolate the characteristic at fault—that is, point to the word mispronounced, to the annoying mannerism, or to the confusing passage.

Good Criticism Is Adapted to the Student

In commenting on speeches, the teacher must consider the emotional maturity of each student. The experienced teacher learns to soften his remarks for those who seem to feel injured when faults are mentioned—that is, references to bad grammar, unpleasant voice quality, and annoying mannerisms. Making good criticism acceptable requires adroitness and tact.

Good Criticism Is Constructive and Helpful

To many persons the word *criticism* has a negative meaning of faultfinding and censure. But in the classroom and at the speech contest it should have a positive connotation—telling the student how to improve, how to develop better speech habits, how to achieve a greater response. Cromwell has explained that it must be "an integral part of the learning experience. To be effective it should accomplish three objectives: (a) give the student a yardstick for evaluating his success in accomplishing an assignment, (b) provide a basis for the student to discriminate between what is correct and incorrect, and (c) motivate the student toward further achievement."[3] Harry Barnes, who supervised beginning courses at the State University of Iowa for many years, has carried the advice a step further: "The philosophy of criticism which is based on calling attention to bad habits in my judgment is educationally unsound. Criticism should call attention to and emphasize the good response rather than the bad. Standards are thus more effectively developed, good habits become established more firmly, confidence grows with a sense of achievement, and a desire to speak minimizes imperfections, which after all are only relative."[4]

ORAL CRITICISM

Oral criticism has the advantage of immediacy. Before he forgets what he has done, the performer hears an evaluation; and he knows specifically to what the teacher refers. If well stated, such evaluation cannot be ignored. In contrast to the oral critique, written criticism may be vague and mean-

[3] Harvey Cromwell, *Suggestions for the Beginning Course in Speech and Public Speaking*, Glenview, Ill.: Scott, Foresman, 1956, p. 3.
[4] Harry G. Barnes, "Teaching the Fundamentals of Speech at the College Level." *Speech Teacher*, November, 1954, 3:249.

ingless, and may even be discarded by the student in his haste to get to his next class or in his eagerness to talk to a certain girl.

What is the starting point? Before anything can be accomplished, the student must be convinced of the teacher's ability, honesty, integrity, and good will. There is little doubt that a student more readily accepts suggestions from a person whom he trusts and respects than from one about whom he is skeptical or of whom he is afraid. The student must believe that the teacher is impartial and objective; he must be prevented from feeling that he is being picked on.

During the first weeks, when students are struggling to gain self-confidence, oral criticism of several speakers at one time is often highly desirable. After listening to three or four speeches, the teacher comments without mentioning names in order to protect the sensitive students. Hence, some gross faults are eliminated painlessly. Furthermore, these indirect comments involving no names may start class discussion and give the timid student opportunities to ask questions about his given difficulties without associating himself with any of them. Under these conditions he is encouraged to talk about his problems.

Of course, there is no substitute for direct oral criticism aimed at a specific fault of a given student. This is particularly true for a student who is unable or unwilling to recognize his limitations and awkwardness. But directness does not imply harshness or tactlessness. The teacher must always strive to find the least embarrassing way, the most acceptable approach, to giving his critiques. In this regard, the following suggestions may be helpful:

1. Comment on good points in a performance before dealing with weaknesses.
2. Assure the student that you are sincerely interested in his welfare and improvement.
3. Show concern and sympathy for the student struggling to cope with his problem.
4. Point out that the problem is one with which many, particularly important speakers, have had trouble.
5. Attribute criticism to someone else: an authority or textbook.
6. Make the student demand that he be criticized.
7. Present two or more points of view concerning the fault, emphasizing one but giving the student a face-saver.
8. Express doubt as to whether the student can take the criticism.
9. Ask the class whether the criticism is justified in a given case.
10. Put the criticism in a question form—i.e., "do you realize that you are . . ."

Making criticism acceptable should in no sense constitute pampering or playing down to the student. Each speaker must learn to take criticism, to recognize his limitations, and to strive to make the best of them. Every effort should be made, therefore, to move the student toward emotional maturity.

Oral criticism is a valuable way to focus the attention of the entire class on ways to improve. For example, when the unit on organization is under consideration, the teacher may emphasize a point by saying, "Did you notice how Smith used signposts to label his main points? He said, 'The first step involved. . . . The second step involved. . . . The third step involved. . . .'" Or the instructor may say, "Contrast the way Jones and Smith used the blackboard. Smith placed his diagram on the board in clearly defined steps, labeling each part. But Jones had no set order and no labels. Which presentation did you think was clearer?" Remarks of this type guide the members of the class in what is good practice; they learn by seeing others try new techniques.

Should classmates be asked to comment on a speech? Some teachers use this method to great advantage.[5] How class criticism is used will depend on the maturity of the students and on the time available for this phase of class activity. In large classes, permitting class members to comment on speeches must be held to a minimum in order to conserve time. Furthermore, student comments should be carefully controlled, directed to a given aspect of the speaking process, and not permitted to wander to inconsequential points. Class discussion must not overwhelm the awkward or timid performer or make him feel that his case is hopeless.

Group criticism offers the positive advantage of encouraging intelligent listening as well as building esprit de corps. The teacher must instruct the students how to evaluate, how to criticize, and how to accept criticism. Often the teacher should criticize the criticism as well as a performance.

What to Say About Stage Fright

As many as three-fourths of many beginning classes confess that their chief problem is stage fright and that they are most eager to overcome their shyness. A little questioning will reveal that some have put off taking the course perhaps three or four semesters because they could not summon up enough courage even to think of delivering a speech. It is not unusual to have students in class who have never appeared before the public and who have never even stood before a class to give a report. These same persons seek the back row, attempt to remain as inconspicuous as possible, and may even schedule classes that require no oral recitation. Many adults report that stage fright is a real bugaboo; these are the people who enroll in evening classes of public speaking in the hope that they can master their feelings of inferiority.

Handling the person with stage fright involves two tasks: first, giving the student numerous opportunities to speak before the class and, if at all possible, to succeed; second, giving him wise counsel and helpful suggestions. A tactless remark by the teacher may undo weeks of effort and drive

[5] See Chapter 12.

the student into greater frustration and anxiety. It behooves the teacher to word his criticism carefully and wisely.

Teachers differ in how they approach the problem of stage fright. Some advocate the direct approach. They talk about the problem, describe it in detail, minimize its importance, and seek to stir the student through introspection to look at and to face his fears and thereby eliminate them.

Other teachers minimize the problem but seek through carefully arranged assignments to provide the student with a set of experiences that will show him he has nothing to fear, and that a dry mouth, perspiring hands, and shaking knees are not fatal.

There are some helpful hints on stage fright around which the teacher may build his suggestions and which he can subtly work into his criticism. A number of them that are widely recommended and, in most cases, carefully tested are given below:

1. Stage fright is a normal reaction that many persons experience.
2. Even famous speakers and actors confess that on occasions they have stage fright.
3. The speaker need not worry about his listeners knowing about his stage fright; studies show that listeners cannot generally identify the extent of a speaker's fears.
4. The student may remove one source of fear through careful preparation.
5. He can expect to have less difficulty with topics about which he is enthusiastic and well informed.
6. The student can expect his symptoms of stage fright to decrease as he gains additional speaking experience.
7. The student can promote his confidence by oral rehearsal.
8. The student may increase his fear by memorizing a speech—he has the additional fear of forgetting.
9. The student may lessen his fears by engaging in some physical activity while speaking; that is, he will have less difficulty if he has an apparatus to manipulate or a chart from which to speak.
10. The classroom is the best place to eliminate stage fright; here he has a sympathetic, captive audience.
11. Usually understanding the nature of stage fright gives some relief.
12. The student should never let stage fright be his master; regardless of how tense or embarrassed he becomes, he should finish the speech, never giving in to his desire to flee.

The teacher who helps a student to conquer his stage fright will win a lifelong friend and an enthusiastic public-relations representative.

Handle Difficult Problems in Private Conferences

The most serious problems, those that border on serious psychological difficulties, should be dealt with in private conferences, where fear of class ridicule, of public disapproval, and of failure to make a satisfactory grade are less pressing. The informality aids in breaking down reserves and delving into the background of the problems. In some cases an "ice-breaker" may be helpful. One successful teacher keeps a box of chocolates in her desk for this purpose. Perhaps a difficult problem may be discussed over a coke or a cup of coffee. In an informal setting the teacher and student establish greater rapport. The teacher seems more human and the student senses his friendly concern. Under these conditions the student is more likely to open up and talk about his problem freely. Once he starts to discuss his problem and attempts to understand it he has made a step toward improvement; furthermore, he is in a more receptive mood to take suggestions and to attempt to do something about them.

WRITTEN CRITICISM

Most teachers prefer to supplement their oral critiques with some type of written evaluation. Obviously, extended discussion of a given performance is impossible in a large class. Furthermore, the teacher may not wish to discuss certain aspects openly before classmates—for example, a mispronunciation or a slip in grammar.

Many teachers like to keep a record of their day-to-day observations of each student. They are eager to be consistent in what they say and to build each observation on the one before. One successful teacher maintains a manila file on each of his students. Here he keeps a personal data sheet, a copy of each written criticism, and any other pertinent information about the student. He has these materials on hand when he hears a speech or when he holds a conference with the student. The files are also valuable at the time he determines the final grades.

In brief, experienced teachers report the following advantages of written criticism:

1. The teacher has a permanent record.
2. The teacher can hear more speeches because less time is devoted to oral remarks.
3. The student has a record he can study and a way by which he can note his progress.
4. The instructor is likely to be more precise and consistent in his remarks and his evaluation.
5. The written comment is less embarrassing than oral remarks about a speech.

Rating Sheets and Critique Forms

The form that written criticism takes depends on the preference of the instructor. One teacher writes his observations on a 5" by 8" pad. He simply inserts a carbon paper between two sheets; the original goes to the student and he keeps the carbon. Some instructors construct critique forms on which they write their remarks.

PUBLIC SPEAKING CRITIQUE
LSU Baton Rouge

Name _____

Assignment _____

							Poor	Fair	Below average	Average	Above average	Excellent	Superior	
Poor: 6	Above average: 30						
Fair: 12	Excellent: 36						
Below average: 18	Superior: 42						
Average: 24		1 2 3 4 5 6 7					Comments:

Choice of Topic:
appropriate for assignment, speaker,
occasion, audience, time limits

Organization: External and internal:
clear? logical? appropriate?
introduction, conclusion, sign posts,
transitions

Content:
adequacy of support, variety of
support, visual support, use of
detail, sources of support

Language and Style:
concise? clear? appropriate? vivid?
impressive?

Delivery:

Bodily	*Vocal*
eye contact	variety
gestures	loudness
posture	fluency
movement	rate
vitality	pronunciation
facial expression	articulation
use of lectern	vocal pauses
use of aids	

Effectiveness:
Did the speech accomplish its purpose? to inform? other? to persuade?
Was the Speech:
clear? interesting? adapted to the
audience? communicative? enthusiastic?

Total Score _____   Grade _____

The most common practice involves the use of rating blanks or check sheets. To be useful, the rating sheet must provide a clearly defined set of characteristics, understood by both teacher and student; and it must be laid out in a form that is easy to use during the speaking process. When handed to the student, it must be instantly intelligible and sufficiently detailed to tell him wherein he failed or succeeded.

Reproduced on pp. 328 and 330 are rating blanks developed for the public speaking classes at Louisiana State University. On these blanks the rater merely checks the column, from one to seven, that best describes the student's use of the given characteristic. At the close of the speech the teacher sums the items and records the total score. He may provide the student with a set of norms for translating a total raw score into a grade. The norms for the first blank may be on the order of the following:

A: 33 and above   D: 18—22
B: 28—32   F: 17 and below
C: 23—27

If a teacher wishes to emphasize the importance of improvement, he may move his norms up at the middle of the semester to something like the following:

A: 38 and above   D: 23—27
B: 33—37   F: 22 and below
C: 28—32

Obviously, such norms are merely suggestive and subjective. Each teacher should determine his own standards, which he may even vary from class to class. Further, it should be emphasized that the rating sheets like the ones shown here are in no sense exact measuring devices. Actually they give the teacher no more valid or reliable measure than would a simple linear scale for evaluating total effectiveness:

```
     1    2    3    4    5    6    7
   Poor                      Superior
```

The rating sheet used in more advanced classes is found on p. 330. Because it lists eleven characteristics, it permits the instructor to make a more specific and detailed analysis of a speech. The numbers refer to chapters in Giles W. Gray and Waldo W. Braden, *Public Speaking: Principles and Practice*, 2nd ed., New York: Harper & Row, 1963.

The advantage of rating sheets may be summarized as follows:

1. Student and teacher have a common set of understood terms that apply to all assignments.
2. The teacher is forced to render a judgment on all aspects of speaking performance.

RATING SHEET

Name _____

Poor: 11   Above average: 55
Fair: 22   Excellent: 66
Below average: 33 Superior: 77
Average: 44

	Poor	Fair	Below average	Average	Above average	Excellent	Superior	Comments:
	1	2	3	4	5	6	7	

Choice of Subject:
appropriate to speaker, listener,
assignment, time limit (2, 12)

Organization:
clear, simple, orderly, logical (2, 14)

Development of Introduction:
Did it gain an attentive, friendly,
intelligent hearing? (15)

Development of Discussion:
factual and visual support (17 through 22)

Development of Conclusion:
summary, appeal (16)

Bodily Control:
facial expression, eye contact,
gestures, posture, movement (3, 6, 29)

Putting over Ideas:
rapport, communicativeness,
persuasiveness (10, 11)

Language:
clarity, vividness, impressiveness
(25, 26, 27)

Voice and Pronunciation (3, 28)

Attitudes:
toward listeners and speaking
situation—urge to communicate
(1, 3, 4, 5, 7)

Overall Effectiveness (19 thru 22)

Total Score _____

3. The student has a record he may keep for comparison with his own successive performances and with those of other students.
4. The rating sheet reduces the necessity for detailed oral criticism.

Workbooks and Project Notebooks

Many teachers report that their teaching is made more effective by the use of workbooks. These loosely bound paperback booklets, which are often equipped with tear sheets, may contain personal data sheets, outline forms, listening reports, exercise sheets, check sheets, criticism blanks, and rating forms. When he is called on, the student passes his personal copy to the instructor who in turn checks perhaps the speech outline, evaluates the talk on another blank, and returns the book to the student. Thus under one cover the student has a complete record of his speech performance. Following are some of the better known workbooks.

AMRAM, FRED M. AND BENSON, FRANK T., *Creating a Speech: A Student's Workbook*, New York: Scribner's, 1968, p. 199.

CARLILE, CLARK S., *Brief Project Text for Public Speaking*, New York: Harper & Row, 1957, p. 127.

CARLILE, CLARK S., *Project Text for Public Speaking*, rev. ed., New York: Harper & Row, 1962, p. 179.

DICKENS, MILTON AND MCBATH, JAMES H., *Guidebook for Speech Practice*, Harcourt Brace Jovanovich, 1961, p. 163.

EHRENSBERGER, RAY AND PAGEL, ELAINE, *Notebook for Public Speaking*, 2nd ed., Englewood Cliffs, N.J.: Prentice-Hall, 1956, p. 162.

ERICKSON, KEITH V., *Communicative Rhetoric: A Work Book*, Berkeley, Calif.: McCutchan, 1968, p. 80.

HANLEY, THEODORE D. AND THURMAN, WAYNE L., *Student Projects for Developing Vocal Skills*, New York: Holt, Rinehart and Winston, 1962, p. 151.

MILLS, GLEN E. AND BAUER, OTTO F., *Guidebook for Student Speakers*, New York: Ronald Press, 1966, p. 191.

OLIVER, ROBERT T. et al., *Effective Speech Notebook*, Syracuse, N.Y.: Syracuse University Press, rev. ed., 1958.

OLIVER, ROBERT T., ARNOLD, CARROLL C. AND WHITE, EUGENE E., *Speech Preparation Sourcebooks*, Boston: Allyn & Bacon, 1966, p. 106.

QUIMBY, BROOKS, *The Student Speaks and Listens*, Portland, Me.: J. Weston Walch, 1968.

ROBB, MARY MARGARET AND BOWLER, NED W., *Improve Your Speech*, Dubuque, Ia.: William C. Brown, 1965, p. 59.

WISEMAN, GORDON AND BARKER, LARRY, *Worksheets for Speech—Interpersonal Communication*, San Francisco: Chandler, 1967, p. 123.

EXERCISES

1. Prepare evaluation or check sheets to use in evaluating each of the following:
   a. An interpretative reading
   b. An informative speech

   c. A speech of introduction
   d. A persuasive speech
   e. A discussion
   f. A play
2. Write a 500-word defense of the items you include on one of the blanks prepared in exercise 1.
3. Prepare a rating sheet for evaluating oral criticism. Defend your choice of items.
4. Make a collection of rating blanks used in various speaking contests and included in various textbooks. If possible, procure copies of those used in the American Legion Oratorical Contest, the I Speak for Democracy Contest, the speaking contests of the 4-H Clubs, etc. Compare the different items considered in judging.
5. Observe in a high school or college class how a speech teacher gives his oral critiques. Study how he handles several assignments, particularly for different types of speeches. Does he use the same approach on all students? Write a 500-word evaluation of what you observe.
6. Have four or five members of the methods class listen to the same speaker. Within 20 minutes of the close of the speech have each observer record independently what he would tell the speaker. Then listen to all critiques, compare, evaluate, and rank.
7. Discussion questions concerning handling stage fright (speech anxiety).
   a. What are the causes of stage fright?
   b. Is it possible to "cure" stage fright?
   c. During the first assignments of a class, should the teacher ignore stage fright or should he discuss it openly? What are the possible disadvantages of each approach?
   d. When a student manifests signs of excessive anxiety about speaking, what should the teacher do? Excuse the student from completing the performance assignment? Give the student a zero for failing to complete the assignment? Give the student an easier assignment? Express sympathy for the student? Have a private conference with the student? Transfer the student to another section?
8. Investigate attempts at "systematic desensitization" of speech anxiety.

REFERENCES

BASKERVILLE, BARNET, "The Critical Method in Speech," *Central States Speech Journal,* July, 1953, 4:1–5.

BROOKS, WILLIAM D. AND PLATZ, SARAH M., "The Effects of Speech Training upon Self-Concept as a Communicator," *Speech Teacher,* January, 1968, 17:44–49.

CLEVENGER, THEODORE, JR. AND PHIFER, GREGG, "What Do Beginning College Speech Texts Say about Stage Fright?" *Speech Teacher,* January, 1959, 8:1–7.

FURR, H. BEDFORD, "Influences of a Course in Speech Communication or Certain Aspects of the Self-Concept of College Freshman," *Speech Teacher,* January, 1970, 19:26–31.

HARRIS, CHESTER W., "Some Issues in Evaluation," *Speech Teacher,* September, 1963, 12:191–199.

HILDEBRANDT, HERBERT W. AND STEVENS, WALTER W., "Blue Book Criticisms at Michigan," *Speech Teacher,* January, 1960, 9:20–22.

HOLTZMAN, PAUL D., "Speech Criticism and Evaluation as Communication," *Speech Teacher,* January, 1960, 9:1–7.

HUCKLEBERRY, ALAN W. AND STROTHER, EDWARD S., "Saving Time in the Speech Class," *Speech Teacher,* March, 1969, 18:124–128.

MC CROSKEY, JAMES C., *et al.*, "The Effect of Systematic Desensitization of Speech Anxiety," *Speech Teacher*, January, 1970, 19:32–36.

RAGSDALE, J. DONALD (ED.), "Symposium: Evaluation in the Public Speaking Course," *Speech Teacher*, March, 1967, 16:150–164.

ROBINSON, EDWARD R., "What Can the Speech Teacher Do About Students' Stage Fright?" *Speech Teacher*, January, 1959, 8:8–14.

ROBINSON, KARL F. AND KERIKAS, E. J., *Teaching Speech: Method and Materials*, New York: McKay, 1963, chap. 10, "Poise and Emotional Adjustment" and chap. 11, "Diagnoses, Evaluation, Testing and Criticism."

SEIGER, MARVIN L., "The Speech Teacher: Listener and Critic," *Speech Teacher*, November, 1956, 5:259–261.

THONSSEN, LESTER, BAIRD, A. CRAIG, AND BRADEN, WALDO W., *Speech Criticism*, 2nd ed., New York: Ronald Press, 1970. The book is considered the authoritative source in rhetorical criticism. It discusses all aspects of evaluating significant public address.

WIKSELL, WESLEY, "New Methods of Evaluating Instruction and Student Achievement in a Speech Class," *Speech Teacher*, January, 1960, 9:16–19.

16. Innovations

Waldo W. Braden

No one will deny that traditional educational methods have been subjected to considerable questioning and analysis. The persistent cry today is how to handle more students without increasing the staff or the budget. At the same time there is a demand that instruction be individualized. The lecture method and the traditionally arranged classroom have come under repeated criticism. Furthermore present student unrest has necessitated great student involvement and participation. The disadvantaged and the handicapped have presented new challenges to the teacher.

The Committee for Economic Development, an organization of some two hundred educators and businessmen, recently issued a study entitled Innovations in Education: New Directions for the American School (1968). In its description of innovative schools, this report offers a clear view of the "emerging instruction pattern" (pp. 40, 41):

In many advanced schools, the basic instructional unit has been increased from the customary 30 or so students to 90 or even 120 students. The group is housed in a large, open, carpeted area staffed with a team comprised of assistants, interns, and media technicians, who function in subcenters around a learning center containing various instructional resources. The certified teacher-to-pupil ratio is increased to 45 or 50 to one, with staff dollars deployed to employ assistants and to purchase audiovisual and other equipment and materials. Through the more efficient use of lecture and independent study activity, made possible in part by the new instructional techniques, there will be a decreased demand on the teacher's time. This, in turn, makes possible a closer and more personal relationship between teacher and student.

This emerging new pattern of organization for instruction should be developed more rapidly. At the current rate of change it will require decades to transform the classroom teaching system into this more open, adaptive, man-machine system.

We recommend continued and more extensive experimentation in school organization to eliminate the regimentation of students that results from the conventional class units and lock-step method of advancement. We believe that the combination of differentiated staffs, team teaching, and variable student grouping, together with the use of instructional television and other audiovisual media, has much promise for individualizing instruction.

This chapter attempts to explain how some of these new methods have been utilized in speech communication pedagogy. The resourceful teacher may find applications for these suggestions at almost any level of instruction.

PEER GROUP TEACHING

Peer group instruction, that is, having the students teach each other, is as old as education. It is not unusual to have the more proficient help their less fortunate classmates. On almost any college campus many fraternities and sororities sponsor intense peer group instruction programs; unfortunately the goal of these efforts too often may be devoted to how to get around the requirements with the minimum effort or how to recoup after a semester of fun and games. In a bull session, peers share views about teachers, subjects, and the problems of the world in general. This type of instruction is the basis of instruction in many adult groups: toastmaster clubs, garden clubs, creative writing groups, the League of Women Voters, and university women.

The problems of handling increased numbers of students with smaller budgets have forced many educators to consider how to save performance time. In a typical speech class of 20, the instructor must take at least three or more class periods to hear a round of speeches; as a result the speech communication teacher cannot handle as many students per section as the history or sociology departments. Michigan State University, Indiana University, Ohio University and New Mexico State University (Las Cruces)[1] have experimented with having fellow students hear and grade some of the speeches. The method used at Ohio University[2] is as follows:

1. Forty students (two usual classes of 20) became a peer group section under the supervision of one instructor. The section was then divided into two equal parts, each of which was subdivided into four groups of 5.

[1] Gordon R. Owen, "The Beginning Course, Don't Renovate—Innovate," *Speech Teacher*, January, 1970, 19:74–75.
[2] Gordon Wiseman and Larry Barker, "Peer Group Instruction: What Is It?" *Speech Teacher*, September, 1966, 15:220–223.

2. For speaking assignments, the teacher presided over 20 and a student chairman presided over the other 20 in another room.

3. The speaking order, chairmanships, timekeepers, and evaluators were determined well in advance and posted.

4. Five, 8-minute speeches were scheduled for each class period. While the teacher evaluated one panel of 5, in the other classroom the five scheduled speeches were evaluated by appointed student critics.

5. The instructor shifted from group to group on alternate days. For a given assignment he evaluated 20 students; and the other 20 speakers were evaluated by student evaluators.

Larry L. Barker, who has experimented with this method observes:

Peer group instruction appears to function best among teachers who are willing to structure tightly their classroom activities and who view students as individuals capable of responsible action. The peer group teaching method potentially offers the secondary speech teacher the following advantages: (1) development of leadership and responsibility among students; (2) student training and practice in evaluation of communication; (3) aid in helping students adjust to criticism from others; (4) aid in helping students constructively criticize the communication of others.[3]

Peer group instruction may be utilized in many ways. In fact, it may provide a method of giving the more advanced students new insights while at the same time providing less fortunate ones with concentrated tutoring. Many teachers may use such devices as the following:

1. A student may conduct a rehearsal of a speech, debate, discussion, or play before it is presented to the class.
2. A student may assist a fellow student by operating the tape recorder or videotape.
3. Students may direct plays or coach a debate. The seniors may help the novices.
4. The student with a good ear may supervise the articulation drill for a student who wishes to perfect his pronunciation or articulation.
5. Actually, class criticism of a speech or play is in fact a type of peer group instruction.

TEAM TEACHING

In recent years the phrase team teaching has received increased attention. A team, usually made up of two or more teachers, works together in a joint instructional project. In their cooperative undertaking they share duties, plan together, observe each other's teaching, exchange information, give joint examinations, and counsel each other on how to meet student problems.[4]

Under this scheme two or more subjects may be integrated and taught to

[3] Larry L. Barker, "Peer Group Teaching," *Speech Teacher*, September, 1968, 17:260.
[4] Judson T. Shaplin and Henry F. Olds, Jr. (eds.), *Team Teaching*, Harper & Row, 1964, *passim*.

50 or more students. Speech may be teamed with English composition, literature, or social studies. To function efficiently the enlarged class requires a lecture room large enough to accommodate all the students as well as small rooms for conferences and splinter group activities. It is helpful to have a resources material center nearby to supply audiovisual equipment as well as printed materials and to provide material to challenge the student during his released time.

The entire group meets together for orientation, special lectures, films, and demonstrations. Groups are organized in terms of needs or special interests. One teacher may instruct 35 students, while another gives specialized instruction to 15.

Sometimes two subjects are completely integrated. For example literature and oral interpretation work well together: short stories may be dramatized or the student may utilize role playing or sociodrama in the study of a piece of literature.

B. F. Johnston, instructor of speech at Homewood-Flossmoor High School, Floosmoor, Illinois, discusses the combining of the teaching of speech, English and drama.

For example, the objectives of a unit on the novel might very well be achieved through the communicative media of speeches, group discussion, readers theater, and written composition as well as through the usual teacher-lecture and question-answer session. This entails concurrent instruction by the speech expert in the skill of communication, but the subject matter is drawn from the literature. . . .

Integration might include the objectives of a unit on short stories as a basis for the presentation of speeches, group discussions, and written compositions; oral interpretation of poetry, voice improvement, and writing; nonfiction speeches, group discussions, research techniques, logic, reasoning, and writing. . . .

To cite a more specific example of coordinating literature and speech, one might select a unit on drama at the sophomore level, detailing how objectives might be achieved through written and oral experiences. Possible objectives could be concerned with understanding the origin of drama, drama as a visual and oral experience, problems of a play as related to society, structure of a play, types of plays, types of staging, and fundamentals of acting and directing. Methods of achieving the foregoing objectives could include reading a modern play for diagnosis of its dramatic fundamentals; group discussions of its factual, technical, symbolic, and ideational values; readers theater presentations of selected scenes; attendance at a professional or amateur play as a basis for oral and written critiques; group and individual writing of scripts to cast, rehearse, and present; and research papers and informative speeches on aspects of theatre and drama.[5]

Discussion, parliamentary procedure, and debate may become a part of teaching of social problems, economics, sociology, or government. Some

[5] B. F. Johnston, "Team Teaching in Speech, English and Drama," *Illinois Journal of Education*, February, 1967, 58:49–51.

teams operate on the basis that the speech teacher handles the oral skills, while his teammate evaluates the content.

Below are three examples of team teaching. The first involves team teaching of American problems through speech activities at Cleveland High School, Portland, Oregon. Ray Nelson and Ronald G. Hustead report:

In the spring of 1967, the two authors, who teach at Cleveland High School in Portland, Oregon, initiated a new program in the team teaching of American problems through speech activities.

The intent of this program is to make American problems more meaningful by emphasizing communication skills. From this course, both teachers believe that students should be able to develop and understand the concepts of the social studies, develop an appreciation through speech related activities; create and arrive at conclusions relative to the thought processes, develop skills essential to the acquisition of data, and present information effectively in an oral and written manner. The following diagram illustrates the format:

Daily Procedure

1. Informative speech	Sociology	3 weeks
2. Persuasive speech	Propaganda	3 weeks
3. Formal debate	Politics	10 weeks
4. Symposium and closed panels	Economics	10 weeks
5. Parliamentary procedure	International relations	10 weeks

Each of the social studies units is correlated with the speech activities.

Although both teachers have adequate preparation in their own subject matter areas, neither of them is sufficiently prepared in both subjects. Moreover, by team teaching certain advantages exist; e.g., while the speech teacher is working with small groups on communication skills, the social studies teacher is conducting a student oriented discussion relative to the material to be included in the speeches; while the social studies teacher critiques speech content, the speech teacher concentrates on the organization and delivery thus giving a more thorough critique.[6]

The second case involves a project in combined English-speech course at Charleroi (Pennsylvania) High School. Thelma Caruso reports:

English IV-A in our school is scheduled as a modified team-teaching unit involving two English teachers and one speech teacher. The forty-five students of the class may be divided into two sections or three when the speech teacher is involved.

One teacher presents the research paper assignment related to one general subject to the entire class. After writing the theme, the student presents it orally. When the research paper is returned, the student is instructed to familiarize himself with its contents and to review for an oral presentation any notes which he may have. The class is divided into three groups of fifteen each. A teacher is assigned to each group.

[6] Ray Nelson and Ron Hustead, "Team Teaching of American Problems and Speech," *Speech Teacher,* January, 1969, 18:81–82.

The speech teacher sets the pattern for conducting the talk. It is important that an informal, interested atmosphere permeate. Students are seated in a circle, and talk follows the conversational pattern. In addition to his own topic, the student is encouraged to exchange information which he may know relating to any of the other assigned topics. He is encouraged to share visual materials or to use the chalkboard. The teacher remains in the background.[7]

The third case, the teaming of a public speaking teacher and dramatics teacher. The class was conducted at McCluer Senior High School, a 3-year high school of 3000 students at Florissant, Missouri. Martin and Munger report:

In an effort to provide students with comprehensive speech training in a course in fundamentals of speech at McCluer Senior High School, an experiment in team teaching was organized. Two teachers, one of whom had considerable experience in debate and the other with a wide background in interpretive reading and dramatics, combined efforts to provide students with opportunities to observe, compare, and contrast varied demonstrations and to combine for themselves elements of the two examples which appealed especially to them.

The principal . . . scheduled students in two "beginning" classes of speech in a large classroom for the theory sessions. . . .

Through tight scheduling, the class was divided with half of the students in each of two rooms for their practice and critique sessions. At times, the students were grouped according to their abilities or progress, or both.

In setting up the curriculum, approximately 80 class periods were utilized for the combined sessions in which the instructors presented theory, and approximately 105 periods were devoted to presentations by the students and to critiques. In his 33 presentations during the year, each student spoke in different rooms before different instructors, heard different critiques, and adapted to different audience situations.

Instructors collaborated in the writing of test items in an attempt to develop a valid and reliable evaluation instrument, and again on the assigning of quarter and semester grades. . . .

Team teaching permitted each instructor to operate generally in his area of specialization. Thus, he was able to draw from his specialized experience in his presentation.[8]

ROTATIONAL INSTRUCTION

The heart of instruction in speech communication is to train the student to adjust to diverse audience situations. But the normal classroom arrangement in which the student delivers all speeches to the same group is not conducive to preparing the student to meet the demands of several groups.

[7] Thelma Caruso, "Talking the Research Paper," *Speech Teacher*, March, 1968, 17:176–177.
[8] Charles K. Martin and Daniel T. Munger, "Team Teaching in a Course in Fundamentals of Speech," *Speech Teacher*, November, 1965, 14:331–333.

Rotational instruction, although difficult to manage provides a means of adding a dimension to speech instruction. As its name implies, the student rotated to different groups for successive assignments. He may deliver speeches to three or four different groups and receive evaluations from several different critics. Such an arrangement is possible (1) if several sections of the same class meet at the same hour, (2) if the sections keep together on a common syllabus, and (3) if the teachers are teamed or cooperative.

In team teaching with groups of 50 students, rotational instruction would be easier to administer and more effective.

At the University of Illinois an experiment was conducted using five classes and six speaking assignments.[9] The first and the sixth speeches were delivered in the regularly assigned or home room. In rounds two through five, the students moved from class to class in a uniform pattern shown in the accompanying table.

			Round			
Student	I	II	III	IV	V	VI
a	1	2	3	4	5	1
b	1	2	3	5	4	1
c	1	2	4	5	3	1
d	1	2	4	3	5	1
e	1	2	5	4	3	1
f	1	2	5	3	4	1
g	1	3	2	5	4	1
h	1	3	2	4	5	1
i	1	3	4	2	5	1
j	1	3	4	5	2	1
k	1	3	5	2	4	1
l	1	3	5	4	2	1
m	1	4	5	2	3	1
n	1	4	5	3	2	1
o	1	4	3	2	5	1
p	1	4	3	5	2	1
q	1	4	2	3	5	1
r	1	4	2	5	3	1
s	1	5	2	4	3	1
t	1	5	2	3	4	1
u	1	5	3	2	4	1
v	1	5	3	4	2	1
w	1	5	4	2	3	1
x	1	5	4	3	2	1

[9] King Broadrick and Theodore Clevenger, Jr., "Rotational Instruction in the Public Speaking Course," *Speech Teacher*, September, 1965, 14:200–206.

This pattern, probably too complex for most schools, suggests underlying possibilities for planning a rotational pattern.

MODULAR SCHEDULING

In many secondary schools, modular or opening scheduling has been devised to make more effective use of time. In contrast to the traditional schedule with six or seven periods, the modular schedule is divided into segments of 20 minutes called mods. Instead of scheduling a class 5 days per week at some hour for 40 or 50 minutes, the teacher may plan his presentation in one or more mods (20, 40, 60, or 80 minutes). Below is a description of a theater course taught at Evanston (Illinois) Township High School.

A two-semester course entitled Introduction to Theatre met for four mods two days a week. In this particular instance the class meetings was scheduled for Monday and Friday. One can see immediately the advantage of a theatre class meeting for approximately eighty minutes. If the students are working with stage movement, for example, it provides ample time for them to get into rehearsal clothing during the opening moments of the class, to participate in activities, and to change back to street clothes at the close of the period. On the other hand, an eighty minute period requires the teacher to be prepared and to have a variety of activities planned for the students. It requires that the activities be activities, all of which are focused on the teacher emphasis for the day. It requires that the students "show, not tell."

One can also see the problem which can result from a class which meets only on the first day and the last day of the week. Retention by the students of the project in progress or the segment of the unit being covered can become quite difficult. A class which meets for two consecutive days can probably work much more efficiently and be much more conducive to learning. In either case, the idea of preparing learning activities which focus on one major concept for each week can work quite successfully.

At this point, there is still the question of maintaining and motivating interest during the remaining three days of the week when the class does not meet with the instructor. This, of course, is where the mod system introduces that "freedom of movement" and that opportunity for independent study. The opportunities for independent study and research in the theatre class are almost innumerable. Cited below are a few examples which have been found to work well or which are in the process of being prepared for future use:

1. Periodic one-mod conferences with one student or with groups of students who are planning performances or who are creating a play for performance.
2. Assignment of available audio or videotapes dealing with acting techniques or specific periods in the history of theater.
3. Special workshops conducted outside of class time for all interested students in theater classes. (As an illustration, during the past year our dance artist

in residence was asked to teach a dance workshop which was offered to theater students during their unscheduled time.)

4. "Mini-courses," a name given to short term classes offered to interested students of theatre. (To illustrate, a two-week course in stage makeup offered to actors and members of the makeup crew prior to the production of a play.)[10]

The flexible schedule permits the student to have more free time and let him decide how he is going to use it. During a mod the student may confer with a teacher, study at the resource center or library or talk to a friend at the commons. This type of schedule offers interesting possibilities to the teacher of speech communication. He can arrange for a sufficient block of time for many speech activities that do not fit into the traditional schedule. Many extracurricular speech activities, usually pursued in after-school hours, may be fit into free mods.

Modular scheduling and team teaching go hand in hand. Such time can be appropriated to complete projects growing out of integrated subjects such as speech and social problems.

PROGRAMMED INSTRUCTION

At present there is considerable interest in individualizing instruction in order to permit the student to progress at his own rate. In a school using modular scheduling the student has more free time at his disposal. The teacher, of course, hopes that the student on his own volition will go to the resources center for independent study. Programmed instruction provides an excellent way for the student to master a subject without teacher supervision. The essential characteristic of programmed instruction is that a subject is arranged in small sequential *steps*. The student *responds* (pushes a button, or writes in an answer) to the *step* (question: multiple choice or completion). A correct response brings immediately affirmation, and he progresses to the next step. Occasionally the programmer will put in a step repeating information given earlier in order to *reinforce* what has been learned. The student progresses through the program until the body of knowledge is mastered.[11]

The material is presented in three ways: (1) the programmed textbooks; (2) the scramble book; or (3) the teaching machine. Below are three statements which explain each of these methods. L. S. Harms explains the first as follows:

[10] William Waack, "Fexible Modular Scheduling at Evanston, Illinois," *Speech Teacher*, March, 1969, 18:105–108.
[11] Charles J. Torch, "Method of Programming Teaching Machines for Speech," *Speech Teacher*, September, 1962, 11:233–238; L. S. Harms, "Programmed Learning for the Field of Speech," *Speech Teacher*, September, 1961, 10:215–219.

The *Programmed Textbook* outwardly resembles a traditional workbook. The student reads the information, constructs his answer, turns to the following page to check his answer, and then goes on to the next page to the information-question frame. Answers are both required and corrected. This type presentation does not control cheating, but does have the advantage of requiring no laboratory space. It is economical.[12]

Another common method is the so-called scrambled book format. Professor Phillip P. Amato explains this approach:

In the "scrambled" book format each step of the program is presented on a different page. The material (program steps) is scrambled throughout the book to prevent the student from merely reading through the program. Thus, step one may be on page 1, step two on page 12, and so on. The student is given a short discussion of the material to be learned, followed by a multiple choice question designed to test him on the material just discussed. Each alternative leads the student to a different page in the book. . . . If the student selects the correct alternative, he is given additional information and a new problem; if he selects a wrong alternative, he is told why he is wrong and referred back to the problem where he selects another alternative. The shifting of material is contingent upon the student's responses and for this reason the intrinsic or branching method is sometimes referred to as "adaptive programming". . . . The choosing of a wrong alternative leads the student to a remedial level. Thus, the shifting of material difficulty is dictated by the student's response.[13]

Professor Charles J. Torch explains the teaching machine as follows:

As the student uses a teaching machine, he reads an item or paragraph and then is requested to respond to the item in some fashion, perhaps by writing his answer in a blank space provided for him, or by selecting and checking an appropriate answer from a group of alternatives. In either case, he immediately learns the correctness of his response. A main purpose of teaching machines is to guide students individually through a program of statements, questions, problems, or situations of a specific subject matter area in such a way that the method closely resembles that of individual tutoring, where the student is constantly making overt rather than passive responses.[14]

At present the following material has been programmed for ready use of the instructor:

ECROYD, DONALD H., HALFOND, MURRAY H. AND TOWNE, CAROL C., *Voice and Articulation: Programed Instruction*, Glenview, Ill.: Scott Foresman, 1966.
ERWAY, ELLA A., *Listening: A Programmed Approach*, New York: McGraw-Hill, 1970.
GRAY, JOHN W. AND REA, RICHARD G., *Parliamentary Procedure: A Programed Introduction*, Glenview, Ill.: Scott Foresman, 1966.

[12] L. S. Harms, "Programmed Learning for the Field of Speech," *Speech Teacher*, September, 1961, 10:218.
[13] Phillip P. Amato, "Programed Instruction and Speech, Part I: History, Principles, and Theories of P. I.," *Today's Speech*, September, 1965, 13:5.
[14] Torch, *op. cit.*, p. 232.

LEHMAN, WARREN, *Parliamentary Procedure*, New York: Doubleday, 1962.
TOLCH, JOHN, *Programed Phonetics*, Madison, Wisc.: College Printing & Typing Co., 1964.
WIKSELL, WESLEY, *How to Conduct Meetings*, New York: Harper & Row, 1966.

RESOURCE MATERIALS CENTER FOR SPEECH COMMUNICATION

Providing students with more unscheduled time and greater freedom of movement as well as insistence upon individualized instruction has necessitated the development of specialized teaching materials and making them readily available to the students. Of course meeting the problems of exceptional and disadvantaged students requires additional teaching materials. The resource material center becomes a vital part of the educational setting. This type of center is broader in its scope than a speech practice laboratory or a library, for it pulls together a variety of audiovisual machines and specially prepared material. Its usefulness is not limited to any age group or to any particular type of school.

Professor Stafford North of Oklahoma Christian College at Oklahoma City built a basic speech course around the extensive use of recorded materials deposited in the learning center.[15] He prepared 16 taped lectures averaging 40 minutes in length and an accompanying workbook. These tapes were played and discussed by the teachers during the class meeting. They were then deposited in the learning center for the students to listen to as often as they wished. The workbook required the student to fill in definite answers. In addition, each classroom speech was recorded and made available to the student. A part of the assignment was for the student to evaluate his recording and to listen to the teacher's suggestions. Also deposited at the center in recorded form were critiques, illustrations, speeches of famous men, and drill materials. The student could dial for this material from a carrel in the library and listen as long as he wished.

Phoebe L. Dickson, an elementary school teacher in Denver, Colorado, created in one corner of her busy classroom what she called a Speaking-Listening Center.[16] Walled off by a screen, the Center was equipped with a simple tape recorder, eight earphones, eight chairs, and a small table. Under a plan of self-direction her young students in groups of eight used the equipment. They could listen to stories, fables, lessons from the *Weekly Reader*, worksheets for the phonics lessons and, of course, whatever they produced. They recorded speeches, told stories, conducted interviews, and stimulated broadcasts. Interest was no problem in that corner.

[15] Stafford North, "Increasing Teaching Resources Through Tapes!" *Speech Teacher*, September, 1967, 16:212–214.
[16] Phoebe L. Dickson, "Using the Tape Recorder in the Elementary School," *Speech Teacher*, September, 1967, 16:221–224.

These two cases suggest the flexibility of a resources center. The magic of seeing and hearing themselves hooked many otherwise uninterested learners.

Throughout this book are numerous suggestions about teaching materials available for the resources center. The chapters on radio-television and audiovisual materials should stir up many ideas about individualizing instruction. But in case anyone has difficulty thinking about how to set up a center, below are 25 further suggestions:

1. Workbooks and answer sheets
2. Self-administered tests
3. File of old examination questions
4. Programed lessons and necessary equipment
5. Material to teach listening: records, drills, tests, etc.
6. Voice and articulation drill material
7. Models of vocal and breathing mechanism
8. Recordings of famous speeches
9. Readings of famous plays and literature
10. Recorded speeches and readings of former students
11. Recorded interviews with important visitors or former successful students
12. Taped lectures of material for persons missing class
13. Videotapes of students and stage productions
14. Pictures of famous speakers, actors, stage settings, etc.
15. Drill cards and language master
16. Hard-to-find-books or magazines containing pertinent illustrative material (*National Geographic* or *Life*).
17. Slides and film strips of speakers, former theater productions, costumes, or legislative assemblies
18. Supply of empty tapes for recording material for class
19. Scrapbooks prepared by students on speech activities or upon common materials
20. Collection of pamphlets, government documents, on common materials theme
21. Ditto and photo duplicating equipment and supplies
22. Materials for model making (for stage sets, etc.)
23. Large scratch pads, colored chalk, and chart racks
24. Back file of *Vital Speeches of the Day*
25. One or more daily newspapers and news magazines

EXERCISES

1. Plan a team unit using one of the following combinations: drama-debate, speech and English composition, speech and economics, speech and history.
2. Investigate and report on a project of peer group teaching in your school or community. Consider public speaking classes, garden clubs, YMCA or YWCA classes, or investment clubs.
3. Plan a scheme of rotational teaching of public speaking involving three sections of the same course.
4. Investigate modular scheduling in a neighboring elementary or secondary school in

the area. If possible, visit the school, interview the students and teachers, and report your findings to your class.

5. Program a unit of a public speaking or drama class. Limit yourself to subjects like the following: organization, speech criticism, straight thinking, stage movement, or stage lighting.

6. Lay out a plan of a speech resource material center for a high school. Suggest how each item is to be used, and suggest specific free time assignments.

REFERENCES

AMATO, PHILIP R., "Programed Instruction: Its Potential Utility in Speech," *Speech Teacher*, September, 1964, 13:190–196.

BARKER, ELDON E., "An Investigation of the Scrambled-Book System of Programing Oral Assignment in the Beginning Speech Course," *Speech Monograph*, June, 1967, 34:160–166.

BRADEN, WALDO W., "Potpourri," *Speech Teacher*, January, 1969, 18:80–85.

CLEVENGER, THEODORE, JR., "A Rhetorical Jigsaw Puzzle: A Device for Teaching Certain Aspects of Speech Composition," *Speech Teacher*, March, 1963, 12:141–146.

CLEVENGER, THEODORE, JR., "Some Factors Involved in Classroom Procedures for the Acquisition of Verbal Concepts," *Speech Teacher*, March, 1966, 15:113–118.

GORDEN, WILLIAM I., "Academic Games in the Speech Curriculum," *Central States Speech Journal*, Winter, 1968, 20:269–279.

HARMS, L. S., "Two-Person Learning Programs for Speech," *Speech Teacher*, March, 1966, 15:119–125.

KANE, PETER E., "Role Playing for Educational Use," *Speech Teacher*, November, 1964, 13:320–323 (annotated bibliography).

KING, THOMAS R., "A Multi-Media Approach to the Beginning Speech Course," *Western Speech*, Summer, 1970, 34:225–230.

KING, THOMAS R., "Programmed Textbooks in Communication," *Journal of Communication*, March, 1967, 17:55–62.

LEONARDO, MANUEL AND TIFFANY, WILLIAM R., "A Study of Six Machine Programs in Oral Reading Improvement," *Speech Monographs*, June, 1965, 32:192–197.

NEWSOM, LIONEL AND GORDEN, WILLIAM I., "An Exchange of Taped Discussion Between Students of Negro and White Colleges," *Speech Teacher*, November, 1962, 11:317–321.

POTTER, LOIS SHEFTE, "A Plan for Individualized Speech Activities in the Elementary School," *Speech Teacher*, September, 1966, 15:200–206.

REA, RICHARD G. AND GRAY, JOHN W., "Teaching Parliamentary Procedure Through Programed Instruction," *Speech Teacher*, January, 1964, 13:21–24.

RUCKER, JUANITA, et al, "Innovations for the High School Teacher of Speech," *Speech Teacher*, September, 1968, 17:258–267.

SKINNER, B. F., "The Source of Learning and the Art of Teaching," *Harvard Educational Review*, Spring, 1954, 24:86–97.

TUCKER, RAYMOND K., "Computer Simulations and Simulation Games: Their Place in the Speech Curriculum," *Speech Teacher*, March, 1968, 17:128–133.

WISEMAN, GORDON AND BARKER, LARRY, "An Appraisal of Peer Group Instruction," *Central States Speech Journal*, May, 1966, 17:125–130.

WISEMAN, GORDON AND BARKER, LARRY, "A Study of Peer Group Evaluation," *Southern Speech Journal*, Winter, 1965, 31:132–138.

17. Understanding Students with Speech and Hearing Disorders

C. Cordelia Brong and Stuart I. Gilmore

IDENTIFYING SPEECH AND HEARING DISORDERS

If all the students in a public school or college population could be lined up according to their speaking ability, an effectiveness continuum would result. At one extreme would be found category one, the superior speakers. Not only are they richly endowed with native talent; they have also the necessary motivation for translating that talent into brilliant performance. They represent a very small segment of the continuum.

Then there is category two, a long line encompassing the largest portion of the total population—the "normal" speakers. These are the students who in some schools receive no speech instruction. In more progressive schools, where the philosophy of education includes a recognition of the importance of effective communication in a democratic society, numerous curricular offerings are made available for the purpose of raising to the highest possible level the oral efficiency of this group. Some schools provide courses in *speech improvement*.[1] Usually this educational program is concerned with "normal" speakers or with those who have mild speech deviations, and is handled as a whole-class activity.

[1] The speech improvement program, described in "Speech Improvement," *Journal of Speech and Hearing Disorders*, Monograph Supplement No. 8, 1961, involves classroom experiences designed ". . . to permit all children to develop the best speech, voice, and language patterns of which they are capable, correct minor speech and voice difficulties, and express their ideas clearly and effectively" (p. 84). "Speech improvement programs utilize seven speaking activities: auditory training drills, voice and articulation practice, discussion and conversations, dramatic presentations, oral reading, parliamentary procedure, and talks and reports to accomplish these goals" (pp. 84, 85).

The major portion of this book is applicable to the members of categories one and two, the students for whom teachers of speech are primarily responsible. But there is a third category.

At the far end of the continuum are those whose expressive and (or) receptive abilities are reduced in such a way as to set them apart as members of a separate unit requiring a special kind of attention. They have *speech disorders*, and the rehabilitation program for them is referred to as *speech correction*. Since many persons with hearing handicaps have accompanying speech disorders, they are often included in this group; and the educational program is then known as *speech and hearing therapy*.[2] It is with the population of category three that this chapter and Chapter 18 are concerned.

One may ask, "How can a line be drawn between categories two and three?" Certainly there are poor "normal" speakers who could be judged on a par with the mildly affected ones in the defective aggregation. The question is a valid one. Certainly there is no rigid ruling that governs the separation of the two populations. The dividing line is quite unstable and fluctuates somewhat according to such influences as the competency demands of the social group and the vocational aspirations of the individual. For example, the line would tend to move a notch in one direction on a college campus and in the opposite direction in a city's slum district; it would be slightly different for the student whose goal is to become a lawyer and for an agriculture student who plans to work on a farm. Yet, since it is a recognized fact that most speech and hearing defectives require individualized instruction, it is important that this line of demarcation be described. Hence, the question: Under what conditions would a person be classified as having a speech defect rather than as a "normal speaker"?

What Is a Speech Defect?

A widely recognized definition is the one offered by Charles Van Riper: "Speech is defective when it deviates so far from the speech of other people that it calls attention to itself, interferes with communication or causes its possessor to be maladjusted."[3] Let us examine the three facets of this measuring stick: conspicuousness, unintelligibility, and unpleasantness.

[2] The terms most commonly used to denote speech and hearing rehabilitation programs are *speech correction* and *speech and (or) hearing therapy*. The specialists dealing directly with speech and hearing disorders are variously referred to as *speech and (or) hearing therapists, speech correctionists, clinicians*, or *pathologists*—depending on level of training and professional environment. The *audiologist* is the individual who specializes in the assessment and rehabilitation of auditory disorders. The American Speech and Hearing Association, 9030 Old Georgetown Road, Washington, D.C. 20014, has published a brochure, *Speech Pathology and Audiology: Career Information*, which describes the training and activities of seven representative professionals.
[3] Charles Van Riper, *Speech Correction: Principles and Methods*, 4th ed., Englewood Cliffs, N.J.: Prentice-Hall, 1963, p. 16.

It calls attention to itself. James, a severe stutterer, is talking to a fellow student on campus. His speech rhythm is so atypical and his facial grimaces so hideous that the listener becomes amused and walks away. This is a dramatic example. Now consider a more common one. Jane, a lisper, is trying out for the debate squad. She is rejected because the unsightly popping out of her tongue on every s sound attracts the listeners' attention to a flaw in the mechanics of speaking and away from what she is saying.

It interferes with communication. Communication is the *sine qua non* of all speaking. There are few incidences in our social milieu in which persons talk only to hear themselves chatter. Communication is a two-way circuit; it includes not only the presentation of ideas to a listener; it expects also some kind of response in return. According to the second part of the definition under discussion, anything that cuts this circuit may be considered a speech defect. Mary, a cerebral palsy victim, is trying to persuade several of her classmates to attend a community concert. However, because of her many consonant and vowel distortions she is quite unintelligible. She is talking but the symbols she uses reach her listeners as meaningless jargon. There can be no appropriate response since the message is lost somewhere between the sender and the receiver. Or to cite a more common example: George, a comparatively mild articulatory defective, may find himself misunderstood because of an inability to produce two consonants, [l] and [r]. His attempt at communication could sound something like this: "Meet me at the Ayen Hoteu at Wedyand and Eyeventh Stweets. Bing Awy with you." (Meet me at the Allen Hotel at Redland and Eleventh Streets. Bring Larry with you.)

It causes its possessor to be maladjusted. According to the third criterion indicated in the definition, speech may be considered defective if it is a cause of an emotional problem. John is a tall, well-built, handsome young man of high school age. But his voice is high-pitched and sounds like a girl's. Given a sensitive nature and the expected social penalties, the effect of such a problem on his personality can be incalculable.

Relationship to Other Disabilities

It is important not to confuse speech defects with other disabilities.[4] To begin with, the term is not synonymous with poor grammar, or incorrect pronunciation: A student who declares "I ain't got no money" or who says "git" for get is not said to have a speech defect. If he has difficulty in reading from the printed page he does not necessarily fall into this category, though in most instances an individual who has phonetic irregularities in spontaneous speech uses the same errors in reading aloud. Additionally, a reading problem sometimes stems from a cause, such as brain

4 See Wendell Johnson, Spencer Brown, James Curtis, Clarence Edney, and Jacqueline Keaster, *Speech Handicapped School Children*, 3rd ed., New York: Harper & Row, 1967, pp. 11–13.

injury, common to both reading and speech inadequacy. But reading retardation *per se* is a separate entity requiring a different kind of remedial program by another professional discipline.

The "problem child" who is constantly upsetting the status quo of classroom routine is not, because of his personality quirks, a case for the speech and hearing clinic. To be sure, he may also have a communication problem, and if so may be in serious need of a rehabilitation program. Too, the emotional fraction of his problem may be the cause of his speech and hearing difficulties. But behavior irregularities alone will not qualify him for inclusion. Rather he may need the assistance of a psychiatrist.

Visual inadequacy is not usually an intrinsic aspect of a speech disorder. The close functional interdependency between speech and hearing does not exist in the speech-vision relationship. Here again, however, a visual-motor deficiency and a speech handicap may result from a common cause—as brain injury. In this event the visual problem becomes a very real concern of the speech clinician.

Lastly, the individual with a speech disorder is not necessarily a mentally deficient person, though an individual with limited intelligence is quite likely to have a speech problem. Clinical evidence indicates that a mentally retarded population usually has a higher incidence of speech defectives than a normal one. However, speech impairments cover the total range of intellectual functioning. Children with superior intellectual potential often have speech inadequacies that require therapy.

It should be noted that any or all of these other human deficits, though not the major essence of speech defectiveness, can exist side by side in a speech-handicapped individual either with or without a cause-effect relationship.

SPECIAL NEEDS OF THOSE WITH SPEECH AND HEARING DEFECTS

Thus far the problem of individuals having speech disorders has been described essentially in terms of the effect of his output on the listener's ears. Usually his deviation is more glaring than those of "normal' speakers. But this feature alone would not set apart category three for special consideration. This group represents also the more serious disorders in terms of dynamics, causation, and necessary treatment.

The Speech Impaired

If an aspiring debater with otherwise normal speech uses "ketch" for *catch*, it is not because he cannot produce the correct vowel. He uses the short "a" [æ] in other words appropriately. He employs the error vowel in that particular word because it is a part of his language form learned from his associates. If the discrepancy is brought to his attention, and he has sufficient motivation to correct it, he should learn to say *catch* with the accepted pronunciation. Let us turn to another student who talks about his "thithter thailing on the theven theath." Analysis of his articulatory pattern may reveal that he has no [s] in his phonemic repertoire. For some reason he has never learned to produce it. Here just a reminder is insufficient. He must create entirely new neuromuscular patterns of tongue movement, blend them with the movements used for innumerable other sounds, and finally incorporate them into conversation before the [s] can be said to be a newly acquired speech sound. Often if the [s] is defective the other sibilant sounds are also atypical. Each must be learned in the same painstaking manner. If additional consonants are involved, the problem becomes correspondingly more complex.

It may be that the sounds just mentioned have never been learned because of unfavorable environmental conditions during the speech-development period in early childhood. Hence, the origin of the difficulty is now completely in the past and the therapy program consists essentially of establishing new habits. On the other hand, causative factors may still be operating. There may be paralysis of the musculature of the tongue or an opening in the hard or soft palate. There may be a brain injury, a hearing loss, or an emotional disturbance that interferes with the learning process. As the problem becomes more and more involved, the diagnosis increases in complexity and the therapeutic procedures grow more demanding. Often a team of specialists representing several professions (as medicine, dentistry, psychology, and psychiatry as well as speech pathology) is required to isolate the cause and to plan a remedial program.

As the responsibility for helping these individuals increases, the training for carrying such responsibility grows also in both broadening and deepening dimensions. Generally speaking, the functional articulatory case can be handled by a worker with minimal training. As the emotional and organic factors increase, so must the therapist's training become more and more highly specialized to enable him to handle these complexities with competence. A rich background in psychology, physiology, anatomy, neurology, and speech pathology is needed in order that the therapist may deal adequately with the complicated cases.

The Hearing Impaired

Thus far attention has been paid entirely to the speech defective. How does the person with a hearing loss find a place in this discussion? Because of the close dependency of the acquisition of speech on the individual's ability to hear the spoken word, a person with diminished auditory acuity may have a speech disorder. Depending on the amount and type of hearing loss, his speech defect may range all the way from a slight articulatory irregularity to a speech pattern of jargon or grunts. He also is subject to the environmental penalties and consequent emotional upsets experienced by speech-handicapped persons. Certainly he needs individual attention. In addition to the importance of giving the hearing-defective individual specialized therapy, there is also a need to find small hearing problems before they become big ones. Hearing testing of large populations thus becomes highly important. The speech and hearing specialist's training, then, in addition to those areas mentioned earlier, should include a study of audiology, acoustics, and hearing pathology.

Prevalence of Communicative Disorders

Five percent of the public school population (ages 5 through 18) in the United States are estimated to have significant speech disorders. In the same age group, 40,000 have hearing defects so severe that everyday sounds are of little, if any, practical use to them (that is, deaf or deafened) and approximately 360,000 have partial losses (hard of hearing).[5]

MAJOR TYPES OF SPEECH AND HEARING DISORDERS

A discussion of "types" always carries with it an element of risk. It is done here to provide a brief overview of the varieties of speech and hearing problems a teacher of speech may encounter, and to offer suggestions for recognizing and understanding the various abnormalities. It should be remembered, however, that every person having a speech or hearing disorder is really a special and unique individual, with his own peculiar constellation of symptoms and causes. To provide here a survey that would include all the possible aspects of speech irregularity is neither feasible nor desirable.[6] Only the major categories commonly found in high school or

[5] The incidence and significance of the various communicative disorders is presented in National Advisory Neurological Disease and Stroke Council, Subcommittee on Human Communication and Its Disorders, *Human Communication and Its Disorders—An Overview*, National Institute of Neurological Diseases and Stroke, U.S. Department of Health, Education and Welfare, 1969, pp. 18, 19. The prevalence of communicative disorders in the public schools is given in American Speech and Hearing Association Committee on Midcentury Whitehouse Conference, "Speech Disorders and Speech Correction," *Journal of Speech and Hearing Disorders*, June, 1952, 17:129–130.
[6] Since this volume directs itself to those intending to teach speech in the high school or college, communicative disorders found in preschoolers and older adults, the majority of which are of a complex organic nature, are not discussed. Further information on these disorders can be obtained from Lee Travis (ed.), *Handbook of Speech Pathology and Audiology*, New York: Appleton-Century-Crofts, 1971. Robert West and Merle Ansberry, *The Rehabilitation of Speech*, 4th ed., New York: Harper & Row, 1968; and books dealing with specific disorders, e.g. McKenzie Buck, *Dysphasia: Professional Guidance for Family and Patient*, Englewood Cliffs, N.J.: Prentice-Hall, 1968 (Foundations of Speech Pathology Series).

college populations are included. They will be discussed from the points of view of (1) description, (2) cause, and (3) rehabilitation.

Articulatory Disorders

Description.   An articulatory disorder is a phonemic[7] deficiency; that is, it represents a deviation in the production of the distinctive sounds of our language. It usually takes the form of omission, substitution, and (or) distortion of speech sounds. Some authorities include also insertion or addition. If a student in a snack bar who wants a cup of coffee asks for a "up of offee" [ʌp əv ɔfɪ] he is omitting the [k]. If, however, he requests a "chup of choffee" [tʃʌp əv tʃɔfɪ], he is substituting one consonant for another. Or he may distort the [k] sound. Instead of substituting a standard consonant for the [k] which he is unable to produce, he uses a sound not found in the English language. He may, for example, produce the [k] as a fricative instead of a plosive, thus altering its acoustic characteristics. If he should ask for a "clup of cloffee" [klʌp əv klɔfɪ] he would be adding a sound.

It should be pointed out that such error types are not mutually exclusive. In using a substitution, the individual usually does not employ a "perfect" English sound, but rather one that is sufficiently within its phonemic limits to be roughly recognizable. Thus the substitution error may resemble one of distortion. Even omissions are frequently not represented by a complete absence of sound. They are often filled by slight glottal noises or tongue clicks that defy description, thus again approaching the distortion error. However, for most practical purposes these four phonemic irregularities can be regarded as grossly representative attributes of an articulatory disorder. The omission, substitution, and addition varieties lend themselves well to designation through the use of phonetic symbols. Distortion errors must be recorded by means of verbal description. Nor do these types tend to categorize articulatory defectives. Frequently a person who has a minor deviation may employ only one of the forms described. The more severe cases frequently use all of them. They are found in articulatory problems of all etiologies, both functional and organic.

The question may be asked as to the consistency of these errors in the individual's overall vocabulary. If a person substitutes [θ] for [s] in *sister*, for instance, will he use that same substitution in all words containing [s], or may he sometimes substitute *sh* [ʃ], sometimes use a distortion, sometimes omit the [s] entirely, and sometimes produce it correctly? Clinical experience and research reveal varying degrees of consistency—and variabil-

---

[7] For a discussion of the phoneme see Claude Merton Wise, *Applied Phonetics*, Englewood Cliffs, N.J.: Prentice-Hall, 1957, pp. 74–78; and James Carrell and William R. Tiffany, *Phonetics: Theory and Application to Speech Improvement*, New York: McGraw-Hill, 1960, pp. 18–20.

ity—in this respect. Often a sound is produced adequately in certain positions in words and in certain phonemic environments and not in others. The same individual may use a variety of substitutions or distortions for one error sound. In spite of these exceptions, articulatory deviations usually follow a fairly orderly pattern of sound deviation that can be determined, recorded, and used as a basis for therapy. If several consonants of high incidence in the spoken language are defective, or if many sounds are lacking, the individual may be completely unintelligible. According to Van Riper and Irwin, "variable errors are favorable signs; they indicate that the error has not been overlearned or stabilized, that the process of phonemic learning is still in flux." The consistency of error, then, is a way in which the severity of the problem can be estimated.[8]

The severity of an articulatory problem is also influenced by the age of the individual. It is normal for a 6-year-old to have difficulty with [r], [l], or [ð]. However, a student of junior high school age or older who is found to have such speech is in need of specialized help.

Causes.   In respect to cause, speech disorders are often said to be either *functional* or *organic*. If no obvious physical impairment is responsible for the deviation, the defect is assumed to result from improper "functioning" of the speech organs.[9] The cause of a functional articulatory defect, then, lies in some interference in the process of learning the phonemes of the language.

Organic deviations present a more complex situation. If the teeth meet in malocclusion, presenting an overbite, underbite, or open or uneven bite, or if the hard or soft palate is structurally abnormal, the articulated airstream may be misdirected, thus changing the characteristics of certain sounds. If the tongue, lips, and (or) velum are wholly or partially paralyzed, or if they are affected by other neural damage (such as in cerebral palsy), the articulators cannot properly perform their function to create the necessary speech sounds. If the individual has a significant hearing loss, he may lack certain phonetic elements because he has never heard them. Thus obstacles are added to the fundamental problem of learning new speech sounds.

By far the largest number of articulatory problems are thought to be functional in nature. It might appear at first glance that the nonspecialist could offer corrective treatment for most articulatory problems. Two cautions should be given with emphasis. First, a functional deviation is not necessarily an "easy" problem that can be managed in an incidental manner. Even one that is considered "minor" may be the result of intricate

[8] Charles Van Riper and John V. Irvin, *Voice and Articulation*, Englewood Cliffs, N.J.: Prentice-Hall, 1958, p. 19.
[9] See Margaret Hall Powers' discussion of the terms *functional and organic* in her chapter, "Functional Disorders of Articulation—Symptomatology and Etiology," in Lee Edward Travis (ed.), *Handbook of Speech Pathology and Audiology*, New York: Appleton-Century-Crofts, 1971, pp. 837–875.

causes and require special rehabilitative techniques. Inappropriate handling by the classroom teacher can lead to frustration and consequent emotional disturbance on the part of the student. Second, many defects that seem to be completely functional may in reality be organic in origin. Too often cases are classified as functional when no clear-cut etiology has been found. If closer scrutiny were made, a causally linked physical anomaly might be discovered. Even where none is detected by the most sensitive instruments used by medical scientists, there still remains the possibility of a subclinical deficiency of the nervous system that can set up substantial resistance to therapy. Then, too, among those cases whose problems seem to lie completely in the area of faulty learning, hidden clues to rehabilitation are frequently determined when appropriate diagnosis is available. For example, certain research suggests the possibility that flaws in the special auditory perceptive abilities may retard the acquisition of a normal phonemic vocabulary. Perhaps the individual is significantly lacking in the faculty of phonetic discrimination, auditory memory span, or the perception of sound sequences. Moreover, a "functional" disorder can also be a symptom of a deep-seated emotional problem. In such instances the case may not be one for the classroom teacher or the speech correctionist, but may need the services of a psychiatrist or psychologist.

Articulatory disorders are not simple problems. As indicated by Carrell, most have multiple causes. It is preferable to think in terms of neurological, structural, and functional *factors* causing defective articulation, and to classify a given speaker's defect on the basis of what seems to be the predominating cause.[10]

Rehabilitation. Much of the therapy in elementary grades takes the form of assisting the developmental process. In these early years children lose many of their error sounds entirely through the normal course of maturation. A marked decrease in the number of articulatory defects may be observed from first through fourth grades. After that time, however, little change can be expected without specialized assistance.[11] The articulatory deviations of adults may require more skillful methods of eradication, either because their duration has ingrained undesirable habits more deeply or because adventitious defects are usually the result of complex organic causes. Additionally, adults may develop personality problems stemming from embarrassment related to their failure to acquire adequate speech or to its loss following illness, injury, or aging processes.

The majority of adult articulatory disorders require rehabilitation by specialists. Under certain circumstances, however, the informed speech

[10] James A. Carrell, *Disorders of Articulation*, Englewood Cliffs, N.J.: Prentice-Hall, 1968, p. 12.
[11] For further information refer to an interesting study showing the decrease in articulatory problems through the first four grades: Vivian Row and Robert Milisen, "The Effect of Maturation upon Defective Articulation in Elementary Grades," *Journal of Speech and Hearing Disorders*, September, 1949, 14:202–207.

teacher may offer assistance. These conditions and appropriate procedures are discussed in the next chapter.

Voice Disorders

Description. A voice may be considered defective (1) if it calls attention to itself, interferes with communication, or causes its possessor to be maladjusted;[12] (2) if the vocal product is inappropriate to the age or sex of the individual; (3) if the acoustic peculiarity is a result of a pathology of the vocal structures or of a severe hearing loss; and (or) (4) if the atypical pitch, loudness, or quality is instrumental in causing a vocal pathology.

Certainly Van Riper's yardstick can be used in determining the defectiveness of voice as well as that of speech defects in general. In addition, there are other criteria that may help the teacher to decide whether a specific case requires specialized assistance. If a boy's speaking voice is abnormally high, if a girl's voice sounds like a man's, or if a woman is using a child's pitch and intonation, the case may need individual attention. If the voice is hoarse, breathy, or aphonic, the possibility of active vocal pathology should be investigated. Bizarre melodic patterns and an unusual quality may indicate a serious hearing impairment. Also, if extremes in pitch or loudness are such as to run the risk of damaging the vocal structures, the voice is considered defective.

Causes. Let us examine the three major symptoms of voice disorders and indicate some of the causal factors of each.

1. Deviations in pitch. If an adult's voice is either too high or too low in pitch, the possibility of emotional difficulties should be explored. Also, a too-high pitch can be found among high school boys whose voices are going through the normal process of change. The boy who at 16 or older has a juvenile voice may have underdeveloped laryngeal structures or glandular deficiencies. Or his problem may be completely functional; he may be having unusual difficulty in gaining the necessary control of his changing voice. In either event he may need professional help.[13] Then, too, either extreme in pitch is to be regarded as a potential cause of damage to the vocal folds, thus placing both groups in the category of problems that may require specialized attention.

2. Deviations in loudness. If a voice is too weak to be heard easily, the possibility of an emotional disorder, general systemic frailty, or laryngeal pathology should be suspected. If the voice is too soft or too loud, a hearing loss could be the fundamental condition. A too-loud voice may also point to a personality problem. A complete loss of voice may require the attention of a speech pathologist and a psychiatrist.

3. Deviations in quality. Unpleasantness in quality has been described

[12] Van Riper, *op. cit.*, p. 16.
[13] For further information see Van Riper, *op. cit.*, pp. 159–167.

by a multitude of adjectives. Fairbanks,[14] however, has provided four classifications that include the major quality deficiencies. They are nasality, breathiness, harshness, and hoarseness.

The first of these, nasality, is a resonance phenomenon and results mainly from a failure to separate the oral from the nasal chambers in the production of nonnasal sounds. When the velum remains patent, or is too short, or when a hole exists in the hard or soft palate, too much nasal resonance is supplied on nonnasal sounds, especially the vowels. Denasality, according to some authorities, is an articulatory disorder rather than one of phonation, since it is a defect of the [m], [n], and [ŋ]. Here organic cause should be investigated, since the trouble frequently lies in a stoppage in the nasopharyngeal passage.

The other three quality irregularities—harshness, breathiness, and hoarseness, result from some fault in the use of the laryngeal structures or defect in these structures themselves. A *harsh* voice has a noisy, rasping sound that usually reflects excessive tension. It may or may not result from laryngeal pathology. Some authorities use the term *strident* in describing high harshness and *gutteral* or *throaty* when referring to low harshness. A *breathy* voice has an aspirate quality resulting from the failure of the vocal folds to approximate appropriately for phonation. The cause of this failure is often traced to laryngeal pathology. Psychological factors are also important considerations. The quality deficiency that should always wave the red flag of suspicion is hoarseness. Not only is this rough, husky tone frequently the consequence of laryngeal disease; it is often the first symptom of laryngeal cancer.

Hoarseness can result from tumors of the larynx, both benign and malignant, from paralysis of one or both of the vocal folds, or from misuse of the voice which in turn may cause certain pathologies. Jackson and Jackson list and describe more than 50 medical conditions associated with this quality. They emphasize the importance of prompt investigation "because it is frequently an early symptom of serious disease in the larynx or elsewhere."[15] Certainly functional hoarseness does exist. However, one should always treat a hoarse voice as one with organic origin until it is proved not to be. For this reason one should refuse to carry on a speech improvement or rehabilitative program with a student who has a hoarse voice without the approval of a laryngologist. Additionally, hoarseness may reflect a psychogenic problem requiring psychological and (or) psychiatric assistance.

Rehabilitation. In most instances nonstructural conditions that are entirely of the "bad habit" variety can be handled by the teacher of speech

[14] Grant Fairbanks, *Voice and Articulation Drillbook*, 2nd ed., New York: Harper & Row, 1960, p. 170.
[15] Chevalier Jackson and Chevalier L. Jackson, *Diseases of the Nose, Throat and Ear*, 2nd ed., Philadelphia: Saunders, 1959, p. 576.

who understands voice production. Any voice abnormality with organic or emotional origin belongs in the speech therapist's load. In dealing with harshness, breathiness, and hoarseness in speech classes, the teacher should see that each problem is professionally diagnosed to rule out pathologies before planning vocal educational programs.

Cleft Palate Speech

Description. Cleft palate speech is a defective pattern of utterance that results usually from a hole in the roof of the mouth, which frequently is accompanied by a break in the upper lip. These anomalies are commonly known as cleft palate and cleft lip.[16]

Cleft palate speech cuts across the areas of articulatory and phonatory deviation. Because the palatal opening diminishes the pressure-building potentiality in the oral cavity and tends to direct the airstream through the nose, any or all of the individual's plosives and fricatives may be defective. The articulatory aspects of cleft palate speech may include a substitution of nasal equivalents or near-equivalents for plosives and fricatives. For example, a person with such speech may say "man" [mæn] for *bat* or "nee" [ni] for *see*. He may also use glottal stops, back-throat fricatives, or nasal snorts as substitutions for or in addition to any of the consonant sounds. Added to these are articulatory inaccuracies that may include any or all of the error types that have been discussed under that subject. The voice quality may be nasal, with a possible overlay of breathiness, hoarseness, or harshness. In severe cases the speech is unintelligible.

Causes. That a cleft usually results from a failure of maxillary parts to unite during embryonic development has been established; the reason for this failure, however, is still nebulous. Some of the theories that receive consideration are heredity, malnutrition of the mother during the first trimester of pregnancy, maternal metabolic disorders, accidents, illness, and parental age. Though most cleft palates are congenital, a palatal cleft may result from an accident or surgery involving the palate. Also, "cleft palate speech" may be the product of a too-short or a paralyzed velum.

Rehabilitation. Today a cleft palate should not be considered a handicap, but it is always a case for a specialist. Physical restoration is usually accomplished before formal speech therapy is started. This can be done by means of surgery or by prosthodontia[17] or by a combination of both methods. When such a program is started early and carried through to

[16] A relatively short but comprehensive coverage of cleft palate, its associated disorders, and treatment is provided in Harold Westlake and David Rutherford, *Cleft Palate*, Englewood Cliffs, N.J.: Prentice-Hall, 1966.
[17] Fitting of a dental prosthesis, sometimes called an *obturator*, to cover the cleft and aid in the production of speech. For a discussion of both surgical and prosthetic management, see Westlake & Rutherford, *op. cit.*, pp. 75–81.

completion, the outlook for acceptable speech is excellent, especially since chances are about the same as in the normal population that the cleft palate person has average intellectual potential. The adult faces a more difficult situation. Nevertheless, with a satisfactory structural closure followed by speech therapy, vast improvement is possible.

Stuttering

Description. Stuttering may be described as a disturbance in the rhythm of speech characterized by "repetitions of parts of words and whole words, prolongations of sounds, interjections of sounds or words, and unduly prolonged pauses."[18] A definition of stuttering based solely on disfluency is inadequate, however. In the first place, comparison of the speech of stutterers and nonstutterers reveals considerable overlap in both the frequency and the distribution of disfluencies, as well as considerable inconsistency in the speech of stutterers.[19] Secondly, attention only to the audible characteristics of the disorder ignores the complexity and dynamics of stuttering behavior and their implications regarding possible causes, maintaining factors and therapeutic approaches.[20] As stated by Johnson, "Stuttering is a problem of speech behavior involving three definitive factors: (1) speech disfluency . . . , (2) reactions of the listeners to the speaker's disfluencies as evaluated by them as undesirable, abnormal, or unacceptable; and (3) the reactions of the speaker to the listener's reactions, as well as to his own speech disfluency and to his conception of himself as a stutterer."[21]

Causes. Perhaps more research has been carried on in an attempt to understand stuttering than is the case with any other speech handicap. Yet the causes are still in the realm of theory. If a simple one-sentence answer to the question "What causes stuttering?" were requested, it would probably have to be: "No one really knows." Van Riper has suggested that "so far as stuttering is concerned, speech correction is at present in the era of 'authorities' just as medicine was before Pasteur's discovery of bacterial agents in disease."[22] Hahn's compendium[23] presents the theories and

[18] Wendell Johnson's description of disfluency in his definition of stuttering in *Dorland's Illustrated Medical Dictionary*, 24th ed., Philadelphia: Saunders, 1965, p. 1454.
[19] The variability in frequency and severity of disfluencies in the speech of stutterers and nonstutterers is extensively described in "Studies of Speech Disfluency and Rate of Stutterers and Nonstutterers," *Journal of Speech and Hearing Disorders*, Monograph Supplement 8, 1961.
[20] The multiple characteristics of stuttering are summarized in Albert Murphy, ed., *Stuttering: Its Prevention*, Memphis, Tenn.: Speech Foundation of America, 1962, p. 12.
[21] *Dorland's Illustrated Medical Dictionary, op. cit.*, p. 1454.
[22] Van Riper, *op. cit.*, p. 316.
[23] Eugene F. Hahn, *Stuttering, Significant Theories and Therapies*, Palo Alto, Calif.: Stanford Univ. Press, 1956.

therapies of 26 persons whose views are respected; Eisenson's symposium[24] includes six. History has given us many others. We can make a list of the many theories that have been proposed and group them into larger units to get an overview. Ainsworth has made such a classification,[25] organizing the maze of hypothetical material into three main categories: neurotic, developmental, and dysphemic (or constitutional). At the risk of error because of oversimplification, we may say that much of our theorizing is done within this framework.

The developmental or learning theories of stuttering are probably the most significant for the classroom situation. According to these theories stuttering is a learned behavior in which emotional components, if they exist, are secondary reactions to the disfluencies. Speaker-listener relationships and interactions result in speech wariness, uncertainty, hesitation, and struggle, and in consequent shame, guilt, and conflict.[26] Specific stuttering patterns are reinforced and perpetuated as they reduce the speaker's embarrassment or facilitate his avoidance or escape from disfluency.

Rehabilitation. On the clinical level the eclectic view, that stuttering is a multicausal disorder, is widely accepted. Just as a person may have a headache for a variety of reasons, he may stutter from more than one cause. A rehabilitation program, therefore, must be tailor-made to fit the needs of each individual. Stuttering therapy should not be attempted by the classroom teacher. Even for the experienced speech therapist it is a demanding responsibility. Some suggestions for helping students who stutter are offered in the next chapter.

Cerebral Palsy

Description. Cerebral palsy is a condition characterized by paralysis, weakness, or incoordination of the muscular function of the body resulting from damage to the motor nerve tracts in the brain. Because the injury is to that part of the brain subserving bodily movement, a cerebral palsy victim may be so lacking in motional control that he may appear to be drunk or disoriented.[27]

Approximately 75 percent of the cerebral palsied demonstrate some degree of mental retardation on standard tests of intelligence.[28] Their

---

24 Jon Eisenson (ed.), *Stuttering, A Symposium,* New York: Harper & Row, 1958.
25 Stanley Ainsworth, "Integrating Theories of Stuttering," *Journal of Speech and Hearing Disorders,* 1945, 10:205–210.
26 An interesting approach to stuttering as a "disorder of social presentation" is elaborated in Joseph G. Sheehan, *Stuttering Research and Therapy,* New York: Harper & Row, 1970, chap. 1.
27 For a nontechnical discussion of the types of cerebral palsy, refer to Mary Louise Hart Burton in collaboration with Sage Holter Jennings, *Your Child and Mine, the Story of the Cerebral Palsied Child,* New York: Coward-McCann, 1949.
28 Eugene T. McDonald and Burton Chance, Jr., *Cerebral Palsy,* Englewood Cliffs, N.J.: Prentice-Hall, 1964, p. 44.

reduced scores may reflect a real intellectual impairment which, like the muscular impairment, is due to the brain damage. Their scores, however, may reflect other problems secondary to brain damage, such as hearing, visual, perceptual, emotional, behavioral, and learning disorders, or language delays resulting from the reduction in life experiences associated with motor and sensory problems.

The speech problems associated with cerebral palsy include poor respiratory and phonatory (pitch, loudness, and time) control, labored utterance, and severe articulatory defects. Indeed, the speech of the cerebral palsied individual may be unintelligible or he may have essentially no speech at all.

The numerous problems associated with cerebral palsy require a comprehensive diagnostic and rehabilitative approach.[29]

Causes. The direct cause of cerebral palsy is brain injury. The crippling condition was once thought to be brought about in most instances by damage to the infant's brain at birth. Today many other possible causes are considered. Diseases of the mother during pregnancy (especially German measles), genetic factors, Rh blood incompatibility between mother and unborn child, and other conditions interfering with the normal development of the brain in fetal life may cause cerebral palsy. Some cases are acquired after birth due to injuries, poisoning, or asphyxiation.

Rehabilitation. Because of the complexity of the disorder, individuals having cerebral palsy are ideally treated in rehabilitation centers where they can receive well-rounded therapy programs by professional personnel. The cerebral palsy team usually consists of one or more of each of the following: physician, physical therapist, psychologist, and social worker.[30] A cerebral palsy student with a speech defect should be referred to such a center or to a speech therapist.

Impaired Hearing

Persons with normal hearing are not aware of the extra problems encountered by those with hearing disorders. Even if the auditory loss is moderate, the annoyance resulting from a continuing inability to follow the trend of conversation may grow into serious consequences. The individual may give up his struggle to be a social being and become withdrawn and disagreeable. How often students are labeled indolent or belligerent when their real trouble lies in an inability to hear!

[29] A compact but comprehensive discussion of the causes, associated problems, and management of cerebral palsy can be found in McDonald and Chance, *op. cit.* The reader is also referred to William M. Cruickshank (ed.), *Cerebral Palsy, Its Individual and Community Problems*, rev. ed., Syracuse, N.Y.: Syracuse Univ. Press, 1966.
[30] For the role each plays in a rehabilitative program, see Jon Eisenson and Mardel Ogilvie, *Speech Correction in the Schools*, 3rd ed., New York: Macmillan, 1971, pp. 397–398.

Description.   Hearing disorders may be classified according to severity of the loss and time of its occurrence.

Let us consider for a moment the relationship between hearing and speaking. As the infant coos and babbles, he is responding to the inner urge to make vocal noises. At about the age of 6 months the "ear-voice reflex" is begun. Now he makes a sound, hears it, likes it, and happily repeats it. His utterances are like beads on a string: ba-ba-ba-ba-ba-ba-ba-ba-ba-ba. He is preparing for that next stage in which he will pick up the language of his environment.[31] But if Johnny has a severe congenital hearing loss, he will not progress through these normal stages of language development because the ear cannot play its role in the early learning process. Ann, his twin, may have a hearing loss, too; but it is less severe. She can hear when her mother speaks close to her ear. With the help of amplification devices she will learn to talk.

Mary had normal hearing until the age of 10; at this time, due to disease, she lost this prized possession. Although the experience was traumatic, requiring years for adjustment, her loss was not a barrier to language acquisition. Her speech patterns were learned years ago.

The foregoing discussion illustrates three classifications of hearing disorders based on severity of loss and time of its occurrence. Mary, classified as *deafened,* is fortunate to have developed language normally prior to her loss of hearing. Johnny is a profoundly *deaf* child. His hearing is not functional even with amplification. He will not learn to talk except through very special measures. Since the auditory avenue is closed to him, language must be learned through the senses of sight and touch—a long and tedious process. Ann is known as a *hard-of-hearing* child. Since she can hear the speech spoken in the home if it can be made loud enough, she will learn to use it. However, she may hear certain speech sounds improperly, and some phonemes she may not hear at all. Thus the hard-of-hearing child may develop an abnormal articulatory pattern. Some cases are completely unintelligible; others may have difficulty with only a few sounds. The voice also may be atypical.[32] Most hearing losses in the public schools are of the hard-of-hearing variety. Some courageous deaf students who have been unusually successful in schools for the deaf are able to go to college. Deafened students might be found in either population.

Causes.   Hearing disorders usually result from some injury to, or failure in development of, the hearing instrument—the ear. If the injury is in the

[31] For an interesting discussion of the stages of normal speech and language development see Nancy E. Wood, *Delayed Speech and Language Development,* Englewood Cliffs, N.J.: Prentice-Hall, 1964, pp. 4–20.
[32] An explanation of the effects of hearing loss on speech and a discussion of speech training procedures used with the hearing impaired can be found in Raymond Carhart's chapter, "Development and Conservation of Speech," in Hallowell Davis and S. Richard Silverman (eds.), *Hearing and Deafness,* 3rd ed., New York: Holt, Rinehart & Winston, 1970, pp. 360–371.

middle ear, the person has a *conductive* loss; if the destruction is to the inner ear and the nerve is damaged, he has a *sensory-neural* loss. If both the middle and inner ear are involved, he has a *mixed* loss.

Causes of conductive impairments include otitis media (middle-ear infection), an accumulation of wax in the ear canal, congenital malformation of the ossicles or the ear canal, and a bone disease, usually of the middle ear, known as otosclerosis. Purely conductive losses are never total.

Sensory-neural hearing losses may be partial or total, hereditary, congenital, or acquired. A person may lose his hearing for no apparent reason except that his father or aunt or grandmother was hard of hearing. A common cause of congenital nerve deafness is maternal viral disease during pregnancy, especially German measles (rubella) in the first 3 months. Mumps, influenza and other viral and bacterial diseases, inner ear injuries, constant exposure to loud noise, or the side effects of certain drugs can result in sensory-neural losses after birth.

Rehabilitation. A person with a purely conductive loss has a definite advantage over the one with a sensory-neural or mixed type, since the auditory nerve is intact. In some instances surgery may help the situation remarkably, and a hearing aid may prove helpful. But the individual with a sensory-neural loss is not so fortunate. Once the nerve has been damaged it cannot be restored. Moreover, sensory-neural deafness is often progressive, leading to a severe loss of hearing.

Because of the importance of finding the beginnings of hearing disorders before they grow to serious problems, many states require hearing tests of certain grades in the public schools each year. Such a program is known as a hearing conservation program.

Testing and rehabilitation programs for deaf and hard-of-hearing students belong in the hands of specialists. Profoundly deaf students will probably be found in special classes taught by trained personnel or in schools for the deaf. Hard-of-hearing students should have access to therapy programs conducted by speech and hearing therapists or hearing specialists. Such programs will include speech (lip) reading, auditory training, and speech correction.[33]

A POINT OF VIEW

Communication today is the core of all living. When we pause long enough to ponder the wonders of the telephone, radio, television, and motion pictures, we are astounded by the widespread influence of these instruments on our everyday activity. When we add the realization that

[33] For further information see Johnson, *et al., op. cit.,* chap. 8; Davis and Silverman, *op. cit.;* and Louis M. Di Carlo, *The Deaf,* Englewood Cliffs, N.J.: Prentice-Hall, 1964.

our leaders today are striving to settle the major problems of the world by the power of the word instead of the sword, speech takes on the characteristics of a basic social need. By the same token it is also a vital personal need. Consider its importance in interpersonal relationships represented in the classroom, at the soda fountain, or over the back fence. Try to imagine the changes you would have to adjust to if, per chance, the ability to talk were taken from you for, say, a period of six months!

A breakdown in this ability to communicate, then, constitutes a handicap—just as does a breakdown in the ability to use one's hands or eyes. Since the speech defective's problem is often not a visible one, it is not always recognized as a disability—but it is there. The stutterer who blocks on almost every word, the cleft palate or articulatory case who cannot make himself understood, the brain-injured individual who knows he once knew and now cannot find that word or idea—all have disabilities that interfere with normal living.

How does an afflicted person feel as a result of his "difference"? As Johnson puts it, the psychology of the handicapped is basically the psychology of frustration; and the handicap of impaired speech is no exception to this general rule.[34] Every public school speech clinician can cite examples of students of normal or superior intelligence who were failing scholastically until speech or hearing rehabilitation programs were provided. Let us examine the dynamics of this frustration. If a speech-deficient person were to analyze and to verbalize his feelings, his description would probably be something like this. He is constantly torn between two opposing forces: one, a desire to talk, to make his contribution in the speaking situations in which he finds himself, and hence to be accepted by his peers; the other, an urge to remain silent, for experience has shown that talking has an adverse effect on his listeners and seems to result in rejection. The second force often wins; and when he does converse, being unsure of his role he handles the situation clumsily. Then follow more frustration and often a retreat from or a defiance of society.

Fortunately, there is a growing interest today in the personal worth of the individual. We are beginning to see the individual with a speech deviation not only as a "person with a difference" but also as a human being with feelings and aspirations like those of his neighbors. The teacher who can see beneath the false front of the speech-defective student and can interpret his motives is on his way to understanding him as a person. Frequently the student is sullen and refuses to recite in class, even though he knows the information under discussion; or he may be aggressively contemptuous, thus becoming a disrupting influence in the classroom. If the teacher is to react in such instances with empathy rather than with vindictiveness, he must understand the total situation.

[34] Johnson *et al.*, *op. cit.*, p. 74.

If the teacher wishes to develop an improved attitude toward the speech-disabled student in his class, he may well examine his feelings toward handicapping conditions in general. If he digs deeply enough he may find a hidden resentment that colors his relationship with persons possessing any kind of abnormality. It may stem partly from the archaic notion that a defect is always a symptom of mental retardation, or that it is the result of careless living in the social segment "on the other side of the tracks." These impressions are of course erroneous. Handicaps are found among the intelligent as well as the dull, the rich as well as the poor; they are found in all parts of the country and among the various races. They could have fallen to the lot of any one of us. We are obliged to make provision for them.

Because of the importance of communication in our culture and in the lives of individuals, the teacher of speech cannot carry his responsibility to completion without an understanding of the various facets of verbal breakdown just discussed. To *understand*, however, is but a means to an end. The next step is to do. The teacher wants to know how to lead students having speech defects to appropriate services consistent with the best scientific knowledge of the present day. The following chapter is concerned with his role in *helping* these students toward that goal.

EXERCISES

1. Try this experiment. For one day simulate a speech or hearing defect. Become, for that day, a severe stutterer, an articulatory case who can't be understood, a cerebral palsy patient, or a person with a significant hearing loss. Go into at least three stores and carry on conversations with the clerks. On your note pad, indicate the reactions of people toward your pseudo defect and describe your feelings about each of these reactions. What conclusions can you draw from the experience?
2. Read a least one complete chapter referred to in the foregoing discussion in each area of speech abnormality. Write a report of each for your speech notebook.
3. From the incidence statistics given in this chapter and in the references cited in footnote 5, estimate (a) how many speech defectives, (b) how many of each type of speech defectives, and (c) how many hearing defectives are in the public school population of your home town.
4. Visit a speech and hearing clinic or a speech and hearing therapy program in a public school system. Report your impressions to the class.
5. Order films depicting various types of speech and hearing problems and present them to the class. (See list of suggested films at the close of the next chapter.)

18. Helping Students with Speech and Hearing Disorders

C. Cordelia Brong and Stuart I. Gilmore

FINDING THOSE NEEDING HELP

Every teacher can recite the basic principle that stresses consideration of individual differences in the educational process. Such a philosophy becomes a mere platitude if students with speech and hearing disorders are allowed to *just sit* in the classroom. If we are going to "educate the whole person" we must study the background of each individual with a problem and deal with him in the light of pertinent findings. This does not mean mere acceptance with kindness; it means also the adoption of an important premise that may be stated as follows: the person who is "different" needs a different kind of education in addition to his regular course of study. Hence, an important objective of the teacher of speech is to recognize and sort out those students who require specialized attention.

Students with Speech Disorders

In some high schools and colleges an annual speech survey is made by speech and hearing clinicians to discover students who need rehabilitation. Fortunate indeed is the school system with this service! Because of the scarcity of specialized personnel, however, the procedure often does not extend into the upper educational levels. Here, the classroom teacher usually finds and refers those needing help to the therapy program. The teacher of speech, with his trained ear for speech irregularities, should have no difficulty in performing this task.

Usually as a result of the oral opportunities offered as a function of the course, the teacher is familiar with the speech of his students within the first few weeks of the term. If, however, the class is unusually large, or if referrals are to be made to the therapy program before a scheduled deadline, the teacher can find those needing help in a short time by means of a *screening test*. For older children and adults this usually consists of two parts: a reading phase and a speaking phase. The reading portion consists of a few sentences or a paragraph containing all the vowels, consonants, and major consonant blends in the English language. The material is read by each student in the class and the teacher records pertinent information as disorders are recognized. Both articulatory and voice deviations may thus be detected. An opportunity for a minute or two of spontaneous speaking serves the purpose of getting a sample of the student's communicative intelligibility and for finding stutterers who may exhibit no symptoms when reading.

With a modicum of ingenuity, the teacher of speech can prepare the reading test himself. The sounds most likely to be found defective should be used freely in the composition. In surveying the speech of 1998 pupils in grades 7 through 12, Saylor found consonants and consonant blends to be missed in the following order: [ʌ z v ð tʃ ŋ st sk f g s θ l b t str k r p d dʒ f l dr w ʃ].[1] Useful screening tests are provided in various standard texts, especially Avant and Hutton, Eisenson and Ogilvie, Fairbanks, and Van Riper.[2]

Students with Hearing Disorders

Many public school systems conduct hearing conservation programs annually. Through systematic planning (with certain grades included each year), total student populations are tested periodically by professional audiologists or by speech and hearing clinicians. In this way, hearing deviations are determined in an organized way and rehabilitative programs are recommended.[3]

Where no hearing surveys are made, the classroom teacher can make a contribution by finding students with hearing defects. The task is not an

[1] Helen K. Saylor, "The Effect of Maturation upon Defective Articulation in Grades Seven through Twelve," *Journal of Speech and Hearing Disorders*, September, 1949, 14:206.
[2] Velma Avant and Charles Hutton, "Passage for Speech Screening in Upper Elementary Grades," *Journal of Speech and Hearing Disorders*, February, 1962, 27:40–46; Jon Eisenson and Mardel Ogilvie, *Speech Correction in the Schools*, 2nd ed., New York: Macmillan, 1963, pp. 180–189; Grant Fairbanks, *Voice and Articulation Drillbook*, 2nd ed., New York: Harper & Row, 1960, pp. IX–XIX; Charles Van Riper, *Speech Correction Principles and Methods*, 4th ed., Englewood Cliffs, N.J.: Prentice-Hall, 1963, pp. 467–471; 482–484.
[3] For a comprehensive description of such a program see Hayes A. Newby, *Audiology*, 2nd ed., New York: Appleton-Century-Crofts, 1964, chap. 8.

easy one; nor is it possible through observation alone to suspect other than gross losses. In a study reported by Watson and Tolan, teachers were capable of detecting only about 22 percent of the pupils who were subsequently found through audiometric testing to have significant hearing impairments.[4] Most adults with major hearing losses are aware of the disorder. Some may wear hearing aids as a result of previous testing. But a surprisingly large number of persons are not conscious of the problem, especially in its milder forms. While anything the teacher can do is a poor substitute for the professional survey, if he is alert to the signs of hearing deficiency he may be instrumental in helping a student by making appropriate referral for examination.

To organize his suspicions of hearing loss into a "clinical hunch," a teacher may use the following procedure:

I. Observe the student in class.
  A. Does he seem to watch your face very carefully as though he is trying to read your lips?
  B. Does he sometimes turn his head as though he is turning his better ear toward the speaker?
  C. Does he frequently ask the speaker to repeat what he has said?
  D. Does he often make mistakes in following your directions?
  E. Does he frequently not pay attention?
  F. Does he seem unusually restless?
  G. Does he seem excessively shy or overly aggressive?
II. Listen to his speech.
  A. Are certain phonemic elements in his speech omitted or distorted? Does he have special difficulty with the high-frequency sounds such as sibilants?
  B. Is his voice abnormally weak or loud? Does it have a strange quality or unusual intonation pattern?
III. Discuss the matter with him.
  A. Has he frequent earaches, running ears, or colds?
  B. Has he had infectious diseases, as scarlet fever, measles, or influenza?
  C. Has he had a brain disease, such as meningitis, or sleeping sickness?
  D. Has he had a head injury including a skull fracture?
  E. Has he been exposed to unusually loud noise over a period of time?
  F. Does he complain of strange head noises or ringing in the ears? Dizziness or poor balance?

Affirmative replies to any of these questions point toward diminished hearing. This is not to say that the clue implied in each item can conclusively be traced to a hearing loss; other factors may be operating. Nor, in most instances, is one affirmative response sufficient to make a judgment. However, if the information gained from these questions adds only slightly

[4] Leland A. Watson and Thomas Tolan, *Hearing Tests and Hearing Instruments*, Baltimore: Williams & Wilkins, 1949, pp. 236–238.

to the teacher's original suspicion, he should refer the student for hearing tests. If audiological services are not offered in the school, the student can be referred directly to a local otologist.

HELPING STUDENTS WITH SPEECH DISORDERS IN THE CLASSROOM

In Any Classroom Situation

"How shall I treat the speech defectives in my classes?" is a common question asked by teachers. To present a rule-of-thumb reply is impossible. Every situation is surrounded by its own special circumstances which must be examined with the help of all the information that can be accumulated. There are, however, a few general principles that may offer assistance to the beginning teacher of speech.

1. Treat speech defectives in a casual and objective manner. Some teachers, embarrassed by the presence of a handicapped student in the class, go to extremes in exhibiting sympathy; others ignore the disorder completely. Most disabled persons abhor sympathy; they want to be accepted, not pitied. And to treat the problem as though it did not exist is just as unwholesome. When it is necessary to speak of the abnormality, do so with as little emotionality as one might use in referring to Mary's broken arm or Ben's new glasses. Talk about it frankly but always with a sensitive, empathic understanding and a motive of helpfulness.

2. Do not penalize the student for any aspect of his speech handicap that he cannot change as a function of the course. Just as a cripple who walks with crutches is not expected in a physical education course to play tennis or run a race, so the speech or hearing cripple should not be required to carry out the assignments that are impossible for him. If the teacher understands the student's problem, he can often make adjustments that will place his assignments within both the capabilities of the student and the requirements of the course. If such adjustments are not possible, the student should probably find another course.

3. On the other hand, require him to participate in the activities that are within his range of abilities. The articulatory case in an acting course would not be expected to try out for a role in a public performance, but he should be required to participate in class productions. Many adults having speech disorders report that through their public school years they learned to depend on the "generosity" of well-meaning teachers who released them from all oral responsibility. Many of them admit that these teachers performed for them a distinct disservice.

4. In skill courses, expect him to make gains within the boundaries of

his limitations. Often a teacher does little more than carry the speech defective student on the roster, requiring participation in course projects but having no concern about improvement. True, at times it is difficult to find areas in which students with speech disorders can work for improvement without specialized assistance; if no such area exists, he does not belong in the course. Often, however, with some extra consideration of his speech needs on the part of the teacher, the focus of attention can be delineated and the student's gains in specified particulars pointed out. For example, a cleft palate case in a public speaking class should not be expected to work toward articulatory normalcy. But gains in other phases of speaking—such as organization of material, English usage, and audience contact should be expected.

In a School with a Speech and Hearing Therapy Program

If the teacher of speech works in an institution that maintains a remedial program, his role is uncomplicated, yet important. In the first place, the teacher may well investigate certain factors when a student with a speech disorder joins a speech class. He should ask the question, "Is this the appropriate time for the student to take this course?" Let us say that a severe stutterer enters a public speaking class. He cannot talk without long pauses, excessive bodily tension, and distracting facial contortions. Perhaps he should not be taking the course at this particular time. If a concentrated therapy program can be provided for him now, he may in another semester or two be ready to profit from the public speaking activities. The course may then serve a terminal therapeutic purpose, in addition to providing him with an elective. By cooperative planning with the therapist and arranging for schedule changes, a situation that could have been a nightmare for both pupil and teacher becomes at a later time a satisfying experience.

Or the coordination of a therapy program and a speech offering during the same term may be desirable. A functional voice disorder, for example, may be significantly benefitted by a course in interpretation simultaneous with remedial work in the clinic.

The speech teacher can offer the student valuable assistance in the carryover phase of the remedial program. Schooled as he is in the science of phonetics, he should have little difficulty, for example, in helping to stabilize the new speech sounds that are being established in articulation therapy. Usually the therapist periodically informs the teacher which sounds are in need of strengthening and offers suggestions for "holding" the student for the correct production; on the adult level the student himself reports his needs to the teacher.

In a School Without a Speech and Hearing Therapy Program

The role of the speech teacher in the classroom in a school without a remedial program does not differ significantly from that already discussed. Since he has no specialist with whom to coordinate his efforts in behalf of those with speech or hearing disorders, he is in complete charge of all the communication irregularities of his pupils. His role out of the classroom is quite different and is discussed later in this chapter.

HELPING STUDENTS WITH SPEECH AND HEARING DISORDERS INDIVIDUALLY

"Come to my office and we shall talk about the problem." This invitation is the first step toward assisting a speech- or hearing-defective student found in a speech class. The point here is so obvious that it could be overlooked: All conversations touching even remotely on the confidential should be carried on in private. Such a conference, if conducted with warmth and perception, serves several purposes. It assures the student that the teacher is taking a sincere interest in him as an individual. It not only provides an opportunity for a frank discussion of the difficulty in private; it also establishes the necessary rapport between teacher and pupil for future handling of the subject in class. The teacher can thus lay the groundwork for the special program he will recommend.

In a School with a Speech and Hearing Therapy Program

1. Make the student aware of his disorder. Most people with speech disorders are aware of their abnormalities, but not all are. Persons with serious as well as moderate impairments sometimes find their way into high school—or even college—without realizing that they have atypical speech. Junior high school students in particular are often unaware of their substandard utterance until it is brought to their attention. Probably few adults have major speech deficiencies without knowing that they exist, but there are exceptions. Not long ago a student with a history of brain injury entered college and registered in a speech curriculum. When the matter of her own speech problem was mentioned in conference, she was so shocked that she withdrew from college the following week. She knew that the muscles in one arm and leg were affected, but no one had ever told her that her speech was impaired also.

Usually accepting the fact of a speech deviation is not so traumatic as the above illustration may suggest. It does, however, point up the possibility of such a reaction and the need for extreme care in making a student aware of his defect. In most instances, the person responds with gratitude for the information, especially if specific plans for therapy are immediately offered. He must, of course, be convinced that he has a deviation that will require remedial help. The teacher can use a mirror to assist the pupil in observing the visual aspects of the defect, and he can use a tape recorder to point out its auditory characteristics.

2. Motivate him to want help. In some instances, the student is not ready to be referred to the speech and hearing therapist. He may need a planned program to motivate him to want therapy. Because of immaturity he may be unwilling to tie himself down to an extra series of "lessons"; he may object because the scheduled sessions conflict with his football or baseball practice. Sometimes he may resist for more basic reasons. One college student with a juvenile voice required several months of counseling in a clinical setting before actual therapy could begin because of his fear of what he would sound like with a "man's voice."

The teacher should attempt motivation, however, only against a background of understanding of the total problem. Perhaps the disorder is such that little can be done for him. For example, consider a cerebral palsied student with unintelligible speech. The possibility of improvement, given the best rehabilitation program available, may, at his age, be slight. His particular handicap sets up physiological limits that no educational process can transcend. For the teacher to serve as a high-pressure salesman and to convince such a student of the miracles to be expected in a speech therapy program is not only unwise but harmful. On the other hand, speech disabilities with good prospect for improvement may require ingenious devices to create the necessary willingness for tackling the job of changing speech behavior.

In difficult cases, motivation becomes a joint enterprise to be shared by the teacher and therapist. Whenever he is in doubt the teacher should consult the specialist.

3. Make the referral to the therapy program. The teacher of speech should work closely with the speech and hearing clinician. He should know the schedule for making referrals. Usually in the public schools therapy programs are started within the first few weeks of the fall term. In order that students from speech classes may receive maximal benefit, they should be referred as early in the term as possible.

General Suggestions for Schools Without Remedial Programs

1. Refer the severe cases to an established evaluation center for examination. If funds are needed to finance the project, perhaps the assistance of a local civic organization may be enlisted.

2. Try to find therapy services for those who require the help of special-

ists. Try university clinics, nearby public school programs, hospital clinics, and rehabilitation centers.

3. Search for private therapists. If no therapy center can be found, it may be possible to locate qualified therapists in the vicinity who will take private cases. It should be made clear, however, that many private practitioners (as do some centers) charge high prices for their services. Of even greater concern should be the possibility of employing unqualified persons who pose as speech and hearing specialists. Because of the great demand for correctionists, the private practice market is wide open to the charlatan. One way to determine the qualifications of a speech and (or) hearing therapist is to refer to the most recent issue of the American Speech and Hearing Association's annual Directory.[5]

4. If none of these attempts bring results, recommend a change of schools. The parents of a high school student with a severe problem may be willing to send him to a private school that offers a remedial program. Certainly in choosing a college those with speech or hearing disorders should consider the clinical services offered.

5. Use your influence to bring to the school the services of a speech and hearing clinician. Often a school lacks these programs because no one has ever presented the need to administrators. It may be advisable to make a survey to determine the number who require therapy. If financial considerations provide substance for objection, look around for help. In many states the state department of education provides funds for employing speech correctionists in the public schools. Some state departments of health sponsor hearing programs. Also, the state or local chapter of the National Society for Crippled Children and Adults and the state Office of Vocational Rehabilitation may offer assistance.

SUGGESTIONS FOR HELPING STUDENTS WITH MILD ARTICULATORY PROBLEMS

A mild articulatory problem may be defined as a defect known to be functional[6] and to include only several deviant sounds. If organic or personality problems are causally related, if the speech pattern reveals errors in more than several different speech sounds, or if the few errors are strongly habituated, the case may be one for the specialist.

Let us say that you teach in a school system with no therapist. In your speech class you find a student who lisps. You make the necessary investi-

[5] The American Speech and Hearing Association also publishes three journals: *The Journal of Speech and Hearing Disorders, The Journal of Speech and Hearing Research,* and *Asha.* Subscriptions and single copies can be obtained from the Business Manager, American Speech and Hearing Association, 9030 Old Georgetown Road, Washington, D.C. 20014.

[6] See discussion on p. 253.

gation and rule out organic and emotional factors. Here is a student for whom you can plan a remedial program.

Testing Procedures

The first step is to find out as much as possible about the articulatory errors as they exist in the sudent's speech pattern. Judging from your impression in casual conversation, you assume that only the [s] and [z] sounds are affected. But you want to be sure. Before starting to teach a new sound you should know: (1) what sounds are defective; (2) what type of error is made in each instance, (3) in what position in the word each error is made, and (4) how the error is being made.[7]

1. Let the student read sentences or paragraphs loaded with all the sibilants to determine whether others are defective. Let us say that you find no additional deviations. The error sounds may now be recorded as [s] and [z].

2. Analyze these sounds as the student speaks to determine whether they are represented by omissions, substitutions, or distortions. Ask him to read the sentence: "I went to the store to buy celery, lettuce, bananas, and roses for Elizabeth." Suppose he says the nouns as follows: "thtore" [θtɔr], "thelery" [θɛləri], "lettuth" [lɛtəθ], "bananath" [bənæməð], "rotheth" [roðɪð], and "Elithabeth" [iliðəbəθ]. Note that in each instance the substitution error is used.

3. Now determine in what position within each word the error is made. Phonetic flaws may occur in the initial (I), medial (M), or final (F) positions in words. All three positions are here represented. To use Van Riper's system of recording the articulatory errors in these words may be indicated as follows:

store [θt/st] (I)   bananas [ð/z] (F)
celery [θ/s] (I)   roses [ð/z] (M, F)
lettuce [θ/s] (F)   Elizabeth [ð/z] (M)

Examine closely the student's production of the error sounds. Does the tongue tip protrude between the teeth for the [θ] and [ð], or does it touch the inner surface of the upper incisors? Usually it is well for the teacher to learn to imitate the student's production of the error sound so that he will be better able to offer specific assistance in changing tongue movement.

The question of consistency should also be explored. To what extent are these two sound errors ingrained in the student's speech pattern? Does he always use the same substitution, or does he sometimes substitute other consonants and at other times omit the sound altogether? Are his errors

[7] The reader is referred to the section entitled, "Articulation Errors: Their Nature" in Van Riper, *op. cit.*, pp. 218–227.

different as the [s] or [z] enters different phonetic environments? Is there one particular word, or one position in words (initial, medial, or final), or one consonant combination as [st], [sk], or [sn] in which the sound is said correctly? To elicit this information, the student should read material loaded with [s] and [z] sounds in as many different phonetic contexts as possible.[8]

Let us say that this student uses the lingual-protrusion production exclusively for the [s] and [z]. No words were found in which these sounds were said correctly.

The Correction Program

Only one sound is taught at a time. For the purpose of demonstrating the steps to be employed we shall use the [s].

1. Teach the student to differentiate between the [θ] and the [s] sounds. Most persons hear words as "lumps" of sounds. Before a student with an articulatory problem can start the chore of changing the production of a speech element, he must be able to hear and to recognize the difference in the correct and incorrect sounds. Speech clinicians frequently report that where phonics is taught, their work is favorably affected because the students have learned to listen to the phonetic ingredients of words. In the instance of our hypothetical student with the lingual-protrusion for [s] and [z], he must hear the difference between [θ] and [s]. To him a *pencil* is a "penthil." Ask him to pronounce the name of the writing tool as "pencil" and he will probably respond, "Thatth what I thaid—penthil!" He has not developed the ability to listen to his own speech and to match the phonemic components with those of the model pattern presented by another speaker. Before the new sound can be established, "penthil" and all other error words must sound *wrong* to him.

In such ear training procedure some kind of label is usually employed to assist the person in detecting the correct and the incorrect elements. On the adult level perhaps the most effective means of identification is the phonetic symbol. After representing the error sound as [θ] and the correct one as [s], the teacher can provide the following experiences: (a) "Spotting" the [s] *sound*. Present orally a random series of consonant sounds, including [s] at irregular intervals. The student writes the phonetic symbol [s] each time he hears you say the [s] sound. Example: [p t m s f s] etc. Present in like manner a series of nonsense words. In some words use no [s] and in others include it. The student writes [s] each time he hears the [s] in a nonsense word. Example: [ritu soso fʌm ætsu] etc. The same procedure may be used with words and short sentences. (b) Discriminating the [θ] and [s] sounds. Present an irregular sequence of [s] and [θ] sounds.

---

[8] See the section on "Habit Strength and Error Consistency," Van Riper, *op. cit.*, p. 218.

The student writes the appropriate symbol each time he hears a sound. A sequence might be: [s s θ s θ θ], etc.

Present these sounds in nonsense syllables, asking the student to write the appropriate symbol each time he hears a nonsense word containing that sound. For example:

Teacher says, [θaθa]; pupil writes [θ];
Teacher says, [sisi]; pupil writes [s], etc.

Present a series of [s] words, sometimes saying the [s] correctly and at other times using the [θ] error. For example:

Teacher says "sock"; pupil writes [s];
Teacher says "thoap" (for soap); pupil writes [θ].

Another experience may be carried on as follows: The teacher writes on the blackboard in large symbols [s] and [θ]. He then reads aloud a paragraph containing many [s] words. In the reading he sometimes substitutes [θ] for [s]. The student listens carefully and points to the [s] when an[s] word is said correctly, and to the [θ] when it is said with the [θ] substitution.[9]

2. Establish the [s] sound in isolation. The term *establish* emphasizes a procedure of implanting in a person's speech a sound that has heretofore not existed there. He has probably not, even by accident, arranged his tongue, teeth, and soft palate in the proper relationships to produce a standard [s] sound. To build such coordination is his present task. The therapist has at his command many techniques for helping an articulatory case to say the new sound for the first time. If one fails, another and another are tried until success is achieved. This case has been described as having a "minor" impairment, which by implication should respond to treatment without difficulty. Hence, only one method is discussed here. If additional procedures are needed, the student should be sent to a specialist.

Listen-Try Procedure.   Stimulus-response is the natural process of learning to talk. During the early stages of language development the infant repeats, parrotlike, the sounds that are said to him. As mother shows the baby the ball she says "ball," and the little one responds with a fair approximation of the word. The child listens, integrates the heard pattern with the necessary lip and tongue movements, and then produces the word.

Of course, the process is really not that simple. And certainly when a sound that has never before existed in the phonetic repertoire of an adult is to be learned, the stimulus-response event must be fractionated in order to build a sequence of steps to be used in the learning process. Actually, when

[9] For further information see the section on "Ear Training" in Van Riper, *op. cit.*, pp. 249–259.

the stages are analyzed they represent not a simple "listen-try" activity but rather a "listen-search-try-compare" series of steps.

First the learner must *listen* to the model presented by the teacher. Then he must *search* for just the right shape of the tongue, for its proper proximity to the teeth, and for the appropriate distance between the upper and lower incisors to produce a sound like the stimulus. He will probably use a mirror and a view of the teacher's mouth to help him determine possible postures for exploration.[10] With the search terminated and a position located that may bring results, he *tries* the sound. At first the heard product of his attempt is probably far from that of the stimulus. Now he must *compare*. He must hold on to the self-produced sound in his "mind's ear," compare its characteristics with those of the [s] made by the teacher, and decide what articulatory adjustments he can make to bring the product of his next try closer to the model. Only then is he ready to try the entire cycle again. Not until he has said a [s] that is a recognizable facsimile of the standard sound has he "established" the sound in isolation.[11]

3. Strengthen the [s] sound. (a) In isolation: The new consonant is weak and unstable. Sometimes careful positioning results in the desired sound; at other times it does not. Thus, much practice is necessary. As soon as the student has memorized the auditory pattern of the teacher's [s] he can practice alone. By this time the "search" stage can probably be eliminated, and drill takes the form of "listen (to the model [s] in his mind's ear), try, compare." Every try needs an evaluative phase for the purpose of matching the produced [s] against the model [s] and determining the degree of success. (b) In nonsense material: Clinical research and experience have shown that the use of nonsense material assists significantly in strengthening the newly learned sound. Through assimilation in running speech, a sound is changed slightly by the other sounds that come next to it. The muscular coordination required to say [s] in *see*, *soup*, *step*, and *desk*, for example, varies from word to word, and more difficulty may be encountered in certain sound combinations than in others. Then, too, the old phonetic associations with familiar word configurations may stand in the way of correct production of the new sound in words without this

[10] The teacher must know the "standard" positions for the speech sounds he will teach. For discussion of the production of the consonants accompanied by practice materials see; Johnnye Akin, *And So We Speak: Voice and Articulation*, Englewood Cliffs, N.J.: Prentice-Hall, 1958, pp. 83–136; Jon Eisenson, *The Improvement of Voice and Diction*, 2nd ed., New York: Macmillan, 1965, pp. 225–349; Jon Eisenson and Paul Boase, *Basic Speech*, 2nd ed., New York: Macmillan, 1964, pp. 116–148; Grant Fairbanks, *Voice and Articulation Drillbook*, 2nd ed., New York: Harper & Row, 1960, pp. 57–103; Elise Hahn, Donald E. Hargis, Charles W. Lomas, and Daniel Vandraegen, *Basic Voice Training for Speech*, New York: McGraw-Hill, pp. 163–202.

[11] For further information see Charles Van Riper and John V. Irwin, *Voice and Articulation*, Englewood Cliffs, N.J.: Prentice-Hall, 1958, chap. 6.

intermediate stage. To the student, for example, that writing instrument may still be a "penthil." By using nonsense material the [s] can be combined with various vowels and consonants, and it can be practiced in the initial, medial, and final positions in words without meaning. Example: The teacher provides the stimulus; the pupil responds to each nonsense word.

(I) [sa si so su sta spi sko slu], etc.
(M) [asa isi oso usu asta ispi osko uslu], etc.
(F) [as is os us ats ips oks uls], etc.

4. Establish the sound in words. The sound [s] is now ready to be learned in words. The student collects lists of words containing [s] in the initial, medial, and final positions. In practice sessions he listens carefully and evaluates the heard product of each try.

5. Carry the newly learned sound over into everyday speech. The new sound is not yet ready to be relied on in spontaneous speech. It must first be practiced in planned communication situations. By starting with structured phrases and sentences in a natural conversational setting, the sound is blended into normal speaking patterns. Because of the reduced thought content in these small language fragments, the student can concentrate on the mechanics of producing the [s] correctly. As the new sound becomes habituated, less and less structure is used in the practice material.

Sequences ranging from highly structured questions and answers with only one response to loosely structured conversation samples, are used according to the needs of the learner.

Example: Highly structured sequence (almost no thought content):

Teacher: Will our team win tonight?
Student: Yes, I think so.
Teacher: Are you going to the game?
Student: Yes, I think so.
Teacher: Is Mary going too?
Student: Yes, I think so.

Example: Moderately structured sequence (some thought content introduced):

Teacher: Will you meet me at the First National Bank?
Student: I'd rather meet you at Smith's Grocery Store.
Teacher: Will you meet me at the corner of Fourth and Fifth Streets?
Student: I'd rather meet you at the corner of Sixth and Seventh Streets.

Example: Loosely structured situation (more thought content introduced):

The teacher and student carry on a conversation on a chosen topic.

The student will be "held" for the correct production of [s] in certain predetermined words. These words may be written on the blackboard or on paper so that they will be before the student as the conversation ensues. The topic: Building a new house; practice words: cost, first floor, basement, ceiling, sunporch, fireplace, color scheme.

Before the new [s] can be said to be completely stabilized in spontaneous speech, one more step is frequently necessary. This last approach aims to make the student aware of slips into error with the newly learned sound during everyday speech. The student may ask friends to help him catch his phonetic lapses at certain designated times. He may schedule for himself nucleus situations in which he is specifically aware of his faulty [s] sounds and corrects them immediately during conversation. The use of a tape recorder of high fidelity may help him to detect his errors. Any plan that brings to his attention his inaccurate [s] sounds for correction during communication will be helpful in this final stage of therapy.

The [z] sound may be taught in the same way as that outlined for the [s]. The student will probably have little difficulty in mastering this sound, however, since the necessary muscular coordinations have been established while learning the [s].

SUGGESTIONS FOR HELPING STUDENTS WITH VOICE DISORDERS

In the discussion of voice disorders in Chapter 17 it was indicated that nonspecialists should handle only functional voice disturbances not causally linked to emotional problems. What is the role of the teacher of speech in a school where there is no therapist? Here are a few suggestions.

1. Determine which voice disorders can be treated by nonspecialists. One of the most common vocal deficiencies in the school population is excessive nasality. Unless it is caused by some structural deformity, such as cleft palate, the speech teacher with training in voice science should have no difficulty in planning an improvement program.

Though denasality is considered by some authorities to be an articulatory rather than a voice problem, it often demands attention. Frequently it results from posterior nasal obstruction, such as enlarged adenoids. The teacher of speech can adequately handle an improvement program *after the cause has been removed*. The main goal in such treatment is to teach nasal production of [m], [n], and [ŋ].

2. Learn to recognize those vocal qualities that are frequent symptoms of pathology. Actual harm may result from inappropriate handling of certain types of vocal disorders. The qualities deserving special consideration are hoarseness, breathiness, and harshness. The speech teacher should learn to identify each of these.

Of the three disorders, hoarseness is most likely to prove serious. Listen closely to the sound of a voice during an attack of laryngitis. Carry that quality always in your "mind's ear as a potential danger signal when hoarseness persists.

Breathiness, also a possible symptom of organic or personality abnormality, can be recognized as a whisperlike tone, usually weak in volume.

A harsh voice may or may not indicate organic origin; perhaps it more frequently reflects improper vocal usage. Recall the too-loud, tense, rasping voice of the politician for an example of high harshness. To recognize low harshness, listen for a "gravelly" low-pitched tone and note signs of hypertension. To simulate a low-harsh voice, try the following and listen to the resulting quality. Start to swallow, then say a low-pitched [ɑ] just before the swallow is completed. Listen to the tense, noisy tone. Using a hard glottal plosive attack, say words beginning with vowels, like "apple," "eat," and "onion." Or vocalize on an inhalation.

3. Refer to a laryngologist any student whose vocal quality may be a symptom of pathology. A safe rule to follow is to recommend for laryngeal examination *by a throat specialist* any student who has had a hoarse or breathy voice for a period of time. Since hoarseness is frequently confused with harshness, the teacher is on the safe side to make the same suggestion to students with harsh voices.

An incident that allegedly occurred some time ago in a junior high school points up the importance of the precautionary measures just described. An uninformed teacher of speech, noting the hoarseness of one of his pupils, searched for exercises to correct the condition. Realizing that the girl's voice was weak, he chose drills designed to strengthen the voice. Under his direction she read poems demanding excessive loudness to large imaginary audiences. A year later the girl died of cancer of the larynx. Whether the inappropriate procedures contributed to the malady will never be known. This much is certain: if the teacher had recognized the danger potential of a chronically hoarse voice and had sent the girl to a laryngologist for examination, he might have been instrumental in saving her life.

The point that cancer is only one of many possible vocal pathologies cannot be emphasized too strongly. The student is not asked to have an examination for the detection of a dread disease; rather he is asked to seek medical diagnosis to *rule out* the possibility of organic irregularity of any kind. If the teacher makes such procedure a routine matter, there should be no reason for trauma. The student can be advised that in either event he is the winner. If the results are negative, the good news is worth the price of the examination; if a pathology is revealed, the information is invaluable for planning a course of action.

4. Refer for professional help any student whose voice disorder seems to be a symptom of an emotional problem. Since speech and personality are closely interrelated, a deviation in one probably affects the other is some degree. Voice seems to be an especially sensitive index of attitudes and

feelings. Voice irregularities may be related to emotional factors extending on a continuum all the way from minor deviations in outlook to severe emotional disturbances. The point at which psychological or psychiatric assistance should be sought is not easily established, and the classroom teacher may sometimes need professional help in making such determination. Perhaps the school psychologist or a local psychological clinic is available for consultation. Psychogenic voice problems should never be treated by the teacher of speech.

5. Teach improved vocal production to students with uninvolved functional deficiencies. Most voice irregularities result from improper usage— even in the areas of hoarseness, breathiness, and harshness. But only after organic and serious psychological factors are ruled out can an educational program be planned.

This chapter is not designed to provide specific techniques for working with functional voice defects. Excellent voice improvement texts are available. The teacher of speech should be familiar with the ones by Akin, Anderson, Eisenson, Eisenson and Boase, Fairbanks, and Hahn et al.[12]

SUGGESTIONS FOR HELPING STUTTERERS

To cope with stutterers the teacher should know as much as possible about stuttering. This abnormality was discussed in the previous chapter and reading references provided. We are now ready to consider specific suggestions for helping stuttering students in the classroom and in private conferences.

Helping the Stutterer in Class

1. Accept him, stuttering and all, as a worthwhile member of the class. He is probably a normal person except for his speech difficulty. At the upper high school and college levels, chances are more than ever that he is average or above in intelligence. He has probably been considered "different" ever since childhood. The teacher's attitude toward him as a person may be important to him.

2. Encourage him to talk. For many stutterers the speaking experience is one of struggle and anguish. Often they give up and withdraw from social situations entirely. In class they usually prefer not to participate in discussion. Anything the teacher can do to encourage a stutterer to carry on as a normal social being is helpful from a mental hygiene point of view. His

12 Akin, op. cit., pp. 166–214; Virgil A. Anderson, Training the Speaking Voice, 2nd ed., New York: Oxford Univ. Press, 1961, chaps. 1–6; Eisenson, op. cit., pp. 59–121; Eisenson and Boase, op. cit., pp. 80–115; Fairbanks, op. cit., chaps. 11–12, 14–15; Hahn et al., op. cit., chaps. 3–5.

speech may also profit from more talking. In a therapy program the silent person has little chance for improvement, since he has nothing to work with. Willingness to talk will lay the groundwork for rehabilitation.

3. Be a patient listener. Look at the stutterer when he is talking just as you would look at any person who is speaking to you. It is not easy to maintain natural eye contact when he is caught in a block, especially if he manifests secondary symptoms of facial contortion. But to look away may add to his embarrassment.

4. When a stutterer is caught in a block, do not try to help him. Normal speakers talking to a stutterer often supply words for him or pick up the conversation, thus cutting short his contribution. Most conversationalists resent having their sought-for words given them, and the stutterer is no exception.

5. Do not make homespun suggestions for getting the words out. He has probably listened to such "helpful hints" ever since childhood; he may have tried some of them and found them to increase the complexity of his problem. In studying parental attitudes toward stuttering children, Darley found that in 48 cases out of 50, one parent or both had made suggestions to their children for overcoming the stuttering. The most frequent were: "talk more slowly," "stop and start over," "think of what you are going to say," "take it easy," "relax," "take a deep breath," and "repeat." Such helps were given at least daily to 35 of the children, according to at least one of the parents.[13]

6. Do not tell him to try not to stutter. If it were possible for him to turn on and off the blockages at will, he would not be a stutterer. According to Johnson the very crux of his problem lies in his trying too hard not to stutter: "Stuttering is what a speaker does trying not to stutter again."[14]

7. Do not praise his moments of fluent speech. Fluency is his most coveted goal, yet his efforts for gaining it only strengthen the power of the nonfluencies. Consciously or subconsciously he devises schemes to circumvent or to postpone his stuttering blocks. He learns to use "starters" and other tricks to win his freedom from the plague of blocking. When therapy is begun, these devices must be eliminated. Do not make the task more difficult for him than it now is.[15]

[13] Frederic L. Darley, "The Relationship of Parental Attitude and Adjustments to the Development of Stuttering," in Wendell Johnson (ed.) assisted by Ralph R. Leutenegger, *Stuttering in Children and Adults*, Minneapolis, Minn.: Univ. of Minnesota Press, 1955, p. 140.

[14] Wendell Johnson, Spencer J. Brown, James F. Curtis, Clarence W. Edney, & Jacqueline Keaster, *Speech Handicapped School Children*, 3rd ed., New York: Harper & Row, 1967, p. 240.

[15] Excellent suggestions for teachers who have stutterers in their classes are provided in Harold L. Luper and Robert L. Mulder, *Stuttering: Theapy for Children*, Englewood Cliffs, N.J.: Prentice-Hall, 1964, pp. 193–206.

Helping the Stutterer in Private Conference

The rehabilitation of stutterers is an assignment for specialists only. Where they are not available, then next best is a hands-off policy. Too many stutterers have tried nonprofessional "schools," neighbors' recipes, and their own techniques gleaned from suggested readings. Each unsuccessful trial adds to frustration. The best assistance the teacher of speech can provide includes the following steps: (1) determining whether this particular student is a good prospect for therapy; (2) if he is, motivating him to undertake treatment; and (3) helping him find a program. Not all stutterers are good clinical risks; some may need help from a psychiatrist rather than a speech pathologist, and others may be lacking in basic intelligence. But in high school and in college many of them have a high potential for improvement. Make a study of the stutterer as a person. Is he an above-average student? Does he seem to have a wholesome outlook on life? Can he tackle a difficult task and carry it through to completion? (Success in therapy requires strong initiative and hard work.) Does he accept as his responsibility the task of changing his behavior—given the necessary guidance? If these questions can be answered affirmatively, motivate him to search for professional assistance and help him find it.

EXERCISES

1. Ask a friend of yours who speaks a foreign language to teach you to say a consonant sound from that language that you have never heard before. Try to describe the learning process as you attempt to master the new sound. Make a list of the questions you ask as you are attempting to produce it acceptably. From this experience, make a list of steps that you might use to teach a new English sound to a student with an articulatory defect. Compare this sequence of steps with those given in this chapter.
2. An articulatory case was giving the following information to his friend: "Yesterday Charles and I drove to school in his new Rambler. Just as we were approaching Sixth Street a tire blew out and we found ourselves climbing a tree."

    Following is a transcription of his speech as he said it. Indicate in phonetics each error sound and designate the type of error in this way: [θ/s] = a substitution of the [θ] for [s]; − [s] = an omission of the [s]; + [s] = an addition of the [s] sound. Write each word containing an articulatory fault and follow it with a designation of the error or errors found in that word.

    [jɛθtə·de tʃɑrlð ənd aɪ dwov tʊ kul ɪn hɪʒ nu wæmblə·. dʒʌt æʒ wi wə· əpwotʃɪn θɪkθ twit, ə taɪr bju aut ən wi faund aurθɛlvð klaɪmɪŋk ə twi.]
3. Prepare a screening test for discovering students in your class who have articulatory defects using the sounds listed on p. 336.
4. From the text discussion of speech and hearing disorders, make an outline specifying the following: (a) which deviations must be handled only by specialists; (b) which may be attempted by the teacher in situations where specialists are not available; and

(c) which speech irregularities the competent teacher of speech should be prepared to handle whether or not a rehabilitation program is available.

5. What would you do if, after you had accepted a position to teach speech in junior or senior high school, your principal indicated that you were expected also to conduct a therapy program for the speech defectives in the school?

REFERENCES

Selected Readings

American Speech and Hearing Association Research Committee, "Public School Speech and Hearing Services," *The Journal of Speech and Hearing Disorders*, Monograph Supplement 8, July, 1961. Describes the public school speech and hearing program.

ANDERSON, VIRGIL A., *Improving the Child's Speech*, rev. ed., New York: Oxford Univ. Press, 1961. This book discusses for the classroom teacher the speech and hearing problems that may be found in the public schools. It presents an overview of the major areas of speech and hearing disorders and provides a detailed discussion of articulatory defects. A major value is its clear organization and the simplicity of its presentation.   .

EISENSON, JON, AND OGILVIE, MARDEL, *Speech Correction in the Schools*, 3rd ed., New York: Macmillan, 1971. These authors present an overview of speech and hearing problems for the classroom teacher and the school speech therapist. Although much of the material is directed to those working with children, the three chapters dealing with articulatory defects and the chapter on voice disturbances should be helpful to teachers of speech in high school and college.

JOHNSON, WENDELL, BROWN, SPENCER J., CURTIS, JAMES F., EDNEY, CLARENCE W., AND KEASTER, JACQUELINE, *Speech Handicapped School Children*, 3rd ed., New York: Harper & Row, 1967. This is perhaps the most comprehensive survey of speech and hearing disorders designed for the classroom teacher. The book is so well documented with background references that it could be used effectively in specialized courses. It is written interestingly and in language that can be understood by the nonspecialist.

Selected Films Depicting Speech and Hearing Disorders[16]

General

Good Speech for Gary, 22 minutes, Film Library, New York University, 26 Washington Pl., New York 10003. Deals with a second-grade boy with a speech defect; shows its effect on his personality and its improvement through speech correction. Describes the integration of the work of the speech therapist and the classroom teacher.

Introduction to Speech Problems, 27 minutes, Wayne State University Audio-Visual Center, 5448 Cass Ave., Detroit, Mich. 48202. Discusses speech problems caused by physical and emotional factors and what can be done through speech therapy, surgery, and speech appliances. Presents children and adults with articulatory, stuttering, cleft palate, speech retardation, aphasic, and dysarthric problems.

The Speech Chain, 30 minutes, Bell Telephone Laboratories, New York. Available through local Bell Telephone Company business office. General speech production, transmission, and receiving mechanisms are shown with discussions of the physiological and physical functioning involved.

[16] Since both the rental and purchase prices of the following films depicting speech and hearing disorders are subject to change, it is suggested that interested individuals contact the distributor for current prices. In some cases no charges are made for use of the films.

Speech Training for the Handicapped Child, 30 minutes, National Society for Crippled Children and Adults, 2023 West Ogden Ave., Chicago, Ill. 60612. This film presents a summer rehabilitation program in speech and hearing under the direction of the Division of Services for Crippled Children at the University of Illinois. It includes case finding, diagnosis, medical consultation, therapy, and recreational activities.

Your Voice, 11 minutes, Encyclopaedia Britannica Films, 1150 Wilmette Ave., Wilmette, Ill. 60091. Portrays in animated drawings and photography the four elements of speech production: respiration, phonation, resonance, and articulation.

Articulation

Functional Articulatory Speech Disorders, New York University Medical Center, available through National Medical Audiovisual Center (Annex), Station K, Atlanta, Ga. 30324. Discusses and illustrates functional articulatory disorders; traces treatment progress.

Cerebral Palsy

Physiological Aspects of Speech: Speakers with Cerebral Palsy, 25 minutes, Bureau of Audiovisual Instruction, University of Iowa, Iowa City, Ia. 52240. Presents the respiratory, laryngeal, and articulatory deviations occurring in cerebral palsied individuals.

Out of the Shadows, 20 minutes, Audio Visual Department, University of Southern California, Los Angeles, Calif. 90007. A film presenting diagnostic and therapeutic programs for cerebal palsied persons.

Cleft Palate

Physiological Aspects of Speech; Speakers with Cleft Palate, 30 minutes, Bureau of Audiovisual Instruction, University of Iowa, Iowa City, Ia. 52240. Presents the various types of deviations of the velopharyngeal mechanism in individuals with clefts and their effect on speech production. The importance of other physical abnormalities, such as deviant dentition and inadequate lip tissue, are also considered.

Rehabilitation of Patients with Clefts of the Lip and Palate, 28 minutes, State University of Iowa, University Hospitals, Department of Otolaryngology and Maxillofacial Surgery, Iowa City, Ia. 52240. This film points out the causes, therapy, and various services involved in the total rehabilitation of the cleft palate person.

Children with Cleft Palates—A Program of Speech Development, Audio-Visual Education Center, 4028 Administration Building, University of Michigan, Ann Arbor, Mich. 48104. This film illustrates the procedures that may be followed to encourage the development of good speech in children with cleft lip and palate.

Hearing Disorders

Information Series (nine films), 20 minutes each, John Tracy Clinic, 806 West Adams Boulevard, Los Angeles, Calif. 90007. The films cover the function of the ear, language learning in the normal and the deaf child, the development of lip reading skills, the development of expressive language, and the multisensory approach to teaching the deaf child.

The Joy of Listening, 13 minutes, Courtney D. Osborn, Chief, Hearing Conservation Section, Division of Maternal and Child Health, Michigan Department of Health, Lansing, Mich., free loan. A film on hearing conservation produced by the Hearing Conservation Section of the Education Section of the Michigan Department of Health. Traces three children through hearing conservation procedures and outlines followup.

Rehabilitation of Persons with Auditory Disorders, 89 minutes, New York University

Medical Center, available through National Medical Audiovisual Center (Annex), Station K, Atlanta, Ga. 30324. Describes the problems associated with congenital and acquired hearing loss.

Silent World, Muffled World, 28 minutes, Deafness Research Foundation and American Academy of Ophthalmology and Otolaryngology, available through National Medical Audiovisual Center Annex, Chamblee, Ga. 30005. Describes the world of the deaf and hard of hearing, their problems of social acceptance and education, the causes of hearing loss, and progress toward relieving the conditions.

A Time to Sow, 30 minutes, Captioned Films for the Deaf, U.S. Office of Education, Washington, D.C. 20202. A résumé of some of the communication problems of the deaf.

Stuttering

Stuttering, 114 minutes, New York University Medical Center, available through National Medical Audiovisual Center (Annex), Station K, Atlanta, Ga. 30324. Discusses results of years of research at the University of Iowa. Considers stuttering a social rather than a physical defect.

Speech of Stutterers Before and After Treatment, 30 minutes, University of Minnesota, Audio-Visual Extension Service, 2037 University Avenue S.E., Minneapolis, Minn. 55455. Shows how the secondary habit patterns of stuttering can be eliminated in some stutterers; describes cases of improvement and relapse.

New Hope for Stutterers, 28 minutes ("The Search"), Young America Films, 18 East 41 St., New York 10017. This film presents a demonstration of Dr. Wendell Johnson's work with adult stutterers.

Stuttering, an Overview, 42 minutes, Audio-Visual Services, San Jose State College, San Jose, Calif. Presents aspects of therapy with child and adult stutterers, including an interview of a mother of a stuttering child.

Stuttering, 30 minutes, Council of Adult Stutterers, Speech and Hearing Clinic, The Catholic University of America, Washington, D.C. 20017. Presents a discussion of the problems of stuttering by stutterers of the Council of Adult Stutterers. Intent is to expose the public to stuttering and stutterers.

19. Course Planning

Oran Teague

Because course planning encompasses the entire teaching process, it is small wonder that beginning teachers approach it with uncertainty and that many experienced teachers look on it as time consuming, tedious, and frustrating. It can be all of these and more, but the teacher can dispel the frustration and the apprehension by understanding the principles and by undertaking course planning step by step.

The opening chapter of this text points out that the four essential elements of a successful course in speech are (1) a well-trained teacher, (2) a philosophy of speech, (3) a course plan, and (4) a meeting place and equipment. The present chapter considers the principles and procedures involved in course planning. These principles apply to all speech instruction, with special emphasis on the first or beginning speech course.

The principles are presented in this chapter in an order in which they may be applied in course preparation, but you should be warned at the outset that there is no perfect order which will fit every case. For example, student analysis does not need always to precede the formulation of objectives. The two often demand simultaneous consideration, and in reality it makes little difference which comes first. The important thing is that they be considered.

Since course planning is ultimately an individual matter, the author makes no attempt to dictate any one type of plan. Some teachers need detailed plans, while others prepare only broad outlines. Still others, in order to satisfy administrative or curricular requirements, are forced to organize courses in units, with detailed daily lesson plans, or to follow prepared syllabuses. Whatever the specific needs are, the principles remain the same and may be adapted to any set of requirements.

NEEDS AND ABILITIES

Sound planning starts with the desires, needs, and abilities of the students. Speech is inherently bound to personality. All factors that affect the individual, including his physical makeup, his innate abilities, his mother tongue, his previous speech training, and his past and present experiences, may make his speech needs different from those of another person. In a given class a teacher of speech may find some students who are fluent and others who have difficulty executing simple speech skills. In one class there may be a student who lisps, several who use substandard speech, and a few who seem to need little training in voice or pronunciation but who should have instruction in speech organization, control of bodily activity, and the projection of ideas.

One teacher described his beginning speech class as follows:

There are ten girls and six boys in my beginning speech class. The average age is 15 years. They come from homes of various socioeconomic and educational backgrounds. Most of the students seem to be well adjusted emotionally and socially and have only normal speech needs. There are five members of the class, however, who have marked speech problems which demand special attention.

Mike suffers from a sinus condition. I have talked with his mother and his doctor about the problem. The medical reports show that his condition is quite serious. Mike's voice is unpleasant, and at times he seems to have difficulty in speaking. He is extremely self-conscious about his nasal twang and often misses class on the days he is scheduled to perform.

Jim enjoys tremendous popularity with the members of the class by virtue of his position on the football team. In all of his subjects except English he has excellent grades. On his speech data sheet he stated that he wants to be a lawyer. Jim has a pleasant voice, but his grammar and pronunciation are inferior. Thus far in the class he has rejected all criticism of his speech maintaining that he "talks like everybody else."

Charles is a superior student, but he stammers when he speaks before the group. His father, a notable speaker in the state, has talked to me about Charles' problem. Part of Charles' difficulty arises, I feel, from pressures to be as good a speaker as his father. He is a most willing student and is working hard to overcome the stammer.

Beth is one of the most popular girls in the junior class. She is vivacious, intelligent, and attractive. She wants to be an actress. Unfortunately Beth has a lisp which she refuses to acknowledge even though she has heard many recordings of her voice.

Martha, a small, timid girl, has few friends in the class. Usually she sits apart from the group and seems to be in a dream world. This is the second time she has enrolled in Speech I, and thus far she has given only one speaking assignment. Her voice is soft and pleasant in normal conversation, but it becomes high and strident when she is called on to speak in class.

The report just cited is not typical of all classes, because each grade level has its unique problems and each class demands a different approach. It does, however, illustrate the diverse problems that a speech instructor may encounter and for which he must be provided, even in those schools where sectioning according to ability is a curricular practice.

STUDENT ANALYSIS

A beginning step in course planning involves pupil analysis similar to audience analysis. Just as the successful speaker must know his listeners, so the successful teacher must study his students.

Analyze the Community

The first step is to get acquainted with the community. To a large degree, local dialectal habits, colloquialisms, and occupational tendencies will provide some suggestions about what should be taught and, to some extent, how it should be taught. Economic and educational levels of the homes of the students may be contributing factors to speech patterns and to the anomalies that they bring to the classroom. The speech needs of a rural community like Dry Prong, Louisiana, differ greatly from those of a city like New Orleans. The problems of the students of New Orleans will differ from those of New York City. In addition to understanding local mores, you should be aware of the major dialect spoken by the "majority of the educated people" of the area.[1] To insist that students in the deep South or in New England use General American dialect or that Iowans attempt British diction is sure to bring ridicule and, in some cases, even revolution. Of course, such a procedure is the height of folly.

Check Cumulative Records

The second step in preclass analysis is to check the student's personnel records, which most administrators are glad to make available. Even though this file may not contain actual data on speech, it may give you insight into the problems of the student. You may find in the cumulative folder some or all of the following information:

[1] See Giles Wilkeson Gray & Claude Merton Wise, *The Bases of Speech*, 3rd ed., New York: Harper & Row, 1959, chap. 5.

1. Personal data including identifying information; family record; health and physical condition; outstanding personality traits; course preferences; recreational, community service, and extracurricular activities; proposed academic schedules; tentative (or final) vocational abilities, aptitudes and interests; future plan of action
2. Academic record
3. Results of standardized tests such as A.C.T., National Merit Scholarship scores, aptitude, ability, achievement, personality, and interest inventories, together with their evaluation by a qualified person
4. Medical and dental record
5. Subjective evaluations such as rating scales, anecdotal records, etc.
6. Results of special tests such as speech correction surveys, vision and hearing tests
7. Autobiography

Preanalysis, however, is only a first step. If it is to be valuable, the analytical process must be continued throughout the entire course. When a problem arises you may find the answer to it by taking a second look at the student's file or by consulting the school counselor. A fact passed over initially may take on new meaning in the light of subsequent behavior and performance. A note of warning: Remember that students' records are confidential and should be treated as such.

Pretest

The next step in planning should provide methods for determining the specific needs, abilities, and potentialities of the students. The most effective way to learn about the students is to conduct early in the term a pretest, both oral and written.

The Speech Data Sheet. A speech data sheet is a questionnaire to be answered by the student at the first class period. The enrollee is asked to supply important background information. Probably each teacher should design a questionnaire to fit his local situation.[2] A sample data sheet is shown on p. 392.

Oral Pretest. The second step in pretesting may involve a performance test which is designed to reveal students' habitual speech. To assure reliability make the test as unobtrusive as possible, not overemphasizing its importance or in some cases even revealing its purpose. When a test is given undue emphasis, some individuals become nervous and perform in an artificial manner. Learning that they are graded on improvement, others

---

[2] For examples of speech data sheets, see the following: Harvey Cromwell, *Working for More Effective Speech, Speech Projects to Accompany Principles and Types of Speech and Principles of Speech,* Glenview, Ill.: Scott, Foresman, 1955, pp. 1–3; Clark S. Carlile, *Brief Project Text for Public Speaking,* New York: Harper & Row, 1957, p. vii; Ray Ehrensberger and Elaine Pagel, *Notebook for Public Speaking,* 2nd ed., Englewood Cliffs, N.J.: Prentice-Hall, 1956, pp. ix–x; Leroy T. Laase, *Speech Project and Drill Book,* rev. ed., Dubuque, Iowa: William C. Brown, 1950, p. 223.

may purposely do poorly in order to be able later to show greater improvement and thus to make a better grade.

The teacher of speech usually seeks information about the following:

1. Knowledge about speech and speaking
2. Proficiency in original speaking
3. Proficiency in oral reading
4. Proficiency in fundamental processes: (a) voice control, (b) vocabulary and use of language, (c) speech rhythm, (d) pronunciation and articulation, (e) control of bodily activity

A complete diagnosis may require several types of activities. For example, in his workbook that accompanies Alan Monroe's *Principles and Types of Speech*, Cromwell suggests four testing assignments:

1. A short oral autobiography
2. The reading aloud of a poem
3. An articulation test passage
4. An intelligibility test[3]

Each teacher should devise a form on which to record systematically his observations, to be retained for future reference.[4]

Recording the Pretest Speech or Material. A part of the pretesting may include a tape or video tape of the student reading a test passage. The selection should be carefully planned to include all of the speech sounds in various combinations. The passage below is one that has been used widely for this purpose.

My Grandfather

You wished to know all about my grandfather. Well, he is nearly ninety-three years old; he dresses himself in an ancient black frock coat, usually minus several buttons; yet he still thinks as swiftly as ever. A long, flowing beard clings to his chin, giving those who observe him a pronounced feeling of the utmost respect. When he speaks, his voice is just a bit cracked and quivers a trifle. Twice each day he plays skillfully with zest upon our small organ. Except in the winter when the ooze of snow or ice prevent, he slowly takes a short walk in the open air each day. We have often urged him to walk more and smoke less, but he always answers, "Banana Oil!" Grandfather likes to be modern in his language.[5]

The best recordings are obtained under conditions in which the student is not distracted by the process. Video tapes are the most desirable method, but a tape recording permits careful evaluation of problems of voice,

---

[3] Cromwell, *op. cit.*, p. 4.
[4] For examples, see the following: Cromwell, "Speech Proficiency Profile," *op. cit.*, pp. 95–100; Leroy T. Laase, "Diagnosis of Speech Needs and Abilities," *Speech Project and Drill Book*, Dubuque, Ia.: William C. Brown, 1950, pp. 224–225.
[5] C. Van Riper, *Speech Correction: Principles and Methods*, 4th ed., Englewood Cliffs, N.J.: Prentice-Hall, 1963, p. 484.

SPEECH DATA SHEET

Name _____ Class _____ Age _____

Address _____ Telephone _____

Your father's occupation or profession _____

Does any member of your family speak in public? Explain _____
_____

Does any member of your family speak a foreign language? _____
   What language? _____ Can you speak this language?_____

Why did you enroll in this speech class? _____
_____ Is it required? _____

Did someone suggest that you enroll in this class? _____ Why? _____
_____

What do you want to accomplish in this speech course? _____
_____

Have you ever made a speech in public? _____ Give occasion. _____
_____

Have you participated in any speech contests? (debate, oratory, extemporaneous speaking, 4-H Club speaking, parliamentary team,
   Boys' or Girls' State?) _____
   Did you win any contests? _____ Did you encounter any
   problems? _____

Have you participated in any plays? At school, church, in a club? ___
_____

Have you had any previous speech courses? _____

Have you taken speech lessons? _____ Have you ever worked on
   speech improvement? _____ Have you worked with a speech
   clinician (or correctionist)? _____

What kind of problem did you work on? _____

Do you like to listen to speeches? _____ Go to plays? _____

Who are your favorite speakers? _____

Why do you like these speakers? _____

Would you like to speak like any of these speakers? _____

What occupation or profession are you planning to enter? _____
_____

What is your major or favorite subject? _____

Name other subjects in which you excel. _____

Would you like to participate in any of the extracurricular speech
   activities? _____ debate _____; extemporaneous speaking _____;
   oratory _____; radio production _____; plays _____; interpretative
   reading _____; speech club _____; other activities _____

Are you interested in majoring in speech? _____ Why? _____
_____

Additional information obtained during personal interview:

rhythm, pronunciation, and articulation. Either voices or video tapes may serve as the basis of personal conferences. Later they may be compared with subsequent recordings to determine progress and achievement.

STUDENT NEEDS AND TEACHER STANDARDS

The teacher must establish standards that are neither too advanced nor too elementary for students. To gear the course too far above them results in frustration and discouragement; if it is too low they are likely to waste time. A beginning teacher illustrates the point in the following excerpt:

My first three weeks of teaching speech have been a disappointment to me. I planned a wonderful course and started the class with high expectations. The first day I told the students what I expected of them, read them my objectives, and assigned the first speech exercise. Much to my sorrow the speeches were terrible. I have never heard students with such poor speech. Many words are mispronounced, and what's worse, they don't seem to care. Two students refused to speak and consequently dropped after the first week. Finally I checked their records and then had a personal interview with each student. The results are appalling. None of them has ever made a speech before, and most of them admitted that they have never heard a speech. I had no idea that students would take speech if they couldn't even talk. With this class I am not going to be able to uphold any of the standards we talked about in methods class—certainly, none on the level which I feel a speech teacher should uphold. . . . I am now so disgusted that I am giving the class sixth grade assignments. If anything, this has made the situation worse because they feel that the work is so simple that I am wasting their time. . . .

Standards, then, should be determined by the needs and abilities of the students rather than by arbitrary goals that are unrealistic. Start with the students where they are, not where you think they should be.

OBJECTIVES

In the light of student needs and abilities the teacher must determine what he hopes the student will achieve in a course or units. This determination is stated in the form of objectives. From these aims he will select subject matter, teaching methods, and student activities, and he will formulate the several kinds of evaluations to measure outcomes.

National Objectives

There are various kinds and types of objectives for several levels of planning. For example, the broadest, most comprehensive kinds of objectives are those educational aims formulated by national and regional committees. The famous *Cardinal Principles of Secondary Education* of 1918,[6] the Educational Policies Commission's objectives published in 1939,[7] the educational objectives issued by *The Committee for the White House Conference on Education* in 1956,[8] and the statement of the *Phi Delta Kappa Commission on Education and Human Rights*[9] are examples of broad national aims. Each of these statements is of utmost value reflecting the educational needs of the time for which each purports to speak. Briefly interpreted, the *Cardinal Principles* were directed toward needs made obvious by the high illiteracy rate found among World War I American soldiers. The Educational Policies Commission objectives reflected the economic conditions of the country in 1938; the White House Conference's aims sought to clarify the world citizen's role, while the *Phi Delta Kappa Commission on Education and Human Rights* is directed toward educating for social justice.

Even though these broad national aims for education serve as guidelines for regional and state curriculum planning committees and even though every teacher is ultimately affected by them, such statements are too general to be of immediate value to the teacher in planning units and courses. However, no attempt is made here to minimize the value of these national objectives. On the contrary these aims may help the teacher develop his philosophy of education which in turn determines what and how he teaches. For this reason every teacher should acquaint himself with those broad inclusive objectives for education. They are readily available in numerous educational texts and journals.

Institutional Objectives

Another level of educational objectives includes aims formulated by a particular school. Like the various national goals, school objectives are directive in nature. They encompass the school's philosophy and articulate guidelines for the school's several curricula and disciplines. Not only do they reflect national educational aims, but they also are consistent with the purposes of the regional accrediting association in which the school holds membership. Such objectives are formulated by the school's administrators and faculty, and although they may not be classified as instructional objectives, the school's aims have a direct bearing upon unit and course planning.

[6] *Cardinal Principles of Secondary Education*, Bureau of Education (now Department of Health, Education, and Welfare), Washington, D.C., pp. 11–15.
[7] *The Journal of the National Education Association*, February, 1939, 28:48–49.
[8] *The Committee for the White House Conference on Education*, April, 1956, pp. 91–92.
[9] *Phi Delta Kappan*, April, 1968, 48:418–419.

Resource Objectives

Yet another kind of objective directly influencing classroom instructional aims is the resource objective. Usually these aims are general in scope and are prepared by members of a particular department for use in building units and courses. They function to insure articulation or sequence of units and courses, promote consistency of purposes within the department, and aid individual teachers in planning units and courses. Their importance is that they emphasize teaching outcomes rather than learning outcomes. For example, "To discover the speech inadequacies and deficiencies of the student and by a process of reeducation redirect the functioning of his mechanism through a series of progressive speaking experiences"[10] states precisely what the teacher plans to achieve in the course.

In all of the above mentioned kinds of objectives, except the resource objectives, emphasis is placed upon broad, long-ranged educational outcomes and the acquaintance of desirable understandings, beliefs, and attitudes. No one course or even several courses may accomplish completely such objectives. In essence these objectives are the desirable ends of education itself established as guides to direct the planning of the curricula that may lead to their fulfillment.

Instructional Objectives

The remaining kinds of goals, the classroom instructional objectives, apply directly to course planning and are, therefore, of paramount concern for the teacher. One conceivably could teach without considering the other kinds of objectives, but attempting to teach successfully without clearly enunciated instructional aims is virtually impossible. For this reason the remainder of this chapter deals with the theory and application of classroom instructional objectives, usually classified as general instructional objectives and specific instructional objectives.

General Instructional Objectives. Statements of the broad outcomes expected from a particular course or unit are called general instructional objectives. Basically this type of objective should be peculiar to the specific course. For example, the general informational objectives for physics should be different from those of English; those for beginning speech should be different from those for advanced debate. This concept is based on the theory that each discipline has an inherent structure different from any other subject. Nevertheless, every course should include some general instructional objectives, common to all subjects. To illustrate, the general instructional objective *appreciates scholarship* should be a goal for each

10 Harry G. Barnes, "Teaching the Fundamentals of Speech at the College Level," *Speech Teacher*, November, 1954, 3:242–243.

course in the curriculum. The teacher of speech lists it as a general instructional objective the same as teachers of chemistry, Latin, or history. In the scheme of education each course must assure learning outcomes which direct the student toward the achievement of the broader aims of education.

In the process of planning, the general instructional objectives serve a unique function: (1) they state the general outcomes as the desired end product of instruction that serves to fulfill the broad educational objectives, and (2) they result in the derivation of specific instructional objectives that in turn "specify behavior we are willing to accept as evidence of the attainment of that objective."[11]

In writing general instructional objectives the teacher must focus on learning outcomes rather than on the teaching process. For example, "To give the student understanding of a correct attitude toward the speaking situation"[12] clearly emphasizes the teaching process rather than defines learning outcomes. To direct the above objective toward the learning outcome it is necessary to restate it in the following manner: Demonstrates the correct attitudes toward the speaking situation. In the first instance the evaluation would test the instructor's ability to give the understanding; therefore, the teacher is evaluating himself rather than the student. On the other hand the second example focuses on the outcome of learning that requires the student to demonstrate his understanding in an observable way.

The following list of general instructional objectives for a beginning speech course should further illustrate the nature and purpose of these objectives in planning:

1. Recognizes the esthetic interests in oral interpretation.
2. Analyzes propositions of policy in persuasive speaking.
3. Demonstrates control of oral language.
4. Understands speech organization.
5. Appreciates stage direction.
6. Recognizes debate as a democratic process.

From the above list it should be observed that the initial verbs are understood to refer to outcomes on the part of the learner. In writing objectives it is unnecessary to begin such phrases as, "The student appreciates, the student should be able to demonstrate," or "the student should recognize." As Gronlund has pointed out, "There is no need to add such refinements. . . . The less wordy the objective, the better."[13] Furthermore, many of the verbs employed in the general instructional objectives are abstractions that of themselves are incapable of demonstrative learning

---

[11] Norman E. Gronlund, *Stating Behavioral Objectives for Classroom Instruction*, New York: Macmillan, 1970, p. 4.
[12] Barnes, *op. cit.*, pp. 242–243.
[13] Gronlund, *op. cit.*, p. 2.

outcomes. Take, for example, the verb *appreciate*. What does it mean? To paraphrase Stuart Chase, for such words there isn't a referent in a carload.[14] Yet to use the verbs *appreciate, comprehend, translate, evaluate,* or *interpret* in general instructional objectives is quite appropriate. Obviously then the general instructional objectives must be translated into terms that are demonstrative or that give evidence of the behavior implied by the abstraction.

Specific Instructional Objectives. After selecting and developing general instructional objectives the teacher is then able to prepare the specific instructional objectives. Because this class of instructional goals is stated in terms denoting learning outcomes of students they are behavioral objectives. Succinctly expressed, behavioral objectives are instructional goals designed to define and delineate learning experiences that are empirically measurable. To be more specific, behavioral instructional objectives state precisely the behavior (learning experience) expected of the student in language that directs the student to demonstrate overtly that behavior (empirically measurable). As has been seen, the specific instructional objectives are the concrete translations of the general instructional objectives and are the specific behaviors to be achieved by the student through a specific lesson or a series of lessons in a unit or course. The following are examples of the specific instructional objectives:

I. Recognizes the esthetic interests in oral interpretation.
   A. Identifies images described by poets.
   B. Verbalizes passages which are unusual.
   C. Differentiates between rhythmical and nonrhythmical stanzas.
   D. Selects appealing phrases.
   E. Paraphrases author's idea.
II. Analyzes propositions of policy in persuasive speaking.
   A. Differentiates between pertinent and irrelevant material.
   B. Evaluates divisions of the proposition.
   C. Compares material for validity.
   D. Searches for faulty reasoning.
   E. Concludes the worth of the premise.
III. Demonstrates control of oral language.
   A. Imitates the physical activity in the creation of sounds.
   B. Repeats the sounds in isolation.
   C. Structures the words into groups.
   D. Accents through use of volume, rate, and pitch.
   E. Synthesizes sounds into meaningful units.
IV. Understands speech organization.
   A. Formulates main theme.
   B. Categorizes arguments.
   C. Compiles evidence.
   D. Locates deviations in arrangement of ideas.
   E. Arranges material in outline form.

[14] Stuart Chase, *The Proper Study of Mankind,* rev. ed., New York: Harper & Row, 1956, pp. 285 ff.

V. Appreciates stage direction.
   A. Contrasts area movement.
   B. Identifies individual and group posturing.
   C. Compares choreographic movement for comic and tragic themes.
   D. Substitutes movement for open and closed scenes.
   E. Directs stage movement.
VI. Recognizes debate as a democratic process.
   A. Identifies the main issues.
   B. Evaluates evidence.
   C. Formulates logical arguments.
   D. Attends to both sides of the argument.
   E. Deduces that debate is superior to force.

A most significant study of objectives is the *Taxonomy of Educational Objectives.*[15] In its present form it contains two major divisions: the cognitive domain and the affective domain. A third, the psychomotor, domain is incomplete at this writing. The cognitive area is concerned with those goals directed toward intellectual achievement; the affective domain includes objectives directed toward emotional, conceptual, and attitudinal achievements. Psycho-motor objectives categorize the motor skills such as handwriting, typing, driving, and, in general, physical activities and sports. No doubt, when completed, the psychomotor domain will be of tremendous value to speech instruction.

The categories in each domain describe the various levels of learning arranged in hierarchical order proceeding from the simplest thinking processes to the most complex. In each instance learning processes are described in terms of learning outcomes and are, therefore, readily adaptable to the development of behavioral objectives. Taken from the taxonomy, the following categories and their descriptions are simplified:

Cognitive Domain

1. Knowledge: Remembers, recalls, or recognizes previously learned information.
2. Comprehension: Demonstrates understanding of material by translating information into a different language or symbolic form.
3. Application: Transfers learning to different skills, concepts, and situations.
4. Analysis: Resolves material into its parts in order to identify and classify its structure.
5. Synthesis: Relates the parts of information to one another in a meaningful pattern or new structure.

Affective Domain

1. Receiving: Receives and attends to phenomena and stimuli willingly.
2. Responding: Demonstrates interests in scholarship by voluntarily performing obligations and duties beyond minimum requirements.

[15] B. S. Bloom (ed.), *Taxonomy of Educational Objectives Handbook I: Cognitive Domain,* New York: McKay, 1956; D. R. Krathwohl (ed.), *Taxonomy of Educational Objectives Handbook II: Affective Domain,* New York: McKay, 1964.

3. Valuing: Reveals by overt behavior the values, attitudes, and appreciations for objects, phenomena, and actions.
4. Organization: Formulates a life style that is harmonious and internally consistent with abilities and beliefs.
5. Characterization by a value or value complex: Demonstrates over a sufficient period of time behavior that is controlled by a value system and is pervasive, consistent, and predictable.

Since the taxonomy for the psychomotor domain is incomplete no attempt is made here to describe its major categories. Perhaps a few general instructional objectives in the psychomotor domain will suffice to demonstrate its value to speech.

Psychomotor Domain

1. Demonstrates skill in bodily control.
2. Performs oral skills acceptably.
3. Demonstrates control of facial expression.

When the teacher begins to make his plan he should ask himself if the material and the needs of his students warrant the use of all three domains. In most speech courses and units it is desirable to employ all three inasmuch as the three domains give greater scope and satisfaction to the learning experiences and facilitate testing.

The hierarchical arrangement of the learning processes is designed to secure more comprehensive and meaningful outcomes. Using only the knowledge category of the cognitive domain typifies all too many courses. Too often an entire course is nothing more than memorization of isolated facts and the spewing back of that data. Memory alone is frequently irrelevant and unrelated. However, by utilizing both the memory and the comprehension categories a more complex level of learning is achieved. Memory, the simplest level of the cognitive domain, is essential to each succeeding level as are the other four levels. "Each category is assumed to include the behavior at the lower levels. Thus comprehension includes the behavior at the knowledge level, application includes that at both the knowledge and comprehension levels, and so on."[16]

The other types of learning should be and must be employed. The teacher should be aware of the other categories of learning outcomes that may more intelligently satisfy the demands of educational aims. From the taxonomy, then, one chooses the kind of learning desired and formulates general instructional objectives. From those objectives he evolves his specific instructional objectives.

The more definite and concrete the objectives are, the more meaningful and practical they become in the planning process. Francis Bacon's famous exhortation that "writing maketh an exact man" should be remembered when the teacher begins to consider what the course is to achieve. Often

[16] Gronlund, op. cit., p. 19.

he may feel that he has a clear view of the aims of education and of the general instructional objectives, only to find in the process of writing them down that he does not.

Once the objectives have been determined, the teacher should then turn to the principles of course planning that affect directly the selection of materials and activities, teaching methods, and student evaluation. These principles have a dual function. In the first instance, they are principles of planning; in the second, they are principles of teaching. This double purpose demonstrates forcefully that planning and teaching methods are conceived at the same time.

MEANS OF IMPLEMENTING THE OBJECTIVES

Select Materials and Activities That Facilitate Learning and Skills

The teacher should plan for materials and activities that lead directly to the realization of the course objectives. There are no set rules about how many activities or what materials should be used, apart from the nature of the course and the needs of the students. Too, there are no rules for arranging the activities and materials in the course plan except the nature of the content being studied at the time. If, for example, the students are studying the principles of speech organization, the oral activity should provide practice in organization. Materials and activities should be ordered depending on their relationship to the content that they explain or demonstrate. In the study of speech the materials must contribute to the understanding of the principles of speech; the activities must provide the students with a variety of speaking experiences. Harry Barnes warns that "the course should not be divided into units of speaking theory and practice. Such theory should be taught through participation in speaking situations."[17] Under no circumstances should materials and activities be used as mere busywork.

Teach One Principle at a Time

The successful speaker does not emerge full blown from Zeus' head. Nor is there a magic wand that the teacher can wave suddenly to make a student into an effective performer. He becomes an accomplished speaker as he understands the principles and masters the skills that underlie successful oral communication. Usually this process is long and arduous. In course planning the teacher should (1) choose the principle, (2) select the methods and materials, and (3) provide for oral activities by which the student learns and puts the principle into practice. Only in this way can

[17] Barnes, op. cit., p. 244.

the student master each principle and move toward a more complete mastery.

Teach Principles and Practice Progressively

Speech principles should be taught progressively, beginning with the simplest ones and proceeding successively to the more complex. For example, in a beginning unit in public speaking the teacher may wish to consider first how to conquer excessive stage fright—one of the most severe problems for large numbers of beginners. In developing speech organization the teacher may follow a sequence such as the following: (1) the one-point organization, (2) organization of the informative speech, and (3) the organization of the argumentative speech.

Successive assignments may be arranged in the following progressive order:

1. Stage fright
2. Control of bodily activities
3. Simple content analysis
4. One-point organization
5. Organization of informative speeches
6. Organization of argumentative speeches

Throughout the course each succeeding phase is build on the preceding one. As soon as the student demonstrates proficiency in one phase, the next assignment should incorporate all principles previously learned, in addition to the new and more advanced principle.

Base Practice on Theory

The aphorism that practice makes perfect is not necessarily true. Practice may actually lead to imperfection if it is the wrong kind of practice. A "duffer" golfer may be able to hit a golf ball by swinging the club as he would a baseball bat; but until he learns the proper stance, grip, and follow through, his chances of developing an effective swing are doubtful even if he practices every day. The wrong kind of practice serves only to fix bad habits. Golf is a learned sport based on principles that differ greatly from natural inclinations; therefore, the beginning golfer must unlearn many of his previous habits before he can develop skill in driving and chipping. Until he has mastered fundamental principles he will never be anything more than mediocre.

A striking analogy exists between the learning of golf and the learning of speech. In many instances speech, like golf, requires considerable unlearning of previous habits. Because a student has been talking for 15 or even 20 years does not imply categorically that he is an effective oral communicator. Nor will day-by-day repetitions of bad speech habits in the classroom make him a good speaker. The teacher must help him acquire desirable speech habits by providing opportunities for supervised practice. Practice alone, however, is not sufficient; all speech performances must be based on sound theory. Until the student understands the reasons for knowing the principles, and learns them, improvement in speech skills is likely to be superficial. McBurney says, "If practice in speaking is to be useful, it should be informed practice. The practice should involve the application of principles which are known and understood, and it should be followed by competent criticism so that mistakes are identified and methods for improvement suggested."[18]

Provide an Encouraging Atmosphere

Many students enter a beginning speech course with misconceptions of the nature and content of the course, as well as of what is to be expected of them in class. They suddenly find themselves in a situation in which they are required to unlearn some of their old speech habits, learn new ones, and participate in activities that have been wholly or partially foreign to them. Often they become frustrated when they learn that their habitual speech is substandard and that what they have been doing all their lives is considered bad speech practice. Some students become discouraged because they are unable to distinguish between sounds or because they can see no progress in their speech work. Often they complain that they were better speakers before they knew anything about speech. These and many other discouraging problems arise in speech classes and will, if not properly handled by the teacher, develop into major emotional problems.

The suggestions that follow may help in developing an encouraging atmosphere:

1. Make the speech classroom as inviting and pleasant as possible, yet business-like.
2. Explain that speech is a learned art and that everyone profits from a study of speech.
3. Point out that students learn from one another in speech; they should work together to achieve their individual goals.
4. Be friendly, understanding, and enthusiastic toward the students. Let them know that you are interested in them as individuals.
5. Set a good example for the students by your own speech practices.
6. Establish the proper attitude concerning criticism:
   a. Explain that criticism is the process by which the teacher reveals the diagnosis and appraisal of the speech performance, and this enables the student to know his strengths and weaknesses so that he may improve his speech.

[18] James H. McBurney, "Fact and Fancy in Teaching People How to Speak," *University of Missouri Bulletin*, November, 1955, 56:27.

b. Impress on the students that criticism is a significant part of the learning process. It is evaluation directed toward improvement.
c. Stress the fact that criticism is never a personal attack on the individual.

Discouragement is not peculiar to beginning students only, nor is it peculiar to the first few days of class. Students may become disgruntled when they feel that what they are studying is of no value to them or when they are confronted with assignments that seem too difficult. Although possible problems of this nature are infinite, some can be anticipated and provided for. The following suggestions may prevent these difficulties:

1. The teacher should relate the course to the motives of the students.
2. The teacher should provide the students with experiences in which they can be successful and take pride.
3. The teacher should plan activities to carry learning beyond the classroom.

Provide a Challenging Atmosphere

If a student is to be encouraged to do his very best, course materials and activities should challenge, not his minimum, but his *maximum*, level of attainment. Teachers who permit students to "get by" in a course are guilty of malpractice. "Snap" courses are the laughing stock of the school, and ambitious students shun them. Only students looking for an easy way out seek them; the better students who are forced to enroll become dissatisfied and restless, feeling that their time is being wasted.

No teacher worthy of the name would deliberately hold "snap" courses, but teachers often underestimate the capabilities of their students. If the original plans do not provide challenging materials and activities, they should be reevaluated and revised.

Coordinate Classroom with Cocurricular Instruction

Fortunately, speech students can be given assignments both in and out of class that will challenge them to work at their maximum levels. Because cocurricular activities are an integral part of a good speech program, they should be planned in conjunction with the course. Public speaking, debate, interpretative reading, and dramatics provide the motivation for better work in speech, and the rewards are often more stimulating than classroom assignments alone.

FORMULATION OF THE PLAN

Basically there are three types of plans that the teacher may use in building a course—the term, the unit, and the daily lesson plan. Course plans and daily lesson plans are essential to every course; the unit may be optional for college courses, but it is highly recommended for high school speech instruction.

The course plan presents the overall program and should be made before the teacher attempts to prepare either a unit or a daily lesson plan. In reality, the course plan is the broad outline which must be supplemented by units or daily lesson plans.

A unit plan is developed around a significant area of learning. The types of units most generally used are the subject-matter unit, the experience unit, and the combination subject-matter—experience unit. Subject-matter units are centered on a subject topic. Public speaking, discussion, debate, interpretative reading, radio and television, and drama may be developed into units in a fundamentals course. In a course in public speaking a significant area of learning, such as analysis, may be developed into a unit. Units in debate may be built on such topics as evidence, developing the brief, etc. Each course has divisions of content that can be made into units of study.

Experience units are usually social-centered and deal with real problems and situations. For example, students may choose an actual local problem to debate in class, such as improved housing and slum clearance. In one community where there was a campaign under way to raise property assessments, speech students were asked to present their views on the subject before a public meeting of the city council. Such activities provide the student with experiences in dealing with sociological problems which, if handled properly, create interest far beyond purely subject-centered units.

The third type, the combination subject-matter experience unit, provides for both subject content and experience situations. In speech classes where the oral activities are real experiences, members of the class become an audience. This type of unit has found wide acceptance.

Even though the unit may be developed spontaneously, it must achieve the purposes of the term plan. Only in this way can the course have continuity of purpose and direction. The teacher must not permit a class to drift uncharted.

Daily lesson plans are outlines that contain the specific instructional objectives, materials, activities, and methods for specific lessons. Though they are essential to all teaching because they are the lessons to be learned, the activities to be performed, there are no rules concerning how complete daily lesson plans should be. This determination is dictated by the needs and experiences of the individual instructor. Daily lesson plans for units are usually shorter than those for nonunit courses. The unit plan itself should be complete making the development of daily lesson plans an easy task.

Regardless of the type of plan used, the teacher should make a daily lesson plan for each meeting or period. No teacher should attempt to teach a class without first determining exactly what he is going to do, even though he may have a course plan and a unit plan. Teachers who digress in class while they collect their thoughts are wasting valuable time, a commodity the student can ill afford. Formats for the course plan and daily lesson plan and a complete unit are found below.

A Format for the Course Plan

    I. Name of course
   II. Dates, number of lessons, and length of time for course
  III. Statement of philosophy: Educational point of view and speech philosophy
  IV. Objectives for the course
      A. Educational objectives
      B. General course objectives
      C. Specific course objectives. (In the course plan the specific objectives must be tentative.)
   V. An overview of the course—a statement of what the course is to include and how it is to be taught
  VI. Material for the course
      A. Teacher references, etc.
      B. Students' materials
 VII. Tentative activities for the course
VIII. Motivational ideas
  IX. Methods for teaching lessons
   X. Assignments
      A. Number of assignments
      B. Type of assignments

A Format for the Daily Lesson Plan

    I. Name of course
   II. Date and number of the lesson
  III. Statement of the objectives
      A. Educational objective
      B. General course objective
      C. Specific objective
  IV. Materials for the lesson
   V. Activities
  VI. Methods
 VII. Lesson. (In this step the lesson may be adapted to the needs of the individual instructor. Some may use a brief topical outline, others a more complete plan.)
VIII. Assignment

A Complete Unit Plan

   I. Title of the unit: Parliamentary procedure is a democratic process.
  II. Objectives for the unit: In the cognitive domain the categories of knowledge and comprehension are utilized. Within the affective domain the categories of receiving, responding, and valuing are employed.
      A. Cognitive domain
        1. Knows specific data. (General instructional objective)

        a. Describes terms that belong to the parliamentary procedure vo-
           cabulary.
        b. Identifies motions that are designed for specific purposes.
        c. Outlines the steps in presenting motions.
        d. Lists the methods of voting.
    2. Understands the fundamental principles of parliamentary procedure.
       (General instructional objectives)
        a. Explains how parliamentary procedure assures equality of rights.
        b. Gives examples that evidence the rule of the majority and the
           protection of the minority.
        c. Summarizes the rights of discussion and the rights of information.
        d. Defends the idea of fairness and good faith.
 B. Affective domain
    1. Demonstrates interest in the subject. (General instructional objec-
       tive)
        a. Asks questions related to the practice of parliamentary procedure.
        b. Follows discussion attentively.
        c. Chooses correct terminology.
        d. Gives divisions of motions.
    2. Participates in classroom practice of parliamentary procedure. (Gen-
       eral instructional objective)
        a. Presents ideas and motions in proper form.
        b. Answers inquiries of the teacher and classmates.
        c. Conforms to the parliamentary procedure rules.
        d. Presents additional information on the subject.
    3. Applies parliamentary procedure knowledge to other situations.
       (General instructional objective)
        a. Proposes the use of parliamentary procedure in other disciplines.
        b. Initiates the planning and organizing of committees to speak on
           parliamentary procedure.
        c. Follows parliamentary procedure principles in school organiza-
           tions.
        d. Studies procedures used by local, state, and national governing
           bodies.
III. Material to extend and complement the unit
 A. Printed material
    1. Auer, J. Jeffery, *Essentials of Parliamentary Procedure*, 3rd ed., New
       York: Appleton-Century-Crofts, 1959.
    2. Robert, Henry M., *Robert's Rules of Order*, rev. ed., Glenview, Ill.:
       Scott, Foresman, 1951.
    3. Sturgis, Alice, *Sturgis Standard Code of Parliamentary Procedure*,
       New York: McGraw-Hill, 1966.
    4. Wiksell, Wesley, *How to Conduct Meetings*, New York: Harper &
       Row, 1966.
    5. Text
 B. Audiovisual
    1. Films of committees, conferences, and organizations employing
       parliamentary procedure.
    2. Records
    3. Overhead projectors
    4. Tape recorders
    5. Speaker

IV. Overview: This unit will provide the student with theory and practice relating to parliamentary procedure. A knowledge of the development and purpose of parliamentary procedure will demonstrate the value of such a code in a deliberative society.

V. Content of the Unit
  A. Subject matter
      1. Structure of the formal group
      2. Motions
      3. Meetings
      4. Order of business
      5. Debate
      6. Voting
      7. Nominations and elections
      8. Officers
      9. Committees
      10. Minutes
      11. Rules and authorities
      12. Constitution, bylaws, and standing rules
  B. Stages of the unit
      1. Introduction
          a. Discussion of situations where deliberation is essential (2 days)
          b. Organization of four committees paralleling the four classifications of motions (2 days)
      2. Development
          a. Conduct meetings (2 days)
          b. Discussion and practice of order of business (show film; 3 days)
          c. Presentation of various motions and the disposal of those motions (use overhead projector and tape recorders; 3 days)
          d. Analysis of authority for parliamentary procedure; emphasis on members, officers, elections, and minutes (guest speaker; 3 days)
          e. Structure and organization and practice parliamentary procedure (use records; 4 days)
      3. Culmination
          a. Evaluation
              (1) Tests
              (2) Observations
              (3) Critical examination
          b. Transition into following unit

EXERCISES

1. Discuss what you would do if the school's policy were contrary to your philosophy of education.
2. Discuss the following statements which students often make about teachers concerning planning:
    a. The reason I failed was that the teacher did not have her course organized.
    b. The teacher wouldn't answer my questions because it got him off his lesson plan.
    c. The class is interesting, but the teacher never gets around to the subject.
3. Discuss the following attitudes teachers sometimes have about course planning:
    a. Course planning is fine for student teachers, but experienced teachers don't need to plan.
    b. I am so busy teaching I don't have time to make a course plan.

c. If you *know* your subject, planning is a waste of time.
4. Discuss the advantages and disadvantages of using the textbook organization as a substitute for course planning.
5. Discuss the advantages and disadvantages of using a course of study (standardized course plan) as a substitute for your own course plan.
6. Write three general instructional objectives for the cognitive and the affective domains. Subsume two specific instructional objectives for each general instructional object for a unit in speech.

REFERENCES

Books

BLOOM, BENJAMIN S. (ED.), *Taxonomy of Education Objectives Handbook I: Cognitive Domain,* New York: McKay, 1956.

BOROUGHS, HOMER, JR., FOSTER, CLIFFORD D., AND SLAYER, RUFUS C., JR., *Introduction to Secondary School Teaching,* New York: Ronald Press, 1964.

CHASE, STUART, *The Proper Study of Mankind,* rev. ed., New York: Harper & Row, 1956.

GRAY, GILES WILKESON AND WISE, CLAUDE MERTON, *The Bases of Speech,* 3rd ed., New York: Harper & Row, 1959.

GRONLUND, NORMAN E., *Stating Behavioral Objectives for Classroom Instruction,* New York: Macmillan, 1970.

KRATHWOHL, D. R. (ED.), *Taxonomy of Education Objectives Handbook II: Affective Domain,* New York: McKay, 1964.

LEWIS, GEORGE L., EVERETT, RUSSELL, GIBSON, JAMES W., AND SCHOEN, KATHRYN T., *Teaching Speech,* Columbus, Oh.: Charles E. Merrill, 1969.

MC ASHAN, H. H., *Writing Behavioral Objectives: A New Approach,* New York: Harper & Row, 1970.

MAGER, ROBERT F., *Preparing Instructional Objectives,* Palo Alto, Calif.: Fearon,1962.

SANDERS, NORRIS M., *Classroom Questions: What Kinds?,* New York: Harper & Row, 1966.

VAN RIPER, CHARLES, *Speech Correction, Principles and Methods,* 4th ed., Englewood Cliffs, N.J.: Prentice-Hall, 1963.

Magazine Articles

BAKER, ELDON E., "Aligning Speech Evaluation and Behavioral Objectives," *Speech Teacher,* March, 1967, 16:158–160.

CLARK, RICHARD W. AND NELSON, OLIVER W., "Standards for Appraising and Building High School Speech Programs," *Speech Teacher,* September, 1969, 18:181–186.

CORTRIGHT, HENRIETTA, NILES, DORIS S., AND WEIRICH, DOROTHY Q., "Criteria to Evaluate Speech I in the Senior High School," *Speech Teacher,* September, 1968, 17:217–224.

"Fundamentals of Speech: A Basic Course for High School," *Speech Teacher,* March, 1959, 8:93–113.

GRUNER, CHARLES R., "Behavioral Objectives for the Grading of Classroom Speeches," *Speech Teacher,* September, 1968, 17:207–209.

HANCE, KENNETH G. (ED.), "Public Address in the Secondary School," *Bulletin of the National Association of Secondary School Principals,* May, 1952, 36 (187).

KAUFFMAN, ELLEN, "Meeting Specific Speech Needs in the Public Schools: The Speech Program in a Teachers College," *Speech Teacher,* January, 1957, 6:36–42.

KIBLER, ROBERT J., BARKER, LARRY L., AND CEGALA, DONALD J., "Behavioral Objectives and Speech Communication Instruction," *Central States Speech Journal,* Summer, 1970, 21:71–80.

KONIGSBERG, EVELYN, "An Outline Course of Stury in Dramatics," *Speech Teacher*, January 1955, 4:27–31.

MC BURNEY, JAMES H., "Fact and Fancy in Teaching People How to Speak," *University of Missouri Bullein*, November, 1955, 56: 23–30.

SEABURY, HUGH F., "Objectives and Scope of the Fundamentals Course in Speech in the High School," *Speech Teacher*, March, 1954, 3:117–120.

20. Selecting a Speech Textbook

Oran Teague

Recently the author met a teacher who declared with considerable pride that she taught her course without a textbook. To her, this was a sign of good teaching. She said she could find no book that was consistent with her ideas of how her subject should be presented. When asked how she conducted her class, she explained that she let her students develop their own textbook, drawing on newspapers, magazine articles, government pamphlets, and whatever else seemed appropriate. This no-textbook method may work for the teacher who is extremely well informed and who has great stacks of material close at hand, enough to provide each student with an ample supply, and who has the help of a diligent librarian, willing to search for supplementary materials.

But hazards are often encountered in classes conducted without textbooks. Students frequently declare that these courses are not well organized, that materials are not easy to find, and that course requirements are not clearly set forth. At the end of the term they complain that they have difficulty in reviewing and synthesizing what they have learned.

A good textbook makes teaching easier. More important, it provides a common core around which to build a syllabus. Furthermore, it helps conserve precious class time by making available an explanation of principles and of procedures that need not be discussed at length during class period. Likewise a good textbook offers supplementary teaching materials such as speech models and study questions which stimulate class discussion. The wise teacher, of course, adapts the textbook to his local requirements, and supplements weak chapters with outside readings. The begin-

410

ning teacher especially should look to a textbook for guidance in the presentation of his subject.

Whether he settles for a single textbook or a multiple-book approach, he cannot escape the responsibility of a thorough analysis of his materials. Indeed, he will be naive if he relies solely on a publisher's representative to sell him or if he makes his selection on the basis of the sound of the title, the color of the cover, or even the extent of the adoption list, so conveniently available in advance fliers. He must decide whether a book or books advance his philosophy, his course goals, his departmental requirements, and the needs and abilities of the students. He of course will want to determine whether he can adapt the book to his syllabus or prepare a syllabus that fits the book. In studying a new book he will probably follow four steps.

1. Consult as many reviews of the book in leading journals as possible.
2. Read the book from cover to cover.
3. Compare it with other leading books in the field.
4. Make a systematic evaluation.

STUDY THE REVIEWS OF THE BOOK

Before attempting a systematic analysis, it will probably help the teacher to get an overview of the text by consulting several reviews. Some people, however, prefer to reverse this order: that is, they first study the book carefully, and then compare their impressions with those of reviewers. Regardless of which comes first, the book review sections of leading national and regional journals provide reliable insight into values of new publications. Generally, the book review editors have taken care to select reviewers who are recognized for professional competency, intellectual breadth, and balanced judgment.[1] In a good review the reader may expect such information as follows:

1. Who the author is
2. Important bibliographical data including publisher, place of publication, date of publication, number of pages, and price
3. The level of instruction for which the book is planned
4. A statement about the philosophy, purposes, and methods of the book
5. A summary or resume of the contents
6. An estimate of the place of the book in the field
7. An evaluation of supplementary teaching aids and materials
8. Comparison of the book with others in the field
9. The reviewer's opinion concerning outstanding and noteworthy features, chapters, and sections

[1] A. Craig Baird & Gladys Borchers, "What We Expect of a Book Review," *Quarterly Journal of Speech*, February, 1951, 37:81–86.

10. The reviewer's opinion concerning omissions, misrepresentations, and faulty scholarship
11. The reviewer's overall evaluation of the book

DETERMINE THE AUTHOR'S PROFESSIONAL COMPETENCY

A book is the expression of an author's philosophy, purposes, experience, and research. The reviewer will find his task easier if he can first learn something about the background, training, and reputation of the author. In this search he may look for answers to such questions as the following:

Has he expressed and expounded on an educational and speech philosophy?
What is the author's training?
How did the author arrive at his philosophy and conclusions?
What recognition has the author received from professional and honorary organizations?
Is he recognized as a good teacher and thorough scholar?
Do his other writings and professional activities suggest competency in his field?

A brief biographical sketch, often promotional in nature, frequently accompanies the review copy. In addition, the reviewer may locate other facts in association directories, professional journals, and bibliographies. Such information may also be found in *Who's Who in America, Who's Who in American Education*, and similar volumes. When possible, the reviewer will seek opportunities to hear writers at national meetings and perhaps to make their personal acquaintance. He can then ponder whether or not they practice what they preach.

Closely related to the qualifications of the author is the standing of the publisher. The reviewer should consider, if at all possible, the publisher's reputation for careful editing and selective publication. Established companies are likely to issue better books than the unknown ones. The reader should of course be suspicious of privately printed books, those issued under the imprint of unknown firms, and those that show inferior craftsmanship.

ANALYZE CONTENT AND ORGANIZATION

What Does the Preface Reveal?

Many persons believe that there is no point in reading the preface of a book. They think of this section as an afterthought which contributes nothing to the main development. With some books this observation, unfortunately, is true, but with many the preface gives the author's declaration of intentions, his philosophical point of view, and his acknowledgment of sources. The reader needs to look for statements like the following:

This book is for all who are interested in rational decision making. It is designed specifically for the undergraduate course in argumentation, but may be used in any broadly liberal course designed for students who seek self-realization as individual personalities and who desire to prepare themselves for effective participation in a democratic society.[2]

This is a textbook for speech improvement. The aim is to study speaking as a distinctly human activity, which, though varied in its different forms and uses, consists always and basically of certain characteristic processes. These elements are both psychological and symbolic, both mental and organic, both covert and overt. Together they constitute a uniquely human function.[3]

Principles of Speaking is written primarily for the beginning student in speech, whether he is an undergraduate college student or an adult who seeks to improve his skills in oral communication. Its content is related to everyday occasions, not necessarily "large-auditorium" speeches; and it is developed upon the concept that most speaking opportunities arise out of specific occasions rather than out of free choices made by the speaker well in advance of the speaking situation.[4]

My purpose in writing this book is to integrate classical rhetoric and some of the "new" empirically-based communication theories into one coherent body of theory on rhetorical communication. The resultant theory is essentially Aristotelian. The main emphasis of the book is on rhetorical communication in the extemporaneous, oral person-to-group format. The theories presented are also appropriate, however, to rhetorical communication in other formats. Specific references to differences in application of the theories to various formats are made throughout the book.[5]

Thus, we regard human communication as the end product of the social sciences, the culmination of scientific investigation, and the ultimate of artistic expression. The hyphen in the title of this book, *Speech: Science-Art*, indicates that science and art join in the act of communicating; scientific knowledge and artistic skill are synthesized into one. It also implies that there is a unifying basis for the fragmented communication taught today. This unifying basis is the total human personality in interaction with other personalities. Thus, a physiological view, a physical view, a psychological view, a social view, a linguistic view, a performance view, are all, in themselves, insufficient, but, if taken together, they may provide deep insight into what happens when humans face each other in a communication relationship. Speech is a complex science that

---

[2] Austin J. Freeley, *Argumentation and Debate*, Belmont, Calif.: Wadsworth, 1966, p. viii.

[3] Horace G. Rahskopf, *Basic Speech Improvement*, New York: Harper & Row, 1965, p. ix.

[4] Kenneth G. Hance, David C. Ralph, & Milton J. Wiksell, *Principles of Speaking*, Belmont, Calif.: Wadsworth, 1969, preface.

[5] James C. McCroskey, *An Introduction to Rhetorical Communication*, Englewood Cliffs, N.J.: Prentice-Hall, 1968, p. iii.

virtually defies explanation; and it is a high art that represents the best of man's creative powers.[6]

Textbooks for the beginning course in speech tend to concentrate on performance—on the techniques of public speaking, discussion, oral interpretation, and so forth. The authors of this textbook—while not neglecting instruction in skills—have attempted to introduce students to speech as a humanistic study.[7]

In each of these excerpts from prefaces the author gives important information about his material. The reviewer's task is to check the book against such statements to see how well the author has achieved his declared intent.

In summary, the reader is likely to find in the preface information such as the following:

1. The author's purpose
2. For whom the book is intended
3. The type of course for which the book is planned
4. How the book differs from other texts in the field
5. Why the author has written the book
6. Instructions concerning how the book is to be used
7. The list of persons who have reviewed the book in manuscript

What Is the Author's Philosophy?

In addition to the insight into the author's philosophy the reviewer can get by studying the preface carefully, he may also find in later sections additional hints about the educational point of view as well as the author's philosophical attitudes. As suggested earlier, the author may also elaborate his educational and speech philosophy in other publications. The reviewer should seek to measure a book by the yardstick of declared goals. In addition, he must decide whether the author's tenets are consistent with his own basic beliefs, the purposes of the proposed course, and his department objectives. He must determine whether the philosophy is one he cares to endorse. With the philosophy succinctly stated, the reviewer is ready to analyze the content.

What Does the Table of Contents Suggest?

The table of contents presents a preview of what is to be expected, indicating scope and organization. Chapter titles and their sequence should give some idea as to whether the text can be adapted to course requirements and whether it covers what usually are considered the essential elements of the subject.

[6] Elwood Murray, Gerald M. Phillips and J. David Truby, *Speech: Science-Art*, New York: Bobbs-Merrill, 1969, pp. viii–xi.
[7] S. Judson Crandell, Gerald M. Phillips and Joseph A. Wigley, *Speech, A Course in Fundamentals*, Glenview, Ill.: Scott, Foresman, 1963, preface.

Is the Subject Adequately Covered?

Adequate coverage refers to both breadth and depth of the subject, the breadth of material having to do with the extensiveness of the presentation and depth implying adequate and clear treatment of each phase. A book that presents too little information—that is, fails to give sufficient scope—provides little challenge for its student readers. Furthermore, in covering too little, it gives the impression that there is little to be learned in the subject. The author who attempts to cover too great a scope may clutter his treatment with nonessentials. Does the author exercise selectivity? Students may have difficulty with texts that they feel are too extensive. The author who attempts to cover too much sacrifices depth for superficial breadth of coverage. The best textbooks are those that combine judicious selection with thoroughness of content.

Does the Textbook Fit the Course Requirements?

Of paramount importance to any teacher is finding a book that satisfies the needs and abilities of his students as well as the local departmental requirements. He must find a book within the intellectual grasp and experience of the students. He should consider such items as the following:

1. The author's statement concerning for whom the book is planned
2. The sequence of assignments
3. The amount of time devoted to each unit
4. The use of illustrative material
5. Types of exercises and projects

A workbook may be completely adequate for a course that meets once a week and may provide sufficient challenge to the type of students who enroll in the course. On the other hand, the more extensive courses that draw mature students will demand a more extensive discussion of principles and practices.

Is the Book Readable?

Books are written to be read. Like the public speaker, the author must write in such a way that students will understand and will remember the material. In checking readability the teacher should consider carefully the word choice to determine whether it fits the maturation level of the students for whom the textbook is intended. Many writers of high school textbooks select their vocabulary from standard word lists. In actual practice, this procedure sometimes breaks down because some classes may be two or three grades above or below the national norms. Individual differences, too, even among members of a given class, add another dimension.

Important as vocabulary is, it is only one of the factors of readability.

Style and composition are additional criteria. Does the author have a clear, concise, and distinctive quality of writing? One distinguished authority comments: "Style is an increment in writing. . . . Every writer, by the way he uses the language, reveals something of his spirit, his habits, his capacities, his bias."[8] The reviewer of a textbook should attempt to see how well the writer reveals himself. In its broadest sense he should note (1) organization, (2) sentence structure, (3) language, and (4) development.

The text that presents one principle after another, without amplification, makes dull reading. Supporting materials that are trite or development that seems overelaborate are equally bad. By beating a point to death the author defeats his own purpose. Well selected examples and apt illustrations heighten attention as well as create and maintain interest. Naturally, there can be no set formula, apart from the difficulty of the material, as to the amount of elaboration necessary; but a rule of thumb is that clarity, precision, and quality are more desirable than quantity and verbosity.

Does the Textbook Provide Teaching Aids?

A good textbook will probably include these items: (1) suggested course plans, (2) a selective bibliography, (3) exercises and supplementary teaching materials, and (4) a comprehensive index.

Suggested Course Plans. There is no substitute for a syllabus prepared by the teacher who is responsible for the course, but often a course outline included in a textbook provides excellent suggestions about how to teach a subject. The author may include assignments he feels are best taught in a particular way at a particular time. Some writers prepare teachers' manuals containing exercises, outlines, and study questions. These materials are particularly valuable to the teacher who is using a book for the first time.

An Extensive Bibliography. References at the ends of the chapters are sometimes misunderstood. Someone has said that a bibliography is nothing more than a device by which one expert impresses other experts. Likewise, students may take a dim view of lists that mean additional reading. Contrary to such opinions, an extensive bibliography can serve as an important teaching aid. Of course, the reviewer should check the items to make sure that they are pertinent and selected with care. If the selection proves to be nothing more than an inappropriate assortment, a reviewer should seriously question the author's scholarship. The teacher should note what suggestions the author makes for using the bibliography. Does the author integrate it into his development? Does he include items that increase insight and comprehension of the subject? Does he plan assignments that send the students to references for additional reading?

[8] William Strunk, Jr. & E. B. White, *The Elements of Style*, New York: Macmillan, 1959, p. 53.

A carefully made bibliography is the key to research. With it, doors to knowledge are opened. For this reason high school speech texts, as well as college texts, may well include both a teacher's bibliography and a list of readings for the students.

Exercises and Supplementary Materials. Carefully planned exercises, model speeches, outlines, and reading selections are definite assets. Writers often include models and projects that research and experimentation have proved effective in teaching certain aspects. Does the author interweave exercises into his development? The teacher should not plan to rely exclusively on the aids to teach the course for him, but he should remember that they may supplement his plans and activities.

The Comprehensive Index. The index is a matter that reviewers and selection committees frequently pass by. The index, a valuable aid for quick reference, reveals the accuracy of workmanship that went into the preparation and editing of the book. The teacher should check several entries to determine if the subjects, sections, or topics are on the pages indicated. He should make a quick random sampling of several entries to see whether the index helps in locating vital material.

Is the Manufacture of the Book Satisfactory?

Is the Book Well Made? The reviewer should keep in mind that textbooks generally receive hard treatment. A poorly manufactured book or one made from inferior materials is not durable and therefore is a poor investment. Does the book have a good binding? He should examine the spine and the covers. He should be reasonably sure that the book is capable of several years of normal wear.

Is the Book Attractive? Is the book attractive and inviting? Does the cover make the user want to look inside? The teacher should consider seriously the general appearance of the book, remembering that drab-colored and inartistically designed books often have adverse effects on students. Such books make pride of ownership impossible; the students may deface such volumes or even purposely lose them. Attractive books provide no guarantee against all carelessness and vandalism, but investigations on the matter indicate that attractive books are less likely to be mistreated.

Size of the Book. Students also set up barriers against oversized books. A prodigious volume may seem so formidable that the student avoids it. This is a common psychological problem with many high school students. Another aspect that should be considered is the matter of transportation. Is the book heavy and awkward to carry? Many times a large, bulky book remains in a desk or locker simply because the students find it difficult to manage.

Paper and Printing. The teacher should not overlook the paper and printing; he should consider ease of reading. Is the paper tough enough for hard use? He should also observe the gloss of the paper. If it causes glare under normal lighting conditions it is unsatisfactory. The print should be easily read and not crowded. Are there typographical errors? Is there variety in type face and in sizes used? Is there balance of white and black masses? Study line drawings and pictures. Are they carefully selected and sharp? The teacher should also give attention to headings and subheadings. Are the headings consistent? Do these titles guide the student in his study? Do headings and subheadings give sufficient emphasis to subordinate ideas?

RATING SHEET FOR TEXTBOOK EVALUATION

	Inferior	Poor	Fair	Average	Above average	Excellent	Superior
Authorship and publisher							
Speech philosophy							
Coverage of subject							
Adaptability							
Readability							
Teaching aids							
Manufacture							
Overall evaluation							

Total Score _____

Comments:

EXERCISES

1. Compare three or four reviews of the same textbook. You will find reviews in the *Quarterly Journal of Speech*, the *Speech Teacher*, the *Educational Theatre Journal*, *Journal of Speech and Hearing Disorders*, and the regional speech journals.
2. In a given issue of the *Quarterly Journal of Speech*, the *Speech Teacher*, or the *Educational Theatre Journal*, read all the book reviews. Select the five best ones and write a justification for your selection.

3. Prepare a book review in no more than 500 words of a leading high school or college textbook in speech. Carefully polish your style.
4. Carefully analyze 10 leading textbooks in your chosen area. Copy the accompanying evaluation chart and use it to record your findings.

REFERENCES

ANDERSON, PAUL S., "How Teachers Share in Textbook Selection," *Nation's Schools*, September, 1957, 60:57–59.

BLANCHARD, B. EVERARD, "Tentative Criteria for the Selection of Textbooks," *High School Journal*, May, 1955, 38:293–296.

CLEMENT, JOHN ADDISON, *Manual for Analyzing and Selecting Textbooks*, Champaign, Ill.: Garrard, 1942.

GORMAN, BURTON W., "Some Deficiencies of Textbooks," *High School Journal*, May, 1955, 38:289–292.

HOUTZ, HARRY E., "Teachers Can Help Evaluate and Select Textbooks," *Elementary School Journal*, February, 1956, 56:250–254.

PEARSON, RICHARD M. AND SPAULDING, WILLIAM E., "Textbook Publishers Look at Selection," *Educational Digest*, December, 1956, 22(4):27–29.

REEVE, WILLIAM DAVID, "How to Choose a Textbook," *School Science and Mathematics*, November, 1955, 55:601–609.

ROBINSON, KARL F., *Teaching Speech in Secondary School*, 2nd ed., London: Longmans, Green, 1954, pp. 231–264.

ROUSSEAU, LOUSENE, "How to Choose a High School Speech Text," *Speech Teacher*, January, 1968, 17:27–29.

21. Evaluation of Performance

J. Donald Ragsdale

Even in a day when many people question the relevance of the educational system itself, there are few areas of student-teacher relationships that are more controversial than the evaluation of student performance in the classroom. It is an area which at several schools is reflecting the demands of some for pass-fail options for the usual system of letter grades or for simplified letter grading systems. Further, the story of each teacher's method of testing and grading is one of the most common pieces of folklore among the students in any school. For good or ill, there are few things which have so profound an effect on a teacher's reputation for honesty, fairness, and justness than his evaluation of performance.

Unfortunately, an impression which many people, including teachers, have is that evaluation is only a matter of testing and grading, that it is a mere technique. This is analogous to a popular impression of the experimental scientist. There are those who in their thinking reduce the experimenter's method to the use of statistics. To be sure, statistics are nearly inevitable in the scientist's work and their use must be mastered early on. They are, however, only the most visible sign of his endeavor, the proverbial tip of the iceberg. As with the scientist's work and his use of statistics, there is profoundly more to evaluation of performance than the teacher's tests and grades. Before discussing methods of testing and grading therefore, an examination of such things as the teacher's development of his course objectives and his expectations of his students' performance is necessary.

420

THE TEACHER'S OBJECTIVES

One of the major causes of faulty evaluation of student performance in the classroom is the failure of the teacher to specify clearly, for himself perhaps more so than for his students, his course's objectives. Many teachers would reply to such a charge that they most certainly know what they want. They intend for their students to develop "effective oral communication," "effective delivery," "organizational skills," and "critical abilities and standards," among other things.[1] What, however, constitutes effective oral communication, or effective delivery, and what are organizational skills? It is well known that teachers sometimes disagree about such matters, so how will the student, the teacher's colleagues, or perhaps even the teacher himself know *exactly* what is expected in a particular course? Further, how effective must one be to pass a course or to receive a given grade, and how difficult will this be for him? If one wishes to be neither ambiguous nor capricious with his students, not to say if one wishes to produce better tests, then he would do well to pay careful attention to stating his course's objectives clearly. Moreover, Robert L. Ebel, of the University of Iowa's Examinations Service, speaks for virtually every authority on evaluation when he says that "we have little patience with those who assert that many of the important outcomes of instruction are intangible. . . . I strongly suspect that many of those who insist upon the importance of intangible outcomes of education are simply using it as a shield for their relutance, or inability, to describe specifically what a given course of instruction ought to accomplish."[2]

In Chapter 19 are discussed a broad range of general educational objectives and also some specific course-related ones for the field of speech communication. The purpose of the present section is to suggest a method of specifying these objectives in such a way as to allow them to be more easily evaluated. A crucial word in any discussion of evaluation is "objective." Another is "operational." "Evaluation is objective," writes Ebel, "to the degree that equally competent observers can agree in their evaluation of a particular achievement."[3] An operational statement is one which is specific enough to yield objective evaluation. It is one which another teacher could follow without a need for information other than the statement itself. If course objectives are to be specified operationally for objective evaluation, then they must be stated in unequivocal, behavioral

[1] James W. Gibson, Charles R. Gruner, William D. Brooks & Charles R. Petrie, Jr., "The First Course in Speech: A Survey of U.S. Colleges and Universities," *Speech Teacher*, January, 1970, 19:16.
[2] Robert L. Ebel, "How an Examination Service Helps College Teachers to Give Better Tests," in Anne Anastasi (ed.), *Testing Problems in Perspective*, Washington, D.C.: American Council on Education, 1966, pp. 118–119.
[3] *Ibid.*, p. 117.

terms. As Robert F. Mager puts it, "until you describe what the learner will be DOING when demonstrating that he 'understands' or 'appreciates,' you have described very little at all."[4]

Some readers may object that to specify objectives in behavioral terms is to be overly mechanical at best and is to reduce course goals to mere pragmatism at worst. They would be correct if the only result of this suggestion were to be a list of such things as the number of emphatic gestures needed to get a grade of A on a speech. While such a list might well be part of a set of objectives, were it possible to quantify gestures in this way, it would certainly not be sufficient in itself. Furthermore, every teacher, in fact, evaluates his students in behavioral terms whether he recognizes it or not. Every speech, or group discussion, or oral interpretation is an observable behavior as is every test response. Even when the teacher gives some credit for effort, he does so on the basis of some perceptible evidence. It could hardly be otherwise. The problem, then, lies in how unequivocally the behaviors are stated. To the teacher who claims that it is not possible to identify all the conceivable evidences of such things as effort, the question "How then do you know them when you see them?" might be asked.

An example of putting objectives into behavioral terms may show both the reasonableness and the ease of the technique. A widespread goal of beginning courses in speech communication at the college level appears to be the development or improvement of organizational skills.[5] The first thing which the teacher might ask himself is what constitutes "organizational skill." Naturally, there is some disagreement among people as to what they "like" about organization. There is, moreover, only a small amount of research into this variable.[6] It is clear, however, that the teacher should be cognizant of the available research, and that he should at least be unequivocal in stating what he "likes."[7]

One factor which appears to be very important in organization is the use of transitional statements.[8] One course objective stated behaviorally, therefore, might be "to use transitional statements in speaking assignments." Such a statement of an objective is obviously less equivocal than the frequently encountered statement "to exhibit organizational skill," although it is not as inclusive. The teacher would need to enumerate all of the

[4] Robert F. Mager, *Preparing Instructional Objectives*, Palo Alto, Calif.: Fearon, 1962, p. 11. Cf. also p. 53. The ensuing discussion closely follows Mager's suggestions.
[5] Gibson *et al.*, *loc. cit.*
[6] Cf. Wayne N. Thompson, *Quantitative Research in Public Address and Communication*, New York: Random House, 1967, pp. 65–72.
[7] Wayne N. Thompson's book provides a summary of research through 1964. The teacher can supplement this book by consulting the journals used by Thompson since that date.
[8] Ernest Thompson, "Some Effects of Message Structure on Listeners' Comprehension," *Speech Monographs*, March, 1967, 34:51–57.

behaviors which make for organizational skill. The behavioral statement, however, is still incomplete. The teacher should also specify the *conditions* under which the student must operate in fulfilling the objective. Will he be allowed, for example, to use notes or a manuscript as aids? Will he have a time limit? Finally, the teacher should specify the *criterion* by which the student will be measured. Will he be required to use all types of transitional statements? Will he need to use them after every separate idea in the speech, every main point in the speech, or when? A full behavioral statement of this objective might be as specific as the following one:

To use transitional statements, of either the flashback-preview or the internal summary type, in speaking assignments exceeding 3 minutes in length. The student may use a key-word outline but must not use more extensive notes or a manuscript. Although every main point should end with one, a transitional statement for one-half of the main points will be sufficient for a passing score on this variable.

It is clear that the individual teacher alone is responsible for the content of the statement of an objective and that the content may differ from teacher to teacher. What should not differ is the degree of clarity of the statements themselves.

Is it really necessary to be so specific as is the statement in the example? There can really be only one answer to this question. Unless the teacher wants to evaluate capriciously, he must be specific at some point in his course. The only real question is when should he be this specific. The teacher who has his students' best interests in mind will not wait until he is rating their speeches or grading their tests to make his decision. "An additional advantage of clearly defined objectives," notes Mager, "is that the student is provided the means to evaluate *his own* progress at any place along the route of instruction and is able to organize his efforts into relevant activities."[9]

EXPECTATIONS OF STUDENT PERFORMANCE

Another preliminary to the evaluation of performance in the classroom is an understanding by the teacher of what to expect from his students. Such an understanding can go far toward preventing undue optimism or pessimism on the teacher's part as well as frustration among his students over an unrealistically difficult or easy course. One branch of specialization in the field of psychology which provides some understanding of expectations is learning theory. The learning theorist concerns himself with such things as the variables or phenomena which foster learning and the nature of the

[9] Mager, *op. cit.*, p. 4.

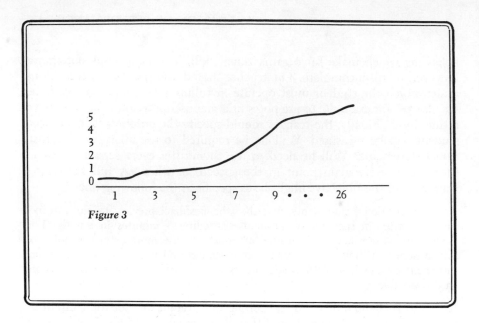

Figure 3

learning process in the individual. Although he has noted many individual differences in learning, he has found that much learning follows a typical pattern.

Suppose one were to observe the early development of language in the child and were to graph the child's acquisition of the correct pronunciation of the word "smoke" over a period of time (see Figure 3). If the vertical axis of the graph were to represent "degree of approximation to the correct pronunciation" and the horizontal axis were to represent time in weeks, then a particular "learning curve" would result. At first, there may be no production of the word by the child, then a period during which the child might produce a very remote approximation, perhaps "thmoke" or just "moke," and continue with this for a time. Next there may be a marked increase in a very short time in the child's accuracy of production followed by a plateau. Perhaps he now would produce something like "sumoke." Finally, the child may show a mild spurt of learning and may appear fully to have acquired the pronunciation of the word.

Not all learning curves would have this exact shape, but most of them would share the features of rapid gain in ability at some point followed by a plateau of slower, perhaps no improvement. Generally, rapid gain will occur earlier if the learner has already acquired behaviors which he can build upon in learning a new one. The student who has had a high-school speech activities course, for example, is likely to make more progress early in a college public speaking course than the student who has not. The performance of both types of students may, however, be nearly the same at the end of the college course. This fact has led some to suggest that speech performances should be graded on improvement in order not to penalize the student with little or no background. Perhaps the most desirable way to handle the problem would be to enroll students with different backgrounds in separate courses or separate course sections. Since this type of selective enrollment is often impossible, the teacher must decide whether he will handle the expected student differences by a grading system based on improvement.

There are at least two ways in which one may grade on improvement. One way would be to grade each assignment by comparison to the one preceding it. Something which may complicate this procedure, however, is the fact that the assignments in a course usually progress in difficulty from one to the other. The teacher is thus faced with deciding how much improvement has occurred in the elements shared by the two assignments, how well the student has done on the new elements of the second one, and how much weight should be granted to each, an onerous task if not an impossible one. Furthermore, the student with prior experience will be penalized by this method of grading. Learning curves suggest that he may exhibit most of his improvement early and show little development thereafter.

A second way of recognizing improvement would be to weight each successive performance more than the one preceding it with each graded in terms of the demands of the assignment itself. If the teacher is careful to construct his assignments, so that his students with little or no background acquire their basic skills before the more heavily weighted ones are due, then the learning "spurts" of all of his students should more nearly coincide. In spite of all he may do, however, the teacher is likely to have students who will differ as to the time when they exhibit their most rapid achievement. There may be occasions when a student will make three grades of C on his assignments and then two grades of A. The reverse of this pattern is not unusual either. When the teacher encounters such patterns as these, he hopefully will couple his knowledge of what he has the right to expect with what he has asked of his students and shun any unduly rigid method of determining their overall grades.

Learning theory is not the only source of information for the teacher about what to expect from his students. There is also a body of research data which has been compiled about the particular behavior of speech students. This data suggests that speech communication ability is not fully explainable as an intellectual activity. The role of personality appears to be very important as well. The technical meaning of the term "personality," of course, has little direct relationship to the popular meaning as a variable indexing someone's popularity or agreeableness. It refers rather to those dimensions of behavior which have to do with a person's adjustment to himself and to others. A person's self-esteem and his introversion-extroversion are two such dimensions. There are several research studies which indicate that a student's intelligence quotient, his scores on standard tests of achievement, and the like, are only weakly correlated with his grades on oral assignments or in speech communication courses. They further show that such personality factors as high self-esteem, extroversion, and social adjustment are much more strongly correlated with such grades.[10] These findings indicate that such usual indicators of scholastic ability as IQs, achievement test scores, standing in school, and grades in other courses, may be misleading when applied to the field of speech communication.

Most teachers have had students who have a high scholastic standing in school but who never seem to excel in their oral assignments, as well as students whose experience is almost the reverse of this. None of these findings should be taken to suggest that speech communication is a "mere knack," a form of "cookery," as Plato once rhetorically called it, and that the good speech communication student will be none too bright. The findings also do not suggest that one is born with speech communication skill. Personality factors are to a large extent learned behaviors. Variations in, say, IQ just do not account for variations in speaking ability as well as variations in some personality dimensions do. Frequently, the bright student will also exhibit the personality characteristics which make for success in the speech classroom. These findings do suggest that there may be some disparity between oral performance and written performance, however. The especially good speaker or group discussant may not do so well when he is given a written examination and vice versa. Greene, in fact, found only a moderate degree of correlation between grades on public speaking assignments and grades on written tests of public speaking principles.[11] The teacher will want to weigh this possibility carefully in assigning proportionate weight to oral and written performances.

THE RATING OF ORAL PERFORMANCE

Only with a clear understanding of his course objectives and of what to expect of his students should the teacher turn his attention to the more practical matters of rating oral performance, giving written tests, and assigning grades. These more familiar tasks, like statistics, are only manipulations of elements. They cannot salvage an ambiguously structured course or alter the effects of unrealistically high expectations. Of all of these tasks, the most frequent and perhaps the most difficult for the teacher is rating.

[10] Cf. Wayne Thompson, op. cit., pp. 186–191.
[11] Guy S. Greene, "The Correlation Between Skill in Performance and Knowledge of Principles in a Course in Speech-Making," Journal of Applied Psychology, April, 1941, 25:232–242.

For the teacher who is willing to do a little advance preparation, though, the task need not be either an unpleasant or a poorly performed one. In this preparation, the teacher should consider the validity, the reliability, and the communicability of his rating sheet.

Validity: The Content of the Rating Sheet

The primary question to be asked of any rating sheet is whether or not it is a valid one. Very simply, does it rate what it claims to? Now rating sheets claim to measure, or to allow evaluation of, speaking performance.[12] The question, then, is what are the elements of speaking performance which should be rated? Scholars in the field of speech do not agree completely on this apparently basic matter. When engaging in what has elsewhere been called *post hoc* criticism, they have tended to emphasize somewhat different things than when they engage in synchronic or classroom criticism.[13] A more serious problem is the failure to distinguish between factors which are *characteristic* of speaking performance and factors which are *crucial* to it. There are a number of phenomena which are typically listed as categories of judgment on speech rating sheets. Among these are speech rate, fluency, voice quality, gestures, citation of sources, clarity of language, use of transitions, and many others. The effects of some of these variables are yet to be determined by research studies. The effect of gestures on persuasiveness, for example, is not altogether clear at this time. It does seem, however, that such things as clarity of language and the use of transitions are important for the speaker.[14] Phenomena such as speech rate, fluency, and voice quality, on the other hand, appear to have little effect on the outcome of a speech.[15] Research on the citation of sources suggests that this may be an unnecessary, although harmless, addition to a speech whose evidence is otherwise satisfactory.[16] The implication seems clear that the teacher who is ignorant of the research evidence may give undue emphasis to virtually irrelevant phenomena and perhaps not enough to more important ones.

There is also evidence from research studies which indicates that there are a number of elements common to classroom criticism but that the number of really distinct elements is small.[17] Becker's 1962 study is one of

[12] The ensuing discussion focuses on public speaking performance for purposes of illustration. It is likely that similar problems would be encountered in rating other forms of speech communication.

[13] J. Donald Ragsdale, "*Post Hoc* and Synchronic Criticism," *Speech Teacher*, March, 1967, 16:161–164.

[14] Cf. Wayne Thompson, *op. cit.*, pp. 72–76.

[15] *Ibid.*, pp. 88–92.

[16] Robert S. Cathcart, "Four Methods of Presenting Evidence," *Speech Monographs*, August, 1955, 22:227–233.

[17] Cf. Wayne Thompson, *op. cit.*, pp. 177–180.

the most interesting in this respect. Using a technique called factor analysis, which is designed to uncover the basic elements actually being discriminated in a large number of cases, he found that there were only three principal ones. These were analysis-content, delivery, and language.[18]

The reader may be surprised at the small number of elements in Becker's study. What this study, and factor analysis in general, indicates, however, is that, where there are many separate elements of evaluation, these are probably resolvable into more general categories. Moreover, it indicates that there are fewer really different, or discrete, categories of speech judgment than many people are inclined to believe. Where the rater has separate ratings for organization and analysis, for example, he may be inclined to rate them similarly. Together they may be considered as parts of a larger whole, in Becker's study analysis-content. If a teacher's rating is to be valid, he should include these three factors on his rating sheet and question seriously the need for others. In the final analysis, however, the problem of validity is one of fidelity to a stated objective. The teacher who is rating an oral interpretation of Shakespeare or an open-ended group discussion of the effects of marijuana may need to emphasize different aspects of performance. For this, his course objectives, based as they should be on the textbook and his supplementary lectures, as well as the research studies are of great value.

One final word of caution appears to be in order before leaving the subject of validity. A few researchers have found disturbing evidence that some raters' objectivity may be compromised by their attitudes toward the topics of their students' speeches. As early as 1935, Knower found that when students were used as raters they gave higher ratings for topics with which they agreed than for topics with which they did not.[19] Bostrom more recently has found that ratings are influenced by the personality factor of rigidity of behavior.[20] The teacher can hardly give up his attitudes when he rates, and probably he can do little about his personality at least by himself. Perhaps an awareness of the chance that he may be influenced by his own attitudes and personality will serve as adequate protection against unusual subjectivity. It should also serve to remind him again of the great importance of clarity in stating his course objectives and in adhering closely to them.

[18] Samuel L. Becker, "The Rating of Speeches: Scale Independence," *Speech Monographs*, March, 1962, 29:38–44. Cf. Theodore Clevenger, Jr., "Influence of Scale Complexity on the Reliability of Ratings of General Effectiveness in Public Speaking," *Speech Monographs*, June, 1964, 31:154n.

[19] Franklin H. Knower, "Experimental Studies of Changes in Attitude: I. A Study of the Effect of Oral Argument on Changes of Attitude," *Journal of Social Psychology*, August, 1935, 6:315–345. Cf. Gerald R. Miller, "Agreement and the Grounds for It: Persistent Problems in Speech Rating," *Speech Teacher*, November, 1964, 13:257–261.

[20] Robert N. Bostrom, "Dogmatism, Rigidity, and Rating Behavior," *Speech Teacher*, November, 1964, 13:283–287.

Reliability: The Consistency of Rating

The aspect of rating which produces the greatest difficulty for the teacher is being consistent. No teacher is immune from the ill effects of fatigue, of poor memory, or of human variability in general. The realiability of a rating is a measure of consistency. *Temporal reliability* is a measure, for example, of the correlation or agreement between two ratings of the same performance at different times. *Interjudge reliability* is a measure of the agreement between several raters evaluating the same performance. In speech communication classes, both types of reliability are necessary. Teachers need to be consistent in rating different speakers—not the same thing as, but essentially similar to, temporal reliability—and their ratings should be reasonably similar to those which their colleagues might give. Both types of reliability will be greatly enhanced by the clarity with which the teacher has understood and expressed his objectives.

At face value, studies of the temporal reliability of speech ratings do little more than confirm that humans are variable creatures. Clevenger found only a modest correlation between his judges' two ratings of the same set of speeches 6 weeks apart.[21] There does seem to be evidence, on the other hand, that when the rater is well-trained in his subject matter or at least in the use of his particular rating sheet, his temporal reliability will increase.[22] Additionally, the raters in Clevenger's study generally did a more reliable job when rating the general categories on their sheets, such as "general effectiveness." These raters had, of course, rated other some less general categories. It is thus possible that their rating of the general categories was enhanced by this fact.[23] Other researchers, however, have noted that a few general categories of judgment seem to produce more reliable results than do many.[24]

On the subject of interjudge reliability, the research evidence also suggests that training enhances reliability. In another study, Clevenger found that judges with heterogeneous backgrounds, including some with no speech communication teaching experience, exhibited very little agreement with each other when rating such general categories as "general effectiveness" and only modest agreement when using six more specific categories.[25] Although not overwhelming, the research evidence clearly implies that the teacher who wants to improve the reliability of his ratings will

[21] Theodore Clevenger, Jr., "Retest Reliabilities of Ten Scales of Public Speaking Performance," *Central States Speech Journal*, Novmber, 1963, 14:285–291.
[22] *Ibid.*, But cf. Wayne Thompson, *op. cit.*, pp. 180–182.
[23] Clevenger notes that his findings in this regard are contrary to expectation based on studies of other judgmental tasks by numerous psychologists.
[24] Cf. Wayne Thompson, *op. cit.*, pp. 177–180.
[25] Clevenger, "Influence of Scale Complexity." Cf. Wayne Thompson, *op. cit.*, pp. 182–185.

study his own objectives carefully and will strive to confine his rating categories to a few general ones.

Another finding in studies of interjudge reliability is that reliability can be enhanced by the use of several raters.[26] The teacher might well want to ask the other students in the class to rate the speaker along with him, a procedure now popularly called "peer rating." The averaged results of the several ratings would be likely to have greater reliability than the teacher's alone. This rating procedure would have the desirable additional effect of utilizing what for many students is a waste of time and of reinforcing their own knowledge of speaking skills. Further, the speaker should rarely have the feeling that he was being graded unfairly. Of course, the teacher would want to train his student critics in the use of the rating sheets so as to minimize unreliability stemming from a lack of training.

One final warning appears to be in order before leaving the subject of reliability. Occasionally, teachers indulge in what has been called "overlap" rating in order to conserve time. As the second and subsequent speakers begin their performance, the teacher continues to fill out his rating sheet for the preceding speaker, sometimes missing the initial comments of the next speaker. While time seems especially to be the teacher's nemesis, this means of conserving it appears to yield dubious results. In general, all of the speakers except the first will be rated somewhat higher, or more leniently, than they would be if time were taken between speeches to complete the rating sheet before the next performance.[27] The careful rater will want to avoid even this relatively harmless source of unreliability.

Communicability: The Rating Sheet as a Teaching Device

In developing or choosing his rating sheet, the teacher should also consider how well the completed form will communicate to the student who receives it. Unless the student understands the markings on the sheet, the instrument cannot serve as a teaching device in any important sense. Again, careful explanation of a rating sheet which embodies a set of clearly stated course objectives will solve many problems of communication when the sheet is used. The suggestions for the makeup of a rating sheet in the previous two sections, however, may not make for optimal communicability. Although the teacher may neither truly discriminate nor reliably judge more than a few categories when he is rating, the student may well profit from a more elaborate form. Perhaps the most practical way to meet this

[26] Alice I. Bryan & Walter H. Wilke, "A Technique for Rating Public Speeches," *Journal of Consulting Psychology*, March–April, 1941, 5:80–90. Cf. Roy V. Wood & Alvin A. Goldberg, "The Effects of Three Styles of Training upon Small Group Effectiveness," *Speech Teacher*, September, 1968, 17:238–245.
[27] Larry L. Barker, Robert J. Kibler, and Eugenia C. Hunter, "An Empirical Study of Overlap Rating Effects," *Speech Teacher*, March, 1968, 17:160–166. The raters in this study were inexperienced ones, however.

need without violating previous suggestions is to provide space on the rating sheet for descriptive materials and for the teacher to write comments.

The form reproduced on p. 330 was developed for use in one of the public speaking courses at Louisiana State University. The major categories down the left-hand side of the sheet have key-word descriptions appended to them in most cases as well as numbers indicating chapters in the course textbook which may be consulted for further help. There are seven steps or scale positions to be checked by the rater. Seven such positions is a widely used number, although some raters prefer five. There is at least one research study which suggests that the use of a seven-position scale will enhance temporal reliability if the rater does not habitually confine his checks to only a few of the seven.[28] Finally, there is space on the right of the sheet for brief comments alongside each judgment category and at the bottom for more general comments.

The form reproduced on p. 432 is one developed by Professor Franklin H. Knower. It approaches the problem of communicability by providing a number of descriptions of faults for the rater to check. Knower found that requiring raters to check faults rather than strengths enhanced interjudge reliability.[29] Although space is allowed for positive comments to be added by the rater, many teachers may feel that the approach of this rating sheet is unsatisfactory at times, especially with the beginning student or with one who is especially troubled by speech fright.

Neither of these two rating sheets is as concise as seems desirable and neither has an indication of the different weights, if any, to be assigned to the several categories. One way to solve the first problem would be simply to regroup the categories into more inclusive units. In the case of the Knower sheet, for example, the first and fourth categories might be left alone, categories two and three might be bracketed together, and the fifth, sixth, and seventh could be combined. This would yield five categories including general effectiveness. Whatever the teacher's decision is with respect to weighting, it could be indicated by percentages for each general category. Category two ("delivery") might be assigned a value of 30 percent, category three ("language") 20 percent, category four ("analysis-content") 40 percent, and so on. There is no reason, of course, why a teacher could not make up his own rating sheet. In several ways, the teacher's own terminology might be more communicative to his students than that of someone else. Further, the effort which he would expend in this preparation would undoubtedly be repaid by the greater ease, and perhaps reliability, which he would experience in using the sheet.

28 Samuel L. Becker and Gary L. Cronkhite, "Reliability as a Function of Utilized Scale Steps," *Speech Teacher*, November, 1965, 14:291–293.
29 Franklin H. Knower, "A Study of Rank-Order Methods of Evaluating Performances in Speech Contests," *Journal of Applied Psychology*, October, 1940, 24:633–644.

GENERAL SPEECH PERFORMANCE SCALE

Name _____ Date _____ Rater _____

Project _____ Time _____

Subject _____ Grade _____

	Rate 1–5	Comments

Speech Attitudes and Adjustments

Indifferent ____	Antagonistic ____
Tense ____	Apologetic ____
Flustered ____	Posed ____
Irresponsible ____	Immature ____

Voice and Articulation

Weak ____	Loud ____
Fast ____	Slow ____
Monotonous ____	Excess vocalization ____
Poor quality ____	Indistinct ____
Poor pitch ____	Dialect ____
Not rhythmic ____	Mispronunciation ____
Poor phrasing ____	Misarticulation ____

Bodily Postures and Action

Indirect ____	Monotonous ____
Inexpressive ____	Not integrated ____
Random ____	Exaggerated ____
Slovenly ____	Weak ____

Language

Inaccurate ____	Monotonous ____
Ambiguous ____	Inexpressive ____
Wordy ____	Stilted—Technical ____
Colloquial ____	Immature ____

Content

Not clear ____	Inaccurate ____
Insignificant ____	Lacks originality ____
Dull ____	Lacks movement ____
Insufficient ____	Abstract ____
Too much ____	Lacks unity ____

Organization

Poorly purposed ____	Weakly supported ____
Questionable central idea ____	Poor transitions ____
	Poor sequence ____
Poorly introduced ____	Poorly concluded ____
Poorly analyzed ____	

Audience Interests and Adaptation

Attention not aroused ____	Beliefs not considered ____
Interest not maintained ____	Obviously solicitous ____
Knowledge not considered ____	Confidence not secured ____

General Effectiveness

Total _____

THE TESTING OF COURSE KNOWLEDGE

In giving written tests, the teacher must also concern himself with validity and reliability. The measure of a test's validity is the degree to which it measures what the teacher has taught with the correct proportion. The teacher's course objectives again should provide the best guide to preparing valid tests. Tests are sometimes measured for their temporal reliability if the effects of learning during the first testing session can be removed or minimized. Occasionally, to check their *intertest* reliability they are also correlated with other tests which purport to measure the same thing. The most important type of reliability for the kinds of tests most teachers will devise for use in class, however, is a measure of their internal consistency. Such a measure, which might correlate the first and second halves of the test or the odd and the even test items, would tell the teacher whether his questions were reasonably consistent. A simple check of *internal* reliability and of test item difficulty will be discussed momentarily. In addition to these overall considerations, the teacher will want to consider the types of tests, or test items, which he can devise and how each of these types should be prepared to yield optimum results.

Multiple-Choice Test Items

Many students and teachers have rather definite opinions about so-called objective tests. When they use the term "objective" they are usually referring to tests which can be scored with the use of a key, which do not require the judgment of the grader as to whether or not the answer is correct. For some people, all but objective tests are anathema, while for others objective testing smacks so much of the mechanical that they would never use it. Neither of these attitudes has very much basis in scientific fact. Objective tests can be devised which are so ambiguous or invalid that they are of little or no use. They can also be devised in such a way as to allow the student to exhibit as much of what he knows as can other types of tests. Similar statements might be made of nonobjective tests. In this discussion, therefore, no one type of test will be advocated as generally better than another. The reader should feel free to use any of the types, singly or perhaps preferably in combination, without fear of being inferior.

   Multiple-choice test items follow a format similar to the following examples:

1. The author of the ancient dialogue on public speaking called *De Oratore* was
   ( ) a. Aristotle   (x) b. Cicero   ( ) c. Plato   ( ) d. Quintilian
2. If the cricothyroid muscles contract, the vocal folds will
   ( ) a. shorten   ( ) c. open near the arytenoid cartilages
   ( ) b. hump up in the center   (x) d. become thinner

Occasionally, the test writer will provide five possible choices rather than four. Because this type of item provides the student with a limited number of responses, care must be taken not to make his task too easy. By guessing alone, he should get 25 percent of the items correct or 20 percent on a five-choice item. All of the choices save the correct one should ideally be "legitimate." They should not be false, but imperfect or inadequate in some way. The correct answer should *clearly* be the "best" one, however, or even the good student may be hampered by the ambiguity. Indeed, one of the most frequently heard complaints of students about multiple-choice tests is that they are ambiguous. Developing so-called distractor choices is a difficult business, however. Frequently the teacher will have to use choices which are clearly wrong, but which have enough association with the correct response to make it less obvious. Both of the examples here use such distractor choices. In preparing test items, the teacher should also randomize the position of the correct response so that no position is the correct one unusually often and so that an unintended pattern of correct responses does not result for the complete test.

It should be emphasized that with enough items and careful attention to validity, the teacher can be quite comprehensive. He can thus avoid the often-voiced criticism of the multiple-choice test, that it does not tap what the student knows but what he does not know. While the teacher is working to avoid this difficulty, he might also strive to develop questions which ask for the student to use his knowledge (example 2) rather than to recall isolated facts (example 1). The former are much less likely to be guessed correctly than are the latter.

One of the more desirable features of the multiple-choice test is that it can be used again if the teacher is cautious about security. Indeed, it is usually only after several uses and progressive revision that such a test becomes highly reliable. One way of checking this as a means of improving whole items or single distractors is to compare the responses of the students who performed in the upper 27 percent of the class on the test with the responses of those in the lower 27 percent.[30] With a group of 50 students, the tabulation of Example 1 above might look as follows:

	1	2	3	4	Total
Upper 27%	3	8	0	3	14
Lower 27%	2	4	1	7	14

Choice 2, Cicero, is correct, and it appears that the question distinguishes well between good and poor students. Twice as many good students responded correctly as did poor students. On the other hand, choice 3 seems not to have been attractive to either group and needs to be revised. A similar tabulation of example 2 might look like this:

[30] Henry E. Garrett, *Testing for Teachers*, New York: American Book, 1959, p. 217.

	1	2	3	4	Total
Upper 27%	3	3	4	4	14
Lower 27%	2	4	3	5	14

Choice 4, become thinner, is the correct one, but more poor students chose it than good students. Further, choice 3 was selected as often by the good students as was the correct one. Perhaps all of the distractors were too attractive, or perhaps the correct choice may be too ambiguous. In any case, the item needs revision. These examples are not exhaustive, rather they are suggestive of the information which the teacher may secure from this sort of a quick tabulation.

Essay-Type Test Items

Perhaps the most widely used type of test item outside the fields of science and the best-known of the nonobjective test items is the essay. In this type of item, a rather general question is put to the student allowing him to exhibit the extent of his knowledge and perhaps his compositional ability. All too often the essay-type item is as ambiguous as some of its detractors claim the multiple-choice item is. Such questions as "discuss the development of early rhetoric" leave room for virtually any interpretation and are only effectively limited by a time limit to the test session. Some teachers will accept nearly any answer as correct, making the item a poor discriminator of student ability, or will accept only one answer, frequently making the correct response a matter of knowing the teacher's preference.

Just as the multiple-choice item need not be mechanical, so the essay-type item need not be vague or all-encompassing. One obvious way of improving essay-type items is to replace the one general question with several more specific ones. Another way is to try for the same degree of clarity in writing these items as was recommended for stating course objectives. The above discussion question, for example, might be broken down into the following more specific ones among others:

1. List and describe the major rhetorical treatises before the appearance of Aristotle's *Rhetoric*.
2. Name and characterize the 10 Attic orators.
3. Compare the essential features of Plato's view of rhetoric with the essential features of Aristotle's.

One of the great advantages of the multiple-choice test is that the teacher spends most of his time in preparing and revising it rather than in grading it. A principal advantage of the essay test, and perhaps one reason it is sometimes an inferior product, is that it is relatively easily and quickly constructed. The time the teacher saves in constructing the essay test, however, is rapidly offset by the time-consuming task of grading it. To make matters worse, the grading is usually done under the pressure of a deadline for turning in grades. Furthermore, the task of reading answers to a question, each of which may be of a different length and viewpoint, is hardly conducive to reliability. The teacher should strive, therefore, to enumerate for himself the elements which constitute an acceptable answer for each letter grade level. The less specific the question is, the more specific he should be in making this list. This procedure will provide the teacher with a sort of key or checklist which should enhance his reliability. He should try to assign proportionate values to each aspect of the answer. It is also desirable from the standpoint of reliability to grade all of the answers to a single question at a time rather than to grade all of the answers on a single test paper before moving on.

There are other types of test items which the teacher may wish to use from time to time. There are matching items, true-false items, completion items, and so on. The considerations for these items are, however, similar to the ones which have been discussed with respect to multiple-choice and essay-type items and should serve as a general guide in preparation. A custom which is prevalent in graduate-level examinations is to use objective-type test items to ascertain quickly the scope of a student's knowledge, then to use essay-type items to determine the student's ability to integrate his information, to make keen discriminations, and to communicate himself cogently in writing. There is no reason, though, why this practice should be confined to the graduate level.

ASSIGNMENT OF GRADES

The assignment of grades on an exam or in a course is by far the most subjective element among the several under discussion in this chapter. There are those who strongly question the reasonability of either a set of five letter grades or a scale of values from 0 to 100. There are others who complain that a student's striving for a particular grade subverts real learning. For these reasons among others, the grading system is currently in a state of flux at many schools. Unless grades are abolished altogether however, the problems which accompany them are not likely to disappear completely. The teacher, then, should consider the viewpoint which he will adopt and which procedures he will follow in grading.

One point of view about grading is absolutist. It holds that there should be a fixed standard of attainment, usually expressed in percentages, at each letter grade level. If the student correctly answers 93 percent or more of the questions on a test, for example, he receives an A, if 85 percent he receives a B, and so on. Of course, there is no magic in a particular percentage and no substantive reason why, say, an A should be defined as a correct answer 93 percent of the time or more. Those who take this viewpoint, if they do not do so arbitrarily, do so for reasons which are inherent in neither the tests which they typically produce nor the sort of performance which their students usually give.[31] Such a view, tacitly or otherwise, assumes that all tests are of equal difficulty, that all classes of students are of equal ability, and that the teacher himself always performs at the same level. The one thing which may be said for this view is that it solves the problem of grading for the teacher who adopts it, but that is a dubious advantage at best.

Some people dislike the expression that "everything is relative." In grading, however, this is the only realistic view available. Tests do vary in difficulty, classes have different distributions of ability, and teachers sometimes do well and sometimes not. It is true that careful development of a battery of tests over a period of time can minimize variability in test difficulty. It is also true that classes with a sufficiently large number of students are often reasonably similar in their ability and that with experience the teacher's performance will be more uniform from term to term. Nonetheless, the careful teacher will want to know and to allow for the extent of each of these variabilities before he assigns his grades.

The first step in dealing with these variabilities is to consider each class on its own terms. One measure which reflects all of the types of variability mentioned above is the class range of scores on a test, the highest score minus the lowest score. Normally, the range should be rather wide. If it is restricted, then the test is probably not discriminating well between the different abilities one would expect to find in a class. When the range is restricted and the scores are accumulated at the higher end of the scale, the test is probably too easy. It could also be that the class is exceptionally able, an additional reason for pursuing the sort of tabulation procedure suggested earlier for determining the difficulty of multiple-choice test items. If the range is restricted and the scores tend toward the lower end of the scale, the test is probably too difficult.

Two other simple measures which will be helpful in assigning grades are the mean score, or the arithmetic average, and the median score, the one which lies exactly at the mid-point between the highest and the lowest score. When these two measures coincide, or nearly do, the distribution of scores is usually very close to normal. This is to say that a large percentage of the scores will cluster around the mean and the median and the percentage of scores as one moves away on either side from these measures will diminish. It is true that a normal distribution as described here is what one would expect of a set of scores or measures drawn at random and that student ability in a class is not necessarily random. Since as the size of any sample of scores increases the sample distribution will increasingly approxi-

31 John E. Horrocks and Thelma I. Schoonover, *Measurement for Teachers*, Columbus, Ohio: Charles E. Merrill, 1968, p. 573.

mate that of a normal curve, there is little reason not to expect such a distribution in most cases for all but very small classes. When the mean lies above the median although the range may not be restricted, then a few students' very high scores may be causing the mean to give a somewhat distorted picture of the performance of the group as a whole. In the same way, a few very low scores might cause the mean to fall below the median.

Some idea about the variability in his set of test scores equips the teacher with guidelines for assigning overall grades. He should also have in mind some reasonable definition of each letter grade. What, for example, constitutes failure? What is average and what is superior? In deciding on an answer to the first question, the teacher might use the highest score made on a test as a point of reference. He might then estimate how much less than that score a particular student could make and still be considered competent to perform the skills for which the course was to prepare him or to pursue other courses for which the present one is a prerequisite. There are no simple answers to these questions. One would expect the passing scores to be higher for some courses, for example, than for others. The passing scores probably would also be higher at more advanced course levels. In the beginning course of a highly technical subject, the student might need to know 65 percent as much as the best student in order to continue in the curriculum. Since there is some attrition of students through failure at lower levels, one would expect the performance of, say, juniors and seniors to be generally better than that of freshmen and sophomores.

In assigning all of the grades, the teacher might also profit from looking for the places in the distribution where the greatest gaps occur between particular scores. One would expect the scores of students with similar abilities to cluster together at various points in the distribution and for these clusters to be better indicators of real differences among the scores in a particular class than absolute percentages would be. Sometimes, dividing the range by the number of letter grades to be assigned will yield a roughly equal and equitable range of scores for each letter. In terms of percentages of students, the distribution of scores in high school and in the first two years of college might appear as follows:

A	B	C	D	F
9%	26%	30%	26%	9%

In the junior and senior years of college, the distribution might be:

A	B	C	D	F
12%	28%	44%	12%	4%

These distributions are nothing more than suggestions based on the kind of performance which is typical.[32] They reflect the fact that "because of the selection factor which operates at the upper academic levels . . . there will be more A's and B's in the advanced classes and a larger percentage of D's and F's at the lower class levels."[33] The reader will note that the percentage of C's also goes up with the academic level. "This would be an evaluation of capability of the student who has survived the selection process but is clearly not outstanding."[34] The teacher should use such suggested distributions as a check against the preceding suggestions for arriving at grades rather than as quotas to be met.

In a few instances, the distribution of scores on a test may be restricted to a particular part of the scale without the test itself being at fault. In an honors course, one in which only the very best students are enrolled, or in some graduate level courses, the lowest score might deserve a grade of C. If for some reason a class appears to be unusually dull, perhaps the best grade should be a C. The teacher should consider the effects of such factors as these in addition to the others.

The final task facing the teacher will be to combine all of the grades in a course, those given in rating speeches, group discussions, and other oral performances if any, as well as those given on written tests. A set of procedures much like those outlined above for grading tests may be followed provided the teacher has some way of converting the letter grades which he may have given for oral performances to numerical ones. Perhaps the easiest way for doing this is to assign a specific number of points for each oral assignment. Another way is to convert all of the letter grades in the course into a grade-point equivalent. An A+ might be assigned 4 points, an A 3.75, an A— 3.5, a B+ 3.25, a B 3, and so on. Each particular grade would need to be multiplied by a number appropriate to its relative weight in the overall grade, the minor assignments of the course carrying less weight than the others.

CONCLUSION

The evaluation of performance in the classroom is no mere technique. It is not merely a necessary evil. It is the logical extension of everything the teacher does in his course, and it is only done well when it is viewed in that perspective. It may well be that the teacher who evaluates poorly is also a poor teacher in other respects.

[32] *Ibid.*, p. 574.
[33] *Ibid.*
[34] *Ibid.*

EXERCISES

1. Formulate specific course objectives for
   a. the first speaking assignment in a public speaking course
   b. a 5-minute informative speaking assignment requiring the use of visual aids
   c. a lecture unit on the vowels of American English
   d. a practicum session on rehabilitation of adult stutterers
   e. an outside reading assignment on the chorus in Greek drama
2. Following the formula from one of the references (see especially Guilford, *Fundamental Statistics*), compute a reliability coefficient for the odd versus the even items of a recent test.
3. Ask several of your students and colleagues to join you in rating a round of speeches or other oral performances. Compute separate interjudge reliability coefficients for the two groups of raters. Which group is the more reliable?
4. Prepare 10 multiple-choice test items on the substance of this chapter.
5. Prepare five essay-type test items on this chapter. Devise a checklist for evaluating the answers to these items.

REFERENCES

The Teacher's Objectives

BAKER, ELDON E., "Aligning Speech Evaluation and Behavioral Objectives," *Speech Teacher*, March, 1967, 16:158–160.

BLOOM, BENJAMIN S. (ED.), *Taxonomy of Educational Objectives: The Classification of Educational Goals, Handbook I: Cognitive Domain*, New York: McKay, 1956.

KRATHWOHL., DAVID R. (ED.), *Taxonomy of Educational Objectives, Handbook II, Affective Domain*, New York: McKay, 1964.

Expectations of Student Performance

BERELSON, BERNARD AND STEINER, GARY A., *Human Behavior: An Inventory of Scientific Findings*, New York: Harcourt Brace Jovanovich, 1964.

DEESE, JAMES, *The Psychology of Learning*, New York: McGraw-Hill, 1958.

Rating, Testing, and Assigning Grades: General Sources

GUILFORD, J. P., *Fundamental Statistics in Psychology and Education*, New York: McGraw-Hill, 1956.

LINDQUIST, E. F. (ED.), *Educational Measurement*, Washington, D.C.: American Council on Education, 1951.

NUNNALLY, JUM C. JR., *Tests and Measurements: Assessment and Prediction*, New York: McGraw-Hill, 1959.

TYLER, LEONA E., *Tests and Measurements*, Englewood Cliffs, N.J.: Prentice-Hall, 1963.

22. Making Effective Use of Audiovisual Aids in Teaching Speech

Wesley Wiksell

For a moment you will think you are not in a classroom, but in a cross between a conference room and a library. There are no rows of tablet armchairs—only tables and straight chairs. On one side are cabinets for films, tapes, models, charts, and equipment for making visual aids. Magazines and newspaper racks stand in one corner. On the opposite wall the bulletin board is covered with an assortment of items. There is the agenda for a class—names of chairmen, recorders, and those who are responsible for class projects. One section of the board is devoted to a display of book covers, a picture of the United Nations in session, an assignment sheet, a calendar of discussions, a cartoon of the President of the United States presiding over his Cabinet, and other notices. At one end there is an enclosed booth for a motion-picture projector, a tape recorder, a filmstrip projector, cassettes, a video recorder, and an overhead projector. This classroom is equipped to make effective use of audiovisual aids in teaching group discussion.

Audiovisual aids are designed to vitalize instruction. While the motion picture is perhaps the most familiar audiovisual aid, the term encompasses also filmstrips, slides, transparencies, bulletin boards, blackboards, exhibits, recordings, models, radio, video, and television. As aids in teaching speech these devices are a means to an end. Properly used, they make speech training interesting, significant, and likely to become permanent. Improperly used, these "aids" are nuisances and wasteful of time, interest, and energy. There is no "best" type of visual aid, for each unit and each subject has its own peculiar requirements. A motion picture may be ideally suited to one project, while a flannel board is better for another one.

Many school systems, as well as colleges and universities, maintain as one of the school services extensive audiovisual aids departments, sometimes with considerable staffs and more than adequate budgets. These divisions purchase new materials, rent specialized items when necessary, assist in preparing art work for charts and flannel boards, and operate projectors and recorders. The teacher who goes to a new school should make early inquiry about the audiovisual aid services and what help he can expect. He should ask about what is available, how to request service, how long in advance to file requests, and what the policy is concerning the purchase of new items, particularly films and filmstrips. When his school has a well-operated audiovisual department, he can save himself much time and worry by calling on the technically trained specialist for help.

The interested teacher may request the help of a technician to operate a recorder, a sound camera, or a movie projector. He may seek advice on what device will best help him present a unit in his course. But this type of service can never take the place of the teacher, for he is the only one who thoroughly understands the students, their problems, the class objectives, and the nature of the subject matter. Teacher and technician must function as a team. If the teacher is to utilize audiovisual materials to their maximum, he must understand the nature and the potentialities of each type. It is the purpose of this chapter to describe the principal types of audiovisual aids, to discuss the advantages and disadvantages of each type, and to suggest how to use each one.

THE BULLETIN BOARD IN THE CLASSROOM

A bulletin board can relieve the bareness and bleakness of a typical classroom. Carefully used, it can be made a focal point of learning; used badly, it is a distractor and an eyesore. The materials that may be posted on a bulletin board depend on the imagination and thoughtfulness of the teacher. Below are several suggestions for the speech teacher:

1. Current items: excerpts from speeches, comments about actors, reviews of plays, reports of speech conventions, statements about famous speakers, designs of costumes, photographs of stage settings, and drawings of the speech mechanism.
2. Conflicting opinions: differing reviews of a play, different interpretations of a speech, contrasting opinions of the effectiveness of a television program, opposing points of view in a debate.
3. Contrasts of past with present: photographs showing the theater in Greece and the theater of today; gestures a hundred years ago and today.
4. Special days: pictures, documents, reports of speeches, and other materials related to holidays and anniversaries.

5. Cartoons and comics: caricatures of long-winded after-dinner speakers, pompous actors, or overenthusiastic television announcers.
6. Outstanding work: outlines, visual aids, photographs, and designs.
7. Announcements, assignments, and agenda: detailed information about class or club organizations, debate schedules, coming plays or films, or class responsibilities.

Many instructors encourage students to submit interesting items and to take responsibility for planning and putting up exhibits. Others assume full responsibility themselves for materials displayed. Regardless of who is in charge, he should keep in mind the following principles:

1. Materials may be found in innumerable places: newspapers and magazines; pamphlets, posters, and displays from many organizations and pressure groups; original drawings and advertisements.

2. Materials should be arranged carefully: decide on a central theme; avoid too much material; try various color combinations; letter carefully; work for originality.

3. Materials should be made an integral part of teaching. Tie the display in with the subject matter by referring to it from time to time. Move to the bulletin board when you mention aspects posted there that relate to the assignment. At appropriate times, encourage the students to gather around the display for detailed study.

4. Materials should not be left on the board too long. Take them down, evaluate them, and file the best for the next semester. Over the years many valuable pictures and items will be added to your collection.

5. Give contributors credit for contributions.

EVALUATION OF BULLETIN BOARD DISPLAY

Name of Display _____

Dates _____ to _____

Purpose _____

Photograph or copy

                        Above or Below Average—Why?

Arrangement
Use of Color
Lettering
Interest to Students
Help in Teaching

Comments:

CHALKBOARD AND PAPER PAD

Chalkboard

The chalkboard is probably the oldest and most readily available of all visual instruction devices; nevertheless, it is often taken for granted and poorly or seldom used. Outlined below are its chief advantages and disadvantages, as well as suggestions for its use.

Advantages

1. It is nearly always available and ready for use at a moment's notice.
2. It is the least expensive of all visual aids.
3. Mistakes can be easily corrected.
4. Student participation can be great; they can demonstrate knowledge about a particular subject on the chalkboard.

Disadvantages

1. Many subjects do not lend themselves to chalkboard display.
2. Properly designed drawings for the chalkboard take too much time.
3. Erasers and crayons may be dusty and untidy, and the dust may cause throat and skin irritation.
4. There is a temptation to play or doodle with chalk.

Suggested Uses

1. Showing the organs of speech
2. Sketching stage setting
3. Plotting the action in a play
4. Outlining details in costuming
5. Noting phonetic symbols in pronunciation
6. Listing new words for vocabulary building
7. Listing principles to be explained
8. Giving brief summaries
9. Pointing up a rule of parliamentary procedure
10. Plotting a discussion
11. Visualizing the progress of a debate or discussion
12. Indicating the agenda for the class period
13. Listing assignments and readings
14. Outlining instructor's lecture
15. Giving a short test
16. Writing questions before the class period to capture the imagination of the students
17. Explanation of formulas
18. Reproducing material not found in class texts

Suggestions for Improvement

1. Work on a clean chalkboard.
2. Letter and draw in advance of the class. In this way you can be sure of the spelling and the details of the drawing.
3. Use color.
4. Use large letters.

5. Get variety and sharpness by flattening, sharpening, or blunt-rounding your chalk.
6. Use a yardstick for straight lines.
7. Make labels simple.
8. Keep the material covered until it is needed. You may use a curtain that slides over it, cover it with a piece of wrapping paper, or pull a map over it.
9. Erase drawings or cover them up when you are through with them.

Things to Avoid

1. Do not give long tests; they should be given through other means.
2. Do not put up drawings that are used repeatedly; it is wasteful of time.
3. Do not stand in front of the material when drawing it.
4. Do not talk to the chalkboard.
5. Do not use drawings that are too small or too complex.

Paper Pad

Paper pads are made up of 10 to 50 different sheets (sometimes plastic), plain or ruled, 24″ × 30″ and larger. This pad is used much like a chalkboard. It can be attached to a wall or placed on an easel. Among its advantages are the following: (1) You need not erase class notes or interesting ideas—simply turn the page to a clean sheet, retaining the old one for future classes. (2) Material used from class to class can be taken down and posted again when needed. This is particularly helpful when other teachers use the room before you meet your students again. (3) A great deal of material can be recorded on it. When one sheet is filled it can be torn off and taped on the wall. The principal disadvantage of the paper pad is that the cost is considerable; unless the sheets are plastic, they cannot be used a second time.

Evaluation of Chalkboard and Paper Pad

Answer the following questions:

Did the use of the chalkboard or paper pad make the explanation clear? Yes_____ No_____
Was the chalkboard information more effective than other accessible or easily arranged materials? Yes_____ No_____
Was the chalkboard material clear and pleasing in appearance? Yes_____ No_____

FLANNEL BOARD AND MAGNETIC BOARD

Like the visual aids just mentioned, the flannel board—sometimes known as a felt board or clingboard—has a definite value in speech instruction. Here you build your presentation step by step by placing previously prepared lettered or illustrated symbols on a portable or permanent background.

Construction

A flannel board may be purchased, or made of thin plywood, heavy cardboard, or similar light material. It is covered with flannel or duvetyn of any color—white, black, gray, dark blue, green, red, etc.—and fastened to the background with thumbtacks, brads, or rubber cement. Although the usual dimensions are 24″ × 36″, the size can be modified to fit the nature of the figures to be attached to it.

Pictures, captions, titles, or other explanatory materials to be attached to the flannel board need to have a special backing glued to their back to make them adhere. This backing may be sandpaper, Flok-Tite or Flock-Craft (commercially prepared materials), or felt or flannel.

A magnetic board is readily constructed by stretching a wire screen over a frame covered with cloth. Small magnets are then glued to the backs of visuals to be used in the presentation. Otherwise it is like the flannel board.

Advantages

1. Items can be prepared in advance and used over and over again.
2. Items can be moved about and arranged in different combinations.
3. This device gets attention and holds interest. Even though it is not new, many students have never seen this type of visual aid used.
4. The speaker can recapitulate at any point. Use of the flannel board encourages him to speak in an extemporaneous manner, adjusting to the overt cues of the class. His pace can be flexible. Parts can be omitted, points can be stressed, and material can be added when desired.
5. A presentation is often easier to understand because the speaker is likely to follow a logical preplanned pattern.

Disadvantages

1. It takes considerable time to plan and make the materials, and they are costly if made by an artist.
2. It is easy to overemphasize a point. Students often wonder about the apparent emphasis the teacher seems to give at certain points.
3. Intrigued by the procedure, students often become more interested in the presentation than in the message.

Suggested Uses

1. Photographs of stage settings, the organs of speech, and speakers may be posted during a class presentation.

2. A stage setting may be built up, step by step, as it is explained.
3. Stage action may be blocked out on the board by using letters or symbols for each character. The parts of a speech may be explained section by section.
4. Pronunciation drills may be dramatized when the words are placed before the students.
5. Words, questions, statements, photographs placed on the flannel board give the students an opportunity to identify and discuss.
6. The students may utilize this type of visual in the presentation of a speech. For example, they may explain safety procedures, economic trends, or shifts in population.
7. This visual aid is useful when the problem is to impart a new concept in a step-by-step cumulative manner. (Use the bulletin board or paper pad if the entire story can be presented at one time.)

Improving Presentation

1. Use as few words as possible; printing can be difficult as well as expensive.
2. Use symbols, pictures, or illustrations often.
3. Plan different sizes of slap-ons to denote different aspects of the presentation.
4. Use a variety of nonglare color to catch attention and to symbolize ideas.
5. Number each item.
6. Practice the presentation many times.

Evaluating a Flannel Board

In checking a flannel board, consider the following questions:

Did the presentation help me above and beyond the more accessible and more easily made visual aids?   Yes_____ No_____
Were attractive headings, captions, or explanations used to tell the story?   Yes_____ No_____
Were the ideas organized around a focal point of interest so that the entire design, when completed, made an artistic and logical pattern?   Yes_____ No_____

RECORDS AND TAPES

Teachers have long used records and tapes because of the great variety of material that has been recorded. Among their advantages are the following.

1. Speeches of important personalities can be brought into the classroom. Students can hear the voices of Churchill, Eisenhower, Franklin D. Roosevelt, Carl Sandburg, John Gielgud—now or ten years from now—with such recordings as *Voices of Freedom* (Victor) and others.
2. Time, place, and distance are no obstacles to the listener. Students

can hear the recorded voices of actors a thousand miles away, at any hour of the day, often recorded years before.

3. Great literary works and scenes from great plays can be heard in the smallest classroom at negligible cost. Events in which speech was important, such as the *You Are There Series* (CBS), are available.

4. The speech teacher can plan and use recordings at appropriate times, or whenever convenient. Records can be stopped or replayed to discuss points or to answer questions.

When you have decided on the subject your students should hear, write your State Department of Education for a catalog of transcriptions or the National Tape Repository, Bureau of Audio-Visual Instruction, Stadium Building, University of Colorado, Boulder, Colorado for a list of tapes available.

Using Records and Tapes

1. Carefully audit material before using it in class. Decide if the recording should be played in its entirety or stopped from time to time for discussion.
2. If you are going to interrupt the recording, plan the questions to be asked.
3. Prepare the students by discussing vocabulary problems and objectives to be accomplished.
4. Plan follow-up discussions, readings, and evaluation.
5. When you play a recording give attention to acoustics, seating arrangements, tone, and volume.
6. You can record many individual and group speech activities such as speeches, discussions, telephone usage, interviews, conversations, remedial training, proceedings of meetings, resolutions, choral readings, acting, debating, pronunciation, and self-evaluation.

Advantages

1. Tape recordings are inexpensive, and tapes can be used innumerable times before wearing out.
2. The instructor can play the recording at any time in or after the class.
3. With proper facilities the student can listen to himself, comparing the instructor's criticisms with his own observations. He thus has a way to evaluate class and instructor criticism of his speech. It is one thing for an instructor to tell a student that he lacks variety in pitch and another for him to hear the monotony of his own voice. With the short magazine type of recording he can utter a word, listen to it, and say it again.

Difficulties

As with most machines, recording can be annoying, frustrating, and downright heartbreaking. Even new machines sometimes fail to work occasionally—the tape is wound improperly on the spool, the volume control is either too high or too low, or the machine (even a portable one) is too heavy to carry around easily.

Evaluating Tapes

Evaluate your recordings, using the form shown here.

TAPE EVALUATION FORM

Title of tape _____ Date used _____

Source _____

Cost _____ Rental _____ Speed _____ Time _____

Where can this tape be best used

	Excellent	Good	Poor

1.
2.
3.

Professional qualities of the tape
1. Sound:
2. Content:
3. Study material with it:

Abstract:

MOTION PICTURES

You may want to use a film in your speech classes; but if you are like most teachers who seldom operate projectors or have no staff to help, you may encounter considerable difficulty. Few will deny that films can assist materially in teaching; the research that followed their tremendous use during World War II proved their value. Yet there are also disadvantages in their use: it takes considerable skill and imagination to select, obtain, and use a film effectively.

Advantages of Motion Pictures in Teaching

1. The movement of an image, especially in color and with narration, projected on the screen in a darkened room stimulates student attention.
2. Motion-picture films can bring into the classroom the past with its great speakers and actors, distant places, and famous personalities and events.
3. Pictures of small objects, such as the cartilages of the larynx, can be enlarged on the screen for better understanding.
4. The action of fast-moving speech organs, such as the vocal cords, can be slowed down.
5. Sound waves, impossible to see with the naked eye, can be represented.
6. Continuity of happenings, such as an entire meeting utilizing parliamentary procedure, can be telescoped into a few minutes.

Disadvantages of Motion Pictures in Teaching

1. The use of films is time consuming. Careful planning is required to order films, reserve a projector weeks or months in advance, check the film once you receive it, and return it after use.
2. Costs for either purchase or rentals are high (though you can sometimes find sources of free films).
3. Films are inflexible. Many date quickly, especially as reflected in style of dress and automobiles. These items may even detract to such an extent that students do not get the main idea of the film.
4. Films are difficult to adjust to different age levels. Often producers attempt to appeal to too many groups, i.e., grades, junior high, high school, and college.
5. No film can take the place of a teacher, nor can a poor teacher use a film as well as a good teacher.

Planning the Use of a Film

1. Know the needs of your class. For example, your students have read and discussed the textual material about the voice mechanism, but they are still unable to visualize the vocal cords in action. They need information beyond the materials they have studied. A film could provide this information.
2. In addition to knowing the needs of the class, you must also know exactly what you want to achieve; and this must be planned for. Let us say, for example, that you would like your class in debate to see some great speakers in action. You find a film showing Roosevelt speaking. While it would be unreasonable to demand that the students attempt to copy his methods of delivery, you could expect them to gain a greater understanding of a different style of speaking.

Selection of Films

With the class analyzed and the goals determined, you are ready to select the film. At this stage catalogs and indexes are important. First, consult the catalogs of the film libraries supported by your state. Then, go to the *Film Evaluation Guide* in the library. This is a guide to films. Look for films in the Subject List of Titles by Dewey Decimal Classification on the last pages of the book. The films you find are listed alphabetically in the guide by title. Note a sample title listing included.

Getting the Film

Once you find a film in the Film Evaluation Guide that seems to meet your needs, you must locate a distributor who will lend it to you. Though ordinarily you cannot obtain a film from the producer, listed in *Film Evaluation Guide*, if you will write to him, he will usually direct you to some of the distributors—a film may be owned by a hundred or more organizations, film libraries, and rental agencies. The addresses of some distributors are listed on p. 465 and in the two following directories: *Index to 16mm Educational Films*, New York: R. R. Bowker Company, *Educators Guide to Free Films*, Educators Progress Service, Randolph, Wis. 53956.

Preparing to Use Film

Once you have requested a film and had your order confirmed, it is sent to you. Always preview it before you use it. Ideally, you should do this many weeks before showing it. However, since there is a rental charge even for previewing, you will have to check it a few hours before showing it. Evaluate the film as you preview it; study the photography, the quality of the sound, its organization and its date. Even though color is more effective than black and white, it has both advantages and disadvantages. Today, with most movies produced in color, educational films in black and white may seem dull in comparison. Color is realistic. Sometimes the content must have color to be meaningful, but it loses its effectiveness unless the room is completely dark. Sometimes the color is too bluish or greenish; sometimes it fades. Black and white can be shown in a room only partially darkened.

The sound of any teaching film should be heard distinctly. Yet as in radio, television, or teacher-to-class communication, many sounds may be distorted or inaudible, making it impossible to listen easily. This is especially the case if the film is an old patched one, if the projector is working improperly, or if the actors in the film are careless in their speech.

10 min., b&w, $60, 1955
Centron Corp. Dist—McGraw-Hill Text Films, 330 W. 42 St., New York, N.Y. 10036

Subject Area: Speech

Evaluator: Hempstead Public Schools, New York

Synopsis: A high school boy asks his faculty advisor why he should study speech. The answer is given with real life situations which portray how good speech training can be important and useful in a variety of ways, such as conversation, speaking to fellow students in school, applying for a job, and talking to civic groups in community activities. Activities involved in speech studies and what one can expect to learn also indicated.

Uses: To show the value of good speech in many daily activities; to introduce the study of speech; guidance and language arts classes

Age Level: Junior and senior high, college, adult

Technical: Sound—good; Photography—good

Comment: Stresses that one's success in life may depend on the ability to speak well. Asks viewers what they are doing to improve their speech.

Rating: Good   EFLA No. 1955. 2736

The film should not be obviously dated unless this has historical value. Most of us are not annoyed with a book that is 10 years old, but a film produced 10 years ago has often lost much of its attractiveness. A preliminary explanation of the date of filming may partially offset this problem. To avoid this problem many producers make films such as *The Voice of Your Business* (AT&T) in cartoon style with abstract figures or puppets playing the roles.

Projecting the Film

Check the machine you are going to use several days before the showing. If it needs a minor adjustment or repair there will then be time to take action. Before threading the film, check the light image on the screen for signs of dust on the lens in the picture aperture or on the gate through which the film slides. Then test the machine for sound and focus. This process is all shown in the film *Facts About Film* (International). It is surprising how often instructors fail to take these precautions. As a result the film is threaded improperly, the sound is fuzzy or will not go on, or the image is out of focus. The projectionist, in dismay and unacquainted with the machine, desperately turns switches on and off. Finally someone in the audience goes back to help him. This person does about the same thing. Result? Much of the film is improperly shown or missed entirely.

You will get more alert attention if you consider the physical properties of the room. Show the film in a classroom rather than in an auditorium. Remove or cover up distracting posters, signs, or chalkboard writing not related to the subject considered. Good ventilation is essential even in darkened rooms.

A totally darkened room is ideal for showing any film, and is practically a must when showing colored films. Covering windows with opaque cloth is better than building frameworks into the windows, because the cloth can be opened for ventilation. The screen should be elevated enough to permit everyone to see the full picture without having to peer around the person ahead. If the screen is a portable one it should be set up before the class meets. Teachers unfamiliar with a portable screen are likely to appear ridiculous when trying to set one up while the class waits.

Study the instruction manual and practice running the machine several times before showing your first film. As it nears the end, turn down the volume and stop the projector before the numerical flashes appear. Do not rewind until after the class.

Methods of Using Films

General Methods.   Seldom, if ever, can a film do a job by itself. Films are not magic. Research has revealed that providing an introduction and a review double the amount of information learned. But there is no one way to use films that is always effective. Following are various ideas:

1. Study the guide for the film (if one is available). Here you will find specific suggestions about student study and preparation, what to include in the introduction, methods of discussing the film, and review and evaluation. Some guides include a list of words introduced in the film. For example, the film, *How Television Works* (United World), contains the following key words, *iconoscope, deflect, cathode ray,* and *scanning.* The guide lists these and many others for study.

2. Prepare the class for the film by announcements, discussions, and assignments. Announcements supplied for films can be placed on a bulletin board, sometimes several days before the showing. Tell the students the name of the film, the reasons for showing it, significant points to look for and to be remembered.

3. Stop the film from time to time to discuss significant points.

4. Turn off the sound and run through a second time, making comments as the film is shown.

5. Stop the film at specific points—for example, where the assistant leaves the sign on the desk in *Production 5118* (Champion Paper). Ask

students what is on the sign. In the film *By Jupiter* (Wilding) stop it right after Poindexter's bad day and ask viewers to demonstrate the best way to handle the situations Poindexter found himself in. Stop the film *Working for Better Public Health Through Recognition of Feelings* (U.S. Department of Health, Atlanta) just as the tractor reaches Barlow and ask the class what he should say and do.

6. Before projecting a film, divide the class into three groups. Ask one to look for ideas that have not been discussed before in class, the second to seek ideas that reinforce material that has been discussed, and the third to find points that need further discussion. At the conclusion of the film ask each group to report.

7. Divide the class into four or five small groups before the showing, and ask each group to agree on one aspect of the film that it feels should be discussed by the class.

8. To get the discussion started, ask two or three members to serve as a panel to discuss among themselves certain aspects of the film.

9. Precede the presentation with a short lecture or panel discussion related to the subject of the film.

10. Give a student test on the film immediately after the showing. Show it a second time and then discuss the answers.

11. Exchange experiences suggested by the film.

12. Conduct a discussion after a brief introduction to the film. Ask the class to think about a subject—telephone courtesy, for example—for a minute, and then have each member tell what he thinks is most important in making a telephone conversation effective. After students have thought a minute, ask for quick answers. If there is time, put the ideas on the chalkboard without discussion. Then show the film *A Manner of Speaking* with the introduction, "It will be interesting to see how many of the ideas they got into the film. Let's take a look."

13. Conduct a discussion before showing such a film as *Stage Fright* (Centron), covering such points as the following:

a. Define stage fright.
b. According to the text, what are the causes of stage fright?
c. What can be done to control stage fright?

Then show the film and review the points brought out in it. Here are some sample remarks to precede the showing of such a film as *Parliamentary Procedure* (2nd ed., Coronet): "*Parliamentary Procedure in Action* is a motion picture that has several purposes: First, to stimulate thought and discussion about the rules of parliamentary procedure. Second, to help you to conduct properly and to participate in a meeting. The film shows a meeting in which the rules of parliamentary procedure are properly followed. Each rule is explained by an observer. Obviously, only a short meeting can be covered in a 15-minute motion picture; many points have been omitted. However, some of these can be discussed later. We'll have questions after the first showing. When these have been answered, we will run the film a second time. If you have any questions at that time, raise your hand and we will stop the film, discuss the point, rerun the scene if necessary, and then continue the film. Several members of the class will then be asked to demonstrate a knowledge of parliamentary procedure by serving as leaders and members. Let's see the film."

A *Detailed Procedure for Using Films in Class.*   Before the film is shown:

1. Explain to the class the purpose of the film.
2. Divide the class into groups of six.
3. Select a question for discussion about the film.
4. Have each group select a chairman and a recorder.
5. Hand each chairman a sheet with the following instructions: *Instructions to group leaders for immediately after showing.* "Make certain that all members of your group understand the question. Have each person state his point of view before there is general discussion. Make certain the recorder writes down each response. Discuss each point and agree on the best one. Leader should not state his opinions, but get the members of the group to express themselves."
6. Hand each recorder the following instructions: "Take down each participant's contribution. When asked by the instructor, read the contribution your group agreed was the best."
7. Hand the participants in each group three or four questions for discussion, varying the questions for each group.
8. Announce to the groups that after they see the film they are to discuss the questions given them for 10 minutes.

After film is shown:

1. Turn the discussions over to the chairman of the groups.
2. After 10 minutes have the recorders briefly report their findings.
3. Encourage the entire class to discuss the reports at the conclusion of the reports.
4. Give a multiple-choice examination on the film.
5. Read the correct answers and have each student correct his own paper.
6. Answer questions.
7. Ask each student to evaluate the film on one of the evaluation forms included in this chapter.

Preview many sound motion pictures in your area of speech, keeping a record of each preview on a master card in an index of films. This record should include the basic material found in the *Film Evaluation Guide* as well as your evaluation on a form similar to the one on p. 456. Record student reactions and questions and results on each master card.

Evaluation of Films

The purpose of film evaluation is to enable you to build up a complete record on each film you preview and show in your classes. Such records will

FILM EVALUATION FORM

Your opinion of _____

Name of Film

Your name _____ Date _____

	Agree	Undecided	Disagree
1. Interesting			
2. Instructive			
3. Forces a person to think			
4. Changed my attitudes and behavior			
5. One students should see twice			

Suggestions:

FILM EVALUATION FORM

Name of film _____

Evaluator _____ Date _____

	Low						High
	1	2	3	4	5	6	7
1. Is the film's story told in such a way that its significance is brought out?							
2. Does the film tell its story effectively?							
3. How valuable is it as a source of information?							
4. How provocative is it of thought, discussion, and controversy?							
5. How useful is it for arousing interest and motivation?							
6. Special comments:							

FILM EVALUATION FORM

Title of film _____ Date used _____
Rental source _____
Cost _____ Color _____ Black and white _____ Time _____
Where can this film be best used?

1.
2.
3.

Professional qualities of this film	Excellent	Good	Poor
1. Photography			
2. Sound			
3. Content			
4. Study material with the film			

Comments:

help in the selection and use of films in subsequent years. Many of the films that you, your co-workers, and your students evaluate will not be used again. Some will need more explanations of one kind or another before being shown again. Others may need a different treatment after the viewing.

One method of evaluating a film is to have regular film-evaluation sessions by those who saw it. Criticisms should be freely given and carefully noted for future study (see film evaluation forms).

Another method is an evaluation form, similar to one of those shown here, filled out by those who saw the film. Each person's opinions are recorded and weighed.

Producing Your Own Film

For many years films have been made of plays, student speakers, debates, discussions, and articulatory disorders. These have been worthwhile both as student experiences and in building a school film library.

Generally the silent film is made first, or a film with a magnetic sound track, either in black and white or in color; recorded explanation is added later. The latter process has been developed in the past few years; it is accomplished by adding a magnetic sound head to the projectors. You and your students can then record the sound and play back the sound track immediately, recording a new one if corrections are advisable.

FILMSTRIPS

The term *filmstrip* refers to a sequence of related 35mm still pictures, in color or black and white, silent or sound, and from two to five feet in length. They are sometimes referred to by such names as *slidefilms, still films, stripfilms,* and *pictorials.* They have both advantages and disadvantages in the classroom.

Advantages

1. A filmstrip does not require a completely darkened room.
2. It is less expensive than motion pictures.
3. It can be shown at any speed.
4. It is compact.
5. It is quite easy to make. You can make a filmstrip of anything photographed, drawn, or written—on conversation, organization of speeches, parts of speeches, stage settings, costumes, etc.

Disadvantages

1. It does not have the dramatic quality of a motion picture.
2. Since there is no movement, use of the filmstrip demands considerable teacher skill.

How to Use Filmstrips

With some exceptions, many of the suggestions for using motion pictures apply to filmstrips. You must become familiar with the filmstrip in advance, study the accompanying guide, preview the film, prepare your class for it, and test the equipment. Like motion-picture projectors, slide projectors are of many types and makes. Never wait until class time to thread and adjust the film—if you do, you may have difficulty in showing it. As with motion pictures, explain why the filmstrip is being shown, what to look for, difficult words and symbols, and what the students will be expected to discuss and remember. Encourage the students to participate during the presentation. This step makes the presentation more meaningful and results in greater insight.

SLIDES, TRANSPARENCIES, DRAWINGS, AND PICTURES

Slides

Slides and transparencies are similar to filmstrips except that they can be shown in any desired order. They may be pictures, cartoons, charts, graphs, or diagrams; they can be projected with slide, overhead transparency, or opaque projectors. Thus they have the advantages of projected images. They can be black and white or in color; they are easy to project, inexpensive, and cover a wide range of subjects. Groups can see the same picture at the same time, and students in the back row have the same opportunity to see the projected picture as those in front. There are many new developments. One is the sound-on-slide system; a sound disc may be placed on each slideholder permitting the student or instructor to record instructions, explanations, or interpretations up to 35 seconds.

Transparency Projectors

Overhead projection with transparencies or opaques is probably the most significant development in still projection techniques of the last two decades. The overhead transparency projector enables the teacher to have the image of what he writes or draws projected on a screen while he stands or sits facing the class. Thus he can observe the reactions of his students and can adjust his pace, selection and emphasis accordingly. The students observe the images above and behind the instructor. The image is bright and can be shown in a fully illuminated room. The instructor does not need to turn away from the class to point out a particular detail; he merely indicates it with a pencil on the transparency on the flat surface of the projector before him. This projector is the only type which permits the teacher to write, mark or draw an image while material is being projected. The teacher can present complex material, step by step, by means of masking and overlays, or break down a whole unit into its component parts. He can project transparent or opaque objects, animated devices and fluids. Color can be used to help students see distinctions or to make the image appear more realistic. The instructor can create his own transparencies with transparency-making equipment and materials that are relatively simple and inexpensive. In addition he can purchase professional transparencies, such as a unit on *The Art of Shakespeare* (with tape) from 3M or a unit on *The Sound Stimulation*, which shows how sounds are formed and produced, from Tecnifax.

The Opaque Projector

The opaque projector is another useful still projector. No slides are needed; materials from books and magazines, photographs, charts, and diagrams can be enlarged. Its chief advantages are the ease and inexpensiveness of operation. On the other hand, the image is less sharp than that of film-strips, slides, or overhead transparencies.

EXERCISES FOR BULLETIN BOARD

1. Visit several classrooms in your elementary school, high school, or college and note the kinds of material on bulletin boards. Make a note of the best ones. What adaptations of these displays can you use in your speech class?
2. Interview several teachers who use bulletin boards. Ask such questions as the following:
   a. Where do you get ideas for your bulletin boards?
   b. What was your best display?
   c. Why was that particular display your best?
   d. What principles do you follow when arranging a bulletin board display?
3. Develop a project for which students are to find material for the bulletin board related to the assignment. This activity could be something like sets of graphs on safety and photographs of programs. Have the class discuss and evaluate the project.
4. Analyze a number of bulletin board displays. In each one consider the significance of different items to the central theme, the relative value of the material, what made it attractive, and what made it interesting.
5. Write to your State Department of Education for its list of educational aids useful for displays.
6. Write to various large companies or organizations for display material related to the material being discussed in class. For example, the class may be studying various kinds of discussion procedures, such as those used in the United Nations. Post material received from the United Nations.
7. Have the class give speeches on "The Most Effective Bulletin Board Display I Have Seen."
8. Study the literature on effective bulletin board displays in industry.

EXERCISES FOR CHALKBOARD

1. Write for information to the manufacturers and suppliers listed on pp. 462–463.
2. Buy a book on practical lettering and practice a style of lettering that suits you.
3. Study and practice making stick figures. Use them in your teaching to heighten interest.
4. Enlarge and transfer a small drawing to a chalkboard, using the grid method.
5. Use an opaque projector to transfer hard-to-draw charts to the chalkboard.
6. Make a large drawing on wrapping paper. With a tenpenny nail, perforate along the lines after it is completed. Tape the paper to the chalkboard before class begins and go over the drawing with an eraser impregnated with chalk. The dots left on the board when you remove the paper can be used in chalking the lines. This technique saves

time and results in a neat drawing. Furthermore, you can employ the original in subsequent classes.

7. List several ways to use the chalkboard in the presentation of a unit on some aspect of speech.

EXERCISES FOR FLANNEL BOARD

1. Accumulate a file of photographs, illustrations, signs, graphs, etc., that will help you design material for flannel board presentations.
2. Study some displays and advertisements for possible ways to visualize a unit in your class.
3. Write to some of the commercial sources listed in this chapter for descriptions of material useful in constructing flannel boards and planning displays.
4. Prepare a ten-minute talk on some aspect of speech in which you make use of a flannel board. Construct your own flannel board, spending no more than a dollar for materials.

EXERCISES FOR RECORDINGS

1. Prepare a bibliography of selected recordings.
2. Listen to and evaluate several recordings.
3. Develop a library of tape recordings. These recordings may be purchased or taped for you at San Jose State College. (See *Speech Teacher*, January, 1955, 4:74 for details.)
4. Study the Audio-Visual Aids section of the *Speech Teacher* for reviews of tapes.
5. Study the latest catalogs of recordings, and make a list of speech recordings available.
6. Prepare for a public speaking or interpretation class a unit in which you make use of several commercial recordings.
7. Prepare a list of study questions to give your students to guide them in listening to recordings of prominent speakers or readers.

EXERCISES FOR FILMSTRIPS

1. Get a catalog of filmstrips from one of the companies listed here and order one in your field.
2. Prepare a bibliography of filmstrips in a special field of speech.
3. Screen one of the filmstrips listed in the chapter.
4. Evaluate your filmstrips with one of the forms suggested for films.
5. Plan a 16-frame sequence to be used in teaching a unit on some aspect of speech. Explain what would be included in each frame and the captions to be used.

EXERCISES FOR PROJECTORS

1. Write for literature relative to opaque, overhead, and slide projectors.
2. When you attend a teachers convention, visit the representatives of projection equipment companies and ask for a demonstration.

3. Select, preview, and plan introduction and follow-up questions for filmstrips to be used in teaching a unit on some aspect of speech. Present this film to a speech class. After the presentation write an evaluation.
4. Observe one of your classmates or an instructor presenting a filmstrip to a class. Prepare a detailed evaluation of the presentation and include several suggestions as to how the presentation could have been improved.
5. Use an opaque projector in the presentation of a unit. Find several pictures in magazines or books to include in your presentation.

REFERENCES

General Background on Audiovisual Methods

Books and Magazines

DALE, EDGAR, *Audiovisual Methods in Teaching*, 3rd ed., New York: Holt, Rinehart & Winston, 1969.

HAMILTON, EDWARD A., *Graphic Design for the Computer Age*, New York: Van Nostrand Reinhold, 1970.

WITTICH, WALTER ARNO AND SCHULLER, CHARLES FRANCIS, *Audiovisual Materials*, 4th ed., New York: Harper & Row, 1967.

Films and Filmstrips

Audiovisual Materials in Teaching, 15 minutes, black and white, sound, Coronet. Shows how a variety of audiovisual materials, when integrated with the curriculum, can facilitate learning.

Communications, 28 minutes, color, sound, Psychological Cinema Register, Pennsylvania State University. Relationship between concept development and the use of cartoons and feltboard presentations.

Instructional Films—The New Way to Greater Education, 15-minute and 25-minute versions, black and white, sound, Coronet. Demonstrates how audiovisual teaching saves time in presenting complex ideas.

New Tools for Learning, 20 minutes, color, Encyclopaedia Britannica. Use of audiovisual aids in education.

Bulletin Boards

Books and Magazines

Better Bulletin Board Displays, Visual Instruction Bureau, The University of Texas, 1969.

HORN, GEORGE F., *Bulletin Boards*, New York: Van Nostrand Reinhold, 1963.

RANDALL, REINO AND HAINES, EDWARD C., *Bulletin Boards and Display*, Worcester, Mass.: Davis, 1961.

Films and Filmstrips

Better Bulletin Boards, 10 minutes, color, Indiana University. Discusses the choice of material, arrangement, and design to catch and hold the viewer's eye.

Bulletin Boards—An Effective Teaching Device, 11 minutes, color, Bailey Films.

Blackboards and Paper Pads

Books and Magazines

Designing Instructional Visuals, Visual Instruction Bureau, The University of Texas.

Educational Displays and Exhibits, Visual Instruction Bureau, The University of Texas.

Instructional Display Boards, Visual Instruction Bureau, The University of Texas.
Lettering Techniques, Visual Instruction Bureau, The University of Texas, 1965.
LIECHTI, ALICE O. AND CHAPPELL, JACK R., *Making and Using Charts*, Palo Alto, Calif.:
  Fearon, 1957.
STIEHL, RUTH E., "Do-It-Yourself Display Letters," *Audiovisual Instruction*, November,
  1968, 6:1004, 1005.

Films and Filmstrips

Chalk and Chalkboards, 17 minutes, color, BNA. Treats at length many techniques
  which can be used to improve everyday teaching.
Charts for Creative Learning, 10 minutes, color, BNA.

Flannel Boards

Books and Magazines

FOX, MARION W., "Try Putting a Flannel Board to Work," *Instructor*, January, 1953,
  62:35.
GRASSELL, E. MILTON, "Flannel Boards in Action," *Educational Screen*, June, 1955,
  34:250–251.

Films

Flannel Boards and How to Use Them, 15 minutes, color, sound, materials demonstrated
  by E. Milton Grassell, Oregon State System of Higher Education, BFA. Shows how
  to make boards, offers ideas for devices that can be used by teachers, suggests the
  arrangement and rearrangement of the illustrations. Demonstrates its different possible
  uses.

Recordings and Tapes

Books and Magazines

Better Communications Through Tape, 3M Company, 1969.
Classroom Recordings: A Handbook, Audio Classroom Services, 323 S. Franklin Street,
  Chicago, Ill., 1953.
Creative Teaching with Tape, 3M Company, 1969.
SALM, WALTER G., *Tape Recording for Fun and Profit*, TAB Books, Blue Ridge Summit,
  Pa. 17214.
Tape Recording Guidebook, 3M Company, Minneapolis, Minn.
WITTICH, WALTER ARNO AND SCHULLER, CHARLES FRANCIS, *Audiovisual Materials*, New
  York: Harper & Row, 1967, chap. 11.

Films and Filmstrips

Recording with Magnetic Tape, 8 minutes, black and white, University of Minnesota.
  Instructions on the use and operation of a tape recorder.
Tape Recording for Instruction, 15 minutes, black and white, Indiana University. Shows
  basic techniques of making good tape recordings and how to utilize them.

Films

Books and Magazines

Better Movies in Minutes, Eastman Kodak Company, Rochester, N.Y. 14650, 1968.
DALE, EDGAR, *Audio-Visual Methods in Teaching*, 3rd ed., New York: Holt, Rinehart &
  Winston, 1969, chap. 14.
Educational Media Index, National Information Center for Educational Media, 1969,
  1346 Connecticut Avenue, N.W., Washington, D.C.

Educators Guide to Free Films, Educators Progress Service, Randolph, Wisc. 53956, annually.

Film Evaluation Guide, New York: Educational Film Library Association, 1965.

Film Library Directory, New York: Educational Film Library Association, 1966.

Index to 8mm Educational Films, New York: Bowker.

Index to 16mm Educational Films, 2nd ed., New York: Bowker, 1969.

Library of Congress Catalog: *Motion Pictures and Filmstrips*, Library of Congress, quarterly.

PETERSON, O. H., *Basic Requirements of Meeting Room Facilities for Effective Audio-Visual Communications*, Association of National Advertisers, Inc., 155 East 44th Street, New York.

Audio-Visual Communication Review, spring, 1954, 2:121–134.

WITTICH, WALTER ARNO AND SCHULLER, CHARLES FRANCIS, *Audiovisual Materials*, New York: Harper & Row, 1967, chap. 13.

Films and Filmstrips

Bring the World to the Classroom, sound, 19 minutes, color, Encyclopaedia Britannica. Explains how the sound film facilitates learning.

Facts about Projection, 17 minutes, sound, color, International Film Bureau. Stresses proper operation in advance of the showing. Operational routines for starting and ending a film are included.

Film and You, 13 minutes, sound, color, BNA. Follows a teacher as he prepares a unit, selects and previews the film and guides classroom discussion.

How to Use a Classroom Film, 15 minutes, color, sound, McGraw-Hill.

New Dimensions Through Teaching Films, 27 minutes, color, Coronet.

Stage Demonstration, 21 minutes, color, sound, Columbia. How to use recent innovations in motion pictures.

The Unique Contribution, 35 minutes, color, sound, Encyclopaedia Britannica. Types of educational films used in a modern classroom.

Filmstrips

Books and Magazines

Educators Guide to Free Filmstrips, Randolph, Wisconsin: Educators Progress Service, annual.

Index to 35mm Educational Filmstrips, New York: McGraw-Hill, 1967.

Index to 35mm Educational Film Strips, New York: Bowker, 1969.

Simple Ways to Make Title Slides Filmstrips, Rochester, N.Y.: Eastman Kodak Company.

Films and Filmstrips

Children Learn from Filmstrips, 16 minutes, color, sound, McGraw-Hill.

Simplified Filmstrip Production, 40 frames, black and white, Teaching Aids Laboratory, Ohio State University. How to make filmstrips with a 35mm camera.

Solving a Critical School Problem, 150-frame filmstrip, sound, 12 in. record, Curriculum Materials.

Tips on Slide Films, 92 frames, black and white, Jam Handy Organization, 2821 E. Grand Blvd., Detroit 11, Mich.

Overhead, Opaque, and Slide Projections

Books and Magazines

Audiovisual Instruction, April, 1962. Entire issue devoted to overhead instruction.

DENNIS, DONALD A., "Preproduction Planning: Key to Successful Slide Shows," *Audiovisual Instruction*, May, 1965, p. 401.

GREEN, IVAH, "Blow It Up with the Opaque Projector," *Teaching Tools*, Winter, 1958, 5:22–23.
Index to Overhead Transparencies, New York: Bowker.
101 Teaching Ideas from Beseler, Charles Beseler Company, 219 South 18th Street, East Orange, New Jersey.
The Opaque Projector, Visual Instruction Service, University of Texas.
Overhead Projection in the English Language Classroom, Instruction Booklet, Visual Products Division, 3M Company, St. Paul, Minnesota.
The Overhead System, Visual Instruction Bureau, The University of Texas.

Films and Filmstrips

The Opaque Projector, 46 frames, color, with supplementary notes, The Ohio State University.
Photographic Slides for Instruction, 11 minutes, color, sound, Indiana University. Shows preparation and use of slides made by the photographic process.
Preparing Projected Materials, 15 minutes, color, sound, BFA.

Distributors

Anti-Defamation League of B'nai B'rith, 315 Lexington Avenue, New York, N.Y. 10016.
Bell System Telephone Offices (consult local Bell System Business office).
BNA Films, 5615 Fishers Lane, Rockville, Md. 20852.
Centron Educational Films, 1621 West Ninth Street, Lawrence, Kans. 66044.
Columbia University Press, Center for Mass Communication, 1125 Amsterdam Avenue, New York 10025.
Coronet Instructional Films, 65 South Water Street, Chicago, Ill. 60601.
Encyclopaedia Britannica Films, 425 North Michigan Avenue, Chicago, Ill. 60611.
Indiana University, Audiovisual Center, Bloomington, Ind.
Pennsylvania State University, Audiovisual Aids Services, University Park, Pa.16802.
Teaching Film Custodians, 25 W. 43 Street, New York 10036.
University of California, Los Angeles, Department of Cinema, University Park, Los Angeles, Calif.
University of Minnesota, Audiovisual Education Service, Westbrook Hall, Minneapolis, Minn. 55455.
Young America Films, 18 E. 41 Street, New York 10017.

Equipment Directories

The Audiovisual Equipment Directory, National Audiovisual Association, Inc., Fairfax, Va., 1970.
Audio Visual Market Place, R. R. Bowker Company, 1180 Avenue of the Americas, New York 10036.

Equipment Manufacturers

Bulletin Boards

Acme Bulletin Board and Directory Co., 37 E. 12th Street, New York 10003.
Bulletin Boards and Directory Products, Inc., 724 Broadway, New York 10003.

Blackboards and Paper Pads

Allied Chemical and Dye Corporation, Barrett Division, 75 West Street, New York 10006.
International Display Equipment Associates, Inc., 71 Lansdowne Street, Boston, Mass. 02215.

Flannel Boards and Magnetic Boards

Florez, Inc., 815 Bates Street, Detroit, Mich. 48226.
Oravisual Co., Box 11150, St. Petersburg, Fla. 33733.

Magnetic Sound Recorder Projectors

Bell & Howell Co., 7100 McCormick Road, Chicago, Ill. 60645.
Minnesota Mining & Manufacturing Co. (3M Co.), St. Paul, Minn.

Film and Filmstrip Projectors

Bell & Howell Co., 7100 McCormick Road, Chicago, Ill. 60645.
Eastman Kodak Co., 343 State Street, Rochester, N.Y.

Overhead, Opaque, Slide Projectors and Transparencies

Beseler, Charles, Co., 219 S. 18th Street, East Orange, N.J.
Eastman Kodak Co., 343 State Street, Rochester, N.Y.
Minnesota Mining and Mfg. Co., St. Paul, Minn. 55101
Ozalid Division, General Aniline and Film Corp., Johnson City, N.Y.
Tecnifax Corporation, 95 Appleton Street, Holyoke, Mass.

Index